Anthropological Studies of Education

Series editor
Amy Stambach
University of Wisconsin, Madison
Madison, WI, USA

This series examines the political, ideological, and power-laden dimensions of education from an anthropological perspective. Books in this series look at how society is defined in relation to education. It delves into the kinds of communities that are imagined through educational policies, curricula, institutions, and programming. Many books in the series use ethnography to capture diverse educational positions and experiences. The series uses concepts such as social practice, myth-making, political organization, and economic exchange to address substantive issues pertaining to education in the moment and over time.

More information about this series at
http://www.palgrave.com/gp/series/14767

Oliver Pattenden

Taking Care of the Future

Moral Education and British Humanitarianism in South Africa

Oliver Pattenden
Greater London, UK

Anthropological Studies of Education
ISBN 978-3-030-09913-8   ISBN 978-3-319-69826-7 (eBook)
https://doi.org/10.1007/978-3-319-69826-7

© The Editor(s) (if applicable) and The Author(s) 2018
Softcover re-print of the Hardcover 1st edition 2018
This work is subject to copyright. All rights are solely and exclusively licensed by the Publisher, whether the whole or part of the material is concerned, specifically the rights of translation, reprinting, reuse of illustrations, recitation, broadcasting, reproduction on microfilms or in any other physical way, and transmission or information storage and retrieval, electronic adaptation, computer software, or by similar or dissimilar methodology now known or hereafter developed.
The use of general descriptive names, registered names, trademarks, service marks, etc. in this publication does not imply, even in the absence of a specific statement, that such names are exempt from the relevant protective laws and regulations and therefore free for general use.
The publisher, the authors and the editors are safe to assume that the advice and information in this book are believed to be true and accurate at the date of publication. Neither the publisher nor the authors or the editors give a warranty, express or implied, with respect to the material contained herein or for any errors or omissions that may have been made. The publisher remains neutral with regard to jurisdictional claims in published maps and institutional affiliations.

Cover © Oliver Pattenden

Printed on acid-free paper

This Palgrave Macmillan imprint is published by Springer Nature
The registered company is Springer International Publishing AG
The registered company address is: Gewerbestrasse 11, 6330 Cham, Switzerland

*For my beautiful wife, Claire
And Barry and Jacqui, my loving parents*

Acknowledgements

Many thanks must first go to George Chant, who made it possible for me to receive a generous Ambassadorial Scholarship from Rotary International, which funded much of the fieldwork at the heart of this book. I am also grateful to his colleagues at the Rotary Club of Berkhamsted Bulbourne and Rotary District 1260, who helped to fund my return to South Africa in 2013. I'd also like to thank members of the Rotary Club of Grahamstown for hosting me so graciously.

During my visits to South Africa, numerous other people also offered unwavering munificence. Every individual I had the pleasure of spending time with at Ngomso School is an integral part of this book. Their warm welcome will stay with me forever, and they taught me a great deal about what it means to inspire others. The experiences we shared have fashioned my life for the better; I only hope that I have been able to repay them in some way. Many of those who demand special mention appear by name in this book (albeit frequently under pseudonyms). I have not had the chance to thank them all personally but hope to do so. I also want to acknowledge the assistance of all my interlocutors who live in the UK.

The Anthropology Department at Rhodes became a home from home for me. Des Bekker's warmth and generosity knew no bounds. Silvana Barbali, Nosipho Mngomezulu, Joy Owen, Patti Henderson, Rose Boswell, and Penny Bernard filled my soul with laughter and my head with stimulating discussion. Jai Clifford-Holmes is one of the world's wonderful humans. I thank him for his friendship and the hours he spent improving my work. Throughout 2011 and into 2012, Chris de Wet had the dubious honour of supervising an inquisitive young man who had never studied anthropology before. His guidance and enviable intellect have helped to sustain my work ever since. With his wife Liz, he also helped me to settle into my surroundings, and I thank them both for that.

If I am Ernie, in Robin Palmer I found Bert. In Grahamstown, he went beyond the call of duty, opening up his house to me and graciously accepting my boundless enthusiasm to talk to him at all hours of the day. Di, Robin's wife, could not have been more giving with her hospitality either. Robin then went further by offering to supervise my research from 2012 onwards. To say that I am incredibly grateful to him for this gesture and the endless hours of support he has given me would be an understatement. I just hope he knows that I have not taken his encouragement, insight, commitment, and patience for granted. Professor Palmer—you are a true gentleman.

Several other academics have helped me along the way too. Amy Stambach took an early interest in my work, extending a much-welcomed invitation to spend the day at the University of Oxford. I am also grateful to Amy for helping me to attend the CIES Annual Conference in Washington and for all that she has done to help me to improve my work at various stages throughout the publication process. My thanks also go to Dalene Swanson, Charles Stafford, Leon Tikly, Charley Nussey, and Jenny Parkes, as well as Leslie Bank, Aleksandar Bošković, and Derick Fay, who not only examined my PhD thesis so thoroughly but also offered incredibly helpful suggestions regarding the transition to publication. Gemma Aellah and Raymond Apthorpe at the RAI have convinced me that there is a little corner of London where I can find intellectual stimulation and friendly conversation. During the writing and editing process, Alexis Belson and Kyra Saniewski at Palgrave Macmillan have both been incredibly supportive. I'm also grateful to the two anonymous reviewers who helped me to improve the manuscript.

As will become apparent, one focus of this study is parental care and nurturance. I have written every word knowing how fortunate I am to have the two most selfless parents anyone could wish for: Barry and Jacqui and Mr and Mrs P. Their unending desire to give everything that they have to their children is the reason that I am now writing these acknowledgements. As a child, they sustained and fed my curiosity with hours of attention and stimulation, and as an adult, they have nourished my ambitions and helped to mend my flaws. I love them both. I am also thankful that my sisters, Lucy, Emily, and Abi, and their families have forgiven my failures as a brother/uncle while I have focused on my research.

In 2010, in the pouring rain, over a year before I began my studies, I met a young lady named Claire Jared (aka Chip) in a queue for a nightclub. We were married in June 2016. Her love fuels my very being, and her mind shapes the way that I see the world. This companionship is evident on every page. Chip has endured years of uncertainty and upheaval to support me each and every step of the way. For every moment that she has sacrificed herself to make me happy, I will be eternally grateful. With the book now complete, I intend to repay her with all the love that she deserves. My warmest thanks also go to Claire's parents, Dave and Faye, and all of her family, for supporting us both. Finally, it is time to shake the paw of my co-author—our cat, Puck. Thank you for walking over my keyboard at inappropriate moments, every day for the last four years. Without your input, I could never have reached the finish line.

Contents

1	Having a Future	1
2	Living in a City, Town, and Location	59
3	Extrinsic Barriers to Learning	99
4	A Loving Education	167
5	Promoting Specialness	219
6	The Politics of Responsibility	273
7	Being Taught How to Hope	337
8	The Way Forward?	389
	Bibliography	409
	Index	453

LIST OF FIGURES

Fig. 1.1	Map of Grahamstown, South Africa (Google Maps)	17
Fig. 1.2	The Cape Colony, 1878 (Source: Molteno 1900: 408–9)	23
Fig. 2.1	Grahamstown, 2011 (Note: The location extended further to the north-east)	64
Fig. 2.2	Sources of surveyed learners' household incomes	65
Fig. 2.3	House in the location	67
Fig. 3.1	Living arrangements of surveyed learners	103
Fig. 5.1	Map of Warwick, UK (Google Maps)	225
Fig. 5.2	Map of Whetstone, London, UK (Google Maps)	235

CHAPTER 1

Having a Future

Mary told Sidima to take his hands out of his pockets. Without protest, he silently moved them behind his back and bowed his head. "You need to learn to behave if you are going to go to high school", Mary continued. Now squinting his eyes and scrunching his face, Sidima remained silent.

Minutes earlier, Sidima had punched his classmate Odwa without provocation. More accurately, the member of staff who brought him to the principal's office was sure this had happened. Sidima's version of events was quite different: he had politely asked Odwa to reopen the stationary cupboard so that their classmates could complete their work, and Odwa had then sworn at him, prompting their scuffle.

Sidima was frustrated that nobody else had witnessed Odwa's misbehaviour. In his opinion, blame was unjustly placed on his shoulders.

When Mary, the principal of Ngomso school, situated in Grahamstown, a small city in South Africa's Eastern Cape Province, encouraged him to accept responsibility for the altercation, Sidima refused her invitation. In response, Mary informed him that he would not be going to the classroom next door to eat lunch with the rest of the learners, but should sit on the floor outside her office to "calm down". For the next 20 minutes, like a frog, Sidima crouched above the threadbare carpet to take pressure off his behind. When Mary returned to ask, "Are you ready to talk?" Sidima didn't answer.

An hour later, Sidima was complaining that his peanut butter sandwich had gone stale, having sat on Mary's desk while he remained on the floor. He asked Mary why she was siding with Odwa and not listening to his version of events. "You say I am not doing my job well—then go to another school", countered Mary. With no resolution on the horizon, Sidima tried to sneak back to his classroom before Mary spotted him and dragged him back by the arm. "She thinks that she can beat me with her mind", he told me, privately. Clearly unwilling to be defeated, another member of staff escorted him back to the residential shelter ("the Shelter") where he lived.

After the weekend, Sidima returned to Mary's office accompanied by Danny, a member of staff from the Shelter. Mary informed him, "I am stressed and unhappy about your behaviour. I am ready to suspend you." She then offered some guidance and a resolution:

> There are times to be serious, [like now], or else you will get into trouble. Some of the cleverest people are in jail. They thought that they were cleverer than the police [and] their teachers. They used their brains for clever crimes because they hadn't learnt discipline. It is stupid for you not to use your cleverness in the right way. You have to decide what you will do with your brain. You might be cleverer than me, but I want you [to stay] out of prison. Do you want me to look after you or must I let you run wild?

Sidima stood in silence, with his back to the wall, as he considered his options. After about 30 seconds, he replied, "Look after me, mam".

Why did I choose to open this book with an account of what can happen when a young man is asked to reopen a stationary cupboard? Because I intend to show how anthropological inquiry can uniquely address important questions about the moral dimensions of education. More specifically, I analyse how both historically constituted moral discourses, such as Mary's claim that one must always speak the truth, and creative, ethical encounters, such as Sidima and Mary's exchange of words and actions, influence the potential futures that individuals conceptualise and strive to create for themselves and others. I also critically examine the extent to which individuals, most especially young South Africans, are able to fashion the lives they had once imagined.

In 2008, approximately three years before the stationary cupboard incident, I encountered similar themes of inquiry in a very different context: the offices of an advertising agency in London; surrounded by glass walls and young men wearing limited edition Nike trainers. A team of 'senior strategists' was interviewing me in an effort to "bring Heineken's creative strategy to life". My desk was downstairs. They had developed a "key insight": many young men, around the world, were disappointed that the lives they had imagined themselves living had not materialised. As children, they wanted to be astronauts, professional footballers, musicians, or prime ministers. However, their hopes and dreams, their best-laid plans, had been thwarted by the realities of life. They had grown up, only to feel unsure of themselves, devoid of a sense of achievement. The "creative strategy" was to ensure they knew, believed even, such hollowness could be countered with a bottle of Heineken. As Epicurus foresaw, the plan was to sell achievement and belonging, not beer. The industry had always made me uncomfortable. It was easy to question its morality. I sat in front of the camera and evaluated my own life. I harboured the aforementioned hollowness. It was time to leave.

My departure and related decision to travel to South Africa to complete the research that features in this book intimately relate to my prior experience of other influential events.[1] While studying at school, I had had no academic interaction with anthropology. When the time came, I opted to study marketing and management at Newcastle University. Although much of my undergraduate experience was uninspiring, the final year brought the opportunity to write a dissertation about "tribal marketing": a model of how informal social networks are affected by marketing. My tribe was that of DJs and their followers. I had bought my first pair of turntables when I was 13, and by the time of university, I was regularly 'DJing' in clubs and bars. After graduating, I continued to DJ and promoted club nights of my own. I was making money from something that I loved while meeting musical heroes and drinking decent rum for free. However, I felt that I wasn't really "doing anything". Perhaps I thought I wasn't doing anything "good". I'd been to South America and Asia. Afternoons were spent researching new destinations. I downloaded a PDF entitled "How to become a travel writer". I won an all-expenses paid trip to Antarctica and spoke to primary school pupils about the experience. Despite all of this, I thought everything was happening in London. "When are you going to get a proper job?" everyone asked. "I should probably get a proper job", I thought.

I was offered a place on the graduate training scheme of the advertising agency in January the following year and agreed to start in September. This was perfect; I had time to travel again. Fortunately, a fellow passenger on the boat to Antarctica operated a company that arranged volunteer projects catering to those on gap years and those old enough to take career breaks. He offered me a paid position in Ghana for six months; I flew out two weeks later. Some volunteers came to work in a hospital or orphanage in Accra; others lived in rural villages, helping to build latrines alongside an NGO funded by Water Aid. As a project manager, I was responsible for their welfare, budgeting, overseeing an "expedition" to Timbuktu, and arranging each project. I met with head teachers in the villages so that we could "help out" in their schools. Some of the young British and American visitors embraced these opportunities, arriving with pens and colouring books; others bemoaned the lack of premiership football and became bored very quickly, especially when there were too many of them and too few latrines to dig. The humidity, music, food, wildlife, beaches, wood fires, and dirt roads drew me in.

Despite my excitement, I had constant niggles, endless questions: "What are we all doing here? Who is this 'volunteering' benefitting? What happens when we leave?" I thought about the answers and discovered more questions. I had developed an interest in the moral and ethical dimensions of charity, development, voluntourism, and humanitarianism and, more specifically, Britain's relationship with her former African colonies; themes of inquiry that are central to this book. I engaged in conversations about wants and needs, hopes and dreams. I observed teenagers helping elderly neighbours without question; work stopping for a game of cards; schools closing when it rained. I was no longer convinced by the discourses of improvement, progress and tradition, schooling, mobility, and knowledge that had first led me to Accra. I came home with more to learn.

I returned to the advertising agency's 25th anniversary and flew to Miami for a four-day conference, which was, in fact, a pool party with a free bar. Blondie played the final night. Floating in the pool, with a cold beer in hand, while getting paid for my troubles, I realised I was in the wrong place. I wanted, or perhaps needed, to attend to the thoughts and ideas that related to my recent experiences in Africa. I shared my sense of discomfort with a new friend as he sat on a sun lounger. Two and a half years later, he wrote on my leaving card: "surprised it took you so long".

In the interim, I had eased my discomfort by helping build the company's Corporate Social Responsibility programme, linking with charities to teach a course that engaged 'the yoof' in radio and video production, script writing, and graphic design. I also snuck away from the world of Blackberries, logos, and focus groups to attend public, and not so public, seminars and lectures, as I desperately tried to engage with ideas that could help me to grasp my own better. Michael Jackson (2012: 15) suggests that my efforts and their outcome are not unique: "[Philosophical and anthropological work is that] of a person struggling to become what she is before she is a thinker, to make sense of her situation, to speak rather than be silent, to act rather than remain passive, and, above all, to connect with precursors and contemporaries and so create a sense of human solidarity in a world that is all too often chaotic, incomprehensible, and divided." In particular, the seminars and reading lists of the Anthropology of Development MA at SOAS introduced me to discussions and literature that shed some light on the unease I had felt in Ghana.[2] I quickly learnt that anthropology had been linked with development practices ever since the period of colonial administrations and missions (Lewis 2005; Olivier de Sardan 2005; Nolan 2002); where the nature of this relationship has long been and continues to be debated extensively. It became clear that anthropologists have asked important questions about development and humanitarianism, and the moralistic claims and conceptualisations that underpin them.

I wanted to learn more by studying for an MA focusing on "youth development", two areas of interest together in one neat phrase. With the help of my parents and George, a close family friend, I secured an Ambassadorial Scholarship from Rotary International to study for a master's degree. Sitting at a computer in my damp basement flat near Kings Cross, I typed the words "Africa university anthropology" into Google. In retrospect, I knew almost nothing about South Africa, a bit about Mandela, apartheid, and the colour of the national rugby jerseys, but little else.

It was 12 months before I was due to fly to South Africa, so, before handing in my notice at the advertising agency, I secured a temporary position as a Learner Support Agents (LSA) within the Inclusion Department of a large secondary school in Westminster. Most of my working days took place in the Learning Support Centre (LSC) and the Re-engagement Unit (no acronym, sadly). The LSC was for students aged 11 to 13, who, for a variety of reasons, had been removed from mainstream classes. Disruption or violent behaviour, of one kind or another, most commonly led to their referral. The Re-engagement Unit accepted students from all over Westminster, aged 14 to 16, who had been suspended or permanently excluded. Again, admission often followed disruptive or violent behaviour, and drug use, absenteeism, or, occasionally, vulnerability and low levels of literacy. These were students that most teachers didn't want in their classrooms or students that didn't want to be in their classrooms.³ Most were adjudged to have special educational needs (SEN), such as dyslexia, dyspraxia, attention deficit hyperactivity disorder (ADHD), Asperger syndrome, emotional and behavioural disorders (EBD), and English as an additional language. Collectively they taught me a great deal about their experiences at school, home, and out there "on the street". I empathised, assisted, and, at times, hindered. I laughed and was troubled.

I was in a privileged position. Teachers, students, parents, psychologists, and other Learner Support Agents spoke to me about each other. I encountered different explanations for, and expectations of, behaviour and interactions. 'Special Educational Needs' began to mean something more than terminology. Again, I had lots of questions. I was learning. I came to see conflicting ambitions, beliefs, judgements, desires, and identities. And dynamics of collaboration, learning, testing, deception, bureaucracy, creativity, love, and violence, as well as contestations of power, authority, accountability, blame, punishment, discipline, freedom, and expectation. Although I could not have articulated it like this at the time, I had become fascinated by the moral and ethical dimensions of schooling and 'special education' in particular. Questions relating to these interests are explored throughout this book.

When landing at Port Elizabeth Airport, in the Eastern Cape Province of South Africa, in March 2011, to begin my funded year of studies at Rhodes University, I had no clear plan as to how I would address my interests. However, when new friends and colleagues learnt of my previous experiences and research intentions, there was a consensus that I had to speak with Mary Burton (pseudonym), the principal, and founder of Ngomso School. They variably informed me that the school catered for "street kids", "drop-outs", or "the kind of children you were working with in London". I gained the impression that this was not an ordinary school, and that Mary was not an ordinary lady. Conveniently, my supervisor at the time had been friends with Mary since they met as undergraduates at Stellenbosch University in the late 1960s. He told me that her life's work followed a rich history of familial involvement in schooling and missionisation in the area. Several weeks after unpacking my suitcase, Mary responded to my interest in the school with great encouragement, and we met at her house. With her short, dark, greying hair, pink blouse, and reading glasses secured around her neck, I judged her to be of similar age to my mother, who had her 60th birthday that same summer. With what

I would come to consider an instinctive, effortless, and heartfelt gesture, she greeted me with a hug.

Mary spoke openly about Ngomso and kindly shared several documents that she hoped would be relevant to my research. I learnt that learners at the school were adjudged to have special educational needs relating to "extrinsic barriers to learning", "psychosocial circumstances", and "severe emotional and behavioural problems," such as being "broken, hurt, disturbed, traumatised, very angry, and violent". My previous school in London used the term emotional and behavioural disorders (EBDs). She described the learners as "street kids", "drop-outs", "out-of-school children", "over-aged children", "severely socially marginalised children and youth", "the poor", and "local black children". Although different, each identification signifies something undesirable, downtrodden, or out of place. "What do all these phrases mean, here in Grahamstown?" I wondered. "How do the learners feel about these labels?" Such lines of questioning comprise the first of several analytic themes running through this book: the 'specialness' of Ngomso learners. I examine how and why various interlocutors judged Ngomso learners to be 'special' or not, and interrogate the meaning of 'specialness/special (education) needs' in the context of South African schooling.

A little later in our conversation, Mary claimed that the majority of learners were enrolling at Ngomso "voluntarily" and "voting with their feet" having considered what was on offer elsewhere, especially in 'mainstream schools'. Given my experiences of working in the field of specialist education in London, I instinctively wanted to know whether this was truly the case. In this book, this line of inquiry is manifest in examinations of the ethical evaluations that were integral to various interlocutors' engagements with Ngomso and other sites and forms of moralised education. Moreover, such inquiry is at the heart of another of the book's key analytical themes: the relationship between experiences of education and modes of self-fashioning. As well as analysing events and evaluations associated with initial and continued engagements with the school and other sites of education, I examine how Ngomso and these other sites (e.g. 'the home' and 'the street') influenced interlocutors' conceptualisations of morality and the respective efforts they made to fashion particular lives for themselves.

As had been the case with many of the teachers and practitioners I had worked with in schools in London, during my initial conversation with Mary, it quite quickly became clear that she was keen to channel learners' lives in particular directions, to open doorways to opportunities. For example, she spoke of a visitation agreement with a five-star game farm that was encouraging learners and other "local black children to love and value wildlife". She imagined how such interventions might influence their lives: "Maybe they might become a game ranger." In later chapters, I analyse other interventions, which were similarly conceived by Mary, other members of staff, volunteers, and donors to transform learners' lives in particular ways. This inquiry incorporates three, interlinked foci: (1) the aims of intervention (i.e. the futures my interlocutors hoped to fashion for themselves, each other, and others); (2) processes of intervention (i.e. how interventions were initiated and maintained); and (3) the moral qualities of intervention (i.e. why particular interventions were initiated and not others). Throughout, I examine the moral and future-oriented qualities of various forms of education, most especially schooling.

Mary told me that Ngomso was registered as a public special (needs) school with the Eastern Cape Department of Education. As such, it could be distinguished from 'mainstream' schools. Such distinctions were familiar to me, and I was enthusiastic about the prospect of learning their meaning in this new locality. The question as to how, exactly, Ngomso differed from other schools in the vicinity is central to another of the book's key analytical foci: the 'specialness' of Ngomso, as an institution. Mary told me she was sure the school's specialness enabled her and members of staff to deliver something "over and above" what the "mainstream school" is offering. In later chapters, I examine the validity and complexity of this claim when detailing my interlocutors' engagements with Ngomso and other 'mainstream' schools.

This line of inquiry has added complexity because Ngomso's institutional specialness not only related to the school's association with the Eastern Cape Department of Education but also the activity of a partner, UK-registered charity called Friends of Ngomso (a.k.a. FOA and 'the Friends'), which did much to facilitate the efforts Mary and her staff made to differentiate the school from others.[4] Mary spoke about the charity's "Christian ethos", a phrase that has also appeared on their website. More recently, searching the UK government's Charity Commission register, I identified other UK-registered charities that fund education and Christian-oriented interventions in South Africa. Consider some of their names: Hope and Light (UK); Hope for South Africa's Children; Hope for the Good of South Africa Charity; Hope Through Action; Clouds of Hope; Friends of Hope for Africa Missions; Build the Nations; Raise the

Children International; and Love Is All We Need, which supports 'The Hope Centre' in South Africa. Similar discourses of 'hope' and 'love', 'building/repairing', and 'raising/improving/developing' are central to the analysis offered throughout this book. Given this overlap, it can be read as a critical investigation of the humanitarian, education, Christianised future-oriented discourses and practices that continue to bind Britain with her former colonies in Africa.

This is a theme of inquiry that had first caught my attention in Ghana: the moral dimensions of humanitarian interventions. Such a study is particularly pertinent because of recent changes to the relationship between the British and South African governments. In 2013, Justine Greening, the Secretary of State for International Development, announced that the UK would no longer provide bilateral aid to South Africa from 2015 onwards, 21 years after the practice began following the end of apartheid. Justifying the decision to remove the £19 m budget, Greening said, "South Africa is now in a position to fund its own development" (Watt and Smith 2013: np). This study provides a counter perspective by analysing the ways that 'ordinary folk' living in the UK and South Africa evaluate this scenario, addressing the question of how political and governmental relations between the two nations are constituted by something far broader and more complex than the policy mandates of relevant government departments (e.g. Department for International Development (DFID)). The fact that the charity at the heart of this study was created and managed by volunteers has enabled this line of inquiry, and distinguishes the book from comparable anthropological studies of development and humanitarian-oriented interventions in Africa that focus on charities and NGOs operated, in the main, by paid employees (e.g. Scherz 2014; Cheney 2007; Bornstein 2005).

When considered together, these analytical foci go some way to answering James Ferguson's (2006: 112) call for "an ethnography of processes and practices of encompassment, an ethnographic approach that would center the processes through which the government of the conduct of others (by state and non-state actors) is both legitimated and undermined by reference to claims of superior spatial reach and vertical height". In other words, this is a study of who or what is in control of political, economic, and cultural formations and emergences in the field of education and humanitarianism, and an examination of the methods and projects through which related forms of governmentality are fashioned and contested. To build further on Ferguson's thesis, I dissect processes of nation or state-building and scrutinise the relevance and formation of modes of collaboration and distinction that exist between state and non-state (i.e. civil or public) actors. As such, in terms of its temporal, geographical, and disciplinary orientations, this research project is somewhat borderless. This format both reflects the intangibility of transnational assemblages and relations of power and produces a novel consideration of them.[5]

As I left Mary's house, I knew I had 'found' my main research site and a key interlocutor. I was keen to commence my research and hopeful of meeting Ngomso learners, past pupils, parents, other members of staff, donors and volunteers, and representatives of the Eastern Cape Department of Education. From this moment on, I challenged myself to follow anthropology's lead: to discard my assumptions and be open to new experiences. The impossibility of fully achieving this position remains, for me, anthropology's strongest pull, and where I locate the discipline's value. The result of this ongoing work on myself, this book, is both a product of the knowledge and interest that preceded my research and that which developed during its completion, which I could never have foreseen.

Anthropological Theory and the Moral Dimensions of Education

Before engaging in anthropological literature, my experience of schooling had led me to see an unfair competition. Initially, I had intended to look for inequalities: the causes of why some individuals do better than others; those related to class, race, age, or whatever. I turned to 'practice theorists' such as Pierre Bourdieu (1977, 1980). Taking influence from Max Weber, his model of cultural reproduction and social practice takes life to be a competition or a game; it focuses attention towards its ends, on winners and losers, rather than its means (Lambek 2010a: 21). His work enables analysis of how schools do or don't do what Bourdieu says that they do; where 'it' is structure and reproduce economic and social inequality. Schooling is visible through the lens of its meritocratic aspirations: showing how winners and losers are the products of racialised, gendered, physical, linguistic, cultural, or whatever kinds of capital and expectations. In short, it leads to analysis of competition—its fairness and practices—but not to considerations of the schooling system in terms of something other than its competitive logic and legitimating practices.

Sharlene Swartz draws upon this field of scholarship, when emphasising the need for more research regarding moral education in sub-Saharan Africa. Swartz considers the morality of young men and women in Cape Town and their social, economic, historical, and political contexts and influences. She offers an account of groups of 'moral persons', such as *skollies* and *ikasi boys*.[6] Having laid this foundation, Swartz (2009: 147–8, 2010a) adapts Bourdieu's (1986) notion of *Forms of Capital* to suggest that being moral is, in the final instance, reducible to economic capital, or "educational, career, and financial success". The foundations or contexts of this particular notion of 'the good life' are not explored, nor does she question the moral basis of a society wherein her notion of moral capital might make sense. Moreover, Swartz (2010a: 315) highlights what we could call a form of 'ethical freedom' when stating: "most seemed to lack the resources to act on their beliefs". She is less keen to examine her interlocutors' freedoms to determine and imagine these beliefs. Instead, it is taken as given that there is an identifiable and historically constituted notion of 'the good' with which the young people can, or cannot, identify and act in accordance with.

Collaborators' 'free lists' and 'mind maps' are analysed with reference to Lawrence Kohlberg's (e.g. 1981, 1984) work; a psychologist who, problematically for anthropologists (Zigon 2008: 102–105), maintains that there is a universal and ahistorical arrangement of moral thought, which can be measured as individuals' levels of 'moral development'.[7] Implicit notions of advancement, which underpin these assertions, can also be found in Swartz's linear interpretation of the temporal nature of moral development on a social level. She (2009: 53–61) maintains that there are "traditional", "modern", and "post-modern" moral codes, such that her young interlocutors are adjudged to have "conventional" and "contested" moralities. Therefore, although she (2011: 55) considers her subjective positioning and informs us, "I had to be careful to distinguish between my own values and those young people revealed", in my view, her analysis doesn't take the epistemological possibilities of this commitment far enough.[8]

When I began to question the linkage between *personalised* ambitions and memories and *shared* culture, history, and surroundings, I found that practice theorists' ahistorical conception of agency did not allow for considerations of how values and actions depend on both sociocultural circumstances and personal interpretations (i.e. individualised processes of thought). Further, when I also began to question conceptualisations of the individualised agent, these practice theories, which are only valid according to this very notion, were no longer useful (Laidlaw 2010). Nor did they allow for a consideration of how recognition of agency is always a (moral) judgement (Durham 2008; Desjarlais 1997). Nor did they encourage accounts of how actors might be concerned with actively inhabiting, rather than resisting, prevailing sociocultural contexts (Laidlaw 2010). If we value something other than winning the game, or can understand that others might, such critique becomes necessary. It opens the door to a consideration of how success—or joy, pleasure, desirability, happiness, doing good, being moral, and so on—might mean something other than capital; that is, it might mean different things to different people.

To move away from particular conceptualisations of agency and towards interlocutors' judgements of normality and desirability, I turned to a field of scholarship variably defined as the anthropology of morality or the anthropology of ethics. Authors have productively shown how the insights of moral philosophers, such as Michel Foucault, Bernard Williams, and Aristotle, among others, can be usefully employed and built upon when attempting to understand a "concrete sense" of "particular ethical [lives]" (Zigon and Throop 2014: 2). This literature encouraged me to see how *autopoiesis*, or the creation of the self, depends on one's ongoing engagements *with* others throughout a lifetime. In this vein, I understand education to mean all those experiences that inform the nature of ongoing, lifelong processes of 'becoming', which are always incomplete projects. Crucially, however, anthropologists of education (e.g. Pollock and Levinson 2011; Wolcott 2011) have suggested that related literature has rarely considered lifelong processes of education. To my mind, the theories of anthropologists more directly concerned with morality and ethics, rather than systems of education, provide incredibly useful ways of addressing this oversight. Yet, despite this claim, I am aware of only a small number of articles and book chapters that marry such theorisations with the topic of schooling/education, and none of these consider the moral dimensions of education in Africa.[9]

In particular, I use the work of Jarrett Zigon (2008: 42–43, emphasis in original), who has constructed a useful theoretical framework for studying how humans "*consciously* work on themselves so as to make themselves into morally appropriate persons". This mode of thinking, which builds on the work of Foucault, among others, is a vision of "ethical practice" distinct from "any ethics that would define itself as an abstract normative code or customary conduct" (Bernauer and Mahon 2006: 152). However, unlike Foucault, whose notion of ethics hinged upon efforts towards self-mastery or authenticity, for Zigon (2008: 18, emphasis added), ethics "necessitates a kind of working on the self so that one can return to the unreflective and unreflexive *comfort* of the embodied moral habitus or the unquestioned moral discourse". Individuals draw upon "multifarious aspects of the three aspects of morality… to *inform*" their responses to and invocations of ethical freedoms (Zigon 2010: 9; see Foucault 1997: 291). Zigon (e.g. 2006, 2009a) links such processes of self-making to personalised experiences of hope.[10] For him (2006: 72), the notion of hope does not concern a desire for a perfect or accomplished life, but the ongoing struggle for a better, sane, normal, or bearable life, both for oneself and for others, particularly those cared for.

Having returned from South Africa to write about my experiences there, I was struck by the applicability of Zigon's work to my own. Zigon (2011) examines a rehabilitation centre for intravenous drug users with HIV, run by an NGO with close ties to the Russian Orthodox Church. Although this research context is clearly not identical to my own, both Zigon and I keenly examine the relationship between particular processes of moralised pedagogy and efforts of self-formation or, more accurately, self-transformation. Like Ngomso, the institution at the heart of his ethnography is concerned with 'assisting the marginalised', and with their treatment and containment. A similar institutional orientation and analytical approach are evident in the work of Robert Desjarlais, which I have also found highly instructive.[11] Desjarlais (1997) offers an ethnography of a homeless shelter in Boston; another institution concerned with 'the marginal' and their treatment/containment. His approach also affords primary importance to interlocutors' experiences, perceptions, and subjective realities. We learn that they are constantly struggling to locate a sense of safety, comfort, peacefulness, and normality (also see Zigon 2014). This struggle is made more difficult as others deem them to threaten these very same societal experiences: they are adjudged to be outsiders—troublesome, dirty, discomforting, dangerous, noisy, and abnormal. With phenomenal phenomenological detail, we learn intricate details about the lives of particular characters and come to understand how these lives are constituted through interplay with "political, economic, biological, and cultural forces" beyond their control (Desjarlais 1997: 25).

In the ethnographies of Desjarlais and Zigon, we find institutions that revolve around the contestation of judgements of normalcy and morality;

and accounts of people attempting to change themselves to be 'other kinds of people', and we learn about those keen to 'rehabilitate' them to these ends. What is fascinating in each account is the variability and contested nature of ideas of what is good, right, desirable, or normal. When revisiting my own ethnographic data, Zigon's work most helpfully enabled me to think through distinctions and relationships between various conventions and conceptions of human well-being, or what he terms *discursive morality*, and individualised moral dispositions, or what he terms *embodied morality*.[12] What he (2008: 17–18, emphasis added) calls "discursive morality" is the combination of "those *public* and *institutionally* articulated discourses, such as those of an organized religion or State structures, of what is considered, by the speaker of this discourse, as right, good, appropriate, and expected".[13] According to Zigon (2008: 19), discursive morality can be thought of as "a socio-historic-cultural range of possibilities" for how one can 'be moral'. These possibilities are acknowledged and legitimated during, and as a consequence of intersubjective interactions and engagements, including those that are most regularly associated with education (e.g. parent to child instruction).

What makes such processes analytically interesting is the fact that different parties frequently disagree about the validity of different discourses. Indeed, having spent time working in various education-oriented institutions before first arriving in South Africa, I already knew that individuals and groups, such as parents, teachers, or mentors, regularly articulate conflicting ideas about how to live a moral life when attempting to educate or direct those under their care. In the anthropological literature, this dynamic has most frequently been cast as a conflict between knowledge or culture learnt at school, and that acquired at home.[14] In African contexts, such contestation has most often been analysed using frameworks that draw a distinction between two oppositional cultures: 'traditional African' (home) and 'modern Western/European' (school).[15] For example, writing about South Africa, Bronisław Malinowski (1943: 649) was concerned that "European education has alienated him [the young African of today] from native traditions and imbued him with the values and expectations of European culture".[16] Like those scholars who followed his attempt to understand processes of cultural change in South Africa (e.g. Gluckman 1958; Mayer 1961, 1980; Wilson 1969, 1971), Malinowski recognised how integral schools were to processes of cultural and social change.[17]

Having worked and conducted research in a boarding school in Uganda, Musgrove (1952) responded to Malinowski's argument. He reported that students encountered a "new Western [culture]" and "an orderly pattern of daily life" that were different to the "old indigenous cultures" and "concrete situations of their home lives" (ibid: 240–8). Musgrove (1952: 244–5, emphasis added) saw schools as "fields of conflict" that offer "the means for fashioning *an* ideal type of self". Similarly, Simpson (2003: 83–8) examined the decisions learners made about their futures when responding to the educative efforts of mission teachers in Zambia. In her study of education in Tanzania, Stambach (2000: 152) uses the phrase "the promise of schooling" when similarly analysing how her interlocutors judged the value and appeal of school-based educations. In these studies, the moral qualities of education are under discussion, even when the concept of morality is not employed explicitly, as the authors are concerned with understanding the relationship between educational experiences and processes of self-fashioning.

For Zigon (2007, 2010), *moral breakdowns* are the most formative moments of social experience, including those that are recognisable as educative. Zigon relates his theorisation of moral breakdowns, drawn most explicitly from Heidegger's notion of 'the breakdown', to Michel Foucault's concept of *problematisation*. In his effort to offer "a history of thought", Foucault (cited in Rabinow 1997: XXXVI) was seeking "to define the conditions in which human beings 'problematize' what they are, what they do, and the world in which they live". With acknowledged debt to Foucault, Zigon (2010: 8–9) suggests humans become ethical during existential moments that comprise "a lifelong process of adjusting and readjusting to the breakdowns of social and moral life". During such breakdowns, the 'right thing to do' is unclear or challenged in such a way that responses require moral judgements (also see Lambek 2010b), often encountered as dilemmas (Zigon 2008: 18). It was during such moments that the embodied moralities of my interlocutors and their deliberations were most evident, and, for this reason, I continually return to this theoretical notion.

Despite the importance of such a focus, however, talk of judgements and dilemmas evokes a particular kind of engagement with the future, a sense of *immediate* potentialities, which are thought *possible*, or even likely. However, positive experiences can also result in considerations of futurity, and individuals can also conceptualise far-reaching temporalities and impossible potentialities. I can close my eyes and attempt to understand what it would be like to wake up tomorrow morning as a goldfish, swimming in a tank, for example. The existence of this ability is perhaps most visible in the creative play of children. However, it is also integral to processes of learning and exploration that extend into adulthood.[18] I have found that the notion of the *ethical imagination*, which again builds on Foucault's philosophy, accounts for such processes (see Bernauer and Mahon 2006; Moore 2011).

Conceptually, the ethical imagination enables one to consider how hopes, desires, dreams, memories, traumas, and emotions are related to personal and shared (i.e. social, economic, and political) histories and circumstances. As Henrietta Moore (ibid: 16) makes clear, ethical imaginations are, to some extent, imposed, and proposed by others, but not absolutely determined by them. Because it allows for this sense of freedom, I employ the concept to analyse how my interlocutors' past experiences and present circumstances influenced the ways they imagined and hoped to influence their futures and those of others. In doing so, I will make a case for inquiry that directly links analysis of morality and ethics with considerations of temporality and futurity. Arjun Appadurai (2013: 5) has recently called for "a full-scale engagement with the variety of ideas of human welfare and of the good life that surround us today and that survive in our archives of the past" when pressing for "a robust anthropology of the future". For those interested in such lines of inquiry, I am hopeful that this study will go some way to constituting such an engagement and building a relevant body of work.

Fieldwork Locations and Locating Interlocutors

I lived in Grahamstown for ten months during 2011 and returned towards the end of 2013 for a further two months (see Fig. 1.1). The first four months of 2011 were spent adjusting to my new surroundings, writing a research proposal and interacting with university students and staff, and setting up my relationships with those at Ngomso. I then spent the final six months of 2011 and my shorter stay in 2013, full-time, in and around Ngomso; developing relationships with staff, volunteers, donors, learners, past pupils, parents, psychologists, police officers, social workers, and individuals at the Department of Education, who all became my interlocutors. Soon after my first day at Ngomso, and following my experience of working in schools in London, I knew I would also have to operate outside of the school to better understand these parties. Additionally, it was essential that I engage with individuals who did not spend time at the school, such as past pupils and staff at the Shelter. Having done so, I can attend to

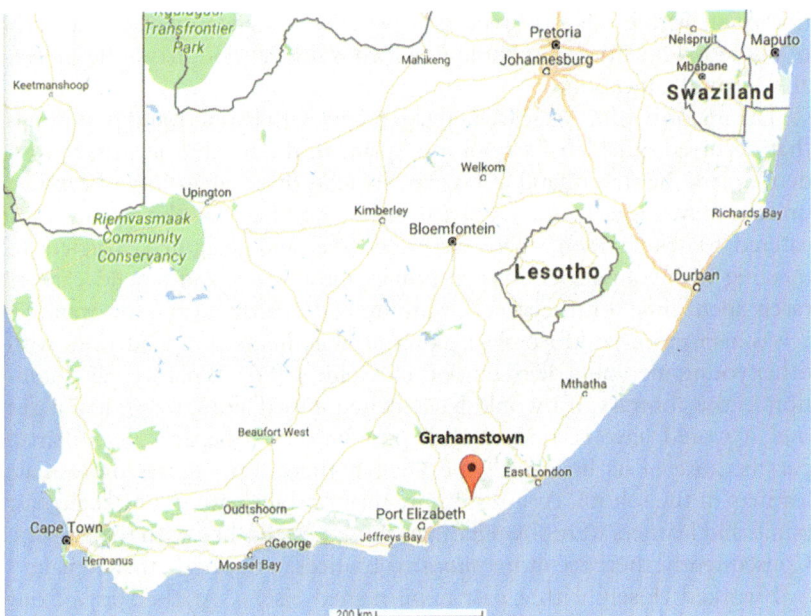

Fig. 1.1 Map of Grahamstown, South Africa (Google Maps)

questions about how individuals encounter conflicting forms of education in various and varying places, and among and between different people and groups of people. Further, with knowledge of moral domains and behaviours outside of school, I can more productively explain events that occurred in the school. Furthermore, the study pays attention to 'past pupils', young men and women who were no longer at Ngomso but shaping their futures as 'young adults'. In my opinion, this is one of its most significant qualities.

This research method is different from those utilised by the majority of anthropological researchers *explicitly* concerned with education, in that the scope of my empirical data extends beyond the 'four walls' of schools.[19] More specifically, Stambach (2000: 12, emphasis in original) recently argued that "there has been no extended [anthropological] look at the ways in which what goes on *inside* schools [in Africa] is related to what goes on in the greater outside". Indeed, if her study of schooling in Tanzania was the first, my comparable work has a limited company.[20] To be clear, then, this book does not solely focus on practices of moral pedagogy that occur within schools. Instead, it perhaps best encountered as a study of the moral qualities of schooling, which is understood, from the outset, as *a* form of education.

The majority of my research engagements with learners and past pupils that occurred outside of school took place in the Shelter, in private residences, 'on the street', and in taverns. In all of these environments, it was, quite simply, easier to interact with males. Additionally, the Shelter only catered to young men; there were less (real and imagined) barriers to meeting with young men in their homes and taverns; and female learners rarely spent time 'on the street', washing and guarding cars, for example. I was also more comfortable making arrangements to spend time with other young men outside of school (cf. Golde 1986). Whatever the intention to the contrary, if I would have invited myself along to a 'girls' night out' it would have carried certain connotations. Moreover, in no small part because of its links with the Shelter, there were always more male learners in the school. As a result, my relationships with young male past pupils and learners were stronger than those I established with the females. Consequently, there are more *young* male voices in this book than female.[21]

I worked closely with a past pupil named Siseko. At the start of our relationship, I asked him if he would like to be "my research assistant" while he soon took to calling me "big brother". In our relationship, he was influential in my coming to know other past pupils, and to a lot of the time I spent in the township.[22] I also paid him a mutually satisfactory fee to complete 20 qualitative surveys comprising 12 open-ended questions with households in the township. He took care to "ask different kinds of people" and we worked collaboratively, meeting to discuss his findings and compose the questions. I also discussed many analytical ideas with him. Siseko was keen to conduct anthropology and auto-anthropology. Our collaboration certainly enhanced this work.

The fact that South Africa has 11 official languages influenced all of these exchanges.[23] IsiXhosa was the 'home language' or 'mother tongue' (concepts my interlocutors commonly used) of the majority of my principal interlocutors in South Africa (e.g. learners, past pupils, and staff). However, by the end of my fieldwork, my ability to speak and understand isiXhosa was very limited.[24] Because it was most difficult to converse with younger learners, I tended to establish stronger relationships with older learners and past pupils.[25] Additionally, some interviews lacked linguistic subtleties and were constrained by limited vocabularies, and, although I could usually speak with individuals, I missed out when groups spoke in isiXhosa. Interlocutors regularly translated for me when they felt something was happening that I should understand. My failings could not have been masked so well if they had not accommodated me so generously.

In addition to my research in South Africa, I have also conducted fieldwork in the UK since returning in January 2012, which allowed me to establish relationships with other, influential interlocutors. Most of these individuals volunteer to work on behalf of the UK-registered charity that was set up to provide financial support to the school and that facilitated the visits of (mostly) British volunteers. Such engagements happened 'organically' after I returned home in 2011, keen to gain a fuller picture of the events I had encountered in South Africa. This mode of working enables me to address Erica Bornstein and Peter Redfield's (2008: 39) call for more scholars to examine how "the field of [humanitarian] intervention is conceptualized and marketed". My research also goes some way to addressing questions that they (ibid: 9) raise about how the historically conditioned "dreams" of volunteers and NGO supporters materialise 'on the ground'. With its UK focus, my study complements anthropological studies that have examined Christian-oriented, transatlantic humanitarian and education-oriented projects conceived in the US and enacted in Africa (e.g. Bornstein 2005; Cheney 2007; Stambach 2010).[26] Following their lead and that of Didier Fassin (2011: 485), another key figure in the growing anthropological literature on humanitarianism, I examine "the moral arguments" that humanitarian workers provide "to explain their intervention" and "the moral and ethical blind spots of their activity". Subsequent chapters also analyse "the inevitable ethical debates and contradictions", "unexpected effects", and "ontological inequalities" of such activity (ibid.). As Fassin (2010: 50.20 minutes; 2012) has argued, "humanitarianism has become our ultimate language to speak of the violence and inequality of the world". This prominence brings impetus to the recognition that humanitarian is both a moral and political phenomenon that should not be immune from philosophically attuned inquiry. With this in mind, later chapters are discursively multi-layered and inter-perspectival.

Quite unknowingly, the religious orientation of the Friends of Ngomso also encouraged me to respond to Bornstein and Redfield's (2008: 9) request for scholarship that considers the theological tenets of humanitarianism and the way that religion factors in the lives of interlocutors with whom we conduct research around issues of care, ministration, philanthropy, and charity. Anthropological research conducted in Brazil (Hecht 1998), Guatemala (O'Neill 2015), Ethiopia (Nieuwenhuys 2001),

Uganda (Cheney 2007), and Tanzania (Stambach 2010) has already enabled us to better understand the interrelated nature of (i) internationally constituted forms of state-funded governance; (ii) humanitarian, charitable, and developmental interventions; and (iii) Christian faith, moral codifications, and eschatological imperatives. This work productively challenges any notion of a distinction between the public and private dimensions of development and education, and between State and Church (i.e. claims regarding the secularisation of governance). The related analytical terrain that this book covers is not so well travelled: Spiegel and Becker (2015: 5) have argued that "Relatively little attention is being paid [in contemporary South African anthropology] to fields such as … state formation, and religion and religious movements". More broadly, Stambach (2010) has argued that studies of the international and 'local' dimensions of faith-led, educationally focused, humanitarian interventions in Africa, and their public/private aspects, are both valuable and scarce.

SHARING EXPERIENCES, DEVELOPING UNDERSTANDING

My methodology is rooted in a form of philosophical inquiry that considers quotidian, ordinary, and circumstantial interactions and lived experiences, paying heed to reflections, dilemmas, judgements, and actions and their intricacies, ambiguities, and complexities. With such a focus, I have come to learn that anthropology is "not so much the study *of* people as a way of studying *with* people" while being open to "other possibilities of being" (Ingold, with Lucas 2007: 287, emphasis in original). By oscillating between states of being attuned to interlocutors or myself, I tested and rethought my expectations, transforming my knowledge of the world and the lives with whom I share it (Jackson 2012). Just as I have learnt in this way, my interlocutors have similarly learnt about me, processes which I have explored in more depth elsewhere (Pattenden 2015; also see Crapanzano 2014). As Jackson (1989: 3, emphasis in original) argues, when highlighting the qualities of a *radically empirical* research method, "anthropology involves *reciprocal* activity and *inter*experience". In this methodological orientation, "there is no constant, substantive 'self' which can address constant, substantive 'others' as objects of knowledge". I follow his (ibid: 4) lead when detailing my experiences, defining "the experimental field as one of interactions and intersubjectivity".

Throughout the research process, my attempts to understand my interlocutors' lives have run concurrently with my desire to contemplate my own experiences. During this process, philosophically attuned anthropological theorisations have pragmatically helped me to come to terms with our shared world, and encouraged me to rethink my assumptions and our collective histories and potential, which is why they feature so heavily in my writing. This realisation leads me to agree with Jackson's (1989: 3, emphasis in original) claim that theorisations are "not mirror images of social reality so much as defences we build against the unsystematic, unstructured nature of our *experiences* within that reality". In this view, objectivity is most likely "a magical token" that bolsters "our sense of self in disorientating situations", rather than "a scientific method for describing those situations as they really are" (ibid.). This line of argument has implications for how different voices—that is, interpretations of the world—are acknowledged and given credence and helps to explain why positivistic knowledge claims do not accompany my work. Instead, this ethnography should be read as *an* interpretation of the situation and lives under discussion.

In line with this orientation, this first person, discursive style of writing continues throughout. If engagements with theorisations, academic or otherwise, are modes by which humans attempt to make sense of their shared world and the experiences they create and encounter within it, which I believe is the case, I can be no different in this regard. By describing some of my personal and professional experiences, which both preceded and unfolded during the research project, I not only intend to inform the reader why I came to recognise the pragmatic value of particular academic works and orientations, but to also argue that personal narratives and accounts of the emotional aspects of fieldwork should not be excluded from anthropological texts in the interests of intellectualised detachment or argumentative surety.[27] Analysis and personal narratives, as relating to both my life and those of my interlocutors, are intertwined throughout as a means of positing that ethnographic research is always constituted during intersubjective engagements and never the outcome of distinctively objective, detached practices of intellectualisation. There is, therefore, an implicit argument that runs through the book that contends that attempts to offer overly intellectualised—that is, definitive, neat, and cohesive—analysis inadvertently separate readers from important layers of meaning and modes of understanding.

A Brief, School-Focused History of the Eastern Cape

As I intend to consider the historically constituted nature of the embodied and discursive moralities I encountered during my fieldwork in later chapters, the next sections highlight relevant political, social, economic, and cultural contestation that preceded my experiences in South Africa. Mirroring and informing the analytical foci of subsequent chapters, the historical analysis focuses on these parties: Xhosas, Anglican Christian missionaries, and South African governments.

In 1795, British military personnel were first sent to secure the Cape of Good Hope, a strategic location on the southernmost tip of Africa, by defeating the incumbent Dutch. On January 4, 1806, several days prior to the Battle of Blaauwberg, which drew Dutch rule to a conclusion, Mary's great-great-great-grandfather, a Captain in the 59th Regiment of Foot, arrived at what was to become Cape Town.[28] Jacob Glen Cuyler, who became General Cuyler, went on to play a crucial role in Britain's activities on the eastern borders of the new colony. It was here, in this role, that he met with the Xhosa.[29] At this moment, Xhosa territories were being expanded, and the Xhosa were generally in a state of confidence about such processes (Peires 1982).[30] However, the Xhosa had already fought three notable wars with those of European descent. Over the next 73 years, they fought six more wars, during what is known as *The Xhosa Wars*, *The Cape Frontier Wars*, or *Africa's 100 Years War*, perhaps the longest conflict in African colonial history (Peires 1982). The fourth war began in 1811 when Lieutenant Colonel John Graham set out to expel the Xhosa from the area just west of the Great Fish River, known as the Zuurveld (see Fig. 1.2).[31] Among these hills, Graham established the city that still bears his name. The period was also marked by the arrival of the British Settlers to the same general area from 1820. Cuyler, Mary's forefather, had persuaded British parliament to fund their settlement. After being allocated farming land that had been under Xhosa rule, they were tasked with helping to maintain stability in the areas that bordered 'Xhosaland' (Lester et al. 2000). During this period, being intent on accelerating their submission, the British practised total war against the Xhosa, decimating crops and livelihoods (Peires 1979). In doing so, they did not spare women and children as the Xhosa did until the last engagements. The Xhosa were pushed back into a smaller strip of land, which reduced grazing space for their most valued asset, cattle, before the Ninth Frontier War of 1887–1879 brought an end to the long and bloody tussle.

Fig. 1.2 The Cape Colony, 1878 (Source: Molteno 1900: 408–9)

Over this same period of time, missionaries were busy introducing the first 'western schools' in the vicinity.[32] More specifically, the proselytising activities of the Church of England were most firmly established when Dr Robert Gray, the first Bishop of Cape Town, arrived in 1848 (Church Chronicle 1880, cited in Anonymous). Anglican missions then received "an unexpected impulse" from the arrival of Sir George Grey, Governor and High Commissioner of the Cape Colony, in 1854 (Anonymous). Grey had already overseen the expansion of churches, schools, public roads, and courts in Australia and New Zealand (Lester 2001; W. Morrell 1969). In the Cape, his task was to "smash the organic structure of Xhosa society and integrate its remnants into the brave new colonial world" (Peires 1989: 54); or, as he (cited in Lewis 1999: 264–265) put it: "[W]e should try to make them [the 'Africans'] part of ourselves, with a common faith and common interest, useful servants, consumers of our goods, contributors to our revenue". For such an endeavour, education was perceived to be cheaper than war (Hlatshwayo 2000: 31).

Between the mid-1850s and early 1950s, state-aided mission schools were the most prominent form of schooling for the Xhosa (Fiske and Ladd 2004: 41). During this time, the country's school system unevenly distributed resources and opportunity (Hyslop 2001; Morris and Hyslop 1991; Dube 1985; Horrell 1963, 1964), and was "sprawling and inchoate" (Kross 2002: 54). There were other notable segregationist practices in the locality too.[33] However, the apartheid policies of the Afrikaner National Party, which returned to power in 1948, were far more divisive than anything that had gone before. Werner Eiselen, an anthropologist at the University of Stellenbosch, supplied their intellectual foundations (Kross 2002).[34] He argued that 'blacks' were "in a state of decline, having been corrupted through their contact with 'white' society", and tried to "demonstrate that integration [between 'African' and 'European' cultures] would bring about anarchy with deleterious consequences" (ibid: 57, 60).[35] Apartheid, or 'total separation', was held to be the solution.

Creating unprecedented levels of educational inequality, the blueprint for state-funded education during apartheid was enshrined when Parliament passed the Bantu Education Act in 1953 (Lewis and Steyn 2003). Although the broader public, especially those racially and politically classed as Black, were (understandably) critical and reacted with strong condemnation (Rakometsi 2008: 81–85), the Nationalists soon took control of public schools (Christie and Collins 1982; Fiske and Ladd 2004: 42; Kruss 2002). Schools for Blacks received comparatively little funding (Crouch 1996; Marais 1995); teacher training, infrastructure and learning resources were limited, and a separate syllabus was mandated (Bloch 2009; Christie and Collins 1982). Authoritarian teaching was encouraged, and critical thinking discouraged (Fiske and Ladd 2004). Further, there remained few secondary schools, and schooling was most often limited to the first four years, which further reduced skill acquisition and employment mobility (Hyslop 1988).

Bantu Education was thus a pivotal aspect of attempts to secure social, economic, and political privileges for the Whites, which also involved housing, health, and recreation departments (Fiske and Ladd 2004: 24). Schools became "part of a broader network of control agencies, including the pass office and police station" (Asmal and James, cited in Fiske and Ladd 2004: 41). Education became "part of the array of apartheid laws" (Bloch 2009: 44). The Group Areas Act, first promulgated in 1950, meant Grahamstown was now legally divided into four Areas, and movement and property ownership were controlled according to the same political categorisations: White, Black, Coloured, and Indian.[36] Schools that catered for each of these Groups were located in the relevant Areas.

Many Black parents and learners faced the unenviable dilemma of inferior schooling or none at all; a situation that understandably gave rise to variable levels of enthusiasm for school-based educations. Among the Xhosa, this dynamic was not new. Conflicting judgements about the appeal of schooling were evident between the mid-nineteenth and twentieth centuries when the 'School Xhosa' and 'Red Xhosa' classification structure emerged as mission schools and churches first proliferated in Xhosa territory (Peires 1982: 164; also see Hunter 1936: 174–179). Relatedly, when conducting research in East London and surrounding areas, 100 miles east of Grahamstown, in the late 1950s, Philip Mayer and his wife, Iona, observed distinct contrasts between 'red people' and 'school people'.[37] Mayer (1961: 4) suggests that the "[Red people] (from the smearing of their clothes and bodies with red ochre) are the traditionalist Xhosa, the conservatives who still stand by the indigenous way of life, including the pagan Xhosa religion". In contrast, he (1961: 4) argues that the 'School Xhosa' were "products of the mission and the school, [who held] up Christianity, literacy and other Western ways as ideals". For these individuals, money and individualised salaried positions, or, at least, wage labour, replaced cattle as signifiers of success and morality (see Peires 1982). Relatedly, Mayer also (ibid: 254, 22) depicts an "official Red morality" and an "official School Xhosa morality".[38] To my mind, he was concerned with analysing personalised navigations and embodiments of such sociocultural-historically constituted moral discourses.[39] While I have no intention of employing the Red/School dichotomy to essentialise the lives of any of my interlocutors, it does provide a useful starting point for my ethnographic analysis.

As the divisive policies of apartheid became more deeply entrenched, the 'Red disposition' became a form of ideological, and to a certain extent actioned and actionable, resistance (Spiegel and McAllister 1991: 2; see Mayer 1961: 63).[40] 'Reds' attempted to live 'outside of the state', to some extent, with actions that were (problematically) facilitated by 'the homelands'. Conversely, Mayer suggests that the School Xhosa struggled against the apartheid government by engaging with its institutions. Their "political desires" (Mayer 1961: 65) or, to quote one of Mayer's (1961: 34) interlocutors, their "programme for the future", involved efforts to reconfigure government policies, including those relating to education, so that they might deliver opportunity rather than limitation.

More broadly, during apartheid, schools served as pivotal sites of political resistance; facilitating emerging imaginations of political freedom and ultimately helping to foster the independence movement (Fiske and Ladd 2004; Hyslop 2001; Ngwane 2001). Initially, counter-inscription was comparatively mundane and symbolic.[41] Later, the policies and curriculum of Bantu Education were transformed and disrupted as teachers and students engaged in alternative educative practices (Hammett 2008: 344; Soudien 2002).[42] Resistance to Bantu Education dramatically came to a head during the Soweto Uprising of 1976.[43] Protest and class boycotts continued into the 1980s, which were led "under the slogans 'liberation before education', 'liberation now, education later' and 'the year of no schooling'" (Prew 2011: 136). A vast number of young people disengaged with schools, in events that led to claims they comprised a 'lost generation' (Abdi 2002: 139).[44]

During this period, Mary "became politicised" while studying at Stellenbosch University, as she told me one afternoon in 2013.[45] Politicisation, as Mary understood it, meant acting politically, on behalf of others. She was a member of student groups actively opposed to the apartheid government and became involved with churches in the township, illegally spending time with their congregations.[46] These churches organised camps for Blacks, Coloureds, and Whites to meet, countering the separatist efforts of the government. When she married, her husband, a minister (from whom she divorced many years later) had the option of moving to the UK, facilitated by his British passport. They "debated the possibility at length, but choose to stay in South Africa", Mary said. "Our work was here." Committed to God and their work, her husband was approached by Special Branch about becoming a spy within the Anglican Church. He turned the offer down. Having shown where their political allegiances lay, the newly married couple were regularly under surveillance: government cars sat outside their home and tailed them as they went about their daily business. As she recounted the story, Mary said, "I was scared at times". Ultimately, such actions, and anti-apartheid resistance more broadly, won through.

As apartheid neared its end, the numbers of young people attending government schools for Blacks drastically increased (Fiske and Ladd 2004). Among the Xhosa, schooling, rather than 'Red isolation', increasingly became integral to hopes of future prosperity. In urban areas, in particular, a rise in labour unionism and the proliferation of social networks unrelated to those found in the 'Homelands' further dissolved Red/School distinctions (Bank 2011). More broadly, in the early 1990s, with the country's first fully democratic election on the horizon, enthusiasm for schooling had become central to hopes of a transition to an egalitarian South Africa.

NGOMSO AND THE POST-APARTHEID TRANSITION

In 1991, the first Ngomso School was founded in East London by a charitable trust with a strong Christian emphasis.[47] The school was incorporated into a "hostel for street children" based in a "traditional mission station dating back from the eighteen hundreds in a big, rural, black owned area".[48] At this time, the term 'street children' had widespread salience, occupying a prominent place in the "social problems marketplace" (Bordonaro 2012; Hecht 1998: 3). Related institutional and public discourses concerning the 'problem with street children' provided ready-made justifications for the removal of young men and women from 'East London's streets' so that they could be housed, educated, and fed elsewhere. However, as the school and hostel were geographically removed from the city centre, many residents did not stay long before returning. As a result, a non-residential school was established in East London in the grounds of a Church. This endeavour was solely funded by charitable support initially because it did not comply with Bantu Education policies. A priest, who represented the charity, soon asked Mary if she would establish the school as its principal.

As the apartheid regime was ending in 1993, the school in East London was registered with the South African government. This process was part of the dismantling of the Bantu Education system and the new government's decision to fund schools that had previously 'sat outside' its remit. Soon after, in 1994, the year of South Africa's first democratic election, Mandela's government (ANC, cited in Fiske and Ladd 2004: 61) were hopeful that they might overturn the educational injustices of the past:

> The journey we are embarking on is long and hard. The educational problems of our country run deep, and there are no easy or quick-fix solutions. But this framework [for negotiated settlement] maps a way toward the transformation and reconstruction of the education and training system and the opening of access to lifelong learning for all South Africans. We need to walk this path together in confidence and hope.

During this same year, the UK began to send bilateral aid to South Africa, pledging $421.6 m between 1995 and 1999 (by 1998 they had released only 30.4% of this figure).[49] With the majority of funds being earmarked for democracy and governance (34.8%), agriculture and rural development (30.6%), and education (19.6%), the arrangement illustrates the UK government's keenness to influence the post-apartheid transition in ways that mirror the key dimensions of the colonial project. Despite the historical significance of such arrangements, however, during this period (i.e. the early 1990s), aid represented less than 1% of the South African government's expenditure (Glennie and Herbert 2013).

Almost immediately after the election, two more satellite Ngomso schools were established in Grahamstown and Aliwal North, an Eastern Cape town 400 km due north. The school in Grahamstown was founded when the aforementioned Christian charity donated two shipping containers to a residential shelter (the Shelter) that catered to young men between the ages of 5 and 18. The Shelter had been founded by a group of theological students who wanted "a safe place for street children" and saw a "need to provide these children with food".[50] Residents were offered beds, shelter, and food on a full-time, live-in basis. After partnering with Ngomso, residents also attended the on-site school.

In 1996, the three Ngomso schools were jointly registered as a special (needs) school by the newly formed Eastern Cape Department of Education (ECDoE), with the intention that the sites would operate under the same managerial and funding arrangements.[51] According to documentation, this joint registration was of a public special school that would cater for "Extrinsically Disabled Learners", whose 'learning disabilities' were "not caused by physical or mental disability" but by "extrinsic circumstances".[52] This unprecedented arrangement meant that the schools were distinguished from 'mainstream' schools. At the same time, the South African Schools Act, 84 of 1996, was passed. It aimed to deliver a schooling system capable of redressing "past injustices in educational provision" by providing "an education of progressively high quality for all learners" (DoE 1996 (preamble)). New policies ushered in hopes of equality, democracy, and universal access (Fiske and Ladd 2004; Chisholm 2002; de Clercq 1997).

By 1997, Ngomso in Grahamstown was contributing to such efforts by offering a school education, up to grade seven, to approximately 25 learners living at the Shelter, where either grade nine or age 15 (whichever comes first) is the final year of compulsory schooling. In 2001, Mary had the opportunity to rent several buildings from Transnet, a government-owned (i.e. parastatal) company. Subsequently, learners who did not stay at the Shelter were able to register, and enrolments grew. The school remained on this site during my fieldwork.

In 2003, the ECDoE registered each of the satellite schools as a stand-alone public special school, and assigned distinct financial budgets and staffing provisions. Having been principal of all three schools, which necessitated a round trip of close to 1000 km, Mary decided to focus her efforts in Grahamstown. Subsequently, the link between this school and the one in East London did not remain healthy. Ties with the school in Aliwal North remained slightly tighter; however, resources and managerial responsibilities were separated. Therefore, other than the history depicted here, Ngomso School in Grahamstown (subsequently referred to as Ngomso) is considered separately from its namesakes. Moreover, during my research, there was no evidence of a relationship with the charity that had formed the first school in East London.

During the weeks that followed my arrival in South Africa in 2011, I was frequently informed that the widespread hopes for a system of schooling that would offer unprecedented equality and accessibility that were prominent in the early 1990s had not materialised.[53] Indeed, the national and, most significantly, Eastern Cape schooling systems were, and have continued to be depicted as being in a general 'state of crisis'.[54] One local newspaper ran a series about the Eastern Cape entitled "schools of shame".[55] Moreover, I encountered anxiety about 'out of school learners' and claims that some parents and their offspring no longer valued school educations (also see Jansen 2012).

Having taken delivery of my new library card, I read *The Toxic Mix: What's Wrong with South Africa's Schools and How to Fix It*, written by Graeme Bloch. It (2009: 17, 58) highlights the country's poor results in internationally standardised examinations, suggests the situation was reinforcing "the social and economic marginalisation of the poor and vulnerable", and argues that "Schooling in South Africa is a national disaster". Academics have considered the state of South Africa's schooling system in relation to levels of poverty and ill-health (Fleisch 2008; Wadesango et al. 2011), unrealised human rights (Spreen and Vally 2006), debates over language of instruction (de Wet 2002; Heugh 1999; Posel and Casale 2011; Webb 1999), and the influence of socio-economic inequalities (Chisholm 2011). Scholars have also considered the 'legacies' of apartheid (e.g. Hendricks 2011), which can be understood alongside older and more recent analyses of 'race' (Hammett 2008; Rakometsi 2008; Christie 1985, 2006; Kallaway 2002; Hyslop 1988, 2001; Glaser 1998; Bennell and Monyokolo 1994; Morris and Hyslop 1991; Christie and Collins 1982; Horrell 1964). In their analysis, the problem lies not with the existence of systems of schooling per se, but the extent to which they unevenly deliver opportunity and prosperity. In this view, schools are interpreted as 'right', and this 'right' is often conflated with the realisation of 'rights' (see Comaroff and Comaroff 1997: 9). In actively interrogating such ideas, this study departs from this work.

During my fieldwork, Ngomso offered primary level schooling—that is, grades one through seven—to approximately 120 registered learners; however, between 20 and 80 attended on any one day. The school offered a programme of Accelerated Bridging Education. Individuals could progress to the next grade at the end of each quarterly term, following an examination; rather than moving between grades at the end of each academic year, which was common practice in mainstream schools. The idea was that Ngomso could bridge transfers to mainstream high schools, following a learner's completion of grade seven. Mary assured me that she had pioneered this system over the past 20 years and that, in South Africa at least, it was unique to Ngomso. Also rather uniquely for a school that offered primary level curricula, learners could enrol up to the age of 19 (i.e. many were 'age-inappropriate') and classrooms were organised by grades, not by age.[56] Each new learner was admitted to a grade according to their adjudged 'academic ability', as measured by "baseline tests" that Mary had developed. For example, a 15-year-old adjudged to be learning at grade three level would have been admitted to that grade, potentially to work alongside a nine-year-old adjudged to be working at this same level. Despite this arrangement, in general, average age did increase through the grades. As a special school, annual funding from the ECDoE was weighed at a ratio of five learners to one: with 118 registered learners in October 2011, for example, there was funding for 18 educators, the same as a mainstream school with 590 learners.

Except for two learners whose mother tongue was Afrikaans, who lived in the locality that had been designated 'Coloured' during apartheid, and a young man who previously lived in the north of the country, all learners appeared to identify with a Xhosa heritage and spoke isiXhosa as their first language. Excluding only two cases that I was aware of, all had grown up in Grahamstown or the surrounding area. Most had been to other schools at some stage before arriving at Ngomso, although a handful had joined at the age of six or seven before doing so. They varied in age (six to nineteen), sex (approximately 75% male), and living arrangements. Approximately one-quarter lived at the Shelter and were known as the "shelter boys", including when speaking about themselves.

Ngomso was a classic, bureaucratic state organisation, with supervisorial hierarchies and chains of command (Weber 1978: 957). As previously stated, Mary had founded the school and was principal during my fieldwork in 2011. She retired in 2013, and Joyce, previously Mary's deputy, became the principal. She had joined the school approximately four years earlier, having been deputy principal of a larger mainstream school in the township. Two head of department posts were responsible for grades one to four and five to seven. Then there were ten subject heads: English, Xhosa, art, and maths for grades one to four, and these subjects plus science and life orientation for grades five to seven. Additionally, there were several educators (the term my interlocutors used in preference to 'teachers') without managerial responsibilities. In total, there were 18 members of "teaching staff" (the terminology used) across these posts, all funded by the ECDoE. Three were men and the rest, including all managerial positions, were women.

There were also "non-teaching staff". The ECDoE funded three "teacher aides" whose duties related more to classroom behaviour rather than assisting educators with lesson content. Additionally, there were two security guards, an LSA (Mrs Noni, described as a "pastoral carer"), a driver (for the bus and minibus), two cleaners, and a finance officer. The teacher aides, security guards, and full-time LSA posts were directly attributable to Ngomso's special school status. As mentioned in the first section of this chapter, the school's partner charity in the UK funded further resources, including full-time "volunteers"—that is, three teacher aides/assistants, a driver, a chef, and an administrative assistant for Mary and Joyce. These individuals were receiving a "stipend" that was less than the wages of those employed directly by the South African government. They also had less holiday, no pension contributions, and fewer training opportunities. There was also a School Governing Body (SGB) that consisted of two parents and two members of staff.

Without notable exception, all members of staff appeared to be Christian, spending each Sunday in church. When I visited the home of Madoda, a security guard, gospel music blasted from the stereo. Framed pictures of Jesus adorned the walls. In the playground one afternoon, I heard a pastor repeatedly singing the word "Amen". It was Madoda's phone. "I like this song", he told me, "it's called Amen; it is praising the Jehovah". When I first rang his mobile, I mistook his gospel song-inspired ringtone as an answerphone recording and hung up. Mr Motsa, the chairman of the SGB, often attended meetings in a cap that read: *I ♥ Jesus*.

Although Mary told me that it was not a determining factor during recruitment processes, Christian faith was integral to the school. However, the staff did not have identical beliefs. An educator named Mrs Zumzi told me: "we are different denominations". She explained that she and Lindiwe, another educator, were Catholics. "The school isn't really a denomination", she continued; "it's Christian." In the past, she said the school had "been closer to the cathedral and Anglican [denominations] because of Mary [and her faith]" and the support that the cathedral gave the school. While one Catholic priest visited during my time at the school, Anglicanism did seem more prominent. Despite these observations, David, who taught art, explained that "Ngomso is not a faith school; public schools cannot be faith schools. It is a Christian school." By "faith schools" he meant those that "teach a different curriculum" and that "are strict with the religion". In contrast, "here [at Ngomso] it is only the prayer, the songs and the Bible readings that are Christian". He put the Christian nature of the school down to the fact that "all teachers here are Christian. It's not that the school itself is a Christian school." In fact, Ngomso was registered as a Christian school with the ECDoE as a consequence of the Christian orientation of its Constitution, as ratified by the SGB. However, it is telling that David didn't need to know this to have an understanding of how Ngomso and Christianity conjoined.

The vast majority of the staff considered themselves to be 'Xhosa', and isiXhosa was the mother tongue of all but two individuals. Only Mary and her administrative assistant Alice, who was also a relative, did not identify with a Xhosa heritage, which was not surprising. While they could both speak isiXhosa, behind English and Afrikaans in terms of fluency, their skin colour was more pale-pinkish-white than a shade of brown. In other words, during apartheid, they were categorised as White, not Black, unlike the rest of the staff. The vast majority of staff had grown up during apartheid, and even the younger ones were born before it ended.

Overview

This book delivers an anthropological consideration of the moral dimensions of education in South Africa, with particular reference to the longstanding relationship between the Eastern Cape Province and the UK. To summarise, I explore four analytical foci: (1) ethical freedoms,

(2) specialness of learners, (3) specialness of Ngomso, and (4) education and self-fashioning. While I hope they will help to guide the reader, it is important to stress that these themes of inquiry will bleed into and inform each other. Certainly, such analytical distinctions were not always apparent during the experiences I shared with my interlocutors, and they did not compartmentalise their lives in this manner.

I introduced foci (2), (3), and (4) earlier in the chapter when discussing my first meeting with Mary. The other analytical focus, 'ethical freedoms', was implicitly introduced when I recalled my experience of the advertising industry and the observation that young men around the world experience the immaterialisation of hope. In later chapters, I examine how 'inherited histories' enable and influence evaluations of potential futures; encouraging individuals to commit themselves to particular projects in the present. I also analyse how inherited political, economic, social, and cultural contexts, and one's relationship to them and relationships with others who relate differently to these shared circumstances, influence the materialisation of such projects. That is, I consider the freedom individuals have to imagine potential futures and to bring them to fruition. This line of inquiry permeates the entire book—I continually shift between temporal scales of investigation when analysing how my interlocutors strived to bring about particular futures for themselves and each other.

Chapter 2 directly considers my interlocutors' experiences of variable ethical freedoms. I highlight divisions that have endured and mutated as South Africa has emerged from apartheid, and consider how these impinge upon ethical freedoms. In particular, the widespread sense of insecurity I encountered in South Africa, which is so integral to subsequent chapters, is addressed. I first examine interlocutors' attempts to evade 'moral decay' and 'corrupting influences' with private schooling. Offering a point of contrast, I analyse how other interlocutors located accountability for 'moral decay' in the increased prominence of human rights discourses, which can limit the freedom parents and communities have to educate their offspring in ways that they see fit (e.g. with corporal punishment). I also argue that the emphasis that the human rights discourse places on the value of liberty can appear misguided in the eyes of those who value hierarchical orderings of generational power. This line of thought illustrates how, in the view of some South Africans, certain aspects of post-apartheid governance have curtailed, rather than extended, certain ethical freedoms. To conclude the chapter, I examine the attempts that other interlocutors made to secure comfort and protection using violence, particularly when access to alternative options was limited. In doing so, I highlight another instance of how enduring economic, spatial, and racial inequalities in South Africa shape the moral dimensions of education in the country.

Chapter 3 brings us more directly to the second analytical focus: productions and contestations of learners' 'specialness'. Its first section focuses upon the judgements that members of staff made about the learners' lives outside of school and their relationships with families/caregivers in particular. I show how the concepts 'extrinsic barriers to learning' and 'street children' gained meaning when the staff considered Ngomso learners to be different from those studying at mainstream schools. Attention then shifts to residents of the township, as I analyse their judgements of Ngomso. In the final two sections, the learners have their say on the matter. I examine their opinions regarding the judgements that others made about their specialness (i.e. abnormality and immorality) and the techniques they employed to transform and evade these judgements. Spinning the discussion back around to the start of the chapter, the final section addresses the question: Why did they attend Ngomso and not some other, mainstream school? In each section, I examine how learners' specialness hinged upon judgements of normality/abnormality and social inclusion/exclusion/marginalisation and consider these judgements in the light of cultural, political, economic, and historical contexts.

Chapter 4 follows straight on by examining how members of staff attempted to address learners' (adjudged) specialness in a bid to include learners in their (i.e. the staff) conceptualisations of a moral society. I explain how and why they attempted to support and guide, or transform, learners with a particular form of moralised education in a bid to enable and encourage them to fashion specific futures for themselves and others. Analytically, this chapter continually revisits the colonial period and draws upon certain tenets of Christian faith to historically and theologically situate the moral qualities of the education that members of staff valued and enacted.

The third analytical focus, Ngomso's institutional specialness, is most directly addressed by Chaps. 5 and 6, which centre on the politics of charity and humanitarianism. Chapter 5 examines how members of staff and The Friends of Ngomso (the partner UK charity) generated funding and support additional to that provided by the South African government. It also highlights the value these parties attached to this financing and the way it was spent. I also analyse how the Ngomso cause was marketed to potential and existing supporters. Questioning the continuing legacy of the UK's historical relationship with Africa and Africans, I interpret supporters and donors' judgements and valuations of promotional discourses, including those concerning 'street children'. Finally, I consider how volunteering provided some UK residents with the opportunity to re-evaluate these discourses in light of their first-hand experiences at the school.

Chapter 6 more explicitly examines what supporters and donors hoped to gain, and did gain, from their involvement with the school. First, I examine discourses concerning Christian obligations, responsibilities, and relationships that were valued by those hoping to fulfil Christian duties. Second, I use the case of Ngomso to examine the ethics of international volunteering. Third, I ask why supporters trusted Mary with their money. Fourth, Ngomso's place in the UK charity sector is considered and problematised. The chapter concludes with a consideration of how prominent supporters evaluated the post-apartheid transition and the capabilities of the South African government. Thematically, the reader will be drawn back to the colonial period, as I question the salience and mutation of historical forms of political interference and paternalism.

The final analytical focus, the relationship between education and self-fashioning, is most explicitly addressed in Chap. 7. I first examine how Ngomso influenced learners' conceptualisations of morality and the respective efforts they made to fashion particular lives for themselves. Second, I examine learners' experiences of high school and attempt to explain why some individuals matriculated, while others did not. Third, I examine how the value of an 'informal' form of education, or socialisation, promoting 'Xhosa masculinity', which had salience outside of Ngomso, was contested during educative experiences in the school. Fourth, I analyse how older past pupils made sense of their experiences of the 'post-school reality'. Finally, I investigate why some learners left the school 'early' (i.e. 'dropped out') to learn how to hustle. Throughout the chapter, I analyse interlocutors' evaluations of and encounters with various opportunities (i.e. forms of educational discourse and possible futures) and consider relevant socio-economic-political contexts that help to explain them.

The book draws to a close with a brief, forward-looking chapter that unites these analytical themes. Discussing the continuing relationship between the UK and former British colonies, I offer some thoughts about how the book's arguments might influence the way that varying forms of education are understood and evaluated. I scrutinise the transformative capacity of schooling and its limits while making broader claims about the relationship between systems of schooling, inequality, and modes of exclusion.

Notes

1. Jackson (2012: 15) makes a similar observation about academic pursuits more broadly, especially those that are philosophically and anthropologically minded. For instance, he (ibid.) explains how "profoundly Foucault's philosophy (*logos*) implicated a biography (*bios*)". This statement is no less accurate in my case.
2. In using the term 'development' in this section and throughout, I follow D. Lewis (2005: np): "'Development' has ... come to be associated with 'planned social change' and the idea of an external intervention by one group in the affairs of another. Often this is in the form of a project, as part of conscious efforts by outsiders to intervene in a less-developed community or country in order to produce positive change."
3. During my time working in government-funded secondary schools in London, the terms 'students' and 'teachers' were most commonly employed by members of staff and the young people in question. To my knowledge, the term 'pupil' is more commonly employed in British private schools. In contrast, 'learner', rather than 'pupil' or 'student', and 'educator', rather than 'teacher', were most frequently used during my research in South Africa. This reflects efforts to move away from the terminology and injustices of apartheid's system of schooling. (Thanks to Dr Dalene Swanson, whose correspondence helped me understand this.) However, 'past pupil' was most frequently used by my interlocutors when speaking of learners who were no longer at Ngomso. Throughout this book, I employ terminology in relation to schooling in each country that reflects these observations.
4. This organisation was the single biggest contributor by quite some margin. In the financial year ending on June 30, 2012, they raised £62,000, or R1,130,840 (£1 = R18, June 2014). Funding had also come to the school directly from individuals based in South Africa, as well as America, Britain, Holland, and Sweden.
5. In using the phrase 'relations of power', I am utilising Foucault's consideration of the historically constituted nature of discourse. Importantly, in his work, power is not synonymous with being wronged, evil, or immorality. Instead, Foucault (1997: 298) argued that society cannot exist without relations of power, in the sense of "strategies by which individuals try to direct and control the conduct of others". It is this kind of strategizing that I mean to describe when using the word 'power' here and in later chapters.
6. Swartz (2009: 160) states that her work is an ethnography; however, it is not anthropological. It is a sociological consideration of moral education (see Swartz 2010b) or, as one reviewer describes it, "arguably the most interesting work in moral psychology of the last few years" (Lapsley 2010:

403). Anthropological literature is almost exclusively cited to affirm her research methods, not to extend and develop an analytical argument. This non-comparative, 'case-only' limitation relates to the increased adoption of ethnographic approaches and research methods by 'educationalists' (Varenne 2007: 1581), which has blurred the line between ethnography of education or, more accurately, schooling and anthropological considerations of education (see Wolcott 2011).
7. Kennedy (2006: 100) argues that the "grand narrative" of evolution is implicit in the work of Kohlberg, who followed Piaget. Their "formulations", he (ibid.) continues, "exemplify the Socializing Mode. Both cognitive and ethical/intersubjective development are constructed as unidirectional, and assume an endpoint from which the fully formed adult looks back, and toward which he brings children through childrearing and education."
8. Swartz (2011: 54) describes herself as being "religiously-committed" at the time of her research. Her work has been funded by the Harvey Fellows Program of the Mustard Seed Foundation (2015: np), which funds "Christian graduate students… in preparation for vocations that are culturally influential, and where there is little Christian presence". Although her study is by no means prescriptive (i.e. it does not call for the teaching of Christianised moral discourses), it is evaluative, in the sense that individuals are placed within a framework of desirable forms and degrees of 'moral development'.
9. Wang's (2013) chapter in Stafford's (2013) volume on *Ordinary Ethics in China* is one relevant example. It builds upon a body of work concerned with education, morality, and childhood/adolescence in China (e.g. Fong 2004; Kipnis 2011; Stafford 2006; Xu 2014). Another example is Qureshi's (2014) article, which appeared in a special edition of the journal *Moral Education*, dedicated to anthropological perspectives on morality and childhood (see Fechter 2014; Zeitlyn 2014, in particular).
10. Similarly, Michael Lambek's (2010a: 4) notion of "ordinary ethics recognizes human finitude but also hope". This includes "attempts in everyday practice and thought to inhabit and persevere in light of uncertainty, suffering, injustice, incompleteness, inconsistency, the unsayable, the unforgiveable, the irresolvable, and the limits of voice and reason" (ibid.).
11. Desjarlais (1997) does not explicitly say that his book is an example of an anthropology of morality/ethics, and it preceded the most concrete efforts to define the field. However, he (2014) recently contributed to a special edition of the journal *Ethnos* that was dedicated to considerations of moral experience and co-edited by Zigon, which, to some extent, shows the compatibility of their theoretical approaches.

12. Embodied morality can be described, following Mauss, as habitus or "unreflective and unreflexive dispositions of everyday social life attained over a lifetime ... [of] socially performed techniques" (Zigon 2010: 8). Zigon (2008: 18) states that he maintains "a position of radical relativism ... [when adopting the stance that] each person to some degree has their own morality based upon their own experiences". Thus, discursive morality "should not be considered as being representative or deterministic of any actually lived embodied morality" (ibid.). However, according to Zigon (2007: 17, my emphasis), it is because "experiences are limited within a range of possibilities structured by a socio-historic-cultural context that makes these various and differing moralities recognizable and translatable to others".
13. Zigon (2010: 6) defines institutions as "those formal and non-formal social organizations and groups that are a part of all societies and wield varying amounts of power over individual persons". Such institutions "often claim to be the bearer and securer of the truth or rightness of a particular kind of morality" and, as a result, "all societies... have a plurality of institutional moralities" (ibid: 6–7). The public discourse of morality, which is "separate and distinct" from but "in constant dialogue with" institutional morality, "is all those public articulations of moral beliefs, conceptions, and hopes that are not *directly* articulated by an institution" (ibid: 7, emphasis in original). One such discourse is "parental teachings" (ibid.).
14. Most famously, Paul Willis (1977: 189) showed how "disaffected working class kids" in 1970s Britain created, and maintained, identities, values, and behaviours when in school, which meant a great deal to them but that staff did not welcome or promote (also see Foley 1990). For more examples of studies that analyse tensions between forms of knowledge taught inside and outside of schools, see Wolcott (2003), Rival (2000), and Howard (1970).
15. Other relevant examples of this theme of scholarship that are not mentioned in the main text include Bledsoe (1992), Bloch (1998), Freeman (2001), Gay and Cole (1967), and Peshkin (1972).
16. In certain respects, Malinowski's observations foreshadow the work of scholars concerned with 'neocolonialism' or 'postcolonialism', and 'cultural imperialism'. Extending the work of Franz Fanon (1967, 1969) and Paulo Freire (1970), among others, these authors are critical of how processes of schooling in South Africa, and across the continent, support 'Western' or 'European' demands and propagate racialised, culturally configured geographical inequalities (e.g. Abdi 2002; Mazuri 1993). They wish to address the way that 'indigenous cultures' were 'decimated' during the colonial era; processes of 'cultural imperialism' that, they argue, are maintained through systems of 'postcolonialism' and 'globalised capitalism' (Abdi and Cleghorn 2005; Shizha 2005; also see, Rizvi 2001). This

corpus raises important questions about the role of schooling on the African continent. However, we rarely learn how 'ordinary Africans' encounter education during their everyday lives. An exception is Dalene Swanson (2013), who conducts empirical research in South Africa and uses personalised narratives to enrich her critical, reflective considerations of the political dimensions of education in the country.

17. Malinowski (1938) laid down his core argument in an introductory chapter to *Methods and Study of Culture Contact in Africa*. Radcliffe-Brown (1952: 202) offered an early critique of his work, specifically referencing South Africa, which suggests that Malinowski's notion of 'culture clash' was "simply a way of avoiding the reality" of "the interaction of individuals and groups within an established social structure which is itself in process of change". For Radcliffe-Brown, the notion of conflict between two forms of culture was simply too simplistic and static, and thus incapable of capturing the reality of the social dynamics unfolding in South Africa during the apartheid period.

18. Paul Harris (cited in Christou 2002: np), whose PhD is in experiential psychology, argues that the "gift for fantasy ... shows itself at a very early age and then continues to make all sorts of contributions to our intellectual and emotional life throughout the lifespan". Moreover, he (2012) argues that, as far as we know, this capacity is unique to our species.

19. Anthropologists have long been keen to recognise other forms of education, particularly where there are, or were, no institutions recognisable as schools (Varenne 2007). For example, Raymond Firth (2011 [1936]: 148) considered education "to include all social processes which serve to fit the human individual more adequately for his social environment", and argued that education is an integral component of daily life and inseparable from experiences outside of schools. However, what emerged in the US from the 1950s onwards (cf. Bonini 2006: 380, for French anthropology) and is most often termed anthropology of education has not only most commonly been concerned with process of schooling but with those activities that unfold inside schools (Pollock and Levinson 2011; Varenne 2007, 2008).

20. Stambach's (2010) other book, *Faith in Schools*, and Freeman's (2001) PhD thesis are two other examples that I am aware of. I would also refer the reader to Amber Reed's (2014) PhD thesis, and the third chapter in particular, which productively utilises ethnographic research conducted inside and outside schools in the Eastern Cape.

21. Such 'male bias' is evident in many of the ethnographies I found helpful when building my own analytical framework—for example, Bourgois (1996), Hecht (1998), Weiss (2009), Willis (1977). While I recognise criticism of anthropology's long-standing masculine focus (e.g. Morgen 1989; Slocum 1975), and do not wish to entrench this gendered inequality, my

research was subject to unavoidably gendered conditions. On a more promising note, Stambach (2000) considers gender in terms of female initiation and schooling in Tanzania while I am able to offer a comparative account of male initiation and schooling in South Africa.

22. I employ the term 'township' throughout to denote the area to the east of Grahamstown's commercial centre, which was first 'reserved' for 'blacks' during colonial British rule and remained so during apartheid. More detailed information regarding geographically defined, racial segregation in Grahamstown and South Africa is provided in later chapters.

23. The 'eleven official languages policy' is a huge topic of debate in South Africa (see Bostock 2002). Moreover, as with Kiswahili and English in Tanzanian schools (Stambach 2004), the language of instruction has been a prominent issue in the politics of South African education. During my time at Ngomso, English was 'officially' the language of tuition after grade three, yet instruction was most commonly a 'mix' of English and isiXhosa (cf. Freeman (Madagascar) 2001: 237–239).

24. There are various reasons for this. Firstly, while speaking isiXhosa might well have led to a certain openness of exchange and increased my understanding (Winchatz 2006), it was not, strictly speaking, essential. All members of staff spoke English while past pupils and learners were proficient to varying degrees. Secondly, my research did not follow the regular format of doctoral programmes in the US and the UK, which often specify language training before fieldwork. Thirdly, some learners said they liked to speak in English with me because it improved their vocabulary and pronunciation. I also read books with them and aided their efforts to write in English (also see Fong 2004: 4–9). Without such dynamics, I might well have been encouraged to speak isiXhosa more regularly.

25. At one stage, I contemplated working with a translator to interview some learners who did not speak English fluently despite the limitations of this approach (Leslie and Storey 2003). However, I decided to interview those who could speak English 'well enough', making it easier to conduct interviews during breaks in the school day. More importantly, an interpreter would most likely have been a member of staff, past pupil or older learner, and all the learners said they preferred to speak with me privately.

26. In the case of Cheney's (2007: 190) ethnography, the staff working for World Vision in Uganda were all Ugandan nationals. However, I have made the assumption that the oversight and planning of their programs was, to some extent, maintained and instigated by the main office of World Vision in the US.

27. Ethnographic research is often shaped "under the shadow of researcher neutrality, objectivity and bias, where emotions are considered to be distortion and noise in the research process rather than part of its potentiality"

(Pullen cited in Warden 2013: 165). This mode aligns with Weber's instruction that we separate impartial scientific thinking from moralised and emotive perceptions, inquiries, and everyday engagements (Geertz 1968). Contrastingly, more in line with my methodological orientation, others argue that socially constituted research processes are laden with emotive dimensions, which, if embraced and analysed, can enhance the research itself (e.g. Blackman 2007; Davies and Spencer 2010; Garifzyanova 2013; Kleinman and Copp 1993; Kleinman 1991; Punch 2012; Spencer 2010).

28. During the Peace of Amiens in 1802, the newly formed British Cape Colony was briefly given back to the Dutch. More accurately, what had been the Dutch Cape Colony prior to British rule now became the Batavian Cape Colony, on account of the fact that, in Europe, the Batavian Republic had succeeded the Republic of The Seven United Netherlands, following the intervention of French forces. However, the imperative to secure it again soon arose with the Napoleonic Wars several years later. The Battle of Blaauwberg, fought on January 8, 1806, re-established British rule.

29. As well as the Xhosa, Cuyler was also to "watch over and conciliate the conduct of the Boers and Hottentots" (Mostert 1992: 343). This directive recognises the groups that had been interacting in the eastern fringe of the Cape Colony long before the British arrived. 'Hottentot' is a problematic term, and 'Khoisan'—referring to San and Khoi, who were hunter-gatherers and pastoralists, respectively—is now used more regularly to refer to the 'non-bantu' speaking people of South Africa who were established here at the time (Mostert 1992: 32). The San had been in the locality for approximately 10,000 years and the Khoi for 2000 (O'Meara 1995: 12). During apartheid, their descendants were politically and racially classified as 'Coloured'. The Boers were the *vertrekkers* who descended from the Dutch settlers and moved inland and along the coast from what is now Cape Town, where successive European governments had greater political influence. While both the Boers and the Khoisan should not be seen as isolated from the events I discuss, they are under-represented here for the purposes of analytical simplicity and because the vast majority of learners at Ngomso identified with a Xhosa heritage.

30. The Xhosa shared a language, isiXhosa, and descend from those who had moved down to Southern Africa following the expansion of the 'Bantu-speakers' out of West and Central Africa. By 800 AD, they had migrated west from what is now the KwaZulu-Natal province, towards the location of my research site (O'Meara 1995: 12). Importantly, the Xhosa cannot be seen as existing in a homogenised and static society, isolated in time as well as place, before prolonged contact with Europeans occurred. According to Jeff Peires (1982: 19), "the Xhosa nation is heterogeneous in origin, rather

than a genetically defined 'tribe' clearly distinct from its neighbours". Tisani (2000) has shown that certain themes and myths have been established and refuted as history and historiography of the Xhosa has developed.
31. The Zuurveld was later renamed 'Albany' after the capital of the State of New York, where Cuyler was born.
32. During the first half of the nineteenth century, 'Xhosaland' "remained an identifiably distinct nation, socially, economically and politically distant from the Cape Colony" (Peires 1989: 53). Xhosa chiefs initially welcomed missionaries on to their land and viewed missionaries as separate from colonialist forces (Mostert 1992: 425). The first permanent mission station among the Xhosa, and all the 'Bantu' speakers of Southern Africa, was established in 1816 (Mostert 1992: 436). However, the presence of such mission stations among the Xhosa became problematical, particularly during times of war.
33. For instance, the Natives Land Act of 1913 "defined less than one-tenth of South Africa as black 'reserves' [a forerunner to the 'homelands' of apartheid] and prohibited any purchase or lease of land by blacks outside the reserves" (Cobbing 2015: np). Together with the Native (Urban Areas) Act of 1923 and the Black (Native) Administration Act of 1927, it also formalised the foundations of the racially segregated townships of apartheid. Additionally, The Mines and Works Act of 1911 and its 1926 successor (also known as the Colour Bar Act), prohibited 'blacks' from taking the better paid, more skilled positions of employment.
34. To some of his contemporaries, Eiselen's plans were ill-conceived because cultural separation was impossible. Many anthropologists at English-speaking universities did not share the same ideas (Sharp 1980). For example, Alfred Radcliffe-Brown of the University of Cape Town argued that attempts to distinguish between 'tribes' and groups with distinct, separate cultures should be discouraged (Kuper 1999). Max Gluckman (1958 [1940]) made a similar argument when analysing *Modern Zululand*. For fuller considerations of the political nature of South African anthropology, see Niehaus (2013), Nyamnjoh (2012), and Spiegel and Becker (2015).
35. From this point forward, I use 'Black' and 'White' in capitalised form in reference to the legal classification structures of the apartheid government. Where these words appear in direct quotations from interlocutors who used them without specific reference to the legal classifications of apartheid, or from academic sources that use them unproblematically in this same way, I have not capitalised the words or placed them in scare quotes. I myself do not use the words 'white' or 'black' without capitalisation or scare quotes anywhere in this book because I feel that this terminology is problematic, ambiguous, and loaded with political implications.

36. The Indian portion of the city was only established in the 1980s, as apartheid was drawing to a close. Previously, this relatively small population had lived on their business premises in the White Areas. The dividing line between the Group Areas of apartheid corresponds to the Kowie Ditch, a geographical divide following the shape of the Kowie River. This ditch is called *egazini*—'the place of blood'—by those who acknowledge the moment when many Xhosa died in its waters at the hands of British forces during the pivotal *Battle of Grahamstown* in 1819 (Peires 1982: 143).
37. Mayer (1961: 23) tells us that his respondents most frequently saw Red/School distinctions as absolute while he depicts "actual behaviour" as sitting somewhere along "a continuum". Despite this caveat, it is, of course, problematic to speak of 'Red or School people', or any generalised group identity for that matter. Indeed, Mayer was accused of helping to validate "ideological", "racist terms" by theorising binaries that did not do justice to the individuals in question (Magubane 1973: 1709). Similarly highlighting the perils of oversimplification, Bank (2011) critiqued Mayer's analytical neglect of internationally constituted cultural changes, suggesting that some young people sought to move away from the politics and entertainment associated with their Xhosa heritage while also rejecting the conservatism associated with the 'White Europeans' of Mayer's typology.
38. In Mayer's (1980: 2) later work, he considered the School/Red divide in terms of "ideologies [that] represented comprehensive patterns of belief, laying down precepts for most aspects of life". Patrick McAllister (2006: 56) revisited this work and suggested that 'School' and 'Red' signify "subjective orientations".
39. To be clear, he does not depict the personalised navigations as they unfolded, in any great detail; perhaps owing to the academic convention of his time and his questionnaire heavy research methodology.
40. Although he was criticised for paying insufficient attention to how apartheid politics (e.g. Magubane 1973), Mayer (with I. Mayer 1961: 283) did speak of "a limiting framework of compulsion", that is, how the apartheid government limited choice and freedoms. His (1980) later work provided more of this kind of contextualisation, targeting separatist and capitalist ideologies, and related policies of forced removal and resettlement, migrant labour stipulations, and urban planning (Bank 2011: 35–36; Spiegel and McAllister 1991: 2).
41. The first school boycotts occurred in the Eastern Cape in 1955, before being abandoned in 1956 (for the time being). Additionally, the ANC initiated schools under the pseudonym 'cultural clubs' as an alternative to Bantu Education. These relied heavily on oral storytelling, songs and games, as well as subjects such as maths and geography (Soudien and Nekhwevha 2002). These were short-lived, however, as the government tightened their power over education and sought to close them down.

42. Critical pedagogy, as outlined by authors such as Paulo Freire (1970), was influential (Nekhwevha 2002). The related philosophy of People's Education established "a new language of resistance and democracy ... [and were] a necessary condition for the political transition of the 1990s" (Kallaway 2002: 7).
43. Young protestors, demonstrating against Bantu Education and attempts to mandate the teaching of Afrikaans in Black schools, fatally clashed with police forces. Subsequently, schools closed and burned down while teachers and students were arrested throughout the country (Pohlandt-McCormick 2000; Glaser 1998).
44. The Soweto protest and subsequent class boycotts "took place largely outside the control of the ANC", which countered students' slogans with "'education for liberation'" (Prew 2011: 135).
45. More broadly, reaction to apartheid politics was not racially determined. Indeed, the End Conscription Campaign (ECC) was necessarily White dominated because the conscripts were White, even if its primary interest was combatting political repression in the townships. In Grahamstown in particular, the White population were mostly of British heritage and less inclined to sympathise with Afrikaner Nationalism compared with Whites in other areas of the country (cf. Dube 1985).
46. In the universities of the Eastern Cape, organisations such as the National Union of South African Students (NUSAS) and South African Students Organisation (SASO), along with other 'oppositional collectives', such as the Black Sash and United Democratic Front, similarly did much to counter the oppressive potentiality of Bantu Education.
47. This charitable trust is no longer associated with the school where I conducted my research nor with the UK-based charity that supports it.
48. The quote in this sentence is from Mary Burton, taken from a website created for the school by a volunteer, which is no longer online. This account of how the school was formed aligns with the one that was relayed to me during fieldwork.
49. In total, "South Africa was pledged approximately $5 billion in foreign development-related aid from 1994-1999, an enormous sum compared to other (more desperate) African countries" (Bond 2001: 25) However, the sum of committed money during this period was much smaller, with the EU, for example, committing only 13% of a pledged $1.75 billion (ibid.). The newly formed and provincially organised South African state was not well positioned to distribute and employ aid money, which goes someway to explaining the shortfall (ibid.).
50. These quotes are taken from the aforementioned web page written about Ngomso that is no longer online.

51. Bantu Education was delivered by separate departments responsible for specific racial categories. Responsibility then shifted to nine departments, representing each province, which could act semi-autonomously under the guidance of National Acts and policies, and a national department. Ruiters (2011: 19) asserts that the Eastern Cape Province itself was formed during "a contested process" that "reflects the outcome of the negotiations around the political settlement of 1993-4".
52. The citations in this sentence are from the ECDoE's registration certificate.
53. There is a body of literature that attempts to identify the failings of 'educational inclusivity' in South Africa. As the researchers are concerned with recommendations for intervention and change, the methodological orientation of this work is very different from my own. However, I would refer the reader to these relevant studies: Bothma et al. (2000), Christie (1999), Engelbrecht (2006), Jager (2013), Landsberg (2005), Lomofsky and Lazarus (2001), Makoelle (2012), Mitchell et al. (2007), Muthukrishna and Schoeman (2000), Muthukrishna and Ramsuran (2007), Naicker (2006), Ngcobo and Muthukrishna (2011), Ntombela (2011), Pather (2007, 2011), Pillay and Di Terlizzi (2009), Polat (2011), Prinsloo (2001), Stofile (2008), and Waghid and Engelbrecht (2002).
54. For example, Allen (2012), G. Bloch (2009), Chisholm (2011), Fleisch (2008), V. John (2012), Modisaotsile (2012), SAPA (2012), and Wright (2012).
55. The series ran in *The Herald* newspaper, based in Port Elizabeth, and details can be found at http://www.blogs.theherald.co.za/schoolsofshame/ (Last accessed on December 01, 2015).
56. On average, in the Eastern Cape, over 65% of learners in public schools are 'age-inappropriate' for their grade and this number increases with each grade. Approximately 80% are age-appropriate in grade one; however, by grade eleven, at the start of matriculation, this falls to approximately 25%. Lewin and Sebates (2012: 517) state that "Over age enrolment is important since it is widely linked to low levels of achievement, premature drop out, and gendered differences in participation."

Bibliography

Abdi, A. A. (2002). *Culture, Education, and Development in South Africa: Historical and Contemporary Perspectives*. Westport: Bergin and Garvey.

Abdi, A. A., & Cleghorn, A. (2005). Sociology of Education: Theoretical and Conceptual Perspectives. In A. A. Abdi & A. Cleghorn (Eds.), *Issues in African Education: Sociological Perspectives* (pp. 3–24). New York/Basingstoke: Palgrave Macmillan.

Allen, K. (2012). South Africa Education Crisis Fuels State School Exodus. *BBC Online*. Retrieved March 4, 2014, from http://www.bbc.co.uk/news/world-africa-17315157

Anonymous. Details omitted in order to maintain the anonymity of interlocutors.

Appadurai, A. (2013). *The Future as Cultural Fact: Essays on the Global Condition*. London/New York: Verso.

Bank, L. (2011). *Home Spaces, Street Styles: Contesting Power and Identity in a South African City*. London: Pluto Press.

Bennell, P., & Monyokolo, M. (1994). A 'Lost Generation'?: Key Findings of a Tracer Survey of Secondary School Leavers in South Africa. *International Journal of Educational Development, 14*(2), 195–206.

Bernauer, J., & Mahon, M. (2006). Michel Foucault's Ethical Imagination. In G. Gutting (Ed.), *The Cambridge Companion to Foucault*. Cambridge: Cambridge University Press.

Blackman, S. J. (2007). 'Hidden Ethnography': Crossing Emotional Borders in Qualitative Accounts of Young People's Lives. *Sociology, 41*(4), 699–716.

Bledsoe, C. (1992). The Cultural Transformation of Western Education in Sierra Leone. *Journal of the International African Institute, 62*(2), 182–202.

Bloch, M. E. (1998). The Uses of Schooling and Literacy in a Zafimaniry Village. In M. E. Bloch (Ed.), *How We Think They Think. Anthropological Approaches to Cognition, Memory and Literacy* (pp. 171–192). Boulder: Westview Press.

Bloch, G. (2009). *The Toxic Mix: What's Wrong with South Africa's Schools and How to Fix It*. Cape Town: Tafelberg.

Bond, P. (2001). Article Foreign Aid and Development Debates in Post-apartheid South Africa. *Transformation, 45*, 25–36.

Bonini, N. (2006). The Pencil and the Shepherd's Crook. Ethnography of Maasai Education. *Ethnography and Education, 1*(3), 379–392.

Bordonaro, L. I. (2012). Children's Geographies Agency Does Not Mean Freedom. Cape Verdean Street Children and the Politics of Children's Agency. *Children's Geographies, 10*(4), 413–426.

Bornstein, E. (2005). *The Spirit of Development: Protestant NGOs, Morality, and Economics in Zimbabwe*. Stanford: Stanford University Press.

Bornstein, E., & Redfield, P. (2008). *Genealogies of Suffering and the Gift of Care: A Working Paper on the Anthropology of Religion, Secularism, and Humanitarianism*. New York: Social Science Research Council Working Papers.

Bostock, W. W. (2002). South Africa's Language Policy: Controlled Status Enhancement and Reduction. In S. Kossew & D. Schwerdt (Eds.), *Re-imagining Africa: New Critical Perspectives*. New York: Nova.

Bothma, M., Gravett, S., & Swart, E. (2000). The Attitudes of Primary School Teachers Towards Inclusive Education. *South African Journal of Education, 20*(3), 200–204.

Bourdieu, P. (1977). *Outline of a Theory of Practice*. London: Cambridge University Press.
Bourdieu, P. (1980). *The Logic of Practice*. Stanford: Stanford University Press.
Bourdieu, P. (1986). The Forms of Capital. In J. Richardson (Ed.), *Handbook of Theory and Research for the Sociology of Education* (pp. 241–258). New York: Greenwood.
Bourgois, P. (1996). *Search of Respect*. Cambridge: Cambridge University Press.
Cheney, K. (2007). *Pillars of the Nation: Child Citizens and Ugandan National Development*. Chicago: University of Chicago Press.
Chisholm, L. (2002). Continuity and Change in Education Policy Research. In P. Kallaway (Ed.), *The History of Education Under Apartheid 1948–1994* (pp. 94–110). Pinelands: Pearson Education South Africa.
Chisholm, L. (2011). The Challenge of South African Schooling: Dimensions, Targets and Initiatives. In J. Hofmeyr (Ed.), *From Inequality to Inclusive Growth: South Africa's Pursuit of Shared Prosperity in Extraordinary Times*. Cape Town: Institute for Justice and Reconciliation.
Christie, P. (1985). *The Right to Learn: Struggle for Education in South Africa*. Johannesburg: Raven Press.
Christie, P. (1999). Inclusive Education in South Africa: Achieving Equity and Majority Rights. In H. Daniels & P. Garner (Eds.), *Inclusive Education*. London: Kogan Page.
Christie, P. (2006). Changing Regimes: Governmentality and Education Policy in Post-apartheid South Africa. *International Journal of Educational Development*, 26(4), 373–381.
Christie, P., & Collins, C. (1982). Bantu Education: Apartheid Ideology or Labour Reproduction? *Comparative Education*, 18(1), 59–75.
Christou, M. (2002). Who Needs Imagination? An Interview with Professor Paul Harris. *Harvard Graduate School of Education* (Online). Retrieved September 15, 2013, from http://www.gse.harvard.edu/news/features/harris03012002.html
Cobbing, J. R. D. (2015). South Africa, History. *Encyclopaedia Britannica* (Online). Retrieved April 12, 2015, from http://www.britannica.com/place/South-Africa/History#ref480694
Comaroff, J., & Comaroff, J. (1997). *Of Revelation and Revolution, Volume 2: The Dialectics of Modernity on a South African Frontier*. Chicago: The University of Chicago Press.
Crapanzano, V. (2014). Must We Be Bad Epistemologists? Illusions of Transparency, the Opaque Other, and Interpretive Foibles. In V. Das, M. Jackson, A. Kleinman, & B. Singh (Eds.), *The Ground Between: Anthropologists Engage Philosophy* (pp. 254–278). Durham: Duke University Press.
Crouch, L. (1996). Public Education Equity and Efficiency in South Africa: Lessons for Other Countries. *Economics of Education Review*, 15(2), 125–137.

Davies, J., & Spencer, D. (2010). *Emotions in the Field: The Psychology and Anthropology of Fieldwork Experience*. Stanford: Stanford University Press.
de Clercq, F. (1997). Effective Policies and the Reform Process: An Evaluation of the New Development and Education Macro Policies. In P. Kallaway, G. Kruss, A. Fataar, & G. Donn (Eds.), *Education After Apartheid: South African Education in Transition* (pp. 142–168). Cape Town: UCT Press.
de Wet, C. (2002). Factors Influencing the Choice of English as Language of Learning and Teaching (LoLT) – A South African Perspective. *South African Journal of Education, 22*(2), 119–124.
Department of Education (DoE). (1996). *South African Schools Act No. 84 of 1996*. Retrieved June 12, 2013, from http://www.education.gov.za/LinkClick.aspx?fileticket=aIolZ6UsZ5U%3D&tabid=185&mid=1828
Desjarlais, R. (1997). *Shelter Blues: Sanity and Selfhood Among the Homeless*. Philadelphia: University of Pennsylvania Press.
Desjarlais, R. (2014). Liberation Upon Hearing: Voice, Morality, and Death in a Buddhist World. *Ethos, 42*(1), 101–118.
Dube, E. F. (1985). The Relationship Between Racism and Education in South Africa. *Harvard Education Review, 55*(1), 86–100.
Durham, D. (2008). Apathy and Agency. The Romance of Agency and Youth in Botswana. In J. Cole & D. Durham (Eds.), *Figuring the Future: Globalization and the Temporalities of Children and Youth* (pp. 151–179). Santa Fe: School of Advanced Research Press.
Engelbrecht, P. (2006). The Implementation of Inclusive Education in South Africa after Ten Years of Democracy. *European Journal of Psychology of Education, 21*(3), 253–264.
Fanon, F. (1967). *The Wretched of the Earth*. London: Penguin.
Fanon, F. (1969). *Towards the African Revolution*. New York: Grove Press.
Fassin, D. (2010). Critique of Humanitarian Reason. *Public Lecture, Institute for Advanced Study, Princeton University* (Available Online). Retrieved July 15, 2013, from http://www.youtube.com/watch?v=jDT2mYg6mgo
Fassin, D. (2011). A Contribution to the Critique of Moral Reason. *Anthropological Theory, 11*(4), 481–491.
Fassin, D. (2012). *Humanitarian Reason: A Moral History of the Present*. Berkeley: University of California Press.
Ferguson, J. (2006). *Global Shadows: Africa in the Neoliberal World Order*. Durham: Duke University Press.
Firth, R. (2011). *We the Tikopia: A Sociological Study of Kinship in Primitive Polynesia*. Abingdon: Routledge.
Fiske, E. B., & Ladd, H. F. (2004). *Elusive Equity: Education Reform in Post-apartheid South Africa*. Washington, DC: Brookings Institution Press.
Fleisch, B. (2008). *Primary Education in Crisis: Why South African Schoolchildren Underachieve in Reading and Mathematics*. Cape Town: Juta.

Foley, D. (1990). *Learning Capitalist Culture: Deep in the Heart of Tejas*. Philadelphia: University of Pennsylvania Press.
Fong, V. L. (2004). *Only Hope: Coming of Age Under China's One-Child Policy*. Stanford: Stanford University Press.
Foucault, M. (1997). *Ethics: Subjectivity and Truth* (The Essential Works of Michel Foucault 1954–1984). In P. Rabinow (Ed.). New York: The New Press.
Freeman, L. E. (2001). *Knowledge, Education and Social Differentiation Amongst the Betsileo of Fisakana, Highland Madagascar*. Unpublished PhD Thesis, Department of Anthropology, London School of Economics and Political Science.
Freire, P. (1970). *Pedagogy of the Oppressed*. New York: Continuum.
Garifzyanova, A. (2013). Research Emotions in the Field: The View from the Other Side. *World Applied Sciences Journal, 27*(8), 1079–1082.
Gay, J., & Cole, M. (1967). *The New Mathematics and an Old Culture: A Study of Learning Among the Kpelle of Liberia*. New York: Rinehart and Winston.
Geertz, C. (1968). Thinking as a Moral Act: Ethical Dimensions of Anthropological Fieldwork in the New States. *The Antioch Review, 28*(2), 139–158.
Glaser, C. (1998). We Must Infiltrate the Tsotsis': Schools Politics and Youth Gangs in Soweto, 1968–1976. *Journal of Southern African Studies, 24*(2), 302–326.
Glennie, J., & Herbert, S. (2013). UK Should Revisit Its Decision on South Africa and Its Concept of Aid. *The Guardian* (Online). Retrieved October 21, 2017, from https://www.theguardian.com/global-development/poverty-matters/2013/may/02/uk-revisit-decision-south-africa-aid
Gluckman, M. (1958). *Analysis of a Social Situation in Modern Zululand* (The Rhodes-Livingstone Papers, 28). New York: Humanities Press.
Golde, P. (1986). *Women in the Field: Anthropological Experiences*. Berkeley/Los Angeles: University of California Press.
Hammett, D. (2008). Disrespecting Teacher: The Decline in Social Standing of Teachers in Cape Town, South Africa. *International Journal of Educational Development, 28*(3), 340–347.
Harris, P. (2012). *Trusting What You're Told: How Children Learn from Others*. Cambridge, MA: Belknap Press.
Hecht, T. (1998). *At Home in the Street: Street Children of Northeast Brazil*. Cambridge: Cambridge University Press.
Hendricks, M. (2011). Eastern Cape Schools: Resourcing and Class Inequality. In G. Ruiters (Ed.), *The Fate of the Eastern Cape: History, Politics and Social Policy* (pp. 254–263). Scottsville: University of KwaZulu-Natal Press.
Heugh, K. (1999). Languages, Development and Reconstructing Education in South Africa. *International Journal of Educational Development, 19*(4–5), 301–313.
Hlatshwayo, S. (2000). *Education and Independence: Education in South Africa, 1658–1988*. London: Greenwood Press.

Horrell, M. (1963). *African Education, Some Origins and Developments*. Johannesburg: Institute of Race Relations.
Horrell, M. (1964). *A Decade of Bantu Education*. Johannesburg: SAIRR.
Howard, A. (1970). *Learning to Be Rotuman: Enculturation in the South Pacific*. New York: Teachers College Press.
Hunter, M. (1936). *Reaction to Conquest: Effects of Contact with Europeans on the Pondo of South Africa*. London: Oxford University Press.
Hyslop, J. (1988). State Education Policy and the Social Reproduction of the Urban African Working Class: The Case of the Southern Transvaal 1955–76. *Journal of Southern African Studies, 14*(3), 446–476.
Hyslop, J. (2001). *Classroom Struggle: Policy and Resistance in South Africa 1940–1990*. Scottsville: University of KwaZulu-Natal Press.
Ingold, T., & Lucas, R. (2007). The 4 A's (Anthropology, Archaeology, Art and Architecture): Reflections on a Teaching and Learning Experience. In M. Harris (Ed.), *Ways of Knowing. New Approaches in the Anthropology of Experience and Learning* (pp. 287–306). Oxford: Berghahn.
Jackson, M. (1989). *Paths Toward a Clearing: Radical Empiricism and Ethnographic Inquiry. Bloomington*. Indiana: Indiana University Press.
Jackson, M. (2012). *Between One and One Another*. Berkeley: University of California Press.
Jager, T. (2013). Guidelines to Assist the Implementation of Differentiated Learning Activities in South African Secondary Schools. *International Journal of Inclusive Education, 17*(1), 80–94.
Jansen, J. D. (2012, September 27). Seven Dangerous Shifts in the Public Education Crisis. Presidential Address, South African Institute of Race Relations. Retrieved June 23, 2015, from http://www.politicsweb.co.za/politicsweb/view/politicsweb/en/page71619?oid=328972&sn=Detail&pid=71616
John, V. (2012). Education in Crisis: Teaching Floored by Lack of Chairs. *Mail & Guardian* (Online). Retrieved, May 26, 2013, from http://mg.co.za/article/2012-10-19-00-teaching-floored-by-lack-of-chairs
Kallaway, P. (2002). Introduction. In P. Kallaway (Ed.), *The History of Education Under Apartheid, 1948–1994: The Doors of Learning and Culture Shall Be Opened* (pp. 1–38). Cape Town: Pearson Education South Africa.
Kennedy, D. (2006). *The Well of Being: Childhood, Subjectivity, and Education*. Albany: State University of New York Press.
Kipnis, A. B. (2011). *Governing Educational Desire: Culture, Politics and Schooling in China*. Chicago: University of Chicago Press.
Kleinman, S. (1991). Field-Workers' Feelings: What We Feel, Who We Are, How We Analyze. In B. Shaffir & R. Stebbins (Eds.), *Experiencing Fieldwork: An Inside View of Qualitative Research* (pp. 184–195). Newbury Park: Sage.
Kleinman, S., & Copp, M. A. (1993). *Emotions and Fieldwork*. Newbury Park: Sage.

Kohlberg, L. (1981). *Essays on Moral Development*. San Francisco: Harper & Row.
Kohlberg, L. (1984). *The Psychology of Moral Development: The Nature and Validity of Moral Stages*. San Francisco: Harper & Row.
Kross, C. (2002). W.W.M. Eiselen: Architect of Apartheid Education. In P. Kallaway (Ed.), *The History of Education Under Apartheid, 1948–1994: The Doors of Learning and Culture Shall Be Opened* (pp. 53–73). New York: Peter Lang.
Kruss, G. (2002). 'Going Where the People Are': The Educational Philosophy of an African Indigenous Church Institute in the 1980s. In P. Kallaway (Ed.), *The History of Education Under Apartheid 1948–1994: The Doors of Learning and Culture Shall Be Opened* (pp. 288–303). New York: Peter Lang.
Kuper, A. (1999). *Culture: The Anthropologists' Account*. Cambridge, MA: Harvard University Press.
Laidlaw, J. (2010). Agency and Responsibility: Perhaps You Can Have Too Much of a Good Thing. In M. Lambek (Ed.), *Ordinary Ethics: Anthropology, Language and Action* (pp. 143–164). New York: Fordham University Press.
Lambek, M. (2010a). Introduction. In M. Lambek (Ed.), *Ordinary Ethics: Anthropology, Language, and Action* (pp. 1–36). New York: Fordham University Press.
Lambek, M. (2010b). Toward an Ethics of the Act. In M. Lambek (Ed.), *Ordinary Ethics: Anthropology, Language and Action* (pp. 39–63). New York: Fordham University Press.
Landsberg, E. (Ed.). (2005). *Addressing Barriers to Learning: A South African Perspective*. Pretoria: Van Schaik.
Lapsley, D. K. (2010). The Moral Ecology of South Africa's Township Youth (Review). *Journal of Moral Education, 39*(3), 403–405.
Leslie, H., & Storey, D. (2003). Entering the Field. In R. Scheyvens & D. Storey (Eds.), *Development Fieldwork: A Practical Guide* (pp. 119–138). London: Sage.
Lester, A. (2001). *Imperial Networks: Creating Identities in Nineteenth Century South Africa*. London: Routledge.
Lester, A., Nel, E., & Binns, T. (2000). *South Africa, Past, Present and Future: Gold at the End of the Rainbow?* Harlow: Pearson Education.
Lewin, K. M., & Sabates, R. (2012). Who Gets What? Is Improved Access to Basic Education Pro-poor in Sub-Saharan Africa? *International Journal of Educational Development, 32*(4), 517–528.
Lewis, A. (1999). *Past and Present Perceptions Surrounding Mission Education: A Historical Metabletical Overview*. Unpublished D.Ed. Thesis, Stellenbosch University. Retrieved May 02, 2012, from http://scholar.sun.ac.za/handle/10019.1/16104
Lewis, D. (2005). Anthropology and Development: The Uneasy Relationship. *LSE Research Online*. Retrieved June 24, 2013, from http://eprints.lse.ac.uk/archive/00000253

Lewis, A., & Steyn, J. (2003). A Critique of Mission Education in South Africa According to Bosch's Mission Paradigm Theory. *South African Journal of Education, 23*(2), 101–106.
Lomofsky, L., & Lazarus, S. (2001). South Africa: First Steps in the Development of an Inclusive Education System. *Cambridge Journal of Education, 31*(3), 303–317.
Magubane, A. B. (1973). The 'Xhosa' in Town, Revisited Urban Social Anthropology: A Failure of Method and Theory. *American Anthropologist, 75*(5), 1701–1715.
Makoelle, T. M. (2012). The State of Inclusive Pedagogy in South Africa: A Literature Review. *Journal of Sociology and Social Anthropology, 3*(2), 93–102.
Malinowski, B. (1938). The Anthropology of Changing African Cultures. In L. P. Mair (Ed.), *Methods and Study of Culture Contact in Africa* (pp. vii–xxxviii). Oxford: Oxford University Press.
Malinowski, B. (1943). The Pan-African Problem of Culture Contact. *American Journal of Sociology, 48*(6), 649–665.
Marais, M. (1995). The Distribution of Resources in Education in South Africa. *Economics of Education Review, 14*(1), 47–52.
Mayer, P. (1961). *Townsmen or Tribesmen: Conservatism and the Process of Urbanization in a South African City* (with Contributions by Iona Mayer). Oxford/Cape Town: Oxford University Press.
Mayer, P. (1980). The Origin and Decline of Two Rural Resistance Ideologies. In P. Mayer (Ed.), *Black Villagers in an Industrial Society* (pp. 1–81). Oxford/Cape Town: Oxford University Press.
Mazuri, A. (1993). Language and the Quest for Liberation in Africa: The Legacy of Franz Fanon. *Third World Quarterly, 14*(2), 348–365.
McAllister, P. A. (2006). *Xhosa Beer Drinking Rituals: Power, Practice and Performance in the South African Rural Periphery*. Durham: Carolina Academic Press.
Mitchell, C., Moletsane, R., & De Lange, N. (2007). Inclusive Education in South Africa in the Era of AIDS: Every Voice Counts. *International Journal of Inclusive Education, 11*(4), 383–386.
Modisaotsile, B. M. (2012). The Failing Standard of Basic Education in South Africa. *Africa Institute of South Africa*, Briefing No. 72, 1–8.
Molteno, P. (1900). *The Life and Times of Sir John Charles Molteno*. London: Smith, Elder & Co.
Moore, H. L. (2011). *Still Life: Hopes, Desires and Satisfactions*. Cambridge: Polity Press.
Morgen, S. (1989). Gender and Anthropology: Introductory Essay. In S. Morgen (Ed.), *Gender and Anthropology--Critical Reviews for Research and Teaching* (pp. 1–20). Washington, DC: American Anthropological Association.
Morrell, W. (1969). *British Colonial Policy in the Mid-Victorian Age: South Africa, New Zealand, the West Indies*. Oxford: Oxford University Press.

Morris, A., & Hyslop, J. (1991). Education in South Africa: The Present Crisis and the Problems of Reconstruction. *Social Justice, 18*(1/2), 259–270.
Mostert, N. (1992). *Frontiers: The Epic of South Africa's Creation and the Tragedy of the Xhosa People.* New York: Knopf.
Musgrove, F. (1952). A Uganda Secondary School as a Field of Culture Change. *Africa: Journal of the International African Institute, 22*(3), 234–249.
Mustard Seed Foundation. (2015). *Overview.* Retrieved June 20, 2014, from http://msfdn.org/harveyfellows/overview/
Muthukrishna, N., & Ramsuran, A. (2007). Layers of Oppression and Exclusion in the Context of HIV and AIDS: The Case of Adult and Child Learners in the Richmond District, Province of KwaZulu-Natal. *International Journal of Inclusive Education, 11*(4), 401–416.
Muthukrishna, N., & Schoeman, M. (2000). From 'Special Needs' to 'Quality Education for All': A Participatory, Problem-Centred Approach to Policy Development in South Africa. *International Journal of Inclusive Education, 4*(4), 315–335.
Naicker, S. (2006). From Policy to Practice: A South-African Perspective on Implementing Inclusive Education Policy. *International Journal of Whole Schooling, 3*(1), 1–7.
Nekhwevha, F. (2002). The Influence of Freire's 'Pedagogy of Knowing' on the South African Education Struggle in the 1970s and 1980s. In P. Kallaway (Ed.), *The History of Education Under Apartheid, 1948–1994: The Doors of Learning and Culture Shall Be Opened* (pp. 134–143). Cape Town: Pearson Education South Africa.
Ngcobo, J., & Muthukrishna, N. (2011). The Geographies of Inclusion of Students with Disabilities in an Ordinary School. *South African Journal of Education, 31*(3), 357–368.
Ngwane, Z. (2001). Real Men Reawaken Their Fathers' Homesteads, the Educated Leave Them in Ruins': The Politics of Domestic Reproduction in Post-apartheid Rural South Africa. *Journal of Religion in Africa, 31*(4), 402–426.
Niehaus, I. (2013). Anthropology and Whites in South Africa: Response to an Unreasonable Critique. *Africa Spectrum, 48,* 117–127.
Nieuwenhuys, O. (2001). By the Sweat of Their Brow? 'Street Children', NGOs and Children's Rights in Addis Ababa. *Africa, 71*(4), 539–557.
Nolan, R. W. (2002). *Development Anthropology: Encounters in the Real World.* Oxford: Westview Press.
Ntombela, S. (2011). The Progress of Inclusive Education in South Africa: Teachers' Experiences in a Selected District, KwaZulu-Natal. *Improving Schools, 14*(1), 5–14.
Nyamnjoh, F. B. (2012). Blinded by Sight: Divining the Future of Anthropology in Africa. *Africa Spectrum, 47,* 63–92.

O'Meara, E. (1995). *Grahamstown Reflected*. Grahamstown: Albany Museum.
O'Neill, K. L. (2015). *Secure the Soul: Christian Piety and Gang Prevention in Guatemala*. Berkeley: University of California Press.
Olivier de Sardan, J. P. (2005). *Anthropology and Development: Understanding Contemporary Social Change*. London: Zed Books.
Pather, S. (2007). Demystifying Inclusion: Implications for Sustainable Inclusive Practice. *International Journal of Inclusive Education, 11*(5–6), 627–643.
Pather, S. (2011). Evidence on Inclusion and Support for Learners with Disabilities in Mainstream Schools in South Africa: Off the Policy Radar? *International Journal of Inclusive Education, 15*(10), 1103–1117.
Pattenden, O. (2015). Relations of Trust, Questions About Expectations: Reflections on a Photography Project with Young South Africans. *Anthropology in Action, 22*(3), 14–26.
Peires, J. B. (1979). Nxele, Ntsikana and the Origins of the Xhosa Religious Reaction. *The Journal of African History, 20*(1), 51–61.
Peires, J. B. (1982). *The House of Phalo: A History of the Xhosa People in the Days of Their Independence*. Los Angles: University of California Press.
Peires, J. B. (1989). *The Dead Will Arise: Nongqawuse and the Great Xhosa Cattle-Killing Movement*. Johannesburg: Ravan Press.
Peshkin, A. (1972). *Kanuri School Children: Education and Social Mobilization in Nigeria*. New York: Holt, Rinehart and Winston.
Pillay, J., & Di Terlizzi, M. (2009). A Case Study of a Learner's Transition from Mainstream Schooling to a School for Learners with Special Educational Needs (LSEN): Lessons for Mainstream Education. *South African Journal of Education, 29*, 491–509.
Pohlandt-McCormick, H. (2000). 'I Saw a Nightmare. . .': Violence and the Construction of Memory (Soweto, June 16, 1976). *History and Theory, 39*(4), 23–44.
Polat, F. (2011). Inclusion in Education: A Step Towards Social Justice. *International Journal of Educational Development, 31*(1), 50–58.
Pollock, M., & Levinson, B. A. U. (2011). Introduction. In B. A. U. Levinson & M. Pollock (Eds.), *A Companion to the Anthropology of Education* (pp. 1–8). Oxford: Wiley-Blackwell.
Posel, D., & Casale, D. (2011). Language Proficiency and Language Policy in South Africa: Findings from New Data. *International Journal of Educational Development, 31*(5), 449–457.
Prew, M. (2011). Socialism and Education: 'Peoples Education for Peoples Power': The Rise and Fall of an Idea in Southern Africa. In T. Griffi & Z. Millie (Eds.), *Logics of Socialist Education: Engaging with Crisis, Insecurity and Uncertainty* (pp. 133–153). New York: Springer.
Prinsloo, E. (2001). Working Towards Inclusive Education in South African Classrooms. *South African Journal of Education, 21*(4), 344–348.

Punch, S. (2012). Hidden Struggles of Fieldwork: Exploring the Role and Use of Field Diaries. *Emotion, Space and Society*, 5, 86–93.

Qureshi, K. (2014). Sending Children to School 'Back Home': Multiple Moralities of Punjabi Sikh Parents in Britain. *Journal of Moral Education*, 43(2), 37–41.

Rabinow, P. (1997). Introduction: The History of Systems of Thought. In P. Rabinow (Ed.), *Ethics: Subjectivity and Truth* (The Essential Works of Michel Foucault). New York: The New Press.

Radcliffe-Brown, A. R. (1952). *Structure and Function in Primitive Society*. London: Cohen and West.

Rakometsi, M. S. (2008). *The Transformation of Black School Education in South Africa, 1950–1994: A Historical Perspective*. Unpublished PhD Thesis, Department of Humanities, Department of History, University of the Free State.

Reed, A. (2014). *Inkululeko: Youth, Non-governmental Organizations, and Discourses of Democracy in Post-apartheid South Africa*. Unpublished PhD Thesis, Department of Anthropology, University of California. Retrieved June 05, 2015, from http://escholarship.org/uc/item/7n75g82z

Rival, L. (2000). Formal Schooling and the Production of Modern Citizens in the Ecuadorian Amazon. In B. A. U. Levinson (Ed.), *Schooling the Symbolic Animal: Social and Cultural Dimensions of Education* (pp. 108–122). Lanham: Littlefield.

Rizvi, F. (2001). Postcolonialism and Globalization in Education. *Cultural Studies*, 7(3), 256–263.

Ruiters, G. (2011). Inventing Provinces: Situating the Eastern Cape. In G. Ruiters (Ed.), *The Fate of the Eastern Cape: History, Politics and Social Policy* (pp. 19–41). Scottsville: University of KwaZulu-Natal Press.

Scherz, C. (2014). *Having People, Having Heart: Charity, Sustainable Development, and Problems of Dependence in Central Uganda*. Chicago: University of Chicago Press.

Sharp, J. (1980). Two Separate Developments: Anthropology in South Africa. *RAI News*, 36, 4–6.

Shizha, E. (2005). Reclaiming Our Memories: The Education Dilemma in Postcolonial African School Curricula. In A. A. Abdi & A. Cleghorn (Eds.), *Issues in African Education: Sociological Perspectives* (pp. 65–83). New York/Basingstoke: Palgrave Macmillan.

Simpson, A. (2003). *Half London in Zambia: Contested Identities in a Catholic Mission School*. Edinburgh: Edinburgh University Press.

Slocum, S. (1975). Woman the Gatherer: Male Bias in Anthropology. In R. R. Reiter (Ed.), *Toward an Anthropology of Women* (pp. 36–50). New York: Monthly Review Press.

Soudien, C. (2002). Teachers' Responses to the Introduction of Apartheid Education. In P. Kallaway (Ed.), *The History of Education Under Apartheid*,

1948–1994: The Doors of Learning and Culture Shall Be Opened (pp. 211–223). Cape Town: Pearson Education South Africa.

Soudien, C., & Nekhwevha, F. (2002). Education Post-1948: A View from Below: Education, Tradition, and Change in the Apartheid Era, In P. Kallaway (Ed.), *The History of Education Under Apartheid 1948–1994* (pp. 259–269). Cape Town: Peter Lang Publishing Inc.

South African Press Association (SAPA). (2012). Our Education System is in Crisis. *IOL* (Online). Retrieved November 12, 2012, from http://www.iol.co.za/news/south-africa/our-education-system-is-in-crisis-1.1355362

Spencer, D. (2010). Emotions in the Field and Relational Anthropology. *Emotions in Anthropological Fieldwork* (Online). Retrieved, April 02, 2012, from http://emotionsinanthropology.blogspot.co.uk/

Spiegel, A. D., & Becker, H. (2015). South Africa: Anthropology or Anthropologies? *American Anthropologist, 117*(4), 1–7.

Spiegel, A. D., & McAllister, P. A. (1991). Introduction. In A. D. Spiegel & P. A. McAllister (Eds.), *Tradition and Transition in Southern Africa* (pp. 1–10). Johannesburg: Witwatersrand University Press.

Spreen, C. A., & Vally, S. (2006). Education Rights, Education Policies and Inequality in South Africa. *International Journal of Educational Development, 26*(4), 352–362.

Stafford, C. (2006). *The Roads of Chinese Childhood: Learning and Identification in Angang*. Cambridge: Cambridge University Press.

Stafford, C. (2013). *Ordinary Ethics in China*. London: Bloomsbury Academic.

Stambach, A. (2000). *Lessons from Mount Kilimanjaro: Schooling, Community, and Gender in East Africa*. New York: Routledge.

Stambach, A. (2004). Faith in Schools: Toward an Ethnography of Education, Religion, and the State. *Social Analysis: The International Journal of Social and Cultural Practice, 48*(3), 90–107.

Stambach, A. (2010). *Faith in Schools: Religion, Education and American Evangelicals in East Africa*. Stanford: Stanford University Press.

Stofile, S. Y. (2008). *Factors Affecting the Implementation of Inclusive Education Policy: A Case Study in One Province in South Africa*. Unpublished PhD Thesis, Faculty of Education, University of the Western Cape.

Swanson, D. M. (2013). Neoliberalism, Education and Citizenship Rights of Unemployed Youth in Post-apartheid South Africa. *SISYPHOS Journal of Education, 1*(2), 194–212.

Swartz, S. (2009). *The Moral Ecology of South Africa's Township Youth*. New York: Palgrave Macmillan.

Swartz, S. (2010a). 'Moral Ecology' and 'Moral Capital': Tools Towards a Sociology of Moral Education from a South African Ethnography. *Journal of Moral Education, 39*(3), 305–327.

Swartz, S. (2010b). The Pain and the Promise of Moral Education in Sub-Saharan Africa. *Journal of Moral Education, 39*(3), 267–272.

Swartz, S. (2011). Going Deep' and 'Giving Back': Strategies for Exceeding Ethical Expectations When Researching Amongst Vulnerable Youth. *Qualitative Research, 11*(1), 47–68.

Tisani, N. C. (2000). *Continuity and Change in Xhosa Historiography in the Nineteenth Century: An Exploration Through Textual Analysis*. Unpublished PhD Thesis, History Department, Rhodes University.

Varenne, H. (2007). Difficult Collective Deliberations: Anthropological Notes Toward a Theory of Education. *Teachers College Record, 109*(7), 1559–1588.

Varenne, H. (2008). Culture, Education, Anthropology. *Anthropology & Education Quarterly, 39*(4), 356–368.

Wadesango, N., Chabaya, O., Rembe, S., & Muhuro, P. (2011). Source of Behavioural Problems That Affect the Realization of the Right to Basic Education Among Children: A Case Study of Schools in the Eastern Cape-South. *Journal of Social Sciences, 27*(3), 149–156.

Waghid, Y., & Engelbrecht, P. (2002). Inclusive Education, Policy and Hope: Mapping Democratic Policy Changes on Inclusion in South Africa. *International Journal of Special Education, 17*(1), 20–25.

Wang, C. (2013). Right or Wrong? A Taoqi Student in an Elite Primary School in Beijing. In C. Stafford (Ed.), *Ordinary Ethics in China today* (pp. 29–44). London: Bloomsbury.

Warden, T. (2013). Feet of Clay: Confronting Emotional Challenges in Ethnographic Experience. *Journal of Organizational Ethnography, 2*(2), 150–172.

Watt, N., & Smith, D. (2013). Hague accuses South Africa of "bureaucratic confusion" over aid cut. *The Guardian* (Online). Retrieved March 01, 2017, from https://www.theguardian.com/politics/2013/may/01/william-hague-aid-south-africa

Webb, V. (1999). Multilingualism in Democratic South Africa: The Over-Estimation of Language Policy. *International Journal of Educational Development, 19*(4–5), 351–366.

Weber, M. (1978). *Economy and Society: An Outline of Interpretive Sociology*. Los Angeles: University of California Press.

Weiss, B. (2009). *Street Dreams and Hip Hop Barbershops: Global Fantasy in Urban Tanzania*. Bloomington: Indiana University Press.

Willis, P. (1977). *Learning to Labour*. Farnborough: Saxon House.

Wilson, M. (1969). Co-operation and Conflict: The Eastern Cape Frontier. In M. Wilson & L. Thompson (Eds.), *The Oxford History of South Africa* (pp. 233–271). Oxford: Oxford University Press.

Wilson, M. (1971). *Religion and the Transformation of Society*. Cambridge: Cambridge University Press.

Winchatz, M. R. (2006). Fieldworker or Foreigner? Ethnographic Interviewing in Nonnative Languages. *Field Methods, 18*(1), 83–97.

Wolcott, H. F. (2003). *A Kwakiutl Village and School.* Walnut Creek: AltaMira Press.
Wolcott, H. F. (2011). If There's Going to Be an Anthropology of Education. In M. Pollock & B. A. U. Levinson (Eds.), *A Companion to the Anthropology of Education* (pp. 97–11). Chichester: Wiley-Blackwell.
Wright, L. (2012). Origins of the Eastern Cape Education Crisis. In L. Wright (Ed.), *South Africa's Education Crisis: Views from the Eastern Cape* (pp. 1–18). Grahamstown: NISC.
Xu, J. (2014). Becoming a Moral Child Amidst China's Moral Crisis: Preschool Discourse and Practices of Sharing in Shanghai. *Ethos, 42*(2), 222–242.
Zigon, J. (2006). An Ethics of Hope: Working on the Self in Contemporary Moscow. *Anthropology of East Europe Review, 24*(2), 71–80.
Zigon, J. (2007). Moral Breakdown and the Ethical Demand: A Theoretical Framework for an Anthropology of Moralities. *Anthropological Theory, 7*(2), 131–150.
Zigon, J. (2008). *Morality: An Anthropological Perspective.* Oxford: Berg.
Zigon, J. (2009a). Hope Dies Last: Two Aspects of Hope in Contemporary Moscow. *Anthropological Theory, 9*(3), 253–271.
Zigon, J. (2010). Moral and Ethical Assemblages: A Response to Fassin and Stoczkowski. *Anthropological Theory, 10*(1–2), 3–15.
Zigon, J. (2011). *'HIV Is God's Blessing': Rehabilitating Morality in Neoliberal Russia.* Berkeley: University of California Press.
Zigon, J. (2014). An Ethics of Dwelling and a Politics of World-Building: A Critical Response to Ordinary Ethics. *Journal of the Royal Anthropological Institute, 20,* 746–764.
Zigon, J., & Throop, C. J. (2014). Moral Experience: Introduction. *Ethos, 42*(1), 1–15.

CHAPTER 2

Living in a City, Town, and Location

In a minibus travelling from the high street to Siseko's home, I instinctively paid for both of us when the young conductor asked everyone for their fare. I didn't ask Siseko before I did it, and he didn't protest or acknowledge my actions. As we hopped out, I set off for the little corner shop up the road, which was already in sight, saying that I wanted to buy a drink. Siseko insisted on coming with me, despite my assurances that I would be fine. The shopkeeper was standing with his stock behind a gated, metal service window. Having asked if I wanted to step inside so that I could more easily make my purchase, he unlocked the door. With a smile that suggested he had never been afforded such treatment, Siseko said that he would also try to enter the service area next time he visited without me.

Bottle of Sprite in hand, we returned to his 'little shack', so that we could listen to a track that Siseko had recorded with his hip-hop group. As they joined us, I became surrounded by Nike and Adidas trainers, and Ecko, Puma, and Zoo York branded hoodies and T-shirts. My attire complied with the unofficial dress code. We planned to finalise the recording before spending the afternoon filming a promotional video. I had joined them in the past to watch music videos and debate the merits of various rappers and producers. They were interested in my career as a DJ, and I wanted to expand my knowledge of the local scene. Our similar taste in music had helped our relationships to develop, and the idea of a collaboratively produced music video was a natural extension of our shared interests

© The Author(s) 2018
O. Pattenden, *Taking Care of the Future*, Anthropological Studies of Education, https://doi.org/10.1007/978-3-319-69826-7_2

and experiences. The plan of action had primarily arisen from their desire to have a promotional film, not any research-led intention on my part to analyse the experience or interrogate the film as a cultural text. My inclusion in the proceedings was, however, cemented by the fact that I owned a digital camera.

Siseko had a semi-dismantled PC next to his bed, which he had built using second-hand parts taken from computers he had fixed in the past. Using a freeware music sequencer downloaded from the internet and a small microphone designed for Skype conversations, not music recordings, they conjoined a sampled female vocal with their own verses, which were delivered in a mix of isiXhosa and English. The track hinged upon the idea that having fun with a girl who then dumps you is a painful thing to endure. They told me they had planned to shoot a video for another song that they had written to highlight the reasons why people were going to prison, but they hadn't organised for "the thugs" to be there for the filming. I asked Siseko if everybody in the locality knew who was and was not a thug. Everyone knew, he said. The difference being that a thug was someone who committed robbery, whereas "other people" did not. I didn't ask for confirmation about which category each member of the group would fall into.

As the recording session drew to a close, eight men crowded around the small screen. Space was tight. A member of the group named Lizo turned to me and said: "Do you want to rent a place like this next time you come to South Africa?" He then looked up at the layer of cardboard that insulated the tin roof and laughed. He didn't know where I lived, but I couldn't honestly tell him that Siseko's place was more inviting. Samkelo said I would be even worse off in the 'shack' next door because rats could slip through the cracks in between the tin sheets and I would have no choice but to "have a shower" when it rained due to holes in the roof. We went outside to take a look, only to see a neighbour from two doors up arrive in the back of a police car, accompanied by a police pickup carrying an undercover officer and a lady in uniform. Siseko's neighbour was handcuffed behind his back but was quite impressively still managing to smoke a cigarette. Siseko told me that he was a "serious thug; very famous here." He said the fact he was handcuffed and still smoking proved that he didn't "care about the police". I'd visited his home two weeks earlier, to speak with a couple that also lived there. They had been drunk, and the lady had spoken of a desire to return to school, one day. I thought it was cramped for two people and didn't know a third resident wasn't at home. The police took very little time to search the property. "They won't find anything," Siseko correctly predicted.

With the pre-show over, we walked towards our first film set, a patch of open public ground next to the main road. We came across a group of Rhodes students who had walked to the site on a 'SlutWalk', an international protest movement concerned with countering sexual violence and "victim blaming" (SlutWalk 2014: np). One held a banner: "A DRESS IS NOT AN INVITATION." As with most of the Community Engagement initiatives at the university, the movement of students into the 'township' (i.e. the Black Area of apartheid) was underpinned by a desire to educate and assist. Their presence was unusual and problematic enough that several police vehicles closely followed them. This response was not evident when large groups of students gathered in areas of the city that had been designated as White during apartheid, nor did I ever see such a police presence during any other event in the 'township'.

Siseko took his position in front of the camera before jokingly saying, "Can you find me a white girl [from that group of students]?" Lizo shut him down almost instantly, "you would never get a white girl". Soon after, a police officer walked up to us and told us it would be better if we filmed nearer the 'SlutWalkers'. I thought he was suggesting that we film with a lot of people in shot to improve the video, but we ignored his advice and carried on. We walked to our second set: a shop covered in graffiti, with rusted metal shutters over its windows. A police car pulled up across the road. The police officer did not say anything or get out of the car; he just watched as I filmed the rappers gesticulating to a recording of their song that played through an unimpressive mobile-phone speaker. It was a collaborative effort. The performers drove matters by changing outfits, picking locations, and ordering retakes. I drew upon my experience in London's advertising industry to offer advice about angles, framing, and continuity. Even though I spent no time in front of the camera, the relations of power between us did not comply with an archetypical notion of an observer/observed dichotomy. Instead, the filming helped to cement the mutual respect and understanding that facilitated subsequent activity that was more explicitly research-led (i.e. recorded conversations and Siseko's interviews).

As the afternoon progressed, it became clear that these dynamics were not visible to everyone. As we walked towards our next film location, the disused railway line, a second police car followed us. The police officer pulled over and told me that he wanted us to rejoin "the main group".

I told him that we were separate from the SlutWalk and were filming a video. He said, "OK", then turned around and drove off. He addressed me and not my companions, just as the first two police officers had done.

As we were filming in front of a derelict church, a fourth policeman appeared. He walked towards me, again without acknowledging my companions. He said that this was "a hot spot" and that I "should not be here with strangers", nor give him "any trouble". I told him that they were not strangers and that I had been working with Siseko for the last two months. I said we were not part of the SlutWalk. He asked me to confirm this, before noting this fact in a small notepad. As he walked back to his car, he turned and addressed Siseko and the others for the first time: he was there on the instruction of his supervisor and was sorry for the confusion. I could sense his embarrassment. We all said that it was OK and that we understood. As we all talked about these events later that afternoon, Siseko said that the policemen probably thought that he and his friends had separated me from the SlutWalk group, with the promise of some interesting pictures, as though to lure me into a trap, like a bunch of lions separating a young buck from his herd before the kill/robbery.

Two years and ten days later, I was again looking at the cardboard sheets and scraps of lino that covered the walls and floor of Siseko's home. Two other members of the hip-hop group and two new acquaintances were there too. The PC had been replaced by a laptop that he had brought for R250 ($24) when a customer couldn't afford to pay for its repair. My coat stayed on, and I could see my breath in front of my face. We shared some bottles of beer and watched music videos; 50 Cent, Lil Wayne, Nas, and Busta Rhymes; penthouses, bikinis, and sports cars. When Times Square appeared on the screen, I took out my phone to show a picture of me standing on the same street several months earlier. When Siseko responded by saying, "Hey, I wish I was you", I regretted my decision. He asked me to take a photo of him posing with a bottle of whisky that must have cost a day's wage.

An older neighbour poked her head around the door: "*Yoh, umlungu!*" she cried. "It's OK, I'm not going to hurt you", I replied, much to the amusement of the young men around me. She ran off, before returning five minutes later, seemingly to inform my drinking partners again that there was an *umlungu* (white man/person) in the room, in case they hadn't noticed already. Siseko explained that there was "this thing in her head" that she couldn't ignore when she saw me. She was "used to white people being in their houses in town, giving her orders as a housemaid".

His cousin went on to say that when I walked with them in the location: "[I am always thinking that people] will be looking at me and thinking, 'Hey, that guy thinks he is better than us [because he is walking with an *umlungu*]'." When we later walked home from a tavern, where I had played pool and chatted with groups of people I had never met before, Cebo, a past pupil, told me that "everyone [in the tavern] was asking us, 'Who is this guy?' It has made us famous [having you with us]." Clearly, in certain places, I stuck out like a sore thumb.

Almost 20 years after the end of apartheid, the legacy of its spatial distinctions was still visible and influential. Movement patterns were no longer enforced on the basis of 'race', at least not officially, but were both symptomatic and productive of socio-economic-political polarities. What had been the Black or Coloured Areas were still most often referred to as the "location" or "township". The formerly White Area was most commonly known as "town", at least by my interlocutors.[1] Most clearly, there remained a noticeable 'racial' divide to population distribution (see Fig. 2.1). Although some households registered as Black in the 2011 census had moved to the town, they remained outnumbered by White ones. I was not aware of any (previously) White households that had made a move in the opposite direction. When walking in the location, strangers would often approach me and ask where I was from and what I was doing there. "I'm from London", I would reply. "You're from London, London? *Yoh*! Sharp, sharp my brother. Go safe", went one conversation. Once I had similarly explained my presence, several others responded with, "You're welcome [here]." Young and old often shouted "*umlungu*" when they saw me, which never happened in town. As I walked with a small gaggle of learners, we passed an albino: "Now there are two of you here", one quipped.

During these fieldwork experiences, I was doing something similar to what Bourgois (1996b: 29, also see Bourgois 1996a) did during his research in Spanish Harlem: "confront[ing] the overwhelming reality of racial and class-based apartheid". Except, the word apartheid had particular connotations in my environment, and I would replace the phrase 'class-based' with 'material wealth'. National income inequality has been increasing: South Africa's Gini coefficient was 63.1% (or 0.63) in 2009 (World Bank 2009), the fourth highest measurement of any country in the world. The Gini coefficient of Makana Municipality, which encompassed Grahamstown, was 0.66 in 2010 (ECSECC 2012a). Although the percentage of those living below the poverty line in the municipality rose from 33.6% in 1996 to

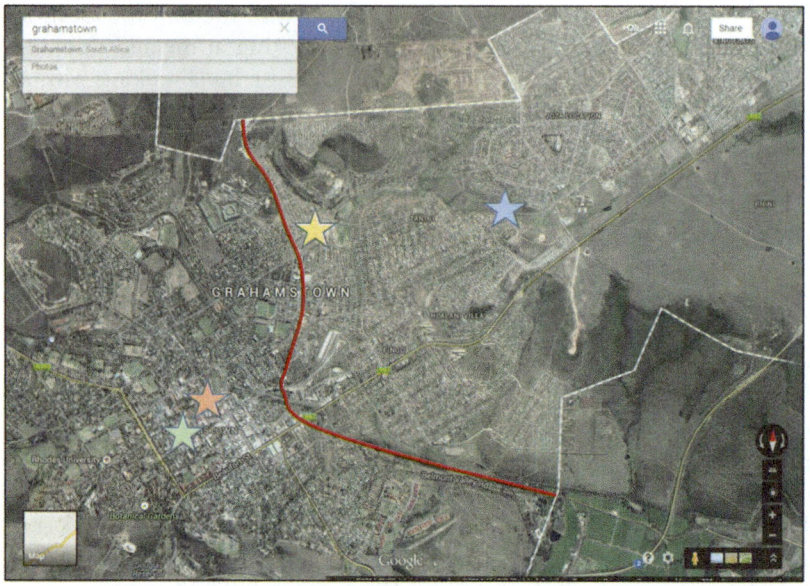

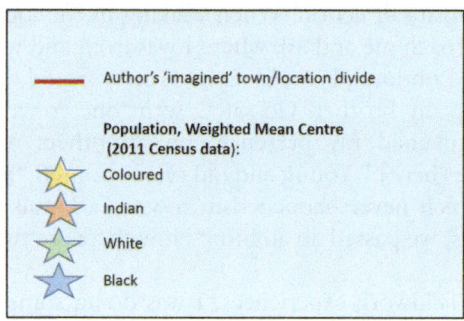

Fig. 2.1 Grahamstown, 2011 (Note: The location extended further to the north-east)

35% in 2011, the poverty gap (a measurement of the 'depth of poverty') increased from R28 million in 1996 to R64 million in 2010 (ECSECC 2012a).[2] In other words, although the percentage of those in poverty has not dramatically changed, those in poverty have become increasingly worse off. South Africa has a relatively high cost of living given its average income levels, in part driven by a market that favours monopolies rather than workers (Barchiesi 2011). Moreover, because there has been little national growth in skilled and semi-skilled job opportunities, employment does not always provide economic stability and a ladder out of poverty (Bank 2011; Barchiesi 2003).[3] In short, during the post-apartheid period, it has become increasingly difficult for many to separate themselves from poverty.

The learners and their families were far from immune to such challenges. Shortly before my arrival in South Africa, Mrs Noni—the school's Learner Support Agent (LSA), who assisted the principal and her deputy with matters relating to health, welfare, and attendance—conducted a survey of 44 learners who lived in the township, rather than the Shelter (see Fig. 2.2).[4] From this sample, 73% of learners said that their parent(s)/caregiver(s) did not work (see Fig. 2.2). If the survey had not excluded those staying at the Shelter, I expect the figure would be higher. The municipal average unemployment rate was 32.55% (SSA 2011). I do not know how the employment status of learners' households would translate into average incomes. However, none could be classed as financially or materially wealthy. There were a handful of exceptions that I knew of, where an employed parent had no trouble providing food, for example, but, to my knowledge, none of the learners' households owned a car.[5] Moreover, most were also not endowed with electrical appliances, furniture, running water, and internal abolitions. As an example, I visited

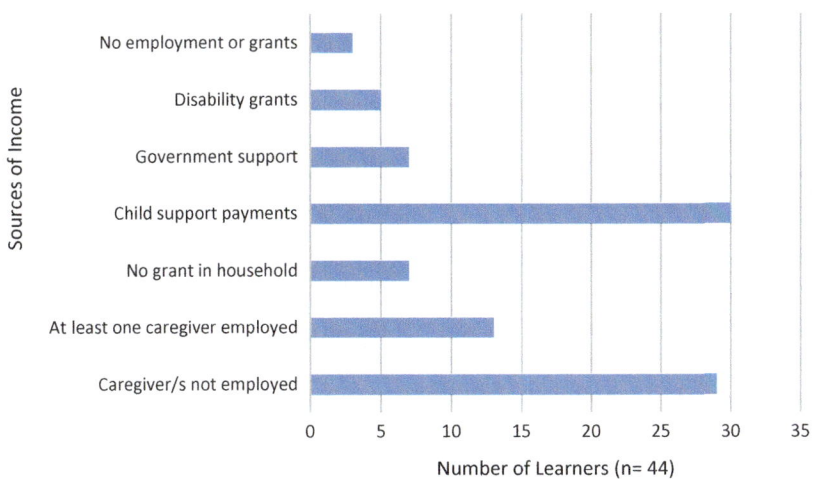

Fig. 2.2 Sources of surveyed learners' household incomes

a learner's home in the hope of understanding why she was not in school. There was a heavy and potent stench in the air. As soon as I walked through the door, I was struck by the lack of ventilation. My eyes were adjusting to the absence of light. The learner's grandmother, who told me that she had problems with her legs and had difficulty walking, lay on a bed, covered in layers of knitted blankets and sheets. Hessian sacks covered the ceiling, which must have struggled to insulate her during winter nights. In the same room, a pair of elderly men sat opposite two males several years younger than me. As we spoke about the learner, a small box TV flickered away as it struggled to find a signal.

The staff at Ngomso and their families represented a more diverse range of household incomes and levels of disposable income. For instance, the school's car park was filled with educators' new 4×4s, ageing hatchbacks, and vehicles with intermediate resale values. In contrast, only one member of the non-teaching staff had a (well-maintained but well-aged) car while others petitioned to be collected by the school bus each morning as the seven-rand taxi (private minibus) fee was prohibitively expensive to them. Similar distinctions were visible in their living arrangements. Four educators—those in managerial roles or with partners in well-paid jobs—lived in the town while the rest lived in some of the township's more desirable homes. Some of the non-teaching staff lived in Reconstruction and Development Programme (RDP) houses, funded by the ANC government as part of a wider socio-economic/poverty alleviation policy framework, with external toilets, chicken wire fences, and no hot water.[6]

It is a fair assumption that all the households in Grahamstown that used paraffin for cooking, had pit latrines or the 'bucket system', and no internal sources of water were in that location.[7] Walking past an open drain with several learners one afternoon, Nyameko, who was in grade six at the time, pointed to it and said, "That thing is dirty." "Do people play in it?" I asked. He responded by pointing a little upstream, towards youngsters running in and out of the sewage. Some homes had roofs made of rusted corrugated iron sheets and had walls that crumbled in the rain (see Fig. 2.3). In contrast to the town, the location had many untarred roads, which had to be navigated like a minefield. These were not mapped by Google Street View, unlike all of those in town. Few residents had internet access and would have been unable to view their front gates, where present, on a computer screen at home regardless.

Fig. 2.3 House in the location
This photograph was taken by Sibusiso, a grade six learner, during the *My Future* project. As he explains, "I was taking a picture of the ducks, but I can see the whole house come out now. Because a lot of black people used to have a lot of chickens and ducks, but not now. Can you see my location? It is not brick houses; we make the houses from soil."

Despite such evident poverty and service-delivery pitfalls, not all households in the location markedly lacked material wealth when compared to those in town. Some had Audi A3s, electric fences, and paved driveways. Even without such luxuries, others had multiple bedrooms and hot showers. Many of these homes were in Extention Four, a relatively small area of housing in the location. Peter, the school's driver, told me that this was where "the professionals" lived. As if to signify how much closer they were to households in town, he added, "some even have their own gardeners". Peter taught me a great deal about the city as we drove around running errands for other members of staff and when dropping learners home after school.

The town hosted the main shopping district and a mall that included a cinema. The public library, high-end restaurants, private schools, Rhodes University, tennis club, and car showrooms were here too. As were many churches and the Anglican Cathedral. Homes and rents were vastly more expensive in the town. The fact that RDP houses have been built far away from former White Areas has served to maintain such distinctions (Bank 2011: 110). As I stood talking to Samkelo, a past pupil, in town one afternoon, at the far-end of the high street near to the school, an unknown man asked him for 20 rand. Samkelo replied: "I'm not from town."

When I asked learners where they lived, none ever answered "Grahamstown". Instead, individuals would say, "Extension Nine" or "Six" (etc.), "Hlalani" or "Joza", which were areas of the location.[8] When recording my surprise that none of the learners in a grade four drama lesson mentioned the word as we talked about their surroundings at home, I wrote, "What is Grahamstown to them? Are Pick n Pay [the expensive supermarket in town] and the cinema, for example, completely alien to them?" Pick n Pay and the city's small cinema were not, of course, unknown. However, they did not regularly visit them. More broadly, movements from the location to the town were patterned, while human traffic more rarely travelled in the other direction. On a daily basis, private minicabs, known as "taxis", ferried maids, cooks, gardeners, security guards, cleaners, petrol attendants, and shop assistants. Once a week, others left their homes in the early morning, walking to the town to pick through the rubbish bags that lay on front lawns ready for the refuse lorries.

Another notable population change occurred in town on the first weekday of each month when there were queues winding down the street from any cash machines that were not already empty of notes. The first time I mentioned this at Ngomso, Mrs Noni explained: "Pension day. It's also when all government grants are paid." South Africa's social security system was already well established before the democratic transition, as 'welfare for Whites' was incrementally expanded to other populations during apartheid (Woolard et al. 2010).[9] The Social Assistance Act of 1992 extended grants and pensions to all South African citizens and social security provisions grew extensively (ibid.). Child Support Grants (CSGs), monthly R250 payments given for each child, were introduced in 1998. By 2010, 29% of the population were receiving at least one form of the government grants, with 9.4 million under the age of 18 receiving CSGs, which "account for 40 percent of household income in the poorest quintile" (ibid: 6). Relatedly, 86% of the surveyed learners reported that their caregiver/s received a government grant of some kind or another, with 68% being aware of CSG payments. Pensions were another major source of income for learners' households and equated to 175% of the annual median per capita income (Woolard et al. 2010: 18). The Shelter received a Foster Care Grant (R710 per month) for each resident.

Perceptions of Danger and Moral Decay in the Location

Like other localities with widespread poverty and high instances of crime and violence, there were concerns about danger and insecurity in Grahamstown and its township in particular (see Bank 2011: 210–214). Sun City, an 'informal settlement' in the location, had "too much crime", according to Peter. With some contrast, Fuzile, a dreadlocked Rastafarian who made pottery in the school's art room and assisted in art lessons, explained where he lived:

> Vucani [an area of the location] is very safe; there are nice guys there, we are not always drinking. We write poetry together and do our hip-hop, write rhymes. We do art. Vucani is very quiet at night: there are three taverns, but they are not as bad as the others [in other areas of the location]. But Thalani [another area] is so dangerous. There are guys there with dangerous guns. There is robbing there every weekend.

In 2011, South Africa's murder rate of 30 per 100,000 population was approximately five times higher than the global average (ISS and Africa Check 2014). With a population of approximately 70,000, there were 35 murders in Grahamstown that same year (Crime Stats 2015). An article in the long-standing local newspaper welcomed the decline from a figure of 42 in 2010, but reported that incidents of robbery had increased: "Grahamstown residents who've felt under siege during the past year haven't been imagining it" (Lang 2011: np).[10] De Souza (2009: 29) refers to the global rise of the 'phobopolis', "a city in which violence has become a very widespread concern, and in which fear has become an almost omnipresent feeling". His consideration of the *intensity* of feelings of fear struck me on my first day in South Africa. With the best intentions and concern for my safety, my interlocutors, young and old, frequently shared their analysis of security issues and offered tips for how I might take care of myself. I soon learnt that my home for 2011 was not considered to be nearly as dangerous as Johannesburg, Cape Town, or Durban. However, talk of safety was so forthcoming that I remember thinking about it as I lay in bed listening to noises that I hoped were birds or creaking gates.

According to conversations I had with members of staff, there was much to be nervous about and suspicious of. Especially the *tsotsis*. Mrs Noni, who was never addressed by her first name, often held my arm when she talked to me and always called me "my friend". She was younger than

Mary, with short, fuzzy hair that she dyed a deep shade of red, but older than many other members of staff. Mrs Noni, Peter, and I arrived at her home one afternoon to find the front door open. "They [the *tsotsis*] are everywhere", Peter informed me. He said they could break into your home "even during the day; they don't care about the neighbours or who is watching".

Swartz (2009: 79) identifies '*tsotsis*' as one of four "moral stances" open to her young interlocutors in Cape Town. As in my experience, she found that '*tsotsi*' was used interchangeably with 'thug' or 'gangster'.[11] Echoing the thoughts of many members of staff, Swartz (ibid: 78) suggests that young *tsotsi* "Were out of school, never at home, and on the streets, except [when in prison gangs]." She (ibid.) continues:

> Crime, substance use, and violence were regular parts of their lives and most had been through the penal system. Their moral positioning was one of ignoring moral codes, unless of course they were in the process of "reforming" – in which many claimed to be.

In reference to his research in East London's townships during the first years of apartheid, Mayer (1961: 73) likened the "tsotsi idea" to "the witch myth" because "both tsotsi and witch embody the same basic concept – the reversal of 'ordinary decent' human values. [Both are] . . . terribly dangerous and terribly unpredictable, so that nobody knows who the next innocent victim may be."[12] Among my interlocutors, those concerned about *tsotsis* were relatedly concerned about societal collectivity. The *tsotsi* did what he liked, without being controlled by teachers, priests, parents, police officers, and, perhaps ultimately, God; and this, they said, meant that they were not free to live without fearing them. Mayer (1961: 73) suggests that some considered *tsotsis* to be different from "ordinary criminals who rob because they are poor" because their criminality is "boundless". They roam the township "with a black heart" (ibid.). Similarly, I learnt that the *tsotsi* was considered to be the most extreme embodiment of what can happen when a young person was not moral, when they had no heart. As Peter and I drove away from Mrs Noni's house, I noted that his warning about ubiquitous *tsotsis* contrasted with the red hearts that Mrs Noni had painted on her door.

More broadly, the staff considered the location to be a site of moral denigration: crime, violence, danger, forced sex or loose fornication, alcoholism, drug use, broken or absent marriages, dirty streets, and dirty talk. The young were considered to be the most troublesome residents. Their concerns are markedly similar to those of academics concerned about 'moral decay' in South Africa who invite more or different, often Christian-oriented, moral education (e.g. Bayaga and Louw 2011; Carl and Johannes 2003; Fry 2012; Louw 2009; Potgieter 1980). The moral judgements of members of staff were most frequently spatialised: the town was different. It was inconceivable that a *tsotsi* should live there. Such considerations are similar to how some European settlers considered the population of 'Xhosaland' to be immoral and 'culturally backward' or 'uncivilised', in contrast to their judgements of the enclave of the colonial 'British town'.

Schooling, Money, and Protection

Holly was head of the department for grades one to four. She liked to ask my opinion on what was happening in her classroom and throughout the school. In their household, her salary was combined with that of her husband, who held a senior post at the ECDoE, and Damba, her daughter, attended a well-regarded, all-girls private school.[13] Money guaranteed access: tuition alone cost R4703 per month (paid volunteers at Ngomso received a monthly stipend of R500). Security guards and electric gates offered safety and protection. I occasionally played tennis on the school's floodlight courts with a friend who worked there. I always cycled past a sea of immaculate blazers and long socks, before setting my bike against a fence. I never felt the need to lock it up. There were no un-plastered breeze blocks and more computers than external toilets. It had an indoor swimming pool and music room. It was in the town, not the location.

Holly said that she was impressed by the increased resources and quality of teaching at her daughter's school. However, I remained curious about what justified the expenditure, especially because the family lived in a well-maintained house in the location, not in the town, and the outlay on fees might have enabled the family to relocate, which was a more typical expenditure.[14] Inversely to how 'low caste' (*asuddha*) children in Nepal learn that their impure touch can pollute pure 'high caste' children (*suddha*) (Larsen 2003), Holly was hopeful that Damba would not be made impure through interaction with "black children" from the location, as she explained:

Oliver: It's expensive to go to [the private school], what's your main motivation for sending Damba there?

Holly: Because not everyone can afford to take a child [there] or [the other private schools in town]. Here, at these schools, there are few [blacks]; it's a white school. . . . When there are more black children than white, it's easy for them to influence the others. Now they are in an adolescent stage, the black children take the things from the location that they see, and they hear, and they do, and then try to influence the others. You see? There [in Damba's private school] it is not easy for them to influence the others.

Oliver: So in [Damba's school] there are fewer influences from the location?

Holly: Yes, there is less there from the location. For instance, maybe there are three or four [black children] from the location there. They can't influence the whites: [they can't tell] all the white kids to 'Do this', or 'Let's start dating', or 'Let's start', [pause] . . . You feel free, even if your child if not with you or your family. [Even when she is with her school friends at their homes in the town] there is not that influence from older girls [living in the location] to not have pure friendship with boys.

In Holly's words, political and economic disparities—legacies of historical injustices and imbalances, such as the segregationist policies of the colonial and apartheid periods, and those in evidence more recently—manifest as fears of moral contamination, particularly regarding sexualisation and chastity. 'The influence' was pervasive and persuasive; without protection, all were held to be under its influence. Any individualised variance was not acknowledged. The agency of the young—their ability to subvert, ignore, discount, devalue, or transform, embrace, and enjoy, what they see, do, hear, and feel—was discounted.[15] Hence, in addition to increased educational opportunity, I felt that Holly saw Damba's private schooling as a necessary means of attaining freedom from impurity. She agreed with me when I asked whether it was "a form of protection". In alignment with claims that racialised fear has predominated in post-apartheid South Africa (e.g. Hansen 2006: 279), the moralised judgements underpinning Holly's actions were racialised (i.e. she equated 'white' with 'the moral'). Her judgements also had a material or economic basis (i.e. she equated material prosperity with 'the moral'). Her understanding of 'the influence' also appeared to hinge upon judgements of spatialised moral possibilities.

Teresa Caldeira considers the favelas of São Paulo, which are similar to South African townships, in being symptomatic of spatialised inequalities of wealth in a highly Christianised post-colony.[16] She (cited in Bank 2011: 213) explains how those living in more wealthy areas of the city fear the favelas: "They seem to think that the spaces of crime are marginal ones . . . and their inhabitants, potential criminals, are people from the fringes of society, humanity and the polity. They also see crime as a phenomenon related to evil, something that spreads and contaminates easily." Bourgois (2002: 22) argues that "the law-abiding majority [in Spanish Harlem] . . . have been pushed onto the defensive, living in fear, or even in contempt, of their neighbourhood. Worried mothers and fathers are forced to maintain children double locked behind apartment doors in determined attempts to keep street culture out." Mayer (1961: 237) tells us that parents similarly "[distrusted the township of East London during apartheid] profoundly as a place where 'girls get spoilt'" and felt that it posed a "threat to [their] virtue". They attempted to control their daughters' movements and encouraged them to stay with a relative or live-in as a domestic servant (presumably in the White Area), in the hope that this would delay "the almost inevitable pregnancy" (ibid; also see ibid.: 252–259). These accounts of 'evil contamination', 'street culture', 'spoiling', and 'threats to virtue' appear to have much in common with Holly's concern about influences from the location, as do the accounts of parents making efforts to protect their children.

Holly's ability to attempt to protect Damba contrasts with one of Mayer's (1961: 72–73) interlocutors in East London, who similarly pondered the dangers and immorality of the location during apartheid: "You can do nothing here about the bad influence on your children." In Grahamstown 50 years on—indeed, from the 1980s when private education was de-segregated—you could do something about it if you could afford to. Moreover, members of staff at Ngomso spoke about locking their doors when the sun went down and not venturing out before morning. Most owned an alarm linked to the control room of a private security firm. Together with their government jobs, pensions, and salaries, and the protection of trade unions, these securities not only provided distinct modes of protection but also distanced them from those who subsisted on a diet of grant money, informal and temporary employment, or, perhaps, crime. Nyquist (1983: 3) considers a *Middle Class Elite* in the township of Grahamstown during apartheid, or the "high ones", the "*abaphakami-leyo*". School inspectors, secondary and primary school teachers, social workers, nurses, and ministers of religion factor in this classification. Apartheid legislation meant that such individuals could not relocate to White Areas. However, Nyquist argues that they still considered themselves to be distinct from other residents in the township.

That tendency persists to this day. Mark Hunter (2010: 115) talks about how the "most privileged elite [in KwaZulu-Natal] has been able to partially insulate itself geographically from the consequences of apartheid's demise". He says that one group classed as Black during apartheid that has since moved to formerly White Areas is teachers. Even if whole families cannot relocate, Hunter argues, those living in the location with 'some money' (e.g. for school fees, uniforms, and transport) send their children to formerly White schools. As elsewhere and for much of recent history, 'the healthy' attempt to distance themselves from 'the sick', guarding, separating, and "not even associating" (Nietzsche 1994: 90). Damba told me that she never interacted with the learners at Ngomso whenever she visited the school. Similarly, those who lived opposite a large secondary school where I worked in London—in multi-million-pound homes that were big enough to house four of the council flats where many learners lived—campaigned for an increased police presence on their street at the end of each school day. They made no effort to interact with the young people they were so fearful of, nor did their children attend our school.

The staff's efforts to isolate themselves from the influence of the location meant that they were, or at least felt, somewhat detached, or untainted, by what might be 'picked up' there. To follow Mary Douglas (1966), they had not allowed themselves to be made 'impure' by the immorality and behaviours of the location. Most that lived in the location considered themselves to be the victims not the creators of its problems. Their sentences contained phrases such as "they don't care" or "those in the location", not collective pronouns such as "we" or "us". Similarly, those living in the town felt separated, if not more so. As I will go on to discuss in more detail, to varying degrees, this meant that they considered themselves to be different from the (potentially impure and dangerous) learners and their families, who were deemed to be 'marginalised' and excluded from *their* society (i.e. the staff's).

Holly and Damba's arrangement was unique. However, those who could not afford the city's private schools did have another option: the former 'Model C' government schools that had catered for Whites during apartheid. Although this terminology was discarded during the post-apartheid transition, these schools continued to be funded by a combination of private and government money. In Grahamstown, heavily oversubscribed former Model C schools offered primary and secondary level schooling and charged fees that were considerably less than those demanded by private schools. Two educators sent their children to these schools, as Mary had done. In contrast, as she cooked mashed potato while I strained to hear above the gospel music that blasted from their 1980s' era hi-fi, Madoda's wife spoke to me about her concerns that her eldest daughter had not got into a former Model C school in the town. She was worried about the unenthusiastic teachers and lack of books at her daughter's current school, but also, because her daughter would have to remain in the township, without the chance to interact with, and learn from, children living in the town. She shrugged her shoulders to say "What can I do?" without opening her mouth.

I spent a day in one of the other private schools in town. My guide was head of admissions and a member of my host Rotary club. He said he found it uncomfortable when parents begged and pleaded for the admittance of their children, despite the fact that they could not afford the fees. Parents wanted to place their offspring in these protected spaces and to give them access to superior resources, relating to sport, music, art, and other areas of schooling. I can imagine their disappointment when it became apparent that the private funding that made such sites so desirable was beyond them and non-negotiable. With this dynamic, private schooling creates an experience of exclusion, both for parents who cannot fulfil hopes for their sons and daughters and for the young people in question who cannot draw from superior educational resources when fashioning their lives.

What are some of the key historical precursors to such experiences? Although the anti-apartheid movement intertwined with People's Education, to some degree at least, centrally defined '(neo)liberal education' came to the fore during transitional negotiations between the ANC and the National Party (Chisholm and Fuller 1996; Salim Vally 2007).[17] Prew (2010: np) argues that this occurred when the "National Party effectively threatened to pull the white middle class out of the public education system" unless it was structured so as to allow "middle class advantage". He (ibid: np) suggests that the structure emerged in response to fears about the potential damage of such an exodus and the benefits promised to the children of "the nascent black middle class sitting around the negotiating table". However, the events also relate to the dissolution of the Soviet Union and the increasing prevalence of market capitalism in post-Mao China, and, relatedly, the ANC's broader move away from socialist economic policies.[18] Organisations, such as the International Monetary Fund (IMF) and World Bank, made concerted efforts to encourage this shift (see Bundy 2014: 31–45). Regarding schooling, private/public funding arrangements were maintained, and private partnerships were welcome (Sayed and Ahmed 2011).[19] In 2012, the Basic Education Minister, Angie Motshekga, sought increased private investment in the public education system (de Waal 2012). Speaking about private and public schools, she (cited in SAPA 2012: np) said, "You cannot compare bananas to apples, a Rolls Royce with a Toyota." Similarly, my interlocutors recognised that hopes for an equal and democratic schooling system, as enshrined in the Schools Act of 1996, had not materialised. They knew there were stark disparities between schools that did and did not charge fees, and those that were entirely private (also see Chisholm 2004; Prew 2010). When fashioning their lives within the confines of this arrangement, they experienced and constituted perpetuating, economically organised forms of exclusion.

Corporal Punishment, Respect, and Moral Education

For some interlocutors, an important explanation for perceived moral degeneration in the location was a breakdown of communitarian, intergenerational structures of power. As we drove away from Mrs Noni's home, Peter was explaining how *tsotsis*, who had not infiltrated Mrs Noni's home as he had feared, were just one outcome of changing disciplinary practices. For Peter, the *tsotsis* were particularly immoral, but many other young people were problematic because they had not been morally educated either and therefore similarly lacked discipline. When he was younger: "You would be beaten by an adult if you were drunk at seventeen; even by an adult that didn't know you." He continued by saying that if you told your parents a stranger had beaten you, "they would then beat you twice as hard because they knew there must have been a reason for the beating and that the adult was right to do that". Mrs Noni nodded and said, "*Ewe*" (yes) with enthusiasm.

Twelve days later, Mrs Noni returned to this topic of conversation when complaining about "many issues" with young people in the location. She said that when she was young "my mother used to beat me and my father used to beat me too," especially if she complained to her father that her mother had done so. She said that this meant she was "disciplined and respectful". She concluded by saying that parents disciplined in this way because they cared about their children and their futures, explaining that "Me and my sister were chosen by our husbands because we were disciplined and our family was disciplined." She argued that this disposition explained why her marriage to a pastor continued to prosper. Although she didn't articulate her argument in quite this way, she was effectively saying that many other marriages 'ended early' as a result of lacking discipline during childhood and adolescence and that these 'failed marriages' explained immorality in the location.

Focusing on the training of males, Mayer (1961: 85) discusses how "rustic Xhosa [men]" would enact "physical chastisement" upon uninitiated boys (*amakwenkwe*) and young men (*umfana*) as a "natural mode of correction".[20] They were "beaten" with "sticks" as a consequence of immoral behaviour (ibid.). "An occasional beating" was thought to be "a good [preventative] 'lesson'" (ibid.). This practice was a 'communal'— that is, not strictly brought about by parents or families—responsibility, considered integral to moral education and societal cohesion.[21] In this light, the conversation between Peter and Mrs Noni, regarding their experience of being disciplined by individuals outside their immediate families can be understood as evidence of their embodiment of related moral discourses. "In the eyes of the average country-born Xhosa", Mayer (ibid.) argues, "it is precisely the absence of this pervasive 'communal' discipline in town that turns the town boy into something much worse than a dog [i.e. uninitiated boy], namely a tsotsi". A "migrant" from "the country" said, "parents are powerless in town" due to this absence (ibid: 86). Another suggested it "spoilt" youngsters living the city (ibid.). I do not know if Mrs Noni and Peter would describe themselves as 'average country-born Xhosas', however, having been disciplined in a similar way as a young lady and an uninitiated boy during apartheid, they were similarly mourning an absence of communal, corporal punishment more than 50 years after Mayer's research.

As with Mayer's fieldwork, the word 'respect' was central to many conversations that I had regarding generational hierarchies, discipline/control, and moral education. Benedict Carton (cited in Ntsimane 2007: 115) defines *ukuhlonipha* as "a custom of deference, male and female youths and married women avoided male elders as means of respect and homage". I came to understand that *ukuhlonipha* could also mean respect for elders of either sex. Being respectful of elders was seen as a cornerstone of being a disciplined, moral young person (also see Monica Hunter 1936; Mayer 1961; Ngwane 2001). Some of my interlocutors thought that changing practices of punishment had compromised this obligation.

During the school's AGM one evening, Mr Mayoni was entertaining the room with a story about how the location had become awash with alcohol and sex. As an elderly gent wearing a royal blue suit, he had laid his pork-pie hat on the table. I later told him that he looked like a dapper trumpeter in a 1950s jazz band. I think he took this as a compliment. Before retiring and joining Ngomso's SGB, he sat on the township council during apartheid. He told the room that he had recently entered a tavern to buy some alcohol to bring back to his house. Seeing that he had some money to spend, a young lady had tried to chat him up, making it obvious that he could expect something in return for buying her a drink. She was decades his junior. This prevalent 'sexual economy' (see Mark Hunter 2010) was not foreign to the staff and SGB members in the room. They all laughed when he said he had been surprised by the offer. This young lady should not have been in the tavern; she should have been at home with her parents, he continued. Such waywardness was a cause for concern. "Parents must not shout at their children [when disciplining them]", he explained. "They must talk to them and ask them to stop [doing such inappropriate things]. Even those that sleep out at their boyfriend's: you must speak to them and not beat them because they will report you to the police."[22]

When I first contemplated Mr Mayoni's account, I felt that he was positive about the potential for parents to control and discipline their offspring with words rather than corporal punishment. However, when I returned in 2013, I added another layer to my understanding. As I sat in the back of the school's minibus, pressed against a closed window while suffering from the heat of the sun through the glass, he and Joyce were talking to me about childrearing. Like others, they were interested in the legality of discipline and government involvement in parental freedoms. "The government has taken over with our children", Mr Mayoni proclaimed, while I struggled to scribble in my notebook as we sped over the pitted, patch-worked tarmac. He continued:

> Spanking is illegal, let alone corporal punishment. These days you can find yourself in trouble if you spank the baby for sucking too hard. The baby can never learn what it is supposed to do or not supposed to do. The government interferes with upbringing; because parents are not allowed to beat their children. These policies come from white people.

Governmental supervision of interactions and relations between adults and children, including parental and caregiver relations, has increasingly been linked with public and institutional discourses of human rights following the demise of apartheid.[23] For instance, the Children's Act No. 38 of 2005 (Republic of South Africa 2005: Title) legislated particular intergenerational relations of power in setting "out principles relating to the care and protection of children" and defining "parental responsibilities and rights". According to Mr Mayoni, young South Africans were protected before these 'white policies'. "Young kids weren't beaten", he argued, or abused or left with permanent marks, they were hit just hard enough so that they wouldn't 'act out' again.[24] With a sense of bafflement and regret, he said, "Now, if you chastise without beating, the child will now open the case. They are laying charges against the father." Luxolo, the driver, and Joyce signalled their agreement. Mr Mayoni continued by saying that children skipped school because they knew their parents could not beat them.

Mark Hunter's (2010: 119–120) interlocutors in KwaZulu-Natal were also concerned that pervasive human rights discourses and associated laws and policies that aim to empower children had diminished the power of "a set of 'traditional' practices justified through *hlonipha* (respect)". Worryingly for such interlocutors, this has meant "individuals [and children especially] can challenge long-established [gender and generational] hierarchies".[25] Some of my interlocutors clearly had similar concerns. They argued that the young had too much power, curtailing their freedom to provide them with moral education.[26] As a result, the young were 'out of control' because they no longer feared the consequences of ignoring adult direction, disrupting moral cohesion. Egalitarianism between children and adults—that is, an absence of respect or *ukuhlonipha*—as promoted by 'the authorities' was thus undesirable.[27] More broadly, the emphasis that the human rights discourse places on the value of liberty can appear misguided in the eyes of those who value hierarchical orderings of generational power in their quest to establish equality (see Robbins 2007). Mr Mayoni analysed the situation by saying, "It's a clash of cultures; we don't like this." In his analysis, it is possible to see how conflicting attributions of moral value are frequently understood and articulated through the idiom of cultural contestation (Moore 2011). As South Africans know all too well, individuals can put forth a moralised case for the generation of a particular future by employing the idea that cultures are both bounded and subjectable to hierarchical judgements of desirability.

In contrast to Mr Mayoni's concern, chastising a suckling baby with 'reasonable' physical force was legal.[28] However, rather confusingly, the national Constitution and UN Convention on the Rights of the Child both 'guarantee' South African childhoods "free from all forms of violence".[29] This contradiction has encouraged institutions—for example, the UN, Human Rights Council, Children's Institute, The Children's Rights Project, and Save the Children—to mobilise human rights discourses and South African constitutional legislation when campaigning to outlaw corporal punishment (Jamieson and Mathews 2013; Owen 2012; STC 2005; UN 2008). These organisations promote alternative forms of 'positive discipline'. Such efforts led the National Portfolio Committee on Social Development, media outlets, and 'the public' to debate alternatives to the 'reasonable chastisement' clause, for example, parents fined for "spanking their children" and plans for "programmes on parenting skills and positive discipline" (Waterhouse 2007: 3). Those campaigning for the amendment cast the debate as 'progressive, modern parenting' versus 'backward, traditional practices'. Perhaps this was the 'white interference' that Mr Mayoni referenced.

Such 'modern' conceptions of moral education reward 'the good and welcome', rather than punish 'the negative and unwelcome'. The method is to control with carrots rather than sticks, Santa's list, and the promise of a new bike. One of the 'special education units' I worked at in London used *Traffic Light Charts*. Students were scored out of five following a lesson, according to their targets, for example, "Ask the teacher for some time out when I get angry"; "Accept when a mistake has been made and accept the teacher's resolution." Red for a bad day, green for a good one. Enough green days and you could earn a prize, either a material reward or a brief return to 'mainstream lessons'. Such mechanisms are a powerful option for educators who have something to offer as a reward. However, material expenditure was beyond many households in the location, especially my young interlocutors'.[30] While you can positively reward with praise, which is free, many of my interlocutors felt that this technique was less powerful than the memory of a smacked bottom or rapped knuckle. They didn't appear to enjoy inflicting harm nor were they 'pining for the past', but were hoping to build and maintain moral collectivity. Such ethical imaginations were inextricability tied to South Africa's socio-economic-political climate and my interlocutors' quotidian experiences and judgements.

Fighting and Justice

In continuing to consider the prevalence of violence in the location, this final section of the chapter interrogates Stafford's (2010: 200, building on Westermarck) claim that "underlying emotional reactions, which call for retribution, are at the root of all ethics and morality". The following statement is something that Siseko told me about a link between habitual conduct at Ngomso and education in the township:

> You will notice at school – the small boy is not afraid of the bigger boy. It is what they are taught in the township. If someone is fighting you, the father will say 'My son, you must fight. There is no need to ask what is going on; you must fight.' They are well trained when they are small. The small boy learns to protect himself.

In short, using positive reinforcement, he said that parents encouraged their offspring, and the males, in particular, to fight back following an altercation. As the father featured in Johnny Cash's song, *A Boy Named Sue* explains: "Son, this world is rough. And if a man's gonna make it, he's gotta be tough."

One afternoon I wrote the word "location" (i.e. township) on the blackboard and filmed a drama performance by four male learners.[31] It first depicted the mugging of an old man. A local drug dealer then stepped in to help him to 'beat' the perpetrators. As we watched the footage of their play, the performers elaborated on some of its themes, inadvertently supporting Siseko's assertion:

Dibana: Our mothers tell us to fight.
Fundani: If this guy beat me, my mother [will] say, 'Go, go, go for revenge.'
Langa: Get revenge.
Fundani: Even my father [and] all my family [will tell me that]. Because [when] he was my age, his mother said 'Go, do revenge.'
Jama: If I am fighting [and] I go home and tell my mother [inaudible] slap me and tell me to go back and fight.
Fundai: *Ja* [yes].
Jama: And then I fight back. If I do that, my mother will say 'Good, good.'
Fundani: If I win she will cook me *umphokoqo*, the meal of milk [a treat], because I am the man. Or she will cook and buy for me a chicken. *Ja*. [And say] 'You are the tough man.'
Fundani: In our culture, it's like that.

Importantly, they told me that their parents did not promote violence for its own sake, nor encourage them to "hit first". They were encouraged to respond to incursions in a particular way, not to instigate them.

I witnessed such a response when walking in the township with three learners one Saturday afternoon. Four men walked towards us. They were searching for someone, clearly in response to some form of intrusion. They held a spade, piece of wood, a large kitchen knife and hockey stick. A group of youngsters and women followed them as they disappeared with purposeful strides. My interlocutors informed me that they had witnessed such events many times before. Even if it was not their primary intention, these men were setting out a pedagogic example of how to 'do revenge'. We might say their response was redressive (Turner 1974). In seeking the perpetrator of whatever had befallen them or someone they cared for, they had taken on the responsibility of responding to the unwelcomed event and were endeavouring to bring a halt to such misfortune (Laidlaw 2010: 149, 156).

To stimulate another drama performance, I wrote the word "*Tsotsi*" on the blackboard. It began with a man, played by Peta, feeding his chickens in the yard of his home, as his friend, Bonani, looked on. When their eyes turned, two other men, played by Jama and Diliza, wrung the necks of four chickens and took them home. Dismayed at the loss of his birds, Peta knocked on Jama's door before throwing the suspects to the floor. After Bonani had located the chickens under the kitchen table, there was an exchange of punches and stamps to the head, before Peta and Bonani whipped the accused with their belts. Peta's "neighbour" then pinned Jama and Diliza back to the floor, accusing them of the theft while striking their heads. Afterwards, I spoke to performers and spectators as we watched footage of the play:

Dumisa (spectator):	The neighbours [had the belts]. They look after the chickens, you see? So they are stopping crime.
Unknown Voice:	When you found me, then you must beat me.
Dumisa:	Because you have a right; I steal your stuff first.
Oliver:	What's the reason that the neighbours are helping?
Dumisa:	They show [i.e. teach] me [the *tsotsi*] to respect [them] and [say], 'You mustn't do that again in this street. . . . Tell the other criminals: "[Avoid] that street, it's too rude [i.e. violent]."' We have street committees [and] if you go to them and say, 'Someone

> stole my stuff", then they call everyone, the neighbours, who stay in the same areas; and try and find out who has it. . . . Everyone is angry about that. When neighbours beat you, they make it sore; so you never steal again. When the cops come [after the beating], they find the truth. [Without it they] will never find the truth.

The rationale for such punishment is, then, both *retribution*, which we might associate with a Kantian morality, and *deterrence*, which we might associate with a utilitarian ethic (Metz and Gaie 2010: 278).[32] These are the same "two dominant rationales for State punishment of adult offenders" (ibid.). Calling the police (immediately), personal revenge, and collective retribution involving neighbours and street committees were moral potentialities with substitutable rationales.[33] The disjuncture lay with the *legal* legitimacy of retribution (Abrahams 1996, 1998). Importantly, most learners weren't confident about the ability of agents of the State, and the police, in particular, to enact justice and deliver security. Such judgements followed colonial and apartheid periods when 'blacks' encountered an underfunded police force (Pauw 1963) that controlled, humiliated, and oppressed rather than defended them (Kirsch 2010: 145; Brogden 1989; Watson 1999). There is evidence that such relationships have continued during the democratic transition (McMichael 2013; Pithouse 2011, 2013, 2014; Tabensky 2012). Additionally, the need for protection and justice has been, to some extent, ceded to the private security sector by those with the means to do so (Comaroff and Comaroff 2007: 216). The financial resources of my young interlocutors and their families excluded them from such 'privatised' possibilities.[34]

'Fighting back' can thus be considered as an orientation, perspective, and discernment about how one might "make efforts to keep going through the vicissitudes of life" (Zigon and Throop 2014: 11). The value and significance of this mode of responding to the world depended on identifiable historical and cultural contexts, relations of economic and political power, and experiences of freedom.[35] Siseko, who was a father to a two-year-old boy, offered insight into his perspective:

> I can't give my baby the love that I want to, [like other men can]. But I can make it that no one will touch him. . . . The only love [I can give] is that I can protect him there in location.

> We are fighting because that is the way that we care at home. You can never touch my child. Love is the fighting. [My son] sees me beat that other man and he feels safe. It is the only thing that I can do for him. . . . Those people who have everything, like the house and the car, have all those things, so they are soft. They are good, but they are soft. And we cannot stand with them because they are too soft.

Given this context, the moral qualities of Siseko's statement about the forms of educative discourse promoted by parents in the township become clearer. He was describing instruction concerned with the son's best interests: an ethical imagining of a brighter future, given an evaluation of "social and historical reality" and a "concrete sense of a particular ethical [or moral] life" (Williams 1993: 197). If being "too soft" meant that others would not "stand" with you, the alternative moral disposition promoted by the parent in his example (i.e. habitually fighting back and being strong) could help the boy avoid social exclusion (Williams 1993: 47–48). To my mind, the spatially defined nature of this collectivity is reflected in the moral judgements that Siseko encountered when he left the township. There was no official curfew, as existed in the colonial and apartheid periods, but he recognised more informal restrictions on movement. He told me that he wore different clothes when he went to town at night because he had been questioned by private security firms and the police many times before:

> I'm not living in town; so why am I there at twelve [midnight]? They are judging my clothes and my face – maybe there are too many scratches on my face [and they will know where I come from]. There are students in town so they must decide [if I am a student or not by looking at these things].

Apartheid's enduring legacies are manifest in Siseko's considered attempt to influence the moral judgements that others made about him. With its increased levels of security and protection, compared to the township, the town was generally presumed to have an opposed tolerance of fighting, as personified by Mama Mary, who always discouraged learners from fighting. Relatedly, having provided love and care to his child using the limited resources at his disposal, most notably his body, Siseko could not dwell amongst the residents of the town without crafting ways to evade the gaze of the security apparatus they put in place to exclude 'young men like him' from their environment. More broadly, the inequalities that shape disparate feelings of freedom and comfort in South African cities, and throughout the world, are tested and configured as a consequence of such ethical encounters.

Notes

1. From this point onward, I employ the terms 'location', 'township', and 'town' as per everyday usage of my interlocutors (i.e. without capitalisation or scare quotes).
2. There is no official 'poverty line' in South Africa. The figures from the ECSECC are based upon R1892 ($177) per month for an average-sized family in Port Elizabeth, Eastern Cape.
3. Eastern Cape industries were supported by government subsidies during apartheid. However, the area experienced pervasive de-industrialisation as activity dissolved along with the subsidies. Indeed, the Eastern Cape has been particularly vulnerable to companies exploiting globalised competition, manufacturing, and distribution procedures (Bank 2011: 211). Other than its university, schools, and shops, Grahamstown has little industry.
4. I helped Mrs Noni organise her data and produced tables and charts that she could use. She was happy for me to use this data, in return for this assistance. The respondents knew their answers were being recorded and I have maintained their anonymity.
5. Car ownership in South Africa stood at 165 per 1000 population in 2010, which is comparable to 809 in the US and 519 in the UK ('List of Countries by Vehicles per Capita' 2015).
6. The RDP programme was replaced by the Growth, Employment and Redistribution (GEAR) programme in June 1996 (Bundy 2014: 61). However, my interlocutors continued to refer to any government-funded housing projects as "RDP houses".
7. In 2011, the Eastern Cape was the highest ranked province for the use of paraffin and wood for cooking, unsafe water for drinking, and inadequate sanitation (ECSECC 2011). Internet access was rare (ibid.). One local civic activist (Kota, cited in Jack 2011: np) suggested that Grahamstown was "one of the worst areas in the province in terms of service delivery". Figures from the Eastern Cape Socio Economic Consultative Council (ECSECC 2012b) state that 71% of households in the Makana Municipality (including Grahamstown) had flush or chemical toilets in 2010.
8. In isiXhosa, Grahamstown is named *Rhini*; a word used by some individuals in the locality to denote the specific area of the city denoted as Black during apartheid (i.e. Grahamstown East). The fact that the city is officially known as Grahamstown is contentious because Colonel John Graham is held to have led a particularly brutal military campaign against the Xhosa. Relatedly, there have been calls for the city to be officially (re)named Rhini. In 2005, President Thabo Mbeki (2005) stated: "Rhini had a place name before it became Grahamstown and if some people say we should return to the traditional name of this place and another says no, we should keep the current name that was born out of the system of colonialism it raises a tension

because we want an inclusive South Africa that belongs to all who live in it." ANC councillors supported a name-change in 2007, which was opposed by members of the Democratic Alliance (DA) (IOL, 'Councillors Pick a New Name for Grahamstown' 2007). In 2013, the issue was still, according to a local journalist (Onceya 2013: np), "arguably the city's hottest topic". More recently, journalists writing in the national press have pressed for the name-change (e.g. Dlanga 2014). These events relate to wider contestation concerning South Africa's colonial past, which has seen a statue of the British colonialist Cecil Rhodes pulled down at the University of Cape Town and a statue of Paul Kruger, former President of the South African Republic, defaced in Pretoria.
9. As the most prominent social security provisions, pensions for Blacks "rose fivefold in real terms between 1970 and 1993" while benefits for Whites "fell by a third" (Woolard et al. 2010: 7).
10. 'Robberies with aggravating circumstances' increased in Grahamstown from 44 in 2004 to 344 in 2011 (Crime Stats 2015).
11. Swartz most prominently uses the word 'skollies' to demark this typified moral stance. However, I do not recall hearing this Afrikaans word during my research.
12. Mayer (1961: 75) argues that other interlocutors, "the townspeople", whose sons may have become tsotsis, "offered more complex and realistic theories" to explain the existence of tsotsis. "They would speak in terms of working mothers, overcrowding, lack of work opportunity for juveniles, the influence of the bioscope and so on", he (ibid.) continues.
13. Three educators who appeared to be wealthier than most had husbands who worked at the ECDoE.
14. In support of my observation, Mark Hunter (2010: 106) argues that in the period following 1994: "Areas denoted as black under apartheid remained sites of the most extreme poverty. As both a cause and a consequence of this, social mobility [for many South Africans] typically required a new form of geographical mobility: a move out of a poor area to a richer one."
15. Swartz (2009: 65) offers a similarly deterministic notion of "morality of inevitability (or located morality)". She (ibid.) writes: "It is not only by placing yourself in a location that determines your moral stance, but also by virtue of merely living in a township that the nature of your moral stance if determined." Swartz (ibid: 75) talks about a spatialised morality that one cannot separate themselves from; it is an uncontrollable force: "[township] youth simply absorbed the morality of the prevailing township culture".
16. In the 2010 census, 86.8% of the Brazilian population declared themselves Christians (64.6% Roman Catholic, 22.2% Protestant), 8% as non-religious, and 5.2% as followers of other religions ('Religion in Brazil' 2014).

17. Following Klees (2008: 312), I take 'neoliberal education' to mean: "the increased use of some form of user fees; the privatisation of more educational activities; and the direct connection of management and financing of education to measurable output".
18. Before and during apartheid, the ANC did not only share ideas about economic policy with the Soviet Union. Josiah Gumede, who was taught by Robert Miller in the early to mid-1880s, was the first ANC president to travel to the USSR. In 1927, he attended "the tenth anniversary celebrations of the Russian revolution" in Moscow and "met the Soviet leader, Joseph Stalin" (Zuma 2012: np). Gumede (cited in van Diemel 2001) returned to South Africa, impressed by his hosts: "I have seen the new world to come, where it has already begun." During apartheid, the Soviet Union supported the ANC and the South African Communist Party, the ANC's partner in the Tripartite Alliance (together with the Congress of South African Trade Unions), with financial aid and military training for their armed wing *Umkhonto we Sizwe* ('Spear of the Nation').
19. Some academics suggest that such arrangements are appropriate when resources remain limited (Rose 2007; Tooley and Dixon 2006). However, others argue that they have resulted in the privatisation of the South African schooling system and maintained, or even increased, inequities and access limitations (Sayed and Ahmed 2011; Motala and Dieltiens 2010). In this view, although government budgets for schools catering to the poorest catchment populations were five times higher than average, schools charging fees were better resourced and provided better educations.
20. One of Mayer's (1961: 86) interlocutors is quoted as saying, "When uncircumcised boys are rude and irresponsible, and have no respect for their elders, beating is our traditional way of training them." In this chapter, I focus on forms of punishment, rather than the specifics of generational categorisations of male Xhosas and their initiations, which are considered in greater depth in Chap. 7.
21. Mayer (1961: 85) argues that "any responsible-minded senior [i.e. initiated man]" could discipline any Xhosa boy or young man "when [the appropriate] occasion [arose]".
22. The following quotation, taken from a teacher working elsewhere in the Eastern Cape (cited in Reed 2014: 83), reflects my interlocutors' concerns: "In our culture, Xhosas, we knew that if you did something wrong, your mother and your father are going to beat you. But children of today, they don't do that. Once you beat him or her, they'll go to the police station. So in that, they are free to do anything."
23. Foucault's (1977a) treatise on changing practices of discipline and relations of power—that is, that bodies are not punished for moral transgressions, instead, individuals are encouraged, or coerced, to govern themselves—is relevant to this analytical point.

24. Mr Draai's comments can be compared with Mayer's (1961: 86) report on a 'vigilante crusade' in the township of East London: "[On] the second day of the beatings, ten youths were treated at the Frere Hospital for lacerations inflicted by sticks. . . . But nobody was killed. The country-born men claimed that they knew how to use their sticks 'to teach a lesson' without inflicting death; and townsmen, who had feared 'massacres', had to admit their admiration of this 'skill'."
25. Others have considered how democratic and 'neoliberal' forms of governance in South Africa and the associated emergence of human rights discourses have been encountered as curtailments of freedom that contribute to 'moral decay', particularly by individuals who value collectively oriented and hierarchically ordered conceptualisations of moral order. For example, Jason Hickel (2015) discusses this topic in relation to rural/urban migration. Nicholas Smith (2015) argues that vigilante groups have proliferated in response to the judgement that human rights have brought about immorality (also see Buur 2008; cf. Mayer 1961: 83–88, who discusses a similar judgement in 'pre-democratic' South Africa). Another interesting debate concerns the constitutional validity of the Witchcraft Suppression Act of 1957, which some South Africans see as a limitation upon freedoms to respond to violence brought about by witchcraft (see Ashforth 2005). I will discuss witchcraft later in the book.
26. Other anthropologists—for example, Ashforth (2005), Hickel (2015), Reed (2014), and Smith (2015)—have similarly maintained that, in the eyes of some South Africans, certain aspects of post-apartheid governance have curtailed, rather than extended, certain ethical freedoms.
27. Reed's (2014: e.g. 83–84) argument about how Xhosa teachers working elsewhere in the Eastern Cape have reacted to the 'democratic politics' of the post-apartheid transition, particularly those relating to corporal punishment, is remarkably similar to some of my analysis in this section. I first encountered her work when she kindly shared an unpublished paper via email in June 2014. I was struck by similarities with my research findings and analysis. For instance, in my upgrade proposal of June of 2013, I argued "There was concern from adults who had grown up with corporal punishment as a normalised practice that immoral behaviour amongst the young was proliferating because corporal punishment was now problematized by law." Hence, while her work provides a fascinating point of comparison, it gave me confidence in my own thinking to a greater extent than it informed it.
28. In 2011, there was "no specific mention of dealing with parental corporal punishment in any policy" (Bower 2012: 3). Under common law (cited in Owen 2012: 2), parents had the power "to inflict moderate and reasonable chastisement on a child for misconduct provided that this was not done in

a manner offensive to good morals or for objects other than correction and admonition". This power could be "delegated to a person acting in the parent's place, though not in the case of teachers" (Bower 2012: 3). This common law principle meant that parents "charged with assaulting their children [could] claim in their defence that they were exercising their right to reasonably chastise their children" (ibid.).

29. The most relevant constitutional statement is arguably Section 12 in the Bill of Rights, which states that "everyone has the right to be free from all forms of violence from either public or private sources; not to be treated or punished in a cruel, inhuman or degrading way; and that everyone has the right to bodily and psychological integrity" (STC 2005: 18). Article 19 of the UN Convention on the Rights of the Child (cited in STC 2005: 16), which South Africa ratified in 1995, states the intention to take "all appropriate legislative, administrative, social and educational measures to protect the child from all forms of physical or mental violence, injury or abuse, neglect or negligent treatment, maltreatment or exploitation including sexual abuse, while in the care of parent(s), legal guardian(s) or any other person who has the care of the child".

30. R. Morrell (2001: 292) similarly considers "official ambivalence about the continuing use of corporal punishment [in schools]" as evidence that teachers and parents continue to favour the practice in the absence of "effective alternatives". He also details various policies that have aimed to address the issue.

31. I facilitated a variety of drama performances by first engaging learners in drama activities and games. I was keen that they communicate, through their performances, subjects that were of interest to them. To this end, their plays were improvised, although I occasionally wrote a prompting word on the blackboard, such as "school", "township", or "police". Many performances highlighted moral and ethical concerns, and all depended on memories of sociality I was not privy to depictions of events learners had witnessed and experienced in social spaces outside of school, before my fieldwork and outside my observational gaze. I filmed some of the pieces and made observational notes on others.

32. Thomas Hill, Jr. (2000: 173–99) offers a considered critique of the claim that Kant was strongly and exclusively concerned with retribution in his work on punishment. I am by no means in a position to offer any insight into this debate. Instead, I use the analysis of Metz and Gaie simply to make a point of comparison between various modes of punishment.

33. In the Eastern Cape, there is a long history of 'alternative' systems of justice and punishment, and attempts to maintain moral order using retributive and, perhaps, restorative violence, in the absence of, or in opposition to, State-sanctioned mechanisms (Bank 2011: 231; Kirsch 2010: 145). On

a national level, the democratic period has brought more recent examples of 'community policing', 'mob justice', 'privatised security', and 'vigilantism' (Smith 2015; Fourchard 2011; Kirsch 2010; Buur 2003, 2009; Bénit-Gbaffou et al. 2008; Comaroff and Comaroff 2007; Bénit-Gbaffou 2006; Dixon 2004; Johns and Dixon 2001; Nina 2000).

34. A monitored home security alarm was equivalent to eight monthly rental payments for Siseko's one-roomed home and 20% more than a monthly governmental child grant, a major source of income for many parents.
35. Anthropological literature is replete with accounts of localities where, in the absence of effective or trusted State institutions, assertions of protection, masculinity and honour/respect depend on (violent) responses to incursion and challenge (e.g. Bourgois 1996b, 2002; Herzfeld 1985; Horowitz 1983; Peristiany 1965; Jane Schneider 1971; Schwandner-Sievers 2001; Wacquant 2008; Whyte 1969).

Bibliography

Abrahams, R. (1996). Vigilantism: Order and Disorder on the Frontiers of the State. In O. Harris (Ed.), *Inside and Outside the Law: Anthropological Studies of Authority and Ambiguity*. London: Routledge.

Abrahams, R. (1998). *Vigilant Citizens: Vigilantism and the State*. Oxford: Polity Press.

Ashforth, A. (2005). *Witchcraft, Violence, and Democracy in South Africa*. Chicago: University of Chicago Press.

Bank, L. (2011). *Home Spaces, Street Styles: Contesting Power and Identity in a South African City*. London: Pluto Press.

Barchiesi, F. (2003). Wage Labor, Precarious Employment and Social Inclusion in the Making of South Africa's Post-apartheid Transition. *African Studies Review*, 51(2), 119–142.

Barchiesi, F. (2011). *Precarious Liberation: Workers, the State and Contested Social Citizenship in Post-apartheid South Africa*. Scottsville: University of Kwa-Zulu Natal Press.

Bayaga, A., & Louw, J. (2011). Moral Degeneration: Crisis in South African Schools? *Journal of Social Science*, 28(3), 199–210.

Bénit-Gbaffou, C. (2006). Police–Community Partnerships in Responses to Crime: Lessons from Yeoville and Observatory. *Urban Forum*, 17(4), 7–32.

Bénit-Gbaffou, C., Morange, M., & Didier, S. (2008). Communities, the Private Sector, and the State: Contested Forms of Security Governance in Cape Town and Johannesburg. *Urban Affairs*, 43(5), 691–717.

Bourgois, P. (1996a). Confronting Anthropology, Education, and Inner-City Apartheid. *American Anthropologist*, 98(2), 249–258.

Bourgois, P. (1996b). *Search of Respect*. Cambridge: Cambridge University Press.

Bourgois, P. (2002). Understanding Inner-City Poverty: Resistance and Self-Destruction under U.S. Apartheid. In J. Macclancy (Ed.), *Exotic No More: Anthropology on the Front Lines* (pp. 15–32). Chicago: University of Chicago Press.

Bower, C. (2012). *Prohibition of Corporal and Humiliating Punishment in the Home*. Topical Guide (Prepared for PAN: Children). Retrieved April 15, 2013, from http://children.pan.org.za/sites/default/files/publicationdocuments/ Prohibition of Parental Corporal Punishment Topical Guide.pdf

Brogden, M. E. (1989). Origins of the South African Police – Institutional Versus Structural Approaches. In W. Scharf (Ed.), *Acta Juridica* (pp. 94–110). Cape Town: Faculty of Law, University of Cape Town.

Bundy, C. (2014). *Short-Changed? South Africa Since Apartheid*. Athens: Ohio University Press.

Buur, L. (2003). Crime and Punishment on the Margins of the Post-apartheid State. *Anthropology and Humanism, 28*(1), 23–42.

Buur, L. (2008). Democracy & Its Discontent: Vigilantism, Sovereignty and Human Rights in South Africa. *Review of African Political Economy, 35*(118), 571–584.

Buur, L. (2009). The Horror of the Mob: The Violence of Imagination in South Africa. *Critique of Anthropology, 29*(1), 27–46.

Carl, A., & Johannes, D. (2003). Critical Elements in the Training of Teachers in Peace Education Within the Context of Outcomes-Based Education. *South African Journal of Education, 22*, 162–169.

Chisholm, L. (2004). Introduction. In L. Chisholm (Ed.), *Changing Class Education and Social Change in Post-apartheid South Africa* (pp. 1–28). London/New York: Zed Books.

Chisholm, L., & Fuller, B. (1996). Remember People's Education? Shifting Alliances, State-Building and South Africa's Narrowing Policy Agenda. *Journal of Education Policy, 11*(6), 693–716.

Comaroff, J., & Comaroff, J. (2007). Popular Justice in the New South Africa: Policing the Boundaries of Freedom. In T. R. Tyle (Ed.), *Legitimacy and Criminal Justice: An International Perspective* (pp. 215–238). New York: Russell Sage Foundation.

Crime Stats. (2015). *Crime Stats* (Grahamstown). Retrieved May 26, 2015, from http://crimestatssa.com/precinct.php?id=954

de Souza, M. L. (2009). Social Movements in the Face of Criminal Power. *City, 13*(1), 26–52.

de Waal, M. (2012). Survival Times: Basic Education Wants Billions from Big Business. *Daily Maverick* (Online). Retrieved July 13, 2014, from http:// www.dailymaverick.co.za/article/2012-04-12-survival-times-basic-education-wants-billions-from-big-business

Dixon, B. (2004). Community Policing: 'Cherry Pie' or *Melktert*? *Society in Transition, 35*(2), 251–272.

Dlanga, K. (2014). Change Town Names That Celebrate Our Oppressors. *Mail and Guardian* (Online). Retrieved December 30, 2014, from http://mg.co.za/article/2014-10-01-change-the-names-of-towns-that-celebrate-our-brutal-oppressors

Douglas, M. (1966). *Purity and Danger.* London: Routledge.

Eastern Cape Socio Economic Consultative Council (ECSECC). (2011). *Service Delivery and Condition of Living in the Eastern Cape.* Retrieved March 17, 2015, from http://www.ecsecc.org/files/library/documents/ECSECCLivingStandardsJune2011.pdf

Eastern Cape Socio Economic Consultative Council (ECSECC). (2012a). *Poverty Social Statistics 2012.* Retrieved July 14, 2013, from http://www.ecsecc.org/statistics-database

Eastern Cape Socio Economic Consultative Council (ECSECC). (2012b). *Access to Services 2012.* Retrieved December 16, 2014, from http://www.ecsecc.org/statistics-database

Foucault, M. (1977a). *Discipline and Punish: The Birth of the Prison.* London: Penguin.

Fourchard, L. (2011). The Politics of Mobilization for Security in South African Townships. *African Affairs, 110*(441), 607–627.

Fry, C. M. (2012). *An Investigation into the Need for Introducing a Moral Education Programme to Adolescents in South African Schools.* Unpublished M.Ed. Research Report, Faculty of Humanities, University of the Witwatersrand, Johannesburg.

Hansen, T. B. (2006). Performers of Sovereignty: On the Privatization of Security in Urban South Africa. *Critique of Anthropology, 26*(3), 279–295.

Herzfeld, M. (1985). *The Poetics of Manhood: Contest and Identity in a Cretan Mountain Village.* Princeton: Princeton University Press.

Hickel, J. (2015). *Democracy as Death: The Moral Order of Anti-liberal Politics in South Africa.* Berkley: University of California Press.

Hill, T., Jr. (2000). *Respect, Pluralism, and Justice: Kantian Perspectives.* Oxford: Oxford University Press.

Horowitz, R. (1983). *Honor and the American Dream: Culture and Identity in a Chicano Community.* New Brunswick: Rutgers University Press.

Hunter, M. (1936). *Reaction to Conquest: Effects of Contact with Europeans on the Pondo of South Africa.* London: Oxford University Press.

Hunter, M. (2010). *Love in the Time of Aids: Inequality, Gender and Rights in South Africa.* Bloomington: Indiana University Press.

Independent Online (IOL). (2007). *Councillors Pick a New Name for Grahamstown.* Retrieved October 21, 2014, from http://www.iol.co.za/news/politics/councillors-pick-a-new-name-for-grahamstown-1.370629#.VfrVIN9VhBc

Institute for Security Studies (ISS) and Africa Check. (2014). Factsheet: South Africa's Official Crime Stats Unpacked. *Mail and Guardian* (Online). Retrieved

May 23, 2015, from http://mg.co.za/article/2014-09-22-factsheet-south-africas-official-crime-stats-unpacked/

Jack, M. (2011). Grahamstown Poised for Mass Protest. *The New Age (Online)*. Retrieved March 03, 2012, from http://www.thenewage.co.za/

Jamieson, L., & Mathews, S. (2013). *Submission on Amendments to the Children's Act: Corporal Punishment* (Policy Submission). Cape Town: Children's Institute. Retrieved June 25, 2014, from https://open.uct.ac.za/bitstream/item/3835/CI_policysubs_corporalpunishment_2013-07.pdf?sequence=1

Johns, L. M., & Dixon, B. (2001). *Gangs, Pagad & the State: Vigilantism and Revenge Violence in the Western Cape*. Centre for the Study of Violence and Reconciliation, Violence and Transition Series, Vol. 2. Retrieved June 02, 2014, from http://www.csvr.org.za/docs/gangs/gangspagadstate.pdf

Kirsch, T. G. (2010). Violence in the Name of Democracy: Community Policing, Vigilante Action & Nation-Building in South Africa. In T. G. Kirsch & T. Grätz (Eds.), *Domesticating Vigilantism in Africa* (pp. 139–162). Oxford: James Curry.

Klees, S. J. (2008). A Quarter Century of Neoliberal Thinking in Education: Misleading Analyses and Failed Policies. *Globalisation, Societies and Education*, 6(4), 311–348.

Laidlaw, J. (2010). Agency and Responsibility: Perhaps You Can Have Too Much of a Good Thing. In M. Lambek (Ed.), *Ordinary Ethics: Anthropology, Language and Action* (pp. 143–164). New York: Fordham University Press.

Lang, S. (2011). Crime in Grahamstown – the Numbers. *Grocott's Mail* (Online). Retrieved, June 29, 2013, from http://www.grocotts.co.za/content/crimenumbers-08-09-2011

Larsen, H. B. (2003). *Children of the City: A Study of Street Children in Kathmandu, Their Social Practices and Territoriality*. Unpublished MPhil Dissertation, Department of Geography, University of Bergen. Retrieved March 02, 2012, from http://rua.ua.es/dspace/bitstream/10045/17395/1/STREET%20CHILDREN.pdf

List of Countries by Vehicles per Capita. (2015). *Wikipedia*. Retrieved May 27, 2015, from https://en.wikipedia.org/wiki/List_of_countries_by_vehicles_per_capita

Louw, J. M. (2009). *The Socio-Educational Implications of the Moral Degeneration of the South African Society: Towards a Solution*. Unpublished D.Ed. Thesis, University of South Africa. Retrieved June 22, 2012, from http://uir.unisa.ac.za/handle/10500/3087

Mayer, P. (1961). *Townsmen or Tribesmen: Conservatism and the Process of Urbanization in a South African City* (with Contributions by Iona Mayer). Oxford/Cape Town: Oxford University Press.

Mbeki, T. (2005). Mbeki: Reply to Debate on the Presidency Dept Budget Vote 2005/2006. *The Presidency*. Retrieved June 03, 2014, from http://www.polity.org.za/article/mbeki-reply-to-debate-on-the-presidency-dept-budget-vote-20052006-26052005-2005-05-26

McMichael. (2013). Footsoldiers in a Social War: The Police, Crime and Inequality in South Africa. *Open Democracy* (Online). Retrieved October 23, 2014, from http://www.opendemocracy.net/opensecurity/christopher-mcmichael/footsoliders-in-social-war-police-south-africa

Metz, T., & Gaie, J. B. R. (2010). The African Ethic of Ubuntu/Botho: Implications for Research on Morality. *Journal of Moral Education, 39*(3), 273–290.

Moore, H. L. (2011). *Still Life: Hopes, Desires and Satisfactions.* Cambridge: Polity Press.

Morrell, R. (2001). Corporal Punishment in South African Schools: A Neglected Explanation for Its Persistence. *South African Journal of Education, 21*(4), 292–299.

Motala, S., & Dieltiens, V. (2010). *Educational Access in South Africa: Country Research Summary.* Johannesburg: University of the Witwatersrand, Education Policy Unit (EPU). Retrieved March 03, 2013, from http://www.create-rpc.org/pdf_documents/South_Africa_Country_Research_Summary.pdf

Ngwane, Z. (2001). Real Men Reawaken Their Fathers' Homesteads, the Educated Leave Them in Ruins': The Politics of Domestic Reproduction in Post-apartheid Rural South Africa. *Journal of Religion in Africa, 31*(4), 402–426.

Nietzsche, F. (1994). In K. Ansell-Pearson (Ed.), *On the Genealogy of Morality.* Cambridge: Cambridge University Press.

Nina, D. (2000). Dirty Harry Is Back: Vigilantism in South Africa – The (Re)emergence of 'Good' and 'Bad' Community. *African Security Review, 9*(1), 8–28.

Ntsimane, R. (2007). The Ukuhlonipha Code of Respect: Gender and Cultural Tensions Around the Zulu Nurses. The Case of the Emmaus Mission Hospital. *Studia Historiae Ecclesiasticae, XXXIII*(2), 115–133.

Nyquist, T. E. (1983). *African Middle Class Elite.* Grahamstown: Institute of Social and Economic Research.

Onceya, T. (2013). No Consensus as Name-Change Workshops End. *Grocott's Mail* (Online). Retrieved January 28, 2015, from http://www.grocotts.co.za/content/no-consensus-name-change-workshops-end-28-01-2013

Owen, S. (2012). South Africa: Briefing for the Human Rights Council Universal Periodic Review (13th Session, 2012). *Global Initiative.* Retrieved July 09, 2014, from http://lib.ohchr.org/HRBodies/UPR/Documents/session13/ZA/GIEACPC_UPR_ZAF_S13_2012_GlobalInitiativetoEndAllCorporalPunishmentofChildren_E.pdf

Pauw, B. A. (1963). *The Second Generation: A Study of the Family Among Urbanized Bantu in East London.* Oxford: Oxford University Press.

Peristiany, J. G. (1965). *Honour and Shame: The Values of Mediterranean Society.* London: Weidenfeld & Nicolson.
Pithouse, R. (2011). On State Violence. *The South African Civil Society Information Service.* Retrieved July 19, 2014, from http://sacsis-org-za.win24.wadns.net/site/article/666.1
Pithouse, R. (2013). Durban Poison. *The South African Civil Society Information Service.* Retrieved March 04, 2014, from http://sacsis.org.za/site/article/1817
Pithouse, R. (2014). Four Bodies in Three Weeks. *The South African Civil Society Information Service.* Retrieved May, 23, 2015 from http://sacsis.org.za/site/article/1888
Potgieter, P. C. (1980). Moral Education in South Africa. *Journal of Moral Education, 9*(2), 130–133.
Prew, M. (2010). The South African Schools Act: Is It Time to Dump It? *The Centre for Education Policy Development* (Online). Retrieved July 20, 2012, from http://www.cepd.org.za/files/pictures/The South African Schools Act - Is it time to dump it by Dr Martin Prew.pdf
Reed, A. (2014). *Inkululeko: Youth, Non-governmental Organizations, and Discourses of Democracy in Post-apartheid South Africa.* Unpublished PhD Thesis, Department of Anthropology, University of California. Retrieved June 05, 2015, from http://escholarship.org/uc/item/7n75g82z
Religion in Brazil. (2014). *Wikipedia.* Retrieved January 19, 2014, from http://en.wikipedia.org/wiki/Religion_in_Brazil#Christianity
Republic of South Africa. (2005). *Children's Act, No. 38 of 2005.* Retrieved March 28, 2012, from http://www.centreforchildlaw.co.za/images/files/childlaw/consolidated_childrens_act.pdf
Robbins, J. (2007). Between Reproduction and Freedom: Morality, Value, and Radical Cultural Change. *Ethnos, 72*(3), 293–314.
Rose, P. (2007). *NGO Provision of Basic Education: Alternative or Complementary Service Delivery to Support Access to the Excluded?* Create Pathways to Access, Research Monograph No.3, June 2007. Retrieved May 29, 2012, from http://sro.sussex.ac.uk/1830/1/PTA3.pdf
Save the Children (STC). (2005). *Ending Corporal Punishment of Children in South Africa.* Retrieved June 19, 2015, from https://test-za.savethechildren.net/sites/savethechildren.org.za/files/Ending%20Corporal%20Punishment%20of%20Children%20in%20South%20Africa.pdf
Sayed, Y., & Ahmed, R. (2011). Education Quality in Post-apartheid South African Policy: Balancing Equity, Diversity, Rights and Participation. *Comparative Education, 47*(1), 103–118.
Schneider, J. (1971). Of Vigilance and Virgins: Honor, Shame and Access to Resources in Mediterranean Societies. *Ethnology, 10*(1), 1–24.

Schwandner-Sievers, S. (2001). The Enactment of 'Tradition': Albanian Constructions of Identity, Violence and Power in Times of Crisis. In I. W. Schröder & B. E. Schmidt (Eds.), *Anthropology of Violence and Conflict* (pp. 97–117). London: Routledge.

SlutWalk. (2014). About. *SlutWalk Toronto* (Online). Retrieved December 13, 2014, from http://www.slutwalktoronto.com/

Smith, N. R. (2015). Rejecting Rights: Rights and Violence in Post-apartheid South Africa. *African Affairs, 114*(456), 341–360.

South African Press Association (SAPA). (2012). Public Schools Don't Match Private Schools. *Times* (Live/Online). Retrieved July 19, 2013, from http://www.timeslive.co.za/politics/2012/12/04/public-schools-don-t-match-private-schools

Stafford, C. (2010). The Punishment of Ethical Behavior. In M. Lambek (Ed.), *Ordinary Ethics: Anthropology, Language and Action* (pp. 187–206). New York: Fordham University Press.

Statistics South Africa (SSA). (2011). *Makana* (2011 Census). Retrieved January 12, 2012, from http://beta2.statssa.gov.za/?page_id=993&id=makana-municipality

Swartz, S. (2009). *The Moral Ecology of South Africa's Township Youth.* New York: Palgrave Macmillan.

Tabensky, P. (2012, January 27). Reign of Thugs – The Easy Option. *Grocott's Mail.* Grahamstown, p. 11.

Tooley, J., & Dixon, P. (2006). 'De Facto' Privatisation of Education and the Poor: Implications of a Study from Sub-Saharan Africa and India. *Compare: A Journal of Comparative and International Education, 36*(4), 443–462.

Turner, V. (1974). *Dramas, Fields and Metaphors: Symbolic Action in Human Society.* Ithaca: Cornell University Press.

United Nations (UN). (2008). *Summary Prepared by the Office of the High Commissioner for Human Rights, in Accordance with Paragraph 15c of the Annex to Human Rights Council Resolution 5/1.* Retrieved April 14, 2013, from http://www.univie.ac.at/bimtor/dateien/southafrica_upr_2008_summary.pdf

Vally, S. (2007). From People's Education to Neo-liberalism in South Africa. *Review of African Political Economy, 34*(111), 39–56.

van Diemel, R. (2001). 'I Have Seen the New Jerusalem': Revisiting and Re-conceptualising Josiah T. Gumede and Jimmy La Guma's USSR Visit of 1927. *What Next? Marxist Discussion Journal* (Online). Retrieved June 13, 2014, from http://www.whatnextjournal.org.uk/Pages/History/Gumede.html

Wacquant, L. (2008). *Urban Outcasts: A Comparative Sociology of Advanced Marginality.* Cambridge: Polity Press.

Waterhouse, S. (2007). Status of Corporal Punishment in the South African Children's Amendment Bill Law Reform Process. Cape Town. *Article 19, 3*(2),

1–3. Retrieved July 23, 2012, from file:///C:/Users/Oli/Downloads/ Volume 3 Number 3 - December 2007 (2).pdf

Watson, K. I. (1999). *A History of the South African Police in Port Elizabeth, 1913–1956*. Unpublished PhD Thesis, History Department, Rhodes University.

Whyte, W. F. (1969). *Street Corner Society*. Chicago: University of Chicago Press.

Williams, B. (1993). *Ethics and the Limits of Philosophy*. London: Fontana Press.

Woolard, I., Harttgen, K., & Klasen, S. (2010). *The Evolution and Impact of Social Security in South Africa*. Paper Prepared for the Conference on "Promoting Resilience Through Social Protection in Sub-Saharan Africa", Organised by the European Report of Development in Dakar, Senegal, 28–30 June 2010. Retrieved April 28, 2013, from http://erd.eui.eu/media/BackgroundPapers/Woolard-Harttgen-Klasen.pdf

World Bank. (2009). *Gini Index*. Retrieved May 24, 2013, from http://data.worldbank.org/indicator/SI.POV.GINI/

Zigon, J., & Throop, C. J. (2014). Moral Experience: Introduction. *Ethos, 42*(1), 1–15.

Zuma, J. (2012). *The Life and Times of Josiah Gumede*. Address by ANC President Jacob Zuma on the Occasion of the Memorial Lecture on the Life and Times of ANC Fourth President Josiah Tshangana Gumede, Durban, April 19, 2012. Retrieved March 23, 2013, from http://www.politicsweb.co.za/opinion/the-life-and-times-of-josiah-gumede--jacob-zuma

CHAPTER 3

Extrinsic Barriers to Learning

One Saturday afternoon, Holly came to my small flat, a converted outbuilding in the garden of a family home in the town. She was accompanied by Damba, her daughter, as I had said I would like to meet her. At 13 years old, she was talkative, confident, and seemingly content to play on her Blackberry while I helped Holly complete some coursework for a degree she was completing as a distance learner. Afterwards, Damba said that she was happy to answer some questions and composed herself as I switched on my voice recorder.

Oliver:	Can I ask you about the school where your mum works? What do you know about it?
Damba:	I know that it's a school for street kids and she works there. Yeah, that's what I know. And I know this: the children there pass by terms.
Holly:	What do you know about their behaviour?
Damba:	I know that some of them bring weapons to school, and some of them take drugs. They are violent and stuff like that. And they swear a lot.
Holly:	And they steal.
Damba:	Yes, they steal.

© The Author(s) 2018
O. Pattenden, *Taking Care of the Future*, Anthropological Studies of Education, https://doi.org/10.1007/978-3-319-69826-7_3

Other than the knowledge that learners can "pass by terms", a reference to the Accelerated Bridging Education programme, Damba's perception was full of moralised, danger-filled imagery. Holly built upon Damba's account having most likely inculcated these ideas. Throughout my fieldwork, I was frequently struck by how my interlocutors' focused on such negative identifications.

Members of staff linked judgements of undesirable or immoral behaviour to the idea that learners at Ngomso were different to those at mainstream schools. Lindiwe was one of the younger female teachers. We often talked on a bench outside the classrooms about her children, love of Mexican food, new Nokia, and life-orientation lessons with grades six and seven. She was talking about the learners being "rude", a word my interlocutors used to mean naughty or badly behaved.

Oliver: Do you think that they are rude?
Lindiwe: Some of them are rude.
Oliver: Ruder than children in other schools?
Lindiwe: Yes, more rude than children in other schools; really. The difference is . . . [pause for thought]; I don't know. It seems as if these children are coming from their own [unique] community; because they are rude alone.

As evidenced by Damba and Lindiwe's use of the word "some", interlocutors rarely said that *all* learners were abnormally rude, or more likely to steal, take drugs, drink alcohol, use weapons, have sex, swear, or be violent, when compared with those in other schools. However, the consensus was that there were more young people behaving in such ways at Ngomso than you could expect to find elsewhere. I only recorded one conversation where a member of staff said that learners were no different from those at mainstream schools.

These judgements did not mean that the staff uniformly disliked them. Learners' 'specialness' encouraged some members of staff to be at the school. One educator, whose name I did not record at the time, told me that she had primarily moved to Grahamstown to be with her family. When she applied for her position, she "did not know what extrinsic barriers were, or behavioural problems". Even though she felt that "the children [were] so rude", she had come to "love them" and would not consider applying for a post elsewhere. In contrast, one security guard decided that the challenges were too great. Complaining of "stress" and a painful chest, he successfully applied to be transferred to a mainstream school.

Madoda, a different security guard, had experienced numerous episodes that would be worthy of attention here. He had trained with the city's largest private security firm, before gladly accepting the offer of a government post.[1] As was often the case, we were in the playground, sitting on small plastic chairs, as Madoda waited for a shout asking him to help to control a learner's behaviour. He was wearing a replica Arsenal shirt, and we talked about how my flat was a five-minute walk from the Emirates Stadium in London. He then recounted a story of how a learner had spat in his face and injured his shoulder by throwing a rock at him. He shook his head and said, "[these learners] are not the same as others". I asked: "Do you think that the children in this school are different than the children in other primary schools?" He replied:

> You see, I can say 'Yes' because this is a special school. These kids do not grow up [properly]. That's why this school is a special school because we deal with kids who are not the same as those in the location [schools].

After I had asked him, "And when you say they are not the same, how are they different?", he continued his explanation:

> Madoda: You see, sometimes, it's their home backgrounds: where they grow up, in a [difficult] situation. Some of them, when they get home, there are no parents there; there's no one, you see? Maybe they are staying with their grandmother, and you ask him 'Where is your mama?' [And he says] 'Mama is passed away.' [You ask] 'Your father?' [And he replies] 'Father does not stay in Grahamstown' or 'I don't know my father.' You see? Things like that.

When explaining their judgements of learners' specialness and special educational needs (SEN), other members of staff also most often referred to the experiences learners had outside of their time in school and, in particular, aspects of their 'home lives' that they deemed problematic. Their conceptualisations relate to the registration category that was effectively enshrined in government policy when Ngomso was first registered as a public special school—that is, (schools for) 'Extrinsically Disabled Learners'. As with policies more generally, the initial employment of this terminology created a new category of "individuals to be governed" (Wedel et al. 2005: 30). For the first time in South Africa, young people could 'officially' be classified 'extrinsically disabled learners' and schooled in government institutions set up to cater for them. During my fieldwork, this institutionalised discourse served as guiding criteria when individuals attempted to determine whether and how Ngomso learners were or were not special. However, although individuals could also invoke other relevant frameworks of meaning and evaluation—for example, emotional trauma, emotional intelligence, marginalisation, psychosocial barriers, and so on—the quality and existence of learners' specialness and their extrinsic barriers to learning remained ambiguous because relevant institutional and public discourses of morality were always evaluated by individuals, according to their knowledge and experience of Ngomso and its learners (Goffman 1963: 12). As a result, no two people thought the learners were special or normal in exactly the same way. Relevant ethical judgements were notably contestable because an identification of the particular special education needs that were most readily associated with Ngomso *always* hinged upon subjective, personalised understandings of societal norms that do not lend themselves to quantification or scales of severity.[2] Yet, despite their variable perceptions of difference and otherness, members of staff did understand and evaluate learners' 'specialness' with *some* degree of continuity. Indeed, individuals could only gain admission to the school having been deemed special in a particular way. As such, relevant discourses were both instructive and malleable, in being applicable to all manner of social phenomena and individualised experiences.

Madoda's concern regarding parental absence was a common discursive theme. During the survey that Mrs Noni conducted of learners who did not live in the shelter, which I mentioned in the previous chapter, approximately one in eight (14%) Ngomso learners said that they lived with both parents (see Fig. 3.1). The provincial average was 22% (SSA 2011). Almost half (45.4%) lived in female-headed households, mainly with their mothers. This figure is similar to the municipal average, which was 44.5% in 2011 (SSA 2011). Mrs Noni completed the survey in response to a mandate from the ECDoE regarding concern about the impact of the HIV and AIDS epidemic upon learners in the province and departmental proposals to address it.[3] Encouragingly, a substantial increase in the availability of antiretroviral treatment, which is now the world's largest programme (Department of Health 2013), has increased the survival rate of HIV-infected individuals in South Africa (Shisana et al. 2014). However, this turnaround came too late for some parents of Ngomso learners, who passed away before my research began.[4] In total, of the 44 learners surveyed, 19 or 43% said that one or both parent(s)

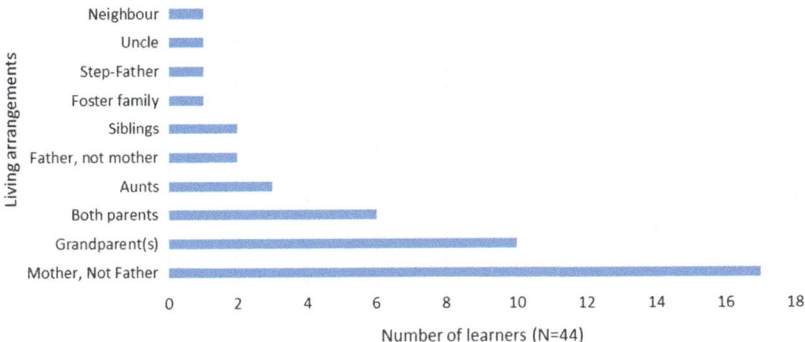

Fig. 3.1 Living arrangements of surveyed learners

had died. If the shelter boys were included in the survey, I would expect this figure to increase (some had lost both parents, while others had a mother, father, or both). As it stands, it greatly exceeds a national census estimate of 18.8% for those aged 18 and under without one or both parents (SSA 2012). Of the 20 learners who lived with neither biological parent, three had lost both parents (6.8% of the total sample), ten had lost one parent and said that the other lived elsewhere (22.7% of the total sample), three had both parents living elsewhere, two had an ill mother but did not mention a father, one did not know their whereabouts, and the final response was unrecorded.

In addition to the prevalence of HIV, the absence of biological fathers in Ngomso learners' homes and across South Africa more broadly—an estimated 50% of fathers do not have daily contact with their children (Richter et al. 2010)—relates to apartheid's labour policies. Men could not legally live with dependents in certain areas, which meant families were separated by the search for employment (Bank 2011; Mark Hunter 2010). Moreover, the slowing economy in the 1970s affected family structures and led to generational and gender conflict (Bank 2011; Ngwane 2001). Migration away from families for employment has been prominent in South Africa more recently too (Richter et al. 2010). One notable form of social change encouraged by such contexts has been a shift from male to female-headed households and to other, intergenerational household arrangements (Anderson et al. 1999; Hunter 2010; Pauw 1963). Relatedly, many learners also lived with other family members, including uncles, aunts, grandmothers, and cousins. This assertion supports existing ethnographic research that highlights how young South Africans have various and variable relationships with a variety of caregivers (Henderson 2012: 85). To my knowledge, the largest household consisted of seven people.

Quantitative research does indicate that "children living with biological parents [in South Africa are] more likely to be in school than those living in other family set-ups" (Shindler 2010: 4; also see Anderson 2005). However, for members of staff, anxiety about the structure of learners' home lives was not simply related to absenteeism. Their concerns went well beyond that dynamic and into the territory of moralised evaluations. For instance, Mary was concerned about "dysfunctional families".[5] Consider the following statement from her. The educators had gathered in a classroom for their daily briefing. Those who attended a training session the previous day were explaining how they had learnt that parental divorce could impact upon attendance and result in poor behaviour in school. After thanking them for sharing this information, Mary responded:

> Here the situation is much worse than a simple divorce; the kids have a right to be angry. It's worse than divorce. Our kids' parents just get up and leave. The kids say that they don't even know their parents.

These comments were a catalyst for discussion about the effect of parental absence upon behaviour and learning. The conversation was one of many where members of staff highlighted the importance of homes having a father and mother. Such concerns also relate to discourses regarding 'broken homes', which have been a central component of 'delinquency theories' that developed as criminology emerged in the nineteenth century, particularly in America and Britain (Wells and Rankin 1991).[6] Mayer (1961: 75) noted similar concerns during the apartheid period in South Africa:

> When tsotsis grow up apparently lacking in the moral faculty, many Xhosa migrants blame the mothers. Tsotsis are said to be children of unmarried mothers; of loose women. . . . The argument is that in the absence of a male head of the family (the natural implanter of morality by traditional Xhosa standards) nobody has taught them the elementary lessons of right and wrong.

Lacking pedagogic influence from men is also a Christianised concern (not exclusively, obviously). It is the *son* of God who is the saviour of Christians and their most revered teacher. It is also the male in each Christianised nuclear family who is closest to Christ and God: "But I want you to understand that the head of every man is Christ, the head of a wife is her husband, and the head of Christ is God" (Corinthians, 11: 3).[7] Without men, so runs the argument, families lack their most direct connection with God and thus direction and instruction from Him.

Although concerns about absent fathers were more prominent than those regarding mothers, for many members of staff, anything other than an idealised, 'nuclear family' or 'patriarchal household'—for example, 'child-headed households', 'single parents', or 'siblings in charge'—was deemed problematic: harmful to the learner and thus a potential cause of 'social danger', criminality, and undesirable behaviour. Similarly, the American missionaries operating in Tanzania considered by Stambach (2010: 109) idealised the "nuclear, monogamous family" and revered such arrangements as "a foundational unit for a Christian community". Ngomso staff thought such units offered the most desirable experiences of love, guidance, protection, nurturance, support, and moral instruction. This perception was also true for colonial missionaries who took umbrage with the polygamy of the Xhosa, seeing it as an impingement to "the advance of Christian civilisation" (Ashley 1974: 202). Although my interlocutors' judgements are not illustrative of an unbroken continuation of these tensions, historically constituted Christianised discourses regarding idealised, gendered structures of familial and caregiver relations were a component of the moral assemblages they could draw from when attempting to understand and explain the situation at hand.

Worries about absent parents also factored in judgements about the behaviour and moral dispositions of individual learners. As we sat in her cramped office, surrounded by walls covered with photographs of learners, motivational quotes, and extracts from the Bible, Mary turned to a visiting social worker and said:

> We are having enormous problems with him [and his behaviour]. He is a child who is very needy emotionally. He feels that no one is fair to him. He is bullied. Then it comes out that he has no family, [which explains it].

Mrs Noni said that the 15-year-old learner was living with "somebody that [was] feeling sorry for him". In their consideration of street children, Ennew and Swart-Kruger (2003: np) relatedly suggest that "popular myth and policy alike act as if there is some kind of ideal entity called 'The Family' – a nuclear form that bears little resemblance to the variety of kinship arrangements within which people have lived and do live". The situation at Ngomso was similar, but not as clear-cut. While the staff had concerns about learners' living arrangements that deviated from this idealised conception, they did acknowledge and value other forms of caregiver relations, such as foster parents, the Shelter, and sibling-headed households. These were evaluated, not arbitrarily discounted as harmful or abnormal. Judgements were frequently put forth with a qualifier, such as "some", "not all", or "most". Moreover, regardless of household arrangements, certain carers and parents were thought to be 'trying their best' or to have gone beyond the call of duty.

I remember learning about two young men who had not been in school for about three months. Mrs Noni and I went to see their mother in the hope that they might be living with her. I walked over the rocks on the road and avoided the geese and dog mess that surrounded a windowless, circular structure made of sticks and mud. The wooden door had fallen from its hinges when three young men had burst in to steal everything that they could carry. The remains of a wood fire smouldered in the middle of the mud floor. Smoke still hung in the air. I bent down to shake the lady's hand, and she raised herself from the sponge mattress that lay on the floor. The weakness of her handshake and the scabs on her body told me that she was ill. She had tears in her eyes as she explained that she tried to encourage her sons to go to school. They had not been to see her for three weeks and did not like to see her in such poor health. When I spoke with Mary, Joyce, and Mrs Noni about the situation later that same day, I don't think that one of us was thinking about parental irresponsibility.

Where learners lived with family and parents, staff were most often disturbed by the form of parental and familial influence and learners' experiences of it. Compretta (2012: 104–110) reports something similar when considering staff at a faith-based after-school programme targeting low-income families in a southern American city, which she names 'Home Mission'. At Ngomso, a lack of material support was a key concern. Madoda said he had "been on a lot of home visits with Mary" and didn't "like to see the living conditions of some of the learners". He was fretful that there was "sometimes no food between school days". He said that when the learners were "rude" to him: "I think about where they come from and know that I cannot get mad at them." I noted widespread anxiety about a lack of food, clothing, warmth, cleanliness, and comfort in learners' homes, including concerns that hungry stomachs impeded learning and that inadequate accommodation meant sleepless nights and poor attendance. Staff also worried about a lack of funds for uniforms, school meals, and transport. They also knew that some learners left school to work, to provide families or themselves with money. During our first meeting, Mary said that financial hardships that might limit engagements with schooling were "why they are at Ngomso in the first place". Survey-driven research suggests that such concerns do indeed affect attendance.[8]

Peter took the time to care for the school's vehicles, polishing and scrubbing, sweeping and tweaking. His house, which he had renovated and extended from its original RDP specification, was immaculately clean. As I passed one Saturday afternoon, he was standing on his front step, looking dapper in a suit and tie having returned from Church. I often accompanied him on errands and asked his opinion on matters of interest. As we drove through the town and location, he often waved at other vehicles or pedestrians walking at the side of the road. We once passed a primary school in the location, and I asked him if it was "different to Ngomso". "It is different", he responded. "The children are quiet; they stay in their class. It is more relaxed." He went on to tell me about the homes of Ngomso learners:

> You will be surprised if you go there. You will feel sympathy. For some of them, there is no money there: you must sit on a paint tin when you visit. There is no food. Their parents are drinking during the day; some of them are. They return home and know that there will be no food there.

Widespread concern about 'absent basics' not only related to considerations of material deprivation but also provisions of care, guidance, and discipline. I once asked Lindiwe "What happens if a learner is away from school for a week?" It was most often because she was "staying at her boyfriend's [place]", she said. This situation troubled her: "How is it that they are young and are staying there when they have parents? That I don't know." It was just this kind of issue that encouraged Holly to send Damba to a private school. For Lindiwe and other members of staff, ensuring school attendance was widely held to be an essential aspect of being a good parent; a judgement that aligns with The South African Schools Act of 1996, which made parents legally responsible for such matters.[9] When parents were understood to have failed this most basic of roles, members of staff regularly took it upon themselves to address the situation.

For example, Peter and I accompanied Mrs Noni as she visited Avu, a learner, at her home to try to understand why she had not attended school for some time. As we arrived, I noticed a couple of neat vegetable patches behind a chicken wire fence. Avu's father had been a gardener for a man in town for the previous three years, who gave him seeds to plant. The living area of her two-roomed home had a South African flag, an ANC poster, a picture of Peter Tosh and an out-of-date 2010 calendar on the wall. The sound of a small TV filled the room. Avu—who had HIV and often asked me to help with her grade six maths and English, which she found more challenging than most—was sitting on the sofa watching a chat show with her mother and younger sister. Mrs Noni introduced herself as a "social worker" and asked her why she had not been in school. "I don't know", Avu replied. Mrs Noni encouraged her to return and spoke about the free uniform, food parcels, and the school meals that Ngomso provided. The mother began to cry as she explained that Avu had ignored her pleas to attend school. She wanted a psychologist "to check" that Avu was "OK". With tear-filled eyes, she said, "I am so worried. She is too young; she is too beautiful". I was playfully distracting the little sister from the emotional conversation by making silent, stupid faces; she was about two years old. Avu got up from the sofa and went to the back of the house. She returned wearing Ngomso's trademark green jumper. Her mother continued crying as she hugged her and Mrs Noni. I was still blowing out my cheeks to try to make the little sister laugh. Peter opened the door to the minibus as Mrs Noni, Avu, and I approached the vehicle.

A week later, Mrs Noni was telling me that there were "problems" with young and old. She had stopped buying clothes for one of her daughters unless she went to church. When her other daughter refused to get out of bed in wet weather, she encouraged her to go to school by saying "it is not raining in the classrooms". "Other parents" didn't do this, she said, which confirmed that "they don't care about their kids". Just like "some" of the parents of Ngomso learners who "don't care about their children", she said, while emphasising the word 'some'. To give me an example, she recalled our visit to Avu's house. The mother had cried about her daughter's refusal to go to school when minutes earlier they had been watching TV together. "How can she do that?" she asked. In her opinion, the mother should have come to Ngomso with Avu to discuss the matter. That evening, as I finished typing notes, I wrote "Mrs Noni has a thing about 'their parents do not care about them'".

The upshot of such judgements was that members of staff fretted about young people who were not in school, especially those who had left prematurely. Following Mary Douglas (1966), there was a polarity of purity and danger between the school and learners' other social worlds (Ennew and Swart-Kruger 2003), hence the numerous home visits designed to locate absent learners. Perceptions that learners didn't acquire appropriate moral knowledge elsewhere compounded enthusiasms for schooling. Schools and churches were adjudged to be the rightful sites of education (cf. De Boeck and Honwana 2005). Their evaluation is evocative of Swartz's (2010: 323) analysis:

> The usual institutions that might inoculate youth against multiple negative influences exert less influence in resource-poor environments than might be the case in a middle-class context. Such consideration shows how township youth have to choose to opt out of the prevailing *ikasi* [or township] culture in favour of moral goodness, unlike their middle-class counterparts, who are protected against harmful moral choices by the presence of normative role models and regulators.

For most members of staff, the normal and good appears as the State and its institutions (e.g. schools, police, and law), Christianity, 'nuclear families', and wage labour. Such judgements are invocations of historically constituted moral possibilities regarding forms of governance (Zigon 2009b, 2010). The promotion of 'normative' regulatory institutions and role models is indistinguishable from enthusiasms for controlling unpredictability or precariousness: normativity is good; the abnormal is harmful, sometimes even evil.

For Lindiwe, lacking parental guidance resulted in criminality:

> They don't get love from their parents. That's why some of them end up doing burglaries. Some parents like to drink. They don't prepare [dinner] for their children [and] the children are hungry. So they must get something to eat; so they become criminals to get money for food. The parents are getting grants, but they are not spending it on their children.

As indicated by Peter's aforementioned statement, the staff often thought that parents and carers drunk because they didn't care about the young people they were responsible for, or that they didn't or couldn't care for them because they were often drunk. As Madoda explained:

One of the mamas of the kids here, she doesn't even see her child, she was drinking. Even if they come for a meeting here, some of them, once they know about the meeting, they will think in that situation [and stop drinking for the meeting]. But it affects us in the school because the kids are dealing with something like that.

During many conversations, members of staff readily offered other moralised judgements about the extent to which learners' parents and carers did or did not match up to their ideals. This was Lindiwe's explanation:

Sometimes [a learner is] angry at you, although you are not the person that makes him angry. He is not angry with you; he is angry with what is happening to him. They are rude because of what is happening [to them outside of school and] the anger inside of them [is because of that]. But some of them are rude: they are naturally rude. They didn't get the basics from their parents; you know?

When continuing his explanation of how Ngomso learners were different, Madoda shared a similar message:

It's not totally that they are all disadvantaged from home; some have parents, but they have parents who are not doing as parents should do. If you are a parent, you have to teach your children the good way.

Appropriate and desirable moral education—'teaching the good way'—was considered an essential determinant of success at school and desirable social interaction; and, as a consequence, its absence was held to explain learners' behaviour and learning barriers. Such judgements were dependent upon the notion that parenting was a skill, with some individuals being better equipped than others to fulfil the role. In certain respects, there are historical precedents relating to the staff's condemnation of learners' parents. In Victorian Britain, during the consolidation of the colonial empire, "mothering became something that was no longer natural but which had to be learned" (Abrams 2001: np). Poorer, working-class mothers were "labelled irresponsible and neglectful" by wealthier philanthropists and agents of the State (ibid.). Individuals made similar judgements about 'native' parents throughout the empire.[10] Missionaries worried about an absence of nuclear families, sexual assaults and exploitation, venereal disease, and out-of-wedlock pregnancies (Jacobs 2009: 92).

The men who surrounded the children at home were thought to be violent and devoid of 'civility'.[11] However, because members of staff deeply embedded themselves into learners' lives, and were privy to a vast amount of information regarding experiences at home and the actions of their parents and caregivers, their judgements are not evidence of their wholesale embodiment of any particular, overarching moral schema. Instead, these historical conditions brought a degree of legitimacy to the ethical judgements they made about parents and caregivers when working in their capacity as an agent of the State, as individuals who had access to relatively substantial material resources.

Joyce was deputy principal in 2011. Her hair was tightly braided, and she always welcomed me by saying, "Hi Oli", with an enthusiastic overpronunciation of the 'lee' sound at the end of my name. A group of journalism students came from Rhodes one afternoon to interview her as part of their studies. Joyce was explaining the challenges faced by her staff: "Our children, some of them, they don't accept rules and regulations because of their backgrounds; no adult has taught them to respect adults, so our rules and regulations are new to them." One student looked up from her notepad to ask: "What children does the school cater for?" Joyce replied:

> Children from the streets, orphans and those with alcoholic parents. Their background is not conducive to raising children in a good way. The school cannot expect help from the parents if they are not even taking care of their basic needs of the children.

Assertions of lacking parental care and, more worrisome, knowledge of violent/sexual abuse in the home frequently linked with considerations of learners' psychological and physical well-being. In 2010, Mary spoke at a public hearing of the Parliamentary Monitoring Group. The following extract comes from the document she submitted:

> Learners at Ngomso have enormous psychosocial problems. Some appear to be suffering from Post-Traumatic Stress. Most are emotionally and psychologically underdeveloped. They have not had the opportunities for normal developmental growth; in fact, their home environments have stunted their emotional, physical and psychological development. Violence is often the only form of conflict resolution many have experienced, and thus the only form they practice. Unscrupulous adults have used many learners for a range of criminal activities, and a number of the children have criminal records. A large number have been sexually abused.

Such assertions were informed by what Mary her staff knew about learners' experiences outside of school. Their evaluations were not abstractions, but reflections upon events whereby learners shared information about their lives. In Mary's office, in particular, learners disclosed enough accounts of stabbings, rapes (including one committed by an uncle), violent robberies, domestic abuse (e.g. an older brother burnt a learner with a cigarette), alcoholism and drug use, and all manner of unenviable experiences, that judgements about extrinsic barriers to learning were made with knowledge of tearful, scared, and shaken victims and reluctant witnesses. There was much evidence that (some) learners were unprotected. Moreover, these same conversations frequently involved (some) learners appearing as denying or remorseful perpetrators. Learners were thus both victims and purveyors of immorality, where such categories were interchangeable and indeterminate depending on how one judged the situation (see Hecht 2008; Honwana and De Boeck 2005). Either way, my understanding is that members of staff felt that learners had been 'made special' by their experiences in the location, at home, and on the streets; that they were spoilt and had become impure/immoral.

CHILD SUPPORT GRANTS AND PARENTAL CARE

As some of the previous quotes indicate, judgements of parenting often involved anxiety about alcoholism, which often interlinked with concern that Child Support Grants (CSGs) were spent on alcohol rather than intended beneficiaries. I asked Mary whether she was aware of any literature, perhaps from the time she prepared for an MA in education, which discussed this. She said she knew CSGs were "often wasted, due to extensive experience" not because she had "read it somewhere". As she mimed someone swallowing the dregs of an empty bottle, she said that the money "goes down [parents'] throats". "They are then drunk, so they beat their kids", she concluded.

A visiting social worker was informed that a learners' mother was not using a CSG to benefit her daughter. "The mother gets the grant but doesn't care about her", as Mrs Noni put it. The visitor then asked, "Why didn't the grandmother say something [to the Department of Social Development] about the mother so that the grant could be transferred to her?" This question suggested that payments were taken away from parents regularly. On another occasion, Lindiwe explained a marked absence of learners by saying that CSGs had been paid the day before. "What difference does that make?" I asked. She answered by saying that some learners collected the grants, which were unconditional cash transfers, with their parents, grandparents, or foster parents so that they could be sure that the money would go to them. She then said that learners spent their portion of the funds on alcohol for themselves and were absent from school for a couple of days as a result.

Claims that CSGs were insecure in the hands of carers were sometimes justified by, or allied with, the judgement that some individuals had wanted to be legally responsible for those under 18, without actually being responsible, in order to get the grant money. As Mrs Mzomba, the school's bursar put it: "some parents are fighting over the child—because of the grant". Mrs Noni visited the home of Phaphama, a learner in grade seven who had missed several days of school but was unable to find his foster mother. Phaphama later explained her absence by saying she had been "drunk" the previous night. The foster mother was intending to take him back to Mthatha, a town close to where he used to live. "He says that she is fed up with him", Mrs Noni explained. When Phaphama didn't attend school again, Mrs Noni returned for a second home visit. The foster mother said that Phaphama had left that morning in his school uniform and that she was unaware he had skipped school. Mrs Noni had her concerns:

> The situation wasn't good. There were two other ladies there. It was early to have other women in the house. It seems as if the mother is drinking. The situation of Phaphama is not right: at his age, sixteen or eighteen, there are girlfriends [staying with him]. It seems that he is 18 now and the [CSG] grant has stopped, so that is why [his foster mother] is annoyed [with him].

In addition to well-founded fears about HIV, conversations with staff about learners' girl/boyfriends, underage sex, and teenage pregnancy repeatedly included their concerns that young women with babies were more likely to drop out of school prematurely. They also felt that boyfriends were viewed as sources of income (also see Hunter 2010), which similarly reduced their enthusiasm for schooling and its promise of employment.

Relating to these same anxieties, I was told that young women were having children because they wanted to secure a CSG. For instance, Holly was debriefing Joyce and Mary following a workshop that she had attended in Port Elizabeth the previous day that focused on "risky behaviours".

One such behaviour, which was a hot topic of conversation among members of staff, was "teenage pregnancies", which were not uncommon.[12] Holly had learnt that the rate of teenage pregnancy had increased fourfold since 2004.[13] Joyce responded by saying: "the child grants are clearly not working". All three women laughed.

Almost three months before this conversation, soon after my first day at Ngomso, I was standing in the kitchen with Bongani, a past pupil who became a paid volunteer and the school's cook, and Madoda. This was the first time that I learnt of the assertion that "young girls", as Bongani put it, were having "up to five children to get the child payments from the government". There were fears that these young mothers would not care for their babies; that the grants encouraged births and gave birth to irresponsible parents. The worry that young men like Phaphama were sharing beds with young ladies because uncaring carers cared more about grants added a perpetual dimension to the problem, which demanded, even more, anxiety.

Such rumours about 'babies for cash' was a pervasive public discourse of morality (Zigon 2010) driven by alarmist news reports (see Solomon 2013) and everyday conversation and conjecture. To my mind, the notion that women (it was never said to be the father's decision) were having children primarily to secure an income of R250 a month (R300 in 2013) conveys more about evaluations of other income prospects than the accuracy of the claim that young women were becoming 'professional mothers'. Indeed, Mark Hunter (2010) suggests that when CSGs were introduced in South Africa, many thought it would encourage 'babies for cash'; however, research doesn't support this imagination (also see Solomon 2013), nor does it confirm the idea that grant money is regularly used to purchase alcohol.[14] Nonetheless, my interlocutors did not think CSGs were capable of providing learners with appropriate care and protection.

Street Children and Children

A typologised, somewhat extreme, image of a young person devoid of parental guidance and material comfort is 'the street child'. Indeed, Ennew and Swart-Kruger (2003: np) argue that street children are "frequently designated as having no family, or as being victims of 'family breakdown'". They are not the "normal (loved) home-based child", but "unloved" (ibid.). Judgements like these meant that members of staff widely saw 'life on the street' as being productive of extrinsic barriers to learning.

The term 'street children' has been inconsistently defined (Panter-Brick 2002).[15] In short, there is little consensus about who street children are, what they do, where they live and how they are distinct from, or similar to, other young people. Relatedly, organisations have struggled to define those targeted by interventions (ibid.). However, broadly speaking, street children are seen to be *out of place* (Connolly and Ennew 1996). Building on Goffman's (1963) consideration of stigmatised outsiders, Scheper-Hughes (1992: 374) argues that when a 'normal' encounters a stigmatised 'other', the "moral economy that governs social relations is unmasked and the society reveals itself in the very phenomena that it disowns, excludes, and rejects". When considering the stigmatised street child, we learn what 'the normals' consider to be normal. Ennew and Swart-Kruger (2003: np) follow Claude Levi-Strauss to argue that such discourses build upon "mutually constructed oppositions":

> Morally-powerful social constructions of family, home, domesticity, and childhood could not exist without the construction of the 'other' – the danger of the street, the amorality of street life and, above all, 'street children' who are outside the domestic sphere and challenge the order of social existence. . . . This is the basis of the assumption that street children must be living antisocial, immoral, chaotic lives and are thus necessarily a public order problem.

In line with this argument, the staff at Ngomso were worried that street children posed a threat to societal order due to lacking adult supervision and time spent outside of the confines of domestic spaces and schools. Colonial missionaries were similarly concerned that young Xhosas were encouraged to contribute to family wealth and that the Xhosa's child-rearing practices had a 'peer-to-peer' quality (also see Mayer and Mayer 1970). They wanted them 'off the fields' and in schools, in front of an adult teacher, placing great emphasis on the notion that it is primarily the mother's responsibility to rear her children and discouraging peer-to-peer type arrangements (Erlank 1999). Malinowski (1943: 658) similarly tells us that when he worked "in tribal areas or in the native townships of South Africa and the Rhodesias", he "constantly came across complaints . . . [from those working in missionary schools that] children are constantly compelled to take part in some economic pursuits or tribal festivities or domestic events". In January 1857, with a sense of disillusionment, Robert Miller (cited in Anonymous) wrote: "There are very few [Xhosas] at school [today], for all are out hunting." In the case of young South Africans and street children today, similar tension persists.

Members of staff were concerned for the welfare of those 'living life on the street', in addition to their concerns about the implication such lives held for society and the upkeep of moral norms. In a statement on the school's website, Mary writes:

> We define street children as profoundly poor children who spend a substantial part of their lives on the street in the city or in the township. This is where they beg, work, eat or just sit. These children are extremely vulnerable to illness and abuse. Most are physically and mentally able but, through no fault of their own, are amongst the most vulnerable people in society. While many people see street children as a social nuisance, we see them as intelligent, resourceful, tough and resilient. They eke out an existence in the toughest of environments and survive in circumstances that most adults only have nightmares about.

In noting the interplay between evangelical Christian faith and development interventions in Zambia, Bornstein (2002: 8) refers to "a common secular list of five development indices". Mary's definition of street children speaks to three of them: "vulnerability", "financial insolvency (material poverty)", and "social isolation" (ibid.). The other two are "powerlessness" and "bodily weakness" (ibid.). Despite the idea of vulnerability to illness, I don't believe that Mary and other members of staff saw the learners as 'weak'. "Most", says Mary, were physically able. Similarly, I don't think that they were thought to be 'powerless' either. Rather, they were thought to be tough and resilient. Mary knew she was dealing with 'intelligent survivors'. Similarly, academic discourses concerning street children have moved away from "ideas of dysfunction, pathology and psychological breakdown" (i.e. individualised deficiencies and weaknesses) and towards analysis of negotiations of social, political, cultural, and spatial environments (Ennew and Swart-Kruger 2003: np).[16] No longer are they depicted as "hapless victims of industrialisation", "passive recipients of adult culture", or 'social deviants', but as adaptive and resourceful individuals (Hecht 1998: 5, 93).[17] I noted this juxtaposition between understandings of the street child as vulnerable and in need of protection and help, on the one hand, and, on the other, resourceful and resilient.

Various members of staff informed me that learners should not have had to learn how to respond to challenges and that they had become capable of overcoming 'adult problems' without learning 'how to live' as adults. In Mary's opinion, in particular, learners transitioned from childhood to adulthood too quickly. They had "seen and experienced what most educated adults have only read about", she said, but had "never truly been children". Mary thought that learners had missed out on key morally educative experiences, such as playing "with real toys". Their transformation from one generational category to the next—their "development"—was thought to be incomplete.

More broadly, Terrio (2004: 10) states that street children "blur the accepted boundaries between the child and the adult". Comparably, Cheney (2007: 189) suggests that staff working for World Vision with former 'child soldiers' in Uganda lamented the loss of "normative childhood". She (ibid: 191) quotes one counsellor who said, "When they were abducted as children, their childhoods were stolen from them". For Cheney (ibid.), "this idea configures life in the LRA [Lord's Resistance Army] as a sort of static environment that either suspends or usurps childhood". The staff at Ngomso thought that life on the street, or early years without appropriate adult supervision and a lack of material learning resources, did the same (cf. Kilbride et al. 2000). Regardless of their age, therefore, learners were most frequently considered to be *children*, in need of protection from their own 'childish choices' and impulses, as well as from illness, abuse, environments, and circumstances. Their potentiality was unbridled: they did not know the right way, even if they could take care of themselves.[18] In this light, to some extent at least, (some of) the learners were considered to be among the 'untrained of the location' who were responsible for much anxiety over public safety.

At Ngomso, judgements and identifications relating to street children—as with orphanhood, child-headed households, and 'children in work, not school'—depended on implicit or explicit interpretations of historically constituted discourses concerning appropriate, normal, or desirable childhoods. Important precursors occurred during the eighteenth century when poets and philosophers fretted about childhoods lost to industry, and childhood began to emerge as a cosseted generational stage. The publication of Jean-Jacques Rousseau's *Emile* in 1762 was influential in 'the Romantic turn', which associated childhood with innate innocence and purity; a moment in life blissfully without the burdens of adulthood (Cunningham 2006). In Britain, the poetry of William Wordsworth that followed, such as *Intimations of Immortality from Recollections of Early Childhood* (1808), and William Blake, such as *Songs of Innocence and Experience* (1789), continued what Rousseau had started

(Burke 2004). At a similar time, in 1811, the *National Society for Promoting the Education of the Poor in the Principles of the Established Church* (NS) was established, which aimed to provide school education to all in the UK who had previously denied one (Gates 2005).[19] From 1833, annual grants were given by the British government to the NS to fund their Christian school project.[20] State-funded education delivered by the Church then proliferated over the course of the century, which ultimately formed the foundations of the mass education system in the UK.[21] In South Africa, the state-funded Anglican mission schools of the colonial period, which, in many ways, prefigured the structuring of Ngomso, emerged alongside these developments.

Discourses concerning childhood and the pivotal role of schooling gained further credence when developmental psychology emerged in the late nineteenth century, along with psychology and sociology more broadly. The evolutionary nature of the separation of adult from child, connected as higher and lower forms of life, was reified as 'the science of childhood'. This notion of evolution "annexed childhood as its proof-text for the human condition just as the doctrine of original sin had done before" (Kennedy 2006: 99). Relatedly, "the law of recapitulation" held that "cognitive, affective, sexual, or moral" aspects of childhood were "merely performative states" (ibid.). Because children were defined as primitive in this way, controlling them by employing 'specialists' in environments such as schools, now had a scientific justification. Child labour became increasingly regulated (amid much contention), and discourses concerning maturity and 'adult knowledge' were increasingly associated with literacy (Burke 2004).

Related, normalising relations of power encountered in contemporary society informed and reinforced the judgements of members of staff at Ngomso. Most specifically, they depended upon productions of knowledge relating to 'child psychology' and 'developmental psychology', that hold children to be developing adults moving along an Aristotelian 'great chain of being' (Kaplan 2006: 11). Nieuwenhuys (2001: 552) argues that such notions of normative or "enlightened" childhoods imply "that the existing diversity in the lives of children results from a lack of understanding and failure to adhere to higher moral values". He (ibid: 543) goes on to suggest that "Western charity workers insist upon imposing a . . . very Western view of what would constitute a 'normal' childhood on the children of the poor". Hecht (2008: 157) similarly argues that "work with street children", such as that done by the NGOs and 'street educators' he encountered in Brazil, "is shaped by moral judgements of how childhood ought to be". This 'ought', he (ibid: 232) argues, relates to "increasingly global notions about . . . [childhoods lived] in the protective realm of school and home, in training as future workers and citizens". Relatedly, Foucault suggested that the objectification of categories of children and adults enables the exertion of power over subjects (Gadda 2008): children can be corrected in ways that adults cannot. For members of staff, any motivation to exert such corrective power was inseparable from their concern for the young people in question.

Proving Abnormality

The notion that Ngomso learners were somehow different from 'normal others' was explicitly tested when the Department of Education sent a fax to all special schools in the province instructing them to report on learners' SEN. Ngomso had to quantify learners with "severe behavioural disorders". The fax stated, "SEN learners have to be tested by an appropriately qualified specialist to be considered". However, such individuals (e.g. psychologists) were in short supply. Instead, Alice, Joyce, and Mary debated whether learners had a "severe behavioural disorder", the label waiting to claim those who matched their conceptualisations of what this terminology meant (McDermott 1993). Learners with SEN were "an advantage", as Joyce put it, because of the weighted funding. They asked my opinion about certain individuals, and I remembered the moral dilemmas of my job in London. They also recognised that it was difficult to determine who was 'disordered' accurately.

The DoE's insistence on an "appropriately qualified specialist" was just one of its attempts to prioritise detached, scientific truths (Foucault 1977a, b). Individuals could also make judgements about the 'specialness' of learners without owning the signifiers of validated forms of knowledge (i.e. qualifications) that the department and its policies acknowledged and validated. The space for alternative opinions relates to Ray McDermott and Hervé Varenne's (1995, 1998) argument that SENs are culturally constituted (also see Bourgois 1996b; Seyer 2002). Certainly, discourses concerning SEN can only materialise and proliferate subject to the existence of encompassing schemes of understanding and expectation relating to behavioural expectations. In turn, these same discourses enable individuals to gain a sense of understanding when encountering the behaviour of others—that is, they enable mechanisms of identification, compartmentalisation, categorisation, grouping, grading, quantification, and qualification. When subsequently employed and validated, these explanatory discourses (re)establish and (re)fashion moral norms and expectations. For instance, notions of appropriate behaviour and explanations for inappropriate behaviour are central to the concept of oppositional defiant disorder, which is, among other issues, associated with resistance to those in positions of authority (e.g. teachers).[22]

Evidence of such dynamics was visible during an exchange between Mary and Nomalizo, a senior educator. Mary explained what she had learnt during a workshop the previous afternoon: "Those with ADHD [Attention Deficit Hyperactivity Disorder] cannot do two things at once. When you say 'look at me', he goes deaf and doesn't hear because he concentrates on looking—so if they're not looking, they're probably listening." Nomalizo, who had not been to the workshop, said, "In our culture, it is not common to look at something". I believe she was referring to the fact that young Xhosas are not encouraged to look their elders in the eye as a sign of respect (*ukuhlonipha*), or deference to their generational status; refraining from eye contact could have signified this moral imperative.

Much like the analysis of corporal punishment and human rights provided in the previous chapter, various moral discourses readily associated with 'Xhosa culture' that offered frameworks of understanding regarding generational hierarchies and behavioural expectations to my interlocutors were somewhat at odds with those promoted by and within the school and its institutional bedfellows (e.g. the policies of the Department of Education). Similar contests are evident in anthropological studies conducted elsewhere that also demonstrate how systems of schooling can function to challenge 'traditional' generational hierarchies because they are conceptualised and managed to promote and legitimise particular forms of discourse at the expense of others (see Ngwane 2001; Stambach 2000; Bloch 1998; Grindal 1972; Peshkin 1972). It was telling that Nomalizo's cultural knowledge was absent during the workshop and that her perspective did not factor in discussions about ADHD again. Likewise, I never recorded an incident where a learner's 'misbehaviour' was attributed to their embodiment of 'Xhosa culture' (to use my interlocutors' parlance) rather than some form of special educational need more readily acknowledged by the policies and surveillance tactics of the Department of Education. More broadly, for the school to receive the additional, weighted funding that comes with a special school status, the staff had to prove that the learners were special in ways that the DoE was prepared to recognise.

The imperative to maintain the claim that Ngomso learners posed particular challenges on account of their special educational needs was constant and unabating. Members of staff knew that the DoE employed modes of surveillance far more subtle than faxes that explicitly set out such intentions. In response, they employed various techniques in an attempt to maintain the school's status and funding. One such technique was the crafting of a *presentation* or an *impression* that supported their claim that learners had SENs (Goffman 1959). As we waited for a delegation from the DoE to visit the school, for example, a grade four learner arrived in the principal's office with bloodshot, glazed eyes. Joyce suspected he had been smoking. She held his fingers close to her nose and smelt the tell-tale notes of burnt tobacco and *dagga* (marijuana). Mary said that she would "normally send him home", but, on this occasion, wanted him to "sit in the passage" outside the office so that the visitors from the DoE could "see the sorts of things that we are dealing with". The young man was to be a physical manifestation of the status attributed to him and his peers. However, he had other ideas for how he should employ himself that afternoon and snuck away from the premises before the delegates arrived, somewhat regaining a mode of power for himself, and taking it away from members of staff intent on galvanising support for their intervention.

A similar technique was employed to convey the message that the school's additional funding did not mean that it was overly well resourced. As the offender sat in the passage, Mrs Mzomba suggested the visitors should not be given any tea or coffee, "so they can see that we are poor here". Mary thought it was a good idea. Soon after, a lady and a man from the national office of the DoE and a man from the provincial office arrived at the gate. Madoda led them to Mary and Joyce's office. I forgot about Mrs Mzomba's recommendation and made six cups of instant Nescafe. "We [staff] buy our own supplies for the office here", Mary told the delegates. I sat on the safe behind the visitors, who lined up close to one another. "The office is like a jigsaw puzzle", said Mary. With two sentences, she had subtly made the visitors aware of the staffs' trustworthiness and the space limitations of the school buildings.

These ethnographic vignettes demonstrate how various discourses relating to specialness were tactically employed to encourage to construct or refashion their conceptualisations of (1) learners' (moral) qualities, including judgements regarding their 'defects' or 'abnormalities', and (2) the school and its (special) needs. Such exchanges most regularly took place 'above learners' heads'. Resultantly, the young men and women in question were somewhat powerless to determine how they and the school they attended was understood and viewed by others. For those motivated to attend the school because it differed from others in the vicinity, this predicament was an inescapable moral bind.

Fearing Specialness

So far in this chapter, I have argued that members of staff thought Ngomso learners were different from learners at mainstream schools because they were special or abnormal. The interviews that Siseko conducted and his explanations of them helped me to understand how other residents of the location made related judgements. Importantly, several respondents said that Ngomso learners were not all alike. For instance, one 26-year-old man said:

> Some of them have good behaviour, some they don't have it. It's not because they are studying there [that there is this difference], it is because they were raised in different homes and other homes that don't have good behaviour.

However, this balanced judgement was not the norm. The majority of Siseko's respondents expressed thoroughly negative judgements, which focused on distinctions similar to those members of staff highlighted: that is, general immorality (e.g. "corruption" or "rudeness") and criminality; offensive and aggressive language; unkempt appearances and poor hygiene; underage sex, promiscuity, and 'teenage pregnancy'; and alcoholism and smoking (marijuana and cigarettes). For instance, when Thembu, a lady in her late twenties, was asked "What do you know about Ngomso School?" she replied:

> It is the rudest school in Grahamstown that I know of. It is for street kids – I mean children who sleep on the street, most of them. And children that are going there are dirty. Especially boys, you can sometimes see them in town begging using the school uniform, and if you say 'No [I won't give you any money]' they are going to say something [to you in response] that you won't like. When you talk with them, [they are] cursing at everyone.

A man in his forties responded to the same question by saying:

They are corrupt and don't have discipline, the majority of them; even the girls are no different: they are all corrupt. Even in their uniform, they are still dirty, most of them. It is the school that takes care of the children that are likely [to be] hopeless, who have no home, some are from the street. I think they don't have parents, some of them.

Siseko also spoke to a man named Sizo, a 28-year-old ANC councillor, and asked him "Can you describe the children that go there?" Sizo responded:

Children who go there, mostly I see them as thugs [and] children who smoke in front of old people. I think that there is no discipline in that school. And I see children in the tavern with the school uniform on, drinking most of the time. . . . They are the same age as the [learners in the] township schools, but they are very *stout* [i.e. naughty]. They are dirty and with the bad behaviour. They are swearing at old people. Their behaviour is very strange; it's not normal like other children. They already know about life, like having babies and smoking, at the small age.

Sizo and several other respondents also argued that Ngomso learners were *stout* (naughty) because corporal punishment was not tolerated at the school. In contrast, judging from numerous accounts, corporal punishment was prevalent in government schools in the location, despite being illegal for almost two decades (also see Morrell 2001; Reed 2014; Veriava 2014).[23] One male respondent said, "I think that [the schools in the location] are *doing good* by beating the child, because black children, in order for them to listen to you, you must use the *sjambok*" (Afrikaans, meaning a stiff whip, originally leather but now more often plastic).[24] Siseko explained: "They think that children come here and become more aggressive [because they don't fear the consequences of violence]." For these individuals, Ngomso was not morally instructive because its punishments weren't tough enough on immoral behaviour.

In line with the analysis of punishment and morality in the township and human rights discourses provided in the previous chapter, such statements and judgements can be seen as evidence of embodiments and invocations of localised, historically and culturally constituted moral discourses concerning the relationship between appropriate and effective forms of punishment, societal production and regulation, and moral education/child-rearing. Philip Mayer and Iona Mayer (1970) highlight the centrality of organised and regulated forms of violence within the system of generationally organised transitions from childhood to adulthood most readily acknowledged and valued by 'Red Xhosas' living in rural areas of the Eastern Cape during apartheid. Amongst my interlocutors, those who equated an absence of corporal punishment with ineffective moral education were positioned in accordance with a similar model. They believed that corporal punishment could be regulated and integrated into a broader scheme of societal organisation and (re)production, in spaces outside of schools *and* within them. This observation aligns with arguments put forward by anthropologists of education (e.g. Simpson 2003; Flinn 2000; Stambach 2000) who have argued that modes of education do not materialise within schools in isolation of the cultural dynamics that shape the world beyond them.

For members of staff at Ngomso, the cultural permeability of Ngomso's perimeter fences created an uneven ethical terrain within them. Competing moral discourses and related behavioural expectations had to be negotiated during their attempts to fulfil their responsibilities as educators. When I spoke with Mr Zamisa in 2011, he provided this perspective:

> Because we are a special school, there are rules and regulations that are similar to mainstream schools, but we differ in terms of enforcing discipline. We talk to them nicely; we beg them not to do things – 'Please do this or please do that.' In high school, they say 'I'm here to teach [you] not to sort out your behaviour.' They will give you one warning; then they will chase you away or [corporally] punish you. If they are chased [away] here, or if a teacher is hitting them, they will go to Mama Mary, and she will back the student up.

Mary did indeed bring disciplinary measures against members of staff who hit learners. Mr Zamisa himself was dismissed for striking a learner in 2012, having diverted from the codified 'softly-softly approach' during an argument on a sports field.[25] His dismissal was confirmed following much negotiation by members of the Disciplinary Committee. Nomalizo, a senior educator, most prominently came into conflict with Mary by leading a group of staff keen to orchestrate Mr Zamisa's reinstatement. Although tensions between loyalty to peers and hierarchical punishment of the breaching of moral criteria are universal in schools (and other similarly organised institutions), they had particular qualities at Ngomso. Nomalizo was a prominent member of the South African Democratic Teachers Union (SADTU). In this capacity, and perhaps more broadly, she said she was "fighting those [same political struggles] of the past". When her colleagues contravened moral criteria laid down by government law and the policies of the DoE—frequently constituted with reference to individualised human rights and accountabilities—she did not strive to uphold this criterion. Instead, she appeared to place greater emphasis upon the moral imperative to assist a colleague, or a "comrade" (to use the terminology of SADTU). Other members of SADTU working elsewhere in the country have reacted in a similar manner.[26]

Any tension that existed between Mary and members of staff who might have otherwise employed corporal punishment without the threat of disciplinary measures from her was not, however, absolute. Instead, some members of staff were evidently well aware of how justifications for the lack of corporal punishment could also draw upon expectations regarding learners' SEN. For instance, consider Madoda's analysis of the situation:

> [Because these learners are different from those at mainstream schools] you can't go straight to them; you must go around [the problem]. You can't say 'You must go to class.' You must talk to him nicely [because] he is going to cross-question you. I must listen [to him and not force him], or else he says 'I will report you to Mama Mary.'

His comments referred to a commonly held perception of the ways that learners engaged with instruction. As such, ethical contestations regarding the efficacy of various forms of discipline had cultural and institution-specific qualities. Staff frequently argued that Ngomso learners were different from 'mainstream learners' who more readily did as they were told (so they thought). Like some of his colleagues, Madoda connected such 'specialness' to the appropriateness of the school's approach to discipline. However, it is impossible to know the extent to which any tendency for members of staff to abstain from practices of corporal punishment related to their belief that other forms of discipline were more suitable and effective given the school's cohort as opposed to a concern that they could be disciplined for crossing the institutional line of expectation that Mary had drawn in the sand.

In Mary's opinion, the colour of her skin and lack of Xhosa heritage made policing corporal punishment and other unsanctioned behaviours more challenging. However, she was not simply more sympathetic to 'Western moral assemblages'.[27] For one thing, she was not anti-corporal punishment per se. For instance, she once told me she had "[carefully] used a wooden spoon" when disciplining her children.[28] "They knew it was there and it made them behave", she continued. Like Mrs Noni's comments about her long-lasting marriage, cited in the previous chapter, Mary then spoke about her son and daughter's well-paid careers and stable families. However, reports of corporal punishment at 'her school' put jobs at risk, including her own. The risk of dismissal from her post for failing to police the 'official line' was not one she was willing to take, especially because she felt that the learners depended on her; it was a policy rooted in pragmatics rather than moral objections.

To return to Sizo's concern about the lack of corporal punishment at Ngomso, Siseko told me he had made only partial notes of his comments. When I asked why, he smiled nervously and said, "He hates this school too much". He told me Sizo thought "normal children" arrived at the school before becoming "a very bad person". I asked Siseko why people thought such things. He replied, "They say that the school corrupts young children and it doesn't help. They [think normal children] are damaged [by their time at Ngomso] because the children at this school are bad". Similarly, a respondent named Xolelwa said "I would never take my child there because the school is different from other schools. [Learners] are very rude, so I think they will spoil my child". I heard a similar judgement while having dinner with a young (i.e. in her early twenties) Canadian lady, who was "volunteering" at an NGO catering for individuals affected by HIV.[29] We had met earlier that week when I visited the NGO with Mary. I was surprised by her comments because this organisation supported several Ngomso learners and past pupils. She explained that her colleagues had recently discussed the schooling of two young sisters, who had been absent from school due to material poverty and parental ill-health. When one colleague suggested they enrol at Ngomso, others had responded with comments about violence, drugs, and criminality at the school. She said that the theme of their opinions was: "We cannot send the girls to Ngomso as they will be lost forever if we do that". In my notes, I wrote, "their view [is that] the school is a breeding ground for criminals and a dead end that no learner ever comes out of". She didn't ask whether this was a fair assessment. Instead, I had to digest her words in silence as the communal conversation moved to the next topic.

Nonkonzo was a prominent figure within the Inclusive Education sector of the DoE's district office, situated 15 minutes' walk from Ngomso. She had unkempt, curly hair that she dyed bright red and frequently called me "my English son". Her relationship with staff at Ngomso shifted between varying degrees of conviviality and antagonism, particularly because she and Mary were both strong characters. When we spoke in 2013, she was adamant that Ngomso "should not be a special school as its learners do not have profound special needs; this is where Mary and we [at the DoE] differ". Learners with "these needs", she said, should be in mainstream schools. She then conceded that some learners at mainstream schools, especially those who were 'age inappropriate' (i.e. working below target levels), could go to Ngomso for three months to "get up to speed" through the Accelerated Bridging programme. However, when I asked if she knew of any suitable learners, she undid the appeal of her suggestion: "No, [I don't know any], they would get polluted by the learners at Ngomso, if I can use the word polluted." In effect, she was saying that, although the learners at Ngomso were not profoundly special, they were special enough to pollute learners from mainstream schools.

Dr Pienaar, Nonkonzo's superior at the DoE, had a different opinion about learners' specialness. She had two psychology doctorates that provided her with relevant and associated frameworks of meaning and explanation:

> Working with Ngomso kids is totally different from other children in other schools because their experiences are worlds apart. These kids go to the streets and develop coping skills far superior to that of other children. That sticks out as totally different from what you would find in normal schools. . . . That type of neurological damage [that results from traumatic experiences and life on the street] does have an impact on learning ability and your way of coping with life.

Despite its 'scientific grounding', Dr Pienaar's statement was, fundamentally, a normalised judgement about childhood, brain development, learning ability, and existential engagements with life. Her analysis became more complicated when she considered "the kids who come to Ngomso who are not street children but are [over-aged learners] who have fallen behind for some other reason". She didn't think these young people had had to develop the same "coping skills" as those who lived on the street and were therefore 'more normal'. For her, this distinction had an important implication, which brings us back to the issue of discrimination:

> I don't know if it is good for them to be in one school; maybe they should be dispersed into other mainstream schools. . . . [Because] it's almost like it is a breeding ground, or reinforcement, for these [problematic behavioural]

strategies; they learn [them] from each other. . . . The main concern, I think, with doing it the way that Mary is doing it, is basically that you are creating a nucleus for bad behaviour to be, sort of, contained. . . . [As a result, you find that] the parents [of those who aren't street kids] will say, 'No, they cannot go to Ngomso' because they do not want them to become like these other children with behaviour problems. [They say] 'We don't want our kids to mix with those kids'.

Ideas that Ngomso learners were capable of corrupting or spoiling (i.e. immorally transforming) others led me to a passage in Mary Douglas's classic text *Purity and Danger*. She (ibid: 114) writes, "A polluting person is always in the wrong. He has developed some wrong condition or simply crossed some line which should not have been crossed, and this displacement unleashes danger for someone". Certainly, in the eyes of some interlocutors, Ngomso learners had crossed a line by enrolling at the school: they had become 'wrong uns', if they weren't already, and were thus a potential source of danger. "Pollution", continues Douglas (ibid.), "can be committed intentionally, but intention is irrelevant to its effect – it is more likely to happen inadvertently". This assertion aligns with perceptions that learners' intentions were irrelevant or at least not worthy of discussion. Instead, it was considered a given that they would pollute others who might come into contact with them. Thus, whereas Ngomso staff thought the location and a lack of moral education outside of school corrupted learners, other interlocutors wished to separate their loved ones from Ngomso. In turn, these 'loved ones' were the same 'black children in the location' that Holly was attempting to separate from her daughter by schooling her privately. All of these moralised fears about pollution were dependent upon individuals acknowledging some form of societal stratification.

I noticed similar concern about separation when talking with Nitin, the principal of a high school in the location, one sunny Saturday afternoon, soon after we had finished a game of mixed doubles at the local tennis club.[30] Nitin told me that the behaviour of learners who had joined his school earlier that year, after passing their grade seven exams at Ngomso, was "worse" than previous years. His teachers were complaining that this intake was "very naughty". "We try to accommodate them", he said, "and in the past, they have integrated well". What did he think was creating this barrier to integration? He said they would attempt to justify their actions by saying educators at Ngomso had allowed them to curse and hit others (including educators).[31] He also said that when he confronted them after they did "something wrong"—he gave the example of a grade ten learner jumping over the school fence to avoid afternoon lessons—they would readily apologise, in a way that other learners would not.[32] For Nitin, the inclination to apologise in the hope of forgiveness merely served to proliferate immorality. "We are not equipped to deal with these children", he said, with a shake of his head. He thought he might have to refuse to enrol next year's cohort.[33] As for the 'wrong and naughty' already enrolled, he suggested they might also have to go elsewhere. (In schools in London, the term "managed move [to an alternative school]" was used to describe this same process.) His comments clearly show how judgements relating to issues of discrimination and fairness (i.e. justice) are central to issues of educational inclusivity.

With analysis that helps explain such efforts to separate Ngomso learners from others, Douglas (1984: 98) writes: "if a person has no place in the social system and is therefore a marginal being, all precaution against danger must come from others". She (ibid.) goes on to consider the difficulty that ex-prisoners have when trying to secure employment: "[This is] a difficulty which comes from the attitude of society at large. A man who has spent any time 'inside' is put permanently 'outside' the ordinary social system." The idea that Ngomso learners exceeded the capabilities of 'mainstream institutions' as a consequence of having been 'inside' a school that ostensibly catered for those 'outside' the margins of 'mainstream society' is an example of this same difficulty. Displays of seemingly unexceptional behaviour—for example, 'skipping class'—were deemed especially problematic because they had once attended a special institution.[34]

As if to explain Nitin's assumption about the next cohort of Ngomso learners, Douglas (ibid.) goes on to say, "With no rite of aggregation which can definitively assign him to a new position he remains in the margins, with other people who are similarly credited with unreliability, unteachability, and all the wrong social attitudes". The staff at Ngomso tried to create rites of aggregation; for example, with exams undifferentiated from those at mainstream primary schools and brand new uniforms on the first day of high school. However, for some 'outside observers', it was not enough: Ngomso learners were and would remain 'abnormal unteachables'.[35] In other words, the fact that Ngomso learners engaged with specialist interventions when attending the school limited the probably that others would judge them to be normal, regardless of their actions.

For Dr Pienaar, this interplay between identifications of marginality/ specialness and resultant practices of separation and ethical imaginations of social or 'mainstream' integration was a source of existential discomfort. In other words, she felt uneasy as a result of the present scenario, but she was not sure if any alternative solutions (i.e. moral possibilities of acting upon the world) were better (i.e. more moral and improved) options. Like my interlocutors at Ngomso, she was keen for social integration, yet, unlike them, she wasn't sure that the school represented was the most effective tactic:

> Look, there is probably much to say for all the views on this matter, but I went to a career exhibition, there in Joza [in the location], and Mary sent her children too. . . . They came in that beautiful new bus of theirs, and when they got out there was outroar from the [mainstream school] kids around them, who were laughing at them; and I felt so disgusted. And I thought 'What are we doing? Are we really giving these kids a chance? What are we doing [when we] keep on telling them that they are different? In trying to help them, are we not marginalising them?' Yeah well, if you talk to Mary, she will definitely disagree.

I agreed with her prediction about Mary. As I have noted already, I knew she felt Ngomso's uniqueness gave 'these kids' a better, if not their only, chance of 'demarginalisation'. In contrast, for Pienaar, psychological theory and neurological research brought meaning to the behaviour of Ngomso learners but did not enable her to come to a conclusion about what was best for them. For this scientist, there remained a need for ethical, philosophical judgement. This necessity was felt by other interlocutors concerned with issues of marginality and redressive intervention. In my experience, at least, such ethical quandaries are inescapable whenever these same issues fundamentally underpin human interaction.

Dealing with Stigma

Ngomso learners and past pupils were well aware of the circulating public and institutional discourses regarding their specialness and negotiated them in the process of fashioning their lives. The following quote was Nyameko's take on the issue; he was 16 and living at the Shelter:

I don't think this is a special school. Mama Mary says that it is a special school, 'Because we give you a grocery [parcel every week].' . . . [But we are like learners] in the location schools: some of them are *stout*, and some of them are not *stout*; some of them in the location are stealing and smoking, like [some of] us, [and some of them] are fighting [like some of us] ... [Those learners in location schools] are the same [as us], my brother.

Some [people say] to us that we are the street kids. Some of them [say that we've got] problems and [suggest we] learn [them] at school. And, also, teachers are talking about street children. *Eh*, my man [that's frustrating]. I told the people, 'No, [you are wrong].' I must show that I am not [one of those] street children. But some of the boys, they are street children, you know, brother? Not me, brother. I will never be the street child. You know? But some of the people say that [I am]. I don't care [about] them. Telling me, 'I am a street child' – do whatever you want. I don't care about them.

Zigon (2011: 63) makes "an analytic distinction between self and person" to better describe the different relationships that individuals have with themselves and others. As per considerations of 'self-fashioning', "self is a way to describe the process by which human bodies are engaged, oriented, and actively attuned to their social world" (ibid.). The outcome of this process is personhood: "the person is the *socially recognized* disclosure of these embodied self processes" (ibid, emphasis added). Similarly, in his discussion of stigma, Goffman (1963: 12–31) uses the terms "social identity" to describe the attributes assigned to individuals according to the perceptions and expectations of others and "self-demands and self" when describing an individual's response to these ascribed identities. Nyameko's sense of self conflicted with public discourses concerning his personhood or social identity. Attuned to this intersubjectivity constituted conflict, he responded to it by "work[ing] to preserve" his "moral integrity" (Crossley 1996: 67). Such responses frequently resulted in observable ethical contestation, as individuals variably judged the validity of socially recognised classifications (also see Desjarlais 1997: 110).

As the quote from Nyameko suggests, one social identity learners encountered was that of 'the street child'. This is an extract from my conversation with Sicelo and Velile, two grade six learners who were living at the Shelter:

Oliver:	You said that other people don't understand the school and that they think it is a school for street children. Do you think that it is a school for street children?
Sicelo:	No, because if you [live at] home and [the people you live with tell you] 'Go [and live] somewhere [else] and don't come here again', you will not go there to town and sleep [there]. You only go to town to get something to eat.
Velile:	[Or to get] some money, you know?
Sicelo:	They are saying that this is a school for street children, and we are not street children – we know that; [so] we can leave them talking.
Velile:	We know that we are not street children.

The sign at the entrance to the Shelter carried the words "Street Children", informing passers-by who to expect behind its gates. As Sidima, a 14-year-old grade six learner and resident of the Shelter, put it, "Here at Shelter there is the sign that says it is for street kids. I hate that because I am not a street kid". He told me that he had a home in the location and stayed at the Shelter because his mother was an alcoholic. Like Sidima, Errol keenly told me that he had never been a street kid either. He was 21 and studying at high school, having spent much of his childhood at the Shelter. He used the word "painful" when recalling how it felt to hear members of staff inform visitors that residents of the Shelter were street children.

Similar conflict, between the socially constituted identity of the 'street child' and learners' understandings of themselves, was also evident during quite ordinary events at the school. Soon after assembly one Monday morning, a group of four female learners stood in the passage outside Joyce and Mary's office. I noted that "they [seemed] pretty worked up about something". It transpired that an educator had said the school was for "street kids" the previous day. In my notes, I wrote:

> The girls are not happy about this label at all. They tell me that they are not street kids and that they are angry to have been told that they are street kids by the teacher. They stand in the corridor waiting to talk to Mama Mary, as do about five other people. Mary is showing some guests around, two women – not sure who they are but they just turn up and start taking photos of the children and stuff, as if they have arrived at a zoo. [Mary] tells the girls that she cannot deal with them now and that they must go back to their classrooms. . . . [Later on] I heard [Mary] say this term ['street children'] to the two volunteers, as she was showing them around: 'They are mostly street kids or orphans.'

In Chap. 5, I will analyse why members of staff used this terminology (i.e. 'street child' and 'orphan'), even though it helped maintain public discourses and social identities that the learners disliked. For the moment, it is enough to say that terminology employed by individuals who are eliciting support for institutions that are ostensibly concerned with assisting 'damaged youngsters' can inflict damage upon these same 'beneficiaries'.

Ngomso's institutional history and significant events of the post-apartheid period help to explain this paradoxical situation. Firstly, Mary recalled that groups of peers were working together and living on the street in 'downtown' East London when she founded the first Ngomso school and began to employ the term 'street children'. To my knowledge, however, in Grahamstown, groups and individuals who 'worked on the street', by begging and car guarding, in particular, slept in the location. This disparity might relate to the fact that East London is bigger than Grahamstown, which would make it more difficult for young people to live in the township *and* commute each day to business and industrial districts. Despite this difference, staff and supporters seemed happy to employ the term 'street children' to refer to individuals who 'worked on the streets' whether they slept there or not. Moreover, some learners had 'worked on the street' before joining the school or did so when absent, whether through truancy or during the holidays. However, learners who regularly attended did not engage in such activity. Adding further ambiguity: in the past, learners had 'lived on the street' in Grahamstown. Indeed, some of the older past pupils who had attended Ngomso when it was at the Shelter readily said they had been "street children" before joining the school. An explanation for this historical shift is that Ngomso was founded when government-funded social welfare provisions were less extensive than they were at the time of my research and the need for some to 'live on the street' has diminished as a result. The stigma attached to such living arrangements probably dates from the early period and had stuck, despite all that had changed.

This ambiguity meant there was room for judgement regarding the validity and appropriateness of the term 'street children'. Consider the 'middling judgement' of Siseko and friends, a group of past pupils:

Siseko: They're from the street, most of them [who are] at Ngomso.
Oliver: What does that mean?
Siseko: They were eating on the street [and] begging in town, most of them. And others, they have been staying at the township, but they can't afford to go to the [mainstream] primary school.

Oliver: But, are all of them from the street?
Mzoxolo: No, not all of them.
Siseko: Not all of them.
Dalumzi: Some of them are from [homes in] the location.
Siseko: But they couldn't afford [cut off].
Mzoxolo: To go to school.
Siseko: Or they don't have parents around.

The distinction they made between learners who ate and begged in town and those who simply could not afford to go to mainstream schools was integral to how many learners constructed their sense of self. For example, when I asked Errol to explain why it felt painful to be misunderstood, he replied, "street kids are those that are eating out of bins and [who] are begging". Implicit in his response was the assertion that he did neither. Other interlocutors also maintained their sense of moral selfhood in opposition to the immorality of begging. After he had spoken of the sign at the Shelter, Sidima responded to my question "What do think about people begging?" by saying:

> They must get to the Shelter because I don't like people begging because they don't know what those other people are saying about them. It's not good to see someone you know that is begging; you must take him to another place and stop him begging. Maybe that will be better [for him].

In his reasoning is the idea that the harm inflicted when individuals *know* you are begging is greater than that inflicted when individuals *assume* you beg because you are a resident of a shelter ostensibly for street children. In other words, it was better to encounter false perceptions rather than valid ones. Some interlocutors thought that those who begged in town were guilty of perpetuating these false, stigmatising social identities because, as a technique of persuasion, they disingenuously informed members of the public that they remained at the school. This was Jikela's perception, who was in grade six:

> I can say that there are no street kids in the school. You see [there is confusion about this because some learners] leave [Ngomso and] then go to the town and beg for money. And then maybe the person that he begs money from will say 'Where is your school? Why are you not at school?' And then he doesn't answer [truthfully with an answer about] why he is not at school;

he answers only that 'My school is Ngomso.' And the other person [will] go 'Ngomso?' And he [replies] 'Yes.' And then [the other person] goes and spreads rumours like 'At Ngomso they are keeping street kids [on their register].'

For Jikela, the rumour (or public discourse) that there were street kids at Ngomso was epistemologically flawed: individuals simply misinterpreted the school and its learners because they didn't know the truth. More broadly, learners thought other public discourses about themselves and the school were inaccurate for the same reason. Velile was one of my closest interlocutors and was 17 and in grade six in 2011. I once asked him "Is this school the same as other schools?" This was his response:

> This school is very good. But other guys think that this school is not good because they have not seen [what happens here] with [their] own eyes. They say this school is [a place of] learning for crime, [and for] smoking. But Mama Mary never tells us or teaches us how to smoke. So when others see [learners of Ngomso] smoking they think that all of the children [here] are smoking. Maybe [also] there is another [learner who is] swearing, and they think that every child here at school is swearing [too]. You know?
>
> Here [at school], [maybe they] saw crime [happening once], maybe another guy there at class slapped a girl and then the policeman came [to the school]. Another guy that is passing there [at the front of the school] is going to say 'Hey, these guys that are here are not learning [anything good] – they are just learning the crime.' But it's not that thing man because we make a decision to [say] 'No, [I won't engage in that kind of activity].'
>
> We can't [do] the foolish things, the stupid things, the swearing – [we can't] do all that stuff [because it won't help us]. Because you make your [own] choices, you know? [For example:] 'Ok, I am here [at school], I want to learn.' I know where I am coming from [and I know where I am going]. You know all the things about yourself.

His friend Sicelo philosophically took up the theme of his argument:

Sicelo: In your life, you've got choose.
Velile: You have to choose.
Sicelo: What is right and what is wrong.
Velile: What is right and what is wrong.
Sicelo: [Will you do] something that will help you, or not?

In sum, Velile and Sicelo knew stigmatic judgements about them and their peers were misplaced because they were exercising their capability to make moral decisions. The problem was, as they recognised it, their moral dispositions were not visible to others. Instead, they were judged according to arbitrary signifiers; the visibility of (other) learners who smoked, for example. Velile spoke of how a member of the public might attend court to collect their possessions, only to see a past pupil from Ngomso on trial:

> [They see that and think] 'That one was learning at Ngomso and now he is in court – so there at Ngomso they are teaching our children the wrong thing.' [Because of things like that] other families don't want their children to come here. They say 'No, no, no – at that school they will teach you the wrong things.' But, there is no one that comes [to this school] and learns the thing that is wrong. [In] this school they teach you the right things for you to survive in life.
>
> So me, I am proud of this school. No matter what the other guys are saying [about it] – 'street kid school' [or whatever]. I like that thing they are saying because I know that it never happen here [i.e. is not true]. They [say] the wrong [i.e. incorrect] thing to other people about something that they don't know [anything about].

According to Velile, misunderstandings arose and solidified because the school was in a very public space—that is, next to the main pedestrian thoroughfare between the location and town. Police cars did occasionally visit, and fighting, swearing, and smoking did occur. However, Velile astutely recognised that these events were especially visible to members of the public, as was not the case at other schools. Mongezi and Jikela, two learners in grade seven, were sure that inaccurate moral discourses, or "rumours" as they put it, were prevalent because passers-by witnessed Ngomso learners play fighting with security staff:

> Mongezi: They say we are the thugs [*tsotsis*]; the enemies.
> Jikela: If you are playing with someone, they get it wrong – they say 'They are teaching the thugs there.'
> Mongezi: [But] there are no thugs here at school. The thug is the stranger that takes peoples' money or is beating someone [up] – [we don't do that].

For these young men, true discourses about the school went unnoticed by observers who misconstrued causality in a bid to reach conclusions. To my mind, their analysis speaks to the epistemological claims of ethnography:

that is, by sharing in quotidian experiences with particular individuals in certain localities, we can become attuned to the intricacy and thus actuality of what we are concerned to understand. These interlocutors made a focused, ethical attempt to ignore such discourses. In line with Goffman's (1963: 22) analysis, they assessed "the limitations of normals" and devalued their false judgements. Moreover, Jikela and Mongezi were making an effort to transform these judgements:

Oliver:	You're telling me that people think that because you are working here, you are rude and you are thugs – how do you feel about that?
Mongezi:	I am not feeling right, but I want to finish school and show them that we are not thugs.
Jikela:	You mustn't listen to them because you must do the thing that you are doing.
Oliver:	So what is the thing that you are doing?
Jikela:	The reason that I am in school is that I want to fulfil my dream and to show [others] that the rumour spreading – [the idea] that Ngomso is for rude children – is not [true].

Sophie Day (2010: 294) builds on Goffman (and others) to consider *private* (i.e. self-constituting) reactions to *public* (i.e. social or 'externally given') expectations of sex workers. Like some of the women in her (ibid: 302) essay, my interlocutors responded to the debilitating, dehumanising qualities of stigma by "battling for justice and recognition". More broadly, populations considered marginal and, to some extent, powerless can locate ethical freedom in the ways they respond to negative judgements directed towards them. For my interlocutors, the possibility of transforming public discourses with ethical contestation opened the door to hopes that they might yet live without the discomfort of being perceived as 'immoral abnormals'. With this ethical imagination and effort to transform inaccurate, socially constituted labels and categorisations, they gained some sense of control over their relationships with the world. The need for this effort was constant and inescapable.

Luzuko, a past pupil who will feature heavily in this book, wanted to talk about the burdens of his effort and I arranged to meet him in my office at the university. He was battling to understand why he encountered stigma, when, like Velile and Sicelo, he knew he was capable of making informed and moral decisions:

Luzuko: [Ngomso learners] are not physically mad in their head. [*Exhales in frustration.*]
Oliver: 'Not mad in the head', what do you mean?
Luzuko: I mean, they can succeed. A person who is mentally mad in the mind needs backup [i.e. support and direction] – [people to say] 'Don't do this, don't do this' – because he is not normal. Right? [Ngomso learners don't need that, so] those children are normal.
Oliver: Do you think they are normal?
Luzuko: Yes. You can tell when someone is not normal, isn't [that right]? One day I was so angry because there were some people who thought I was not right in my mind because I was coming from Ngomso. I told them that the learners at Ngomso are 100% normal – I am normal.

Other interlocutors keenly distinguished their material poverty from the idea they were somehow psychologically abnormal.[36] Similarly, Desjarlais's (1997: 109) interlocutors at a homeless shelter in Boston "did not welcome the awkward identity that came with being considered mentally ill". Like Luzuko's feeling of anger, an interlocutor named Henry (cited in ibid.) informed Desjarlais: "It kinda hurt me to be called a psychotic." Desjarlais (ibid.) argues that such discomfort arose because "The implications [of such identifications] were moral: to be psychotic [or crazy] was to be something less than fully human, without control over one's actions, and set apart from the social and ethical realities of others". To counter such judgements, Luzuko fought to assert the idea he was "100% normal" because he was living without "backup".[37]

Other interlocutors attempted to evade rather than correct stigmatic judgements. As discussed earlier, Sidima hated to be engulfed by stigmatic discourses. In a shipping container at the Shelter, used as a homework room, we spoke about his response to them:

Oliver: So are you happy to say that you are at Ngomso?
Sidima: *Ja* [yes]. But not to someone like a Xhosa. *Yoh, yoh* [exclamation of the point]. I will say 'I am from [a mainstream primary school in the township].' [Otherwise] they will [know that] I'm going [to Ngomso] and [because they think] 'Those [Ngomso] boys are swearing', they are going to think that I am swearing [too].

I interpret "someone like a Xhosa" to mean individuals living in the location, some of whom harboured negative opinions about Ngomso and its learners, like Sizo for example.[38] Like some of the other sex workers Day (2010: 302) considers, when encountering particular audiences, Sidima was adept at "hiding" or "concealing" his stigmatic status to present himself as an untainted person. Day (ibid.) argues this tactic of partitioning one's life can enable individuals to avoid feelings of dishonour. In other words, it is a mode by which individuals can mediate between their aspirations and the judgements of others.[39] Sidima was aware that stigma carried dishonouring potential during particular social exchanges. In avoiding the need to respond to, or fight against, such discrediting judgement, I presume he was able to dwell more comfortably in the world.

In a similar analytical vein to this discussion of concealment, some learners, male and female, complained about their skin tone and took steps to lighten it. Their actions relate to Goffman's (1963: 19) consideration of how a "stigmatized person" might respond to those who do not accept him with "respect and regard" with "a direct attempt to correct what he sees as the objective basis of his failing". Upon seeing a group of young men at the Shelter wearing a thick layer of white cream (calamine lotion) on their faces, I asked them to explain.[40] One of them replied, "It's to stop my face from the sun so that the skin is not too black". I saw Liani, a grade five learner, wearing similar cream one Saturday in the location. The following week, I gave her a copy of a photograph I had taken that afternoon. Upon seeing it, Ntombekhaya (an educator) questioned her about the cream and told her that she shouldn't be using it. Ntombekhaya may have been aware of the health risks associated with the practice, or perhaps she wanted Liani to be proud of her appearance.[41] Liani responded with an embarrassed smile and ran back to the playground.

The potential for contestation over such significations and practices of aesthetic transformation was also noted by Mayer during his research in the locality during apartheid. He (1961: 62) cites a 'Red Xhosa', who says:

> White people have a white skin and their women therefore use white powdery stuff on their faces, to look perfectly white I suppose. . . . Some African girls, black as they are, have copied this style, and very foolish they look. Have you ever seen a black car after it has rolled in a heap of wood ash? It is neither black nor white and it looks very ugly.

During my research, approximately five decades later, judgements premised upon a white/black binarism, and the respective symbiotic relationship between visible signifiers (e.g. skin colour) and assumptions regarding moral qualities, were not only evident to me but were also central to my interlocutors' existential reflections. In other words, they both enabled and limited their ability to comprehend their past experiences and futuristically reimagine and (re)fashion their lives.

Errol and I were talking on the high street when he told me that I had it "easy" because "whites" don't have to go "to the bush" for initiation. He then said he wanted "to be white—like how Michael Jackson was black but then became white". Earlier, he said he had "dark days" when "struggling for things" or when having "to fight". I assumed he was hopeful that lighter skin would mean fewer dark days. Similarly, Simpson's (1999: 7) interlocutors, male learners at a Catholic mission school in Zambia, revealed "an ambivalence to their own blackness". Simpson considers this observation in light of Franz Fanon's (1970) treatise on colonialism and the violence inflicted by discourses of 'white superiority'. Errol's ethical imagination should not be considered independently of such history either. His comment was also a response to his experiences. He told me that "[being a] young black man means that, if you brush against a white lady in the street [accidently], she will think that you are stealing her bag". Although he thought "other black boys [were] stealing", he was not one of them. Much in the same way that subjectivities were fashioned in opposition to the perceived immorality of the practice of begging, Errol wished to disassociate himself from the immorality of theft, only to be hampered by the tone of his skin.

Siseko was not immune from such stigma either. His appearance raised suspicion if he left the location at night. There was no official curfew, as existed in the colonial and apartheid periods, but there were informal restrictions on movement. He told me he wore different clothes when he went to town at night because he had been questioned by private security firms and the police many times before:

> I'm not living in town; so why am I there at twelve [midnight]? They are judging my clothes and my face – maybe there are too many scratches on my face [and they will know where I come from]. There are students in town so they must decide [if I am a student or not by looking at these things].

Siseko and Errol's discomfort in their own skin analytically relates to something Siseko told me about his neighbours.[42] When confronted/ interrupted by "white people" while conducting a burglary, they would scream and cry to confuse and disorient the house owners, before running off. They also used the tactic of grabbing a puppy and threatening to stab it to death unless the house owners complied with their demands.[43] Errol expected 'white women' to react to him as though he were a thief. The 'screaming black man' and 'puppy threat' techniques purposefully invoked other racialised reactions—that is, *surprise* that 'black intruders' would scream and cry and *fear* that they would fulfil their threat to kill a pet. Presumably, Siseko's neighbours employed such techniques to escape arrest without resorting to physical violence. In this way, their actions maintain a particular moral quality, no matter how questionable. In a city, the size of Grahamstown, retellings of such events became public moral discourse. Thus, an effective technique of power for Siseko's neighbours was constitutive of the racialised expectations that informed Errol's perception of his self and his desire to alter his way of being in the world.

Hoping to Find Hope

Given that learners had to encounter and deal with the stigma of attending Ngomso, the question arises as to why they attended *this* school when there were (potentially) other options open to them. To some degree, learners evaluated Ngomso's specialness against what it might offer them. Individuals preferred the smaller class sizes and increased attention they received from members of staff. The lack of corporal punishment was also appealing, particularly to those who had experienced it at previous schools; supporting the claim that corporal punishment in South African schools "makes learners unhappy" and "contributes to absenteeism and learners dropping out of school" (Veriava 2014: 7). However, other learners bemoaned the absence of corporal punishment. On one occasion, a grade four learner asked to 'be beaten' while having to sit on the floorboards outside the office. I compared his logic to the decision to rip off a plaster quickly. Some past pupils thought that the lack of corporal punishment impinged upon educators' abilities to assert authority and gain respect, and maintain discipline and moral order; encouraging learners to "do whatever [they wanted]" (as Mzoxolo put it).[44] Such judgements might appear as evidence of my interlocutors' individualised embodiments of locally and historically constituted moral discourses concerning the interplay between violence and generational hierarchies of respect (*ukuhlonipha*), similar to those which informed my interlocutors' debates about corporal punishment more broadly. Certainly, notable historical precedents to their judgements are identifiable. For instance, consider the words of a 20-year-old *mtshotsho* (adolescent Xhosa man), recorded in the 1960s:

> If a man is beating a boy even for the wrong reason the boy does not hit back – just runs away. This is respect… If we did not learn to respect punishment by seniors there would be fights daily. (Cited in Mayer and Mayer 1970: 175)

To some extent, the decision to enrol at Ngomso, or not, hinged upon an evaluation of these potentialities. Some individuals were greatly appreciative of the fact that they could avoid beatings by attending Ngomso, while others were worried that this absence—that is, the freedom to operate without fear of physical reprisal—were impinged upon their ability to ethically fashion a moral, societally rewarded future.

The material provisions on offer at Ngomso, which were not available in mainstream schools, were also a big draw. Consider the conversation I had with a small group of past pupils in Siseko's cramp 'tin shack' one afternoon:

> Oliver: In your opinion, your view, what makes [Ngomso] special? How is it different to other schools?
> Mzoxolo: For me, you go to Ngomso to go and sit in a chair at a table with a pen and just write what they want you to write – you don't have to pay school fees, buy a uniform or books. You don't have to pay anything; you just go to school to write.
> Dalumzi: And then you get something, [like] food.
> Mzoxolo: And then you get something from them. That's why Ngomso is special.
> Siseko: And it's special because it is for people that don't have money. You get food in the morning, the [porridge] at ten O'clock, and then the four slices [of bread a bit later], and [hot food] after school. That's why it's special.

I began to learn about the value of these forms of specialness during my first day at the school. In my notes, I wrote: "Food is a huge part of the day. The day, in terms of time, seems to revolve around meal times."

I also noticed the school had a new bus, unlike mainstream schools: "It is essential for children who live a long way away. It does a route and picks them all up." One learner, whose name I had not had time to learn, said, "It would take me three hours to walk home". Another told me "If I miss the bus in the mornings I just go home". A third simply said, "If there was no bus and no food we wouldn't come". Another told me that he came to Ngomso because he got a free uniform and shoes, unlike his experience at a mainstream primary school. "I come here because my mother is not working", he explained. A learner named Dumisa later told me that he sometimes came to school for electricity as well as food when both were absent from his home.

In sum, many learners came to Ngomso due to material poverty.[45] However, given their variable home environments, they did not uniformly value the material provisions available at the school. The morning porridge was eaten by approximately half of them, although some said that they didn't like it or that they weren't hungry when I asked why this was the case. Moreover, attendance dramatically fell when there were no lessons (e.g. post-exam season), suggesting that few learners turned up *solely* for food. However, it is impossible to know how important the food was because stigmatised judgements and managements of pride and shame hid its value. To me, it seemed that some learners did not eat the porridge to signify the idea that they didn't need the school's food. This dynamic reminded me of my schooling. I took care to banish products from supermarket value ranges from my lunch box to avoid ridicule. The free school meal vouchers provided at the schools where I worked in London were not paraded like trophies either. At Ngomso, I was mocked in the playground for the cheapness of my mobile phone, even though most of my tormentors did not have one at all.

I foresaw this line of argument on my second day at the school when an exchange between Samkelo, a learner in grade six, and Bongani, the school's cook, forced me to rethink the judgements I had made on my first day. Bongani made a joke after Samkelo threw some rice into the bin. Samkelo turned to me and said:

> He thinks I am hungry. He thinks that I want food. No – I am not hungry. Go to my home; there is lots of food there. Because I come to this school, he thinks that I am a hungry street kid. No. I come here because I like it here. I could go to a different school, but I like it here.

Samkelo was clearly keen that I would not make the same error of judgement. When I visited his home some months later, his mother kindly gave me an ice-cold glass of Coke as I sat on a comfy sofa in their living room. She was working as "a cleaner for a family in town", and I assumed she purchased their flat screen TV with her wages. Samkelo's grandmother lived in an adjacent building. She told me, with a slightly odd mix of sadness and amusement, that Samkelo would return from school and not eat the food she had cooked for him until much later in the evening because he always ate at school.[46] As Samkelo had said, there was food at his home. However, in truth, he could not attend another school because he was 18 years old and in grade six due to a spell in a prison for young offenders. He had enquired, but no other school would enrol him. Other learners were also 'too old' for mainstream primary schools, and many appreciated The Accelerated Bridging Education programme, as it meant they could quickly graduate to high school. Given these constraints, Samkelo attended Ngomso and did his best to maintain his sense of pride.

These markers of 'institutional specialness' were important motivating factors. However, young men and women did not attend Ngomso as a consequence of simplistic value calculations. More accurately, attendance was interwoven with, or a consequence of, unique life experiences: meetings, relationships, projects, reactions, hopes, regrets, successes, failures, and a multitude of other words I could use to describe the experience of human life. As I contemplated this fact during my research, I often asked learners "What's the reason you came to Ngomso?" Almost without fail, they responded with an answer that had little to do with an enthusiasm for a school education. While sitting in the disused shipping container at the Shelter, I asked Sidima this question. He replied:

> My mother was dying, there in the location. She was drinking and she [would] beat me all the time. When I was there, I was walking alone in the road at night, and I was so scared. She was beating me, so I stayed there in the street alone. Then, my brother was here [at Ngomso], and I came here [too]. And they gave me food and bread, so the next day I stayed. I talked to Mary, and she said that I must come [every day].

While Sidima's response was one of the more troubling, many interlocutors spoke about their early days at Ngomso and their continuing attendance in terms of problem-solving efforts to fulfil immediate needs and limit undesired experiences, such as hunger and violence. For many individuals, experiences of an absence of hope, rather than the specific hope offered by schooling, preceded school attendance in the first instance.

The words of Velile and his classmate Sicelo help explain the individualised nature of such processes of self-fashioning with great poignancy. I asked them "What was the reason you chose to come to Ngomso?" then said nothing more as they answered:

Sicelo: There are many problems at home. Maybe your mother is drinking, or she beats you and does not let you sleep at her house; maybe you must go and sleep outside at a friend's. That's why we come here. We want to solve our problems.

Velile: [As for] me, firstly my mother was not drinking [at the beginning]. But her sister was drinking – she took her to the tavern, showed her how to drink. At that age, I was not of that mind where [one] can know what is going on that is right. So my mother, all that time she drinks and drinks and is not coming home. I ask my grandmother, 'Where's ma?' But mum didn't come. Every day [she was] doing that. So I thought 'Maybe my mum is where? Maybe she is dead?'

Me and my brother, we were going to the town to ask for money to buy the bread. We arrived there in town [and] Mama Mary picked us [up] and asked us 'Do you want school? Want to learn?' Me, I said 'Yes'. But my brother said 'No, I don't want to go.' Mama Mary said that tomorrow I must come here to Ngomso. So I came to Mama Mary and shared my problems with her.

When I came home, I heard that my mother has HIV – so she is there at hospital and is very sick. So we take a taxi car and go there to the hospital, and I saw her there. I was so shocked. 'Hey man, this is my mother?' I have never seen her like this. . . . Another day, we are at back home, and they phone us there at hospital and say that my mother is dead. Why? Why is she dead now? I still can't believe it.

Then my family is starting to fight. My big sister [i.e. aunty] said all the children of my mother are not to live there at that family [home]. So my father take me to his house. Then I say, 'No, I want to learn.' But my father say he has no money for school fees, clothing, shoes, everything. Because my grandmother was [having] the [pension], [but] even her, she can't buy all those things.

When my big sister threw us away, my grandmother say 'No, no, these are our children, you can't throw them away.' My big sister

> say 'No, I don't need them anymore, their mother is dead.' So who is going to take care of [us]?
>
> Another day we arrived at the home where my grandmother [was staying] and she was not there. 'Where is grandmother now?' I ask my big brother? He said 'She is dead.' I asked 'How?', because I didn't remember that she has a disease.
>
> So I come back here again at Ngomso. I come to Mama Mary again: 'I want to learn.' My father is not working, and my mother is dead, and my grandmother is just dead. So me, I have nowhere to go because at my home they throw me away, at my mother's home they throw me away, [and] my father can't afford all the things that I want. Even the Christmas clothes – nothing. We were just walking with my shorts when I come here to Ngomso.
>
> So *ja*, that is my life, my man. So many things that are happening. Now my big brother has a job; now he is looking forward. I will never give up. I will push again and push again. That is my life man.

One important observation that I took from this conversation and several others is that when fulfilment was elusive and despair predominated, my interlocutors hoped for an alternative life. This hope appeared to sustain them during such challenging times and inform their intentioned efforts to fashion better, more desirable lives (Zigon 2009a). Their attendance at Ngomso was a component of such efforts.

To give further credence to this analytical point, I'd like to share a shorter extract from a conversation that I had with a past pupil. When we met in 2011, Lindela had recently moved on to high school having completed his final year at Ngomso. As we shared a curry one afternoon, he told me that at his first school, a mainstream primary, he was bullied for not having any shoes. Lindela then left because he could not afford to buy a pair (a problem Ngomso addressed with free shoes). Like some of his peers, he then made a living by begging and washing cars in the town.

> Lindela: I was walking in town and [Mary] saw me. She said that I must go to Ngomso for food and clothes.
> Oliver: How old were you?
> Lindela: I was twelve.
> Oliver: And how long was it since your last time in school?
> Lindela: It was maybe one year.
> Oliver: Why didn't you stay there [in town]?

Lindela: At that time, I was talking about hope. It was my dream that day to move on with my life; to see different things and different situations. 'I deserve more'; that's what I was thinking.

In the sense that they concern reactions to undesired and unenviable changes in circumstance, the events Velile and Lindela describe correspond with those that occurred in the area during the nineteenth century. Historians have argued that land, refuge, and material charity, frequently found at mission stations, tended to be more attractive to potential Xhosa converts than Christian theology itself (Peires 1989). More certainly, while the Xhosa were interested in debate and interaction with missionaries from the start, early missions struggled (Mostert 1992: 433; Peires 1989).[47] Indeed, those attracted to missionaries and Christianity "in the early years were misfits and refugees from Xhosa justice" (Peires 1982: 76).[48] Early converts were "often . . . outcasts, the dispossessed . . . [and] those accused of witchcraft . . . [who] were often not very highly regarded by the missionaries" (Mills 1976: 112; also see Deliwe 1992: 60–5).[49] However, as The Cape Frontier Wars raged on, an unprecedented event altered this scenario considerably.

The Great Xhosa Cattle-Killing (April 1856–May 1857) saw the Xhosa destroy their cattle and crop stocks following the vision of a prophetess named Nongqawuse that foresaw "the resurrection of the dead" and "the regeneration of the earth and the re-enactment of the original Creation" (Peires 1987: 45). Much ambiguity still surrounds the events.[50] They were the result of conflict among, and between, the Xhosa and British over the previous half-century, and lung sickness in cattle, which was unknown before. Although some isiXhosa speakers did not subscribe to the prophecies, sparing some cattle, the effect was massive and devastating.[51] The movement decimated food supplies and families, wreaking unprecedented dispossession and destitution (also see Deliwe 1992: 61–3).[52] Droughts exacerbated the seriousness and longevity of this imperative.[53] Bereft of cattle, sustenance, land, and numbers, the Xhosa ceded the vast majority of their remaining land to "white settlers or black clients of the Cape government", not least because they fled it for mission stations or farms owned by European settlers in search of sustenance (Peires 1982, 1987: 43; also see Crais 1992). In particular, mission stations provided welcomed, if not essential, humanitarian assistance and an alternative to the swift, negative turnaround in the fortunes of 'Xhosaland'.

As a "road to mobility, to the achievement of aspirations", mission schools became appealing like never before (Ashley 1974: 200). Subject to this new assemblage of moral discourses and possibilities (Zigon 2007), Xhosas began to attend mission stations and schools in greater numbers. For example, Jennifer Wenzel (2009: 49) makes this assertion with reference to the mission station of Tiyo Soga, the first Xhosa to be ordained to the Christian ministry. Similarly, on October 1, 1856, as the Cattle-Killing was beginning, Mary's forefather Robert Miller (cited in Anonymous) wrote in his diary: "The native schools for children, to which I ride every few days, are being very poorly attended." Upon visiting Bishop Gray's station on July 9, 1857, he (ibid: 37) noted: "A great many natives have come there, in a dying state, to settle on the station." Then, towards the end of 1857, "300 destitute children were in the hands of the missionaries", including Robert Miller himself (Anonymous). Then, as during my fieldwork, individuals with pressing needs turned to schools operated by individuals with Christianised ambitions to assist and save, presumably in the hope of finding reasons to be hopeful again.

More broadly, levels of school attendance in Africa are inextricably dependent upon forms of political, economic, social, and cultural change that do not explicitly concern education in the first instance. For example, my analysis of Ngomso and the vicinity during the colonial period reflects Nathalie Bonini's (2006: 391) account of events in Kenya during the early 1990s, when, she argues, increased numbers of the Maasai attended schools as a result of "socio-economic shifts confronting [them], such as the need to diversify their sources of income, partly due to decreasing herd sizes" and the increased usefulness of studying Kiswahili (taught in school). Similarly, Andrew Epstein (2010: 19) argues that "Dinka school Enrollment [in Sudan] increased gradually over time because families came to use it as a security net and a way to strengthen a weakening pastoral enterprise". School-based educations were "particularly sought after by the growing number of Dinka households whose entitlements within the pastoralist political economy had been eroded over many decades of imperialism, war, famine, and disease, and who felt increasingly vulnerable to destitution" (ibid.). In this comparative light, we can better understand the socio-economic and political contexts that conditioned levels of enrolment at Ngomso and my interlocutor's existential evaluations of the opportunities it represented. The school was *one* avenue of possibility and probability, which was conceptualised differently depending on individuals' experiences and evaluations of other potential avenues of engagement.

Notes

1. In South Africa, government posts frequently offer pension contributions, private healthcare, and relative security. Over 120 applications were received when Peter's post as the school's driver was advertised.
2. Perhaps the only 'barrier' that can be measured is material poverty. However, even this has to be relativised.
3. An estimated 12.2% of the South African population were HIV positive in 2012, and 11.6% was the comparable figure in the Eastern Cape (Shisana et al. 2014: XXVI). National HIV prevalence rates have been particularly high among "black African females aged 20–34 years" (31.6%) and "black African males aged 25–49 years" (25.7%) (ibid: xxix). The prevalence of HIV infection among pregnant women rose from 2.2% in 1990, when the eldest learner enrolled at Ngomso during 2011 was born, to 30.2% in 2005, when the youngest registered learner was born (Sishana 2008: 3).
4. In 2006, the Department of Health (2007: 43) estimated that 66% of South African orphans were orphaned as a consequence of HIV-AIDS. I cannot estimate how many Ngomso learners lost parents to HIV-AIDS. However, several individuals spoke to me about such a loss. Likewise, I do not know how many learners were among the estimated 410,000 individuals aged 0–14 living with HIV in South Africa, frequently as a consequence of mother-to-child transmission (Shisana et al. 2014). However, I know that several learners were HIV positive. Encouragingly, in 2012, an estimated 280,000 women received the Prevention of Mother-to-Child Transmission (PMTCT) programme and such interventions continue to widen (Department of Health 2013: 66).
5. An article by Wadesango et al. (2011) uses this same terminology and speaks to many of the concerns of members of staff.
6. While the terms 'broken homes' and 'juvenile delinquency' have become unfashionable, the argument that young people (males especially) who grow up in single-parent households are more likely to engage in criminality and have 'psychological and behavioural problems' appears in a vast array of (US- and UK-focused) sociology and psychology literature (e.g. Blankenhorn 1995; Demuth and Brown 2004; Flouri 2005; Herzog 2013 [1983]; Paquette 2004; Popenoe 1996; Rohner and Veneziana 2001). To my mind, this research raises many concerns about causality. Caution must also be exercised when attempting to relate this research to the situation in South Africa.
7. Unless otherwise stated, all references from the Bible in this book are taken from the New International Version.
8. Shindler (2010: 4) argues that "a higher proportion of children in poorer households [are] more likely to be out of school than children in higher

income households"; access to transport, school uniforms, meals, fees, books, and stationary are all factors in this situation.
9. The Act states that "every parent must cause every learner for whom he or she is responsible to attend a school" from the ages of seven to fifteen, or until they reach the ninth grade (DoE 1996: Chapter 2, section 3). It continues by saying that any parent failing to ensure compulsory attendance "is guilty of an offence and liable on conviction to a fine or to imprisonment for a period not exceeding six months" (ibid.).
10. For instance, Margaret Jacobs (2009) provides an account of 'American Indians' and Aborigines in colonial America and Australia, respectively.
11. Barbara Ramusack (1990), writing of missionising British women in India, and Jean Allman (1994), writing of the same in Ashanti (now Ghana), both provide similar accounts of how the 'indigenous Other' was thought to be 'child-like' in their naivety and lack of civility and thus incapable of parenting their own children.
12. Despite Robert Morrell's (2013: np) report that "rates of teenage pregnancy [in South Africa] have actually been dropping since the 1980s", elsewhere he (Morrell, Bhana and Shefer 2012: 5) writes: "Teenage pregnancy is common in South Africa. Nearly a third of women have children before they reach the age of 20."
13. I do not know the source of Holly's information so cannot confirm its validity. However, I have found no information supporting it. In contrast, according to the Health Systems Trust (HST 2011), the percentage of pregnant women aged 15 to 19 increased from 11.9–15% in 2003 to 19.2% in 2011, and the General Household Survey of 2011 (SSA 2011) suggests a 'teenage pregnancy rate' of 4.5%.
14. A substantial report found that CSGs have "reduced sexual activity" among adolescents and reduced pregnancy rates (DSD, SASSA, and UNICEF 2012: v). More broadly, fertility rates in the Eastern Cape declined from 4.6 (average per woman) in 1991 to approximately 2.75 in 2011 (HST 2011). The report also found that the CSGs "reduced alcohol and drug use, particularly for females, and with the effect strengthened by early childhood receipt of the CSG" (DSD, SASSA, and UNICEF 2012: v).
15. Definitions of the term 'street children' "generally have three main elements in common: (1) these children live or spend a significant amount of time on the street; (2) the street is the children's source of livelihood; and (3) they are inadequately cared for, protected, or supervised by responsible adults" (Le Roux and Smith 1998: 915). However, there is room for ambiguity within each of these elements, and each can be prioritised or ignored, which results in variable and inconsistent usages of the term.
16. Examples of this shift can be found in Connolly (1990), Ennew (1994), Hecht (1998), Kilbride et al. (2000) Magazine (2003), Markus and Free

(2008), Márquez (1999), Scheper-Hughes and Hoffman (1997), Schernthaner (2011), Swart (1990), and Turnball et al. (2009).
17. The assertion that street children in South Africa and elsewhere can be, and have often been, associated with 'social nuisance' or 'social deviance' is supported by the work of Konanc (1989), Mangwana (1992), Swart (1988), Swart-Kruger and Donald (1994), and P. Wilson and Arnold (1986).
18. In reference to his research in Cape Verde, Bordonaro (2012) argues that street children are thought to have the 'wrong kind of agency': their freedoms from adult supervision are not welcomed, but seen as risky and potentially disruptive.
19. Grammar schools, civic foundations, dame schools, and public schools, such as Eton, Harrow, and Westminster, also existed at this time but none educated the numbers that the Church schools did.
20. Other societies such as *The British and Oriental School Society for the Education of the Labouring and Manufacturing Classes of Society of Every Religious Persuasion*, which favoured non-denomination Christian-based schools, and the *Central Society of Education*, which favoured schools with no reference to religion (a tiny minority at the time), also received some, but less, funding (Gates 2005).
21. This arrangement was problematic for those who wanted more secularised schools, and the voice for secularisation later triumphed in 1902, when the Balfour Bill stipulated a secular curriculum, without "expectation of conformity to religious belief of ritual" (Gates 2005: 19). In reality, however, in the UK the debate over the relationship between faith and schooling remains as vivacious as ever (see Gardner et al. 2005).
22. In this paragraph and the one that follows, I am making an analytical observation about the formations and functions of SENs, considered as a publically and institutionally constituted moral discourse, rather than a moral judgement about the validity of the notion of SENs or any particular 'needs', 'disorders', or 'disabilities'.
23. Two sets of data suggest that the use of corporal punishment is highest in Eastern Cape schools, with an estimated 30–67% of learners experiencing it (Veriava 2014). However, Chapter 1, Section 10 of the South African Schools Act (DoE 1996) clearly states that "No person may administer corporal punishment at a school to a learner". Any person who does so "is guilty of an offence and liable on conviction to a sentence which could be imposed for assault" (ibid.).
24. Reed (2014) also discovered that corporal punishment was widely practiced in schools and argues that its prominence is evidence of conflict between the emergence of human rights discourses during the democratic transition and 'cultural valuations' of physical chastisement. In a more

prescriptive paper, Smit (2013: 347) similarly considers "the compatibility of democracy (which incorporates human rights) with the maintenance of order and discipline in schools". Comparable and contradictory assertions can be found in Cicognani (2004), Maphosa and Shumba (2010), Mthanti and Mncube (2014), and Shaikhnag and Assan (2014).

25. As I discuss in more detail in the penultimate chapter, 'softly-softly' punishments took the following forms: exclusion (e.g. a two-day suspension or no outing), isolation or another limitation of freedom (e.g. to sit on the floor in the corridor), humiliation (e.g. cleaning the girls' toilets), and the denial or delay of otherwise expected provisions (e.g. food or school shoes).

26. For example, in 2005, the provincial secretary of SADTU in Mpumalanga, Shamba Mthembu (cited in Yende 2005: np) said, "We feel that dismissal in these cases is harsh and need to find a way of rehabilitating guilty teachers." In 2011, John Maluleke, the national secretary of SADTU, said that the ban on corporal punishment had increased violence in schools and forced some teachers to resign (Matlala 2011). Additionally, when the chairman of SADTU's Gauteng region was due in court to defend allegations of assault against a learner, other members of SADTU attempted to block access to the court and sung 'struggle [i.e. anti-apartheid] songs' (SAPA 2011). However, as an organisation, "SADTU condemns acts of corporal punishment in line with the Union's code of conduct" (SADTU 2015: np). A senior representative of SADTU (Maphila, cited in Chauke 2014: np) recently said that "SADTU is not going to protect anybody dismissed for administering corporal punishment."

27. Anderson-Levitt (2003: 11) suggests that "an official ban on corporal punishment [in schools]" might be considered as an outcome of the 'isomorphism' (i.e. globalised convergence) of institutionalised forms of education, together with the emergence of human rights more generally and the 'right to education' especially, as promoted most vigorously by the UN. More specifically, "The prohibition against corporal punishment in schools in South Africa follows the trend adopted by many democracies such as Sweden, Norway, Denmark, Finland, Australia, the United Kingdom and Namibia [the first African country to introduce a ban, in 1991]" (Veriava 2014: 6). R. Morrell (2001: 292) states that during the post-apartheid transition of the 1990s, South Africa more definitively took "a lead from legal precedents in the European Union" when the practice of corporal punishment became unlawful. It is these kinds of processes that I am referring to when using the simplifying, and thus inadequate, term 'Western moral assemblages'.

28. R. Morrell's (2001: 296) paper considers an "elite, single-sex, formerly white, rugby and cricket playing school" and corroborates the argument

that it is too simplistic to say that 'blacks' have been pro-corporal punishment while 'whites' have been anti. To this point, corporal punishment was integral to Christian National Education during apartheid (Vally 1998). More recently, a voluntary collective of 196 Christian schools recently took to the South Africa's Constitutional Court to argue that the legal ban on corporal punishment contravened parents' religious and cultural rights as the practice aligns with biblical instruction (i.e. not 'Xhosa culture'). (Judge Sachs did not rule in their favour, and the legal ban was maintained.)

29. We were two of approximately 20 guests invited to the restaurant by a member of my host Rotary club, who worked at Rhodes and coordinated an exchange programme for South African and Canadian students.
30. Nitin was himself considered 'different' by some members of the tennis club. With his Asian heritage, several individuals suggested he represented the "[membership] diversity" that the club wanted to increase. To my knowledge, he was the only member who regularly worked in the township.
31. I knew of a handful of incidents were members of staff had been injured by learners, but they did not regularly direct physical or verbal abuse at them, nor did any such events go unpunished. Likewise, 'bad language' was not openly tolerated by the staff.
32. On numerous occasions, I observed Mary and Joyce encourage learners to apologise for their misdemeanours and to shake hands or 'hug it out' with those wronged by their actions. Such education was inseparable from the promotion of notions of Christianised love and forgiveness.
33. It is worth noting that the South African Schools Act (DoE 1996, Chapter 2, 5.1) states that "A public school must admit learners and serve their educational requirements without unfairly discriminating in any way." Nitin's plans clearly contrast with this directive.
34. Offering another example of this analytical theme, Douglas (1984: 98) revisits research that suggests the behaviour of individuals "admitted to a mental hospital" – a 'marginal space', not unlike Ngomso in this respect – was tolerated before their admission but "judged to be abnormal" afterwards.
35. As an interesting point of comparison, McCarthy, Wiener, and Soodak (2010: 3) inform us that during the twentieth century in America, "students with disabilities were categorized as 'educable,' 'trainable,' 'untrainable,' or 'uneducable'". Those "labeled 'educable' and 'trainable' were schooled at the public's expense but usually in isolation from their nonclassified peers—either in separate [special] schools or classrooms". In contrast, those "labeled 'untrainable' or 'uneducable' were excluded from public schools".

36. Only one learner at Ngomso, Zamekile, was 'officially classed' (i.e. by a medical practitioner) as having 'mental health problems'. He was diagnosed as having ADHD, as I discuss elsewhere in the book.
37. Such claims were especially value-laden because another special needs school in Grahamstown catered for the 'severely intellectually disabled' or '(mildly) mentally handicapped'. Its learners were also heavily stigmatised. As I walked past the school with two grade six learners they were not disparaging about them, but keenly pointed out they were different from Ngomso learners.
38. I think Sidima would have said those 'unlike a Xhosa' were 'wealthy whites living in town'. I would guess that he thought this group would react differently when hearing that he attended Ngomso because individuals who lived in the town generally had positive things to say about the school and the efforts of Mary in particular.
39. This sentence was inspired by the following statement from Pitt-Rivers (1968: 503): "[The] psychological and social functions [of honour] relate to the fact that it stands as a mediator between individual aspirations and the judgment of society."
40. My observation should not be confused with the fact that young men wear *ingceke* (white clay) when undergoing initiation into Xhosa manhood, even though calamine lotion might replace the clay should it be hard to obtain or too expensive (Vivian 2012: 31). An interesting comparison can be made, however, as *ingceke* signifies the transformative state of the initiate and is ritually washed-off when one graduates to manhood (Mhlahlo 2009: 118). In using the lotion, my interlocutors were similarly attempting to alter the pigmentation of their skin, albeit permanently, to signify something about their moral qualities and transform how they were perceived by others.
41. Research conducted at the University of Cape Town found that approximately one-third of South African women use skin-lightening creams, including those that are illegal and contain chemicals that harm human skin ('Dying to be White' 2014). The health implications and decision-making processes related to this issue are currently being investigated by an interdisciplinary team at the same institution.
42. I cannot be certain, but I believe that Siseko did not engage in the activities he described. When the police came to arrest his neighbours one afternoon, they paid no attention to him, and, as far as I know, he never came into contact with the law about their conduct.
43. I learnt about a similar technique while talking to a student friend. She was approached on a night out by a man with a dog, who said he would kill the animal unless she bought it from him there and then, which she did.

44. R. Morrell (2001) found that some students in Durban welcomed the prohibition of corporal punishment while others were concerned about a lack of 'harsh consequences'. Similarly, in the Eastern Cape, Reed (2014: 86) found that "students were often proponents of corporal punishment, recognizing it as a critically important method of social control, cohesion, and learning".
45. According to the General Household Survey of 2010, "a lack of money" was the main reason (39% of cases) why those aged seven to twenty-four in the Eastern Cape did not attend school (ECSECC 2011: 6). The percentage of learners attending school without paying fees (on a national level) increased from 0.7% in 2002 to 55.6% in 2011 (SSA 2011: 1).
46. In reference to how some 'orphans' in Botswana are increasingly fed by NGOs rather than family members, Dahl (2006: 637) considers a "feedback loop of threatened kinship". I do not know just how perturbed Samkelo's grandmother was by the situation; however, the school did step in when he took time off from school to care for an aunt, which speaks to Dahl's analysis of a tension between NGOs and the families of young beneficiaries.
47. Despite the statement in the main text, Christianity, in varying forms, was by no means absent from Xhosa society at this time, and was perhaps most notable in the prophecies of the Cattle-Killing movement (see Peires 1987: 45).
48. The significant exception was the amaFengu (now Mfengu). In return for their military services to the British, these isiXhosa speakers were allowed to settle in the Colony and rapidly converted to Christianity.
49. Gendered relations of power and spiritual aspects of Christianity also factored in processes of Christianisation among the Xhosa (Erlank 1999; Hodgson 1983). It has been argued that women were initially attracted to mission stations because they found a preferable societal arrangement (Gaitskell 1990). Women were the labourers in Xhosa society (Peires 1982: 104), while missionaries encouraged them to leave the labour to men and save their energies for domestic roles, including a distinct concept of motherhood. This may have had its own appeal for women who experienced 'the double shift' long before 'modernity' brought this to 'Western women'.
50. It is argued that the British administration did not intervene in the Cattle-Killing as it served to reduce the political influence of the chiefs over the Xhosa and limited the terms of "pastoral patronage" (Stapleton 1993: 356). Adding further ambiguity, Stapleton (1993: 369) suggests that the Cattle-Killing movement was as much about the Xhosa contesting their material subjection within Xhosa chiefdoms as it was a spiritual move-

ment. S. Davies (2010) provides an analysis of numerous accounts of the movement that highlights the diverse meanings and interpretations which have been assigned to the events.
51. According to Peires (1987: 43; also see 1989), "about 85 per cent of all Xhosa adult men killed their cattle and destroyed their corn in obedience to Nongqawuse's prophecies. It is estimated that 400,000 cattle were slaughtered and 40,000 Xhosa died of starvation. At least another 40,000 left their homes in search of food."
52. There are reports from the period of cannibalism and filicide that were completely against the beliefs and value systems of the Xhosa (Mostert 1992). Infants were offered to men of the Church (Mostert 1992: 1231). The destitute Xhosa also began labouring on public works in increased numbers (Peires 1989: 58).
53. Crais (2011: 77; also see Spinage 2012: 190) argues that "the second half of the nineteenth century was an especially turbulent and dry period" in South Africa, with "no less than eighteen years of serious drought" between 1850 and 1870.

BIBLIOGRAPHY

Abrams, L. (2001). Ideals of Womanhood in Victorian Britain. *BBC Online*. Retrieved September 24, 2015, from http://www.bbc.co.uk/history/trail/victorian_britain/women_home/ideals_womanhood_07.shtml

Allman, J. (1994). Making Mothers: Missionaries, Medical Officers, and Women's Work in Colonial Asante, 1924–45. *History Workshop Journal, 38*, 23–47.

Anderson, K. (2005). Relatedness and Investment in Children in South Africa. *Human Nature, 16*(1), 1–31.

Anderson, K., Kaplan, H., Lam, D., & Lancaster, J. (1999). Paternal Care by Genetic Fathers and Stepfathers II: Reports by Xhosa High School Students. *Evolution and Human Behavior, 20*(6), 433–451.

Anderson-Levitt, K. (2003). A World Culture of Schooling? In K. Anderson-Levitt (Ed.), *Local Meanings, Global Schooling: Anthropology and World Culture Theory* (pp. 1–26). New York: Palgrave Macmillan.

Anonymous. Details omitted in order to maintain anonymity of interlocutors.

Ashley, M. (1974). African Education and Society in the Nineteenth Century Eastern Cape. In C. Saunders & R. Derricourt (Eds.), *Beyond the Cape Frontier* (pp. 199–212). London: Longman.

Bank, L. (2011). *Home Spaces, Street Styles: Contesting Power and Identity in a South African City*. London: Pluto Press.

Blankenhorn, D. (1995). *Fatherless America: Confronting Our Most Urgent Social Problem*. New York: Basic Books.

Bloch, M. E. (1998). The Uses of Schooling and Literacy in a Zafimaniry Village. In M. E. Bloch (Ed.), *How We Think They Think. Anthropological Approaches to Cognition, Memory and Literacy* (pp. 171–192). Boulder: Westview Press.

Bonini, N. (2006). The Pencil and the Shepherd's Crook. Ethnography of Maasai Education. *Ethnography and Education, 1*(3), 379–392.

Bordonaro, L. I. (2012). Children's Geographies Agency Does Not Mean Freedom. Cape Verdean Street Children and the Politics of Children's Agency. *Children's Geographies, 10*(4), 413–426.

Bornstein, E. (2002). Developing Faith: Theologies of Economic Development in Zimbabwe. *Journal of Religion in Africa, 32*(1), 4–31.

Bourgois, P. (1996b). *In Search of Respect.* Cambridge: Cambridge University Press.

Burke, C. (2004). Theories of Childhood. In P. Fass (Ed.), *Encyclopedia of Children and Childhood: In History and Society* (p. 818). New York: Macmillan Reference.

Chauke, P. (2014). Union Won't Protect Corporal Punishers. *The Citizen* (Online). Retrieved December 19, 2015, from http://citizen.co.za/187784/no-union-protection-for-corporal-punishment-dismissals/

Cheney, K. (2007). *Pillars of the Nation: Child Citizens and Ugandan National Development.* Chicago: University of Chicago Press.

Cicognani, L. (2004). *To Punish or Discipline: Teachers Attitudes Towards the Abolition of Corporal Punishment.* Unpublished M.Ed. Research Report, School of Human and Community Development, University of the Witwatersrand.

Compretta, C. E. (2012). *Growing Gaps: Children's Experiences of Inequality in a Faith-Based Afterschool Program in the U.S. South.* Unpublished PhD Dissertation, College of Arts and Sciences (Department of Anthropology), University of Kentucky. Retrieved April 8, 2014, from http://uknowledge.uky.edu/anthro_etds/4/

Connolly, M. (1990). Adrift in the City. A Comparative Study of Street Children in Bogotá, Colombia and Guatemala City. *Child and Youth Services, 14,* 129–149.

Connolly, M., & Ennew, J. (1996). Introduction: Children Out of Place. *Childhood, 3*(2), 131–146.

Crais, C. (1992). *White Supremacy and Black Resistance in Pre-industrial South Africa: The Making of the Colonial Order in the Eastern Cape, 1770–1865.* Cambridge: Cambridge University Press.

Crais, C. (2011). *Poverty, War, and Violence in South Africa.* Cambridge: Cambridge University Press.

Crossley, N. (1996). *Intersubjectivity: The Fabric of Social Becoming.* London: Sage.

Cunningham, H. (2006). Re-inventing Childhood. *OpenLearn* (Open University Online). Retrieved March 28, 2015, from http://www.open.edu/openlearn/history-the-arts/history/re-inventing-childhood

Dahl, B. (2006). "Too Fat to Be an Orphan": The Moral Semiotics of Food Aid in Botswana. *Cultural Anthropology, 29*(4), 626–647.

Davies, S. (2010). *History in the Literary Imagination: The Telling of Nongqawuse and the Xhosa Cattle-Killing in South African Literature and Culture (1891–1937)*. Unpublished PhD Thesis, St John's College, University of Cambridge. Retrieved August 9, 2012, from https://www.repository.cam.ac.uk/handle/1810/238313

Day, S. (2010). Ethics Between Public and Private: Sex Workers' Relationships in London. In M. Lambek (Ed.), *Ordinary Ethics: Anthropology, Language and Action* (pp. 273–291). New York: Fordham University Press.

De Boeck, F., & Honwana, A. (2005). Introduction: Children & Youth in Africa. In F. De Boeck & A. Honwana (Eds.), *Makers & Breakers: Children & Youth in Postcolonial Africa* (pp. 1–18). Oxford: James Curry.

Deliwe, D. (1992). *Responses to Western Education Among the Conservative People of Transkei*. Unpublished MA Thesis, Department of Anthropology, Faculty of Humanities, Rhodes University.

Demuth, S., & Brown, S. L. (2004). Family Structure, Family Processes, and Adolescent Delinquency: The Significance of Parental Absence Versus Parental Gender. *Journal of Research in Crime and Delinquency, 41*(1), 58–81.

Department of Education (DoE). (1996). *South African Schools Act No. 84 of 1996*. Retrieved June 12, 2013, from http://www.education.gov.za/LinkClick.aspx?fileticket=aIolZ6UsZ5U%3D&tabid=185&mid=1828

Department of Health. (2007). *HIV & AIDS and STI Strategic Plan for South Africa 2007–2011*. Retrieved October 24, 2014, from http://data.unaids.org/pub/ExternalDocument/2007/20070604_sa_nsp_final_en.pdf

Department of Health. (2013). *The 2012 National Antenatal Sentinel HIV & Herpes Simplex Type-2 Prevalence Survey in South Africa*. Retrieved May 22, 2014, from http://www.health-e.org.za/wp-content/uploads/2014/05/ASHIVHerp_Report2014_22May2014.pdf

Desjarlais, R. (1997). *Shelter Blues: Sanity and Selfhood Among the Homeless*. Philadelphia: University of Pennsylvania Press.

Douglas, M. (1966). *Purity and Danger*. London: Routledge.

Douglas, M. (1984). *Purity and Danger: An Analysis of the Concepts of Pollution and Taboo*. London/New York: Routledge.

DSD, SASSA, & UNICEF. (2012). *The South African Child Support Grant Impact Assessment: Evidence from a Survey of Children, Adolescents and Their Households*. Retrieved February 12, 2014, from http://www.unicef.org/southafrica/SAF_resources_csg2012s.pdf

Dying to Be White. (2014). *Daily News* (University of Cape Town). Retrieved October 15, 2015, from http://www.uct.ac.za/dailynews/?id=8821

Eastern Cape Socio Economic Consultative Council (ECSECC). (2011). *Service Delivery and Condition of Living in the Eastern Cape.* Retrieved March 17, 2015, from http://www.ecsecc.org/files/library/documents/ECSECCLivingStandardsJune2011.pdf

Ennew, J. (1994). Parentless Friends. A Cross-Cultural Examination of Networks Among Street Children and Street Youth. In F. Nestmann & K. Hurrelmann (Eds.), *Social Networks and Social Support in Childhood and Adolescence* (pp. 409–426). Berlin: De Gruyter.

Ennew, J., & Swart-Kruger, J. (2003). Introduction: Homes, Places and Spaces in the Construction of Street Children and Street Youth. *Children, Youth and Environments, 13*(1). Retrieved July 25, 2012, from http://www.colorado.edu/journals/cye

Epstein, A. (2010). Education Refugees and the Spatial Politics of Childhood Vulnerability. *Childhood in Africa, 2*(1), 16–25.

Erlank, N. (1999). Re-examining Initial Encounters Between Christian Missionaries and the Xhosa, 1820–1850: The Scottish Case. *Kleio, 31*, 6–32.

Fanon, F. (1970). *Black Skin, White Masks.* New York: Grove Press.

Flinn, J. (2000). Transmitting Traditional Values in New Schools: Elementary Education of Pulap Atoll. In B. A. U. Levinson (Ed.), *Schooling the Symbolic Animal: Social and Cultural Dimensions of Education* (pp. 123–136). Lanham: Rowman Littlefield.

Flouri, E. (2005). *Fathering & Child Outcomes.* Chichester: Wiley.

Foucault, M. (1977a). *Discipline and Punish: The Birth of the Prison.* London: Penguin.

Foucault, M. (1977b). The Political Function of the Intellectual. *Radical Philosophy, 17*(Summer), 12–14.

Gadda, A. (2008). *Rights, Foucault and Power: A Critical Analysis of the United Nation Convention on the Rights of the Child.* New Directions in Sociological Research Working Paper Series, The University of Edinburgh. Retrieved July 22, 2014, from http://www.cas.ed.ac.uk/__data/assets/pdf_file/0010/13015/WP31_Gadda.pdf

Gaitskell, D. (1990). Devout Domesticity? A Century of African Women's Christianity in South Africa. In C. Walker (Ed.), *Women and Gender in Southern Africa to 1945* (pp. 251–272). Cape Town: David Philip.

Gardner, R., Cairns, J., & Lowton, D. (2005). *Faith Schools: Consensus or Conflict?* New York: RoutledgeFalmer.

Gates, B. (2005). Faith Schools and Colleges of Education Since 1800. In R. Gardner, J. Cairns, & D. Lowton (Eds.), *Faith Schools: Consensus or Conflict?* New York: RoutledgeFalmer.

Goffman, E. (1959). *The Presentation of Self in Everyday Life.* London: Penguin.

Goffman, E. (1963). *Stigma: Notes on the Management of Spoiled Identity.* New Jersey: Prentice Hall.

Grindal, B. (1972). *Growing Up in Two Worlds: Education and Transition Among the Sisala of Northern Ghana*. New York: Holt, Rinehart and Winston.
Hecht, T. (1998). *At Home in the Street: Street Children of Northeast Brazil*. Cambridge: Cambridge University Press.
Hecht, T. (2008). Globalization from Way Below: Brazilian Streets, a Youth, and World Society. In J. Cole & D. Durham (Eds.), *Figuring the Future: Globalization and the Temporalities of Children and Youth* (pp. 223–243). Santa Fe: School of Advanced Research Press.
Henderson, P. (2012). *A Kinship of Bones: AIDS, Intimacy and Care in Rural KwaZulu-Natal*. Scottsville: University of KwaZulu-Natal Press.
Herzog, J. (2013). *Father Hunger: Explorations with Adults and Children*. New York: Routledge.
Hodgson, J. (1983). *The God of the Xhosa: Study of the Origins and Development of the Traditional Concepts of the Supreme Being*. Oxford: Oxford University Press Southern Africa.
Honwana, A., & De Boeck, F. (2005). *Makers and Breakers*. Oxford: James Curry.
HST. (2011). Total Fertility Rate. *Health Systems Trust, Demographic Indicators* (Online). Retrieved, March 04, 2013, from http://indicators.hst.org.za/healthstats/5/data
Hunter, M. (2010). *Love in the Time of Aids: Inequality, Gender and Rights in South Africa*. Bloomington: Indiana University Press.
Jacobs, M. D. (2009). *White Mother to a Dark Race: Settler Colonialism, Maternalism, and the Removal of Indigenous Children in the American West and Australia, 1880–1940*. Lincoln: University of Nebraska Press.
Kaplan, S. (2006). *The Pedagogical State: Education and the Politics of National Culture in Post-1980 Turkey*. Stanford: Stanford University Press.
Kennedy, D. (2006). *The Well of Being: Childhood, Subjectivity, and Education*. Albany: State University of New York Press.
Kilbride, P., Suda, C., & Njeru, E. (2000). *Street Children in Kenya: Voices of Children in Search of a Childhood*. Westport: Bergin & Garvey.
Konanc, E. (1989). Street Children and Children Working in the Street: Preliminary Results of a Field Study in Turkey. *The Child Care Worker, 7*(11), 13–15.
le Roux, J., & Smith, C. S. (1998). Is the Street Child Phenomenon Synonymous with Deviant Behavior? *Adolescence, 33*(132), 915–925.
Magazine, R. (2003). Action, Personhood and the Gift Economy Among So-Called Street Children in Mexico City. *Social Anthropology, 11*(3), 303–318.
Malinowski, B. (1943). The Pan-African Problem of Culture Contact. *American Journal of Sociology, 48*(6), 649–665.
Mangwana, T. (1992). Working with Street Children: Hints for Child Care Workers. *The Child Care Worker, 10*(5), 14–15.

Maphosa, C., & Shumba, A. (2010). Educators' Disciplinary Capabilities After the Banning of Corporal Punishment in South African Schools. *South African Journal of Education, 30*, 387–399.

Markus, B., & Free, W. (2008). Theoretical Reflections on the Life World of Tanzanian Street Children. *Anthropology Matters, 10*(2), 1–24.

Márquez, P. C. (1999). *The Street Is My Home. Youth and Violence in Caracas*. Stanford: Stanford University Press.

Matlala, A. (2011). Teachers Quit over Lack of Discipline. *The Sowetan (Online)*. Retrieved April 25, 2013, from http://www.sowetanlive.co.za/news/2011/12/21/teachers-quit-over-lack-of-discipline

Mayer, P. (1961). *Townsmen or Tribesmen: Conservatism and the Process of Urbanization in a South African City* (with Contributions by Iona Mayer). Oxford/Cape Town: Oxford University Press.

Mayer, P., & Mayer, I. (1970). Socialization by Peers: The Youth Organization of the Red Xhosa. In P. Mayer (Ed.), *Socialization: The Approach from Social Anthropology* (pp. 159–189). London: Tavistock.

McCarthy, M. R., Wiener, R., & Soodak, L. C. (2010). Vestiges of Segregation in the Implementation of Inclusion Policies in Public High Schools. *Educational Policy, 26*(2), 309–338.

McDermott, R. (1993). The Acquisition of a Child by a Learning Disability. In S. Chaiklin & J. Lave (Eds.), *Understanding Practice: Perspectives on Activity and Context* (pp. 269–305). Cambridge: Cambridge University Press.

McDermott, R., & Varenne, H. (1995). Culture as Disability. *Anthropology & Education Quarterly, 26*(3), 324–348.

McDermott, R., & Varenne, H. (1998). *Successful Failure: The School America Builds*. Oxford: Westview Press.

Mhlahlo, A. P. (2009). *What is Manhood? The Significance of Traditional Circumcision in the Xhosa*. Unpublished MPhil Thesis, Department of Sociology and Anthropology, the Stellenbosch University.

Mills, W. G. (1976). The Taylor Revival of 1866 and the Roots of African Nationalism in the Cape Colony. *Journal of Religion in Africa, 8*(2), 105–122.

Morrell, R. (2001). Corporal Punishment in South African Schools: A Neglected Explanation for Its Persistence. *South African Journal of Education, 21*(4), 292–299.

Morrell, R. (2013). SA Broods Over Teen Pregnancies. *Mail & Guardian* (Online). Retrieved July 03, 2015, from http://mg.co.za/article/2013-04-12-sa-broods-over-teen-pregnancies

Morrell, R., Bhana, D., & Shefer, T. (2012). Pregnancy and Parenthood in South African Schools. In R. Morrell, D. Bhana, & T. Shefer (Eds.), *Books and Babies: Pregnancy and Young Parents in Schools* (pp. 1–30). Cape Town: HSRC Press.

Mostert, N. (1992). *Frontiers: The Epic of South Africa's Creation and the Tragedy of the Xhosa People*. New York: Knopf.

Mthanti, B., & Mncube, V. (2014). The Social and Economic Impact of Corporal Punishment in South African Schools. *Journal of Sociology and Social Anthropology*, 5(1), 71–80.

Ngwane, Z. (2001). Real Men Reawaken Their Fathers' Homesteads, the Educated Leave Them in Ruins': The Politics of Domestic Reproduction in Post-apartheid Rural South Africa. *Journal of Religion in Africa*, 31(4), 402–426.

Nieuwenhuys, O. (2001). By the Sweat of Their Brow? 'Street Children', NGOs and Children's Rights in Addis Ababa. *Africa*, 71(4), 539–557.

Panter-Brick, C. (2002). Street Children, Human Rights, and Public Health: A Critique and Future Directions. *Annual Review of Anthropology*, 31(1), 147–171.

Paquette, D. (2004). Theorizing the Father-Child Relationship: Mechanisms and Developmental Outcomes. *Human Development*, 47(4), 193–219.

Pauw, B. A. (1963). *The Second Generation: A Study of the Family Among Urbanized Bantu in East London*. Oxford: Oxford University Press.

Peires, J. B. (1982). *The House of Phalo: A History of the Xhosa People in the Days of Their Independence*. Los Angles: University of California Press.

Peires, J. B. (1987). The Central Beliefs of the Xhosa Cattle-Killing. *Journal of African History*, 28, 43–63.

Peires, J. B. (1989). *The Dead Will Arise: Nongqawuse and the Great Xhosa Cattle-Killing Movement*. Johannesburg: Ravan Press.

Peshkin, A. (1972). *Kanuri School Children: Education and Social Mobilization in Nigeria*. New York: Holt, Rinehart and Winston.

Pitt-Rivers, J. (1968). Honour. In D. L. Sills & R. K. Merton (Eds.), *International Encyclopedia of the Social Sciences* (pp. 503–511). London: Macmillan.

Popenoe, D. (1996). *Life Without Father: Compelling New Evidence That Fatherhood and Marriage Are Indispensable for the Good of Children and Society*. New York: The Free Press.

Ramusack, B. (1990). Cultural Missionaries, Maternal Imperialists, Feminist Allies: British Women Activists in India, 1865–1945. In N. Chaudhuri & M. Strobel (Eds.), *Western Women and Imperialism: Complicity and Resistance* (pp. 109–150). Bloomington: Indiana University Press.

Reed, A. (2014). *Inkululeko: Youth, Non-governmental Organizations, and Discourses of Democracy in Post-apartheid South Africa*. Unpublished PhD Thesis, Department of Anthropology, University of California. Retrieved June 05, 2015, from http://escholarship.org/uc/item/7n75g82z

Richter, L., Chikovore, J., & Makusha, T. (2010). The Status of Fatherhood and Fathering in South Africa. *Childhood Education*, 86(6), 360–365.

Rohner, R. P., & Veneziana, R. A. (2001). The Importance of Father Love: History and Contemporary Evidence. *Review of General Psychology*, 5(4), 382–405.

Scheper-Hughes, N. (1992). *Death Without Weeping: The Violence of Everyday Life in Brazil*. Berkeley: University of California Press.

Scheper-Hughes, N., & Hoffman, D. (1997). Brazil: Moving Targets. *Natural History, 106*(61), 34–43.

Schernthaner, M. (2011). *Coming of Age on the Streets: An Exploration of the Livelihoods of Street Youth in Durban*. Paper Presented at the International RC21 Conference 2011 (Amsterdam), Session 30, Diversity and Space: Youth Geographies and Spatial Identities. Retrieved from http://www.rc21.org/conferences/amsterdam2011/edocs2/Session%2030/30-1-Schernthaner.pdf

Seyer, I. (2002). *Smart on the Under, Wise to the Streets: Mapping the Landscapes of Urban Youth*. Unpublished PhD Dissertation, The School of Education, Stanford University.

Shaikhnag, N., & Assan, T. E. B. (2014). The Effects of Abolishing Corporal Punishment on Learner Behaviour in South African High Schools. *Mediterranean Journal of Social Sciences, 5*(7), 435–442.

Shindler, J. (2010). *Characteristics of Out-of-School Children of Compulsory School Age in South Africa: What the Community Survey 2007 Shows*. CREATE Working Paper No. 1. Retrieved September 21, 2012, from http://www.createrpc.org/pdf_documents/Working%20paper%201-%20Out%20of%20school%20children.pdf

Shisana, O., Rehle, T., Simbayi, L. C., Zuma, K., Jooste, S., Zungu, N., Labadarios, D., Onoya, D., et al. (2014). *South African National HIV Prevalence, Incidence and Behaviour Survey, 2012*. Cape Town: HSRC Press.

Simpson, A. (1999). The Labours of Learning: Education in the Postcolony. *Social Analysis: The International Journal of Social and Cultural Practice, 43*(1), 4–13.

Simpson, A. (2003). *Half London in Zambia: Contested Identities in a Catholic Mission School*. Edinburgh: Edinburgh University Press.

Sishana, O. (2008). *HIV/AIDS and Society* (Paper Prepared for The Presidency). Cape Town: HSRC Press.

Smit, M. (2013). Compatibility of Democracy and Learner Discipline in South African Schools. *De Jure, 1*(46), 345–365.

Solomon, M. (2013). The Myth of Teenage Pregnancy and Child Support Grants. *Africa Check*. Retrieved January 24, 2014, from http://africacheck.org/2013/05/30/urban-myths-and-teen-pregnancy/

South African Democratic Teachers Union (SADTU). (2015). *Statement of SADTU NEC Following Its Meeting Held in Durban*. Retrieved October 14, 2015, from http://www.sadtu.org.za/show.php?id=3023

South African Press Association (SAPA). (2011). SADTU Block Court Entrance. *Times* (Live/Online). Retrieved, July 24, 2014, from http://www.timeslive.co.za/local/2011/03/14/sadtu-blocks-court-entrance#

Spinage, C. (2012). *African Ecology: Benchmarks and Historical Perspectives*. Heidelberg: Springer.

Stambach, A. (2000). *Lessons from Mount Kilimanjaro: Schooling, Community, and Gender in East Africa*. New York: Routledge.
Stambach, A. (2010). *Faith in Schools: Religion, Education and American Evangelicals in East Africa*. Stanford: Stanford University Press.
Stapleton, T. J. (1993). Reluctant Slaughter: Rethinking Maqoma's Role in the Xhosa Cattle-Killing (1853–1857). *The International Journal of African Historical Studies, 26*(2), 346–369.
Statistics South Africa (SSA). (2011). *General Household Survey* (Statistical Release P0318). Retrieved July 10, 2014, from http://fraser.stlouisfed.org/docs/releases/e34/e34_19680629.pdf
Statistics South Africa (SSA). (2012). *Census 2011 Statistical Release*. Retrieved July 19, 2013, from http://www.statssa.gov.za/publications/P03014/P030142011.pdf
Swart, J. (1988). 'Street-Wise': Opening the Way to Self-Actualization for the Street Child. *Africa Insight, 18*(1), 33–41.
Swart, J. (1990). *Malunde: The Street Children of Hillbrow*. Johannesburg: Witwatersrand University Press.
Swart-Kruger, J., & Donald, D. (1994). Children of the South African Streets. In A. Dawes & D. Donald (Eds.), *Childhood and Adversity: Psychological Perspectives from South African Research* (pp. 107–121). Cape Town: D. Philip.
Swartz, S. (2010). 'Moral Ecology' and 'Moral Capital': Tools Towards a Sociology of Moral Education from a South African Ethnography. *Journal of Moral Education, 39*(3), 305–327.
Terrio, S. J. (2004). Violence: Prosecuting Romanian Street Children at the Paris Palace of Justice. *International Migration, 42*(5), 5–33.
Turnball, B., Hernández, R., & Reyes, M. (2009). Street Children and Their Helpers: An Actor-Oriented Approach. *Children and Youth Services Review, 31*(12), 1283–1288.
Vally, S. (1998). Spoil the Rod, Spare the Child. *The Educator's Voice, 2*(9), 4–5.
Veriava, F. (2014). *Promoting Effective Enforcement of the Prohibition against Corporal Punishment in South African Schools*. Pretoria: Pretoria University Law Press.
Vivian, L. M. H. (2012). *Psychiatric Disorder in Xhosa-Speaking Men Following Circumcision*. Unpublished PhD Thesis, Department of Psychiatry and Mental Health, University of Cape Town. Retrieved June 01, 2013, from http://uctscholar.uct.ac.za/PDF/91520_Vivian_L_M.pdf
Wadesango, N., Chabaya, O., Rembe, S., & Muhuro, P. (2011). Source of Behavioural Problems That Affect the Realization of the Right to Basic Education Among Children: A Case Study of Schools in the Eastern Cape-South. *Journal of Social Sciences, 27*(3), 149–156.

Wedel, J. R., Shore, C., Feldman, G., & Lathrop, S. (2005). Toward an Anthropology of Public Policy. *The ANNALS of the American Academy of Political and Social Science, 600*(1), 30–51.

Wells, L. E., & Rankin, J. H. (1991). Families and Delinquency: A Meta-Analysis of the Impact of Broken Homes. *Social Problems, 38*(1), 71–93.

Wenzel, J. (2009). *Bulletproof: Afterlives of Anticolonial Prophecy in South Africa and Beyond.* Chicago: University of Chicago Press.

Wilson, P., & Arnold, J. (1986). *Street Kids: Australia's Alienated Young.* Victoria: Collins Dove.

Yende, S. (2005). Teacher Hit Kids, is Suspended. *News 24* (Online). Retrieved January 25, 2014, from http://www.news24.com/SouthAfrica/News/Teacher-hit-kids-is-suspended-20050908

Zigon, J. (2007). Moral Breakdown and the Ethical Demand: A Theoretical Framework for an Anthropology of Moralities. *Anthropological Theory, 7*(2), 131–150.

Zigon, J. (2009a). Hope Dies Last: Two Aspects of Hope in Contemporary Moscow. *Anthropological Theory, 9*(3), 253–271.

Zigon, J. (2009b). Within a Range of Possibilities: Morality and Ethics in Social Life. *Ethnos, 74*(2), 251–276.

Zigon, J. (2010). Moral and Ethical Assemblages: A Response to Fassin and Stoczkowski. *Anthropological Theory, 10*(1-2), 3–15.

Zigon, J. (2011). *'HIV Is God's Blessing': Rehabilitating Morality in Neoliberal Russia.* Berkeley: University of California Press.

CHAPTER 4

A Loving Education

I first met Warrant Officer Maleku during an "interdisciplinary meeting" held during my first week at the school. She was the linchpin between Ngomso and the South African Police Service, fulfilling her duties within the Social Crime Prevention Department and occasionally speaking with learners when they were absent from school. Maleku explained her methods to the room:

> I meet them [the children and young people] on the street. They know me now. We share stuff together. I am showing them how to do things. Showing them love and support because they lack it, and maybe it will change their attitudes. They don't get [love], not by their choice but by their situation; I tell them that it is not their fault. It is their situation and circumstance that put them there.

As we stood in the art room during my second week at the school, David told me something similar:

> All we can give is love. We are not trained [to be] teachers for these kids. I don't think that there is a teacher anywhere in the Eastern Cape trained to deal with these children with behavioural problems. They lack parental love. We must teach manners and respect, thank you and please. All those things that they have missed. We are not shouting [at them]; we must stay calm. Maybe there is a reason from God why I am here, but I don't know yet.

Mrs Noni attended monthly meetings with other Learner Support Agents working in mainstream schools in the surrounding area. The Eastern Cape Department of Education (ECDoE) had only recently introduced these posts. I asked her what she had learnt about their job roles. She told me that most wanted to care for the learners at their schools but that many had struggled to gain the support of their principals. As she explained their efforts, it was as though she was summarising the care I had witnessed at Ngomso, which she felt was path-breaking. This was her concluding remark:

> Some are dealing with rape. [Others are dealing] with parents that are not talking the truth, who are hiding from the problems [with their children]. Some notice that the child has problems, they are sitting alone [in class, for example], then they find out that they are abused. Some help with grants, where there is no grant. Some learners have no food at home, so cooking in the school is helping.
> One [colleague] bought a table and a chair so that a learner who is not feeling well can sleep there. She has a mirror so that, after [a learner has been] crying, she can say 'You are so beautiful'. But I feel lucky when they are talking about their schools that do not care. It happens here already; it's easy for me.

Other members of staff similarly spoke of efforts to address abuse and sexual violence, parents who hid from problems, access to grants, hunger, and medical needs. They wanted to care for the learners, and encouraged them to value themselves. Mary used the term "self-esteem". The school's mission statement highlights a plan "To provide a happy, relaxed learner friendly, yet secure and stimulating environment in an atmosphere of caring and concern". Effectively, members of staff wanted to step into the gaps that (they felt) were left behind by absent and uncaring parents/caregivers.

At Rhodes University's student radio station, Mary and I were being interviewed for a programme about "special needs education". One question was: "What can parents do to assist with their child's learning?" I answered first with some ideas about reading at home, healthy relationships with teachers, and helping with homework. It sounded like I was reading from a parenting handbook. Having listened attentively, Mary then responded by saying, "Give them love". She emphasised the importance of "encouragement", "care", and "support". The disparity of our answers encouraged me to think about our understandings of education and schooling. Mary had already said, "We love, we care, we support, we don't discriminate" when speaking about learners with AIDS who "dropped out" of other schools. Mother Teresa (cited in Bornstein and Redfield 2008: 13) made a similar distinction: "Government agencies accomplish many things in the field of assistance. We must offer something else: Christ's love."

Fuzile was a new face at the school in 2013. He was crafting a candlestick that featured a lion. I guessed that it was representative of the Lion of Judah, on account of his faith as a Rastafarian. His attention to detail and the delicacy with which he crafted his block of clay conferred something of his gentle character. He explained his relationships with the learners: "My character is to be nice. Some of them share stories; it helps me to understand them." He took his hands away from the clay and said, "They see me as a father or brother". Gesturing towards the building, he added, "This is their home". His comments took me back to my first stage of fieldwork in 2011. A week after my visit to the student radio station, I attended a conference at Stellenbosch University. I drove back to Grahamstown in a minibus with my then-supervisor, studying the landscape as the other students slept in the seats behind us. I was talking about the radio interview and the realisation that members of staff wanted to create a family-like and homely environment at the school. Returning to Ngomso the following day, I propped my bike against the fence. Mary shouted at me through her car window, "Welcome home". That evening I wrote, "It smacked me in the face, this is what the school is all about: providing a home for kids—a place of shelter and support". During a conversation with Lindiwe, two months later, she said, "They feel at home when they are here at school".

Ennew and Swart-Kruger (2003: np) suggest that "Hygiene, both physical and social, is the key to the modern social construction of 'home' in developed countries, and increasingly penetrates child welfare discourses in international aid activities". The word 'home' once connoted "a place, a village, a group of kin, a state of being" (Jackson 1995: 86). It was a dominant idea "inextricably tied to the rise of the bourgeoisie in the seventeenth century" (ibid.), which "became the keystone for a code of domestic morality" (Berkhout, cited in Jackson 1995: 86). The idea of 'a home' infers security because, as a place and an idea, it is considered to be substantive: capable of housing and holding belongings, relationships, and ideas (Jackson 1995: 85). A plaque on the wall of the Shelter—an institution understood via this same concept—captured this sentiment: "A house is made of bricks and beams, a home is made of love and dreams."

In the playground, months later, I asked Lindiwe if I could interview her. I said that I wanted to "understand what is happening at the school". Without further prompting, she said, "We are trying to be parents to them; to give them love because we know that they don't have love at home. We are trying to share how we are with our own children so that they feel loved [liked they do]". In the interview itself she further explained her ideas:

Lindiwe: Firstly, I am an educator, teaching natural sciences and life orientation. The other role here is to be a parent to these children because I am a parent myself. How am I a parent here? In most cases, these children come to me when they have a problem that they don't want to discuss with their peers. They want to discuss it with me. And I discuss [it] with them. And sometimes, if it is easy for me to solve their problem, I solve it for them. If it is beyond me, I consult the principal and tell her what is happening to the child.

Oliver: Can you give me an example of a time when you have been a parent here at school?

Lindiwe: Most of them are coming from difficult situations. Most of their parents are drinking; most of their parents don't care about them, some of them died. So they don't have that mother, they didn't receive the mother-child comfort, you know? So, in most cases, I am giving them the love that they need. Because sometimes, most of them, some of them, are angry. They don't know why [they are] angry, but I discover that they need love. So I make it a point that I take maybe one of them and chat with them and give them what I have. I give them what I have. I want to be a role model, somebody that they can look up to. To say 'No, your life doesn't have to go that way [towards criminality].'

One night, Mary was at the hospital until two in the morning for the birth of a past pupil's baby. During the staff meeting later that morning, she said that one of the educators had "become a grandmother". The past pupil had stayed at the educator's house when "she needed somewhere to stay", Mary later explained. This event meant that the learner was "like her daughter". The new baby was "her grandchild".

Soon after a bell had signalled the end of lessons one afternoon, the metal door protecting the school's electrical fuse box was pulled off its hinges. I knew enough to presume it had been sold to the scrap dealer behind the school. As I spoke to Mary about this, an elderly man entered her office. He was worried about the danger posed by the exposed wires. After he had left the room, Mary said, "He is our role model. He used to be our driver but [when he became too old for that] we didn't have the heart not to keep him on". At 76, he came to the school sporadically, perhaps once a week on average. He spent most of his time with the learners in grades one and two and received a small stipend to supplement his pension. Mary then showed me a photograph that was glued to the wall in her office. He was sitting with a young man who had been murdered the year before. Mary and I were both looking at the image in silence when she said:

> That is what he is so valued for. He's our grandfather, and that's his role; to be a role model of what a man can be. He is a real old gentleman. We feel that you cannot put a price on that for these kids who have grown up only with drunken men.

On several occasions, I saw this elderly man sitting with younger learners on his lap. We smiled at each other when we passed on the playground, and he often put both thumbs in the air at the same time. When I wrote a draft of this chapter before returning to the school in 2013, I regretted not speaking to him more often, nor learning much about his life. He was no longer there when I returned.

The idea that a school and its staff might provide a 'family-like-environment' and 'parental-style' relations appear to be quite common. During the Mexican Revolution of the 1930s, female teachers were seen to nurture children in schools and were perceived as role models (Vaughan 1992). More recently, female members of staff have been cast in this light in schools in Vietnam (Rydstrøm 2003). Much like the staff at Ngomso, teachers at the special education institute where Seyer (2002: 244) conducted research in San Francisco described their students as "emotionally needy", with "problems and needs" that they linked to "situations 'at home'". A metaphor they used to describe the institute was "that of a family" (ibid: 229). Bornstein (2002: 26) found Christian faith to be a determining factor in how her interlocutors—those 'rehabilitating child soldiers' at the Harare offices of World Vision—compared their work environment to a "caring family".

At Ngomso, learners' parents and caregivers were rarely invited to contribute to moral pedagogy.[1] When temporally excluded for 'bad behaviour' for example, learners who lived in the location left the school alone and could choose to hide the incident from caregivers and parents. When returning to Ngomso, they engaged in processes of reconciliation with Mary and Joyce without any form of parental/caregiver input. In contrast, several past pupils said that high schools in the location invited collaboration with parents and caregivers during similar events and suggested that such partnerships contributed to improved discipline in these schools.[2] Such cooperation was evident in the case of relationships between staff at Ngomso and the Shelter, who were legal guardians and caregivers of some residents. Staff from the Shelter were party to disciplinary procedures at Ngomso involving the shelter boys and escorted them off-site when they were temporally suspended. More broadly, Mary and Joyce frequently collaborated with the staff at the Shelter to control the learners' behaviour inside and outside of school. In other words, those staying at the Shelter were subject to 'total surrogate parenting'.[3]

I heard the phrase "in loco parentis" on many occasions and two journalism students used it for the title of a short film that they made about Mary. Moreover, members of staff, learners, parents, volunteers, and donors referred to her as Mama Mary. Although '*umama*' literally means 'mother' in isiXhosa, the isiXhosa word can be used differently. Similarly to how many isiXhosa speakers use the word '*Tata*' (father) when speaking about Nelson Mandela, 'Mama' can be used to address a respected woman, most often an elder, and need not imply a biological or 'legal' (e.g. adoptive) mother/child relationship. Instead, it can be used figuratively to mean 'one who mothers' ('Mother' 2014). One of the "housekeepers" at the shelter was called Mama Rose. In this context, 'Mama' may indicate frameworks concerning 'communitarian care' associated with moral discourses of ubuntu.[4] However, in the case of Mary, usage of 'Mama' related more explicitly to enactments of Christian duties.[5]

When I visited her home, Mary continually attended to my sense of comfort. She would ask "Are you OK?" and "Have you had enough food?" The first time I had dinner at her home, she told me I was two years younger than her son. "Treat my house as your own", she continued. On another occasion, I went to the fridge for a bottle of beer. Mary had been to the liquor store that afternoon to buy my favourite brand. Two teenaged volunteers from the UK were staying with her at the time. As she handed me the bottle opener, Mary said "I just love having all these young people in the house; it's so much fun", especially because her own children had moved out. She gave me a tight hug and said, "It's just so lovely". When a young man, her cousin's son, came to stay with her during a troubled time at boarding school, Mary told me that her parents had often fostered children. Her enthusiasm for caring for the young was not a charade or merely her job, but central to her life.

The Reverend Susan Dibb was a vicar who lived in a small village close to Shakespeare's birthplace, Stratford-upon-Avon. When I met her, she had already volunteered at Ngomso on several occasions. During these visits, Susan stayed in Mary's home. She also returned the gesture by hosting Mary during her fundraising trips to the UK. They shared a friendship and understanding of each other built upon a shared sense of humour and Christian faith. During Susan's visit to Ngomso in 2011, I took the opportunity to record two conversations with her. She offered this analysis of Mary: "I think that she does all this direct mothering of people because that is who she is and what she wants to do." When I then asked Susan "What's the role of religion in the school?" she provided me with this assertion:

> I think that the role of religion in Ngomso is essential in that it is Mary's motivating force. It is what got Mary involved with street children and got her involved in the school and this kind of school work to begin with.

Mary's desire to give motherly, agapeic love was rooted in her embodied moral habitus—"who she is and what she wants to do"—but it was also an application of her faith.[6]

Mary's positionality and the institutional emphasis on care and nurturance are not without precedent. The Comaroffs (1986: 16, emphasis added) argue that it was by *"patiently nurturing* the Protestant subject in South Africa [that] the missionary [of the colonial period] made it possible for him to become a colonial object". More specifically, the colonial subject was also 'nurtured' by feminine enactments of notions of motherhood, in addition to the 'firm hand of the male colonial State and Church'.[7] Nancy Lutkehaus (1999: 208) characterises the Holy Spirit Sisters, a German Catholic order of missionary nuns active in New Guinea since 1899, as "maternal". She (ibid.) highlights "a focus on caregiving and nurturance, on the upbringing and socialization of children, and on the development of 'inner' qualities for morality and spirituality, all pursued in a compassionate manner". She (ibid.) argues that this orientation contrasts with the more common idea that missions "replicate the hegemonic values, beliefs, and practices of the patriarchal Western societies and churches of which they are a part". Similarly, Prevost (2010) argues that female British missionaries in Africa, specifically Uganda and Madagascar, used 'pacifistic maternalism' and humanitarianism to counteract the imperialist and patriarchal underpinnings of the Church and State. In the process, they established notions of 'Christian internationalism' that framed 'motherly charity' as an antidote to imperialism, war, and gendered domination.

In her book *White Mother to a Dark Race*, Jacobs (2009: 288) details a "maternalist sense of mission". She (ibid: 88) argues: "Many white women reformers cast themselves as important political players who would solve the Indian and Aboriginal 'problem' by metaphorically and literally mothering indigenous people and their children." They "claimed a role for themselves as surrogate mothers who would raise indigenous children properly in more wholesome environments [than their parents were adjudged to be providing]". Jacobs (ibid: 287) tells the story of Ida Standley, a lady who established a home and school for children in Alice Springs, Australia, from 1914 to 1929.[8] Mrs Standley was awarded the MBE (Member of the British Empire) for "spread[ing] a maternal wing about the unwanted half-castes who were in a sorry plight" and was praised by reporters for "slaving her life out for those girls".[9] As in the case of Mother Teresa, who I mentioned earlier, Standley's maternalism served as a form of identification. She was called the "mother of Alice Springs", "'Ma' Standley", and "To the native 'boys,' in fact to the entire male population, [she] was affectionately known as 'Mum'".[10] When I read this, I instantly thought of Mama Mary.

Having returned to South Africa in 2013, I spoke to Mary about my interest in the history of the Eastern Cape, which had grown considerably since my last visit 18 months earlier. Mary responded by telling me a story about a car she had once had, which "was tied together with string". She recalled someone telling her: "you look like a missionary in that". She laughed as she recounted his observation: "I don't know if he knew anything about me." As she then recounted her family history, Mary said, "It's in my bones", an analogy for her embodiment of a historically constituted way of being in the world (Zigon 2007, 2009). Her positionality has roots that reach back to the seventeenth and eighteenth centuries, when her ancestors, the Miller family, operated a 'charity school' in Wiltshire for well over a century. As well as being teachers, some of the family were also clergy. In 1854, the parents of 16-year-old Robert John Miller arranged for their son to accompany John Armstrong, the first Bishop of the Anglican Diocese of Grahamstown, on his journey from the

UK to the Cape's eastern frontier to work with him as a catechist.[11] Building on his experience of the family's charity school and his father's work as a minister, Robert established schools at St. Luke's Mission, hosted by Chief Mhala of the Xhosa.[12] Mary enthusiastically directly traced her ancestry back to Robert, and she kindly gave me a copy of his diaries in 2011.[13]

In 1857, the first Church of England mission school opened in Grahamstown's 'location'.[14] Bishop Armstrong, with whom Mary's forefather Robert Miller travelled to South Africa, planned for it but did not live to see it materialise.[15] The Rev. E. Cornford (cited in SPG 1858: 13–16) reported the school's opening to readers of *Global Missionary* (printed in London):

> We found the Kafirs[16] in groups, and told them that now some one [*sic*] was come who would care for them; that they were to have a school for themselves, which would begin to-morrow [*sic*], that they should be taught what was useful and good. They were very pleased to hear this, and some of the children clapped their hands with delight.

The moralised nature of this endeavour, and, in particular, an interplay between discourses of humanitarianism and education, is evident in this report, especially within the notions that the missionaries had arrived to "care for them [the unbelievers]" who were to "be taught what was useful and good". As Ashley (1974: 201) argues, with specific reference to the Eastern Cape, missionaries knew that "schools could do more than impart knowledge and skills. They could also effect a change in values and habits". In other words, they dealt heavily in processes of moral education.[17] In 1831, William Thomson, a missionary working 130 km from Grahamstown, suggested that mission schooling dealt in the "disciplining of the disposition" (cited in Ashley 1974: 201). Considered in this way, missionary schooling is distinguishable as an exertion of power concerned with the governance of the Xhosa and their behaviour.[18] It is from this same line of thought that this chapter puts forward the argument that the 'loving education' on display at Ngomso during my research was similarly directive-oriented, with a political-fashioning quality, in addition to any care-oriented or rescue-type qualities.

Harriet Mary (Jennie) Miller, Robert's wife, was a devoted Christian. Only two months after arriving in South Africa in 1862, she (cited in Anonymous) wrote a letter to her father:

My Kafir [i.e. isiXhosa language proficiency] is improving, I teach the little children in school every day in Kafir, it seems so strange to see a lot of little things in sheepskins before me, all very much afraid! We are quite King and Queen here, and have much more of our own way than in a parish in England. All the people in the [mission] station are obliged to do as they are told, and come to chapel and send their children to school; if they are not all there, we send a boy to the different huts to hunt them up!

Her sense of surety that the young should be in school and the technologies of power she and Robert implemented to ensure school attendance (i.e. the relatively autonomous 'King and Queen' sending a boy to hunt the strays) shares some similarities with my experience of travelling with members of staff to learners' homes to encourage them to reattend the school. Likewise, the motivation behind such actions was not only connected to valuations of religious or linguistic education but also recognition of the requirement to provide those less fortunate with material and emotional assistance. In this same year (1862), for example, there was an especially harsh drought.[19] The effects of the Great Xhosa Cattle-Killing lingered on. "Jennie was saddened by the hunger of the [Xhosa] children [who arrived at their mission station in increasing numbers] and Robert accused her of giving away all they had [to help to feed them]" (Anonymous). In other words, Jennie enacted her agapeic love for others, even if it compromised her family's access to food, while Robert was concerned to find the healthy limit of her altruistic love.[20]

From 1864 onwards, having left the mission station to settle permanently in Grahamstown, Jennie's maternalistic endeavours continued. Miller's family home housed their own family of 14 children as well as pupils of the 'Native Branch', a path-breaking section of Grahamstown's oldest private school, founded in 1859 for young Xhosa males, mostly the sons of chiefs (Poland 2013: np).[21] It also "became a 'home from home' for dozens of [pupils of this private school] over the years, who boarded under the care of the devoted [Jennie]" (ibid.).[22] Jennie also co-founded the Grahamstown branch of the Ladies Benevolent Society in 1867.[23] As per my consideration of Mary, Jennie embodied and enacted Christianised notions of *agapē*.[24] She gave her motherly love to others, in order that they might also experience His love.

Despite the significance of this historical context, I am not suggesting that my interlocutors simply regurgitated or blindly followed paths others had laid decades or centuries earlier, nor am I making the claim that practices of moral education and humanitarianism I observed are identical to those enacted during the nineteenth century. For one thing, at the time of my research, notions of saviour and rescue interweaved with the psychological/scientific discourses concerning 'trauma' and mental health I examined in the previous chapter. Moreover, the interplay between modes of care and knowledge-oriented education (e.g. learning the English language) had a very different quality in the twenty-first century because standardised criteria and curricula, and a formalised progression structure leading to matriculation, distinguished these dynamics from the more autonomous structure enjoyed by colonial missionaries such as Robert and Jennie Miller, who reported to the Church rather than government ministers.[25] Instead of a wholesale continuation of a colonial mission education tradition, then, it is more appropriate to claim that moralised practices of education and care at Ngomso, and the moral dispositions of those who enacted them, were possible by local and globalised historical events, and that this history did not *fully* determine such formations. To be clearer still, the actions and beliefs of colonial missionaries were an integral component of the assemblage of moral discourses that circulated publically and institutionally in the locality from which my interlocutors could and did draw from every day when fashioning their lives and conceptualising and enacting models of assistance and interaction.

Mary's moral habitus can thus be understood as an individualised embodiment of historically constituted, localised possibilities of moral personhood, most especially those relating to discourses regarding Christianised forms of education, care, and nurturance. Can the same be said of her colleagues at the school? Certainly, at least to my knowledge, their family histories cannot be connected so directly to the emergence of missionisation during the nineteenth century. However, this does not mean there is no significant linkage. Broadly speaking, as soon as those who identified with a Xhosa heritage began to missionise during the colonial period, and congregations of converts expanded, any clear distinction between Xhosa and missionaries, or an articulation of solidity and uniformity within these groups, dissolved.[26] These events are an essential precursor to the emergence of the possibility that individuals with a Xhosa heritage could enact Christianised forms of education and nurturance during the twenty-first century. However, in line with the theorisation of historically constituted possibilities of personhood put forward already, the dynamic whereby certain interlocutors espoused qualities of both Xhosa and Christian traditions was not one of absolute historical continuation, but, instead, evidence of an intersubjectively constituted discursive platform from which individuals could and did construct imaginations of possible futures for themselves and others, and ethically (i.e. inventively) enact relevant behaviours and interactions when attempting to bring these futures to fruition.

Independence, Interdependence, and Restored Childhoods

When working in 'special education' in London before my first visit to South Africa, two female colleagues spoke about their roles using analogies of mothering. Further, during a staff induction day at a different school, which I attended in 2012, the principal said, "Students spend more time with us than their parents, it's our job to socialise them". She concluded her talk by saying that she wanted the school "to be like a family". The staff aimed to differentiate their 'learning space' from learners' other social worlds. The school's motto was "The street stops at the gate".

At Ngomso, the staff similarly wanted to differentiate the school from the street, which, as I have already argued, was seen as dirty and morally impure, even more so than homes in the location. They wanted the school to be physically and morally hygienic: a defined space, closed-off from the influence of, and difficulties associated with living in the location. However, the staff also wanted learners to bring their problems in 'from the street' so that they might mother them away. Any separation of these social environments was tenuous, tested, and permeable. However, the effect of their intention was clear to see. I noted that sitting on a bench outside the classrooms—watching the constant traffic of bodies, bicycles, shopping trollies, and donkeys moving along the railway tracks—was "like looking out from inside a fishbowl". Fuzile once said, "For those that come from a poor background, it's more nice here than the township". David described Ngomso as a "mini-society". He said that the staff were "preparing" the learners for "the society out there".

Betty and Sally spent one month at the school. The sisters travelled from Suffolk as unpaid volunteers. Both had attended a private school in Southwold, a small town with pristine beach huts, tea rooms, and a thriving pier. (My sisters and I gave our parents a two-night break there for their golden wedding anniversary.) As we sat in the sunshine one afternoon, Sally was speaking about the learners: "They're safe here." I responded by saying, "So it is like a sanctuary? Like, a place . . .", before she cut me off to agree:

Sally: Yeah, sanctuary. Yeah, sanctuary.
Betty: With barbed wire.
Sally: But it's still a sanctuary, though. Like a haven for the school kids.

Because they continued to talk about barbed wire, I asked, "What has the barbed wire got to do with anything?" With a giggle, Sally said, "Betty hates barbed wire; she hates 'being barbed in'".

Oliver: Do you?
Betty: It's just a shame that there is not a nicer way. It's just a constant reminder of where you are.
Sally: It makes you feel like you are in a concentration camp.
Betty: That's true, it does.
Oliver: What do you mean, a reminder of where you are? Explain that to me.
Sally: Danger. Not safe.
Betty: It's that you are safe, just until you go outside [of the school].
Sally: Keeping the danger out through using barbed wire.
Betty: Or keeping the danger in.
Sally: Yeah [laughing a little], keeping it in. I hate barbed wire anyway. Looks dangerous, feels dangerous.
Betty: It's like a constant reminder. All I'm saying is that they are told, 'You should come to school, you are safe', or whatever, but you're not really safe.
Sally: Outside you're not. That's what I am saying about a haven. Like, in Hackney, you have that St Josephs Hospice, where my nan was, and Hackney is, like, awful, and then you have like a haven within this awful place. I am not saying that all of Grahamstown is awful, cos I'm not but . . . [Betty cuts her off].
Betty: You're not from Hackney are you?
Oliver: I live in Hackney.
Sally: Oh. Do you live in Hackney?
Oliver: Yes, but that's fine [laughing].
Betty: You see, I have nothing against Hackney, I was just checking that [you don't live there].
Sally: I don't have anything against Hackney.
Betty: Dig, dig, dig.

For Foucault (1976: 81), dreams that are integral to practices of institutionalised education are removed from the reality of the conditions and miseries they create for adults. In observing distinctions between the safety and appeal of the spaces inside and outside of the school, my interlocutors inadvertently supported his observation.

Zigon (2011: 10–11) suggests that "shelters, rehabilitation centres, camps, and various health and law-enforcement institutions", and I would add Ngomso, are "spaces of inclusion-exclusion" where subjects "receive 'one more chance' to work on themselves to become acceptable citizen-subjects" (also see O'Neill 2015). Colonial mission stations, like those of Robert Miller, were physically and politically included and excluded from, or a bridge between, the colonial State and 'Xhosaland'. Unhinged from either institutionalised arrangement of power, they were perfectly situated to offer the excluded—the 'wayward heathen'—a chance to ethically cultivate the sensibilities acceptable to Christian, colonial society. At Ngomso, education was delivered in a space separate from the trained, accepted citizen-subjects of 'mainstream' schools. The staff hoped that the groups would be reunited once Ngomso learners went to high school or found employment.[27] The school was a space that served desires for integration, rehabilitation, transformation, and 'demarginalisation'.

On my third day at the school, during the "interdisciplinary meeting" with various government agencies, Joyce said:

> We don't just chase them away because we cannot control them. If we can help, it will speed up a long process [of the child changing]. Social workers and probation workers are part of what the school does; [they are there] so that the teaching and learning can go smoothly. [There is] a SECOND CHANCE because they can change, but it takes months and months to transform a child.

I put the words SECOND CHANCE in capital letters when I typed my notes that evening. I would encounter conceptualisations of second chances and last chances throughout my fieldwork. The staff wanted to deliver them. With words that highlight the value she placed upon discourses of Christianised love and forgiveness, Mary once said, "We never reject a child; we can hate what the child does, but we cannot hate the child".

Like Nitin, the high school principal considered in Chap. 5, some past pupils, Luzuko and Siseko especially, expressed concern that unlimited opportunities for reconciliation limited the seriousness of disciplinary consequences, inadvertently encouraging learners to ignore school rules and regulations, and thus behave immorally, without the threat of permanent exclusion. In this view, the value accorded to forgiveness actually reduced the imperative that learners alter their way of being in the world (i.e. become a 'model pupil') in order to engage with the school. In other words, the endeavour to always accommodate every young person, no matter their past 'errors' or 'misbehaviour', limited the efficacy of the school's transformative potential because it reduced the institution's power over learners. The moral quandary is that permanent exclusions would have halted some school educations indefinitely, including Luzuko's, because Ngomso was the only school suitable for, or accessible to, many Ngomso learners (see Chap. 5). For these individuals, if there were no more chances at Ngomso, there were no more chances of schooling at all.

As if to speak to this point, during a staff briefing one morning, Mary told the room: "there is not a rubbish bin for these children; we must give them a chance". As is the general argument of this book, this chance did not only concern school attendance and matriculation. According to Zigon (2011: 10–11), final chances are given to those who have not been "ethically worked upon". He (ibid.) refers to "the homeless, refugees, the poor, drug users, convicted criminals, and the mentally and physically ill". These individuals are "exposed as *bare life* in societies increasingly unwilling to accept or support such 'untrainable' subjects" (ibid, my emphasis). Mary's 'rubbish bin' imagery evoked the idea that others were unwilling in this way and enabled her to highlight the moral qualities of acceptance and support.

Before this last chance, or if they failed to take it, the learners were seen as bare lives: something other than the moral citizen-subject. For instance, Fuzile spoke about learners who came "from the street", not those living with "adults at home", as those who "grow up with friends—with no elders, no big brother". With deft anthropological insight, he declared "There is no generational structure there. [As a consequence] they behave like they don't have responsibilities". David interjected by saying "We find them raw". Likewise, during apartheid, the *Gcaleka*—a term used to describe Xhosas born in the 'heartland' of the Eastern Cape—were adjudged to be "*irwau*" (from 'raw') because they 'did not understand' the "ways" of the 'civilised town' (Mayer (citing an interlocutor) 1961: 76). Similarly, in Mongolia, "'negative exemplars'" are "often called 'mad ones' (*soliot*), that is, human beings who are one of us, but who exist as it were in a natural state, without having developed the particular characteristics of mind and conscience cultivated in the Mongolian way of life" (Humphrey 1997: 39). Likewise, judgements of learners' 'rawness' related to the idea that they had psychological barriers to learning, that is, had not fully developed a capable and moral consciousness, most especially as a result of traumatic experiences and challenging circumstances.

Given such 'rawness', in a written statement, Mary says that the school's "mission" is to "provide an environment in which severely socially marginalised children may develop into confident, productive, independent and inter-dependent [sic] members of society, ready to enter the world of work". As David put it: "We are building them up: we do everything with love." Aspects of the "mission", as stated in the School Constitution are:

- to foster self-esteem and encourage the independence of each child
- to meet the developmental needs of each individual learner, enabling them to develop acceptable and competent social skills for meaningful integration into society
- to prepare each individual to be meaningful members of adult society, by the promotion of vocational, recreational and leisure-time skills
- to assist each individual [so that they learn] the value of self-discipline, self-awareness, good manners and courtesy

The fact that this ethical imagination was, quite firmly, premised upon notions of "self-esteem", "independence", "self-discipline", and "self-awareness" is evidence of historically constituted moral discourse. South African missionaries of the colonial period encouraged converts to exercise "free choice" and informed them that "personal achievement" equated to "moral worth" (Comaroff and Comaroff 1986: 16). In a chapter entitled *Moralities*, Monica Wilson (1971: 93) argues that "[Protestant and Catholic] Missionaries [in South Africa] stressed the need [for] 'initiative' and self-improvement". When "preaching the gospel [of work]", they "stressed the responsibility of the individual. A man must choose life or death, good or evil for himself" (ibid.). This moralistic, education-driven endeavour was antithetical to the Xhosa notion of communitarian interdependence (ubuntu). An aspect of the mission at Ngomso was interdependence, but the directive given to learners was the idea that one contributes to the welfare of others by being self-disciplined and productive. As in the case of the rehabilitation programme in Zigon's (2011) ethnography, although it was God that had the power to restore, it was the responsibility of those being transformed to integrate, or not.

Zigon (2011: 14) argues that in "the contemporary world that is increasingly characterized by more and more competing discursive traditions" it is "responsibility" that "is a foundational moral disposition that allows for a normal and sane life". The disciplined self is a cornerstone of

Foucault's (2008) understanding of 'governmentality': how we are responsible for our own 'meaningful societal integration' as both a consequence and a composite component of the 'modern, liberal sovereign State'. According to Foucault (ibid: 63–64), liberal forms of governance, like that which has come to define the post-apartheid period in South Africa, work by managing and organising "the conditions in which one can be free". As Mitchell Dean (2010: 193) has usefully put it: "in order to act freely, the subject must first be shaped, guided and molded into one capable of responsibly exercising that freedom through systems of domination". In line with Bornstein and Redfield's (2008: 13) consideration of humanitarianism more broadly, similar discourses were evident at Ngomso as "a secularized narrative of transformation – from destitute to self-sufficient". This focus ran alongside promotions of Christianised agapeic love and religious salvation. Perhaps more accurately, and given the centrality of Christianity in the formation of 'secular' South African politics, these discourses were interwoven and mutually constitutive so as to be distinguishable only analytically.

This integrative mission had added importance because 'street children' and those without parental guidance were held to have the wrong kind of freedom—that is, misdirected agency that resulted in marginalisation. Lorenzo Bordonaro (2012: 413) has helpfully considered the relationship between enthusiasms for discourses of 'youth agency' and concerns about control, suggesting that those working with street children in Cape Verde weave practices of "protection and correction" together. Similar practices were evident at Ngomso.

It is not surprising that the staff at Ngomso wanted the learners to fashion sane or normal lives analogous to those they (the staff) wished to live or were already living. They believed that fostering self-discipline and independence as a mode of 'societal preparation' would allow the young people to live happily in their society. As Bernard Williams (1993 [1985]: 47–48) articulates it, "the formation of ethical dispositions" requires "education or upbringing" that is attentive to "[moral] convention" and a "conception of human well-being".[28] The staff at Ngomso were attentive to the moral conventions, dispositions, and notions of human well-being that they valued. They thought that young people would be better off if included in *their* society, rather than left out of it. In this light, their educative efforts to fashion normality conjoined with enthusiasms for, and practices productive of, social reproduction.

This enthusiasm for preparing the learners for adult society, or hopes of enabling them to 'properly develop', materialised as efforts to give learners childhoods that they had not had, or would not have, elsewhere. Programmatic literature regarding 'street children' has "frequently referred to 'giving children back their childhood' as if children from impoverished homes had ever 'had' the socially constructed 'Western' childhood of play, school and absence of responsibility" (Ennew and Swart-Kruger 2003: np). Similarly, in the case of refugee children, for the World Bank (cited in Epstein 2010: 22), "schools are seen as key institutions that will play the major role in rebuilding core values, in instilling new democratic principles, and in helping children recover a lost childhood". In this same vein, Cheney's (2007: 190) interlocutors at World Vision in Uganda, who worked with child soldiers, wished to encourage their young 'students' to "rise" to the "ideals" of a "'normal' state of childhood". Education was "the very nexus of this return to normality" (ibid.). At Ngomso, members of staff similarly wanted learners to engage in particular kinds of moralised learning experiences. As Mary says in a short promotional video, "we slowly unlock the child inside the hard little adults". This extract from her submission to the Parliamentary Monitoring Group explains this process in more detail:

> Unlocking of the child within is one of the keys to the holistic rehabilitation of these children. It enables them to go through the developmental stages they have missed.... Free play time with toys allows the children to enter imaginary worlds – to get lost in play, indeed to be children.

'Restoring lost years' or 'unlocking the child inside' was akin to setting 'cognitive development clocks' back, as close to zero as possible, so that learners could start afresh from the stage of childhood innocence, no matter their age. They could be 'born again', or, at least, grow again. Members of staff hoped that transitions to adulthood might then run smoothly. In attempting to offer such experiences, they were optimistic that learners could realise their potential, to the benefit of learners, themselves, and society (Comaroff and Comaroff 2005: 19).

Guide Them to Employment, Guide Them to God

At Ngomso, the ethical imaginary regarding learners' potential had two complementary, but distinct, components. One was their potential to be Christians, joyfully filled with His love. The second was their potential to be productive members of society by contributing to the economy, while not having to endure material poverty. Like the American missionaries that Stambach (2011: 20.45 minutes) came to know, members of staff expressed their "theological faith that schools should be at the centre of creating and educating a global world united through New Testament Christianity". They also had "a secular modernist faith [that] schools can [and] should ameliorate social inequality and help people move out of poverty" (ibid.). Bornstein discusses (2002) a similar arrangement when examining faith-driven non-governmental organisations (NGOs) in Zimbabwe and desires for economic development and religious conversion.

A secular modernist faith was very much evident at Ngomso. In particular, I know that Mary and Joyce were troubled by the social and economic inequalities in South Africa, and did not conceptualise learners' 'lack of innocence' and material poverty in isolation of such contexts. They hoped to address such inequalities by widening access to quality schooling. They planned to insulate learners from material poverty and reduce their desires/need to work by providing them with clothes, food, and money for rent, as a means to integrate them into the economy as acceptable citizen-subjects, that is, as taxed labourers or entrepreneurs, at a later date. In this analytical light, members of staff did not hope to facilitate a radical alteration of the unequally structured economy that gave rise to their hopes of change.

Pejoratively, unemployment was considered on individual rather than societal levels; as such, there was hope that schooling and qualifications would lead to employment. The word 'Career' in the full name of the school is illustrative of this observation. Madoda affirmed the value that he placed on schooling:

> There is a more challenging life as you grow up, because if a job needs qualifications, then you will be upset if you don't have them. Township people are complaining [about a lack of jobs], but they punished themselves by not learning at school. Don't cry for anyone, *cry for yourself*.

As well as preparing learners for transitions to high school, members of staff also told me that "vocational education" was a promising route to employment. Especially for individuals who could not "go the academic route", as Mary put it. Governor Grey had built *Schools of Industry*, upon thinking that mission schools were too "bookish" (Lester 2001: 186). At Ngomso, there was the option of being academic or industrious.

When I first arrived at Ngomso, I met with Joyce and told her that I had run an evening class on "creative marketing" for young people in London who were not in education, employment, or training. Joyce outlined plans to offer learners "panel beating", "mechanics", "domestic skills", and "driving instruction". She was keen for the panel beating to start that term and had been speaking to a local company. "I share this vision with the learners", she said, "to show them that there is a future out there for them". However, she thought that vocational training might not appeal to all: "[We want to] give them the choice; those that want to carry on, can." From her enthusiastic tone, I knew that she thought that vocational training would be a good choice for many.

As I spent more time at the school, I came to understand that pottery was the most active of these vocational routes. Mary hoped learners might acquire knowledge and skills that could be "directly applied in the workplace". Historically, several potteries did offer employment in Grahamstown, but since 1994, all have closed down. The school had links with a potter working outside of the city, and there were hopes that one past pupil, who was focusing on pottery, might begin an apprenticeship with him, however, to my knowledge, this did not happen. While the lack of employment opportunities in this field, locally speaking, at least, might suggest that pottery training was a misplaced and obsolete offering, there were plans to sell pottery directly to visitors and supporters to generate incomes for the school and the young craftsmen.[29]

The pottery training was in David's hands. "We cannot just teach the skills", he told me. "We must also teach the maths and the figures so they can run a business." He was fully behind the plans for a self-funded enterprise. "We must also teach English so that they can talk with customers", he continued. His comments echo, in reverse, those of a settler-historian (Theal, cited in Hlatshwayo 2000: 33), who, in 1892, did "not see much use in teaching the natives to read and write without teaching them how to make use of their hands as well". David was not the only one to associate speaking and writing English with hopes of employment.

As mentioned already, such enthusiasms for economic development conjoined with those for spiritual development. The hope that learners would find God, as well as jobs, united members of staff. After demonstrating how hard it was to use the potter's wheel because it was crammed into a corner, Fuzile started to talk about the learners. He said, "few love clay" and suggested that most preferred to talk about "stories from the location" rather than concentrate on their pottery. "They have potential", he continued, "but it is hard for them to pay full attention [because] they want to be free". In his experience, a favourite topic of conversation revolved around tactics for how to make money out of other people; Oliver Twist style. He pointed to a tin of metal objects next to the candlestick he was making: "They have witnessed violence, so when they are angry we can see that they have problems. They look at these tools for stabbing, but I tell them to use them for creating art." Having spoken about the positive effects of working with clay, he said, "They are getting redeemed here". Compretta (2012: 108) suggests that staff at 'Home Mission' in the US similarly position "themselves, not guardians or other family members, as the redeemers of children". In juxtaposing the image of learners wanting to be free against their redemption, Fuzile nicely articulated the marriage between enthusiasms for Christian salvation and control.

Mary and several other members of staff also relayed information about the "therapeutic" qualities of clay. Referring to his research in Russia, Zigon (2011: 63) argues that therapeutic processes "are aimed at transforming the moral personhood of the rehabilitants [i.e. drug users] into what the Church would call spiritually moral persons". At Ngomso, it was hoped that art therapies would enable and encourage learners to craft themselves in a similar way. Several lecturers and students from the psychology department at Rhodes voluntarily offered such interventions after school. One of them told David that their sessions would mean learners' "behaviour [would] be less destructive with time". David was not allowed in the room. "I can teach art skills", he explained, "but cannot do the therapy, it is psychology". Interested in this distinction, I asked, "Can't clay making be good too?" David said that it could and told me that Mary had introduced pottery classes for this reason.

Mary and Joyce both expressed a desire to have more extensive and regular access to professional psychologists. When talking in London about five learners who all witnessed murders during 2013, they spoke about their relationship with the psychology department at Rhodes. Mary quickly pointed out that it would "not be enough". "They all need counselling", she said, "not just the five in question". They tried to fill the gap themselves.[30] Joyce had studied psychology at university and felt she had to be "a teacher, a parent and a psychologist" in her role at Ngomso. Mary had not had such training and spoke of her endeavours by using the term "counselling".[31] Writing about concerns regarding *Violence in South African Schools* over a decade ago, Salim Vally (with Dolombisa and

Porteus 2002: 87) suggested that "well-liked and trusted teachers" should be relieved "of teaching hours to provide counselling services". Asanda, one of the few teaching assistants employed on a government contract, implied that the Department of Education (DoE) had taken such advice on board when he told me that they occasionally offered training opportunities in such services. He was hopeful that Ngomso staff would soon have their turn, so he could help to "council" learners when they spoke to him "about their problems". Mrs Noni similarly said that she was "trained in therapy" by the DoE alongside other Learner Support Agents. She also said that people came to her "with their problems" because she was the wife of a pastor and was hopeful this training would also help her in this role. The way she linked counselling to her Christian duties is not unique. For instance, during a tour of one of the private schools in Grahamstown, my guide said that the Chaplain was the school's "counsellor" and "responsible for pastoral care". Similarly, the website of another private school in the city says that the Chaplain "is the spiritual leader of the school and is available for counselling and guidance to pupils at all times". Quite clearly, within South African education, promotions of Christianised moral transformations conjoin with practices of counselling.

According to Nietzsche (1994: 94), Christianity is "a great treasure-chamber of ingenious consolation". When the priest offers the "mitigation of suffering" and "every kind of 'consoling'", he is the saviour who combats "only the actual suffering, the discomfort of the sufferer" and "not its cause, not the actual state of sickness" (ibid). Consoling intertwines with counselling when the mitigation of suffering conflates with the promotion of particular frameworks of explanation and restorative, ethical direction. In the case of Ngomso, the terms 'counselling', 'psychologist', and 'therapy' were ostensibly secular or scientific frameworks of meaning that rationalised the staff's efforts to heal and guide 'the broken children of God'.[32] Similarly, Cheney (2007: 191) observed that World Vision in Uganda aimed to offer 'ex-child-soldiers' "psychosocial services for the recuperation of a sense of normalcy", which included "individual and group counselling". As Nietzsche predicted, during such restorative efforts in South Africa and Uganda, the emphasis was placed on suffering individuals and their ability to overcome their discomfort.

Having worked in schools in London, the prominence given to psychologists, counselling, and therapy was not new to me. During the twentieth century, "education, and socialization" moved into "the hands of a battery of new professions" (Ennew 2002: 339). This has certainly been the case in the field of refugee-oriented intervention. As Epstein (2010: 22) argues, "Recognizing the trauma, stress, depression, and psychological adaptation of children who experienced war and flight – a 'lost childhood' – the provision of psychological, psychiatric, and social services were added to the basic physiological services". "Refugee camp schools", he (ibid.) continues, "eventually became central not only to fulfill a right to education, but to physical, psychosocial, as well as cognitive forms of refugee protection". When working with 'at-risk youth' in London, I myself had training in cognitive behavioural therapy, which effectively offers practitioners a framework of questions that encourages 'rehabilitants' to formulate solutions to their problems and to take responsibility for enacting them. Some specialists at my school also promoted something called 'circle time', where students are encouraged to share all manner of personal thoughts and concerns in a 'safe space'. Such observations are evidence of the increased attention that schools in the UK and South Africa have paid to learners/students' 'emotional well-being' and 'self-esteem'. Kathryn Ecclestone and Dennis Hayes (2009) critic this development, and processes of victimisation more generally, in a book called *The Dangerous Rise of Therapeutic Education*.[33] Fassin and Rechtman (2009) have similarly probed the fact that interventions that occur in the name of 'responses to trauma' most frequently appear as morally inconspicuous entities, rather than questionable ones. Certainly, in promoting particular techniques of the self, or ideas about how individuals should encounter and transform their being in the world, instructional practices like counselling powerfully serve to legitimate particular moral discourses and truth claims. Individuals are comforted, but also simultaneously refashioned as a result of being encouraged to fashion themselves in particular ways. The rise of therapeutic education and its techniques is thus not unlike the 'civilising mission' of the colonial period, in that it concerns processes of moral transformation. The point of distinction, however, is that the discourse employed by religiously motivated individuals in the last decade reflects the emergence of professionalised and psychological models of care-oriented educational interventions, especially those aimed towards 'marginal' and 'at-risk' populations.

I have already compared concerns about 'moral decay' in the location to academic arguments about "street culture" in America (Bourgois 2002: 22) and "ikasi [or township] culture" in Cape Town (Swartz 2010: 323). In 2011, Peter told me that the behaviour of young people in the township, which concerned him, could be explained differently: their drinking, underage sex, drug use, and violence were evidence of "Sin". Thus, for Peter, like Fuzile, addressing immorality was inextricably tied to issues of redemption. A few weeks later, he extended his evaluation:

> Kids are not following their parents to church anymore. They are not inheriting the family belief. They are in the shebeens at the weekend now, not in the church.

When I returned in 2013, I saw him at the front of the school, washing the minibus. As I walked over to him, with a cup of coffee in my hand, he wiped down a plastic chair for me to sit on. We spoke about his wife and son. That weekend he was due to attend the funeral of a man from his congregation. They had been building a new church together that he hoped would be ready at the end of the month. I took the conversation as a cue to ask him about his Christian faith. I told him that I had visited Holly's congregation that weekend and wondered if his church "allowed for [belief in] ancestors". With this prompt, he launched into ten minutes of passionate conversation, halting the cleaning of the minibus to focus his attention on me. I had never seen him this animated before. I asked him if he had ever wanted to be a pastor and he said that he often spoke at his church. I was not surprised; it felt like I was sitting in front of a pulpit.

Belief in ancestors was not encouraged at his church, nor should it be, he contended. This position distinguished him from some of the other members of staff. He drew my attention to Matthew (5:9): "Blessed are the peacemakers, for they will be called sons of God." He spoke about being peaceful to other people and "doing right by them", in order to become "a son of God" and go to "the Promised Land". There would be "no problem here on earth if we did right", he said. He prayed for this: he wanted everyone to take God as their guide and follow His instruction. "There would be no crime, no stealing, no rape [if people did that]", he continued. "You would be able to leave your wallet behind and know that it would be there when you got back if only people were Christian and followed God." After I had left my camera on a pew in Holly's church, a young man ran out from the service to return it to me. I wanted to tell Peter this story, but I couldn't get the words out. He hardly paused for breath as he continued to proselytise.

I was interested in the way that Peter shifted effortlessly between a consideration of how Christian faith would create moral and desirable sociality on earth, here and now, and how adherence to such ideas throughout the course of one's life would result in passing to the Promised Land. When I later read how the missionaries of the nineteenth century had conjoined moral salvation in 'this life' with the eschatological imperatives of Heaven, his words made more sense to me.

Peter was now pointing at my bike, which I had locked to the fence. "That thing is yours, so I mustn't take it", he said, suggesting that people should ask others how they "got their things" so that they could "make plans to get it too". Because "asking questions is not a Sin", he said, but "stealing is". His advice was simple: "Pray, and with God's help, you might get it." David had similarly told me that "kids [should be] patient" and not take things from supermarket shelves without paying for them. Mary was concerned that learners struggled to delay their gratification. Processes of schooling are dependent upon such discourses: that you work now, to secure your future. As Nietzsche (1994: 27) wrote of 'goodness' and obedience to God, "[the] forced necessity of waiting, gain here fine names, such as 'patience' which is also called 'virtue'". For members of staff, the learners could become moral if they could learn to wait. David told me that "the Xhosa believe in the Bible" because of Heaven and the chance to "erase your sins". There is "something at the end", he told me. As I scribbled some notes about our conversation, I underlined the words '<u>something at the end</u>'.

Peter continued to ignore his cleaning duties and turned his attention to "the Promised Land" again. "Everyone is happy there; there are no problems, no crime, never getting old. You do right in this life: you go there." His conviction was empathic. In my notes, I wrote, "he wants, needs, desires me to believe it too". I was not sure how to react. It was during such moments of silence—when my interlocutors understandably expected a response after sharing personal information about their lives— that I often flitted between noncommittally smiling and asking another question to defer attention away from me. I took a sip of my coffee and said nothing. Peter appeared to sense that I was unsure of how to react to his words. "Believe me Oli", he implored, before dipping his dried-up cloth in the bucket and turning back to the minibus.

On our way to pick up some groceries from town one afternoon, Peter and I drove past a small group of past pupils who appeared to be selling some scrap metal at a yard behind the school. I knew that Peter thought this was an inappropriate way to make a living. He told me that he occasionally bought food for them. "I preach to them too", Peter continued. He tried not to be disheartened if they did not "respond straight away".

He was not looking for immediate gratification: "I know that I have planted the seed [by preaching to them]. There is hope that they will remember my words; especially in jail, they will do that." His use of the word 'seed' nicely mimics the concept of a 'bare life' with the *potential* to blossom. The act of planting seeds is a form of power. Peter had this power as one of the faithful, as one of the 'already saved' (Elisha 2008; Bornstein 2002). Once planted in bodies and minds, he hoped that his 'seeds of faith' would have the power to transform the lives of others.

Peter recognised that God might particularly appeal to those in jail. Not dissimilarly, in the UK, the Salvation Army posts chaplains in many prisons (The Salvation Army 2014). Jails are spaces of inclusion-exclusion: life is constricted, isolated, and stripped back (see Agamben 2005). Perhaps Peter thought that those most in need of redemption are most easy to redeem. Transformations—being 'born-again'—appear possible when human life is at its lowest ebb. As Bornstein and Redfield (2008: 7) suggest, "suffering" can offer "the possibility of [religious] purification". Empty vessels are ready for filling: There is no risk of contamination, nothing to spoil one's purity of faith or embodiment of Christianised morality when there is no sediment left in the bottle.

When addressing the room during the "interdisciplinary meeting", Lieutenant Maleku said that, during her patrols, she posed a question to young people "on the street": "Why do you not go freely to church?" She then explained the usual response:

> They tell me that they cannot go; they cannot go with the clothes that they have. I tell them that they can go and wash their clothes. They will be pleased to see you. I hope that maybe there is a little spark for them; that it will do something for them. [I say to them:] 'Maybe the church will give you money.' We need to refer them to church, where they are preaching the salvation. We cannot give up.

A spark has the potential to bring light, warmth, and energy. In 1855, soon after the Church of England was established in South Africa, Bishop Armstrong detailed a similar endeavour when he (cited in SPG 1856: 5) wrote to supporters in the UK: "We hope to see ... those who now live in the darkness of unbelief brought into the fold of CHRIST, lightened with His marvellous light, and taught to know that Saviour's love which passeth knowledge."[34] Before embarking on his travels, during an address to

The Society for the Propagation of the Gospel, Armstrong (cited in Carter 1857: 266) said:

> Africa is given to us, if we will first do our part. It is sowing the small seed, that shall by God's blessing be a mighty tree. Africa lies before us as a great field for spiritual enterprise, and the day I trust will come when native ministers, taught by us, will again teach the tribes beyond them, and so go on widening and widening the blessed empire of our Lord and Saviour, till the light reaches from north to south, and from east to west.

Something similar to Armstrong's hope of an enlightened Africa appeared to sustain Maleku.[35] She had taken up the challenge. If Peter hoped that his sown seeds might germinate in jails, she was hopeful that the sparks she ignited would mean that the unwashed would not end up there. "They need to be kept busy", she continued.

> And we urge you, brothers, warn those who are idle, encourage the timid, help the weak, be patient with everyone (Thessalonians 5:14).

I don't know if Maleku has read this section of the Bible. However, she came to mind when I read it. Due to ambiguity concerning the translation from Greek (i.e. the word ἀτάκτους), the word 'disorderly' appears in place of 'idle' in other versions of the Bible.[36] I think that Maleku's desire that the young would be 'kept busy' was a concern for both idleness and disorder. When she visited the school to speak to the learners about drug use, approximately two months after our initial meeting, she told me:

> Those kids can stop everything that is going on out there [in their troublesome lives] because they don't want to do it.... I'm going to meet people that I can change to be better people. And it can happen as long as everyone who touches them does the same thing: show them love. It will stop. Every day, I believe that if I can just change one...

During an interview for a short film made about the school, Mary articulated her hope:

> I find it an enormous privilege to have been called and equipped to work with God's broken children, God's hurting children. And there are times when ones gets very frustrated, and there are times when one feels a total failure, but His love is new every morning, and I long for them to learn and know that as well.

The staff at Christian Care and World Vision in Zimbabwe spoke to Bornstein (2005: 44) about the importance of relations between faith, love, and well-being. Similarly, for some of my interlocutors, to have faith was to feel His love, which was held to be an antidote to being hurt and broken. Having faith was to live well, in 'complete comfort'. Christianised frameworks of meaning also provided the staff with models of how to 'do good' and 'be good'; offering solutions, and a sense of control over their lives and those of others, or the possibility of resolutions to experiences of discomfort. In believing that God has the power to bring about justice, their ethical imaginary—like all missionaries, Christian or otherwise—foresaw collective prosperity following the unanimous acknowledgement of, and subjection to, God. "Lead me to the rock that is higher than I" (Psalm 61: 2). He reduced their vulnerability and exposure to chance, and, understandably, they wanted the learners to have similar protection.

> The LORD is a refuge for the oppressed, a stronghold in times of trouble. (Psalm 9:9)

Peter did not get disheartened. Lieutenant Maleku would not give up. Mary's frustrations and failures could not dampen her enthusiasm. Indeed, His love transformed her each morning. She knew that Christianity can provide hope during times of crisis (Bornstein 2005) and she hoped the learners would come to know this too. In line with Bornstein's (ibid: 44) consideration of Christianised development interventions more broadly, my interlocutors "identified conversion as a process, embodied in human form through the potential for transformation". In their hopes for learners, they "linked faith to love, to hope and success, to wellbeing, to peace of mind and body, and to a utopian absence of struggle" (ibid.). This possibility starkly contrasted with their judgements of how learners struggled without their intervention. To my mind, this disparity gave impetus to their transformative mission.

This transformative potential was held to be a process of becoming a full or whole human. Two more elements of the "mission" stated in the School Constitution are:

- to develop the unique potential of each child to the fullest in every sphere of his or her life
- to develop spiritual awareness and acceptable moral attitudes and cultural attitudes and knowledge

Where "Ngomso School's Mission" is articulated on the website of the Friends, it includes:

- Practice and teach the Christian principles of love and forgiveness
- Develop a holistic approach to each child

On a website promoting voluntourism in the municipality, it is Ngomso's "Mission ... to develop the whole child, body, mind and spirit" (Edutourism n.d.: np). After David had explained the Christian orientation of the school, he said, "It helps us to teach the learner; to help us *fully teach them*". Reverend Susan Dibb articulated something similar during our conversation in the playground:

> Mary believes in [contributing to the] transformation of lives, and [in] the power of the Spirit. I don't know how it fits in with the curriculum, only in that the curriculum is about enabling people to grow up as fully-rounded, whole human beings, which is a spiritual sort of a thing and is a Christian understanding of what it is to be human. So the education provided here, I think that it is about getting them to high school and vocational opportunities, but it is about, *essentially about*, enabling them to be fully human beings.

For Mary, Susan, David, Peter, and others, coming to know Him was akin to being transformed, healed, saved, or restored.[37] Becoming full, not empty. With, rather than without. No longer hurting, but loved. Whole, not incomplete. Strong, rather than vulnerable and weak. "The righteous person may have many troubles, but the Lord delivers him from them all; he protects all his bones, not one of them will be broken" (Psalm 34: 19–22).[38] The staff thought that those who lacked Christian faith fell short of an imagined, potential limit of the human condition: a 'fullness' or 'wholeness'.

The idea of conflating immoral behaviour and values with 'half-baked humans' was already well-established during the colonial period in South Africa: "The gulf between the saved and the fallen was epitomized by the contrasts between the civil and the savage" (Comaroff and Comaroff 1997: 64). Consequently, "the revitalization of the African soul required a 'revolution in habits'" (ibid: 8). The core premise of such assertions conjoined Christian faith with evolutionary development: "White Western bourgeois subjectivity ... [was] reified as a normative ideal" and 'the native' was "the manifestation of the 'childhood' of the species" and "treated as a child" (ibid: 99). 'The heathen' were thus thought incomplete without faith. The origin of 'heathen' is "generally regarded as a specifically Christian use of a Germanic adjective meaning 'inhabiting open country'" ('Heathen' 2014: np). This Germanic adjective also relates to 'heath': that wild, uncultivated, and untamed land. Similarly, we now talk of *savage*, inhospitable places, if we talk less about 'the savages'. In the UK, wild and wayward vagrants were thought to be sons of Belial: worthless or, definitely, worth little as social outcasts than those who had found God and did not disturb the weal of the realm.[39] Concerns about a lack of faith have long conjoined with concerns about a lack of control and predictability. Enthusiasms for acknowledgements of God's love relate to acts that narrow the potentialities of life: guiding waywardness, taming the untamed. Perhaps the staff wanted the learners to know His love because He could guide them to the moral path: His love lighting the way through prayer.

Seyer (2002: 148–149) uses the conceptualisation of "pathways"—"avenues extending across time and space"—when she discusses the "future orientation" of 'youth' "enmeshed in the street life" of San Francisco. Preachers wished to guide or lead "Christians down the right path" (ibid: 149). Similarly, the staff at Ngomso wanted to guide those that they felt had strayed furthest from 'the good life'. They were role models, who modeled embodied moral possibilities, and educators, who led, conducted and guided; attempting to draw out the potential inside the young.[40] They knew that learners were going *somewhere*; they wanted to work with them to determine the destination; drawing them away from certain, possible lives while encouraging them to construct others. It was a common perception that learners had gone astray as a consequence of their choices and the environments, relationships, and experiences that constituted their lives. And that, without the school, the right path would remain hidden from them or inaccessible to them.

Creating Space to Do His Work

The faith that members of staff placed in the 'promise of schooling' interweaved with sentiments of anxiety regarding the future that would transpire without Ngomso and other similar interventions. In her submission to the Parliamentary Monitoring Group, Mary wrote: "The cost to South Africa of not intervening with appropriate rehabilitation, education and preparation for the world of work cannot be over-estimated." Mary came to mind when I learnt of Nietzsche's claim that concerns about human vulnerability and exposure to chance are central to Christianity (Fraser 2008). Zigon (2008: 52) suggests that "one of the primary ways in which religion influences morality is by providing a conceptual framework within which moral experience makes sense" (also see Weber 1991: 281, 352–3). Although their faiths were not identical, religion certainly enabled members of staff to explain events, environments, and interactions. To my mind, Christianity, and especially the possibility of Christian salvation, provided them with an antidote to their concerns about "the world's imperfections" and its unpredictability (Weber 1978: 519). As Mary put it, "Sometimes we must bow before the Lord and accept that things [do just] happen". On the phone one afternoon, she greeted me with a barrage of "good news", saying, "It feels as those God is really pulling the strings". Although the staff agreed with governmental plans to prepare young people for adulthood with experiences of schooling, they placed their faith in God, not the post-apartheid 'secular State' (also see Bornstein 2005; Stambach 2010). Ultimately, society was seen to be in His hands, and they wished to do His work at Ngomso.

Throughout my fieldwork, I observed how this conceptualisation of the relations of power between God and the South African government related to conflicts that emerged between the school and the offices of the Department of Education. Most obviously, the school's registration status (i.e. Public Special School) was regularly questioned and endangered by individuals working at the provincial and district offices of the DoE. In some important respects, the two 'sides' were aligned in their aims. For instance, although the terminology they employed differed slightly, the DoE planned to address extrinsic barriers to learning by creating a Care and Support for Teaching and Learning (CSTL) programme, which unwittingly proposed mainstream schools become more like Ngomso. The scheme of work developed through partnerships with MIET Africa (a human rights-oriented NGO), the Southern African Development Community, and UNESCO, institutions with familiar ethical imaginaries of human rights oriented, human capital approaches to education.[41] The intervention focuses on "societal barriers [to education] (such as household poverty, high levels of violence and teenage pregnancy)" (DoE and MIET Africa 2010: 4). To address them, documentation recommends a 'multisectoral' model of "care and support" for "vulnerable children" (ibid: 6, 4, 55).[42] This territory clearly overlaps with Ngomso's institutional orientation.

One aspect of this overlap is the school's relationship with donor funders, NGOs, and community-based organisations (CBO). In the case of Ngomso, partnering agencies were often also classifiable as faith-based organisations (FBOs), which is not a delineation covered by the programme model explicitly. Such relationships facilitated interventions that the DoE did not fund, but which Mary and her staff felt were integral to their transformative efforts. For instance, charitable incomes that flowed into Ngomso were funding several full-time "volunteers", free school shoes and uniforms, three free meals a day, and a weekly "food parcel". Additionally, past pupils studying at high schools were "sponsored" and "supported" with monthly grocery packages, school shoes and uniforms, and, less commonly, money for rent. The Friends of Ngomso (a.k.a. FOA and 'the Friends') funded the majority of these benefits. Financial donations and bequests also came from individuals based in America, Britain, Holland, and Sweden. Assistance from overseas had also provided the school with musical instruments, clothing, books, sports equipment, toys, and games. In 2013, for example, donated pottery equipment was sent from the UK with the help of Tools With a Mission (TWAM), a Christian organisation that aims to encourage a "switch from aid dependency to self-sufficiency" (TWAM 2014: np). More recently, the chairman of the Friends placed various donations, including books and clothes, in shipping containers he procured to ship several sports cars out to South Africa. One of the trustees of the Friends has regularly coordinated a group of elderly churchgoers in Sussex, who knit hats and scarves in the school's colours.

The diversity of institutions and individuals based in the local (i.e. Grahamstown) area that supported the school was also impressive. Shops donated bread, fruit, and vegetables. Individuals gave second-hand clothes, books, and classroom materials, such as pens and paints. My host Rotary Club purchased a new pottery kiln for the school through a 'matching grant' with a club in Canada. Additionally, with the Friends and Rhodes University's Community Engagement Programme acting as facilitators, unremunerated short-term volunteers had visited the school for stays of anywhere between two weeks and one year from South Africa, Sweden, America, Australia, the UK, and Canada. Mary told me that two volunteers had recently visited as part of the "experiential programme" of the United Society for the Propagation of the Gospel (USPG, formerly SPG). This organisation has been "sending missionary workers [to South Africa] for over three hundred years", said Mary. The school also received lottery grants, most notably when a UK-based supporter paid for Joyce to attend a training day regarding the application procedure. During our first ever conversation, Mary informed me that this 'third-party support' meant Ngomso delivered something "over and above" the 'mainstream school offering'. Given my knowledge of the provisions available to learners at schools in the location, it is hard not to agree with her.

Although these forms of inter-organisational partnership fit within the CSTL model, they were by no means as widespread or extensive elsewhere. Indeed, although Mary and Joyce certainly welcomed Mrs Noni, whose stipend was funded by the CSTL programme, beyond this conviviality, they were sure that the DoE's plans had not materialised sufficiently because mainstream schools did not care for vulnerable learners. As Mary put it, "There is not mainstream inclusion going on but mainstream dumping, [because] they don't get the support that they need there".[43] Similarly, Mrs Noni told me about a young lady enrolled at a primary school in the location who no longer wanted to go to school because "others were teasing her" because she could not afford school shoes. Having explained that her school had not offered assistance, Mrs Noni said, "They are not interested in the soul; they don't care [about their learners]". Mary told me she would be "delighted if there was no need for a school like Ngomso". However, as it was, she was adamant that there was a need.

Ultimately, it was DoE policy to limit the number of special schools by ensuring all mainstream schools become capable of addressing moderate barriers to learning (see DoE 2005, 2010).[44] This ambition ties in with a globalised discourse that is traceable to the South African Schools Act (DoE 1996)[45] and a UN World Conference in 1994, which raised concerns about the cost of special schools and discrimination.[46] In line with this institutionalised train of thought, Nonkozo, my interlocutor from the Inclusive Education sector of the DoE, suggested that Ngomso learners should be in mainstream schools under the guidance of staff who would assist them by "embracing them" and "nurturing them", much like the model promoted at Ngomso. However, she recognised this wasn't happening because "classes are overpopulated" and "the teachers are unable to work with individuals, as their needs [warrant]". Recognising that her initial suggestion was, therefore, misplaced, she then proposed a course of action that followed departmental policy for learners "requiring moderate support" (DoE 2001: 15).[47] "[Ngomso] should be a full-service school", she said. In effect, these are mainstream schools that have more resources than 'ordinary mainstream schools' but are not as specialised as special schools. However, this proposal did not marry with the situation either: there were no full-service schools in the district, ten years after relevant plans were first laid out in DoE policy. The departmental policies that Nonkonzo saw as an ideal had not materialised, as she recognised herself (also see Engelbrecht 2006; Ngcobo and Muthukrishna 2011; Pather 2011; Pillay and Di Terlizzi 2009). This disjuncture between idealised, proposed scenarios and the situational reality of South Africa's system of schooling created space for experiences of uncertainty and ethical imaginations of alternative solutions, which might explain why Nonkonzo and some of her colleagues at the DoE vacillatingly gave support to Ngomso.

My interlocutors at Ngomso were adamant that the 'multisectoral' approach of the CSTL model did not reflect the day-to-day reality of how learners were cared for by other government agencies, despite the considerable expansion of the national welfare system (see Patel 2005). When Holly shared a PowerPoint presentation from a DoE workshop she had attended about the CSTL programme with Mary and Joyce, Joyce flicked through it and said, "They talk about it but don't see that it is implemented". A speaker had told Holly that schools should contact the Department of Social Development so that learners could be wormed. "We can work with them to get the [learners'] grants and ID [documents] too", she said. "It's easy to go there", replied Mary, "but not easy to get these things from them". She said it was simply "quicker to do things ourselves" and "better for us to try first and then involve the DoE if it doesn't work out". I knew that she had attempted to work alongside other departments in the past. However, it was apparent that a productive 'multisectoral' approach remained elusive. For instance, a relationship with a social worker from the Department of Social Development petered out after several meetings, leaving Mary and Joyce questioning her commitment. The social worker complained to me about her bulging workload, poorly trained colleagues whose mistakes she had to rectify, lack of funding, and preference for working with infants rather than teenagers.

In 2013, Mary told me a story that suggested this interdepartmental relationship had not improved. A learner had witnessed somebody stab his mother's boyfriend to death in the family home. Mary then explained how events developed:

> Another boyfriend was jealous she had been with another man and came round to kill her [but didn't find her].... The community then blamed her for having two boyfriends and said they needed blood from two families, so went looking for the mother. She went into hiding, so they threatened the children and were going to hurt them to get back at her.

When Mary had called the Department for Social Development, she was informed that the social worker responsible was "away for two days" and invited to "call back another time". As she recounted this conversation, Mary shook her head and repeated the words "call back another time", as though she wanted me to understand the implication of the instruction. "I mean", she continued, "the children were threatened with murder; there is no caring with civil servants". The son, who was not at Ngomso, went to stay at the Shelter and the learner and her younger sister spent two nights at Mary's home.

In her moving account of those living with HIV in rural KwaZulu-Natal, Patricia Henderson (2012: 30) writes:

> Care is not one thing, nor is it stable. It is ongoing work, a commitment in which some people succeed and others fail to sustain one another and themselves, and in which the state is sometimes absent and sometimes present, but seldom reliable.

Much like their responses to concerns about learners' parents and caregivers, staff at Ngomso set out to fill the vacuums of care left by other ineffective, inappropriate, absent or inferior State agencies, including other schools. As in the example above, this regularly meant that they pushed ahead to find solutions without the assistance of other departments of government. This observation and the school's partnerships with FBOs strengthens Bornstein and Redfield's (2008: np) claim that "In the case of weak or deteriorating states, religious organizations at times fill gaps of responsibility for the social welfare of citizens". However, in the case of Ngomso, individuals absorbed responsibilities as government employees and individuals funded by charitable support. As their intervention was driven by their Christianised ethical imaginations, more than some form of enthusiasm for following government protocol, my interlocutors frequently strayed from their remit, as prescribed by official policy and the directives of the DoE, inventing their own, pioneering methods. As one visitor from the district office of the DoE put it: "The school is abnormal. The way that it functions is abnormal." Joyce once said, "We are a *special*, special school". For members of staff, this institutional uniqueness positively evidenced their record of going above and beyond the call of duty. For those at the DoE, tasked with building an inclusive system of schooling more broadly, this scenario represented an affront to efforts to consolidate practices and procedures during the post-apartheid transition, which underpinned much of the debate regarding the suitability and capabilities of mainstream schools and the desirability of Ngomso's existence.

During a conversation in her office, Dr Pienaar concisely described the two sides of the 'institutional abnormality' coin:

> [At Ngomso] other departments do render service, but it is initiated by the school. And [yet] the policy says that it should be initiated by the Department of Social Development, because it is, in essence, a social problem, not an education problem. [This] is one of the reasons why the Eastern Cape Department [of Education] says that Ngomso shouldn't be a special school... But we can't take away the fact that what happens at Ngomso is pioneering work in a lot of ways.

Those who valued regulatory legislation and policy as a conceptualisation of what *ought* to happen, over and above any other moral framework (e.g. the Christian discourses most valued by Mary and her staff), were reluctant to support the Ngomso's special school status and the related additional funding. Much like the stigmatic judgements of its learners, in their eyes, the school was teetering beyond the brink of acceptable degrees of marginality. They encountered 'institutional uniqueness' with scepticism and concern. As I argued in the previous chapter, this same predicament was also integral to the stigma that learners faced every day. Underpinning all of these dynamics was the uneven and, in the eyes of many, unsatisfactory materialisation of South Africa's schooling system during the post-apartheid period. That said, to my mind, the key driver of the scenario was discordant action and idealisations relating to conflicting moral dispositions (i.e. individualised embodiments of an assemblage of moral discourses): variations in the degree to which individuals believed they were accountable to God and responsible for being a conduit for the delivery of His love or accountable to the government that employed them and responsible for fashioning the policies and programmes of the Department of Education. That such a situation should exist at all is evidence of the long-standing, often tempestuous and always ambiguous, relationship between the power of the Church and the power of the State in South Africa. This dynamic most relevantly first emerged during the colonial period when mission schools began to receive government grants[48] and continually emerges when religiously motivated educators similarly secure resources from the state in order to fund their missions.

Notes

1. There was dialogue between parents and the school, however. During a parents' evening for example, Joyce encouraged the parents and caregivers in the audience (approximately ten individuals) to take more responsibility for learners' education and welfare outside of school. More generally, parents frequently came to the school, but rarely because they had been invited by members of staff. Instead, like many of the learners, they appeared to visit when there was a problem that the school could assist with. For instance, on several occasions, when a parent or caregiver wanted to communicate something to the Police Service, such as a missing child or an incident of violence at home, they came to the school first so that staff could act as a conduit, especially because of the school's links with Maleku and her colleagues at the local station. As another example, when a learner was arrested for his part in a violent robbery, the mother came to the school to discuss his imprisonment.
2. For some individuals, especially those without 'active' parents or caregivers, Ngomso staff acted in loco parentis during such events.
3. This assertion is reflected in the fact that, generally speaking, the shelter boys attended school more regularly than other learners. Relatedly, many Ngomso learners who matriculated from high school had stayed at the Shelter at some stage and often for many years. As they recognised it themselves, staying in the Shelter—where movements were controlled (e.g. mandatory visits to the cathedral every Sunday) and various after-school activities encouraged school-related learning—increased one's commitment to schooling and the likelihood of matriculation.
4. Thaddeus Metz and Joseph Gaie (2010: 274, 273, emphasis in original) draw attention to "*an* (not *the*) African theory of morality", which they call "'Afro-communitarianism'" and relate to the notion of 'ubuntu'. Metz (2007: 341) argues that this conceptualisation of morality focuses on "relationships, as opposed to self-development". In line with this idea, I'm suggesting that women who are not biologically mothers to young people may be considered to have a relational basis for taking some form of responsibility for their personal development. Hence, they may be called 'Mama' in acknowledgement of the idea that parental-type responsibilities befall all adults.
5. Ashforth (2005: 85) offers an interesting discussion of how discourses concerning ubuntu differ from Christian notions of 'brotherly love'. My statement should not be read as a statement that one was in evidence while the other was not, I am simply saying that each discourse was prevalent but that their influence was often ambiguous.
6. I will link my interlocutors' enactments of care and concern for others to the notion of 'agape', or '*agapē*' (or '*ἀγάπη*') on several further occasions,

and will define particular qualities of Christianised appropriations of *agapē* in more detail where appropriate. For the moment, I employ the word to connote the Christian imperative to unconditionally and unselfishly provide charitable love to others as an enactment of one's love for God (i.e. taking Him to heart), in acknowledgement of His love for humankind on earth and in Heaven. As Spicq (2006: v) puts it: "It is impossible ... to read the word agape in any of the apostolic writings without becoming aware of its extremely full theological content. The most practical moral exhortations make sense only if their call to love refers to God's own charity and its infusion into the Christian's heart."

7. For instance, Ramusack (2005: np) has spoken about the 'civilising missions' of British women, or "maternal imperialists", in India: "like many mothers, [they] adopted a mother-knows-best attitude and, like most imperialists, used their power to impose ideas and programs on their daughters [i.e. Indian women]". Allman (1994) argues that British missionaries attempted to teach 'Christianised motherhood' while 'mothering' women in Ashanti (now Ghana).

8. In Australia, during the 1920s, there were very public and institutional moral discourses that hinged upon the judgement that 'half-caste' or 'part-European' children were growing up in a "filthy, immoral, superstitious, and degraded Aboriginal world" (Manne 2004: 225). These judgements were employed to justify practices of 'child removal' (i.e. of Aboriginal children from their families). This practice began in the late nineteenth century and continued into the 1970s. Practices before the First World War were driven by "ideas about the biological absorption of mixed-descent Aborigines", and post-war ideas were more concerned with "the possibility of their assimilation" (ibid: 217). Events in Australia should not be compared to those in South Africa without acknowledging the fact that the removal of children from the care of parents was legislated by the Australian Parliament according to ideas of racial purity, in a biological rather than cultural sense, much more extensively than was the case in South Africa. In Australia, policies and practices, particularly during the pre-war period, were concerned with "the elimination of Australia's Aboriginal population" (ibid: 220) and 'breeding out the colour' of 'half-caste' children (Jacobs 2006: 214). I hope it is clear that I am not suggesting anything I witnessed during my fieldwork is equivalent to such events.

9. The quotations in this sentence are taken from Jacobs (2009: 288). Jacobs (ibid.) is quoting directly from the following sources: M.H. Ellis, *Black Australia. Alice Springs Bungalow. A Place of Squalid Horror*, clipping from Adelaide Advertiser, n.d. [ca. 1924]; *Clipping, Honoured by Royalty*, ca. 1929, in Scrapbook and Visitor's Book, Ida Standley; and *Royal Recognition*, Melbourne Herald, November 9, 1929.

10. The quotations in this sentence are taken from Jacobs (2009: 288). Jacobs (ibid.) is quoting directly from the following sources: *Mother of Alice Springs*, Smith's Weekly (Sydney), July 13, 1929; and, *The 'Beloved Lady' of Alice Springs*, Melbourne Herald, May 31, 1929.
11. The Xhosa referred to such individuals, and those involved in the missions more broadly, as *umfundisi* or 'teacher' (SPG 1858: 15). "The ambiguity of the term [*umfundisi*] was fitting", argues S. Davies (2010: 96), "for it encompassed both ... efforts to impart the Christian doctrine and (in order to facilitate Xhosa conversion) more conventional instruction in the form of literacy and numeracy."
12. Initially, missionaries were effectively under the rule (and protection) of Xhosa chiefs and their influence was intertwined with political contestation between them (Erlank 1999: 9). Xhosa men brought into the Clergy were in a position of novel allegiance and influence (Mills 1995). When those who identified with a Xhosa heritage began to missionise, and congregations of converts expanded, any clear distinction between Xhosa and missionaries, or an articulation of solidity and uniformity within these groups, dissolved.
13. Robert's diaries were first compiled and edited in the 1950s, and the editor also attended to much writing by Robert's wife and correspondence between family members. Mary gave me a copy of the second edition of the book, which has been edited further by another relation. Throughout this book I use the 'Anonymous' reference style to maintain anonymity.
14. Citations from this period refer to the "Kafir location", an area of land to the east of Grahamstown's centre. As Pettman (1913: 298) explained some decades later: "In the Eastern Province of the Cape Colony, the 'location' is a portion of land set apart by a municipality somewhere on the outskirts of the town, upon which natives are allowed, under certain regulations, to reside." This locality would later also be known as 'the township'.
15. In February of 1855, Armstrong (cited in Carter 1857: 314) wrote to Rev. E. Hawkins, the then secretary of the SPG, about his plan for "The formation of a school in the Kafir location close to Grahamstown." He (ibid.) continues: "Mr. Lange, lately a Berlin missionary, a most excellent man, whom I ordained at Christmas, and who has a perfect knowledge of the Kafir character and language, has offered to take charge of the proposed school of Kafirs at the outskirts of Grahamstown; and as we propose making it a kind of chapel-school, he will also hold divine service in it on Sunday." Armstrong died in the May of 1856. Robert Miller received Lange, along with Bishop Cotterill, Bishop Armstrong's successor, at his mission station on the 20th of August 1858 (Anonymous).

16. The connotation of the word 'Kafir' or 'Kaffir', as used at the time, was 'unbeliever' and related to the non-Christian and non-Muslim belief systems that Europeans and Arabs (who initiated usage of the word in Eastern Africa) encountered in Southern Africa. While this word is historically important, it is now a term of racial abuse and I do not use it outside of direct historical quotation.
17. Colonial missionaries have been criticised for serving to establish economic and labour inequalities, subordination based on gender or race, supporting imperialism, cultural domination and the decimation of 'indigenous cultures', and using their activities to benefit themselves materially (Christie 1991; van der Walt 1992). Some authors, like A. Lewis and Steyn (2003: 103), suggest that missionaries negated "indigenous people's cultural identities" and education practices and set out to use their own educational practices to "replace" them (also see Abdi 2002, 2006; Deliwe 1992: 50–69; Keto 1990). A full analysis of such arguments is clearly beyond the scope of this book. However, it is important that the explicitly political and moralistic nature of their endeavour is acknowledged.
18. Thomson's (cited in Ashley 1974: 201) phrase "disciplining of the disposition" reminded me of Foucault's (1982) theorisation. In particular, I recalled Foucault's play on "the double meaning in French of the verb conduire, 'to lead' or 'to drive', and se conduire, 'to behave' or 'to conduct oneself'" (Sawyer (translator), cited in Foucault 1982: 789). Moreover, conducting others, as with the process of disciplining, is to lead or guide them, which is akin to the ducere component of the Latin educare (to educate); and the notion of conducting oneself is akin to the notion of being disciplined.
19. Clifton Crais (1992: 211) argues that "The drought of 1862 was the worst in the living memories of both African and European in the Eastern Cape. This time of want when corn withered on the stalks and stock died a slow death occurred during a more general economic crisis in the Cape Colony."
20. Jennie's willingness to give food away might be compared to Neil Cooper's (cited in Oord 2005: 932) example of two men in the desert pass a cup of water between themselves – each altruistically wanting the other to drink first – until the water in the cup evaporates in the sun, killing them both. This story highlights something that Robert seemed to recognise: the limit to altruism is imposed by the imperative to sustain the self.
21. Bishop Armstrong established the 'Native Branch' and the main section of the school. Armstrong was also responsible for Zonnebloem or the 'Kaffir College' in Cape Town, founded in 1858, which similarly aimed to educate a 'new black elite' (Collis 2013: 6). These institutions laid foundations for the school educations of many leading figures in South African politics and literature.

22. Their family home is, at the time of writing, still fully integrated into the facilities of the private school.
23. The first branch of the Ladies Benevolent Society was established by Mary Philip, the wife of a minister in Cape Town, in 1822 and it is perhaps the oldest charitable/philanthropic organisation in South Africa (Bradlow 1991).
24. Frankena (cited in Oord 2005: 931) defines agapē as "the principle of benevolence, that is, of doing good". The Ladies Benevolent Society, which was founded by Christian women, might therefore be understood as an organised, collective enactment of agapeic love.
25. This claim is less clear-cut when the emergence of government grants to mission schools during the latter half of the nineteenth century is considered (discussed in more detail in the previous chapter). However, even during this period, the formalisation of curricula and government targets was not nearly as extensive as it was during the course of my research.
26. For example, Bradford (2012: xii) discusses a Xhosa who "fashioned new definitions of ... [his] own 'nativeness,' given ... [his] status as [a] Christian ... [missionary] with ties to a global British Empire". Mills (1995) details early ordinations of Xhosa to the ministry in the Cape Colony and argues that this played an important role in the reactions to Christianity that followed.
27. An important parallel is the "form and function of international protection measures for refugee children", as described by Andrew Epstein (2010: 21). Practices such as "education and repatriation" are "intended not only as a shield from further harm engendered by their age and homelessness, but also to commence a path back to normalcy by repair from within" (ibid). Whereas refugee children may return to their 'home countries' once this process of repair is completed (subject to political and security conditions), Ngomso learners could return to mainstream schools.
28. Williams and Zigon use 'moral' and 'ethics' differently, as do many anthropologists (Zigon and Throop 2014: 12). This is because Zigon's theoretical and methodological framework draws inspiration from Foucault, who differs from Williams in his articulation of the relationship between ethics and morality (Laidlaw 2013: 180).
29. This began to happen during my visit in 2013, when I sold some pieces to members of my host Rotary Club. Part of the funds went back to the school, to help pay for materials, and the potters kept the rest. The problem with this arrangement, for the young men in question anyway, was the inconsistency of income.
30. Fort England Hospital, based in Grahamstown, is arguably the country's leading forensic hospital. However, it could only offer 'therapy' in Afrikaans or English, but not isiXhosa. Mary and Joyce felt this compounded the issue.

31. The line between psychology and counselling is not as clear-cut as this statement might suggest. The national statutory body, the Health Professions Council of South Africa, recognises counselling as one of five categories of registration in psychology, and professional registration most often follows the completion of an honours degree in psychology and internship training (Republic of South Africa 2003).
32. It is perhaps unsurprising that the "Christ-centred, Biblically based, and God honouring" *Association for Christian Counsellors in SA* (2014: np)—which does not have statutory power but offers training to its members, having been formed in 1993 following the lead of the *American Association of Christian Counsellors*—speaks of trauma and emotional wellness, in tandem with the belief that "the Holy Spirit is the agent of regeneration and renewal for believers in Jesus Christ". The conflation of enthusiasms for spiritual, moral, and psychological transformation is evident.
33. One of my colleagues at the school in London where I used to work pointed me in the direction of this text before I began to study for my PhD. Although he himself had relevant qualifications, he was worried that other members of staff, most especially teachers, were appropriating relevant knowledge and practices without having the necessary level of experience and professionalism. In their hands, he was concerned that psychotherapy could have unexpected and damaging consequences.
34. Although Armstrong does not acknowledge a source, the latter part of his statement appears to draw from Ephesians (3:19): "and to know this love that surpasses [or passeth] knowledge—that you may be filled to the measure of all the fullness of God". His words reflect wider discourses prevalent at the time. "Together with the assumption of western superiority"—argue A. Lewis and Steyn (2003: 103) in their discussion of the foundations of mission education in South Africa—"went the conviction that God had chosen missionaries to 'bring the Christian light to heathen countries', known as manifest destiny".
35. I find it interesting that the word 'enlighten' can be employed to both assert the idea that something akin to illumination is central to experiences of spiritualisation and promote reasoning counter to religion, for example, the 'Age of Enlightenment'. In other words, the analogy of illumination can be employed to describe differing experiences of knowing (i.e. of feeling knowledgeable about reality or truth). Further, to enlighten someone is to educate them. Following this linguistic trail, religious conversion might be understood as being an outcome of educative, illuminating, experiences.
36. In this particular passage, the word ἀτάκτους, the accusative masculine plural form of ἀτάκτος ('ἀτακτους' 2015), is, in the first instance, directed towards soldiers who do not remain in rank and file, then to individuals

who do not comply with regulations, and finally to members of the Thessalonian church who not apply themselves to their calling and have instead become ideal and disorderly ('Thessalonians 5:14', 2015).

37. The website of the Church of England ('Pastoral Services, Introduction' 2015: np), which offers guidance on pastoral services, provides a useful build to my ethnographic observation: "Salvation, wholeness, healing and peace with God are part of the same family of words, revealing the same essential theological themes as both incarnation and crucifixion: vulnerability and powerlessness, identification and suffering, being put right, made whole and restored as part of a new creation." For instance, in Matthew (9:22), Jesus heals a woman who has been bleeding for 12 years. The Greek account uses the word 'ἐσώθη' (was saved) to describe the women's transformation. In contrast, the New International Version of the Bible uses the words "was healed" to describe it, and the King James Version uses the words "was made whole". Between these different versions of the same passage, it is clear to see how Christian notions of saviour, healing, and wholeness intertwine.

38. Crucially, the Christian notion of 'healing', discussed here in relation to the image of broken bones, can relate to both physical and spiritual repair/health (Church of England 2015), as per the account of the healed women discussed in the previous footnote.

39. In the early seventeenth century, John Gore (cited in Beier 1987: 51) said that 'masterless' vagrants were "children of Belial, without God, without magistrate, without minister". The origin of the word 'Belial' is the Hebrew *bəlīyya`al*, a composite of *bəlīy*, meaning 'without', and *ya`al*, meaning 'worth' ('Belial' 2014).

40. The Latin word *educare* is constructed from two words: *ex* and *ducere*, where *ex* means 'from, out of, from within' and *ducere* means 'to lead, conduct, guide'. So the word *educare*, which became 'educate', refers to the idea of 'guiding out from within' or 'leading out' ('Educate' 2015).

41. MIET Africa is not Christian oriented in its publicity or programme material; however, given the similarity between the aims of my interlocutors at Ngomso and those at MIET Africa, it is worth mentioning that their chairman was previously principal of the Cornerstone Institute (2014: np) in Cape Town, which "is a community of learning, committed to a Christ-centred, Biblically-shaped worldview, preparing leaders for service in churches and communities". MIET also partners with World Vision, the Christian-oriented NGO that Bornstein (2002, 2005) considers in her research on faith-driven development projects in East Africa.

42. The programme focuses upon nine "priorities" that the DoE is obligated to deliver: nutrition, health promotion, social welfare services, psychosocial support, safety and protection, curriculum support, co-curricular sup-

port, material support, and, finally, infrastructure, water, and sanitation (Department of Basic Education and MIET Africa 2010: 29).

43. Her observation aligns with this statement within the National Model for the CSTL programme: "In the absence of these basic provisions [of care and support], the education system in itself constitutes a barrier to learning" (DoE and MIET Africa 2010: 28).
44. In particular full-service schools were planned to cater for "barriers [that] might arise from factors within learners, such as impairments, psychosocial problems, different abilities, particular life experiences or socio-economic deprivations. [And] Barriers [that] might also be related to a learner's environment" (DoE 2005: 10).
45. Chapter 3, Section 12 (4), reads "The Member of the Executive Council must, where reasonably practicable, provide education for learners with special education needs at ordinary public schools and provide relevant educational support services for such learners" (DoE 1996).
46. In the preamble to departmental guidelines for full-service schools, the director general of the DoE confirms the importance of the Salamanca Statement of the UN (DoE 2010). This Statement (UNESCO 1994: viii) states "those with special educational needs must have access to regular schools which should accommodate them within a childcentered [*sic*] pedagogy capable of meeting these needs". The statement continues: "regular schools within this inclusive orientation are the most effective means of combating discriminatory attitudes, creating welcoming communities, building an inclusive society and achieving education for all; moreover, they provide an effective education to the majority of children and improve the efficiency and ultimately the cost-effectiveness of the entire education system" (ibid: ix).
47. The full quote from White Paper Six reads: "learners who require low-intensive support will receive this in ordinary schools and those requiring moderate support will receive this in full-service schools. Learners who require high-intensive educational support will continue to receive such support in special schools" (DoE 2001: 15).
48. Cape mission schools first received small amounts of State funding in 1841 (Lewis 1999). However, after the arrival of Sir George Grey in 1854, who was Governor and High Commissioner of the Cape Colony, these contributions were made to look insignificant. Grey oversaw the expansion of State-funded grants to mission schools, which began to proliferate as part of his 'pacification policy' (Hodgson 1997; Molteno 1984; Morrell 1969). For Anglican missionaries, who did not otherwise have finance in abundance, the grants were a welcome aid to their efforts to convert the Xhosa (Mostert 1992: 1167). However, one cannot assume that this new partnership represented cohesion of ideology or motivation between the mis-

sionaries and the colonial government. In this case, as with others, "acquiescent neutrality [in response to colonial policy] may have been the price to be paid for the opportunity to proselytise" (MacKenzie 1993: 49). The ambiguous relationship between State and Church did not end with the new deal: while the missionaries welcomed funds, they maintained much influence over what happened in the schools.

BIBLIOGRAPHY

Abdi, A. A. (2002). *Culture, Education, and Development in South Africa: Historical and Contemporary Perspectives.* Westport: Bergin and Garvey.

Abdi, A. A. (2006). Culture of Education, Social Development, and Globalization: Historical and Current Analyses of Africa. In A. Abdi, K. P. Puplampu, & G. J. Sefa Dei (Eds.), *African Education and Globalization: Critical Perspectives* (pp. 13–30). Oxford: Lexington Books.

Agamben, G. (2005). *State of Exception.* Chicago: University of Chicago Press.

Allman, J. (1994). Making Mothers: Missionaries, Medical Officers, and Women's Work in Colonial Asante, 1924–45. *History Workshop Journal, 38,* 23–47.

Anonymous. Details omitted in order to maintain anonymity of interlocutors.

Ashforth, A. (2005). *Witchcraft, Violence, and Democracy in South Africa.* Chicago: University of Chicago Press.

Ashley, M. (1974). African Education and Society in the Nineteenth Century Eastern Cape. In C. Saunders & R. Derricourt (Eds.), *Beyond the Cape Frontier* (pp. 199–212). London: Longman.

Association of Christian Counsellors in South Africa. (2014). *ACC in SA (Homepage).* Retrieved January 18, 2013, from http://www.accinsa.co.za/

ἀτάκτους. (2015). *Glosbe, The Multilingual Online Dictionary.* Retrieved May 24, 2015, from https://glosbe.com/el/en/%CE%AC%CF%84%CE%B1%CE%BA %CF%84%CE%BF%CF%85%CF%82

Beier, A. (1987). *Masterless Men: Vagrancy Problem in Britain, 1560–1640.* London: Methuen.

Belial. (2014). *The Collins English Dictionary* (Online). Retrieved April 11, 2014, from http://www.collinsdictionary.com/dictionary/english/belial?showCoo kiePolicy=true

Bordonaro, L. I. (2012). Children's Geographies Agency Does Not Mean Freedom. Cape Verdean Street Children and the Politics of Children's Agency. *Children's Geographies, 10*(4), 413–426.

Bornstein, E. (2002). Developing Faith: Theologies of Economic Development in Zimbabwe. *Journal of Religion in Africa, 32*(1), 4–31.

Bornstein, E. (2005). *The Spirit of Development: Protestant NGOs, Morality, and Economics in Zimbabwe.* Stanford: Stanford University Press.

Bornstein, E., & Redfield, P. (2008). *Genealogies of Suffering and the Gift of Care: A Working Paper on the Anthropology of Religion, Secularism, and Humanitarianism.* New York: Social Science Research Council Working Papers.

Bourgois, P. (2002). Understanding Inner-City Poverty: Resistance and Self-Destruction under U.S. Apartheid. In J. Macclancy (Ed.), *Exotic No More: Anthropology on the Front Lines* (pp. 15–32). Chicago: University of Chicago Press.

Bradford, T. (2012). *Prophetic Identities: Indigenous Missionaries on British Colonial Frontiers.* Vancouver: University of British Columbia Press.

Bradlow, E. (1991). 'The Oldest Charitable Society in South Africa': One Hundred Years and More of the Ladies' Benevolent Society at the Cape of Good Hope. *South African Historical Journal, 25*(1), 77–104.

Carter, R. T. T. (1857). *A Memoir of John Armstrong, D.D., Late Lord Bishop of Grahamstown.* Oxford/London: John Henry and James Parker.

Cheney, K. (2007). *Pillars of the Nation: Child Citizens and Ugandan National Development.* Chicago: University of Chicago Press.

Christie, P. (1991). *The Right to Learn: The Struggle for Education in South Africa.* Johannesburg: Sached Trust & Ravan.

Church of England. (2015). Wholeness and Healing, Theological Introduction. Retrieved September 18, 2015, from https://www.churchofengland.org/prayer-worship/worship/texts/pastoral/healing/healingintro.aspx

Collis, V. (2013). *Anxious Records: Race, Imperial Belonging, and the Black Literary Imagination, 1900–1946.* Unpublished Ph.D. dissertation, Department of English and Comparative Literature, Columbia University. Retrieved July 23, 2014, from http://academiccommons.columbia.edu/catalog/ac:161742

Comaroff, J., & Comaroff, J. (1986). Christianity and Colonialism in South Africa. *American Ethnologist, 13*(1), 1–22.

Comaroff, J., & Comaroff, J. (1997). *Of Revelation and Revolution, Volume 2: The Dialectics of Modernity on a South African Frontier.* Chicago: The University of Chicago Press.

Comaroff, J., & Comaroff, J. (2005). Reflections on Youth. In F. De Boeck & A. Honwana (Eds.), *Makers & Breakers: Children & Youth in Postcolonial Africa* (pp. 19–30). Trenton: Africa World Press.

Compretta, C. E. (2012). *Growing Gaps: Children's Experiences of Inequality in a Faith-Based Afterschool Program in the U.S. South.* Unpublished PhD Dissertation, College of Arts and Sciences (Department of Anthropology), University of Kentucky. Retrieved April 8, 2014, from http://uknowledge.uky.edu/anthro_etds/4/

Cornerstone Institute. (2014). *Cornerstone: Learn to Change the World.* Retrieved October 1, 2014, from http://www.cornerstone.ac.za/about.php

Crais, C. (1992). *White Supremacy and Black Resistance in Pre-industrial South Africa: The Making of the Colonial Order in the Eastern Cape, 1770–1865.* Cambridge: Cambridge University Press.

Davies, S. (2010). *History in the Literary Imagination: The Telling of Nongqawuse and the Xhosa Cattle-Killing in South African Literature and Culture (1891–1937).* Unpublished PhD Thesis, St John's College, University of Cambridge. Retrieved August 9, 2012, from https://www.repository.cam.ac.uk/handle/1810/238313

Dean, M. (2010). *Governmentality: Power and Rule in Modern Society.* London: Sage.

Deliwe, D. (1992). *Responses to Western Education Among the Conservative People of Transkei.* Unpublished MA Thesis, Department of Anthropology, Faculty of Humanities, Rhodes University.

Department of Education (DoE). (1996). *South African Schools Act No. 84 of 1996.* Retrieved June 12, 2013, from http://www.education.gov.za/LinkClick.aspx?fileticket=aIolZ6UsZ5U%3D&tabid=185&mid=1828

Department of Education (DoE). (2001). *Education White Paper 6: Special Needs Education, Building an Inclusive Education and Training System.* Retrieved June 16, 2014, from http://www.education.gov.za/LinkClick.aspx?fileticket=gVFccZLi/tI=

Department of Education (DoE). (2005). *Conceptual and Operational Guidelines for the Implementation of Inclusive Education: Full-Service Schools.* Retrieved March 14, 2013, from http://www.education.gov.za/LinkClick.aspx?fileticket=LgU29rjb2Hg%3D&tabid=452&mid=1036

Department of Education (DoE). (2010). *Guidelines for Full-Service/Inclusive Schools.* Retrieved March 12, 2013, from http://www.education.gov.za/LinkClick.aspx?fileticket=WbxRkIOFaok%3D&tabid=617&mid=2372

Department of Education (DoE) & MIET Africa. (2010). *National Support Pack.* Retrieved June 30, 2012, from http://www.education.gov.za/LinkClick.aspx?fileticket=TPD7RfXMw/U%3D&tabid=675&mid=2517

Eccelstone, K., & Hayes, D. (2009). *The Dangerous Rise of Therapeutic Education.* Abingdon: Routledge.

Educate. (2015). *Online Etymology Dictionary.* Retrieved January 11, 2015, from http://www.etymonline.com/index.php?allowed_in_frame=0&search=educate

Elisha, O. (2008). Moral Ambitions of Grace: The Paradox of Compassion and Accountability in Evangelical Faith-Based Activism. *Cultural Anthropology, 23*(1), 154–189.

Engelbrecht, P. (2006). The Implementation of Inclusive Education in South Africa after Ten Years of Democracy. *European Journal of Psychology of Education, 21*(3), 253–264.

Ennew, J. (2002). Future Generations and Global Standards: Children's Rights at the Start of the Millennium. In J. MacClancy (Ed.), *Exotic No More.*

Anthropology on the Front Lines (pp. 338–358). Chicago: University of Chicago Press.

Ennew, J., & Swart-Kruger, J. (2003). Introduction: Homes, Places and Spaces in the Construction of Street Children and Street Youth. *Children, Youth and Environments, 13*(1). Retrieved July 25, 2012, from http://www.colorado.edu/journals/cye

Epstein, A. (2010). Education Refugees and the Spatial Politics of Childhood Vulnerability. *Childhood in Africa, 2*(1), 16–25.

Erlank, N. (1999). Re-examining Initial Encounters Between Christian Missionaries and the Xhosa, 1820–1850: The Scottish Case. *Kleio, 31*, 6–32.

Fassin, D., & Rechtman, R. (2009). *The Empire of Trauma*. Princeton: Princeton University Press.

Foucault, M. (1976). *Mental Illness and Psychology*. New York: Harper Colophon Books.

Foucault, M. (1982). The Subject and Power. *Critical Inquiry, 8*(4), 777.

Foucault, M. (2008). In M. Senellart (Ed.), *The Birth of Biopolitics: Lectures at the Collège de France, 1978–1979*. New York: Palgrave Macmillan.

Fraser, G. (2008). On the Genealogy of Morals, Part 4: Is Christianity Cowardly? *The Guardian* (Online). Retrieved May 11, 2012, from http://www.theguardian.com/commentisfree/belief/2008/nov/17/philosophy-religion

Heathen. (2014). *Oxford Dictionaries* (Online). Retrieved May 15, 2015, from http://www.oxforddictionaries.com/definition/english/heathen?q=heathen

Henderson, P. (2012). *A Kinship of Bones: AIDS, Intimacy and Care in Rural KwaZulu-Natal*. Scottsville: University of KwaZulu-Natal Press.

Hlatshwayo, S. (2000). *Education and Independence: Education in South Africa, 1658–1988*. London: Greenwood Press.

Hodgson, J. (1997). A Battle for Sacred Power: Christian Beginnings Among the Xhosa. In R. Elphick & R. Davenport (Eds.), *Christianity in South Africa: A Political, Social and Cultural History* (pp. 68–88). Los Angeles: University of California Press.

Humphrey, C. (1997). Exemplars and Rules: Aspects of the Discourse of Moralities in Mongolia. In S. Howell (Ed.), *The Ethnography of Moralities* (pp. 25–48). London: Routledge.

Jackson, M. (1995). *At Home in the World*. Durham: Duke University Press.

Jacobs, M. D. (2006). Indian Boarding Schools in Comparative Perspective: The Removal of Indigenous Children in the United States and Australia, 1880–1940. In C. Trafzer, J. Keller, & L. Sisquoc (Eds.), *Boarding School Blues: Revisiting American Indian Educational Experiences*. Lincoln: University of Nebraska Press.

Jacobs, M. D. (2009). *White Mother to a Dark Race: Settler Colonialism, Maternalism, and the Removal of Indigenous Children in the American West and Australia, 1880–1940*. Lincoln: University of Nebraska Press.

Keto, C. (1990). Pre-industrial Education Policies and Practices in South Africa. In M. Nkomo (Ed.), *Pedagogy of Domination* (pp. 19–42). Trenton: Africa World Press.

Laidlaw, J. (2013). Ethics. In J. Boddy & M. Lambek (Eds.), *A Companion to the Anthropology of Religion* (pp. 171–188). Chichester: Wiley.

Lester, A. (2001). *Imperial Networks: Creating Identities in Nineteenth Century South Africa.* London: Routledge.

Lewis, A. (1999). *Past and Present Perceptions Surrounding Mission Education: A Historical Metabletical Overview.* Unpublished D.Ed. Thesis, Stellenbosch University. Retrieved May 02, 2012, from http://scholar.sun.ac.za/handle/10019.1/16104

Lewis, A., & Steyn, J. (2003). A Critique of Mission Education in South Africa According to Bosch's Mission Paradigm Theory. *South African Journal of Education, 23*(2), 101–106.

Lutkehaus, N. (1999). Missionary Maternalism: Gendered Images of the Holy Spirit Sisters in Colonial New Guinea. In M. Taylor Huber & N. Lutkehaus (Eds.), *Gendered Missions: Women and Men in Missionary Discourse and Practice* (pp. 207–235). Ann Arbor: The University of Michigan Press.

MacKenzie, C. G. (1993). Demythologising the Missionaries: A Reassessment of the Functions and Relationships of Christian Missionary Education Under Colonialism. *Comparative Education, 29*(1), 45–66.

Manne, R. (2004). Aboriginal Child Removal and the Question of Genocide, 1900–1940. In A. Moses (Ed.), *Genocide and Settler Society: Frontier Violence and Stolen Indigenous Children in Australian History* (pp. 217–243). New York/London: Berghahn Books.

Mayer, P. (1961). *Townsmen or Tribesmen: Conservatism and the Process of Urbanization in a South African City* (with Contributions by Iona Mayer). Oxford/Cape Town: Oxford University Press.

Metz, T. (2007). Toward an African Moral Theory. *Journal of Political Philosophy, 15*(3), 321–341.

Metz, T., & Gaie, J. B. R. (2010). The African Ethic of Ubuntu/Botho: Implications for Research on Morality. *Journal of Moral Education, 39*(3), 273–290.

Mills, W. G. (1995). Missionaries, Xhosa Clergy and the Suppression of Traditional Customs. In H. Bredenkamp & R. Ross (Eds.), *Mission and Christianity in South African History* (pp. 153–171). Johannesburg: Witwatersrand University Press.

Molteno, F. (1984). The Historical Foundations of the Schooling of Black South Africans. In P. Kallaway (Ed.), *Apartheid and Education: The Education of Black South Africans* (pp. 45–107). Johannesburg: Raven Press.

Morrell, W. (1969). *British Colonial Policy in the Mid-Victorian Age: South Africa, New Zealand, the West Indies.* Oxford: Oxford University Press.

Mostert, N. (1992). *Frontiers: The Epic of South Africa's Creation and the Tragedy of the Xhosa People*. New York: Knopf.
Mother. (2014). *Glosbe: The Multilingual Online Dictionary*. Retrieved March 4, 2014, from http://glosbe.com/en/xh/mother
Ngcobo, J., & Muthukrishna, N. (2011). The Geographies of Inclusion of Students with Disabilities in an Ordinary School. *South African Journal of Education, 31*(3), 357–368.
Nietzsche, F. (1994). In K. Ansell-Pearson (Ed.), *On the Genealogy of Morality*. Cambridge: Cambridge University Press.
O'Neill, K. L. (2015). *Secure the Soul: Christian Piety and Gang Prevention in Guatemala*. Berkeley: University of California Press.
Oord, J. (2005). The Love Racket: Defining Love. *Zygon, 40*(4), 919–938.
Patel, L. (2005). *Social Welfare and Social Development in South Africa*. Oxford: Oxford University Press.
Pather, S. (2011). Evidence on Inclusion and Support for Learners with Disabilities in Mainstream Schools in South Africa: Off the Policy Radar? *International Journal of Inclusive Education, 15*(10), 1103–1117.
Pettman, C. (1913). *Africanderisms: A Glossary of South African Colloquial Words and Phrases and of Place and Other Names*. London: Longmans, Green and Co.
Pillay, J., & Di Terlizzi, M. (2009). A Case Study of a Learner's Transition from Mainstream Schooling to a School for Learners with Special Educational Needs (LSEN): Lessons for Mainstream Education. *South African Journal of Education, 29*, 491–509.
Poland, M. (2013). Graham House – Fifty Year Jubilee. *St. Andrew's College* (Online). Retrieved September 23, 2015, from http://www.oldandrean. co.za/uploads/files/graham_house_brochure_50th_final_(low_res).pdf
Prevost, E. E. (2010). *The Communion of Women: Missions and Gender in Colonial Africa and the British Metropole*. Oxford: Oxford University Press.
Ramusack, B. (2005). Q&A: Barbara Ramusack (Conducted by Billie Dziech). *University of Cincinnati* (Online). Retrieved September 17, 2015, from www.uc.edu/news/NR.aspx?id=6579
Republic of South Africa. (2003). *Health Professions Act 56 of 1974 Regulations Relating to the Registration of Registered Counsellors*. Retrieved June 24, 2013, from http://www.hpcsa.co.za/Uploads/editor/UserFiles/downloads/legislations/regulations/psychology/regulations/regulations_gnr1820_2003.pdf
Rydstrøm, H. (2003). *Embodying Morality: Growing Up in Rural Northern Vietnam*. Honolulu: University of Hawaii Press.
Seyer, I. (2002). *Smart on the Under, Wise to the Streets: Mapping the Landscapes of Urban Youth*. Unpublished PhD Dissertation, The School of Education, Stanford University.
Society for the Propagation of the Gospel (SPG). (1856). *The Global Missionary for 1856* (Vol. 6). London: Bell & Daldy.

Society for the Propagation of the Gospel (SPG). (1858). *The Global Missionary for 1858* (Vol. 8). London: Bell & Daldy.

Spicq, C. (2006). *Agape in the New Testament, Volume 2: Agape in the Epistles of St. Paul, the Acts of the Apostles and the Epistles of St. James, St. Peter, and St. Jude*. Eugene: Wipf and Stock.

Stambach, A. (2010). *Faith in Schools: Religion, Education and American Evangelicals in East Africa*. Stanford: Stanford University Press.

Stambach, A. (2011). Education and Evangelism in Africa. *Public Lecture* (Available Online). Retrieved July 25, 2012, from https://www.youtube.com/watch?v=pl9AhRwLjIo

Swartz, S. (2010). 'Moral Ecology' and 'Moral Capital': Tools Towards a Sociology of Moral Education from a South African Ethnography. *Journal of Moral Education, 39*(3), 305–327.

The Church of England. (2015). *Pastoral Services, Introduction*. Retrieved September 18, 2015, from https://www.churchofengland.org/prayer-worship/worship/texts/pastoral.aspx

The Salvation Army. (2014). *Social Work*. Retrieved March 23, 2012, from http://www.salvationarmy.org.uk/uki/HeritageSocialWork

Thessalonians 5:14. (2015). Bible Hub. Retrieved September 24, 2015, from http://biblehub.com/commentaries/1_thessalonians/5-14.htm

Tools With A Mission (TWAM). (2014). *About Tools with a Mission*. Retrieved July 15, 2014, from http://www.twam.co.uk/aboutus.html

United Nations Educational, Scientific and Cultural Organization (UNESCO). (1994). *The Salamanca Statement and Framework for Action on Special Needs Education*. Retrieved July 29, 2014, from http://www.unesco.org/education/pdf/SALAMA_E.PDF/

Vally, S., Dolombisa, Y., & Porteus, K. (2002). Violence in South African Schools. *Current Issues in Comparative Education, 2*, 80–90.

van der Walt, J. L. (1992). The Culturo-Historical and Personal Circumstances of Some 19th-Century Missionaries Teaching in South Africa. *Koers, 57*(1), 75–85.

Vaughan, M. K. (1992). Women School Teachers in the Mexican Revolution: The Story of Reyna's Braids. In C. Johnson-Odin & M. Strobel (Eds.), *Expanding the Boundaries of Women's History* (pp. 278–302). Bloomington/Indianapolis: Indiana University Press.

Weber, M. (1978). *Economy and Society: An Outline of Interpretive Sociology*. Los Angeles: University of California Press.

Weber, M. (1991). In H. H. Gerth & C. Wright Mills (Eds.), *From Max Weber: Essays in Sociology*. Abingdon: Routledge.

Williams, B. (1993). *Ethics and the Limits of Philosophy*. London: Fontana Press.

Wilson, M. (1971). *Religion and the Transformation of Society*. Cambridge: Cambridge University Press.

Zigon, J. (2007). Moral Breakdown and the Ethical Demand: A Theoretical Framework for an Anthropology of Moralities. *Anthropological Theory, 7*(2), 131–150.
Zigon, J. (2008). *Morality: An Anthropological Perspective*. Oxford: Berg.
Zigon, J. (2009). Within a Range of Possibilities: Morality and Ethics in Social Life. *Ethnos, 74*(2), 251–276.
Zigon, J. (2011). *'HIV Is God's Blessing': Rehabilitating Morality in Neoliberal Russia*. Berkeley: University of California Press.
Zigon, J., & Throop, C. J. (2014). Moral Experience: Introduction. *Ethos, 42*(1), 1–15.

CHAPTER 5

Promoting Specialness

In retrospect, it was telling that so many people informed me about Mary and the school during my first weeks in the city. Everyone seemed to know who she was and something about what the school did and who its learners were. None of the schools in the location was so prominently on the radar of residents of the town. Such awareness appeared to result from years of seemingly disparate events and communications that served to bring these 'kids from the location' across the railway tracks and into the town. For example, Ngomso learners ran with the former Model C schools and the private schools during a fun run in town one afternoon. No schools from the location did so. Their second-hand trainers, bare feet, and school shoes contrasted with the lightweight Asics and Nike running shoes of the other competitors. Residents of the Shelter were also invited to attend numerous events organised by university students, and the school had strong links with the Community Engagement Division at Rhodes. These events and relationships exposed the school and its learners to residents of the town, providing mechanisms through which they could offer support to young residents of the location, without having to set foot in the location itself.

Ngomso featured in the city's newspaper as frequently as schools based in the town while reports from schools in the location were rare. Although the school did not have a PR department, the intervention did not lack exposure, and this circulating public discourse was integral to the continued support that the school received. In 2013, Nomalizo and I were reading a

© The Author(s) 2018
O. Pattenden, *Taking Care of the Future*, Anthropological Studies of Education, https://doi.org/10.1007/978-3-319-69826-7_5

newspaper article about the school's celebration of Heritage Day. She was "frustrated" that it did not carry a photograph. She liked the wording but felt that the coverage was not as impactful as it might have been. Such media was integral to how the residents of Grahamstown perceived the school. Nomalizo appeared to recognise this and said, "we must [improve the way we] market our kids [and the school]". I had begun to think about how the fundraising efforts of my interlocutors at Ngomso related to my marketing and management degree and my experiences working in the advertising industry in London during my first visit to South Africa. Nomalizo's employment of related discourse told me that my interlocutors viewed their activity in a similar light.

I understand this process of 'marketing' as the imperative to inform external audiences about the school and its learners, while ensuring that this communication promoted particular imagery and ideas, in the interests of generating support and funds.[1] It overlaps with Bornstein's (2012: 73) analysis of "rituals of verification", whereby those who work on behalf of NGOs orchestrate performances "that validate the institution", lending credibility to claims of programmatic efficacy in spite of lacking resources when encouraging support and funding. In August 2011, for example, a representative of an organisation that supports school governors phoned to ask why the school had not renewed its membership. Mary informed him that the school didn't have the necessary funds. "[The school's] finances are tough, and [our DoE] subsidy is small", she said. Indeed, the learners had not been given their annual supply of new underwear as the requisite funding was not available. Mary told the caller about the predicament: "We must put the need to buy clothing for the children first, [before paying the membership fees]." When the district coordinator of the President's Award (South Africa's version of the Duke of Edinburgh's Award scheme that is prevalent in the UK) visited three days later to encourage the school to join the programme, Mary spoke about missing socks. Both men granted the school a concession.

I once drove to the house of a retired couple with Mary and Asanda, one of the teacher aides. The husband had been a librarian, and his wife had worked at the university. Mary knew them because they also entered the city's annual gardening competition. They were downsizing, before moving to Cape Town and had written a neat list of everything they planned to give to the school. We collected a BBC computer made in the year I was born. Mary hoped that it might be useful for maths or literacy games; however, as I struggled to set it up at the school, Mr Zamisa kindly said, "it belongs in a museum". When I told Mary, she said that she never refused a donation, for fear it would communicate the message that the school did not need assistance. Besides, anything the school didn't use was given to other local charities. Months later I helped to organise the overflowing donations cupboard. It took Daniel, a volunteer from the UK and later a trustee of the Friends, several weeks to categorise all the donated books that had lain in boxes for years; many were entirely unsuitable for the learners.

When managing the idea that the school was in need of assistance during such interactions with potential and existing supporters, members of staff frequently conveyed something about the judgements they made about learners' specialness and employed similarly subtle techniques of power. An article in the local paper states that "Ngomso caters for 130 children, including street children, who cannot be admitted to mainstream schools due to their disruptive behaviour" ('Talented and Proud' 2012). As I stated in Chap. 3, Joyce told journalism students, positioned to convey a depiction of the school to wider audiences, that Ngomso "[caters for] children from the streets, orphans and those with alcoholic parents". Other visitors to the school encountered similar descriptions and heard about learners' experiences of "sexual and domestic violence" and their "material deprivation", "psychosocial barriers", and "drug addictions". Such claims align with the judgements members of staff made about learners.

Fassin (2010: 17.42 minutes) argues that "moral sentiments enter the political sphere"—as they frequently did in the case of Ngomso—as a mode of governance that is not limited to "extreme and remote situations such as disaster areas, war zones, refugee camps, famines, epidemics", but is "also at work in misery close to home, whether it affects the homeless or the immigrant, women who have suffered violence, or children living in poverty, all conditions [that] are often referred to by the bureaucratic word 'vulnerability'". What I take from Fassin's work is the idea that the mobilisation of sentiment, as relates to identifications of vulnerability, is political when it results in the controlling or governance of particular populations. The discourses used to represent Ngomso's target beneficiaries (e.g. orphanhood, street children, addiction, etc.) were certainly employed to elicit moral sentiments and mobilise political interventions, most especially those members of staff enacted. These representations also reflect the stigmatic discourses learners regularly faced when engaging with members of the public in the local vicinity. In short, discourses that propelled the mission by generating empathy among certain audiences produced resistance to the mission from other parties. The fight to secure support from various parties was like a social version of Newton's third law of motion. The continued employment of sentiment-generating representations occurred with the learners' interests in mind, but materialised with unintended outcomes.

Mary kindly diverted past my house one morning so that I didn't have to cycle to school in the pouring rain. As I sat in the back seat of her old but reliable E-Class Mercedes, she told me about a seminar she had attended at Rhodes University the night before, regarding a research project about poverty in South Africa. She was frustrated that "street children were not discussed" because "they never are". She explained that she had pushed the issue by questioning one of the speakers, a lady representing the Department of Social Development, saying, "If they were dogs the SPCA would pick them up." To some extent this exchange relates to concerns regarding the capabilities of other government departments, also discussed in the previous chapter. However, here I want to attend more directly to the observation that notions of vulnerability are so explicitly central to this claim. The words "if they were dogs" invite comparison but also encourage renderings of alternative futures. The audience is invited to wonder: If they were dogs, would they be better off? What does it say about us, collectively if we have not done everything in our power to bring about such interventions? This technique of eliciting imaginings of alternative futures was employed extensively. For instance, in her submission to the Parliamentary Monitory Group Mary wrote:

> Many argue that they are a lost cause, beyond help, or that the interventions needed are just too expensive. I find this appalling. If they were dogs, the SPCA would pick them up, give them a warm, dry place to sleep and clean food.

Mary was appealing to the moral value of obligation by clearly sharing details of her moralised judgement: our obligation to street children is greater than, or, at least, equal to, our obligation to dogs. This evaluation hinges on the conceptualisation that both 'stray dogs' and 'stray children' are similarly in need of being picked up, housed, and fed. Uninitiated Xhosa men are similarly considered to be dogs (*inja* or *inqambi*), meaning they are regarded as an "unclean" (i.e. morally impure) or "half-witted person of whom no good can be expected" (van Vuuren and de

Jongh 1999: 144), incapable of living independently as adults who can care for, and protect, themselves and their families. Stray dogs are often thought to be dirty and unhygienic. Mary was concerned about the squalor of life on the street. I draw out these comparisons to draw attention to the interweaving of discourses of regarding vulnerability and societal order. In inviting her audience to consider whether they too *felt* appalled by the situation (i.e. were emotionally moved), Mary mobilised moral sentiment to push for interventionist action. Similar methods are an integral component of the constitution of humanitarianism more broadly. Miriam Ticktin (2006: 36) states that "humanitarianism was initially a form of religiously inflected charity" that morphed into "an industry of NGOs" with claims to both religious and secular orientations, which advocate "action on the basis of emotion". Such mobilisations are political in the sense that they speak on behalf of others. They are also political in the sense that support is sought for historically constituted reordering of society and inter-human relations.

Marketing activity in the UK revolved around the employment of similar techniques and moral discourses, bringing about the constitution of increased support for the endeavours of my interlocutors working at Ngomso. Events were facilitated to a great extent by volunteers, most especially those who worked on behalf of the school's partner charity, The Friends of Ngomso (a.k.a. FOA and 'the Friends'). The organisation was established when a British couple spent 12 months in Grahamstown volunteering at the College of Transfiguration and Ngomso. As Mary put it, "It was their vision to start fundraising in the UK", and they organised her first fundraising trip and registered the FOA as a charity. When I met her in 2011, she had visited the UK for approximately one month during each of the previous eight years. She visited churches, schools, Rotary clubs, and prominent donors. Although the original founders were no longer active, the Friends still funded Mary's travels. Andy, a prominent trustee who had attended the private school in Grahamstown with historical ties to Mary's family, before moving to the UK, organised the tours and provided support to Mary during her visits. To some extent, these events mirror those that occurred centuries earlier. Mary's forefather, Robert Miller, first met John Armstrong, the first Bishop of the Anglican Diocese of Grahamstown, when he was touring England "to awaken interest in the new venture [i.e. expansion of mission stations], and preach in many parts of the country to collect funds" (Anonymous). In light of this, this section of the book can be read as a demonstration of how fundraising activity, driven most specifically by Christianised discourses, has continued to maintain a bond between British residents and those living in her former colonies.

I introduced Reverend Susan Dibb in the previous chapter. In 2013, she kindly hosted Joyce, Mary, and me at her vicarage in the heart of England's picturesque Cotswold region for several days. She later became a trustee of the FOA. During our first evening together, we shared a green Thai curry and fresh fruit salad and talked about the river at the bottom of her garden. Afterwards, we walked to the church at the top of her driveway because Susan had invited her congregation to meet with Mary and Joyce. About 15 men and women had greeted us before they sat in the pews. A youth worker who was probably in her late twenties was the youngest member of the audience by some distance. Susan opened by explaining that Mary and Joyce were travelling the country to meet those who had supported the school during the previous year and to raise additional funds. Although this was Joyce's first visit to the UK, Mary had already visited the congregation on several occasions, and they had transferred sizable donations in the past.

Using a PowerPoint presentation, Mary explained that Ngomso "is a school for street children and children with psychosocial barriers to learning". She went on to speak about "poverty", "homelessness", "hunger", and "rape". Learners "have issues with their home life or lack thereof", she continued.[2] Having established this context, Mary then focused on "three boys" who held "a guy at gunpoint" but were "now at drug rehab". The audience learnt that this was "the first of this kind of [gun] crime at the school", however, Mary said, "40% of the learners are drug addicts". Mary concluded this particular account by saying "These are desperate children."

On the following day, we travelled to the sixth form of a private girls' school in Warwick, a historical town situated approximately 100 miles north-west of London (see Fig. 5.1). According to its website, the school promotes "Christian principles" and provides its learners with a "caring environment". We parked on the high street, among its quaint Tudor beams, tea rooms, delicatessens, Italian restaurants, and health food stores. The new sixth form building had cost over £2 million. Its large windows contrasted with the historic nature of the listed buildings throughout the rest of the site. The classroom assigned for Mary and Joyce's presentation was soon filled with young ladies aged 17 and 18, complete with manicured nails and cared-for hair. They sat in silence while watching a short film about Ngomso.

Fig. 5.1 Map of Warwick, UK (Google Maps)

The film opens with the words, "Street children: hungry, filthy, begging; the victims of extreme poverty, social disintegration, physical violence and sexual abuse". In the film, the narrator explains that Mary can be seen hugging a 15-year-old "with full blown AIDS" visiting Ngomso in a bid to source antiretroviral medication. The footage then depicts Mary's concern that a learner is about to commit suicide by jumping off a roof.

In Warwick, the film brought the 'other world' of South Africa into view (Rabbitts 2013: 98). Individuals who sought support for charity endeavours during the colonial period used visual media ('magic lanterns') too (Lidchi 1999); however, modern technology permitted the inclusion of interviews with 'young natives', who spoke about the school. To my mind, this gave a visible and audible layer of credence to Mary and Joyce's assertions. When we learn about something that we have not experienced, we must imagine it.[3] The film encouraged audiences, especially individuals who had not visited the school, to imagine 'a world' in South Africa where similar events to those depicted were happening 'now'. The 'real events' of the film also encouraged audiences (at least this audience member) to deliberate future potentialities; to visualise how their involvement could affect events that would come to pass in that world (also see Wark 1995). Such imaginative processes, which are both constituted and limited by the consumption of media, can construct relationships, even when individuals share no 'direct' experiences with each other.[4]

Similar depictions of 'desperate victims' were evident when we visited the studios of a regional BBC radio station in Coventry (approximately ten miles north-east of Warwick) later the same day. Susan, Joyce, and Mary were interviewed as part of a music and conversation programme. The host asked Mary "Do many of [the learners] not have a family?" Mary replied, "There are some AIDS orphans, but most are children of single mothers who are alcoholics, who have a series of boyfriends." She explained that these mothers "have children with multiple men" and "sugar daddies", all of whom are "not willing to support other peoples' children". As a consequence of such arrangements, "the children experience verbal abuse and rejection". Mary's depiction of the challenges faced by one learner, in particular, supported this assertion. She then told the radio presenter that "[learners'] social needs come from the funding of the Friends, it's a wonderful charity". She continued by saying that the Friends provided clothes and food because "dirty, smelly, hungry, frightened children can't learn". These were not only narratives about material poverty but moralised narratives about how families, carers, and parents were failing their children, the learners, in one way or another, especially as a result of their actions and choices.[5] The implicit claim is that some other party, namely the school, should step in and offer assistance in their place; to isolate the young learners from their surroundings and their fate. In arguing for support to this end, then, discourses concerning 'needy learners' promoted the reconfiguration of their relationships with parents, carers, and families.

Fassin (2011: 487) argues that "moral inflection" is generated when humanitarian organisations humanise their communications. In particular, he suggests that targets of humanitarian interventions appear as victims of trauma, which is a concept that appeared in Ngomso's marketing activity, to evoke compassionate reactions (pathos) rather than as oppressors, which would likely elicit reactions of indignation. (Especially in the case of younger Ngomso learners, the latter was not really an option.) Relatedly, in her article on 'orphans' in Botswana, Dahl (2006: 629) draws from the work of Fassin and his colleague Paula Vasquez to claim that legitimations of aid rely "on a spectacle of misery, which renders recipients as pure victims and authorizes engagement".[6] Most relevantly, charities and NGOs compete to secure donations by 'shocking audiences into compassion' with imagery of malnourished, suffering children (Bornstein 2005), who provide "innocent representations of common humanity" (Malkki 2010: 65). The continued dissemination of such images "fuels a conscience industry of global proportions" (Wark 1995: 40). This effective marketing technique has been the target of many critiques, yet appears evident on posters every time I negotiate the London Underground.

Similarly, newspaper articles, 'school tours', radio interviews, and presentations were laden with imagery and narratives that drew attention to and made claims about learners' desperation, hunger, rejection, abuse, and experiences of traumatic events. They were depicted as disrupted, deprived, damaged, and inhibited victims, devoid of care and support (especially parental). Their need was *especially* great, the situation in South Africa *especially* troublesome. There is nothing new or unique in this. Raymond Apthorpe (2013: np) suggests that the need to brand "a new humanitarian emergency . . . as nothing less than the 'world's worst'" when appealing for funds is as evident today as it was when the Romans offered "humanitarian assistance (*susciperetur humanitate*) to the Goths two millennia ago". The fact that my interlocutors emphasised the severity of the situation when attempting to galvanise support is not surprising. Why would potential supporters be told that the school and its learners needed no assistance during attempts to secure support?

A Continent in Need?

In the context of UK-based marketing activities, assertions that Ngomso and its learners were in need of assistance meshed with discourses presenting Africa as a continent in need. These permeate all manner of public and institutional arenas and dovetail into the fabric of everyday life; they are learnt and embodied during everyday experiences. The promotional activities of other charities and NGOs provide one obvious source. Additionally, young Britons learn about the continent during their time in school. Remembering that I did so during my GCSE geography studies, I typed "GCSE geography Africa" into Google. The third link from the top offered me a short film about South Africa hosted on the BBC's Bitesize (revision) website. This is the description given to the footage:

> AIDS is widespread across Africa. The disease has been spread across the continent by soldiers, truckers and prostitutes. Women often cook meals for weary truckers and then climb into the cabs to have unprotected sex. AIDS is so widespread in Africa because of poverty; *people in Africa are too poor to stay alive.* (BBC 2006: np, emphasis added)

In 2013, I visited a primary school with Susan, Mary, and Joyce, during a session set aside for Susan's regular "Christian time". As we stood in the entrance, Susan turned to Joyce and me and asked, "Is 'race' the right way of saying [that Mary is different from Joyce]?" During the three days that I spent in the Cotswolds, 'race' was discussed so often that I was transported back to my time in South Africa. We walked into the school hall. Two classes of pale-skinned boys and girls, aged six and seven, sat with their legs crossed and arms folded. Once they had finished singing *He's Got the Whole World in His Hands*, Susan introduced Joyce: "You can see she is from Africa; her hair and her skin are a different colour [from yours].... Her surname is Mthengana – that is a word that you won't have had to say before." The learners were then encouraged to ask questions. One wanted to know about animals. A conversation ensued about "Africa's big five". I remembered how an 11-year-old at my old school in London had warned me about "lions in the street" when I told him I was going to South Africa. "Do you live in mud huts?" asked one of the boys. "Is your water clean?" enquired a young girl with blonde pigtails. Joyce, who had only recently flown outside of South Africa for the first time, was amused by their questions. She answered with warm smiles and giggles: No, she did not live in a mud hut, and her tap water was only dirty when there was a problem with the municipal supply.[7] Perhaps because she recognised the disjuncture between Joyce's life and the questions, Susan explained that the students had recently completed a project about "some very poor people in Africa".

The way that the young learners imagined Joyce's life did not surprise me. I thought that the brief exchange was a neat summation of the representations of the continent that many audiences in England, adult ones included, would offer if pushed to convey something of their understanding of Africa. In my experience, many would fail to make a distinction between Africa and its composite countries.[8] Moreover, despite all and any evidence to the contrary, this imagined land is frequently understood and depicted as being needy and underdeveloped, devoid of the means and ability to look after itself. Of course, this is a generalisation. However, separating the facts and fictions offered by the British media is not always an easy task. Representations of the continent are so often misplaced or simply untrue that websites like africacheck.org try to set the record straight (see Mark 2014). The young learners in the hall didn't ask about government corruption or dictators, child soldiers or hi-jacking, famine or malaria, yet, as they grow up, and become privy to pervasive exoticised discourses concerning Africa, they will probably learn about such things. From what I witnessed in other situations, Joyce and her 'Africanness' was not uniformly encountered and understood by those she met on her tour. However, those who encountered Ngomso without visiting the school, South Africa, and the continent had to make judgements about their potential involvement and imagine its impact in light of their understanding of similar, circulating, somewhat overarching, discourses.

As we sat in Ngomso's playground one afternoon, Susan conveyed something of this assertion when she spoke about the events that led to her involvement:

> I was having a sabbatical of three months, and I just felt that I wanted to do something with children in Africa; AIDS-related children particularly. Because it was a Dawn French, Vicar of Dibley documentary thing [that I saw on the TV]. And I was really shocked to see how badly treated children orphaned by AIDs were because I had assumed that in African society children were looked after by the extended family. But the stigma of AIDs and the fear of AIDs means that a lot of children are abandoned and older children [are then] looking after younger children. And I found the documentary very moving. I thought that if I could just get involved a bit, and do something.

Like other prominent supporters now living in the UK, Susan had previously lived in Africa. She was born in England but conceived in Nigeria, when her father was teaching engineering at the time of the independence in 1960. During this same conversation, she said, "I have a love of Africa". Clearly, these experiences and this judgement provided foundations to the events she depicted in her statement.

As she mentioned, Susan was affected by an episode of *The Vicar of Dibley*, a BBC sitcom, which aired in 2005; it transformed her, she hoped to "get involved". During the episode, Dawn French, who plays the vicar, is trying to get her friends and parishioners to write to Tony Blair in support of the Make Poverty History campaign, which marked the twentieth anniversary of the Live 8 concert and received a vast amount of British media coverage. Britain used to send 'needy children' to her colonies.[9] More recently, much emphasis has been placed on bringing 'similar youngsters' back under her care through the extension of charitable and developmental interventions. At the end of the episode, a plea for assistance towards such ends is made. The characters gather around a laptop, and the vicar shows them an extract from the documentary film *The Orphans of Nkandla*, a town in KwaZulu-Natal, South Africa, which subsequently gained notoriety for President Jacob Zuma's expensive rural home in the same area. The footage focuses on two young brothers whose mother has died of AIDS (Woods and Shipley 2004). An interviewer asks the brothers "Do you miss your mum?" They answer, "Yes … she did everything [for us]". Because their Dad is also dying, they say that they now have to "do everything" (Dennis 2005: 44–48). Susan told me that when she learnt of Ngomso sometime later, during a presentation in Birmingham, Mary's words resonated with her because of the programme. Her engagements with the film and Mary's presentations relate to Bornstein and Redfield's (2008: 1) consideration of the compassionate and empathetic "impulse to alleviate suffering known as humanitarianism [that] constitutes a central element in international moral discourse". This discourse, they (2008: 4–5) argue, has a "temporal tendency … to focus on the present, and the immediate needs of living humans in distress", while emphasising "the physical (and increasingly the psychological) condition of suffering people above all else". In being moved to react compassionately to the film and later to Mary's depiction of the suffering learners at Ngomso, Susan wanted to "do something" to alleviate their distress.[10]

Anthropologists and ethnographers have considered 'orphans' and relationships of care in South Africa (Henderson 2012; Weckesser 2011), Ethiopia (Abebe 2008), Tanzania (Stambach and Kwayu 2013), and Botswana (Dahl 2006). This work problematises the narrative of the programme that encouraged Susan to "get involved" (also see Bornstein 2012: 87–111; Hosegood 2008; Meintjes and Giese 2006; Riley 2013). The term 'orphans' is an "unstable category" that unravels with an understanding of its applicability to individual lives, social contexts, and culturally specific notions of vulnerability and kinship (Green 2011: 35; also see Dahl 2006; Henderson 2012). Similarly, Susan's concerns relate to ongoing contestation regarding generational orderings and child rearing. Such assertions do not lead me to claim that the words and emotions expressed by the young brothers who feature in the documentary are somehow false or unreal. Rather, they form part of an edited, constructed depiction of their lives—a selective truth employed to promote a moralised and political cause (much like the accounts of learners' lives provided by those promoting Ngomso).[11] This technique is akin to what O'Neill (2013: 208) terms "straining the ethics of representation". Narratives that depict a 'continent in need' connote the idea that the individuals who can offer assistance, who are capable of saviour and rescue, live beyond Africa's borders (i.e. Africans need help from you, the British audience).[12] These promotional discourses justify the judgement that intervention is 'the moral thing to do' by helping to perpetuate the discourse that such justifications depend on (i.e. Africa will flounder and suffer if left to its own devices).

Judging from Susan's reaction, as a technique of power, this form of communication is effective.[13] However, in trying to secure support for a particular intervention, such communication limits the scope of explanation and understanding (also see Clissold 2010; Sankore 2005). Perhaps more accurately, the explanatory scope is limited so that support might be secured; 'please react now, questions later'. "There is", writes McKenzie Wark (1995: 42) in his discussion of politicised media representations and humanitarianism, "an inverse ratio between clarity and significance. In the absence of clarity about who has power over whom, a story appealing to the emotions will have to do." Similarly, Bornstein (2009, 2012) considers the tension between impulsive humanitarianism, knee-jerk reactions to end the suffering of others (e.g. to just 'do something'), which the film clearly encourages, and our obligation to ensure that such reactions are well targeted and rationally conceived. She argues that both are necessary components of humanitarianism but that care must be taken to find a balance between them. In reality, of course, such a balance is hard to find.

Prevention

It is children, in particular, who can be portrayed as being especially vulnerable and innocent, but also as having the potential for brighter futures; as they have many decades before them, especially if they live responsibly (Freidus 2010; Malkki 2010; Wark 1995). This conception of childhood configures ethical imaginations of humanitarian interventions and can legitimise these same interventions (Manzo 2008). However, because members of staff also worried that learners had misguided agency, they were concerned that they also had the potential to be disruptive and dangerous. When eliciting support, they depicted this 'troublesome potentiality' and made the claim that it had to be addressed (although victimisation was a more prominent theme).

One newspaper article discusses the fact that a learner once broke Mary's finger, before it says, "Drugs, violence, kids being dragged off in handcuffs – all these are daily realities" (de Klerk 2012: np). When the principal of another school rang one afternoon, Mary apologised for not giving her more time by saying, "I am dealing with a big knife at school today; a very sharp knife." A learner had indeed brought a knife to school, however, at the time, it struck me that Mary focused the conversation on this aspect of the day. Her attention and time had been pulled in various directions that morning, yet it was this controversial event that she emphasised. Similarly, "kids being dragged off in handcuffs" was not a daily occurrence by any means. During the following months, I continued to note similar dynamics. Violence, drink, and drugs featured prominently in the depictions of daily goings-on shared with 'external audiences' both in the UK and South Africa.

Such depictions did appear to evoke indignant reactions, as Fassin's (2011) argument suggests. During the presentation in Susan's church, for example, a picture of Nyameko, a young man of 17 who was staying in the Shelter, appeared on the screen. I knew him quite well and smiled when I saw his face. "He is a drug addict", Mary explained. "As you can see from the photo he is a troubled boy", she continued. She told the audience that he had recently been found guilty of "statutory rape". The audience appeared to be shocked when Mary said the girl was nine: exhalations of air and tutting sounds accompanied their shaking heads.

***

As I have argued already, the term 'street children' captures this double-sided judgement of vulnerability and potential disruption.[14] In his ethnography of street children in Brazil, Hecht (2008: 232) states: "street children offend a modern awareness of the vulnerability and rights of children while also raising alarm over public safety". Street children are also depicted as being independent and especially capable of looking after themselves (i.e. the resourcefulness my interlocutors attributed to them). This attribute makes them ideal candidates for interventions that focus on long-term, sustainable change; discourses that have become increasingly important to NGOs (Nieuwenhuys 2001), as visible in the 'mission' to provide Ngomso learners with self-sustaining employment and skills. The term 'street children' could, therefore, communicate a great deal of information about Ngomso's target beneficiaries, and the purpose and format of the intervention, by simplifying all manner of moral judgements (also see Hecht 2008: 231). It is concise but also catalytic of imagery and connotations, which are attributes of effective marketing communications more broadly. Other terminology—such as "the poorest of the poor", "the severely socially marginalised", and "those with extrinsic barriers to learning"—did not offer the same level of 'persuasive power'. For those who were marketing Ngomso, the term 'street children' was useful for this very reason. Without it, more explanation—a different way of staking a moral claim about the need for intervention—would have been necessary.

The genealogy of the term reveals much about its qualities. Initially, the term was "widely adopted by international agencies in an attempt to avoid negative connotations for children previously known as street urchins, gamines, rag-pickers, glue-sniffers, street Arabs, or vagrants" (Panter-Brick 2002: 151). This 'original' terminology emerged in Europe from the thirteenth century, as ex-soldiers and inactive workers—no longer serfs bound to a feudal lord—wandered from place to place, notably in urban areas. Poverty became disassociated with holiness and associated with danger and disorder, vagabondage, and beggars (Beier 1987). In England, social control and moral cohesion were at stake: 'masterless vagrants' had no part in idealised patriarchal households and "broke with accepted norms of family life"; they were adjudged to be promiscuous and held "responsible for a multitude of crimes" (ibid: 51, 6). They "were no ordinary criminals" but "corrupt" individuals. These "social outcasts", on the fringes of society, were free to roam without supervision (ibid: 6).[15] They knew no God nor were they disciplined by the law (ibid: xxi).[16] With obvious linkages to the concerns of Christian missionaries, vagrants were identified as the dirty and the unwashed: those without morals.[17] Such concerns sound remarkably similar to how *tsotsis*, as well as street children, were conceptualised by my interlocutors.

After the emergence of 'masterless vagrants' in England came desires to suppress and control. In the fifteenth century, the idea of "law abiding citizens against anti-societies of rogues" emerged, as vagabondage became an offence, premised upon "a new concept of collective crime" (Beier 1987: 12). Vagrancy laws and examination procedures were introduced to control the 'rogues'.[18] This development extended the government's remit and was, arguably, the birth of the welfare state, which laid the groundwork for State-funded education in the UK and Grey's mission schools in South Africa. Following the industrial revolution, "the artful dodgers of the Dickensian inner city", who "were often left to survive … independent of paternal or patrician control", inspired "a civilizing crusade" (Comaroff and Comaroff 2005: 23). This development gave unprecedented momentum to the forms of intervention that had commenced in the thirteenth century.

Nieuwenhuys (2001: 552) argues that "the term [street children] introduces a semantic analogy between the past poverty of children in industrialising Europe and America and that of today's developing world". Given the links between South Africa and the UK that were integral to Ngomso's fundraising and the personal histories of those who facilitated such efforts, this history might be understood as a precursor to, and thus a constitutive component of, the 'crusade' or mission for which funding was sought. Ngomso, as an intervention, is intelligible as a historically constituted, moralised endeavour.

Through their employment of the term 'street children' and their enthusiasm to address 'the street child problem', my interlocutors refashioned historically constituted moral discourses and possibilities; they ethically encountered the modes by which they could understand and describe the school's target beneficiaries, particularly when marketing the school. Reflecting on his decades-long experience of the humanitarian sector, Apthorpe (2011: 209) tells us that "service-delivering agencies 'target' according to only their own ideas of vulnerable groups". These groups "exist only in the project personnel's imagination and report" (Nyamwaya, cited in Apthorpe 2011: 209). In the case of Ngomso, this wasn't strictly true. Some UK-based supporters knew something about how the idea of the 'street child' related to the learners because they had spent time with them. They were aware that the categorisation did not only exist on the FOA website or Mary's PowerPoint slides but that it was contested as a circulatory discourse during everyday experiences and interactions at the school. As a consequence of such knowledge, they debated the validity of the term (i.e. the extent to which it accurately described target beneficiaries) and the morality of its usage.

Andy was an active member of a congregation in Whetstone, North London (see Fig. 5.2). Trustee meetings were sometimes held in the vicarage. We sat on floral patterned armchairs, in a large living room with double-height sash windows. The adjacent church was built in 1832 and designed by the Bishop of London, Charles Blomfield. Blomfield was "primarily responsible for creating the [Colonial Bishoprics' Fund]" that "was vital to the spread of the Church of England throughout the [British] empire" (Faught 2003: 143). This Fund was responsible for the appointment of Robert Gray as the first Bishop of Cape Town (Demissie 2012: 242). Gray hosted Robert Miller, Mary's forefather when he arrived at the

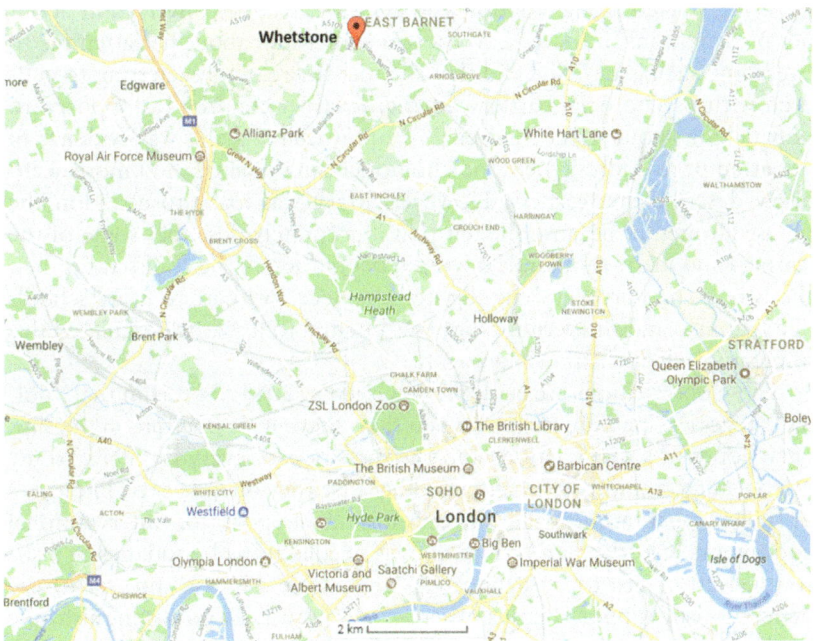

Fig. 5.2 Map of Whetstone, London, UK (Google Maps)

Cape of Good Hope in 1854 (Anonymous). This setting says much about how terminology is always laden with historical meaning; words shift in and out of fashion even when the politicised ends to which they are mobilised change little.

The trustees discussed the wording of a banner that was to be used to promote a fundraising concert in a church in Derby. Jenny, a teacher working in London who had volunteered at Ngomso some years before, said that the learners did not "like to be called street children". Daniel, who had recently volunteered at the school, agreed with her. They suggested that different descriptive terms could be used. However, after some discussion, it was agreed that the term would not be dropped from marketing materials because it was a valuable component of fundraising efforts and integral to the identity of the charity. This deliberation shows how the meaning and usage of terminology takes shape as a result of moralised judgements. Although Daniel and Jenny worried that it jarred with learners' self-identities, the term was maintained for fear it would hinder attempts to aid and assist them.

As we walked along London's Regent's Canal, in conversation about her presentations in the UK, Mary said something about her attempts to overcome such issues. She said that she was "increasingly referring to children with psychosocial barriers, *including* street children [as opposed to only talking about street children]".[19] In my opinion, this was evidence of her attempt to address the term's homogenising qualities and more accurately describe the learners. However, Mary was loath to abandon the phrase altogether because she felt that it accurately describes some of the learners and many thousands of young people across the country. For her, the 'street child problem' highlighted the need for there to more schools like Ngomso and this terminology was integral to how she articulated this imperative when eliciting support.

These observations are evidence of Green's (2011: 34) claim that "policy categories" perpetuate even when they "have little traction on the slippery slopes of social relations and the messiness of everyday life". To my mind, categorisations are maintained because they operate as technologies of power that are capable of galvanising support for interventional endeavours. Clearly, *some* terminology is needed if the boundaries of institutional effort are to be delineated. This process is also integral to the generation of support because there is always a need to distinguish one potential course of action, or one NGO/charity/project, from another. Without a conceptualisation of a target beneficiary—which, in being a group identity, can never do justice to the individuality of the individuals in question—the possibility of *social* intervention falls away. It is hard to see how such tension, which was experienced as ethical dilemmas and debate by Daniel, Jenny and other trustees, and Mary, might be avoided.

***

When conveyed to potential and existing supporters, fears about unbridled freedoms and immoral potentiality (linked to a discussion of street children or otherwise) conflated with further imaginative projections of what might materialise if this potentiality remained unchecked. These imaginings concerned the futures of the young people in question but also that of humanity and society more generally. During the interview at the radio station, for example, Mary explained that charitable funding paid for the children of "teenage mothers [at Ngomso]" to go preschool so that the mothers could return to school. "[Otherwise] they would just fall back into a cycle of illiterate, untrained mothers from which they were born", she continued. The Friends of Ngomso website talks about "Breaking the cycle of poverty". When the interviewer asked Mary to "explain a little bit about the school", she responded:

> The problem with street children is large in South Africa. The gap between the rich and poor is so large. With a gap that large, some drift onto the street and engage in petty crime, or sometimes not so petty. They become victims of pimps and drug lords – it is either an early death or prison.

Highlighting similar assertions of problematic potentiality, this is an extract from Mary's submission to the Parliamentary Monitoring Group:

> We are justifiably horrified when old women and young girls and boys are raped or murdered, yet we fail to understand that our neglect of lost, hopeless children can be the underlying cause of such brutality.

The message is clear: when learners lack care and direction (i.e. moral education), they pose potential 'social dangers'. As another example of this assertion, Mary and I were driving to school one morning when she spoke about the lack of attention South Africa was paying to Ngomso's target beneficiaries, shook her head, and said, "These street children are tomorrow's prisoners, the next fathers of fatherless children". In his work regarding American-funded, Christianised child sponsorship programmes in Guatemala, O'Neill (2013: 209) offers a quote from a missionary who was reacting to a deadly shooting: "if someone would have been by their side . . . being supportive while they were little children suffering traumas, if only someone had loved them and helped them, then they would not be who they are today". The missionary continues, "A lack of love causes them to become like monsters that extort, kill, rob, and rape. And only the love of God can heal and prevent" (ibid.). O'Neill (ibid, emphasis added) summarises her thoughts: "Presence, not absence; love, not hate; affection, not aggressions – these practices assemble *the subject of prevention.*" Clearly, there are similarities here. For Mary, it was important for society to embrace and support the lost, hopeless, and neglected so that love could prevent further catastrophe.

Such projections of continuing 'moral depravity' were sometimes conveyed to audiences as being akin to the threat of different forms of humanitarian disaster, which are similarly capable of disrupting 'normal life'. During an interview, recorded for the short film about the school shown to audiences in the UK and South Africa, Mary says, "I just wonder what sort of tsunami is waiting for us if we as a nation continue to talk about street children and child-headed households as if these things are normal".[20] Her words convey an apocalyptic prediction: foreseeing a failure to act now as an invitation to disaster. Such orientations to the future match Mikael Karlström's (cited in Moore 2011: 137) observation of "most popular imaginaries": they contained "visions of light as well as murk, hope as well as fear, aspiration as well as anxiety". For Mary, there was no time for questioning, "the imminent forth-coming [was] present, immediately visible, as a present property of things" (Bourdieu 2000: 207); the tsunami *was* coming. She was not concerned with shaping a "contingent future" with her "ordinary action", "but [defeating] something which [was] already there in the configuration of the [social] game and in the present positions and postures of team-mates and opponents" (ibid: 208). Implicit in her statement is the claim that disaster can be averted if the 'problem' of street children and child-headed households is addressed. This assertion cleared the conceptual space into which Ngomso could be presented as a necessary intervention.

In the UK media, I constantly learn about 'waves of migrants' arriving in Europe to overrun us with their immorality and demands upon resources. David Cameron recently spoke of a "swarm" of migrants, which carries the same kind of warning about being overpowered and consumed by 'something other', a 'natural, unhuman force'. Those of a conservative political orientation have responded with calls for increased defences and security. In contrast, Mary sold the possibility of quashing the imminent waves of trouble before they could rise from the seabed. Audiences were not encouraged to push street children or youngsters living in child-headed households away, but to embrace them by supporting and enhancing the transformative potential of the school. Emphasising this potential was another cornerstone of communications with potential supporters. I will offer an examination of this technique in the next section.

Turning It Around

The counter-assertion to claims that learners' were especially needy and potentially problematic was that Ngomso did, and had to do, something extraordinary to reach them. In other words, in the hope of bringing 'normative transformations' to fruition, those marketing Ngomso emphasised the abnormality of the school. (During my undergraduate marketing degree, there was constant talk of unique selling points or USPs.) Such assertions were important because financial resources available to 'charitable causes' in the UK and South Africa have been diminishing.[21] Ngomso had to stand out among the plethora of competing recipients, and money finds its way to those selling something unique. Emphasis was placed on details about Accelerated Bridging Education, the overage admissions policy, extra staff, and support for past pupils. Moreover, audiences were informed that it was charitable funding that most significantly enabled Ngomso staff to differentiate the school from other avenues open to young South Africans. However, pronouncements of 'Ngomso's special qualities' clashed with the need to maintain its normative credibility. Alice once told me about "ridiculous donations" sent to the school. She was particularly confused about some used tea bags: "Sometimes I think they think we are a dumping ground." She and her colleagues fought against the idea that the school was a dumping ground for learners too. In a newspaper article celebrating Zamuxolo, a learner selected to run for the provincial cross-country team at a national competition in Nelspruit, Mary says, "Grahamstown and the whole district [can] see that Ngomso is a real school that produces real champions". More broadly, while there was constant pressure to highlight institutional specialness, the claim that Ngomso was just as effective as 'real' (i.e. mainstream/normal) schools, if not more so, also had to be made.

In line with this assertion, throughout the school's marketing activities, Ngomso was presented as a transformative solution, capable of channelling and harnessing learners' potential for good rather than ill. The first slide of the presentations that Mary delivered in the UK was entitled "Hope for the Lost". This phrase was also the title of her MA thesis, which she began to write before she had to sideline her studies due to her commitments as principal. During an interview with some visitors to the school Joyce said, "If there was no school like this in Grahamstown, they would be in the streets. Some of them would be dead by now from sniffing glues [or] petrol, or [from] robbing people."[22] These same words were placed on the FOA website shortly afterwards.

Crewe and Axelby (2013: 1–2) argue: "Set against situations of hopelessness, development agencies offer potential supporters an imagined future that will bring miraculous improvements in people's lives". Alex de Waal (2002: 253) talks about the "famine story" used to raise charity funding. "It has a similar symbolic structure to a fairy-tale", he (ibid.) argues; "with a victim (usually a black child), a villain (the weather, a frightening warlord, a complacent bureaucrat) and a savior (a white aid worker equipped with Western technology and traditional Judeo-Christian compassion)." In the case of Ngomso, the villain was unloving parents and immorality in the township/streets and a dysfunctional DoE. The saviour was Ngomso and Mary in particular. The notion that members of staff operated as a surrogate family was also shared. The 'victims' (i.e. learners and young South Africans more generally) provided "the human scenery before which the melodrama of middle-class redemption [could] be enacted" (Wexler, cited in O'Neill 2013: 210). However, for my interlocutors, this 'scenery' was not fabricated with abstracted stereotypes but built with knowledge of individuals with event-filled lives. To be clear, then, the stories that were shared with existing and potential supporters (i.e. the accounts of learners' lives) weren't fictional but were narrated versions, or 'retellings', of 'real events'—reconstituted as purposeful, discursive truths. As Jackson (2005: 11) argues, events "quickly and imperceptibly blur into and become stories", and, in the case of my research, like stories premised upon historical episodes more generally, this process of blurring was a creative one, whereby memories and perceptions were presented as fact only once they had been reconstituted into digestible formations of discourse.

In particular, stories about how individuals were transformed by their experiences at the school supported the claim that Ngomso provided hope. One article in Grahamstown's local paper juxtaposes the words "street children" and "disruptive behaviour" with a photograph of the *Talented and Proud* Aviwe, who is holding a teapot and cup that he has made using the school's pottery resources. These words sit alongside details of a recent donation from the College of the Transfiguration (a subtle hint of the impact of support). In the story about Zamuxolo's running talents, Mr Zamisa, a teacher at the time, says, "[I am] very pleased that Zamuxolo was chosen to represent the province, especially [because he comes] from a school that deals with children with behavioural problems". Such articles carried a targeted message to those residents most likely to have the resources to contribute to the cause (the newspaper had 30 distribution points in the town and only two in the location). Together with Mary's campaigning at local social clubs, the university and cathedral, and private schools, they provided an understanding of the school's interventions and invited readers to contribute to them.

Similar narratives of 'success against the odds with the help of Ngomso' were also central to communications in the UK. During Mary's presentation at Susan's church, for example, she commented on a photograph of two female learners aged nine and ten. She explained that they were "small" because they had not had "enough food" when they were young. "But", she continued, with an inflexion in her voice that signified a positive counter-narrative, "if we get them at ten [years of age] it is OK [we can address that by providing food at the school]. We have had some learners go on to play first-team rugby." Such claims were evident when Mary's ancestors were operating a charity school in England, at the time when British settlers were establishing Grahamstown:

> Charity schooling [in England, 1700–1850] generally promised recipients and benefactors long-[term], rather than short-term benefits. If the trustees are taken at their word, the children learnt how to support themselves in useful trades in the future. In the meantime, their parents or 'friends' kept them, with [the] occasional provision of food and some clothing to offset the expense. (King and Tomkins 2003: 104)

In Susan's church, a picture of another learner, who I did not recognise, then appeared on the screen. He had joined the school in 2012 after my return to the UK. Mary explained a little about him to those of us who were sitting in the pews in front of her:

He came to school at seventeen, illiterate and only speaking Afrikaans. Now he is learning to speak Xhosa and to speak and read English. He has passed grade one and will likely have passed grade two. [Looks at Joyce, who nods to confirm he has.] He's just soaking it up.

Mary then said that she had recently asked him if he was "OK". A smile took over her face, and she raised both thumbs in the air as she acted out his response; telling us that he had replied, "*Baie, baie, baie* alright." When she explained that '*baie*' means 'very' in Afrikaans, the audience laughed with approval. Literacy is an "essential component of the nonconformist mission" (Comaroff and Comaroff 1986: 14). In learning to read, the young man was one step closer to being able to commit to a "textualized truth" (ibid.). I recalled a moment from 2011 when I had told Mary that Liani had been reading the Bible while waiting for a lesson to begin. I simply meant to highlight the fact that she was waiting patiently. Mary replied by saying "She has come a long way." It is helpful to compare these events with the wording of a letter written in Grahamstown in 1857, addressed to an unnamed "Child" in the UK (E.W., cited in *SPG* 1858: 26). Its author (ibid: 31) reports on her visit to the first, newly opened mission school in Grahamstown:

> I was not a little astonished and delighted with the intelligence [the learners] displayed, and with their evident desire to improve. . . . These poor children have but few advantages, but they appear to me to make the most of them; and the visible results are most gratifying to their kind friends and teachers.

One assumes that the young recipient of the letter had not visited the school herself and learnt about the school's transformative qualities from the judgements and assertions conveyed by its author. Similarly, like the other audience members in the church, I knew nothing about the young man who was "soaking it up" beyond the information that Mary provided. We, the audience, did not find out if he was 'very alright' before joining the school. However, because Mary's account began with his illiteracy and singular language proficiency, and then depicted him absorbing knowledge like a sponge and smiling with raised thumbs, I didn't need to know this to understand the claim she was making about Ngomso's transformative power.

The story of Nyameko's troubling statutory rape conviction contrasted with this positive, smile-filled imagery. It ended with the audience being told: "now he's opted for the street [and left the school]". This story depicted a young man that the school had not been able to help. I was left wondering what had happened to him. However, it's easy to see how the take-home message for those without such a relationship would have been the proposition that there was now 'another rapist out there'. Such depictions highlighted the limits of the intervention and its inability to always succeed. A losing battle demands more resources, more firepower.

During the radio interview in Coventry the following afternoon, Mary continued to promote the school by sharing the story of Luzuko:

> He was arrested at thirteen for armed robbery and spent three years in prison. He was sodomised and has the prison [gang] tattoos. [After leaving prison] he came to school, and he said to me 'I don't know what will happen, I don't want to go back there.' I was nervous about letting him come back to school ... but he ended up as head boy of a mainstream school.

Mary shared Luzuko's story with me when we first met at her house in Grahamstown. He had given her permission to talk about him, and his story was perhaps the most convincing evidence of Ngomso's transformative power. The depiction of Luzuko's life before Ngomso's intervention focuses on the danger-filled imagery of immoral behaviour; he posed a threat, both real and imagined, to others. Audiences also learnt of Luzuko's fears at that time: he did not want to return to prison, to sodomy; he wanted out. Similarly, O'Neill (2013: 208) argues that potential donors in the US are encouraged to help "create a context" in which beneficiaries "might choose God over gangs". He (ibid.) claims that this "is a technique, a mode of governing, that tethers security to Salvation to subjectivity". In the message conveyed by Luzuko's story, we can see something similar: his transformation to head boy contained the threat he once posed to others, and he benefitted from this same process.

When news reached the Friends that Luzuko found work in a local supermarket following his matriculation later that year, details of his continuing renewal were quickly put on their website, as affirmation for those who already supported the cause and a potential draw for those who might yet do so. The website details five more "success stories": past pupils who secured various forms of (low-wage) employment.

A statement about the high unemployment rate in Grahamstown helps to present this information as evidence of exceptional achievement. With ethnography that reminded me of Luzuko and Siseko, O'Neill (2013: 216) shares the story of Ronald, a young Guatemalan man supported by evangelical sponsors. In their eyes, Ronald became "a true success [story]" and avoided the clutches of gangs, prison, and violent death, by moving himself into the arms of Holy support and taxable employment (ibid.). When speaking about fundraising for "the battle against poverty", Crewe and Axelby (2013: 2) argue that "Guarantees of a better world are supported with evidence of previous success stories, the tangible outcomes and past achievements that illustrate mastery and competence". In the case of Ngomso, accounts of masterful moral transformations validated the intervention's effectiveness.

Audiences in the UK and visitors to the school were also frequently informed about the life of my research partner Siseko: how his mother's alcohol addiction meant he had lived in the Shelter during his teenage years before matriculating and becoming head of the marimba band at the cathedral. The Christian orientation of the school was especially pronounced during fundraising activity in churches and religiously orientated schools: Siseko's story helped to bring the idea of religious transformation into view. As I learnt from my time in South Africa, many learners and past pupils experienced very different journeys. Likewise, not all of the learners were illiterate at the age of 17, nor were they charged with committing acts of sexual violence and rape. I wrote this reflective statement in my notes as I sat on a fold-up bed in Susan's spare room, hours after Mary and Joyce's presentation in the church:

> It was like an emotional roller-coaster – the pain of the bad stories and the elation of those [young people] that are doing well because of what the school is doing.

From my professional experience of the advertising industry, I already knew that 'selective truths' are more persuasive than the whole picture. The value of such selectivity finds its counterpoint in "the ethics of representation" (O'Neill 2013: 208). In the case of Mary and Joyce's presentation, real lives were represented, not fabricated tales of fancy. Moreover, while these lives were not typical, I would struggle to present an example of what was; there was no uniform pattern. However, what the selected stories have in common is their ability to illustrate the kind of transformations that members of staff valued. The ethical issues relate most readily to what was missed out rather than the truthfulness of what was included. Those who attended church, matriculated, and found employment following their experiences at Ngomso were shown to be living a better, more desirable and moral, life. There were two stark alternatives: the (normal/moral) lives and futures that Ngomso made possible and the (abnormal/immoral) lives that materialised without its interventions. This dynamic supports Escobar's (1997: 497) assertion that "Development entails the simultaneous recognition and negation of difference". Bornstein (2001: 595) follows Escobar to argue that the "evangelical narratives" of "Christian humanitarian programs of child sponsorship", such as the activities of World Vision in Zimbabwe, "simultaneously transcend difference and exacerbate it". For my interlocutors, highlighting differences in a bid to eliminate them meant delicately negotiating and manipulating the perceptions of others. It was a communicative balancing act with very 'real' consequences, which they recognised but always had to evaluate and judge.

Huxley (2004: 30) (ibid: 30) provocatively said that "It is in the social sphere, in the realm of politics and economics, that the Will to Order becomes really dangerous." With even greater applicability to humanitarianism, under discussion here, he (ibid.) also argued that "The Will to Order can make tyrants out of those who merely aspire to clear up a mess." To my mind, Mary, Joyce, and other members of staff were not tyrants, despite their desires to 'clean up' society. The word 'tyrant' appears to be antithetical to their will to love and care. However, their conceptualisations of assistance were bound up with concerns about uniformity and freedom. We can see this in the narratives that they presented to potential supporters. Huxley (ibid.) suggested that "the only safe course" to chart between freedom and organisation "is in the middle, between the extremes of *laissez-faire* at one end of the scale and of total control at the other". By sharing accounts of extreme (moral) disorganisation and extreme (moral) freedom, my interlocutors attempted to show that such a middle ground remained elusive, that there was much work to do.

Buying into the Promise

All potential supporters had to make judgements about the information presented to them during fundraising activity, most specifically concerning learners' circumstances and potential futures. These evaluations hinged upon their embodied moralities and related conceptualisations of normality and desirability. Were the learners without hope and incapable of becoming normal/moral without Ngomso's intervention? Could they become normal/moral subject to the attention of Ngomso? Did they want to see this particular 'form of normal' materialise for the young people in question and humanity more broadly? The generation of support required a full house of positive answers.

After Mary's presentation in the church, I told the audience about my research and asked them several questions. Why did they offer their support? One elderly lady responded by saying "We love the personal stories about where they are in their lives." Afterwards, I asked Susan if "empathy" was at the heart of her continued involvement with Ngomso and that of her congregation. She agreed that empathy was important but also said: "we like to hear about the resolutions [to the problems in their lives], the turnarounds". I would argue that this usage of the word 'turnaround' is reflective of the ethical imaginaries presented during fundraising activity. 'Turnaround' was shorthand for specific forms of transformation that align with the historically constituted moral discourses pertaining to the reordering of society and inter-human relations that were employed to galvanise support for the school.

A year earlier, as we spoke in the playground at Ngomso, Mary had considered some important components of this ethical imaginary:

> I like knowing their stories; it is what happens in the lives of individuals that motivates me to come back [and volunteer each year]. [I especially like] hearing what has become of the older children, the ones that I have known since 2008; it matters to me, what becomes of them. One of the things that is distressing is that I think nearly all of the girls have dropped out of high school. Some of the boys are getting on and doing it but the girls have babies, or they get AIDs and are sick. There were some really bright girls, they were just lovely when I was here in 2008, and I think that have all got AIDs. It's ... [*pausing for her next words, before a brief silence*]. So I don't see them.

As with engagements with humanitarianism more broadly, the unfolding of individual and collective futures were integral to evaluations of the desirability of forms of intervention. Mary visited Susan's church each year to update the congregation on the progress of learners' lives. Narratives stretched over many years, and individuals could follow the impact of the money and support they sent. The quarterly Friends of Ngomso newsletter included "updates" and "stories" about particular individuals too.

Evidencing the effects of support with feedback loops of information is an integral component of relations between donors and humanitarian charities more broadly. Rabbitts (2013: 67), for instance, talks about the "opportunity (or feeling) of witnessing the transformation achieved by [your] donation". I once sponsored a snow leopard as a present for my girlfriend. We received a quarterly update about 'our' animal. Similar forms of communication are integral to organisations that offer child sponsorship opportunities (see Bornstein 2001; O'Neill 2013; Rabbitts 2012). Such material answers the question: What did my money do?

Susan told me that her annual visits to the school enabled her to observe such transformations first-hand. She positively evaluated the school's efforts. Like O'Neill's (2015) interlocutors, who engage with transformative projects in Guatemala rather than those on their doorstep in America, Susan was drawn to the 'polarities of life' in post-apartheid South Africa and related opportunities for transformation:

> One of the things that attracts me to Ngomso is the intensity of the life. Everything is extreme – the poverty is extreme, the behaviour is extreme – [so] you see change and what is done [by the school], what is making a real difference; whereas in a more diffuse situation in England, you just don't see things changing significantly for people.... Even though when they go to high school they still have a long way to go, you still feel that they made big progress, and there has been a big change happen to them. That is why I like to hear about individual lives. I mean they do go up and down ... [but] yes, *it's good*.

Ethical imaginations of what was, and would be, good for the young people in question had to align, to some degree at least, with those of Mary and her staff. Individuals explained these judgements in different ways, and decisions depended on their differing experiences of, and interactions with, Ngomso; however, they had commonality nonetheless. Positive opinions fundamentally hinged upon (1) the problematisation of lives lived without school educations, which linked with concerns about moral, political, and economic disorder, and (2) faith in the claim that schooling and charity, and especially this school and charity, are generative of desirable change, on individual and societal levels, running counter to such disorder. Like the supporters and employees of the FBOs in Zimbabwe considered by Bornstein (2005) and those in Tanzania considered by Stambach (2010), I also encountered enthusiasms for evidence of religious and economic transformations, for salvation combined with progressive, individualistic materialism, in line with a familiar moralised way of being in the world. However, when individuals most readily described their evaluations, explicit considerations of religious transformation slipped into the background, regardless of whether the individuals in questions were openly attuned to Christian discourses.

To support this analysis, I can consider a conversation that I had with Sally and Betty, the two sisters from England who volunteered at the school for a month. This is something that Sally said:

> Mary is achieving something [by] getting the kids off the street, which is the main thing.... She wants them to understand that they do have prospects and that they don't have to live in the township all their lives and that they need to work hard. They need to get their English learnt. Socialising, cos this is a massive thing, for them to be able to socialise with foreign people, and like, not be scared. They're confident – I think that is really good. To be able to just talk to anyone, I think that is a really good thing.

Her judgement hinged upon a conceptualisation of 'the street' and life in the township, which she contrasted with time spent in school. The way she suggested that neither was a desirable locality in which to live was by no means unique. I responded by asking her "And why is that a great thing?" She replied with a challenging question of her own: "Do you want them on the streets?" Her assertive tone suggested that I should either know the answer to my question or would have to fight to suggest that it was better that they were 'on the street'. I took an anthropological, non-committal stance: "I'm just playing devil's advocate; I'm not saying 'I don't [want them off the streets]', I'm just saying 'Why is it a great thing [that they are kept off the streets]?'" Sally then said:

> Oh right. I think it's because it's giving them a reason to get up in the morning. If they didn't, they probably would be getting into trouble and all that sort of thing. I mean they are drinking a lot earlier than a lot of people over in England. I know that you get troubled kids and everything [in England], I do understand that, but I mean [here it's] twelve or ten [years old] – that's scary. I mean, what does the township give you? Do you know what I mean? I might be totally, like, naive or ignorant, but I figure if the kids stay at home [they will do that kind of thing]. They need prospects, they need ambition, that's what Mama Mary is creating by taking them off the streets, giving them education.

Anthropologists have tried to understand how social life is framed as culture, and then how culture is objectified, reproduced, and transformed in homes and schools during processes of contested 'culture clash', and have shown how schooling can create social and cultural discontinuity, for example, among family members or between generations (e.g. Bonini 2006; Collier 1973; Howard 1970; Rival 2000; Wolcott 2003). In contrast, Sally was adamant that schools are valuable because they encourage young people to move away from knowledge, values, and behaviours they might come to embody as a result of learning experiences 'on the street' and at home. According to her, the township and 'the street' offered drugs, alcohol, and trouble; in contrast, the school provided moral education (e.g. about drugs and drink), prospects, social skills, and the English language. Most strongly, she thought that Mary and 'her school' gave learners "a reason to get up in the morning". Later in our conversation, Betty told me about the importance of the school instilling "an attitude that will make them get up every morning and go to work and do it well". In her words, we more clearly glimpse an accompanying ethic of personal responsibility and hard work. Her words clearly reflect accounts of the learners and the school that appeared in promotional discourses. Betty and Sally agreed with them, trusted them, and, as ethical evaluations, saw the school's intervention, and that of Mary in particular, as a good thing.

Stambach (2000: 10) argues that the notion that "schooling changes social life ... is an optimistic model of socially planned change that is often incorporated into international development policies". This model relates to the 'modernisation theories' of developmental and educational literature, including, I would argue, much of the sociological considerations of schooling in South Africa.[23] Stambach (ibid: 11) playfully calls these "'school-to-the-rescue-models'". As if to speak directly to Betty and Sally's assertions, Stambach (ibid: 11) asserts that such "models turn on a particular assumption that 'becoming modern' stems from outside cultural forces, mostly from Western states, and that modernity is a unidirectional process that moves people towards a common end". There is "a commitment to 'improving' old social forms and to moving people on to a 'better world' through a system of classroom instruction and examinations" (ibid.). Here, pedagogy "is a matter of transmitting knowledge from 'more' to 'less' educated groups and of assisting underdeveloped peoples and countries in securing basic needs" (ibid.). The sisters did not explicitly talk about modernity, only mentioning the idea of "prospects"; however, their words do convey something of the desire to better learners and their social relations with experiences of schooling. For Sally and Betty, there was 'an end' that learners could be helped towards—away from the immorality of the township and away from trouble. Like those individuals operating an orphanage in Tanzania, who Stambach (with Kwayu 2013) considers elsewhere, Sally was sure that schooling could provide learners with the experience of such expectation and anticipation as she articulated when using the word "ambition". For her, schooling could shape learners' imaginations of, and relationships with, their own futures while simultaneously providing the necessary resources to them so that they could fashion this same future. In other words, for this supporter of Ngomso, schooling offered the prospect of a life lived away from the township and the street and was the process whereby the value of this prospect had to be learnt.

It is telling that Sally hoped that the school might draw the young people away from their homes. Her ethical imagination reflects the school's promotional discourses (i.e. that presented learners' parents and carers as being ineffective or absent), and she seemed content with the idea that carers and parents would be circumvented with care and support given directly to the learners. This dynamic aligns with an argument about humanitarianism more generally: when adults take the blame for the challenging circumstances faced by 'the young', supporters and donors are encouraged to direct their assistance directly to the young people in question (see Weckesser 2011: 103).[24] Compretta (2012: 192–3) similarly reports a "focus on individual, not societal, reform" at a faith-based after-school programme in America. She claims that members of staff "ideologically and programmatically" separated "children from guardians [and families]" to focus on their "social and moral transformations". In contrast, services were rarely offered to guardians.

Weckesser and Compretta both discuss their findings by evoking the 'neoliberal' discourse, which has been inescapable while reading about (1) schooling and development and (2) South Africa's post-apartheid 'political transformation' (e.g. Bundy 2014; Bond 2000). Weckesser (2011: 103), for example, asserts that adults "are not perceived as blameless within neoliberal imperatives of personal responsibility and choice". This assertion is also relevant to my research. To some extent, the tendency to direct assistance to children and young adults parallels modes of devolution and decentralisation, which circumnavigate the most senior levels of government, not 'irresponsible parents'.[25] In the neoliberal model, local and low-level bureaucrats can be trusted with finance and responsibility, much like the judgement that young people are best placed fashion their own destinies. However, the strategy of directly funding the 'next generation', children and youth, not only disempowers all levels of government, but it also threatens models of familial and community responsibility that might otherwise be associated with neoliberalism.[26] In Africa, Ferguson (2006: 38) argues that neoliberal shifts have meant that "functions of the state have effectively been 'outsourced' to NGOs, [creating a situation where] state capacity has deteriorated rapidly". One might also argue that the practice of distributing aid and assistance directly to young people would have the same effect upon the capacities of families and communities. In other words, such strategies may actually contribute to the conditions that motivate such measures in the first instance. Moreover, such scenarios would mirror other processes on the continent, whereby engagements with schooling, which is premised most explicitly on the *personal* development of children and young adults, have estranged the 'next generation' from family and community structures (Freeman 2001; Stambach 2000). To a certain extent, such arguments are reflected in the concerns and complaints of Ngomso's staff and donors, who were specifically anxious about a breakdown in the cohesion and (re)productive strength of these very arrangements.

So, the hope that interlocutors like Sally placed in the idea that learners could be separated from their home environments is fully attributable to neoliberalism, right? Well, not quite. In the context of South Africa, the blame ascribed to parents and caregivers cannot be isolated from historical discourses regarding 'the native capacity for child rearing'. Likewise, desires to separate learners from the township relate to the rich history of maternalistic missionisation in the vicinity. More broadly, as Catherine Kingfisher and Jeff Maskovsky (2008: 121) have argued, the term 'neoliberal' might well be useful when one is trying to understand and explain "some of the most egregious forms of inequality, poverty, exploitation and oppression in the world today", but I would argue that this discourse is insufficient when one wants to also understand how experiences and processes, which are always subject to specific histories, are both localised (i.e. distinct) and globally united (i.e. interdependent). Moreover, as in the case of 'native child rearing' and benevolent missionisation, patterns of uneven distributions of power—be they nationalised, gendered, racial, generational, or whatever—did not first emerge with the rise of the 'neoliberal world order', even if the neoliberal discourse captures something of their essence (ibid.). Instead, the tendency to class something as 'neoliberal' is a mode of sensemaking that enables individuals to isolate mechanisms of causality and attribute them to a distinct historical moment. The conceptual framework is an example of how the enthusiasm to strip away nuance from modes of analysis in order to bring about theoretical uniformity and existential security, which are intimately connected, removes the disorderliness of specificity from formations of understanding. This totalising way of working compromises our ability to comprehend the conditions that both unify and distinguish populations struggling for improved conditions, inadvertently imposing a methodologically reductionistic mode of power that reflects the same homogenising qualities that critics of neoliberal governance regularly set out to address.

Certainly, none of my interlocutors spoke about neoliberalism, and it did not appear to help them make sense of their experiences or ethically imagine alternative scenarios. For Sally, successful intervention would result in learners' becoming separated from their present circumstances; understood, ultimately, as some form of transcendence of place. She hoped they would interact with individuals who did not live locally and learn a 'foreign' language. Only then might they have the freedom and confidence to move, communicate, and earn money within the world beyond—'out there somewhere'—the one she thought they were confined by and to (i.e. the township). Unpaid volunteers, such as Sally and Betty, were integral to the enactment of such hope. This is how Daniel articulated the idea, as we sat in the playground one afternoon with my recorder between us:

> I think volunteers do useful work – not just the one-on-one [reading] but just by chatting with the kids. [They are] making the kids used to talking to white people, making the kids aware that people from other countries and overseas can be sympathetic and supportive; just widening their horizons really. And the kids do just accept the volunteers being here. Look at Neo [the university student taking photographs for her project] – she is coloured, really, OK she is from Botswana, and she [only] looks fairly white, but she is a visitor taking photos with an expensive camera, and the kids don't bat an eyelid really.

While Neo was using her (digital) exposures to capture images, Daniel saw this activity as a positive example of learners' exposure to 'foreigners' with different skin colours and expensive material possessions. Daniel first spent time in southern Africa in the 1970s when visiting his aunt and uncle, who were missionaries. In his words "widening their horizons" we glimpse something of the parallels between their endeavours.

My ability to speak English contributed to the welcome I received at the school.[27] Mary was also keen that learners learn about "different cultures". She said that volunteers enabled learners to have "a comprehensive view of globalisation". While she and other members of staff tried to ensure that the school was separate from the township, there was hope that visitors from 'outside it' might open learners' eyes to the 'possibility of life beyond it'. Such ethical imaginaries are comparable with those of the 'civilising project' of the colonial period; when missionaries similarly hoped to separate young Xhosas from their families and villages by hosting them in their schools and mission stations, to shift them away from their 'pre-colonial' and 'undesirable' prior existence. Then, the hope was that the Xhosa would transcend their locality and history, and reorder their understanding of the world and their interaction with it. European settlers brought their language, material consumption, faith, behaviour, clothing, and education. During my research, the language that described and informed such hopes had changed, there were no 'uncivilised savages' anymore. However, the roots of this form of progressivism still appeared to be in good health.[28]

To further this argument, I can consider the embodied moralities of Betty, Sally, Daniel, and Susan, who all visited the school for extended periods of time. Throughout our conversations, I learnt that their analysis of the school's interventionist qualities did chime with discourses concerning modernisation and related efforts to 'bring them forward to where we are', which again parallels the 'civilising project' to some extent. However, they evaluated the extent to which Ngomso provided the hope promised by its marketing activities in light of their knowledge of the intricacies of the school day and had an understanding of the efficacy of the institution and its staff that did not come from public discourses. While these individuals certainly appeared to have bought into the promise (i.e. the hope Ngomso offered), they also expressed concern that the school could improve, and debated the extent to which they should contribute to such improvement.

As we stood in the playground in 2011, Daniel told me that the school reminded him of something that might have existed in "an English village at the start of the nineteenth century". He spoke about the boarding school depicted in *Stalky & Co.*, Rudyard Kipling's book, first published in 1899.[29] Daniel said that "99% [of the learners] are incredibly well behaved", and he was "thinking about the causes of that". He suggested that "there is still much more of a traditional respect for your elders than there is say in Britain, which I think has a lot to do with it". He compared Ngomso's "zero tolerance for trouble in the classroom" and the role of security guards to the discipline regimes and "school sergeants" detailed in Kipling's book:

> I suspect possibly that the security guards have almost come out of the same tradition because quite a lot of the things that happen in South African schools are quite familiar to someone who grew up in England fifty years ago in English schools – they haven't changed in the ways that our own schools have. Now whether that is a lesson that can be learnt back in Britain I don't know.

Although Daniel was keen to consider what England could learn from South Africa, his more prominent theme of analysis construed this relationship in reverse. His analysis of his first months in the country soon shifted to his concerns about what he had seen:

> The culture shock that I did find was the attitude of some of the teachers, which, in summary, is much more laid-back, much more inclined just to do the minimum to keep the class occupied. They are inclined to be happy running traditional – very didactic lessons – probably writing on the board and talking and then doing a written exercise. There is very little variety from that standard pattern.

On his blog, which he wrote to inform friends and family about his experiences, he says that "the Xhosa culture is much more laid back [*sic*] than ours". The Bible tells us that God does not speak to those laid on their backs: "And he said to me, 'Son of man, stand on your feet, and I will speak with you'" (Ezekiel, 2:1). Susan described one of her favourite 'transformation stories' by saying: "[Some make progress], like Vuyani [did]. [I've seen him] coming back, standing up, straight and tall, and [now] he is not the lost little boy that he was four years ago." In place of the words 'laid-back', I more often heard complaints from Mary and volunteers about the 'laziness' of staff.

Reading back over Daniel's words I can see that he was finding it difficult to judge the right course of action in the face of such issues, especially given his enthusiasm for treading lightly. He continues the discussion on his blog and addresses pressing questions regarding economic prosperity, functions of government, and racism, by saying:

I tend to worry ... [but] it can be difficult to know where to stand. On the one hand as visitors we want to respect the local culture however laid back [*sic*] it might be, but on the other the SA government clearly expects the black population to hold a fair share of senior management posts [especially due to Black Economic Empowerment] and the economy to keep on growing. This will not happen unless black children are pushed academically, which of course they are if they happen to have a place at many of the ex-white schools [i.e. former Model C schools] or the British-style independent schools.

He went on to say that "some of the laid-backness" might help learners who were not "disciplined [enough]" to concentrate "every minute of the day". However, he was still unsure whether this approach was "a bad thing" or not. Overall, he clearly felt that substandard school educations posed a threat to successful post-apartheid transformations more broadly. Can 'black children' grow up to hold senior management posts and drive the economy forward without the impact of education delivered by schools managed, in the main, by white adults? Daniel was convinced that the answer is no. According to his judgement, the 'local culture' was ill-suited to the demands of economic growth and better suited to some other ends.

Daniel said that Mary had told him that this 'laid-back culture' "led on from the riots in 1976 and the go-slow [protests]; all the teachers grew up in schools seeing this kind of attitude from their own teachers". The issue of temporal rigidity was, in fact, already an issue before apartheid. The Comaroffs (1986: 2) analyse the missionising endeavour as the "subtle colonization, by the missionary, of indigenous modes of perception and practice".[30] They (ibid: 14) argue that missionaries of the colonial period paid attention to promoting individualistic industry and Christian morality by ordering annual, weekly, and everyday routine and practice "in both its secular and sacred dimensions" (i.e. with school and church bells, clocks, and timetables). In a relationship with moral and material accumulation, this practice served to objectify time and futurity and condition its commoditisation.[31]

When I first sat down with Betty and Sally, holding my MP3 recorder, the sisters were half way through their month-long visit to South Africa. I knew that they were not finding their time at the school particularly enjoyable or comfortable, so I was not surprised when they enthusiastically took time out to speak with me. I opened with the question:

Let's start with the good stuff. [Let's talk] of what you are enjoying or liking. [It can be] anything to do with being in South Africa or being in the school, or....

My voice trailed off as the sisters looked at me with smiles that suggested I was barking up the wrong tree. Sensing that they wanted to take the conversation in a different direction I asked:

Or is there not really much [good] stuff? Does that silence say a lot? Do you want to start with the bad stuff? Is that easier?

Without another word from me, they began to explain their most immediate thoughts:

Sally: Structure
Betty: Lack of structure.
Sally: That is a massive [one]. Pees me off.

Before this conversation, the sisters had complained to me that they were not given timetables when they arrived at the school and had been unsure of what activities they could do. In the UK, they lived at home with their parents and had recently finished their own schooling. The fact they had lived their lives, predominantly, in two environments where they would have been subject to adult supervision and control perhaps explains why they found the lack of structure—that is, the freedom to navigate numerous possibilities of action and interaction—they experienced at Ngomso somewhat uncomfortable, even alien. Their experience contrasted with Daniel's, who, with years of experience working as a member of staff in schools, located and created time and space to involve himself in classroom and playground activities more readily.

Initially, I found it surprising that interlocutors like Daniel, Sally, and Betty craved structure. As a consequence of the work that I read while writing my MA research proposal, especially 'practice theory' literature (e.g. Bourdieu 1977, 1980; Giddens 1984; Ortner 2006), I had come to understand structure as limiting agency, as a curtailment of a universal want for individual freedom. In contrast, my interlocutors were actively promoting structure as 'good stuff' (see Laidlaw 2010). However, they were referring to a particular form of structure, a valued component of an identifiable moral assemblage. Tightly structured activity was held to be an essential element of educational experiences and, relatedly, the formation of moral dispositions. Such an interpretation of the structuring qualities of education aligns better with Foucault's analysis of power: schooling doesn't simply limit individuals' agentive capacities and curtail their freedoms, although to some extent it certainly does. Instead, individuals are encouraged or taught, disciplined even, to employ themselves, their bodies and minds, in certain ways and to particular ends. The ethical imaginaries that underpin the schooling project, most especially those relating to obedience and self-regulation are threatened by the absence of such modes of power. As Sally explained it:

> I know they have set periods, but the bell goes, and they are quite relaxed to get to the next class.... The children are all well behaved and polite in some ways, but in other ways, you know, [they're] just standing up and walking out of class. That's rude, and I think they should be picked up on it. [Otherwise] they are not going to learn. Like, in my first high school, we were taught that as soon as a teacher walked into a classroom, you stood up, and you greeted them. It's just manners. And I think that the teachers [here] are not teaching the kids manners. There's no [structure]. I don't think that they are accustomed to how, you know, other schools would be taught.

I believe that when she referred to "other schools" she was speaking of those in the UK, as, to my knowledge, she didn't visit any others in South Africa. However, it is possible that she was referring to the fact that Ngomso was a 'special school' and, therefore, different to 'mainstream' schools. Either way, Sally considered adherence to the rhythm of the school bell and confinement to the classrooms as being constitutive of desirable moral dispositions: having "manners" and being "well behaved and polite" rather than "rude". She valued authoritative adults and teachers, and institutional regulations and expectations. From what I understand, Sally experienced schooling at a private school in Norfolk that runs on Christian principles. While she was judging events at Ngomso, she seemed tied to a moral habitus that I would expect to find interweaved in the education at such an institution.

While Daniel spoke of "Xhosa culture" or an "attitude", the sisters went on to contrast their understanding of structure with the idea of an "African way":

Sally: [At our school] you respected the teacher, you weren't allowed to just walk out of the classroom.

Betty: I think that is because they are just generally relaxed [here]. But general behaviour is better [than I was expecting].

Sally: It's fine to say that the African way is laid-back, but that's not the British way. And if they are wanting these kids to grow up and do well, they need manners. If they are going to go into an office type job or anything like that, you don't [learn to] just walk out.... That's just so easy to be taught and I think that the teachers are too laid-back, and I just don't think that is acceptable, and I don't think it's an excuse, this laid-back Afrikaans kind of living way.[32] Do you know what I mean? It is only an excuse so far.

Not only were the sisters habitually attuned to the idea that education concerns preparation for disciplined employment, but they were also keen for others to learn the importance of such a disposition too. They wanted education to work on others in the way that it had worked on them. The ease with which they associated a particular conceptualisation of a way of being in the world with an entire continent (i.e. the notion of 'the African way') demonstrates how public and institutional discourses concerning Africa that circulate in the UK feed considerations of 'a people' united by inferiority. Although the sisters were now there, in Africa, in person, the grip of mass generalisation was hard to shake off. As she continued her explanation it became clear that Sally thought there was one member of staff who was doing the right thing and bringing some structure to proceedings:

[This laid-backness] needs to be fought [against] and it needs to be [stopped]. You know? Mama Mary needs to succeed. Because it's sad for Mama Mary, sometimes [she struggles with it]. Like, one of the kids was a bit stand-offish with her, so she called for the three security guards to come and help her and, this is another [example of] them being laid-back, they just looked and then just sauntered over.... She is the only white teacher at the school; I know that as volunteers we are white and what not, but, in the school itself she is the only one. And I think that it is difficult for her, you know? She can speak the language, but the men – the security guards [especially] – still seem really laid-back, and it's rude.

Betty: It's just their whole general attitude that's laid-back.

Sally: Their whole mannerisms are laid-back.

Mary told me that she sometimes struggled to direct and instruct the security guards because they, as initiated or "fully-fledged" Xhosa men (*indoda*), were not inclined to publically take orders from a woman (Ntombana 2011: 79). This observation suggests there were tensions between gendered and generational structures of power associated with *ukuhlonipha* (i.e. a convention of deference) and bureaucratised arrangements of power associated with schooling and Mary's position as principal in particular. Sally and Betty may well have witnessed this tension before interpreting their observations as evidence of a lack of structure and respect altogether. Although they told me that the school was insular from the 'culture' (i.e. practices and moral discourses) of the township, this clearly was not the case. Given this permeability, Ngomso's supporters were keen to transform members of staff as well as learners. As yet, this has not been their primary focus. However, I recently contributed to a debate among trustees of the Friends about the prospect of funding training courses for 'volunteer' teaching assistants who could not attend those offered by the DoE. On his blog, Daniel tells us that he offered subtle forms of 'staff training' himself:

> I try to turn up promptly for lessons, and if I am teaching my lesson finishes on time. It may be only a nominal signal that I am sending out, but it's a start.

Daniel's particularly considered approach when educating 'the black population' was *his* contribution, but it followed the efforts of many others who have, for centuries, tried to convey the value of hard work and diligence to 'the locals'. Christianity and governance have never been far away from such endeavours. In his diary, on May 5, 1855, Mary's forefather Robert Miller (cited in Anonymous) wrote:

> I am busy teaching the natives to work at building with stone, use picks, and turn over the ground for sowing. I find them very lazy except on piece work and need continual watching.... Kaffirs are very obstinate, whenever they do not wish to obey an order, they tell me they are only waiting for an excuse to make war, and then they will kill me, but I take no notice.

As a catechist, it is possible that he may have read one of these extracts:

> Diligent hands will rule, but laziness ends in forced labor (Proverbs, 12: 24).
> A sluggard's appetite is never filled, but the desires of the diligent are fully satisfied (Proverbs, 13:4).

> Whatever you do, work at it with all your heart, as working for the Lord, not for human masters (Colossians, 3:23).
> One who is slack in his work is brother to one who destroys (Proverbs, 18: 9).

Daniel was inclined to send signals rather than give orders. He hoped to counter idleness with modelled behaviour: an instructional technique that presented awareness of the clock as a most valuable embodied moral disposition, ripe for imitation. To my knowledge, he was not concerned about the prospect of war or murder. However, his worry about where to stand suggests that he was aware of the potential for conflict with these 'cultural others'. His deliberation is indicative of the existential angst he experienced when trying to act moralistically towards others.

As far as I can understand, Daniel's anxieties relate more to the effectiveness of his methods and the welcome his intervention might receive, rather than any existential crisis regarding the desirability and configuration of his moral project or the respective orientation of the school and the education it offered. More broadly, these ethnographic insights demonstrate that individuals who came to support the school—as a consequence of PowerPoint presentations in churches, radio interviews, or any other communicative touch points—valued institutional discourses of moral and technologies of power associated with schooling, especially those that regulate and produce experiences and understandings of time, place, futurity, and movement. They also shared concerns regarding 'normal childhoods' and 'normal families'. Moreover, those supportive of the cause saw themselves as being integrated into the same mainstream society that was held to have excluded the young people and thought that the learners would be better off if they were included in it. In short, supporters were united by the hope that the recipients of their support could be steered towards, and enabled to live, a life more like their own. They had learnt to positively evaluate their own embodied moral dispositions; ethically imagining an alignment of moral dispositions and the materialisation of prosperous individualised and collective futures. The fact that their positionality overlapped, to some extent at least, with members of staff is evidence of how historically constituted links between the two localities (i.e. South Africa and the UK) unfold into a form of conceptual cohesiveness that unites individuals living great distances from one another. Conversely, such cohesion is an integral component of the bonds that enjoin these two countries. The ethnography presented demonstrates that it is not only government policies and diplomacy but also humanitarianism that fashions the qualities of political transformations that are most readily described using rubrics such as postcolonialism or post-apartheid.

At play here is something akin to the notion of "politics as a process of world-building", as conceptualised by Zigon (2014: 760). In line with this idea, I have argued that individuals enact processes of marketing and volunteering to bring about "new possibilities, new worlds" for themselves and others (ibid: 759). Donors and supporters of charity invest something of themselves in the possibility that an alternative world to the one that potential beneficiaries currently endure can be created. By doing so, the probabilities and formations of alternative futures are to some extent brought under their influence. Zigon (ibid.) suggests that the motivation to enact such processes emerges after experiences of some form of enlightenment. The context of his research is different to my own, but it is difficult not to recognise how this terminology is also applicable to discourses readily associated with the colonial project and enactments of missionisation in particular. I would argue that the differences between forms of politics as a process of world-building associated with schooling and missionisation during the nineteenth century and those brought about as a consequence of the marketing activity I observed are linguistic distinctions not fundamentally alternative states of affairs.

Processes of world-building emerge as a consequence of ethical demands placed upon individuals during particularly uncomfortable experiences (Zigon 2014: 762). In Zigon's analysis, it is the experience of living as a drug user in a world where such a way of being in the world is unsustainable and unliveable that motivates individuals to enact such processes. In the case of my research, the ethical demands placed upon supporters and donors were quite different. In various ways, they were living possibilities for being in the world that they wished to open up for target beneficiaries so that they could fashion alternative ways of being in the world. However, although they fundamentally wanted to refashion or turnaround the lives of others, the enactment of such process made their own ability to dwell within the world possible. Thus, the lives of those adjudged to be living the unliveable (i.e. young South Africans experiencing vulnerability) and those who wished to intervene to alter these lives intertwined in such a way that the existence of one and the other was integral to the existence of both. In other words, the lives of humanitarianism's supporters cannot exist in any present or potential formations without the existence of other lives caught up in their imaginings of alternative states of affairs, and these 'other lives' (i.e. those of beneficiaries) are to some extent beholden to same imaginations for their formation.

Notes

1. Hecht's (2008: 240) discussion of 'commodification'—that is, how the lives of Brazilian street children have been "photographed and written about", and "in whose name money is raised and social movements galvanised"—has much in common with this notion of 'marketing'. Similar notions have been articulated in reference to fundraising efforts concerning 'orphanhood' and orphanages (see Bornstein 2009; Weckesser 2011). As Cheney (2010: 7) argues, with reference to these same contexts, "children themselves become the commodities that circulate to produce new forms of vulnerability".
2. Dahl's (2006: 636, emphasis added) ethnographic research in Botswana yields a similar observation: "the European man who founded Bathusi [a day-care orphanage] had a particular knack for fund-raising, and he began to *market the stories* of hungry orphans (and greedy relatives) to donors".
3. Paul Harris (2000: 8–9) argues that we do not use our imagination to withdraw "from the world" but as a way of "engaging and learning about it".
4. It is difficult to provide more ethnographic data to back up this point. Imaginations cannot be seen and can only be explained to others after the fact of their formation (i.e. as a memory of an imagination that once was). Moreover, individuals can be selective about the aspects of their imaginations that they share with others, and there are always limits to what can be shared because recollections of what was imagined differ from experiences and forms of initial imagining. Nonetheless, when we observe interactions between others, such as those I saw in Susan's church and at the school in Warwick, we can see how others act upon their imaginations, and deduce something about the qualities of these imaginations.
5. The 'mothers who sleep around' narrative was not, to my knowledge, explicitly linked with the issue of 'AIDS orphans' during fundraising. However, these issues were frequently referenced, leading me to think that members of staff saw a connection between the threat of AIDS and the 'lifestyle choices' of those affected.
6. Crewe and Axelby (2013: 1) make a similar assertion: "Fundraising drives and awareness-raising campaigns … rely on the evocation of despair to provoke a reaction. Shocking images are accompanied by passionate pleas for support."
7. Dirty tap water was frequently offered to Grahamstown residents due to irregularities in municipal expenditure and nepotism in the appointment of unqualified staff, but Joyce didn't mention this.
8. This assertion is made to comic effect in a parody of the quiz-show *Who Wants to Be a Millionaire*. For the "chance to save Africa" the contestant is

asked "How many countries are there in Africa?" (*Who Wants to Be a Volunteer?*, 2014: 1.17 minutes). She 'correctly' answers: "one" (ibid: 2.40 minutes).
9. The London Common Council sent 100 'vagrant children' from Britain to North America as early as 1619 (Higginbotham 2012). This instigated the practice of 'organised emigration and resettlement' for 'abandoned', 'orphaned', and 'gutter children' from Britain to her colonies. Most pointedly, a party was sent to the Cape of Good Hope in 1832 (Merseyside Maritime Museum 2014). The most expansive practice was the Home Children scheme, initiated by Annie Macpherson, a devout evangelical Christian, who also opened the Home of Industry in London (Frost 2005: 325–6). Her organisation was later incorporated into that of Dr Thomas John Barnardo (now Barnardo's) (ibid.). As in the case of Barnardo, "the impulse to rescue children from dangerous or morally undesirable situations informed child migration as practiced by all the major children's societies" (Lawrence and Starkey 2001: 5–6).
10. What might appear to be impulsive reactions to appeals for immediate assistance were, however, rarely impulsive acts. More accurately, they were mobilisations of historically constituted ethical imaginations, which were dependent upon individuals' life courses and resources. Supporters frequently said that their involvement fulfilled a hope for self-transformation of some kind. As mentioned, Susan wanted to work with children in Africa in order to fulfil her obligations as a Christian Vicar. Betty and Sally, two sisters who volunteered at the school, went to South Africa in an attempt to improve their relationship by separating themselves from the UK. Their parents were keen for them to do so and funded their trip accordingly. A man named Daniel volunteered at the school because he met Mary when planning to take time away from his professional commitments in the UK.
11. The episode in question was a component of a bigger effort to construe a particular relationship of responsibility between the G8 nations and the 'developing world' (Africa in particular). The programme in question was criticised for breaching the BBC's stance on impartiality: the writer, Richard Curtis, also founded Comic Relief and the Make Poverty History campaign and helped to organise the ten Live 8 concerts of 2005 (Holmwood 2007).
12. This statement holds true even when the promoted cause is an intervention that aims to bring about self-sufficiency because such notions suggest that the individuals in question have been unable to sustain themselves prior to such interventions, which is clearly not the case if they are alive.
13. Beyond Susan's reaction, consider the words of an American who also watched the programme and was moved to volunteer for the ONE Campaign, an advocacy organisation that focuses its attentions on Africa,

including the promotion of school attendance (ONE 2015): "I couldn't watch it and not do anything.... I told my wife I had to do something" (Reuters 2008: np).
14. Weckesser (2011: 20) suggests that orphans have been portrayed in a similar way.
15. Beier's (1987) book is entitled *Masterless Men: The Vagrancy Problem in England 1560–1640*, which echoes D.H. Lawrence's ([1923] 2011: 41–47) *Spirit of Place*. Lawrence (ibid: 44) was concerned that America had become a republic of "The masterless". He (ibid.) wrote that "Liberty is all very well, but men cannot live without masters" (see McClay 1994). In the Cape, where slavery officially ended between 1834 and 1840, people were once property and many escaped slaves, like stolen goods, were in a different and more desperate situation than mere masterless vagrants, for they knew what awaited them if they were apprehended.
16. For example, in 1654, Richard Younge (cited in Slack 1974: 360) argued that these 'rogues' were "an uncircumcised generation, unbaptized, out of the Church, and so consequently without God in the World". Henry VIII (cited in Nicholls, [1904] 2007: 115) was concerned about the Godless, idle and immoral who disturbed the "common weal of this realm".
17. It is in relation to the 'priestly caste' that Nietzsche (1994: 15) argues "'clean' and 'unclean' confront each other for the first time as badges of class distinction; here again, there develops a 'good' and a 'bad'".
18. For example, the Vagabonds and Beggars Act of 1495 was passed during the reign of Henry VII. It states: "Vagabonds, idle and suspected persons shall be set in the stocks for three days and three nights and have none other sustenance but bread and water and then shall be put out of Town" (King's Norton History Society 2004: np).
19. Cheney (2010) discusses a similar terminological shift in Uganda: from 'orphans' to 'vulnerable children'.
20. Academic accounts of orphanhood have similarly offered warnings of tidal waves in relation to concerns about political security (see Weckesser 2011: 20).
21. In 2012, there were reports in Grahamstown that corporate donations to NGOs had dropped by 42%, National Lottery funding by 38%, and individual donations by 37% (Davis 2012). Between 2010 and 2011, UK donations to charities fell by 20%, from £11bn to £9.3bn (Butler 2011).
22. Recall, from earlier in the chapter, that the term 'street children' has generally succeeded 'glue sniffers'.
23. For instance, Wright (2012: 14) claims that the proliferation of schooling has "intrinsic human value", and that schools "are the only institutions in the [Eastern Cape Province] that have the social and intellectual reach to build the country's long-term future". In this view, schools are interpreted

as 'right', and this 'right' is often conflated with the realisation of 'rights' (see Comaroff and Comaroff 1997: 9). A corpus that provides an interesting counter to such assertions is associated with studies of 'neocolonialism' or 'postcolonialism', and 'cultural imperialism'. Scholars are critical of how processes of schooling in South Africa, and across the continent, support 'Western' or 'European' demands and propagate racialised, culturally configured geographical inequalities (e.g. Abdi 2002; Mazuri 1993). They wish to address the way that 'indigenous cultures' were 'decimated' during the colonial era; processes of 'cultural imperialism' that, they argue, are maintained through systems of 'postcolonialism' and 'globalised capitalism' (Abdi and Cleghorn 2005; Shizha 2005; also see, Rizvi 2001).

24. Kathryn McHarry (2013) made a similar, ethnographically informed, point during her presentation at the American Anthropological Association meeting of 2013, which was entitled *Sponsoring the Future: Marketizing Children's Potential in Senegalese Preschools*.
25. I would like to thank Derick Fay for this insight and his helpful comments regarding this section of analysis, in particular, and my PhD thesis as a whole.
26. For instance, when considering anthropological engagements with neoliberalism as a series of paradigms, one of which is most clearly "influenced by post-structuralism", Kingfisher and Maskovsky (2008: 118) highlight "the shift in governmentality whereby a modality of government based on social intervention and Keynesian welfare statism is transformed into a modality in which the operations of government … are autonomized and economized in accordance with an entrepreneurial model that emphasizes personal, familial and community responsibility and risk, and the proliferation of NGOs". It is with knowledge of this argument that I make a claim in the main text regarding the commonality of associations of neoliberalism with devolutions of power to families and communities, as well as NGOs.
27. English language proficiency was an important aspect of education: matriculation depended on it, and many interlocutors thought it was integral to employment prospects, a view widely held in South Africa (de Wet 2002; cf. Stambach 2010).
28. Harrison and Crewe (1998: 30) make a related point when they argue, "For those working in development, whether they seek modernity or greater respect for local people, 'primitive' has been replaced by 'traditional' or, more recently, indigenous and local, and 'civilized' by 'modern'".
29. Incidentally, Kipling was good friends with Lord Roberts of Kandahar, who led British forces during the second Boer War (1899–1902) and was uniquely the subject in three Kipling poems (Moore 2013). Kipling distributed supplies this same war (ibid.), providing the setting for many of his 'Barrack-Room Ballads'.

30. Their analysis is made with reference to Bourdieu's (1977) theorisation of how domination and control are achieved through the imposition of indirect, subtle everyday practices.
31. Simpson's (2003) ethnography of a mission school in Zambia also directly examines schooling in terms of everyday orderings of time and futurity.
32. I don't know if Sally's shift between "African" and "Afrikaans" was a slip of the tongue or whether her choice of words illustrates a lack of understanding. I only noticed when listening to a recording of our conversation and did not ask her for clarification at the time.

Bibliography

Abdi, A. A. (2002). *Culture, Education, and Development in South Africa: Historical and Contemporary Perspectives*. Westport: Bergin and Garvey.

Abdi, A. A., & Cleghorn, A. (2005). Sociology of Education: Theoretical and Conceptual Perspectives. In A. A. Abdi & A. Cleghorn (Eds.), *Issues in African Education: Sociological Perspectives* (pp. 3–24). New York/Basingstoke: Palgrave Macmillan.

Abebe, T. (2008). *Ethiopian Childhoods: A Case Study of the Lives of Orphans and Working Children*. Unpublished PhD Thesis, Norwegian University of Science and Technology, Faculty of Social Sciences and Technology Management, Department of Geography, Norwegian Centre for Child Research. Retrieved June 9, 2014, from http://www.diva-portal.org/smash/get/diva2:123904/FULLTEXT01.pdf

Anonymous. Details omitted in order to maintain anonymity of interlocutors.

Apthorpe, R. (2011). Coda. With Alice in Aidland: A Seriously Satirical Allegory. In D. Mosse (Ed.), *Adventures in Aidland: The Anthropology of Professionals in International Development* (pp. 199–219). New York/Oxford: Berghahn Books.

Apthorpe, R. (2013). *Post-pieties Humanitarianisms, International Relations, Ex Ante Evaluation, and Anthropology*. Retrieved May 4, 2015, from http://www.raymondapthorpe.com/

BBC. (2006). The Spread of AIDS in Africa. *BBC Online*. Retrieved August 12, 2015, from http://www.bbc.co.uk/education/clips/zcdnvcw

Beier, A. (1987). *Masterless Men: Vagrancy Problem in Britain, 1560–1640*. London: Methuen.

Bond, P. (2000). *Elite Transition: From Apartheid to Neoliberalism in South Africa*. London: Pluto Press.

Bonini, N. (2006). The Pencil and the Shepherd's Crook. Ethnography of Maasai Education. *Ethnography and Education, 1*(3), 379–392.

Bornstein, E. (2001). Child Sponsorship, Evangelism, and Belonging in the Work of World Vision Zimbabwe. *American Ethnologist, 28*(3), 595–622.

Bornstein, E. (2005). *The Spirit of Development: Protestant NGOs, Morality, and Economics in Zimbabwe.* Stanford: Stanford University Press.

Bornstein, E. (2009). The Impulse of Philanthropy. *Cultural Anthropology, 24*(4), 622–651.

Bornstein, E. (2012). *Disquieting Gifts: Humanitarianism in New Delhi.* Stanford: Stanford University Press.

Bornstein, E., & Redfield, P. (2008). *Genealogies of Suffering and the Gift of Care: A Working Paper on the Anthropology of Religion, Secularism, and Humanitarianism.* New York: Social Science Research Council Working Papers.

Bourdieu, P. (1977). *Outline of a Theory of Practice.* London: Cambridge University Press.

Bourdieu, P. (1980). *The Logic of Practice.* Stanford: Stanford University Press.

Bourdieu, P. (2000). *Pascalian Meditations.* Stanford: Stanford University Press.

Bundy, C. (2014). *Short-Changed? South Africa Since Apartheid.* Athens: Ohio University Press.

Butler, P. (2011). Donations to Charity Fall 20% in a Year, Study Finds. *The Guardian* (Online). Retrieved March 3, 2013, from http://www.theguardian.com/money/2012/nov/13/charity-donations-fall-uk-survey

Cheney, K. (2010). Expanding Vulnerability, Dwindling Resources: Implications for Orphaned Futures in Uganda. *Childhood in Africa, 2*(1), 8–15.

Clissold, M. L. (2010). 'Pornography of Poverty': An Anthropological Perspective into Humanitarian Fundraising Campaigns. Unpublished MA dissertation, Social Anthropology of Development, SOAS, London. Retrieved January 14, 2014, from http://www.melissaclissold.com/uploads/2/5/8/8/25889170/2010_melissa_lara_clissold_soas_dissertation_pornography_of_poverty.pdf

Collier, J. (1973). *Alaskan Eskimo Education: A Film Analysis of Cultural Confrontation in the Schools.* New York: Holt, Rinehart and Winston.

Comaroff, J., & Comaroff, J. (1986). Christianity and Colonialism in South Africa. *American Ethnologist, 13*(1), 1–22.

Comaroff, J., & Comaroff, J. (1997). *Of Revelation and Revolution, Volume 2: The Dialectics of Modernity on a South African Frontier.* Chicago: The University of Chicago Press.

Comaroff, J., & Comaroff, J. (2005). Reflections on Youth. In F. De Boeck & A. Honwana (Eds.), *Makers & Breakers: Children & Youth in Postcolonial Africa* (pp. 19–30). Trenton: Africa World Press.

Compretta, C. E. (2012). Growing Gaps: Children's Experiences of Inequality in a Faith-Based Afterschool Program in the U.S. South. Unpublished PhD Dissertation, College of Arts and Sciences (Department of Anthropology), University of Kentucky. Retrieved April 8, 2014, from http://uknowledge.uky.edu/anthro_etds/4/

Crewe, E., & Axelby, R. (2013). *Anthropology and Development: Culture, Morality and Politics in a Globalised World.* Cambridge: Cambridge University Press.

Dahl, B. (2006). "Too Fat to Be an Orphan": The Moral Semiotics of Food Aid in Botswana. *Cultural Anthropology, 29*(4), 626–647.
Davis, R. (2012). The Great NGO Funding Crisis, Part II. *Daily Maverick* (Online). Retrieved July 15, 2013, from http://www.dailymaverick.co.za/article/2012-10-23-the-great-ngo-funding-crisis-part-ii/#.VCFzAPldV8F
de Klerk, M. (2012). Legacy of Selflessness. *Grocott's Mail* (Online). Retrieved, March 4, 2014, from http://www.grocotts.co.za/content/legacy-selflessness-08-11-2012
de Waal, A. (2002). Anthropology and the Aid Encounter. In J. MacClancy (Ed.), *Exotic No More: Anthropology on the Front Lines* (pp. 251–269). Chicago: University of Chicago Press.
de Wet, C. (2002). Factors Influencing the Choice of English as Language of Learning and Teaching (LoLT) – A South African Perspective. *South African Journal of Education, 22*(2), 119–124.
Demissie, F. (2012). *Colonial Architecture and Urbanism in Africa*. Farnham: Ashgate.
Dennis, M. (2005). *Happy New Year* (Television Programme). Britcom and Tiger Aspect Productions.
Escobar, A. (1997). Anthropology and Development. *International Social Science Journal, 49*(154), 497–515.
Fassin, D. (2010). Critique of Humanitarian Reason. *Public Lecture, Institute for Advanced Study, Princeton University* (Available Online). Retrieved July 15, 2013, from http://www.youtube.com/watch?v=jDT2mYg6mgo
Fassin, D. (2011). A Contribution to the Critique of Moral Reason. *Anthropological Theory, 11*(4), 481–491.
Faught, B. C. (2003). *Oxford Movement: A Thematic History of the Tractarians and Their Times*. University Park: Penn State University Press.
Ferguson, J. (2006). *Global Shadows: Africa in the Neoliberal World Order*. Durham: Duke University Press.
Freeman, L. E. (2001). *Knowledge, Education and Social Differentiation Amongst the Betsileo of Fisakana, Highland Madagascar*. Unpublished PhD Thesis, Department of Anthropology, London School of Economics and Political Science.
Freidus, A. (2010). 'Saving' Malawi: Faithful Responses to Orphans and Vulnerable Children. *NAPA Bulletin Special Issue: Intersections of Faith and Development in Local and Global Contexts, 33*(1), 50–67.
Frost, N. (2005). *Child Welfare: Historical Perspectives*. Abingdon: Routledge.
Giddens, A. (1984). *The Constitution of Society: Outline of the Theory of Structuration*. Cambridge: Polity Press.
Green, M. (2011). Calculating Compassion: Accounting for Some Categorical Practices in International Development. In D. Mosse (Ed.), *Adventures in Aidland: The Anthropology of Professionals in International Development* (pp. 33–56). New York/Oxford: Berghahn Books.

Harris, P. (2000). *The Work of the Imagination*. Oxford: Blackwell.
Harrison, E., & Crewe, E. (1998). *Whose Development? An Ethnography of Aid*. London: Zed Books.
Hecht, T. (2008). Globalization from Way Below: Brazilian Streets, a Youth, and World Society. In J. Cole & D. Durham (Eds.), *Figuring the Future: Globalization and the Temporalities of Children and Youth* (pp. 223–243). Santa Fe: School of Advanced Research Press.
Henderson, P. (2012). *A Kinship of Bones: AIDS, Intimacy and Care in Rural KwaZulu-Natal*. Scottsville: University of KwaZulu-Natal Press.
Higginbotham, P. (2012). *The Workhouse Encyclopedia*. Stroud: The History Press.
Holmwood, L. (2007). Dibley Criticised for Campaign Plug. *The Guardian* (Online). Retrieved March, 26, 2015, from http://www.theguardian.com/media/2007/jun/18/bbc.broadcasting1
Hosegood, V. (2008). The Effects of High HIV Prevalence on Orphanhood on Living Arrangements of Children in Malawi, Tanzania, and South Africa. *Population Studies, 61*(3), 327–336.
Howard, A. (1970). *Learning to Be Rotuman: Enculturation in the South Pacific*. New York: Teachers College Press.
Huxley, A. (2004). *Brave New World Revisited*. London: Vintage.
Jackson, M. (2005). *Existential Anthropology: Events, Exigencies and Effects*. New York: Berghahn Books.
Kingfisher, C., & Maskovsky, J. (2008). Introduction: The Limits of Neoliberalism. *Critique of Anthropology, 28*(2), 115–126.
King, S., & Tomkins, A. (2003). *The Poor in England 1700–1850: An Economy of Makeshifts*. Manchester: Manchester University Press.
King's Norton History Society. (2004). *Timeline: Poor Laws, Workhouses, and Social Support, King's Norton*. Retrieved, September 6, 2013, from http://www.kingsnorton.info/time/poor_law_workhouse_timeline.htm
Laidlaw, J. (2010). Agency and Responsibility: Perhaps You Can Have Too Much of a Good Thing. In M. Lambek (Ed.), *Ordinary Ethics: Anthropology, Language and Action* (pp. 143–164). New York: Fordham University Press.
Lawrence, D. H. (2011). *Studies in Classic American Literature*. Exeter: Shearsman Books.
Lawrence, J., & Starkey, P. (2001). Introduction: Child Welfare and Social Action. In J. Lawrence & P. Starkey (Eds.), *Child Welfare and Social Action in the Nineteenth and Twentieth Centuries: International Perspectives* (pp. 1–14). Liverpool: Liverpool University Press.
Lidchi, H. (1999). Finding the Right Image: British Development NGOs and the Regulation of Imagery. In T. Skelton & T. Allen (Eds.), *Culture and Global Change* (pp. 88–104). London: Routledge.
Malkki, L. (2010). Children, Humanity, and the Infantilization of Peace. In I. Feldman & M. I. Ticktin (Eds.), *In the Name of Humanity: The Government of Threat and Care* (pp. 58–85). Durham: Duke University Press.

Manzo, K. (2008). Imaging Humanitarianism: NGO Identity and the Iconography of Childhood. *Antipode, 40*(4), 623–657.
Mark, M. (2014). Get Your Africa Facts Right: Websites Seek to Stem Flow of Misinformation. *The Guardian* (Online). Retrieved September 24, from http://www.theguardian.com/world/2014/sep/27/africa-websites-fact-check-misinformation
Mazuri, A. (1993). Language and the Quest for Liberation in Africa: The Legacy of Franz Fanon. *Third World Quarterly, 14*(2), 348–365.
McClay, W. M. (1994). *The Masterless: Self & Society in Modern America*. Chapel Hill: University of North Carolina Press.
McHarry, K. E. (2013). *Sponsoring the Future: Marketizing Children's Potential in Senegalese Preschools*. Conference Presentation. The Anthropology of Potentiality in Africa (Panel), American Anthropological Association, Annual Conference, Chicago.
Meintjes, H., & Giese, S. (2006). Spinning the Epidemic: The Making of Mythologies of Orphanhood in the Context of AIDS. *Childhood: A Global Journal of Child Research, 13*(3), 407–430.
Merseyside Maritime Museum. (2014). Child Emigration. *Merseyside Maritime Museum* (Online). Retrieved November 18, 2014, from http://www.liverpoolmuseums.org.uk/maritime/archive/sheet/10
Moore, H. L. (2011). *Still Life: Hopes, Desires and Satisfactions*. Cambridge: Polity Press.
Moore, J. (2013). Kipling and Lord Roberts. *The Kipling Society* (Online). Retrieved February 6, 2015, from http://www.kiplingsociety.co.uk/rg_lor-droberts_moore.htm
Nicholls, G. (2007). *A History of the English Poor Law in Connection with the State of the Country and the Condition of the People*. New Jersey: The Lawbook Exchange.
Nietzsche, F. (1994). In K. Ansell-Pearson (Ed.), *On the Genealogy of Morality*. Cambridge: Cambridge University Press.
Nieuwenhuys, O. (2001). By the Sweat of Their Brow? 'Street Children', NGOs and Children's Rights in Addis Ababa. *Africa, 71*(4), 539–557.
Ntombana, L. (2011). *An Investigation into the Role of Xhosa Male Initiation in Moral Regeneration*. Unpublished PhD Thesis, Faculty of Arts, Nelson Mandela Metropolitan University.
O'Neill, K. L. (2013). Left Behind: Security, Salvation, and the Subject of Prevention. *Cultural Anthropology, 28*(2), 204–226.
O'Neill, K. L. (2015). *Secure the Soul: Christian Piety and Gang Prevention in Guatemala*. Berkeley: University of California Press.
ONE. (2015). *About One*. Retrieved February 3, 2015, from http://www.one.org/international/about/

Ortner, S. B. (2006). *Anthropology and Social Theory: Culture, Power and the Acting Subject*. Durham/London: Duke University Press.
Panter-Brick, C. (2002). Street Children, Human Rights, and Public Health: A Critique and Future Directions. *Annual Review of Anthropology, 31*(1), 147–171.
Rabbitts, F. (2012). Child Sponsorship, Ordinary Ethics and the Geographies of Charity. *Geoforum, 43*(5), 926–936.
Rabbitts, F. (2013). *'Nothing is Whiter than White in This World': Child Sponsorship and the Geographies of Charity*. Unpublished PhD Thesis, University of Exeter.
Reuters. (2008). 'One Campaign' Stresses Voters to Focus on Africa. *Dawn* (Online). Retrieved 26 October 2012, from http://www.dawn.com/news/282686/one-campaign-stresses-voters-to-focus-on-africa
Riley, L. (2013). Orphan Geographies in Malawi. *Children's Geographies, 11*(4), 409–421.
Rival, L. (2000). Formal Schooling and the Production of Modern Citizens in the Ecuadorian Amazon. In B. A. U. Levinson (Ed.), *Schooling the Symbolic Animal: Social and Cultural Dimensions of Education* (pp. 108–122). Lanham: Littlefield.
Rizvi, F. (2001). Postcolonialism and Globalization in Education. *Cultural Studies, 7*(3), 256–263.
Sankore, R. (2005). Behind the Image: Poverty and 'Development Pornography'. *Pambazuka News*. Retrieved from http://www.pambazuka.net/en/category/features/27815
Shizha, E. (2005). Reclaiming Our Memories: The Education Dilemma in Postcolonial African School Curricula. In A. A. Abdi & A. Cleghorn (Eds.), *Issues in African Education: Sociological Perspectives* (pp. 65–83). New York/Basingstoke: Palgrave Macmillan.
Simpson, A. (2003). *Half London in Zambia: Contested Identities in a Catholic Mission School*. Edinburgh: Edinburgh University Press.
Slack, P. (1974). Vagrants and Vagrancy in England, 1598–1664. *The Economic History Review, 27*(3), 360–379.
Society for the Propagation of the Gospel (SPG). (1858). *The Global Missionary for 1858* (Vol. 8). London: Bell & Daldy.
Stambach, A. (2000). *Lessons from Mount Kilimanjaro: Schooling, Community, and Gender in East Africa*. New York: Routledge.
Stambach, A. (2010). *Faith in Schools: Religion, Education and American Evangelicals in East Africa*. Stanford: Stanford University Press.
Stambach, A., & Kwayu, A. (2013). Take the Gift of My Child and Return Something to Me: On Children, Chagga Trust, and a New American Evangelical Orphanage on Mount Kilimanjaro. *Journal of Religion in Africa, 43*, 379–395.
Talented and Proud. (2012, August 14). Talented and Proud. *Grocott's Mail*, p. 10.
Ticktin, M. (2006). Where Ethics and Politics Meet: The Violence of Humanitarianism in France. *American Ethnologist, 33*(1), 33–49.

van Vuuren, C., & de Jongh, M. (1999). Rituals of Manhood in South Africa: Circumcision at the Cutting Edge of Critical Intervention. *South African Journal of Ethnology, 22*(4), 142–156.

Wark, M. (1995). Fresh Maimed Babies: The Uses of Innocence. *Transition, 65*, 36–47.

Weckesser, A. M. (2011). *Girls, Gifts and Gender: An Ethnography of the Materiality of Care in Rural Mpumalanga, South Africa*. Unpublished PhD Thesis, School of Health and Social Studies, University of Warwick.

Wolcott, H. F. (2003). *A Kwakiutl Village and School*. Walnut Creek: AltaMira Press.

Woods, B., & Shipley, D. (2004). *The Orphans of Nkandla* (Film). True Vision Productions Retrieved April 14, 2014, from http://truevisiontv.com/films/details/83/orphans-of-nkandla

Wright, L. (2012). Origins of the Eastern Cape Education Crisis. In L. Wright (Ed.), *South Africa's Education Crisis: Views from the Eastern Cape* (pp. 1–18). Grahamstown: NISC.

Zigon, J. (2014). An Ethics of Dwelling and a Politics of World-Building: A Critical Response to Ordinary Ethics. *Journal of the Royal Anthropological Institute, 20*, 746–764.

CHAPTER 6

The Politics of Responsibility

During interactions between those learning and working at Ngomso and potential and existing supporters of the institution, there was always the possibility that relationships could be established, maintained, or severed. If they were to establish or continue a relationship with the school, benefactors had to be sure that *they* should provide assistance or intervention. This process necessitated ethical judgement: they had to decide if they should take *responsibility* for 'the problem' and its resolution, or not (Zigon 2006). Most explicitly, when confronted with images of learners' faces during fundraising activity, and when learning about their mortality, which was comparable with their own, and their destitution, which might have been their own, audiences were summoned to make a judgement about their responsibility for them (Levinas 2002: 537). Mobilisations of sentiment and the possibility of 'turnarounds' did enjoin supporters and donors with those working and learning at the school, as demonstrated in the previous chapter. However, beyond these initial processes of transformation or enlightenment—that is, those that pulled individuals into awareness of the plight of the institution and its target beneficiaries—the continuing constitution of Ngomso as an institution materialised as a consequence of specific relational forms that bound individuals together for months or even years. The dynamic in question makes the difference between an impulsive or one-off gesture of charitable giving and a long-term commitment to a particular cause or institution. In this chapter,

I will demonstrate that various moral discourses that we might describe as being related to conceptualisations of responsibility are integral to the establishment of continuing processes of humanitarian intervention.

Before taking this dialogue further, it is important to state that the wording of the previous sentence, most especially the words 'we might describe', has a significance that may not be immediately obvious. Throughout this chapter, I employ the word 'responsibility' because my interlocutors employed it in ways that had a meaning for them, and I recognise that this meaning was their own and subject to the specificities of their lives and experiences and not some abstraction of a meaning that would hold true for all situations or apply in each and every locality where individuals engage with each other ethically. To put this another way, the word 'responsibility' or the related notion of 'obligation' are employed to describe something that can exist independently of knowledge of these terms or any equivalent term in a different dialect, should such a thing exist at all. That is, the discourse helps us to grasp something specific about ethical imperatives that humans experience when they consciously consider and enact relations with others regardless of whether it is called responsibility or obligation or something else. Zigon (2014) explores this line of thought more thoroughly, extending the argument out to terminology readily associated with morality/ethics more broadly (e.g. dignity). As he puts it, "moralities/ethics, and the politics they may demand, are not intrinsic to language and social activity, but emerge from the ontological conditions for being-in-the-world" (ibid: 762). It is precisely this emergence—that is, the experiences and interchanges that lead individuals to continue to attempt to construct alternative futures for themselves and others—that I consider in this chapter.

Mary and Joyce, and other interlocutors who supported and constituted the Ngomso cause, employed a variety of discourses in their attempt to explain how and why they felt obliged to take responsibility for others, where obligation, following Sykes (2009), is understood in terms of moralistic reasoning and judgement. Staff, volunteers, and the Friends, explicitly acknowledged the idea that Christians have a responsibility to Him and, relatedly, other humans. Mary conveyed this conceptualisation of responsibility in a statement on the school's website; she writes: "They are God's children, and we have a responsibility to protect them." In this statement, we can see that her sense of obligation links with her obligations as a Christian. She was clear that this was the most important aspect of her moral reasoning. Although she often also spoke about absent human rights, this moralised framework was not as powerful as those that were *overtly* Christian. The learners were, ultimately, seen as God's children and to be in need of, and entitled to, His protection. God, the male father figure, was seen as the ultimate parent. Similarly, the Holy Spirit Sisters in New Guinea that Lutkehaus (1999: 208) considers "subscribe to a notion of maternalism based upon the model of Jesus as the caretaker for humanity in general". Like Mary and other interlocutors (male and female), they left space for 'God the Father' (and only Him) to fulfil the 'ultimate paternal role'. At Ngomso, there was room for the staff to do His work.

> For nothing will be impossible with God. (Luke, 1: 37)

Disseminating this idea of divine assistance, Mary told audiences in the UK that she had heard the words of Joel (2: 25): "I will restore to you the years that the locust has eaten." As one audience member explains: "[Mary] talked to us about how the locust in these street children's lives is the abuse, the poverty, the drug addiction and neglect that has eaten up their childhoods. God is restoring those lost years through what is happening at Ngomso."[1] The seeming ease with which she co-opted or reinterpreted the initial conceptualisation of what Ngomso was doing is illustrative of the explanatory qualities of the discourse in question. Those who understood their support of Ngomso as being supportive of the work of God inserted this specific institutional formation into a framework of meaning that could exist independently of it. In a sense, these were metaframeworks of understanding. More broadly, when institutions and political enactments of humanitarian assistance are conceptualised with reference to a biblical framework, they are situated within a temporal frame of reference that suggests that enactments of related conceptualisations of responsibility are integral to the continuation of a moral humanity.

If individuals acknowledged the notion that He was restoring lost lives through the work of Ngomso, they could, in turn, enact their obligations to Him by supporting the school. Again, this possibility for moralised engagement is underpinned by biblical discourses:

> Rather, give as alms what is inside, and then everything will be clean for you. (Luke, 11.41)

There is hope, then, for those who give to hopeful causes. As Susan articulated it: "For me, change for the good is a big motivation in my life, so I find that [my involvement with Ngomso] fulfils this to quite a large extent." The fact that the possibility of "change for the good" motivated her most likely relates to the central role of 'hope' in Christianity.[2] Zigon (2009: 256, emphasis added) explains this assertion very clearly:

> On the one hand, as one of the fundamental virtues of a Christian life, hope is a disposition that must be *actively* acquired, maintained, and perfected. Hope must be embodied, or perhaps better put, ensouled. On the other hand, Paul writes of hope as a *passive* patience or endurance. As he writes in his letter to the Romans about the hope for immortality: 'if we hope for something we do not yet see, then we look forward to it eagerly and with patience'. (Romans, 8:25)

Susan was motived to *be actively* hopeful (i.e. to embody hope): "change for the good is a big motivation in my life", as she put it. Through her involvement with Ngomso, she fulfilled this motivation—that is, the school enabled her to be hopeful—because, I believe, this involvement empowered her to feel that she was bringing hope to others. In other words, she did not passively wait for hope but was actively creating its existence by investing herself in the task of constituting the hope that Ngomso offered (i.e. the notion of hope that Mary 'sold' to supporters). This action helped her to fulfil one of her key duties as a Christian. I would suggest that it also enabled her to become virtuous (according to this same conceptualisation of virtue). I am quite sure that Mary experienced something similar in devoting her life to giving "hope" to "the lost".

Mrs Noni found fulfilment by similarly enacting her Christian obligations to God. Throughout the course of my fieldwork, she gave slices of bread and jam to her young neighbour, whose family were poor. When I asked why she did this, she replied, "You must give thanks to the Lord: you give [to others], and you get good for yourself". Then, with a slight shake of her head and a subtle tutting click of her tongue, she concluded: "Some people are only thinking about themselves; uh-uh, that's not good. You must think about the other people." Her words suggest that she thought God provided her privileges (e.g. the fact she could buy bread and jam when others could not) in recognition of the fact that she took responsibility for others. This belief appeared to help her come to terms with her situation, and, in particular, to *dwell* with some comfort amidst the inequality of the world (Zigon 2014).

As much as she was motivated by the possibility that beneficiaries might experience His love, her own positive experiences of giving to others fuelled her own continued engagements. She once told me about a scenario whereby she had accompanied a university student on a trip to the location to photograph shebeens (taverns). A group of drunk young men joined them briefly, saying they wanted to protect them. One was a past pupil who had stolen "so much from the school" and had broken Mary's finger during an altercation some six years earlier. He asked Mary if she could forgive him for what he had done. "I never thought he would say sorry", she said, "but I told him, 'It's easy [to forgive you now] because I forgave you a long time ago, but thank you for saying "sorry"'. "That forgiveness thing got into him at school", she continued. "It must have done." She explained the events by saying: "You get this experience of grace in life; that was an incredibly healing thing for me, even though I had forgiven him long ago." I would argue that 'grace' is a discourse that both enables conceptualisations of ethicality and conditions the formation of ethical exchanges. In other words, it both orients and describes ethical engagements, most especially acts of giving. To quote one of Omri Elisha's (2008: 161) interlocutors, an evangelical activist and former pastor in Tennessee, grace is a standard of accountability "enacted according to biblical principles". This mode of accountability catalyses and configures humanitarian intervention, carrying with it the potential for the ethical transformation of both those accountable and accounted for. In turn, discourses relating to grace bring a God-given legitimacy to interventions conceptualised accordingly.

As we shared a coffee one afternoon in London, Mary conveyed the idea that she promulgated related conceptualisations of responsibility when communicating with others. She endeavoured to transform individuals she hoped would help her to transform the learners. 'Promoting the cause' was an educational endeavour in its own right.[3] She told me that her father taught her the phrase "there but for the grace of God". Nobody chooses their circumstances, she said. As was the case for Mrs Noni, belief in the notion that He is responsible for privilege/misfortune appeared to give Mary comfort. She told me she had shared the words "there but for the grace of God" during a fundraising presentation the previous day when speaking to a group of privately educated young men in Devon. Stirring her coffee, she explained that she had wanted them to understand that they had not chosen their privilege, just as Ngomso learners had not chosen their misfortune, so should "not feel guilty about it".

However, she had added the caution that they must recognise the maxim that "with great privilege [from God] comes great responsibility [to others]".[4] The inverse, somewhat implied assertion is that the audience should have felt guilty when taking their privilege for granted and failing to respond to the need of others (including Ngomso learners most specifically).[5]

Mary's instruction in Devon came to mind when I read the aforementioned letter written to an unnamed 'child' in the UK, informing her about Grahamstown's first mission school, which had recently opened in the location (i.e. township). Its author (E.W., cited in SPG 1858: 31) sets out to educate her young reader:

> You have much reason to thank GOD, my dear child, that you were born of Christian parents, and in a Christian land. Oh! Learn to estimate your privileges aright, and pity those of your fellow-creatures who are less favoured than yourself. Do not forget the claims of your young Kafir brethren among whom I dwell.

Just as the young recipient of the letter is encouraged to orient herself towards her 'fellow-creatures', during her exchange in Devon, Mary encouraged potential supporters to transform their sense of self (i.e. their (assumed) sense of guilt) by recognising their responsibilities and acting accordingly. In both instances, compassion is promoted as the moral counter to privilege. I don't know how the young men in Devon responded, beyond the fact that a donation later came from the school. Those who contributed to this effort had ethically responded to Mary— that is, as "a process of working on oneself in order to remake oneself, even if ever so slightly, into a new moral person" (Zigon 2011: 5). Such engagement with Ngomso learners was a mode by which individuals could become involved in the world that they shared with others. More accurately, it was a mode by which individuals could readjust their ways of being in the world. Concern for others intertwined with concern for the self.

Speaking directly to this analysis, O'Neill (2013: 205) argues that "evangelical Christians ... self-consciously craft their subjectivities through their participation in gang prevention – as ministers, missionaries, and mentors".[6] At the same time, "at risk youths" are "acted upon" by these same individuals (ibid.). O'Neill (ibid: 208) suggests that child sponsorship programmes similarly offer donors "a principled technique for ethical self-formation". That is, donors encounter the claim that they can become virtuous by supporting such interventions. He (ibid.) asserts that such 'calls to action' are evidence of an "era of evangelical Christianity", which emerged in America during the early 1980s. In this movement, "faith [is] not so much [framed] as a religion but rather as a *relationship* – between you and God, between you and your neighbour, and (most importantly) between you and yourself" (ibid, emphasis added). As we walked around Coventry Cathedral, before our visit to the radio station, Susan informed me of her conceptualisation of having a "real relationship with people in the world". She said that they had informed the learners at the primary school that Mary and Joyce "loved the children that don't get any love elsewhere" because "they love God". This logic, she explained, followed her belief in incarnation; the "worship of a God in human form", as she put it. This disposition meant that she, like Joyce and Mary, had a connection "to God but also to community". She had encouraged (i.e. as an educative technique) the primary school learners to "love other people", "to love God" and "to love yourself because you can't love others without also loving yourself". Following O'Neill's (2013) analysis, we might understand her words as an observation of how shifting moral discourses associated with Christianity are quite similarly embodied on both sides of the Atlantic.

More broadly still, humanitarian interventions rely on the establishment of relationships, which hinge upon some idea of shared humanity. Bornstein (2001: 598, emphasis added), for example, argues that "World Vision's publicity materials describe child sponsorship as a humanitarian *connection* that manifests transcendent love for a stranger". In this case, the humanitarian organisation is a Christian one. However, inter-human bonds drive processes of humanitarianism even when He is not held responsible for them. Similarly, Ticktin (2006: 45) has argued that the "regime of humanitarianism is based on engaging other people in relationships of empathy and in this way demonstrating one's common humanity". Fassin (2010: 14.30 minutes) speaks of humanitarianism as a compassionate "collective emotion" that enables "acts of solidarity". For Ngomso supporters, the school certainly offered the chance to join—emotionally and imaginatively, as well as, for some, physically (e.g. with hugs)—with others. However, the potential for a relationship with Him and the opportunity to His work most forcefully drove the sustained engagement of the most active volunteers and donors.

Faith-Filled Meshworks

At the end of my second stay in South Africa, in 2013, Mary and I discussed her historical involvement with the school and its supporters while sitting in her living room. Before becoming principal of the first Ngomso school in East London, she had been teaching isiXhosa and other subjects at a leading private school in Grahamstown, which has long been integral to the childhoods of children of clergy as well as wealthy local residents and boarders from across Southern Africa. Mary's forefather, Robert Miller, and many more members of the family had also held positions of influence at the school. While teaching one afternoon, a learner had asked Mary: "Why do we have to learn this 'Kaffir' language?" Mary handed in her notice soon afterwards. She then moved to East London with her husband and spent time "praying about what [she] should do with [her] life". Her experience is illuminated by Zigon's theorisation of moral breakdowns. The young learner's use of racist language to question Mary caused to experience one of those "difficult times, and troubles" when we humans must "step-away and figure out, work-through and deal with the situation-at-hand" (Zigon 2007: 137). Mary prayed for a resolution. Similarly, during my time at Ngomso, I noticed that Mary and other members of staff prayed when moral paths were not visible or well-defined, or when ways forward appeared treacherous; when they were unsure, confused or lost. Their prayers occasionally reminded me of the Lord's Prayer, which I memorised as a child in a Church of England primary school: "lead us not". Prayer showed the way but did not deliver one to the end of the journey. It informed ethical responses—that is, modes of self-fashioning—without determining them. Aleksandra, one of Zigon's Russian interlocutors, understood and utilised prayer in a similar way. It was not "just God telling her what to do", it created the possibility that she could "resolve the dilemma herself" (Zigon 2007: 145). In this way, prayer provides a technique whereby communication with God gives way to meaningful action.

Mary took a sip of her coffee and explained the outcome of her prayers. This is a similar version of the story that she shared with me that afternoon, as told by her during a short film about the school:

> A priest called me and said, 'Mary, I have a proposition to make; could I come and have a cup of tea with you?' And he arrived, and we passed a few pleasantries, and then he said, 'I've come to ask you to start a school for the

street children.' And my adrenaline just rushed right through my body, my heart started palpitating, I was perspiring, and I just knew this was what I was going to do with my life.

On a now expired web page she writes, "Energy just ran from my toes to my head and from my head to my toes and I nearly jumped out of my skin". This moment was clearly integral to her commitment to Ngomso and its learners. The prayers, the priest and the energy suggest divine intervention; the will of God. When faced with a moral dilemma about who she should be and what to do for herself and others, the act of prayer worked. "I just knew", she says in the film.

Mary's new moral disposition, her responsibility for 'schooling the street children', meant that answers to further dilemmas were clearer to her (cf. Zigon 2008: 57). Almost immediately after the priest had visited, for example, she was offered a fully paid role at a different school in East London. Unusually, she spoke English, Afrikaans, and isiXhosa, skills that the post required. Her would-be employer "said that I would be perfect", she told me. However, she disappointed him: "I told him that I was committed to these street kids; God has put me here to do this. I think that he thought that I was crazy." This position was her *calling*; her faith the motivation for her actions. This life was chosen for her, by Him. Commenting on Weber's notion of 'calling', Zigon (2008: 39) states that "To have a calling . . . is to live according to a faith in a certain set of values". Mary had faith in Christian values. More than that, however, she was determined to live according to such values. Her faith in divine intervention, I believe, has kept her committed despite overwhelming challenges. When I returned to the UK feeling somewhat battered by my experiences at Ngomso, Mary said that her faith helped her to overcome such existential angst, which might have otherwise thrown her off course. Weber ([1930] 2001) suggests that this kind of commitment brings about a moral life (see Zigon 2008: 39). When I spoke with others about Mary and her ongoing commitment to the school, it was clear that many individuals, in the UK and South Africa, felt that she had achieved such a life.

Such perceptions of Mary were integral to many of her successful attempts to accumulate support, and her religiosity was central to many of the relationships she enjoyed with donors and volunteers. After her presentation at Susan's church had concluded, I asked the audience about the Friend's website. Several individuals had visited it. Many received their quarterly newsletter too. However, when I asked how important these communication materials were, they told me that Mary's visits cemented their commitment to Ngomso to a much greater extent. Mary told me that she raised R30,000 during her trip in 2012, which equated to approximately £1700. Moreover, she said that each visit had "a knock on effect" throughout the year as they helped her to establish and maintain relationships. Technology might allow individuals to communicate with each other across greater distances, at increased speed; however, supporters valued personalised, unmediated interaction.[7] In Susan's village and elsewhere, 'real' social gatherings, such as carol concerts, cake sales, dinner parties, and prayer groups, were essential to the generation of support. Bishop Gray would have recognised the importance of such activity when he sailed back to England in 1852 to canvas support for the Anglican mission in South Africa and, in particular, a new See in Grahamstown, instead of taking the opportunity to write letters to interested parties. The same is true of Bishop Armstrong, who was touring the UK to raise funds for the new See when he met Robert Miller, Mary's forefather, who 'volunteered' to assist him. Similarly, support for Ngomso from UK residents, in the form of money and volunteers, was especially forthcoming after Mary began her fundraising trips. Her visits were funded by an anonymous donor who had been taught by her grandfather at the aforementioned private school where she herself had worked, as Mary informed me: "He said he would not be the man he is today without that [experience]." The social capital provided by her family's history enabled her to build further relationships and (social) capital (Bourdieu 1986). Audiences who knew nothing about this history were similarly inspired to contribute to the continuation of her mission.[8] When she met potential supporters, she engendered trust and inspiration.

I would argue that Mary's inspirational qualities relate to Weber's (1978) notion of the charismatic leader. He (ibid: 1111–2) talks of charismatic leaders who possess "specific gifts of body and mind" that not "everybody could have access to". People openly marvelled at Mary's extraordinary, inspiring commitment and it galvanised supporters. As her friend and my first supervisor said to her during dinner one evening, "You put us all to shame". He was responding to Mary's tearful account of how she had attended to a past pupil as he lay dying in a hospital with stab wounds. She emotionally and physically suffered for others on numerous other occasions too, putting her well-being at risk. An article in the local paper carries the title "A legacy of selflessness" (de Klerk 2012: np). It details the fact that Mary was due to retire "after 22 years helping destitute children on the edges of society" (ibid.). This piece echoes an article written about Jennie Miller when she died in 1924:

> Her life was an inspiration to the women of South Africa. She was a vivid personality, full of good works.... She gave herself freely and cheerfully to others, expecting no return. (Goodwin, cited in Anonymous)

As for her foremother, Mary's selfless disposition was inseparable from her Christian faith and agapeic love for others.[9] For audiences with similar faith, the shame they experienced when reflectively comparing themselves to Mary might be understood as their acknowledgement that Mary's selfless deeds produced a closeness to God that their lesser commitment to His teachings could not deliver. Thus, joining with her as an Ngomso supporter offered the prospect of being enjoined more closely with Him, in this life and the next, and, as a result, experiencing a reduced sense of shame.

Weber (1978: 1117) argues that "the bearer of charisma enjoys loyalty and authority by virtue of a mission believed to be embodied in him". In this vein of thought, it was telling that Mary alluded to divine intervention when frequently sharing the story of how "energy" ran through her body so that she nearly "jumped out of [her] skin" when a priest asked her to establish the school. God inspired her.[10] In addition to the notion that God worked through Ngomso, the message was given to potential and existing supporters that Mary had a direct, inescapable, relationship with Him. Giving her money was thus akin to entrusting it to Him: the most secure and trustworthy of recipients.[11] Given this configuration, during the transition period when Joyce became principal, supporters were asked to trust someone else. A "prayer request" from an FOA newsletters reads: "Mary retires in April – please pray for all the staff and students at Ngomso, as well as for Mary at this time of transition."[12] After 20 stress-filled years, the trustees thought that Mary deserved and needed a break. However, they were hopeful that her absence would not undo her efforts.

After Mary had been forced to return to South Africa from her fundraising trip, following the death of her father, the trustees discussed how well Joyce had coped in her absence. Raymond, the then chairman, said, "She performed very well indeed. She is capable of standing on her own feet, thank you very much". Goffman (1963) said that people can be surprised when a 'stigmatised other' does a good thing. Clive, another trustee, was relieved that Joyce had addressed audiences "so well". Jenny, the teacher who worked in London, responded by saying "We shouldn't be surprised [that she could do so well]. For her to have got to where she has got to in South Africa, she has to be a very capable professional". Clive replied, somewhat defensively, "Yes, but it is also good news that she is a head teacher that can perform well; not all are good at public speaking". The trustees rarely debated the capabilities of Ngomso staff. Although it was never explicitly said, their anxiety that Joyce was not Mary underpinned the discussion. She had not worked in private schools, and English was not her 'mother tongue', nor did she have any British heritage. For some more than others, it had been a learning experience to see that she was capable of being an ambassador for the school. When the trustees later wrote a letter in support of her application for the position of principal, it was confirmation that they had become allied with someone more 'Other' than Mary. This development was significant, given that those who funded Robert Miller to establish relations with the Xhosa 160 years earlier did not, to my knowledge, do so in the hope that a Xhosa would succeed him.

I have had more time to learn about Mary's role in this capacity in comparison to Joyce's relatively recent transition. Initially, I understood her activity in light of analysis of 'development brokers', who, through a process of "translation", generate the "mutual enrolment and the interlocking of interests" between parties (Bierschenk et al. 2002; Lewis and Mosse 2006: 13). Certainly, those who volunteered and donated, communicated with Mary far more 'deeply' and frequently than they did with learners. Like American missionaries working in Tanzania (Stambach 2011: 40.30 minutes), they also did not speak to parents nor hear any of their concerns. However, the notion of 'translation' does not sufficiently explain Mary's role. She did creatively (re)produce stories from 'source material' (i.e. events), similar to how translators interpret and reconfigure words and ideas, but she did not simply offer a 'translation service'. Her relationships with supporters and those that existed between supporters and others at the school were more knotty than this analogy would suggest.

I initially found it helpful to consider Stambach and Ngwane's (2011) concept of *Global Networks*, which they offer as a framework for understanding the international relationships that constitute schooling in Africa. Similarly, when Mary explained how the local game park owner had come to offer free visits to the learners, she said, "it was [an example of] seemingly random [support], from this incredible network". When a German lady persuaded authorities in Dresden to fund a school based on her experiences at Ngomso, Mary spoke to me about "interconnectedness". However, perhaps because I worked for an IT firm for nine months after leaving school, the word 'network' conjures up the image of uniform and organised connections. This representation jars with my understanding of the various relational forms and temporalities that individuals involved with Ngomso maintained; an arrangement that, in turn, sustained the institution.

Helpfully, Ingold (2011: xii) examines human life and its organisation, socially speaking, using the term "wayfaring". Our lives are "one strand in a tissue of trails that together comprise the texture of the lifeworld.... [This is] a relational field ... not of interconnected points but of interwoven lines; not a network but a *meshwork*" (ibid: 69–70). Instead of nodes or some other definitive object separated from its surrounding by a perimeter, as per the notion of networks, human lives are understood as lines or trails.[13] These interweave as humans conduct their lives socially, such that each line is constitutive of others and constituted by its enmeshment with others. Connections are lives; something external to these lives cannot connect them.

When Mary told 'her stories' in the UK, her words provided a path that audience members *could* trace (Ingold 2013: 110). She encouraged them to embark on certain journeys: to donate, volunteer, or pray. With these options, she offered to make their discomfort (in hearing about the learners' lives) manageable.[14] Their responses were self-constituting engagements; they enacted themselves in a bid to bring about imagined futures (for themselves and the learners). When audience members traced Mary's paths—just as Susan had done after hearing her speak "inspirationally" in Birmingham—connections were established between them and Mary, and all those who engaged with Ngomso, in one way or another, including the young people who featured in her stories. These connections were not independent of the lives that made them possible or that materialised as a result of them. In this sense, Mary did not merely act as a translator between learners and donors. Rather, she constituted particular qualities of their lives, just as her relationships with them constituted qualities of her life. What we can *understand* as networks and connections are imagined and experienced, mutually constitutive enmeshments of fashioned human lives. In other words, the 'Ngomso network' was constitutive of and constituted by humans lives. The hope that Ngomso offered to learners, which Mary promoted, generated the relationships that constituted Ngomso as an institutional arrangement and was also generative of the lives of supporters.

For example, two American volunteers visited the school as part of a university exchange programme with Rhodes, before volunteering again after graduation and then starting a literacy project in the location with the assistance of past pupils. One of them moved to Grahamstown in 2011 having married a South African. Explaining a more subtle impact, one lady at Susan's church told me that she prayed for the learners "every day". Susan's relationship with Mary had come to fruition, in one aspect, as this lady's ritualistic movements of her body and organisation of her time and mentality. For those involved experientially, their lives extended beyond and were subject to the impact of enmeshment in the Ngomso project. These human lives—the interwoven lines—were individual and ephemeral. They had histories and trajectories that, for whatever reason and for however long, overlapped with other lives that maintained some relation to the material and imagined materialisation of their overlapping (i.e. the school).

As Mary said, such events and connections are "seemingly random", yet less random when we understand the individual lives and shared histories of those who make such connections. Clearly, shared Christian faith was integral to many of the relationships. Before the Wrights (i.e. the couple that founded FOA UK) established their connection with Ngomso they had "taken young people [i.e. volunteer missionaries] from the UK to live like the people lived in southern Africa", as Mary put it. Both parties were proselytising their Christian faith. Mary said that her first fundraising talk in England was enabled by "the trust that [Mr Wright] set up [with the congregation that hosted her]". As she explained, "They had this network of people that had lived with ordinary black people in Southern Africa [that they could call upon to extend my fundraising activities out to wider audiences]". In other words, without the Wrights and their past lives, the continuing support Ngomso received from the UK may not have existed.

At the end of the Q&A session at the school in Warwick, one potential recruit asked Mary "Is it a Christian school?" It was the first time this particular 'C word' was spoken that afternoon. More broadly, Christianity was not uniformly acknowledged during fundraising activities. Mary replied by saying that it was a Christian school but assured the young lady: "We accept people of all and no faith; it's not a problem." I never saw

Mary exclude non-Christians. Likewise, when I spoke to her about the importance of Christianity among supporters, she keenly pointed out that some were not Christian; like Susan's next door neighbour, she said. This lady (whose name I never noted) sold paintings and greeting cards from the garage outside her immaculately presented Georgian house, which doubled as an art gallery. She then shared the profits from each sale with Ngomso. I spoke to her while looking at her paintings, which were intriguing but beyond my budget. I gained the impression that she supported the school because she wanted to 'do something' for those less well-off. However, every *prominent* supporter was openly Christian.

Despite these assertions, to say that individuals were supporters because they were Christians would miss the point. Religious belief was merely *one* obvious, but important aspect of their collective arrangement. In her brilliantly original book *Ordinary Affects*, Kathleen Stewart (2007: 42) writes:

> Shifting forms of commonality and difference are wedged into daily interactions. There are hard lines of connection and disconnection and lighter, momentary affinities and differences. Little worlds proliferate around everything and anything at all.

Some interchanges and relationships that proliferated around Ngomso were fleeting; others endured for years. The school impacted upon some lives lightly; for others, it was central to who they were and what they did. This 'little world' confounds diagrammatical representation. It was comprised of and by sentiments such as trust, empathy, love, desire, anger, pain, joy, regret, and satisfaction. This collection of individuals had stories of their own and a collective story to tell. They touched each other's lives because of who they were individually and because they continued to create something together.

For Mary and Joyce, such intangibles—this immutable randomness—were not helpful to the task of building and strengthening the Ngomso mission. Again, Christian faith provided a framework for understanding uncertainty and a sense of determinate power over it. For them, the money and support that flowed from this meshwork of human lives were the work of God, rather than arbitrarily shifting connections and disconnections. "You never know when money will appear", Mary told me, "but you just put your faith in God and pray that it will". When receiving a large donation, she said she had been "rewarded for [her] faith". She provided evidence by speaking about the anonymous donor who regularly sent large sums of money. "I rang him when the school [funds] had hit rock bottom, and we were in a bit of a pickle", Mary explained. God's intervention, she said, then provided the necessary funds (via the donor). After a lady from the UK had funded Joyce to attend a training course about how best to apply for Lotto funding, her first application was successful. Mary said such immediate success was rare. "God is great", Joyce answered. "We have been praying a lot."

In sharing her understanding of a care home, or 'orphanage', for children in Uganda run by Catholic sisters, Scherz (2014: 133) offers analysis that helped me to understand Mary and Joyce's positioning:

> Although [the sisters] feel they are working within God's divine plan, they do not see themselves as able to bring about social change without divine intervention. In their embrace of the simple intention, they believe that only God can complete and perfect their imperfect worlds, which are always broken and always partial, as they believe themselves to be. It is thus we find that the giver of charity is not the complete human who strategically distributes surplus to the broken poor. In the sisters' understanding, the giver is also broken, and her actions can be completed only through divine grace.

As already mentioned, divine intervention was most obviously sought through the act of prayer. There were hopes that this endeavour would generate better lives for learners and past pupils, who were most frequently the subject of such attention. In offering their prayers, supporters in England appeared to recognise that their money required the accompaniment of God's attention if it was to have the desired impact.[15] They appeared to pray with hope that it would encourage Him to take a special interest in their lives and those of the recipients of their prayers. Given the power attributed to God, this was an *active* way of hoping. Like Zigon's (2009: 257) Russian interlocutors, who also prayed, my interlocutors were endeavouring "to create the best possible situation for the contingent realization" of hope. For those who do not see Him as having power (or existing at all), this enactment of hope might appear *passive*—akin to lying underneath a tree with your mouth open waiting for a falling apple (Zigon 2009: 255, quoting one of his interlocutors). However, for my interlocutors, prayer was a gift, a productive gesture of assistance, that both connected them to young South Africans and generated transformations that reduced the disparity between their ways of being in the world.

Trust in Charity

Beyond the option of looking at their faces on computer screens, supporters could also relate to recipients of their cold hard cash by visiting the school. To my knowledge, all of the key individuals tasked with operating the Friends had already visited the school and could enact their relationships with learners and staff subject to memories of these experiences. This ability contrasted with the engagements of individuals who could only consume heightened and edited images and stories about the school 'second hand'. The experience of 'being there'—smelling, touching, feeling, hearing, and seeing—appeared to cement relationships (also see O'Neill 2013). This observation aligns with Rabbitts' (2012: 284) claim that "a vast array of embodied, visceral sensibilities and dimensions of interaction [that are] not usually associated with charitable action [are integral to it nonetheless]". He (ibid.) terms this arrangement "the thematic of proximal encounters".

Daniel became a trustee after volunteering for a full academic year and recently returned to the school. Susan has travelled to Ngomso several times. She said that she "fell in love with the place and the children" (also see Conran 2011).[16] She also built a strong friendship with Mary. In the playground of the school, I asked her "What keeps you coming back?" She replied:

> Having said that I am not a particularly mothering type of a person, it is the relationships with the children. That they feel in some sense my children [giggling], which is really bizarre. We don't have a great deal to say to each other, we don't have deep, meaningful conversations, but I know that they are glad to see me, and I am glad to see them. Our lives are somehow connected. I care about what happens to them.

Her words speak directly to Rabbitts' (2013: 274) argument that "networks" that sustain 'Compassion' (a pseudonym for a prominent Christian child sponsorship charity) owe much to "romantic ideological valorisations of 'personal relationship' (read friendship, familial care and Christian love)". As with members of staff, Susan was keen to be a "mothering type of a person"—"caring about" and "caring for [the learners]" (McKie 2005: 3)—in a capacity that appeared to surprise her. This moralistic positioning was inseparable from her Christian faith and connects with discourses concerning Christian maternalism and *agapē*. Her relationship with the school and those attending it delivered such an opportunity.

By praying for the school and its staff, learners, and past pupils, supporters constituted and illustrated their belief in the triangular relationship between self, God, and other. Prayer appeared to bring a sense of immediacy to their relationships that could not be found in the act of sharing money alone. Christians living in the UK have been encouraged to pray for the prosperity of mission schools in Grahamstown since their inception.[17] As if to adhere to such instruction, the Friends saw prayer as one of their two main tasks (providing finance being the other). In setting up a direct debit with (most) charities, you see that money leaves your account each month, but there are no obvious means by which you can communicate with its beneficiaries.[18] In contrast, prayer provided Ngomso supporters with a bridge of communication: through dialogue with God, they could 'speak to' the recipients of their prayers.

The search for authentic connections is integral to the humanitarian/charity sector more broadly, in ways that need not be so *explicitly* tied to religious discourses (even if something of them lies dormant in the roots of ethical imaginaries). In reporting preliminary findings of their study of how audiences in the UK react to the marketing materials of humanitarian NGOs, for example, Shani Orgad and Bruna Seu (2014: np), who have expertise in media and psychology, respectively, argue:

> People want an embodied, direct and meaningful relationship with those whose suffering they are being asked to alleviate. However, this desire differs considerably from how NGOs frequently address the public: as monetary donors, not carers. The discrepancy between how NGOs approach the UK public and the way the public wants to relate to and help people far away, increases a sense of alienation, both between the public and the far-away sufferers, and between the public and NGOs.

This statement suggests that Susan's enthusiasm to feel connected to 'far-away sufferers' is integral to humanitarianism.[19] Scherz (2014: 141) asserts that "such approaches are increasingly rare in the contemporary moment, when so many organizations, including those run by the Catholic Church, are focused on a kind of sustainability [e.g. discourses of empowerment and capacity building] that encourages them to imagine themselves as separable and separate from those living in the places where they work". In contrast, the appeal of Ngomso, for potential and existing supporters, was that it offered an opportunity for meaningful, connected relationships (immediately) and for them to witness learners' self-sustaining independence (in the long-term).

My interlocutors contrasted the importance of 'authentic relationships' with the professionalised relationships and bureaucratic forms of accountability offered by other organisations. Bornstein (2012: 63) observed similar dynamics during her ethnographic fieldwork in India. I would contend that such commonality may well point to some kind of universal, or, at least, non-context-specific, imperative that individuals must evaluate various mechanisms of trust and accountability when establishing themselves as compassionate givers. Susan's church supported three organisations each year, raising about £800 for each one. "The church is asked to support many things", a lady in her congregation explained, "but we [make sure that we] have a real relationship with those that we support". Susan herself explained it similarly when saying "[In supporting Ngomso] *my church was looking to have a real connection with somewhere else in the world, rather than just supporting an organisation*". Another lady agreed: "The personal relationship [we have with Mary and the school] is incredibly important. It is different from what you would have with the big charities." Her words are evidence of what Bornstein (2012: 59) has termed "a nexus of suspicion", which functions in the sphere of humanitarian. More broadly, despite increasingly logical modes of accountability and audit cultures, modes of trust engendered through inter-human recognition pervasively function to orient individuals towards the future, reducing risk and providing a sense of confidence that events will materialise in expected ways (Moore 2011). In the context of humanitarianism, which is premised upon future-oriented projects, such mechanisms are fundamental to the organisation of projects, interventions, and institutions.

To my mind, the fact they distrusted other organisations relates to pervasive public discourses regarding the 'aid relationship' between Britain and Africa. Readers of national newspapers, especially those that lean towards the political Right, are told that DFID employees misspent foreign aid budgets on business class flights (Sherman 2014). Headlines read: "How your money is squandered on foreign aid" (Foreman 2013: np). And: "Wasted, the millions Britain has poured into aid for Congo" (Drury 2013: np). Articles have also informed the public that Band Aid money has been used to buy guns (Brennan 2010). In 2013, when a UK Independence Party (UKIP) politician bemoaned the 'fact' that corrupt foreign politicians have misspent aid sent to "Bongo Bongo Land" on Ferraris and Ray-Bans, his statement was covered by BBC Radio, Channel 4 News, and national newspapers. The media didn't focus on the questionable validity of his contention, but rather on his refusal to apologise for his 'racist language' (e.g. BBC 2013; Mason 2013; Shipman et al. 2013). The implicit message was that aid *is* misspent, just don't be racist when talking about it. Such discourse is so pervasive that when people I meet, in the pub or at a wedding, for example, learn that I am writing about a charity that supports a school in Africa they frequently move the conversion on to the topic of 'wasted aid money'.

Contrasting with UK supporters who implicitly trusted the Friends and staff at Ngomso, some parties in South Africa were wary of them. Siseko told me that Sizo (a respondent to his questionnaire) was sure that Mary was "running the school to collect money from overseas" and was "keeping some for herself".[20] Another respondent named Themba similarly told him that "[Mary] protects [the learners], even in court, even if they are wrong because she is getting money out of them". Mary knew that some members of staff at Ngomso circulated similar discourses and that, in particular, there was conjecture about her relationship with the FOA. Given my experiences in South Africa during my visit in 2011, I initially assumed that this illustrated some form of racialised distrust of Mary and her 'white, European partners'. However, when Joyce took over as principal in 2013, she was also accused of benefitting from the school's coffers. This development encouraged me to link the situation with public discourses about corruption in public office (discussed later in this chapter). However, I have not been able to speak with the relevant parties to confirm this hypothesis. What is clear, however, is that some individuals were unconvinced about the integrity of those who managed Ngomso. On a visit to the school in 2014, Raymond, the treasurer of the Friends, attempted to quell the rumours by sharing his financial accounts during a parents' evening. I do not know whether this mechanism of accountability travelled well from the UK to convince the cynics and sceptics among the audience.

These dynamics of misappropriation and mistrust also extended to interactions between members of staff and learners, who were, to some extent, similarly suspected of being 'on the take'. Such suspicion was rooted in undercurrents of both conjecture and proof. For example, a young man and his sister dropped into Joyce's office one afternoon to tell her that they wanted to enrol. Mrs Noni then spoke to the brother, who confirmed that he didn't know his home address. This claim was not too unusual, or a cause for concern as many learners constructed knowledge of their home environments without recourse to street names and house numbers. The young man said that he lived with an elder sister because his mother had died in 2005, and his father had passed away some weeks earlier.

He also told Mrs Noni that he had previously attended a school in the location but left because they could not provide him with a uniform, books, and food in the way that Ngomso could. Having validated his claim to a position at the school, he attended for a couple of days, but only until Mrs Noni spoke with a fellow Learner Support Agent during a meeting organised by the Department of Education (DoE). Having asked her why she and her school had not "looked after" the young man when he was in attendance, Mrs Noni was told that his mother was, in fact, very much alive.

Upon hearing this story, I guessed that the young man was clever enough to know that such a personal narrative was exactly the kind of plight that Ngomso staff happily attempted to alleviate with material support. He presented himself as the 'model victim' in line with the criteria of institutionalised policies (e.g. extrinsic barriers to learning) and fundraising discourses (i.e. the 'needy victim'). As Fassin (2007: 512) argues, those who successfully secure aid often do so by "willingly [submitting] to the category assigned to them: they understand the logic of the construction, and they anticipate its potential benefits" (also see Cheney 2010; Epstein 2010). This wilful submission may be inauthentic—that is, the adoption of an identity can secure resources, even when the individual cannot legitimately lay claim to the qualities ascribed to her. Similarly, Epstein (2010) argues that some young men and women adopt a 'refugee identity' in Sudan in the hope of securing the school educations on offer in refugee camps. In each example, the malleability of truth provides welcome relief to those encountering limited fields of ethical possibility. However, in turn, these same limitations make it harder for them to maintain a state of moral integrity—that is, the extent to which others may or may not view them as honest is compromised.

In the sense that potential aid recipients selected discourses in the knowledge that they would be likely to resonate with audiences, such techniques of persuasion have much in common with those Mary and Joyce employed when they were similarly attempting to secure resources in English churches. However, in Mary and Joyce's hands, the truth was less malleable. I noticed that young learners or potential learners were more likely to employ false narratives in the hope of securing resources, with varying degrees of success. I would argue that they had less power to maintain their moral integrity because fewer moral possibilities of personhood were open to them, most especially on account of their limited political and economic resources. In other words, they had fewer options.

A relevant theorisation of this scenario is provided by James Scott (2015: 5, 25), who highlights the ways that 'the peasantry' and 'subordinate groups' actively interpret and reconfigure forms of institutionalised dominance, most relevantly through practices of "false compliance" and "the pervasive use of disguise" (i.e. concealment or anonymity). For these individuals, Scott (2015: 24) argues, "everyday forms of resistance have been the only resort short of rebellion".[21] In a sense, those who falsely complied with the criteria of the school in order to secure resources, most notably by disguising themselves in some way (e.g. keeping their home address secret), were able to gain or regain a mode of power from a systemic arrangement of institutions and institutional discourses that would otherwise have refused their claim.[22] However, such techniques were not foolproof. When seeking humanitarian assistance, some lives were recognised as being worthy of attention and others were not (see Fassin 2007). Cabot (2013: 453) usefully employs the term "eligibility practices" to theorise such interchanges between potential aid recipients and those empowered to distribute humanitarian resources.

For members of staff, eligibility practices and the possibility of 'false claims' created uncertainty whenever an individual first arrived at the school or attempted to claim some form of resource, perhaps a new school uniform or a food parcel, for example. Mary once gave a learner some extra money to buy paraffin so that he could cook the food contained within his food parcel one weekend. She told me that she wasn't 100% sure that the funds were legitimately required, but said she had decided to distribute the money because the alternative scenario—that is, the young man was telling the truth and would have gone hungry for two days—did not bear thinking about. The anxiety she experienced in the face of the unknown is an example of how aid workers more generally face an "epistemological problem" whenever they must judge the eligibility of a potential recipient (Cabot 2013: 452). It is, quite simply, often difficult to *really* know whether a claim is legitimate. When resources are limited, and ineffective patterns of distribution carry troubling health and well-being-related consequences, the pressure experienced during such ethical dilemmas is substantial.

As donors placed great emphasis on the trust they attributed to their relationships with members of staff, all efforts to police the ambiguity of eligibility practices were integral to the maintenance of the school's revenue streams; funding could have been held back or limited at any time, subject to anxiety regarding its effective and legitimate distribution. Mary continually took measures to maintain the eligibility of the school's claim on charitable resources. For instance, she did not use the school's coffers to pay the young man who asked for money for paraffin, choosing instead to take money from her own purse, most likely because such payments were not sanctioned by the school's agreement with the partnering UK charity. Through such intricate, almost unseen gestures, lines of communication between the school and existing and potential donors maintained the honesty and transparency that drew many individuals to support the case in the first instance.

In 2013, in a bid to extinguish the possibility that individuals could secure new uniforms through practices of false compliance (e.g. the young man who claimed orphanhood), which were, on occasion, successful, Joyce imposed a new rule, whereby newly enrolled learners had to wait for two weeks before being given new uniforms, no matter how genuine their claims of need. The imposition of this rule was driven by members of staff, most especially Alice, Joyce's administrative assistant, who were keen to ensure their eligibility criteria were not manipulated. Eighteen months later, during the charity's AGM in a church hall in central London, several trustees spoke to Joyce about their concern that some beneficiaries were selling their uniforms for a profit soon after receiving them. Joyce replied by confidently detailing the new eligibility procedures, the two-week 'commitment test window', and said that such misappropriation did not happen anymore. As in the case of the original exchanges between potential beneficiaries (i.e. those securing uniforms) and benefactors (i.e. members of staff), the benefactors in this case (i.e. the trustees) could not have known, for sure, whether the potential beneficiary (i.e. Joyce) had provided an accurate story. Perhaps she had stripped uncertainty and ambiguity from the scenario in a bid to maintain their confidence? Having not visited South Africa for 18 months, I did not know. Much like those who had asked the question of her initially, I could only evaluate the extent to which I trusted Joyce and the truthfulness of her claim. Having presumably done likewise, the audience appeared collectively content with her answer and, to my knowledge, such anxieties have not threatened to disrupt their distribution of assistance again. As a consequence of such engagements, the school lived to fight another day, much like those young men and women who successfully adapted to the demands placed upon them when securing humanitarian assistance.

Trustees of the Friends regularly addressed the suspicion of external audiences by explaining that their funds are sent directly to the school (under the custody of Mary and God) and illustrating breakdowns of expenditure, including very low administration costs. Such transparency, I believe, engendered trust in their activities. Similarly, in 2011 Mary told me that donors liked to meet with her "to know where their money [was] going". As per Bornstein's (2012: 63) analysis of the NGO sector in India, when giving is relational and direct, "social networks [function] as the guarantor". Mary said that the value of such relationships helped to explain why nobody had ever cancelled a direct debit payment plan.

Key parties in the charity also know the importance of this assertion. When Raymond, who was the charity's chairman at the time, first established contact with me soon after I returned to the UK in December 2011, he wanted to know my opinion about their plans to expand the scope of the charity. In an email to members, he wrote: "do we stay small and 'family' or do we try to expand to meet Mary's and the school's future ambitions [for more learners and vocational opportunities]?" He added, "We are nervous of losing our main appeal to many of our generous donors which is that we know exactly where each £1 given will go – which cannot be said of some of the larger charities". This moral dilemma was brought about, most pointedly because the Friends had had an application for a large corporate-funded donation turned down on account of the fact they targeted a relatively limited number of beneficiaries. Their deliberations were attempts to best construe relations of trust and accountability with different audiences (also see Bornstein 2012, for evidence of similar techniques in India). The funding body wanted more detailed and thorough long-term plans, complete with timings and expenditure breakdowns than the Friends had to provide for those who placed their trust in the word of Mary and her (Christianised) good intentions, and their 'real relationships' with the school. Ideally, the Friends did not want to cater for 'the mass-market'—that is, to move their attentions and funds between numerous sites of intervention and groups of benefactors—for fear it would 'thin out' these carefully constructed social and material relationships (also see Scherz 2014). The imperative to maintain 'real relationships' thus limited the potential scope of their work, and the funding channels open to them, while these same relationships simultaneously made their work possible. The key argument here is that the scope and form of humanitarian interventions are constituted as a consequence of how relationships and obligations are maintained. In other words, the emergence of various institutionalisations of humanitarianism is a product of the human requirement for experiences of trust and accountability.

For some potential and existing supporters, knowledge of the fact that the school's transformative qualities were limited in this way met with troubled, ethical deliberation. Compared to her sister, whose judgement about the school was incredibly positive, Betty, for example, was less sure that the hope offered by the school would materialise:

> The thing is, it's sad. Because talking to [the learners] today, [I learnt that] they do all have dreams, things they want to be; like a fashion designer or a bus driver.... It is just whether this is actually [possible]. [I wonder] whether, maybe as well, they have been getting their hopes up. [Have they been] thinking [and believing], you know, [what they are told] – 'If you get through grade seven, you're then going to be able to do this and that' – [even though it might not happen for them]?

The sisters then spoke about Samkelo, a 19-year-old in grade seven. They knew he wanted to be a bus driver but were anxious that he would not finish high school because he was comparatively old for his school year. This conversation was an example of how they deliberated on the distinction between the accounts of turnarounds that were shared with potential supporters, which I assume they had encountered at some point, and the reality that such hope did not materialise for every learner. Betty was not only concerned for those who 'did not make it' but for how becoming hopeful, in the first instance, can imbue later experiences of disappointment with heaviness.

Having heard her sister's concerns, Sally offered this response: "But [despite all that], I think Mama Mary is achieving a great thing, I do, [by just] keeping the kids off the street." This conversation was not the first time I encountered judgements about trade-offs between the value attributed to long-term 'success stories' and the imperative to 'rescue' the learners from their daily existence 'in the now'. While the FOA trustees collectively hoped that the free school meals would encourage learners to stay in school and transform into 'success stories', they felt that it was important to feed the 'hungry learners' regardless of this future pay-off. As Scherz (2014: 141) argues, interventions that focus on alleviating the impact of inequality in the short term, "will [not] bring about an end to global poverty, but they do represent possible responses to the ethical problem of a world shaped by inequality". Ngomso's supporters were ethically responding in this way. However, as Betty's statement indicates, the knowledge that the transformative potential of the intervention was limited could be a source of unease.

Quite recently, I made arrangements for Joyce to speak to the Rotary Club that sponsored my Ambassadorial Scholarship. One of the first questions from the floor was from a Rotarian, who wanted to know how many past pupils had secured employment. Joyce replied by saying that several were employed, and stressed the high unemployment rate and the need for improved vocational opportunities. At the end of proceedings, another Rotarian praised her efforts: "You are providing some hope where there is little." He seemed content that the school was not countering global inequality or poverty per se but providing opportunities for some individuals to escape its clutches. Judging from his frowned expression, I suspected that the man who had asked for quantifiable evidence of employment was less convinced that this was sufficient.

This form of deliberative contestation, regarding Ngomso's transformative power, was inseparable from the fact that the institution *most explicitly* paid attention to the transformation of individuals, rather than collective or structural arrangements, such as labour inequalities.[23] Arguably, this focus did not address the ill-distributed opportunities of employment that limited the potential number of 'success stories'. In other words, by focusing on the transformation of individuals, interventions help to maintain the conditions whereby societies—including the one learners were adjudged to be excluded from but were so very clearly included in—are, for the most part, comprised of 'the marginalised' (also see Zigon 2011). In turn, it was the predominance of 'marginal statuses' in South Africa that fuelled the sentiments of fear and compassion that drove the school's supporters and staff to attempt to act on behalf of the learners.

A Duty to Intervene

The political situation in South Africa and, in particular, the Eastern Cape Department of Education's (ECDoE) 'state of crisis' provided further, more *overtly* political incentives for UK-based individuals to entrust Mary with their money and offer their assistance to the school. Without such intervention, they were concerned that the ANC and its Department of Education would not deliver the quality and kind of support and schooling that, in their opinion, learners deserved and needed. Such judgements were particularly forthcoming from those who had once lived in South Africa before witnessing its post-apartheid transformation from afar. I also encountered similar discourses while living in South Africa. Many individuals who were (or would have been) classed as White during apartheid and who were classed as such by the post-apartheid government, which has maintained the racial categories of apartheid for various purposes, keenly blamed the ANC for the country's failings. For those working on behalf of Ngomso from the UK, this political climate fed into a debate about how best to act on behalf of the learners at the school.

In both South Africa and the UK, I was often told that South Africa had gone downhill since the end of apartheid because the government was ineffective or untrustworthy. There were fears that this trajectory would continue. Likewise, Besteman (2008: 118) details "a vision of decline" that she "heard widely repeated by white people in Cape Town". She (ibid.) listened to concerns about falling standards in schools, as I did. Individuals directed the same discourse at universities during my stay in South Africa. Like me, Besteman (ibid.) also encountered an "insistence that black rule inevitably means civilizational decline" and "constant talk of crime and disorder". And, like me, she heard "the argument that affirmative action programs [e.g. racial quotas, preference in appointments, and Black Economic Empowerment] are promoting incompetence by advancing the unskilled too quickly". In my experience, such sentiments were most often qualified by a caveat that such frustration and concern for the future was not an endorsement of apartheid ideology. Rather, the general thrust of such narratives was: 'Apartheid wasn't good, but, at least, stuff worked (for 'us', at least).'[24]

This is what Daniel wrote on his blog during his stay in 2011:

> Litter is the thing that strikes you as you drive through the locations. One of the biggest problems of the new South Africa is the incompetence and corruption of the local municipalities. One of the Ngomso staff said to me, 'I wouldn't want to go back to the apartheid days, but I will say that the councils did a better job of running the town back then.'

Several UK-based supporters visited South Africa during my writing process here in the UK. They all similarly remarked on the water shortages in the city when they returned. In knowing Daniel, I don't believe that his statement indicates an endorsement of apartheid, rather, I think he was telling his readers (i.e. friends and family in the UK) that he was not alone in thinking that certain functions of government had deteriorated since 1994. He showed particular regret for the disused public railway lines in front of the school, which were slowly being covered by plants and gravel: a visual, somewhat symbolic illustration of decay.

Concern about the government's capabilities was heightened by supporters' knowledge of mismanagement and corruption in its departments, and the ECDoE in particular. David and Fuzile spoke to me about RDP houses that were "made with more sand than cement" in order, they said, that government officials could line their pockets. The poor quality of residential roads in the township, they continued, was evidence that the municipality only maintained those roads that were used by dignitaries during visits to the township. "There is a lot of robbing and corruption [in the ANC]", David continued. Fuzile agreed: "[A group of artists that I work with] have been writing to the local councillors about our plans for re-using the old arts centre [as a communal space for artistic projects]. They say they are listening, but nothing happens." Later that morning, a Catholic priest who was visiting to deliver the morning's assembly was speaking to the staff in the classroom that doubled up as their staffroom during break times.[25] He welcomed their efforts before telling them: "[In their speeches and policies] our government says that 'education is number one', but they are using the young people for votes. 'Using', that's the correct word: they've been getting rich [without making sure that education is number one]."

Since its inception approximately two decades ago, the ECDoE has been subject to "charges of official corruption, mismanagement, and administrative chaos" (Fiske and Ladd 2004: 76). For example, "thousands of school pupils in the Eastern Cape" started 2011 "without stationery [and books] after irregularities were detected in the Department of Education's multi-million rand tender" (Sokopo 2010: np). Thousands more were "forced to walk to school ... after the Department of Education suspended scholar transport" (Maqhina 2011: np), with the then Superintendent General Modidima Mannya (cited in ibid.) quoted as saying "We have run out of funds ... [and] owe a lot to service providers". As Mannya (cited in ibid.) explains, "People were not doing their work properly". In the same year, the ECDoE also "overspent R625million on its salary bill" and "in a bid to cover up the over expenditure ... terminated the employment contracts of 6000 temporary teachers despite a need for their services" (Mokone and Kgosana 2011: np). In March 2011, the National Cabinet decided, for the first time in history, to invoke the terms of the Constitution and hand administrative control of the embattled provincial (i.e. Eastern Cape) education system to the national department. A year after this intervention, the Basic Education Minister (Motshekga, cited in John 2012: np) said, "I have found a human resource development programme that is clearly in total disarray, evidence of financial mismanagement and maladministration".[26] Later, in June of 2015, President Zuma authorised a Special Investigating Unit (SIU) to investigate "serious maladministration", "improper or unlawful conduct", and "unlawful appropriation or expenditure of public money" in the ECDoE (The Presidency 2015: np). Clearly, misspent and unaccounted funds have gone some way to creating the current 'crisis'.

Such considerations have also been on the minds of members of the public, circulating nationally as very public moral discourses:

> The problems in education lie squarely at the feet of the inept ANC government (and not Apartheid!) who are far more concerned with lining their own pockets than in educating youngsters.

> Shall we buy our president another airplane or pay for another minister's ridiculously expensive cars/hotels/entourage or … realize that education is key to unity and a prosperous South Africa?

> So this [failure of public education] is how the mighty ANC looks after 'it's [sic] people'[?] … Fat cats who give each other multimillion contracts despite budget limits. Sheer unmitigated failure and treason against the people of South Africa. Betrayal of the charter, the [Constitution], the oath of office, the dignity of office, the trust of the trusting people.[27]

The Herald newspaper, based in Port Elizabeth, has run a series of articles detailing charges of corruption and misappropriation of funds under the banner *Rotten to the Core: Why Eastern Cape Education Is in Crisis*. In line with the claim that multiple discourses held that there were numerous 'villains' at work, one article claims: "[the ECDoE] is stealing our children's future" (Admin 2014: np). The media has frequently portrayed a duel between 'evil' department officials (led by the Minister of Education) intent on disrupting the schooling system with their 'greed and ineptitude' and the 'forces of social justice' represented by civil organisations, NGOs, and (some) teachers (Chisholm 2012). Needless to say, the DoE has rarely appeared in a favourable light.

These events are evidence of the emergence of what Ferguson (2006: 95) has called the "state-and-society paradigm", which, he argues, has become central to the study and constitution of African politics since the

1980s. This "paradigm sees development not as the project of a developmentalist state, but as a societal process that is held back by the stifling hold of the state" (ibid.). In contrast to the alternative conceptualisation of a 'nation-building' approach, "the state (now conceived as flabby, bureaucratic and corrupt) begins to appear as the chief obstacle to [development]". In contrast, there is "an unmistakable tone of approval and even celebration – not of the nation-building state, but of a liberated and liberatory civil society" (ibid: 96). My research clearly reveals the extent to which such discourses flow freely between institutionalised settings (e.g. the books and journals of the academy or the reports and policies of NGOs and development banks) and public deployments—that is, they both describe and orient political practice. When considered from a certain angle, terms such as civil society, development, charity, and even government are "concept metaphors" in that they "retain an indeterminate status both as theoretical abstractions and as a set of process, experiences and connections in the world" (Moore 2011: 142). In the case of my ethnography, related models of state-and-society distinctions clearly resonated with individuals living in Africa and Europe. To some extent, they were united by the idea that the national and provincial departments of the South African government, and its district municipalities, could not be trusted to operate in the best interests of its people, unlike themselves and other 'organisations of the people'. The complication in this case, however, which reveals the limitations of the state-and-society paradigm, is the fact that the institution in question received financing from a UK-registered NGO and the South African state. What transpires is not so much a clearly defined separation but blurred terrains of responsibility that were continually navigated and refashioned with each and every contestation of political power. This demonstration supports Ferguson's (2006: 103) thesis: "it might make sense to think of the new organizations that have sprung up in recent years not as challengers pressing up against the state from below but as horizontal contemporaries of the organs of the state – sometimes rivals, sometimes servants, sometimes watchdogs, sometimes parasites, but in every case operating on the same level and in the same global space". Certainly, in South Africa, as in the case of my research, NGOs funded by foreign or domestic money or even by the state itself were somewhat engaged in a relentless and metamorphosising scramble to fashion emergent and transnationally constituted political dynamics of responsibility and accountability.

According to their frameworks of rectitude, the FOA were positioned among 'the trustworthy' and 'the just'. When President Zuma used public money to upgrade his private residence, it was deemed a breach of both the Constitution and the Executive Ethics Code by the Public Protector (Madonsela 2014: 439). The report was entitled 'Secure in Comfort'; words that are antithetical to how supporters understood the lives of the learners. Major UK media outlets covered the events (e.g. BBC 2014; Flanagan 2014; Laing 2012; Smith 2013). They were also discussed by the trustees during a monthly conference call when they had a conversation about the fact it had taken the ECDoE 12 months to confirm the appointment of Joyce as Mary's successor.[28] If this was the situation 'over there', the imperative to 'step in' remained clear. Prominent supporters in the UK were not only concerned about the education of learners at Ngomso but for the future of a beloved country, and of family and friends who lived there, all of which were caught up in these issues of governance. Moreover, as well as these sentimental or emotional reasons, the implication of a diminishing currency and the respective, comparative value of their property investments in the country was a topic of concern-ridden conversation.

Among such discomfort they searched for explanation and understanding, ultimately as a means to find a solution. Similarly motivated academics have offered explanations of their own. I will briefly consider some of these before moving back to the evaluations of my interlocutors, identifying commonalities where appropriate. In the Eastern Cape, the post-apartheid "challenge of establishing new departments of education was immense" (Fiske and Ladd 2004: 77). There was, and perhaps still is, an "absence of managerial capacity in many provinces [that has] generated a huge gap between the policies developed at the national level and the ability of provincial departments to implement them" (ibid.). While it is conceivable that mismanagement relates to apartheid legacies—that is, inherited limited capacity and resources, as well as fragmented administrative structures (Hendricks 2011)—the link between the effects of apartheid and the subsequent charges of corruption and mismanagement (which are not to be confused) is contestable. For example, Dr Mamphela Ramphele (2012: np), a well-known South African academic and founder of the Black Consciousness Movement and, recently and fleetingly, an opposition political party, argues:

> It is no longer plausible to blame apartheid for our appallingly poor education and the shocking conditions under which teaching and learning occur in our society.... Our teachers and pupils deserve better. Our country deserves better.... We need to focus on radical change in our education system.... Citizens, parents, the private sector and the government must step up to the plate and lead the education system out of its present dismal state.

To me, it appeared as though the country was going through a transitional period of political blame, as well as reform. As apartheid and colonialism chronologically become more distant, the inheritance narrative will perhaps continue to become less persuasive, regardless of the profoundly negative legacy of 'Bantu Education'. Meanwhile, for some academics, the past has not so easily been forgotten. Laurence Wright (2012: 12) suggests that corruption in the ECDoE is "the ethical residue from transitional life in small-scale pastoral societies". He (ibid: 14) argues that in such societies "it is deemed legitimate to enhance your share of the cake, provided you are not found out, and the 'victim' is not one of your own". While the idea that corruption can be explained with analysis of social networks, relationships, and the moral imperative to 'look out for your own' has appeal, explaining it with recourse to the issue of scale and modernity doesn't, in my opinion, hold up to scrutiny. Wright essentially argues that people who engage in corruption in the ECDoE haven't been able to 'move on and become modern'. His argument hinges upon judgements of progression and superiority that are left hanging as ideological attacks brought to bear on an abstracted locality and history. Corrupt practices 'in and around' the State, including in localities that have been 'modern' from the beginnings of 'modernity', certainly extend beyond the vicinity and population addressed in this analysis.[29]

Alternative arguments and more compelling answers are evident elsewhere in the literature. The following factors come to the fore. One, the blurred line between State, civil, and private interests (see Das and Poole 2004). Two, State adoption of 'business' practices and State management rather than service as a method of governance. Three, an absence of rigorous accountability procedures (a condition perhaps resulting from limited resources and capacity in the department). Four, the undermining of effective State services resulting from efforts to move away from the legacies of colonialism, and related conflicts within government over its purpose. Five, a dominant-party system, tied to histories of racial conflict and oppression, resulting in a lack of political accountability and "scope for misbehaviour" (Matshiqi 2010: 10; also see Lodge 2002). Six, individuals who have been keen, for a multitude of reasons, to exploit these arrangements.[30]

So how did my interlocutors understand and explain the situation? A supporter living in Grahamstown emailed the trustees in the UK to report on the process of registering a partner charity in South Africa (more on that later). She said, "The Deeds Office is in disarray and has virtually ground to a halt, which is sad because it used to be one of the few arms of government that worked efficiently". Clive thanked her for the update, saying "clearly, 'this is Africa', I'm afraid". During my time in Ghana, some volunteers from the UK and the US took to saying the same thing when a bus was late, or the water cut out for an evening: "TIA" (it has an acronym so it must be true). During conference calls and meetings with the trustees, similar explanations—that is, the problems at hand reflected a continent-wide reality—accompanied anxieties about the performance of the ECDoE. To my mind, 'TIA' is shorthand for 'It's how they, the blacks in Africa, do things.' It is a racial discourse that both asserts the idea that 'nothing works in this place' and provides an explanation for it.

One Sunday morning I took the Tube to Green Park in Mayfair. It's the same station I use when I 'DJ' at a private members' club, where bottles of whisky can cost tens of thousands of pounds and Prince Harry drinks alongside David Beckham. (If I have been immersed in my field notes during the day or think too much about my studies, I both laugh and despair at my surroundings.) I walked past cigar and umbrella shops, leather shoes on sale at £325, and a sign advertising a tasting session hosted by a world-renowned cheese expert. Clive had arranged to hold a trustees meeting at The Naval & Military Club, which was founded in 1862 to cater for Naval and Army officers but now has a more open, if still expensive, membership policy. As I entered the meeting room, I saw shelves filled with books about Admiral Nelson and Nelson Mandela, Francis Drake, and Napoléon Bonaparte. On the wall, there was a Parliamentary Recruiting Committee Poster from 1914 of Lord Frederick Sleigh Roberts of Kandahar, dressed in full military uniform.[31] Roberts fought in India, and during the Boer War in South Africa (1899–1902). The poster presented the caption: "He did his duty. Will YOU do YOURS?"

Ian had previously told me about his relationship with the anthropologist Elizabeth Colson.[32] Clive had met Colson as a young boy when his father was working for the (colonial) British government during the construction of the Kariba Dam between Zambia and Zimbabwe in the late 1950s (see Colson 1960). Colson, Clive told me, came to the family home to speak to his father about the Gwembe Tonga, as there were concerns that their resettlement had compromised relationships with burial grounds. As I took my seat in Mayfair, I thought more about how the legacies of colonialism and missionisation, which have helped me to understand the activity of the Friends, are interwoven with an anthropological legacy that has made my research possible.

Ian had recently returned from Cape Town, where he lived for part of each year. It was January 2015. "Government efficiency is declining," Clive reported. "It really was quite shocking to see." He told us about a "lack of skills" and said that those working in government departments were "feeling lost". In Grahamstown, the local municipality had been placed under administration. After the meeting, we retired to another room for some lunch. Most attendees left, leaving Clive and me to talk. He wanted to learn more about my anthropological research and, in return for my explanation, shared his understanding of the situation in South Africa. He told me about water treatment plants that had stopped working due to poor maintenance and individuals who had not ordered emergency diesel. He spoke about the "African way". He told me his concerns that "local tradition" and "Xhosa culture" are ill-suited to processes of "strategic" governance, and he wondered whether "evolution" explained this "lack of impetus" and "inability to plan strategically". He had recently visited the Cradle of Humankind World Heritage site near Johannesburg and told me that Ethiopia was, in fact, "the birthplace of humanity". He had read an argument (somewhere) that suggested that those who went south from Ethiopia did not have to compete for resources as keenly as those who went north to the colder climes of Europe. He wondered whether this history could explain the lack of "competitiveness" in the Eastern Cape (i.e. desire to make things work and to plan strategically!). Despite being worried that his words "might sound racist", he was clearly searching for an explanation about why those working for the South African government did not possess his abilities as a capable administrator. From the tone of his voice and keenness to ask my opinion, I got the impression that he was not thoroughly convinced he had found one.

I responded with a babbled argument about how the notion of societal evolution is flawed because increased competitiveness is not evidence of progress. During my journey that morning, I had been reading *Fragments of an Anarchist Anthropology* by David Graeber. He (2004: 41) writes: "'societies' are constantly reforming, skipping back and forth between what we think of as different evolutionary stages". In my response to Clive, I was following tradition: "[Anthropologists] have been trying for decades now to convince the public that there's no such thing as a 'primitive,' that 'simple societies' are not really all that simple, that no one ever existed in timeless isolation, that it makes no sense to speak of some social systems as more or less evolved; but so far, we've made very little headway" (ibid.). Evidently, these considerations did not influence the analysis Wright (2012) offers either. Usually, in person, I am less forthcoming with such opinions and keener to listen. It was perhaps fortunate for us both that the looming debate never materialised because it became clear that the waiters were impatient to clear the room.

I have included this vignette because this was the most striking conversation that I had with my interlocutors whereby they combined judgements of evolution, progression, and modernity with concerns about issues of governance. However, numerous other, more subtle exchanges were already informing this chapter before this exchange with Clive in Mayfair. Given such understandings about 'the abilities of Africans', and the ANC government and its DoE, in particular, the ability to provide support to Ngomso functioned as a mode of political criticism and intervention. It was a way of governing—that is, influencing the fashioning of the schooling system tasked with morally transforming the next generation—without being elected into office or electing the political party in power. The same is true of the vast majority of South African supporters who did not also support the ANC government. As I understand it, by supporting the school, people in both countries were attempting to reverse, in a small way, the feared 'decay of South Africa' so that the country might again progress back up the hill they were sure it had once begun to climb. Hence, while external funding and support (i.e. that not provided by the ECDoE) facilitated the maternalistic ambitions of staff and their attempts to step in for ineffective or absent parents and carers, it was also paternalistic in the sense that it was driven by desires to reduce the autonomy of the ruling party 'for the good of the country and its young'. It was an echo of the similarly politicised nature of colonial missionisation two centuries before.

Further, because the charity (i.e. FOA) was accountable to UK law (e.g. the Charities Act of 2011) and the UK government's Charity Commission, which both limit the terms of 'acceptable' expenditure and activity, Ngomso could not be run independently of the aims and directives of the UK government. In this way, the efforts of supporters again echo the politicised nature of colonial missionisation; when relationships between those motivated by Christian faith to voluntarily intervene in the affairs of the Cape Colony and those on the payroll of the British government were similarly ambiguous and contestable, but, to some degree at least, amicable. In working to fund activities endorsed by the UK government's criteria, supporters of the FOA went some way to fulfilling her foreign policy objectives and to extending her control upon educational, and thus moral and epistemological, reform globally.

Litigation and Human Rights

Before my fieldwork, interlocutors at Ngomso had been trying to secure funding and approval from the DoE for relocation. For a number of reasons, which I will not explore in any great depth here, they were sure that the school's building and facilities were substandard and not fit for purpose.[33] As Lindiwe put it: "We have been battling with the government for many years [to get our new school]." In 2006, a move looked likely when the DoE listed Ngomso as a priority construction project. Eskom, the electricity public utility company, donated surplus land and buildings and agreed to fund necessary renovations. However, the buildings were demolished without explanation. Two years later, the DoE had not developed any alternative plans, despite staff and the SGB pursuing them with letters and phone calls. Ngomso was then removed from the list of priority construction projects. According to Mary, this was done on the instruction of the provincial director of Inclusive Education, Mrs Nozulu. Although they knew it threatened to upset their relationship, individuals at Ngomso then simultaneously tested and produced the democratic processes of the post-apartheid State and South Africa's judiciary when they resorted to taking legal action against the DoE. Those who instigated the action—that is, Ngomso staff and the SGB—were constitutive of the same State education system they held to account (Chisholm 2012). However, they frequently distanced themselves from the (ANC) government when complaining about government-funded provisions. They had an idea about an underperforming government "as a metapolitical concept" (Abrams 1988; Kaplan 2006: 13). As evident in Lindiwe's explanation, it was this "government" that they were battling.

Mary made contact with Julie Cox, the daughter of an old friend, who was regional director of Law for People (LFP; pseudonym), a leading public interest litigation or human rights NGO. The organisation was always looking to take the DoE to court to challenge their record of managing educational infrastructure. Lodging a complaint on behalf of Ngomso's School Governing Body, they argued that the DoE had failed to provide the school with adequate facilities, in violation of constitutional promises of quality educations for all South African children. The complaint invoked human rights discourses that were already integral to schooling in 'Western democracies' before they replaced the segregationist policies of Bantu Education and influenced South Africa's Constitution, which reads "Everyone has the right to a basic education" (*Republic of South Africa* 1996: s29(1a)).[34] Importantly, human rights discourses also promote conceptualisations of childhood and care that align with those that Ngomso staff valued.[35] Like a multitude of social, cultural, and political movements (see Zigon 2013), it is, therefore, unsurprising that such rights were both a motivation for and intended outcome of Ngomso's litigation and the school's mission more generally.[36]

Those at the LFP provided their professionalism to articulate moralised judgements using terminology recognised by the courts (Weber 1991: 196–244). Those at Ngomso were willing participants and facilitated the LFP's *raison d'être*. I better understood this arrangement after meeting with Julie and her colleagues at a workshop hosted by the Oxford Human Rights Hub, affiliated with the Faculty of Law at the University of Oxford, in December 2014. In a meeting room at the University of Oxford and a local pub afterwards, they told me the LFP both accepted calls for assistance and sought out potential litigation cases. The likelihood of success drove the selection process. As Michael from the Cape Town office put it, "We ask for what we think we can get".[37] They also relished the chance to set legal precedents. As with relations with the FOA, Ngomso's partnership with the LFP was established when individuals' lives and ambitions intertwined. Again, Mary was integral to this collaboration. Such linkages, which are fundamental to civil rights movements throughout South Africa, are at odds with a view of liberal individualism prominent in a great deal of human rights literature and policy (Robins 2008).

Das (cited in DiFruscia 2010: 141) states that the political transpires when "very ordinary individuals in their ordinary acts manage to produce specific newness, precise possibilities" as they attempt to affirm "ordinary things". Individuals at Ngomso and the LFP were trying to secure the possibility of new premises. They were seeking recognition when asking the State to support their endeavours and making a moral claim regarding the best interest of the learners (ibid). Through the courts, they tried to claim something that, in their opinion, rightly belongs to all: a school education (Jackson 2005). They wished to make the DoE *responsible* for the unrealised hopes of the transition to democratic governance—the disjuncture between the education system imagined, as articulated in the Constitution and policy documents, and the one that had materialised—and *accountable* for ensuring the materialisation of these hopes.

This is an extract from the complaint submitted in 2009:

> [The school caters for] impoverished, often abused and neglected children marginalised by the legacy of apartheid and by current South African society.... All have dropped out of traditional school because they face extrinsic barriers to learning that are not – and cannot be – addressed in a traditional classroom setting.... [The national and provincial departments of education have a] constitutional and statutory obligation to provide appropriate and adequate basic education for all children in the Eastern Cape, including learners who ... cannot be successful at a mainstream school.... The school's facilities do not meet the minimum standards for a mainstream school, let alone the standards set out for a special needs school.

There are three implicit judgements in the complaint that need highlighting. First, because mainstream schools do not address their needs, it is in the interest of Ngomso learners to attend a special school. Second, these learners are not receiving a specialised education due to Ngomso's substandard facilities. Third, these facilities need to be of a higher (i.e. specialised and more expensive) standard than mainstream schools. A subclaim of these judgements is that learners should be subsidised at five times the rate of those in mainstream schools. Hence, the affidavit made extraordinary claims upon departmental finances. More broadly, the political contestation between the DoE and Ngomso hinged upon moral possibilities and ethical judgements regarding the allocation of scarce resources (Jackson 2005). As evidenced by the terminology of the complaint, much like the mobilisations of sentiment employed during fundraising activity, actors drew upon discourses of vulnerability and marginalisation in an attempt to legitimise their claims and demands for acknowledgement. However, actors invoked frameworks of constitutional and statutory obligations when conceptualising and emphasising modes of ethical responsibility, rather than the conceptualisations of God's grace that were regularly employed during fundraising.

Such events are evidence of "an explosion in the postcolonial world of law-oriented NGOs" (Comaroff and Comaroff 2007: 142). The Comaroffs (ibid.) suggest such NGOs are "civilising missions of the new century" that "actively encourage citizens to deal with their problems by legal means".[38] With their rise, "the court has become a utopic site to which human agency may turn for a medium in which to pursue its ends" (ibid: 145). Indeed, my interlocutors at Ngomso and their supporters were hopeful that the court would empower them to continue their mission to reach the Promised Land and bring learners with them. Although this legal action was not overtly religious, it was inseparable from their concerns about immorality and conceptualisations of sin.[39] By co-opting the power of human rights, "the dominant moral-political language in the world today" (Zigon 2013: 717), they were able to justify the moral qualities of their intervention. In overtly political contexts, such discourses, relating to legal mandates and the universal attainment of human rights, which chime with the country's Constitution, were powerful, whereas discourses concerning the Bible and His instruction (e.g. agape), which promote the universal embrace of the Christian faith, were fruitfully employed in overtly Christian settings, such as churches in the UK.

These events and the narrative of a law-oriented NGO pitted against the South African government might be taken as further evidence of the emergence of the "state-and-society paradigm" (Ferguson 2006: 95–97). Again, however, real-world events demonstrate the limitations of this explanatory framework. In line with Ferguson's (ibid: 111) argument, what might appear to be a 'local' or 'grassroots' operation (i.e. the school joining with a law-oriented NGO based in the same city) was, in fact, directly linked to "transnationally distributed fields of interest and power". Consider (1) a school linked with a Christian-oriented, UK-registered charity operating subject to the laws of the UK government, joining with (2) a South African NGO linked with a research centre in Oxford funded by the British Academy and the Open Society Foundations (OSF), founded by George Soros, a billionaire financier who established the Foundations to "help countries make the transition from communism" (OSF 2017). When these connections are made salient, it becomes very difficult to articulate an interpretation of the 'society' that had mobilised itself politically. Moreover, relevant invocations of universalising human rights discourses complicate matter further still. I would argue that the interventionist projects of Ngomso and its partner organisations are evidence of a mode of governmentality that "fuses the grassroots and the global in ways that make a hash of the vertical topography of power on which the legitimation of nation-states has so long depended" (Ferguson 2006: 11). Indeed, the court action might be viewed as a transnationally constituted employment of modes of accountability that set out to disrupt the DoE's ability to manage its own affairs. Crucially, the entire scenario was dependent upon particular formations of government fashioned during the transition from apartheid, most specifically the installation of a judiciary independent from the executive and legislative branches of government, and the primacy given to the Constitution of South Africa.

Those who have faith in Constitutions believe them to guarantee, or be capable of producing, equal and moral politics and economics (Comaroff and Comaroff 2007: 141). As the Comaroffs (ibid.) argue, the striking "promulgation [of Constitutions in postcolonies] marks a radical break with the past, with its embarrassments, its nightmares, its torments". When the South African Constitution emerged, enthusiasms for new beginnings, of equality and democracy, were certainly pronounced. However, as I have said, for many South Africans, the pervasive, hope-filled ethical imaginary of 1994—captured in, and fuelled by, constitutional promises—has not satisfactorily materialised. Resultantly, participatory forms of governance have proliferated, especially because South Africa's dominant-party system limits the extent to which dissatisfactions might shift voters' allegiances (Matshiqi 2010; Piper and Nadvi 2010; Handley et al. 2008; Southall 2005). Especially since 2004, there has been widespread protest and demonstration (Atkinson 2007) triggered by frustrations related to poor service delivery, unemployment, corruption and mismanagement, and unrealised government targets and promises (Ballard et al. 2006; Desai 2002; Madlingozi 2007; Marais et al. 2008). Regarding education, various increasingly prolific and wide-ranging public interest litigation cases have been mounted against the DoE, specifically in the interests of systemic reform. The LFP has been central to many of them.

In South Africa, participatory governance is particularly salient because of the 'public action' of the anti-apartheid movement (Tapscott 2007; Friedman 2006). A photo illustrating Mary's part in a protest rally during the 1980s was stuck to the wall in her office. I once looked at it when she was on the phone with Julie. She put the receiver down and rubbed her eyes as if to relieve pressure in her head; the fight with the DoE was taking an emotional and physical toll. She said she was "close to burnout". The court case was constitutive of the lives of those involved. In demanding something from the State, my interlocutors demanded something of themselves: the need to endure the stresses and strains of conflict. Elisha's (2008: 155–156) interlocutors in the US, evangelicals engaged in 'civil society' projects and 'faith-based activism', experienced something similar, which they also termed "burnout". For them, stresses and strains emerged most prominently as a result of engagements with "irresponsible and unrepentant beneficiaries of charitable aid" (ibid.)—that is, something similar to the experiences of my interlocutors when engaged directly with some young learners and potential learners—and not uncooperative government agencies. However, I would argue that the essence of their experiences is very similar. In both cases, the 'burnout discourse' describes, as Elisha (ibid.) puts it, contemplation of "the gaps between one's moral ambitions and the conditions of existence that reinforce and simultaneously threaten to undermine them at every turn". It is the feeling of trying to run forward but being continually tripped up or pulled back or swimming against the tide until you contemplate giving up. An abundance of such experiences constituted the collective 'fight' that my interlocutors felt they were waging against the government.

Although it was demanding, emotionally exhausting even, compared to events during apartheid, when the Constitutional Court did not exist, this fight or 'struggle' was not violent. Relatedly, as we drank coffee in London in 2014, Mary told me her eyes had "really stung" when security forces used tear gas in a church to disrupt an anti-apartheid student protest. Now, through her link with the LFP—just one component of her extensive social capital (Bourdieu 1986; Bourdieu and Wacquant 1992)—she could acquire the technologies (e.g. knowledge and language) necessary to locate power within and through the judicial system. This system inherits much from the one established by colonial settlers; tear gas is still used to quell the disquiet of those who do not possess the appropriate technologies (e.g. BBC 2012; SAPA 2014). Addressing such discrepancy is at the heart of what the LFP sets out to achieve. Without such 'legal aid', the promises and mechanisms of democratic, legalised justice unjustly favour those who *already* possess the necessary technologies.

Similarly, Mark Hunter (2010: 120) argues that although "rights have an egalitarian flavour", it is "the emerging middle class [in South Africa], as elsewhere in the world, [that] is often able to shout the loudest" when "arguing that rights should be realized". However, even if such mechanisms of justice were open to all, the transformative potential of the Constitutional Court would remain muzzled. For, as Zigon (2013) argues, human rights-oriented protest strengthens the State apparatuses confronted. This, he (ibid: 719) continues, "ultimately marks a limit for possible political and moral activity since it merely repeats in differential form the very socioeconomic-political conditions it attempts to overcome". This analysis condemns human rights-oriented civil action for not going *far enough* in trying to alter structures of power in the "fight for moral progress" (ibid: 732). The demand placed upon the State by Ngomso and its supports did indeed endorse and strengthen the State's claim to be *the* rightful educator of South African children. The *form* of the schooling system, not its existence, was under scrutiny.

Relatedly, the staff's embodied moralities and ethical imaginations to some extent align with the language of the Constitution. Tellingly, the personal histories of many key figures of the anti-apartheid movement and post-apartheid transition—such as Walter Sisulu, Oliver Tambo, Thabo Mbeki, Steve Biko, Desmond Tutu, and Nelson Mandela—involve mission schools and universities associated with the Anglican Church. Some also studied at universities in England. Moreover, apartheid resistance saw a relationship between the views of 'liberal Whites'—such as Mary and members of the Black Sash, who opposed the National Party, often shared Christian faith, and were more likely to be (but were not exclusively) of British rather than Afrikaner descent—and 'Blacks', such as those of the Black Consciousness Movement, who were also linked to the Church. Arthur Chaskalson, the founder of the LFP, was a close ally of Mandela, defended him during the Rivonia Trial, and became President of the Constitutional Court in 1994 upon his recommendation. In 1996, the newly formed DoE awarded the Daily Bread Trust, which was still closely linked with Ngomso, its Premier Award for Innovation. Mandela was present when Mary collected the prize at a banquet in Pretoria. This fundamental moral conviviality had not died off during my fieldwork. As was the case with the staff at Ngomso, those at the DoE also appeared to hope for economic development through schooling, Christian salvation and personalised responsibility. The fight with the DoE was therefore not a fight between two camps with antithetical ethical imaginaries or discordant epistemological conceptualisations of possibility.

Zigon (2013: 732) argues that human rights-based movements "may succeed in occasionally making the lives of a select lucky few a bit better in the current state of affairs", but cannot deliver more pervasive change. Individuals working for the LFP acknowledged such limitations. In Oxford, Julie spoke about only being able to "place the spotlight on one issue", which only "encourages [the DoE] to take money away from other areas". Jimmy Taylor, her colleague, shared a similar concern: "The [education] department puts out the fire depending on where the litigation is; they throw money at the problem without having a plan for the broader picture."[40] Addressing the room of academics and lawyers, Julie somewhat rhetorically asked, "Are we not [merely] re-laundering [government] money?" Stressing her frustration, she continued by saying "We are asking the courts to make the government do its job, but we're not in the government's shoes to do this job". Julie and Jimmy knew there were limits to what they could achieve with litigation and experienced existential doubt about the potential for transformation and their influence upon it.

So why did they continue? I believe that (1) they desperately wanted *some* power over the constitution of the South African schooling system, especially given their judgements about the capabilities of the DoE and improper, even immoral, practices; and (2) were not prepared to give up on the hopeful ideals of 'a new South Africa' enshrined in the Constitution. Individuals working on behalf of the FOA were similarly motivated. Michael, from the Cape Town office, spoke about using "litigation for social change" towards "just and equitable outcomes". He went on to say that "the LFP deals in enforcement and remedies". This focus on control and redress is evocative of Ngomso staff and supporters' hopes that they might channel learners' potentiality and heal the morally corrupted. The distinction is that, in their attempt to rescue the nation's collective future, individuals at the LFP focused on curing broken government departments, rather than children.

Like any educative effort, litigation took decision-making powers away from those adjudged to be incapable of managing their affairs. Julie said, "The LFP make the government do their work". Michael spoke of how the court "monitored" the DoE and enforced "consequences" for "non-compliance".[41] As the journalist Veriava Faranaaz (2014: np) has put it, "[South African] courts are schooling the state". Jimmy revealed plans to litigate against "teacher absenteeism" and "the outcome of education", such as low literacy rates. In other words, there were hopes that the LFP might extend its control over the DoE.

In response to Zigon's assertion that such effort is not constructive of widespread redress, Julie and her colleagues and my interlocutors at

Ngomso might say that it is pragmatic. Moreover, their endeavour was not 'more radical' because they had *faith in schools* because they figured in their hopes for a moral, egalitarian, and prosperous society (Stambach 2010). Abandoning this faith would have meant transforming the embodied moralities that enabled them to encounter the world and imagine their futures and those of others. As Zigon's statement suggests, the value of anthropology is its ability to highlight alternative possibilities for living (Ingold and Lucas 2007; Jackson 2005). However, we must always live a moral life, and the possibility of living one focused on the exploration of other moral possibilities is, understandably, not valued by all.

Distrust and Responsibility

Some individuals in vicinity encountered the intentions and methods of Ngomso's staff and supporters with great scepticism, recognising their desire to condition modes of responsibility with a distrusting eye and seeing something of this historical legacy in their actions and ambitions. Perhaps unsurprisingly, some individuals working at the DoE were especially unwelcoming of the interventionist projects of Ngomso, its partner institutions, and other agencies who similarly contested the terrain of governmentality in the field of public education and related services. For instance, in 2013, through court action and public protest, a coalition of education-oriented NGOs pushed the DoE to issue Regulations Relating to Minimum Uniform Norms and Standards for Public School Infrastructure. In effect, when these new regulations were promulgated into law they created a framework of expectation and responsibility regarding the DoE's infrastructure programme, including stipulations about the replacement of deficient buildings. The Minister of Basic Education, Angie Motshekga (cited in Nkosi 2013: np) issued a statement, saying:

> It is interesting to note the sudden interest that Equal Education [and the LRC] is taking in the education of the African child ... Suddenly the NGO knows all about the challenges that African children face against the privileges they [i.e. the white adults at the NGO] have enjoyed. The struggle for black children to receive a decent classroom in which to learn has been ongoing for many decades, even before the days of Bantu education.... However, to suddenly see a group of white adults organising black African children with half-truths can only be opportunistic, patronising and simply dishonest, to say the least.

Motshekga (ibid.) refused to retract her statement following widespread criticism, arguing "It's not racist to mention history". It is telling that she claimed "white adults" were organising "black African children" but did not suggest this power dynamic could work the other way round. Clearly, there is evidence of an inherent degree of mistrust in those seeking to secure modes of governmentality, especially those relating to the education and upbringing of 'black African children'. Moreover, the discourse is evidence of how politicised contestation in South Africa is undergirded by historically constituted racial discourses regarding accountability and justice.

In his ethnography of a formerly Indian township in Durban, Thomas Hansen (2012: 5) articulates his observation about how central such racialised frameworks of meaning are in South Africa:

> Today, no statement, no sentence, and no gesture can acquire its full meaning and significance in South Africa without being linked to, and invariably qualified by, the phenotypical classification of the speaker. An individual's pigmentation is what can be seen by the eye but is also always/already inserted and framed by a larger gaze, a schema of racial ideology that makes bodily pigmentation the very root cause of intrinsic social qualities and cultural propensities.

As I wrote in my notes one evening: "ideas about race always seem to be bubbling beneath the surface". For example, when two police officers arrived at Mary's office after a learner had threatened a security guard, their questions suggested they were also concerned about Mary's enthusiasm to take the reins. They asked her, "Are you reporting these cases to the Department of Education? Are you working with psychologists?" Mary replied by saying "Am I just another white women who hates black people?" One of the officers had responded with something inaudible before Mary said: "I have laid down my life [for black people] for twenty years." The exchange upset Mary, and she called Joyce to the office so that she might help to defuse the situation. Perhaps she thought the police officers would not question Joyce's motivations and practices in the same way.

Significantly, this schema influenced Mary's relationship with Mrs Nozulu, the provincial director of Inclusive Education who, in Mary's opinion, had immobilised the school's claim for improved facilities. As we had lunch in a pub in the Cotswolds during 2012, Mary told me that

Nozulu had once said "Where are all the white children at Ngomso? You are giving black children an inferior education to the whites", which provides an insight into her reluctance to support the school's relocation. As she recounted this accusation, Mary put down her cutlery and pursed her lips together, saying "I was so angry. I am trying to get a better school education for young black children; she must know that there are no poor white children in Grahamstown". I never met Mrs Nozulu, so cannot know her interpretation of events. Nor do I know if she did not lend support to the school's campaign for new infrastructure because she made judgements about a worrisome link between Mary's skin colour and the morality of her intentions. However, it seems unlikely, if not impossible, that racialised distrust of Mary was not a factor in these events. It certainly influenced the way that Mary experienced and made sense of her fight with those at the DoE.

Cebisa, a university student who completed her honours in anthropology in 2011. She had volunteered at Ngomso before I arrived in South Africa but stopped visiting after she, like Dr Pienaar and her colleagues at the DoE, recognised that the school went beyond its remit. In particular, she was concerned that Mary was too keen to take responsibility for learners' welfare away from parents and families. She had learnt about a particular case whereby a past pupil named Luthando had sought compensation for an accident with the assistance of Mary, who had then governed his usage of the funds by keeping his debit card in the safe at the school.

In Mary's opinion, the action was warranted because it protected the Luthando from the exploitative intentions of those who surrounded him in the location. In simple terms, she was concerned that he would be taken for a ride and would see nothing of the finances, much like the concerns members of staff had about misappropriated child grants in the location. In contrast, Cebisa had heard the complaints of the members of Luthando's family who were convinced that Mary's intervention and continued control (i.e. technologies of power) had only served to divide family members and turn Luthando away from them. Similarly, for Cebisa, Mary's dominance over the situation represented something quite sinister. In my opinion, her embodied morality and related opinion of historical processes of social, cultural, political, and economic change, which differed from those I have associated with Ngomso's staff and supporters, meant that she was particularly open to accepting the validity of their viewpoint. She was interested in postcolonial literature and theory, particularly the work of Franz Fanon (e.g. 1970), which she utilised in her own analysis of interracial adoption in the country. In this vein of thought, one can see how Mary and her supporters in the UK might represent the continuation of unwelcomed influence and governance. Supporting this argument further, Nonkonzo didn't seem to appreciate the fact that Mary was always vocal during meetings hosted by the DoE and once told her, "I don't just want to hear from London". Mary became visibly tense when I later mentioned this comment. "I was born in South Africa", she insisted. "My family has been here for as long as the Xhosa have been here. I am not from London." Cebisa once introduced me to a member of Luthando's extended family, who was studying at Rhodes. At the time, I thought she was quite standoffish with me and not too forthcoming with her take on the situation. In retrospect, I think that she may have already made up her mind about which side of the fence I would have been sitting on.

In South Africa, such anxiety and contestation—that is, the tension between atomised and shared conceptualisations of responsibility—have a particular quality on account of very salient moral discourses. Consider Siseko's explanation of how Sizo, a 28-year-old ANC councillor he interviewed as part of his research programme in the location, articulated his evaluation of the school:

> He thinks that [Ngomso] should be closed and the kids should be sent to other schools, as the kids here are given food and uniforms but [he thinks] the social worker should do that with the government and with councillors. [He says that] the whole community must grow the child; it takes two people to make it. Why is there someone like Mama Mary who wants to own a school herself, who doesn't want to take children to other schools? Why? He says they can solve these problems in the township [without her].

Sizo's judgement of the situation reflects the efforts that Ngomso staff made to separate the school from the township and the education offered by its residents; in considering learners to be children of God first, members of a 'local community' second. For him, Mary and the school represented something other than communitarian child rearing—a moral discourse frequently associated with ubuntu in South African contexts, although, of course, not uniquely attributable to ubuntu (see Enslin and Horsthemke 2004). Dalene Swanson (2009: 10) has called for more research exploring how notions of ubuntu might compare to an "obsessive Western focus on individualism". Sizo was wondering why an individual should want to own her own school and take responsibility for individuals when this burden should and could be shared among others. He spoke about social workers, the government, and councillors, and discussed the idea of "the whole community", indicating a framework of meaning that recognises that agents of the state can enact communitarian responsibilities in the course of their employment. As in the case of individuals enacting Christianised interpretations of human rights through their roles as employees of the DoE, in Sizo's conceptualisation of responsibility, the state-society distinction is not of primary importance but encompassed or superseded by a moral discourse (i.e. ubuntu).

As is the case with any other moral discourse, ubuntu has governmental power and is political. For example, on one occasion, Mr Mayoni shrewdly employed discourses concerning ubuntu in an attempt to appease residents of the location who had reacted with concern to a short-lived DoE proposal to relocate Ngomso close to their homes. During a meeting in a small hut opposite the proposed site, he said, "In our culture, your child is my child". Here, on top of the hill overlooking the town—from where the Xhosa launched a sizeable, almost victorious, assault on the British Army in 1819—discourses concerning human rights or a universal, Christianised sense of obligation were absent. To gain the support of this particular audience, Mr Mayoni invoked a moral discourse that would not have had much salience in the UK. His technique appeared quite successful. An audience that had keenly organised the meeting to raise concerns about the school and its rightful place in their locality opened up to discussions about the format of the proposed relocation, as opposed to contesting its very existence, as had initially been the case.

Just like the transnationally constituted constructions and employments of discourses relating to neoliberalism, human rights, and Christian grace discussed elsewhere in this chapter, I would argue that ubuntu is a malleable framework of meaning that orients understanding and action in numerous locations throughout the world.[42] In particular, I have demonstrated that these discourses fashion ethical exchanges that are described and understood through utilisations of the terms responsibility and accountability. As such, they are both descriptive and productive of dynamics of obligation, influencing the extent to which individuals and collectives retain or acquire control over processes of (moral) education and childrearing.

Although the discourses have a universal quality, both in the sense that individuals claim that their frameworks are applicable to and relevant for individuals living in numerous locations across the world and in the sense that the discourses emergence in numerous locations across the world to inform and orient social interaction, my ethnography clearly demonstrates that they retain a specific character on account of the historically constituted assemblage of moral discourses salient in any one particular locality. Yet, what this chapter has done, I hope, by switching backwards and forwards between social settings in the UK and South Africa, is demonstrate how the notion of locality itself is compromised by the flows of lives and discourses that emerge and reform when individuals travel to and communicate across different localities. As such, the foundations of any ethical exchange are both located and unlocatable.

Notes

1. I recorded this quotation and the reference to Joel (2:25) from a website (Marszalek 2008: np) written by a lady who had heard Mary speak in London during 2008.
2. In offering this analysis, I am running on the assumption that Susan would understand this assertion about the link between hope and Christianity in her capacity as a vicar and theologian.
3. In my experience, the processes of planning and delivering advertising pitches and school lessons are remarkably similar. You have an objective and a lesson/pitch plan. In each case, audiences need convincing that you have the right answers and that they should buy into the ideas that you're selling. There is room for questions, but not too many. The audience has to appear interested even if they, perhaps like you, have no real investment in what is being discussed. As one colleague said, advertising "is all smoke and mirrors", not unlike (bad) teaching. It is perhaps unsurprising that both domains have increasingly drawn from psychology and psychologists in their efforts to convince audiences—be they six-year-olds staring at screens in classrooms or living rooms—to want what is being sold, be that a qualification or new toy.
4. She didn't say 'from God' and 'to others', however, I have inserted the words to emphasise the fact that her Christianised reasoning factored in the promotion of such logic.
5. The idea that intervening in the affairs of 'disprivileged Africans' is a means by which individuals can come to terms with their own privilege is not a new one. In his widely shared and published series of tweets on 'The White Savior Industrial Complex' – "the power relations that privileged outsiders

and their African agents try to enforce on the continent" (James Schneider 2015: np) – Teju Cole (2012: np) asserts that the endeavour "is not about justice. It is about having a big emotional experience that validates privilege."
6. Similarly, Allahyari (2000: 4) asserts that Christian-oriented social service agencies for the homeless in America offer volunteers the opportunity to pursue "self-betterment" and to craft "a more virtuous, and often more spiritual" disposition, through a process that she terms "moral selving".
7. Rabbitts (2012: 274) similarly recognised "the importance of face-to-face inspiration and embodied evangelistic performances in environments where friendship and rapport can be fostered over time" while researching the fundraising techniques of a well-known Christian child sponsorship agency. She (ibid.) says that such exchanges "not only [stimulated] charitable action, but also [offered an] antidote to the corporate feel of [the charity's] large-scale, professionalised appearance".
8. Rabbitts (2013: 281) similarly expresses how important "the charismatic inspiration of key individuals" is to evangelical, emotionally laden appeals for charitable funds.
9. It was Jesus who, in his martyrdom, originally suffered most for God (and humans on earth): "he was pierced for our transgressions; he was crushed for our iniquities; upon him was the chastisement that brought us peace, and with his wounds we are healed" (Isaiah, 53: 5). The notion that Christians can similarly enact their faith and become enjoined with God, in this life and Heaven, by enduring suffering and selflessness is conveyed numerous times in the Bible. For example: "it has been granted to you on behalf of Christ not only to believe in him, but also to suffer for him" (Philippians, 1: 29). And: "Whoever finds their life will lose it, and whoever loses their life for my sake will find it" (Matthew, 10: 39). Peter the apostle (2: 20) conveys the doctrine clearly when stating "if when you do what is right and suffer for it you patiently endure it, this finds favor with God". He (4:16) continues: "if you suffer as a Christian, do not be ashamed, but praise God that you bear that name". The promised outcome of such endeavour? "After you have suffered for a little while, the God of all grace, who called you to His eternal glory in Christ, will Himself perfect, confirm, strengthen and establish you" (Peter, 5:10).
10. I use the word 'inspired' in this sentence, with knowledge of its Latin origins (i.e. *inspīrāre*), to argue that Mary was alluding to the idea that God had breathed life into her body.
11. Likewise, the Catholic sisters in Scherz's (2014: 115) ethnography "place their trust [regarding the expenditure of charitable funds] in cultivated virtue and in their invisible accountability to God". In the case of Susan's relationship with Mary, this dynamic was similarly effective, but reversed,

as Susan explains: "Mary just took me on trust [when I asked to volunteer], which in a way [is not surprising], being a priest [means that I am not demanding of] an enormous amount of trust [from others]."
12. It is perhaps significant that Joyce was left to step into Mary's sizeable shoes without the assistance of personalised prayer. This fact may illustrate that UK supporters were more concerned about Mary's experience of the transition. However, the statement could also be read as a suggestion that prayers should be offered for all of the staff remaining at the school, including Joyce, and that Mary was singled out because she would soon be excluded from this group and would, therefore, require prayers that had been extended out to her individually.
13. Rabbitts (2012: 266) offers similar analysis when she writes "charitable space does not consist of autonomous, coherent entities each with their own consistent, stable properties, but of fluid, intertwining 'tangles'". However, her interest lies more in the extent to which institutional forms of organisation are understandable as networks, rather than the extent to which lives caught up in 'charitable space' are mutually constitutive.
14. Mary's provision of such opportunity might well be an integral component of fund- and support-generating activities in the charity sector more broadly. Orgad and Seu (2014: np) argue that "If the upset is not manageable, it is followed by a switching off and further distancing from humanitarian issues."
15. Kathryn McHarry (2013) suggests that 'sponsors' of Senegalese preschool children engage in prayer in a similar way (i.e. as a means to bring about particular futures for the young recipients of their donations).
16. This statement is all the more telling because her congregation in the UK were fearful they were not 'reaching out' to young people in the local area. Perhaps, to generalise, a dismantled 'sense of community' and the promotion of individualism in the UK (similar to those discourses fostered at Ngomso) added to the allure of connections with young people in South Africa.
17. When reporting the opening of the first Church of England school in Grahamstown's location during 1857, Rev. Cornford (cited in SPG 1858: 16) elicited support from British-based readers of Global Missionary: "we pray, and ask your prayers, that [the school] may, by GOD's blessing, prosper". In the aforementioned letter written in 1857, regarding the opening of the same school, the young UK-based recipient is told "If you really pity [the young 'natives' living in Grahamstown], you will pray for them; and if you are sincere, when you pray for them, you will willingly and cheerfully do what you can to help them" (E.W., cited in *SPG* 1858: 31).

18. The dialogue between child sponsors and those sponsored is an obvious exception to this, which, I believe, works in a similar way to how prayer provides a bridge between donor and beneficiary.
19. Geographers have increasingly been concerned with similar themes of scholarship (e.g. Lee and Smith 2014; Proctor 1998; Smith 1997), following a 'moral turn' in the discipline, comparable to that of anthropology. Scholars have considered how the geographical distance between individuals, which has often been (problematically) conflated with difference or 'otherness', influences relations of care, including humanitarian ones (Barnett and Land 2007).
20. Bornstein (2012: 65) argues that public discourses such as these, which surround NGOs and those who work for them in clouds of suspicion, "have a dual moral function: they circulate suspicion in attempts to keep corruption at bay, and they express (more indirectly) suspicion of contemporary institutions". In the case of my research, they were also intimately intertwined with historical discourses relating to colonialism and racial oppression.
21. Cabot (2013: 452), following De Certeau, describes such "modes of agency" as a "kind of tactical manoeuvring". De Certeau's consideration of negotiations of structures imposed by those more powerful, most notably understood as processes of readjustment and 'making-do', is, indeed, helpful. During my research, those securing resources were not fully responsible for the conditions within which their attempts to secure aid/schooling took place, but they were very capable of navigating them. Further on in this book, I consider the related notion of 'hustling' by invoking Lévi-Strauss' (1962) theorisation of 'bricolage', which ties into the discussion here.
22. The fact that particular formations of individuality and personhood were validated or invalidated every time the members of staff made a judgement about a potential enrolment, a processes which served to maintain the very structures that the young benefactors had to navigate, was not, I believe, a consciously enacted mode of dominance. Similarly, I do not believe that they actively set out to dominate others through their impositions of exclusionary criteria. However, like those seeking enrolment, the staff were bound to engage with others according to these same structures of uneven power.
23. The exception to this claim is the attention that my interlocutors paid to transforming South Africa's schooling system more broadly. However, there were also transformative limits of this endeavour.
24. The focus here is the relationships that supporters of the Friends had with the ANC government. However, the 'complete picture' is more complicated. The ANC have been under increasing pressure for service delivery

across all sectors of government and from populations that cross the racial divides of apartheid. Sudarsan Raghavan (2012: np), of the *Washington Post*, recently penned an article entitled "South Africa loses faith with the ANC." During my research in 2011, Julius Malema was on the rise as a very public critic of the administration. At the time of writing, he is currently the leader of the Economic Freedom Fighters, a political party that appealed to some of my interlocutors, who were disgruntled with the ANC but who had not enjoyed the privileges of apartheid.
25. It was rare for Catholicism to be so prominent in the school. Mary explained his presence by saying "we worship the same God [so I am happy for him to be here]."
26. See Basopu (2010) for a review of the ECDoE's accounting irregularities that preceded my research in 2011.
27. These three quotes are all comments that have been posted beneath articles in online newspapers by registered users of each site, who, as far as I know, were not employees of the publications when responding to the articles. The first statement is by a user named 'Gladiator71' (written in response to "Our Education System is in Crisis," 2012). The second is by a user named 'Monique Goosen' (written in response to SAPA & M&G Online Reporter 2012). The third is by a user named '*Shaman sans Frontiers' (written in response to* ibid.*)*.
28. My friends and colleagues in South Africa, especially those I met through Rhodes University or the Rotary Club, also keenly questioned Zuma's credentials and political achievements. Unlike Mandela, who was educated in the missionary tradition and had professional credentials as a lawyer, Zuma did not matriculate from high school. He practices polygamous marriage and turned down an invitation to visit the UK in order to attend the wedding of President Mugabe's daughter. Moreover, he frequently acknowledges the importance of his Zulu heritage and has pushed to enshrine a Traditional Courts Bill into law, as a means of providing 'traditional leaders' with 'African' judicial and legislative powers (Mnisi 2015). Beyond his (alleged) misappropriation of public money, there was, in other words, much about him that didn't sit well with many critics of his government, especially those who did not share his preference for 'African tradition'.
29. Wedel (2004: np) cites the example of two Harvard University employees, including a noted economics professor, who (it was ruled in court) conspired to defraud the US Government. She goes on to detail similar networks and practices of corruption in Poland and Russia. I might also cite the example of the 'expenses scandal' regarding UK politicians.
30. Several of these factors are drawn from the analysis of Chisholm (2013).
31. A copy of the poster can be found at http://www.iwm.org.uk/collections/item/object/1435 (accessed 11.02.2015).

32. In 2011, when I first started to talk to Chris de Wet, my supervisor at the time, about my research interests, he recommended Colson's books. In 2013, he also visited the 97-year-old as part of a research project.
33. At present, it is my intention to write a separate paper about the specific problems associated with the school's building and facilities, which will analyse the specificities of the DoE's response to the court action in more detail. In this chapter, I am more concerned with understanding how and when human rights discourses entered into the equation as a mode of conceptualising responsibilities and obligations.
34. Similarly, Article 26 of The Universal Declaration of Human Rights declares that "everyone has the right to education [i.e. schooling] and that elementary education shall be compulsory" (UN 1948: np).
35. De Boeck and Honwana (2005: 3) argue that the portrayal of "Children and youth ... as innocent and vulnerable, in need of adult protection ... predominates in international law on children's rights". The Universal Declaration of Human Rights (cited in Ennew 2002: 338) informs us that children are "entitled to special care and assistance" and to "grow up in a family environment, in an atmosphere of happiness, love and, understanding". South Africa's Children's Act (Republic of South Africa 2005: np) similarly insists that "children ... should grow up in a family environment and in an atmosphere of happiness, love and understanding".
36. In particular, such discourses are employed to morally justify the activities of other charities and NGOs that promote 'poor children's rights' (Nieuwenhuys 2001: 541–3; also see Pupavac 2001).The mandate of World Vision, for example, "tries to bring disadvantaged children into line with international discourses about appropriate lives for children" relating to human rights and access to education (Cheney 2007: 191).
37. According to notes taken during the workshop, only two cases brought by the LFP have not been settled with the DoE. However, in the Ngomso case and others, the terms of settlement have not been met.
38. Elsewhere, the Comaroff and Comaroff (1997: 9) have argued that the foundation for the human rights movement was established during the "civilising mission" of colonialism, when "right became rights".
39. Zigon (2013: 722, 734) argues that "the realization of human rights entails constant and continuous moral struggle and vigilance", which he compares to "the continuous struggle and vigilance advocated by some Christianities against sin". This analogy is apt for the staff, however, I know that at least one key actor from the LFP was not motivated by Christian faith. Moreover, as far as I can see, the LFP does not associate itself with a religious tradition and its legal arguments are certainly not put forth with religious justification. However, the founder of the LFP was religious and his mother was an active supporter of religious charities.

While it would therefore be inaccurate to separate religious faith from the activities of the LFP, given also the inseparability of South African schooling from Christianity, religious imperatives were not central to their activities.
40. In an article that I cannot quote from directly because it would compromise their anonymity, Jimmy Taylor and a colleague similarly say that they are aware of the fact that litigation alone cannot overcome systemic issues of failing school infrastructures or issues relating to the schooling system in South Africa more broadly.
41. This arrangement resulted from the fact that the LFP most regularly pursued *structural interdicts* in its dealings with the DoE, including in the Ngomso case. This results in the court "supervising government plans to remedy rights violations" (Ebadolahi 2008: 1568). The government is ordered to provide a remedial plan of action to the court, laying out how it will rectify any lacking access to constitutional rights. The court then ratifies the plan, or seeks revision(s), and finally oversees and legally enforces its implementation (ibid.; Mbazira 2009: 164–223).
42. For instance, in 2015, I attended the Annual Conference of the Comparative and International Education Society, which had the theme: "Ubuntu! Imagining a Humanist Education Globally".

Bibliography

Abrams, P. (1988). Notes on the Difficulty of Studying the State (1977). *Journal of Historical Sociology*, 1(1), 58–89.

Admin. (2014). Rotten to the Core. *Herald Live* (online). Retrieved April 25, 2015, from http://www.heraldlive.co.za/rotten-to-the-core/

Allahyari, R. A. (2000). *Visions of Charity Volunteer Workers and Moral Community*. Berkeley/Los Angeles: University of California Press.

Anonymous. Details omitted in order to maintain anonymity of interlocutors.

Atkinson, D. (2007). Taking to the Streets: Has Developmental Local Government Failed in South Africa? In S. Buhlungu, D. Johnson, R. Southall, & J. Lutchman (Eds.), *State of the Nation South Africa*. Cape Town: Human Science Research Council Press.

Basopu, P. M. (2010). *Assessing challenges of corruption in the Eastern Cape Department of Education*. Unpublished MPA thesis, the University of Fort Hare. Retrieved February 04, 2018, from https://www.academia.edu/14886280/ASSESSING_CHALLENGES_OF_CORRUPTION_IN_THE_EASTERN_CAPE_DEPARTMENT_OF_EDUCATION

Ballard, R., Habib, A., & Valodia, I. (2006). In R. Ballard, A. Habib, & I. Valodia (Eds.), *Voices of Protest: Social Movements in Post-apartheid South Africa*. Scottsville: University of KwaZulu-Natal Press.

Barnett, C., & Land, D. (2007). Geographies of Generosity: Beyond the 'Moral Turn'. *Geoforum*, *38*(6), 1065–1075.
BBC. (2012). South Africa Mine Strikes: Police Fire Tear Gas. *BBC Online*. Retrieved March 15, 2013, from http://www.bbc.co.uk/news/world-africa-20137096
BBC. (2013). 'Bongo Bongo Land': UKIP Bans Use of 'Outdated' Phrase. *BBC Online*. Retrieved April 5, 2015, from http://www.bbc.co.uk/news/uk-23597233
BBC. (2014). Zuma's South African Nkandla Home Upgrade 'Unethical'. *BBC Online*. Retrieved June 24, 2015, from http://www.bbc.co.uk/news/world-africa-26645400
Besteman, C. (2008). *Transforming Cape Town*. Berkeley: University of California Press.
Bierschenk, T., Chauveau, J. P., & Olivier de Sardan, J. P. (2002). *Local Development Brokers in Africa: The Rise of a New Social Category*. Working Paper No. 13, Department of Anthropology and African Studies. Mainz, Germany: Johannes Gutenberg University.
Bornstein, E. (2001). Child Sponsorship, Evangelism, and Belonging in the Work of World Vision Zimbabwe. *American Ethnologist*, *28*(3), 595–622.
Bornstein, E. (2012). *Disquieting Gifts: Humanitarianism in New Delhi*. Stanford: Stanford University Press.
Bourdieu, P. (1986). The Forms of Capital. In J. Richardson (Ed.), *Handbook of Theory and Research for the Sociology of Education* (pp. 241–258). New York: Greenwood.
Bourdieu, P., & Wacquant, L. J. D. (1992). *An Invitation to Reflexive Sociology*. Chicago: University of Chicago Press.
Brennan, Z. (2010). Sorry Bob, Band Aid Millions DID Pay for Guns: Charity's Man in Ethiopia Tells His Disturbing Story. *Daily Mail Online*. Retrieved March 3, 2013, from http://www.dailymail.co.uk/news/article-1259061/Sorry-Bob-Geldof-Band-Aid-millions-DID-pay-guns.html
Cabot, H. (2013). The social aesthetics of eligibility: NGO aid and indeterminacy in the Greek asylum process. *American Ethnologist*, *40*(3), 452–466.
Cheney, K. (2007). *Pillars of the Nation: Child Citizens and Ugandan National Development*. Chicago: University of Chicago Press.
Cheney, K. (2010). Expanding Vulnerability, Dwindling Resources: Implications for Orphaned Futures in Uganda. *Childhood in Africa*, *2*(1), 8–15.
Chisholm, L. (2012). *Corruption in Education: The Textbook Saga*. Paper Presented to a Symposium Hosted by the Public Affairs Research Institute (PARI) and Innovations for Successful Societies, Princeton University (at the University of the Witwatersrand, Johannesburg). Retrieved March 1, 2014, from http://pari.org.za/wp-content/uploads/Chisholm-Corruption-in-education.-The-textbook-saga-Aug20121.pdf
Chisholm, L. (2013). The Textbook Saga and Corruption in Education. *Southern African Review of Education*, *19*(1), 7–23.

Cole, T. (2012). The White-Savior Industrial Complex. *The Atlantic* (Online). Retrieved July 27, 2014, from http://www.theatlantic.com/international/archive/2012/03/the-white-savior-industrial-complex/254843/

Colson, E. (1960). *The Social Organization of the Gwembe Tonga*. Manchester: Manchester University Press.

Comaroff, J., & Comaroff, J. (1997). *Of Revelation and Revolution, Volume 2: The Dialectics of Modernity on a South African Frontier*. Chicago: The University of Chicago Press.

Comaroff, J., & Comaroff, J. (2007). Law and Disorder in the Postcolony. *Social Anthropology*, 15(2), 133–152.

Conran, M. (2011). They Really Love Me!: Intimacy in Volunteer Tourism. *Annals of Tourism Research*, 38(4), 1454–1473.

Das, V., & Poole, D. (2004). State and Its Margins: Comparative Ethnographies. In V. Das & D. Poole (Eds.), *Anthropology in the Margins of the State* (pp. 3–34). Santa Fe: School of American Research Press.

De Boeck, F., & Honwana, A. (2005). Introduction: Children & Youth in Africa. In F. De Boeck & A. Honwana (Eds.), *Makers & Breakers: Children & Youth in Postcolonial Africa* (pp. 1–18). Oxford: James Curry.

de Klerk, M. (2012). Legacy of Selflessness. *Grocott's Mail* (Online). Retrieved, March 4, 2014, from http://www.grocotts.co.za/content/legacy-selflessness-08-11-2012

Desai, A. (2002). *We Are the Poor: Community Struggles in Post-apartheid South Africa*. New York: Monthly Review Press.

DiFruscia, K. T. (2010). Listening to Voices: An Interview with Veena Das. *Altérités*, 7(1), 136–145.

Drury, I. (2013). Wasted, the Millions Britain Has Poured into Aid for Congo: Damning Report Reveals EU Projects Have Failed to Deliver Any Results. *Daily Mail* (Online). Retrieved June 13, 2014, from http://www.dailymail.co.uk/news/article-2441580/Wasted-millions-Britain-poured-aid-Congo-Damning-report-reveals-EU-projects-failed-deliver-results.html

Ebadolahi, M. (2008). Using Structural Interdicts and the South African Human Rights Commission to Achieve Judicial Enforcement of Economic and Social Rights in South Africa. *New York University Law Review*, 83(5), 1565–1606.

Elisha, O. (2008). Moral Ambitions of Grace: The Paradox of Compassion and Accountability in Evangelical Faith-Based Activism. *Cultural Anthropology*, 23(1), 154–189.

Ennew, J. (2002). Future Generations and Global Standards: Children's Rights at the Start of the Millennium. In J. MacClancy (Ed.), *Exotic No More. Anthropology on the Front Lines* (pp. 338–358). Chicago: University of Chicago Press.

Enslin, P., & Horsthemke, K. (2004). Can Ubuntu Provide a Model for Citizenship Education in African Democracies? *Comparative Education*, 40(4), 545–558.

Epstein, A. (2010). Education Refugees and the Spatial Politics of Childhood Vulnerability. *Childhood in Africa, 2*(1), 16–25.
Fanon, F. (1970). *Black Skin, White Masks*. New York: Grove Press.
Faranaaz, V. (2014). Our Courts are Schooling the State. *Mail & Guardian* (Online). Retrieved May 14, 2015, from http://mg.co.za/article/2014-03-14-our-courts-are-schooling-the-state
Fassin, D. (2007). Humanitarianism as a Politics of Life. *Public Culture, 19*(3), 499–520.
Fassin, D. (2010). Critique of Humanitarian Reason. *Public Lecture, Institute for Advanced Study, Princeton University* (Available Online). Retrieved July 15, 2013, from http://www.youtube.com/watch?v=jDT2mYg6mgo
Ferguson, J. (2006). *Global Shadows: Africa in the Neoliberal World Order*. Durham: Duke University Press.
Fiske, E. B., & Ladd, H. F. (2004). *Elusive Equity: Education Reform in Post-apartheid South Africa*. Washington, DC: Brookings Institution Press.
Flanagan, J. (2014). South African President Jacob Zuma Must Pay Back £14 Million of Taxpayers' Money Used to Build a Swimming Pool, Football Pitch and an Amphitheatre at His Private Compound. *Daily Mail* (Online). Retrieved April 5, 2015, from http://www.dailymail.co.uk/news/article-2584611/South-African-President-Jacob-Zuma-pay-14-million-taxpayers-money-used-build-swimming-pool-football-pitch-amphitheatre-private-compound.html
Foreman, J. (2013). How Your Money is Squandered on Foreign Aid. *Daily Mail* (Online). Retrieved November 19, 2014 from http://www.dailymail.co.uk/news/article-2255838/How-money-squandered-foreign-aid.html
Friedman, S. (2006). *Participatory Governance and Citizen Action in Post-apartheid South Africa*. Discussion Paper, International Institute for Labour Studies, Geneva. Retrieved September 14, 2013, from http://www.ilo.org/wcmsp5/groups/public/---dgreports/---inst/documents/publication/wcms_193613.pdf
Goffman, E. (1963). *Stigma: Notes on the Management of Spoiled Identity*. New Jersey: Prentice Hall.
Graeber, D. (2004). *Fragments of an Anarchist Anthropology*. Chicago: Prickly Paradigm Press.
Handley, A., Murray, C., & Simeon, R. (2008). Learning to Lose, Learning to Win: Government and Opposition in South Africa's Transition to Democracy. In E. Friedman & J. Wong (Eds.), *Political Transitions in Dominant Party Systems: Learning to Lose* (pp. 191–210). Abingdon: Routledge.
Hansen, T. B. (2012). *Melancholia of Freedom: Social Life in an Indian Township in South Africa*. Princeton: Princeton University Press.
Hendricks, M. (2011). Eastern Cape Schools: Resourcing and Class Inequality. In G. Ruiters (Ed.), *The Fate of the Eastern Cape: History, Politics and Social Policy* (pp. 254–263). Scottsville: University of KwaZulu-Natal Press.

Hunter, M. (2010). *Love in the Time of Aids: Inequality, Gender and Rights in South Africa*. Bloomington: Indiana University Press.
Ingold, T. (2011). *Being Alive: Essays on Movement, Knowledge and Description*. Abingdon: Routledge.
Ingold, T. (2013). *Making: Anthropology, Archaeology, Art and Architecture*. Abingdon: Routledge.
Ingold, T., & Lucas, R. (2007). The 4 A's (Anthropology, Archaeology, Art and Architecture): Reflections on a Teaching and Learning Experience. In M. Harris (Ed.), *Ways of Knowing. New Approaches in the Anthropology of Experience and Learning* (pp. 287–306). Oxford: Berghahn.
Jackson, M. (2005). *Existential Anthropology: Events, Exigencies and Effects*. New York: Berghahn Books.
John, V. (2012). Right to Education: Pupils Can Wait, Says Motshekga. *Mail & Guardian* (Online). Retrieved, May 26, 2013, from http://mg.co.za/article/2012-08-03-pupils-can-wait-says-motshekga
Kaplan, S. (2006). *The Pedagogical State: Education and the Politics of National Culture in Post-1980 Turkey*. Stanford: Stanford University Press.
Laing, A. (2012). Jacob Zuma's £15m Home Upgrades Prompt Calls for Inquiry. *The Telegraph* (Online). Retrieved May 24, 2013, from http://www.telegraph.co.uk/news/worldnews/africaandindianocean/southafrica/9579538/Jacob-Zumas-15m-home-upgrades-prompt-calls-for-inquiry.html
Lee, R., & Smith, D. M. (2014). *Geographies and Moralities: International Perspectives on Development, Justice and Place*. Chichester: Wiley-Blackwell.
Levinas, E. (2002). Beyond Intentionality. In S. Hand (Ed.), *The Phenomenology Reader* (pp. 529–540). London: Routledge.
Lévi-Strauss, C. (1962). *The Savage Mind*. Chicago: University of Chicago Press.
Lewis, D., & Mosse, D. (2006). *Development Brokers and Translators: The Ethnography of Aid and Agencies*. Bloomfield: Kumarian Press.
Lodge, T. (2002). *Politics in South Africa: From Mandela to Mbeki*. Cape Town: Kenilworth.
Lutkehaus, N. (1999). Missionary Maternalism: Gendered Images of the Holy Spirit Sisters in Colonial New Guinea. In M. Taylor Huber & N. Lutkehaus (Eds.), *Gendered Missions: Women and Men in Missionary Discourse and Practice* (pp. 207–235). Ann Arbor: The University of Michigan Press.
Madlingozi, T. (2007). Post-apartheid Social Movements and the Quest for the Elusive New South Africa. *Journal of Law and Society, 34*(1), 77–98.
Madonsela, T. (2014). Secure in Comfort: Report on an Investigation into Allegations of Impropriety and Unethical Conduct Relating to the Installation and Implementation of Security Measures by the Department of Public Works at and in Respect of the Private Residence of President Jacob Zuma at Nkandla in the KwaZulu-Natal Province. *Public Protector, South Africa*. Retrieved July 04, 2014, from http://www.publicprotector.org/library\investigation_report\2013-14\FinalReport 19 March 2014.pdf

Maqhina, M. (2011). School Transport Chaos. *Daily Dispatch* (Online). Retrieved June 03, 2012, from http://www.dispatch.co.za/news/article/321

Marais, L., Matebesi, S., Mthombeni, M., Botes, L., & Grieshaber, D. (2008). Municipal Unrest in the Free State (South Africa): A New Form of Social Movement? *Politeia, 27*(2), 51–69.

Marszalek, R. (2008). Introducing You to a New Website – Amasango. *Revising Reform.* Retrieved from http://hrht-revisingreform.blogspot.co.uk/2008_08_17_archive.html

Mason, R. (2013). Ukip MEP Godfrey Bloom Criticises Aid to 'Bongo Bongo Land'. *The Guardian* (Online). Retrieved June 29, 2014, from http://www.theguardian.com/politics/2013/aug/06/ukip-godfrey-bloom-bongo-bongo-land

Matshiqi, A. (2010). The One-Party State and Liberation Movements in Africa: Lessons for South Africa. In N. Misra-Dexter & J. February (Eds.), *Testing Democracy: Which Way is South Africa Going?* (pp. 2–22). Cape Town: Idasa.

Mbazira, C. (2009). *Litigating Socio-Economic Rights in South Africa: A Choice Between Corrective and Distributive Justice.* Pretoria: Pretoria University Law Press.

McHarry, K. E. (2013). *Sponsoring the Future: Marketizing Children's Potential in Senegalese Preschools.* Conference Presentation. The Anthropology of Potentiality in Africa (Panel), American Anthropological Association, Annual Conference, Chicago.

McKie, L. (2005). *Organisation Carescapes: Policies, Practices and Equality in Business.* Unpublished (Working) Paper. Presented at Public Policy and Equality Seminar, Cardiff. Retrieved June 19, 2014, from http://www.docs.hss.ed.ac.uk/education/creid/Projects/07xxvi_ESRC_Seminar3_PaperLMcKie.pdf

Mnisi, S. (2015). Traditional Courts Bill Contradicts Constitution. *Daily Dispatch* (Online). Retrieved December 29, 2015, from http://www.dispatchlive.co.za/news/traditional-courts-bill-contradicts-constitution/

Mokone, T., & Kgosana, C. (2011). Pretoria Takes Over EC Education. *Daily Dispatch* (Online). Retrieved July 26, 2013, from http://www.dispatch.co.za/news/news/article/620

Moore, H. L. (2011). *Still Life: Hopes, Desires and Satisfactions.* Cambridge: Polity Press.

Nieuwenhuys, O. (2001). By the Sweat of Their Brow? 'Street Children', NGOs and Children's Rights in Addis Ababa. *Africa, 71*(4), 539–557.

Nkosi, B. (2013). Motshekga Won't Retract 'Racist' Attack on Equal Education. *Mail & Guardian* (Online). Retrieved June 23, 2014, from http://mg.co.za/article/2013-06-19-motshekga-wont-retract-racist-attack-on-equal-education

O'Neill, K. L. (2013). Left Behind: Security, Salvation, and the Subject of Prevention. *Cultural Anthropology, 28*(2), 204–226.

Open Society Foundations (OSF). (2017). *Open Society Foundations (OSF).* Retrieved February 04, 2017, from http://www.osisa.org/open-society foundations-osf

Orgad, S., & Seu, B. (2014). Caring in Crisis – Why Development and Humanitarian NGOs Need to Change How They Relate to the Public. *Polis: Journalism and Society at the LSE* (Online). Retrieved March 02, 2015, from http://blogs.lse.ac.uk/polis/2014/07/08/caring-in-crisis-guest-blog/

Piper, L., & Nadvi, L. (2010). Popular Mobilization, Party Dominance and Participatory Governance in South Africa. In L. Thompson & C. Tapscott (Eds.), *Citizenship and Social Movements: Perspectives from the Global South* (pp. 212–238). London: Zed Books.

Proctor, J. (1998). Ethics in Geography: Giving Moral Form to the Geographical Imagination. *Area, 30*(1), 8–18.

Pupavac, V. (2001). Misanthropy Without Border: The International Children's Rights Regime. *Disasters, 25*(2), 95–112.

Rabbitts, F. (2012). Child Sponsorship, Ordinary Ethics and the Geographies of Charity. *Geoforum, 43*(5), 926–936.

Rabbitts, F. (2013). *'Nothing is Whiter than White in This World': Child Sponsorship and the Geographies of Charity*. Unpublished PhD Thesis, University of Exeter.

Raghaven, S. (2012). South Africa Loses Faith with the ANC. *The Independent* (UK, Online). Retrieved July 14, 2014, from http://www.independent.co.uk/news/world/africa/south-africa-loses-faith-with-the-anc-8303778.html

Ramphele, M. (2012). Time for Radical Change in Education. *The Star* (Online). Retrieved June 23, 2013, from http://www.iol.co.za/the-star/time-for-radical-change-in-education-1.1362669#.VgqLnN9VhBc

Republic of South Africa. (1996). *Constitution of the Republic of South Africa*. Pretoria: Government Gazette. Retrieved January 02, 2012, from http://www.gov.za/DOCUMENTS/CONSTITUTION/CONSTITUTION-REPUBLIC-SOUTH-AFRICA-1996-1

Republic of South Africa. (2005). *Children's Act, No. 38 of 2005*. Retrieved March 28, 2012, from http://www.centreforchildlaw.co.za/images/files/childlaw/consolidated_childrens_act.pdf

Robins, S. L. (2008). *From Revolution to Rights in South Africa: Social Movements, NGOs and Popular Politics After Apartheid*. Scottsville: University of KwaZulu-Natal Press.

SAPA & M&G Online Reporter. (2012). Failure of State Teachers Boost Private Schools. *Mail & Guardian* (Online). Retrieved September 30, 2013, from http://mg.co.za/article/2012-07-22-failure-of-state-teachers-boost-private-schools

Scherz, C. (2014). *Having People, Having Heart: Charity, Sustainable Development, and Problems of Dependence in Central Uganda*. Chicago: University of Chicago Press.

Schneider, J. (2015). Inside the White Saviour Industrial Complex. *New African* (Online). Retrieved August 16, 2015, from http://newafricanmagazine.com/inside-white-saviour-industrial-complex/

Scott, J. C. (2015). Everyday Forms of resistance. In F. Colburn (Ed.), *Everyday Forms of Peasant Resistance* (pp. 3–33). Abingdon: Routledge.
Sherman, J. (2014). Aid Group Mis-spent Flight Cash. *The Times* (UK, Online). Retrieved July 23, 2015, from http://www.thetimes.co.uk/tto/news/politics/article4138092.ece
Shipman, T., Cohen, T., & Chorley, M. (2013). UKIP Man in 'Bongo Bongo Land' Aid Row Storms Out of TV Interview After Channel 4 News Presenter Keeps Asking Him if He is a Racist. *Daily Mail* (Online). Retrieved, July 25, 2015, from http://www.dailymail.co.uk/news/article-2386488/Godfrey-Bloom-Sending-aid-Africa-treason-says-unrepentant-UKIP-man-Bongo-Bongo-land-storm.html
Smith, D. M. (1997). Geography and Ethics: A Moral Turn? *Progress in Human Geography, 21*(4), 583–590.
Smith, D. (2013). Jacob Zuma Accused of Corruption 'on a Grand Scale' in South Africa. *The Guardian* (Online). Retrieved June 14, 2014, from http://www.theguardian.com/world/2013/nov/29/jacob-zuma-accused-corruption-south-africa
Society for the Propagation of the Gospel (SPG). (1858). *The Global Missionary for 1858* (Vol. 8). London: Bell & Daldy.
Sokopo. (2010). Bad Start for Class of 2011. *Daily Dispatch* (Online). Retrieved June 15, 2013, from http://www.dispatch.co.za/news/news/article/226
South African Press Association (SAPA). (2014). Tear Gas Used to Disperse Grabouw Protesters. *News 24* (Online). Retrieved June 25, 2014, from http://www.news24.com/SouthAfrica/News/Tear-gas-used-to-disperse-Grabouw-protesters-20140916
Southall, R. (2005). The Dominant Party Debate in South Africa. *Africa Spectrum, 39*(1), 61–82.
Stambach, A. (2010). *Faith in Schools: Religion, Education and American Evangelicals in East Africa*. Stanford: Stanford University Press.
Stambach, A. (2011). Education and Evangelism in Africa. *Public Lecture* (Available Online). Retrieved July 25, 2012, from https://www.youtube.com/watch?v=pl9AhRwLjIo
Stambach, A., & Ngwane, Z. (2011). Development, Postcolonialism, and Global Networks as Frameworks for the Study of Education in Africa and Beyond. In B. A. U. Levinson & D. Holland (Eds.), *Companion to the Anthropology of Education* (pp. 299–315). Hoboken: Wiley-Blackwell.
Stewart, K. (2007). *Ordinary Affects*. Durham/London: Duke University Press.
Swanson, D. M. (2009). Where Have All the Fishes Gone? Living Ubuntu as an Ethics of Research and Pedagogical Engagement. In D. M. Caracciolo & A. M. Mungai (Eds.), *In the Spirit of Ubuntu: Stories of Teaching and Research* (pp. 2–22). Rotterdam: Sense.

Sykes, K. (2009). Adopting an Obligation: Moral Reasoning About Bougainvillean Children's Access to Social Services in New Ireland. In M. Heintz (Ed.), *The Anthropology of Moralities* (pp. 1–19). New York: Berghahn Books.

Tapscott, C. (2007). The Challenges of Building Participatory Local Government. In L. Thompson (Ed.), *Participatory Governance? Citizens and the State in South Africa* (pp. 81–94). Bellville: African Centre for Citizenship and Democracy, University of the Western Cape.

The Presidency. (2015). *President Zuma Signs Special Investigating Unit Proclamation to Investigate Eastern Cape Department of Education*. Retrieved October 3, 2015, from http://www.presidency.gov.za/pebble.asp?relid=19986

Ticktin, M. (2006). Where Ethics and Politics Meet: The Violence of Humanitarianism in France. *American Ethnologist, 33*(1), 33–49.

United Nations (UN). (1948). *The Universal Declaration of Human Rights*. Retrieved October 5, 2015, from http://www.un.org/en/documents/udhr/index.shtml

Weber, M. (1978). *Economy and Society: An Outline of Interpretive Sociology*. Los Angeles: University of California Press.

Weber, M. (1991). In H. H. Gerth & C. Wright Mills (Eds.), *From Max Weber: Essays in Sociology*. Abingdon: Routledge.

Weber, M. (2001). *The Protestant Ethic and the Spirit of Capitalism*. London: Routledge.

Wedel, J. R. (2004, June 12). *Transactorship in Transition: The Shifting World of Aid and Advice in the U.S.-Russia Relationship*. Presentation, Conference on Comparative Transitions, London Business School. Retrieved April 14, 2016, from http://janinewedel.info/presentations_London04.html

Wright, L. (2012). Origins of the Eastern Cape Education Crisis. In L. Wright (Ed.), *South Africa's Education Crisis: Views from the Eastern Cape* (pp. 1–18). Grahamstown: NISC.

Zigon, J. (2006). An Ethics of Hope: Working on the Self in Contemporary Moscow. *Anthropology of East Europe Review, 24*(2), 71–80.

Zigon, J. (2007). Moral Breakdown and the Ethical Demand: A Theoretical Framework for an Anthropology of Moralities. *Anthropological Theory, 7*(2), 131–150.

Zigon, J. (2008). *Morality: An Anthropological Perspective*. Oxford: Berg.

Zigon, J. (2009). Hope Dies Last: Two Aspects of Hope in Contemporary Moscow. *Anthropological Theory, 9*(3), 253–271.

Zigon, J. (2011). *'HIV Is God's Blessing': Rehabilitating Morality in Neoliberal Russia*. Berkeley: University of California Press.

Zigon, J. (2013). Human Rights as Moral Progress? A Critique. *Cultural Anthropology, 28*(4), 716–736.

Zigon, J. (2014). An Ethics of Dwelling and a Politics of World-Building: A Critical Response to Ordinary Ethics. *Journal of the Royal Anthropological Institute, 20*, 746–764.

CHAPTER 7

Being Taught How to Hope

During a grade six life orientation lesson, Lindiwe, the enthusiastic educator who loved Mexican food, was speaking about sex and relationships. She promoted "prevention", "protection", "abstinence", and "patience" before turning attention to "education" (i.e. schooling). She told learners that boyfriends and girlfriends did not replace the "need to make time to study". "Education", she continued, "is more important than sex." She then asked them to repeat the phrase "The most important thing in my life is education." They obliged in unison.

On another occasion, Zamekile, the grade three learner diagnosed with attention deficit hyperactivity disorder, encountered a similar educative discourse. Having been absent for several days, Joyce and Mary called him to their office. Alice, their administrative assistant, questioned him, asking "[Why have you been] working [instead of being here]?" Seemingly confused about this interrogation, Zamekile explained he had been raising funds for an outing organised by his church.[1] He asked, "Isn't God number one?" Joyce and Mary had replied in the affirmative before Mary advised Zamekile how best to consummate his relationship with God: "God wants you to be here, in school, as He is here; you don't always need to go to church."

Some weeks later, I joined grade six and their peers from grade seven at a "Careers Day" organised by the Department of Education (DoE). We sat in a sports hall with several hundred teenagers from "mainstream"

© The Author(s) 2018
O. Pattenden, *Taking Care of the Future*, Anthropological Studies of Education, https://doi.org/10.1007/978-3-319-69826-7_7

township schools, who were sporting striped ties and coordinated V-neck jumpers. The master of ceremonies delivered two Christian prayers after a school choir had sung several hymns. The first informed the audience that "worshipping God makes you wise" and that "you will remain foolish [if you do not]".[2] The second told us that "this side of heaven is not perfect", but that "God helps us to have an abundant life here regardless". These events did not surprise me. As argued in Chap. 4, most particularly, Christianity was a central tenet of educative activities at Ngomso and was explicitly acknowledged during school/education-related events elsewhere. As with Stambach's (2005: 212) research in Tanzania, "[modes] of instruction [involved] daily rituals that [created] conditions for religious conversion". During assemblies, staff delivered Bible readings. When it was his turn, Ndothusile, a cleaner, changed from his overalls into a shirt and tie. This transformation subtly claimed pedagogical power and modelled the kind of transformation learners were encouraged to fashion. Learners also sang hymns. In line with the staff's hopes of illumined pathways to the Promised Land, two common songs were: *We Are Marching in the Light of God* and *We Are Marching Over to Jerusalem*, which carries the repeated phrase "I want to be there, I want to be there forevermore." Mary pedagogically mouthed these lyrics, and some learners were held in the room until they sang with more gusto.

On one occasion, Wonga, a grade five learner, took the assembly. Clutching an isiXhosa Bible, he passionately encouraged his peers to respect members of staff, much to their vocalised delight. Drawing from discourses concerning the differential respect shown to 'elders' as a young, uninitiated Xhosa, he said learners should respect their elders in school as they would when in the location (also see Pattenden 2015). "Like a young pastor" (quoting field notes), he held his Bible aloft and vigorously shook his head. Learners should worship God and stop smoking, he said. "There are two paths [you can take] – the blessings or the wrong things", he continued. When several shelter boys were Confirmed at the Cathedral, a young lady gave a reading with the similar instruction: "Count yourself dead to sin and alive to God."[3] Likewise, in line with the ethical imaginations of members of staff, Wonga read from Psalm 30: "LORD my God, I called to you for help, and you healed me." Some of his peers supportively and jestingly shouted "Amen." Educators stood next to those who giggled and told them to be quiet and listen. With such disciplinary power, soon only Wonga's voice would be audible once more. After the assembly, another learner said he had taken away this message: "If you are smoking *dagga* [marijuana] you can't hear the word of God; so you are going nowhere if you are smoking." He said Wonga had made those who smoked feel uncomfortable. In other words, Wonga had encouraged learners to contemplate their moral habitus and the possibility of transforming it (Zigon 2010).

Returning to the sports hall, the next speaker, Dr Pienaar (of the DoE), evidently struggled to maintain discipline. She asked the audience to stop chattering and said, "You were not quiet when [the Master of Ceremonies] was speaking to God, this is very worrying indeed." Once their voices subsided, she addressed them:

> Close your eyes, look into your soul. Visualise yourself once you have finished school, with your matric certificate in hand. I want you to think about who you are going to be five or ten years from now. If you haven't thought about this already, then you are in trouble. The youth must build their own futures: no one will build it for you. Not parents and not teachers; you cannot have their matric certificates. What you become in life will be your own doing, nobody else's. Today is the day to build your future.

Dr Pienaar's message *may* have been future-oriented because the event itself was oriented in this way, yet learners were encouraged to consider their futures during events that were not ostensibly concerned with such matters. Such situations most often occurred when learners experienced moral breakdowns—that is, when something problematic happened to them, or they did something that was problematised (Zigon 2007). One such event concerned Khuzani, aged 17 in 2011. He had sporadically attended Ngomso for seven years and was struggling to confirm living arrangements with his social worker, having returned from a residential Reform School for 'young offenders'.[4] Mary was helping to resolve his problems in her office, when Khuzani became aggressive, leading her to suspend him temporally. As he ran across the railway tracks, he threatened to return to throw rocks at the school. Mary and I discussed the seriousness of his predicament and the lack of assistance from the Department of Social Development. I said, "It sounds like he's not sure where he's supposed to be going and who he is supposed to be seeing." Mary replied, "Yes, [that's true,] but [the whole situation] is all of his own making." In this answer, her judgement of his responsibility is clear.

Two days later, Khuzani was standing in Mary's office again, smiling at me because I saw him drop his serious expression to blow a flirtatious kiss to Liani (the grade three learner) when she popped her head around the door. On Mary's invitation, Khuzani then considered his suspension and said he had ruined his 'second chance' and should not have threatened to throw stones. Turning to me, Mary said, "Unfortunately he gets overpowered by the negative side of himself. I don't know if it's the drugs [he uses] or what that overpowers him, but the school isn't strong enough to deal with it anymore." She then faced Khuzani to discuss why she would not re-admit him to the school.[5] She told him:

> I have a bad back, and if violence breaks out [because of you] I am worried it will be damaged, and then I will not be able to be there for the other children. . . . I forgive you [for everything you've done], but being forgiven does not mean that you can be back in the school. . . . This does not change how much I love you. I love you. I tell you that [all the time]. Even after you have been on the streets for six months, I pray for you. I have used your name in churches in England so that they pray for you too. You are clever, artistic – you have gifts. I want you to be a winner, but sometimes we have to be tough in the way that we love; when we are soft, we are not helping. . . . We need you to decide, 'I will not let these drug demons rule my life.' The fact that you are here tells me that you are more than half-way there. You're thinking [about your future]; you're on the road, which is good. Hang in there. Pray. When you go back to [the Reform School], if you're praying and asking God for help, you can become the head boy of [that school]. You have the brains [to do that]. It is a choice, choice, choice.

In short, she encouraged him to believe he could decide to avoid demonic drugs and embrace His love to fashion a victorious moral transformation, worthy of 'head boy status'.[6] He was encouraged to reconsider the enmity that had arisen between them and to recognise that Mary's intentions and his punishment were just (Williams 2006: 81).

Bornstein (2005: 41) details the "destabilising" experience of being mugged in Harare while conducting research. An interlocutor working for a Christian NGO prayed for her, hoping it would alleviate her understandable feeling of unease and vulnerability. Her rocky disposition shares some similarities with that of Khuzani. Both individuals were unsure of how to ethically respond to the world in order be more comfortable again in it. In each case, Christianised forms of care and the power of prayer were offered as antidotes. Christian discourses offered ways to understand their predicaments and directions to enticing resolutions. Timing was crucial. As Bornstein (ibid: 44) says, "The hope offered in that moment of crisis carried with it the potential for embodiment [of Christian faith] that was appealing." The idea of 'a moment of crisis' closely relates to Zigon's (2007, 2009a, 2010) theorisation of the transformative potential inherent in experiences of 'moral breakdown'. Individuals look for stability—something, someone, or some words to grab on to—during experiences of existential instability, so that they might prop themselves back up. They might pray that He will give them strength. At Ngomso, learners were encouraged to do so, particularly when they lacked strength or were due to embark on some form of transformative experience (e.g. when transitioning from a drug rehabilitation programme at the psychiatric hospital to 'the temptations' of the location or collecting results from an HIV test).[7] As I argued in Chap. 4, when examining Peter's hopes that his 'seed of faith' would flourish in the minds of those in jail, transformations appear possible when human life is at its lowest ebb.

Perhaps because it provided comfort, Khuzani was holding a small knitted soft toy, which Mary acknowledged by saying:

> I am glad that you have a little toy to love. Do you know why? Because it says that there is a place in your heart that is very soft. You've got a future [because] your heart isn't all hard.

Steven Parish (cited Zigon 2008: 52) suggests concepts like 'soft hearts' "render the mind capable of the moral knowing required for persons to live a moral life". Mary evoked the concept when attempting to mould Khuzani's moral conscience and consciousness.[8] It contrasts with concepts of the hardened, blackened hearts of *tsotsis*; "Blessed is the man who always fears the LORD, but he who hardens his heart falls into trouble" (Proverbs, 28: 14). Soft hearts can be penetrated, purified even; "Blessed are the pure in heart, for they will see God" (Matthew, 5: 8).

As I have argued throughout this book, education at Ngomso was enacted in the hope that learners would lead a particular kind of moral life, worthy of (a conceptualisation of) societal inclusion rather than exclusion. As Mary told Khuzani, her tough (Christian, agapeic) love was for his benefit. These (well-meaning) educative efforts, as with those of Lindiwe and Dr Pienaar, become clearer in light of Michael Lambek's (2010a: 2) argument that ethical dimensions of life become "explicit" when "the right thing to do is unknown or hotly contested" and "priestly classes [are] attempting to rationalize and educate". Although fashioning oneself by spending time in school and embracing Christian faith is *a possibility* for how one might live a moral life, this possibility was promoted as though it were truthful or right (Zigon 2010). Put another way, pedagogic technologies, such as visualisation (Dr Pienaar) and repetition (Lindiwe), were employed to convince learners that school educations and Christian faith were, and would be, good for them. The fact that educators were compelled to offer such direction suggests they were aware of the possibility that learners may have been unaware of such judgements, or may have had their own, different or even antithetical, judgements, as indeed some did (see below).

Two important aspects of this moral possibility are conceptualisations of (1) betterment and (2) responsibility. To the first point, schooling was most frequently promoted in terms of its purported ability to better—that is, to improve *and* make 'more moral'—individual lives, nations, or humanity as a whole; its utility judged as an end external to its practice, namely fulfilment through gainful employment. Relatedly, the predominant political frame of schooling during the post-apartheid period has been 'human capital development' (Sayed and Ahmed 2011). Such conceptualisations contrast with Aristotle's notion of "actuality", understood as "life as lived for itself" (Lambek 2010a: 3), but concur with what Stambach (2010: 183) has termed "Christian-modern faith in schools". They have foundations in the eschatological imperatives of the religion: work/effort and piety/restraint as a mode of fashioning oneself *now* with concern for betterment in this life and the Promised Land.

Turning to the second point, I follow Zigon (2006) in using the concept of *responsibility* when considering individuals' responses to and attempts to deal with the successes and failures of their efforts to bring about an alternative state of affairs. That is, individuals can take responsibility for who they become and what becomes them, or they can (attempt to) locate such responsibility elsewhere. This issue brings us on to Lambek's (2010a: 16) assertion that intersubjectivity—that is, "how much each of us is part of others and how much my self is determined by the self-making projects or the acts of others"—is variably recognised and occluded in different localities and, I would add, by the logic of different conceptualisations of being in the world.

Signalling a particular conceptualisation of responsibility that aligns with educators' ethical imaginations, learners were told that, as self-disciplined *individuals*, they could design and build their own futures, somewhat independently of their personal histories, relationships with others, and the political, socio-economic situations in which they were enmeshed. The related notion that misfortune is merited was frequently articulated with reference to Christianised sin. This logic concerns God's benevolence and His ability to deliver a good and fair world (Laidlaw 2010a), which the master of ceremonies spoke of during his prayers. Learners were encouraged to believe they would lead better lives if they recognised that God created the conditions for such transformations and that they, as individuals, were responsible for bringing them to fruition.

This conceptualisation of responsibility was especially explicit when Mary spoke to Zamuxolo, the talented runner in grade three, after he had absconded from the shelter to visit his family:

> You must be right here [pointing to her head] and set [yourself] goals. God helps those who help themselves: when you get up and help yourself, God has something to work with [so that He can] help you – but you can't just sit there [waiting for something good to happen to you].[9]

More generally, although educators recognised all manner of causal influences, they rarely shared understandings of responsibility that involved third parties (God excluded) with learners. For example, while educators made a causal link between the material poverty of learners' homes and academic underachievement, and made efforts to address it, they did not encourage learners to acknowledge or critically examine this link. Instead, they encouraged them to acknowledge total responsibility for their academic progression or lack thereof, in the hope that their learning to do so would ultimately enable them to disentangle themselves from or overpower causal influences and conditions.

This analysis concurs with Swartz et al's (2012: 35) argument that the 'myth of meritocracy' is "a major tenet of the post-Apartheid South African narrative". It also relates to discourses of empowerment and human rights, which, as I have argued already, were in evidence at Ngomso and had been integral to much recent activity concerning schooling and charity/development in South Africa (and elsewhere). These discourses all rest upon historically constituted, individualised conceptualisations of agency (Durham 2008; Laidlaw 2010a; Zigon 2011: 231–2, 2013).

I began to think about how such moralised discourses could be learnt (i.e. embodied as dispositions following interactions with those who 'had faith') when I noticed disjuncture between the accounts that learners gave of their first days at Ngomso (i.e. the fulfilment of pressing needs, as discussed in Chap. 3) and the evaluations of those in grades six and seven, who had attended for some time.[10] Regardless of their initial circumstances and reasons for joining the school—like the 'School Xhosa' described by Phillip Mayer (1961)—schooling was integral to who they wanted to *be* and to how they envisaged themselves *fulfilling* their hopes. For example, in grade seven, a 16-year-old named Cebisa told me "school is the only way of living nice". A male peer chipped in: "by going to school, maybe I will get a better job". He nodded as he thought about his statement, before concluding "I can do anything". The way they linked their investment of themselves and their resources in schooling to expectations of a pay-off in the future reflects the discourses promoted by educators at Ngomso, which were, in many cases, gradually internalised by the learners.

Errol was not only pondering the possibility of following Michael Jackson's lead, but he was also hoping to become a pastor so that his family would be "proud of [him]". As if to speak to my observation that members of staff espoused the virtue of habitual patience, Errol explained how this moral disposition had been shaped by his time at Ngomso:

> Mama Mary would say to me, 'My child, if you want something, search for it. [For example,] if you want education, search for it. Education won't look for you; you have to look for it. [Everything is like that.] Everything you want, you can have; you just have to be patient. [Take it] step by step.' [So I now know that] patience is very important. Even if you ask God for something, you have to be patient and wait [for it].

Errol was pursuing and crafting his future in line with such direction, while patiently awaiting the fruits of his endeavours. Lindela similarly encapsulated the themes of this section when describing his transformation:

> It is five years now that I have been with Mary [at Ngomso]. Now I have seen my life; I must finish school. Maybe I can go to University. Maybe I can get a job. . . . She took me [when I was] on the ground and now [raises his hand from the table to a position above his head] I can see something. That's why I say *uThixo unceda abazincedayo* [God helps those who help themselves].

Like Errol, following his experiences at Ngomso, Lindela was hopeful of a *better*, possible life: one with school/university and employment. He also knew how to fashion such a life (i.e. by 'helping himself' while recognising His agency). In other words, he had come to embody the hopeful moral discourses that educators like Mama Mary, Lindiwe, and Dr Pienaar articulated. Due to his transformative experiences of schooling, he was now committed to a specific way of being in the world and could acknowledge the person he had become. Confirming Lambek's (2010b: 47) insistence that "temporality is critical" to such *ethical* commitment, Lindela's transformation had taken several years.

Much of the work that schools and their supporters do can be understood as attempts to encourage such commitment. Schools are powerful in this regard. However, learners engage with them *ethically* (i.e. judgementally (Lambek 2010b: 42–3)), with a degree of ethical freedom to evaluate numerous options and opportunities, and they thus have transformative *potential*. As with events at educationally and religiously oriented institutions more generally, particular truth claims were powerfully made at Ngomso, at the expense of others. Members of staff continually endeavoured to establish moral possibilities they valued and brought into question those they did not. However, faith in schools and Christianity was not inevitable because learners consciously evaluated these truth claims. The power that educational experiences exercised upon them was, therefore, not absolute; they could subtly separate themselves from particular educative efforts and moral discourses. For example, when two police officers, Mrs Maleku and a colleague, spoke about the "dangers" of various illegal drugs, the majority of learners listened attentively, and some asked questions. When Maleku then suggested drug use was evidence of a problematic lack of Christian faith, four male learners immediately voiced their frustration and walked out of the room. More broadly, learners did not necessarily embrace educative discourses 'wholeheartedly', as members of staff hoped they would; especially those who engaged with the school only fleetingly, before continuing to live life without it. I will discuss some of these individuals in a subsequent section.

Manhood and Care

The previous sections of this chapter considered the emphasis that members of staff placed on the imperative to have patience and a soft heart, and the completion of school to attain the status and respect accorded to those who matriculate. In this section, I want to consider, more directly, learners' encounters with a different notion of moral personhood.

Siseko told me that he first befriended "the thugs"—who robbed others but left him alone—when walking the streets looking for food at the age of 12. "Those that have food in their homes don't walk late at night; so they don't learn to fight", he said. In other words, Siseko learnt how to look after himself because his circumstances demanded it. During *ukwaluka* or *isiko lokwaluka*, the Xhosa initiation ceremony that guides transitions to manhood (see Mayer 1971; Mhlahlo 2009; Ngxamngxa 1971; Ntombana 2011), initiates similarly endure (orchestrated) hardships when learning how to live independently (i.e. without the care and support that sustained them during childhood).[11] The imperative that one must learn how to be a man, capable of caring for himself and loved ones, was evident leading up to initiation, as well as during the process itself. Velile captured this idea when telling me "All the things we do, we do as culture." He said:

> As a man, you must have the guts to stand on your own. The Xhosa grow up hard, [but] the man never gives up. He knows [what it is like] for something to be hard [and] he gets used to that. No matter [what the] challenge, you do not give up after [going to the] bush [i.e. Xhosa initiation]. That's why he's a man. That's why we have pride. It's the creation of that black person. It's a way of life. It's like [you're] born a new baby: you born again. [In contrast], if you grow up soft, then when life becomes hard, you give up. There is not that freedom [to deal with whatever might come at you]. If someone takes care of you – with money, clothes, eating and takes you places – when that person is passed away, and life is different then you are on your own, but you can't care for yourself [because you are soft].

When speaking of the "creation of [a hard, resilient] black person", Velile was, in his own words, saying that initiation is an educative and ethical experience that results in embodiments of a particular possibility of moral personhood (Zigon 2008: 61). That is, individuals are created and create themselves when, as he put it, they are reborn when learning to adopt a particular "way of life".[12] Initiation is thus a process whereby *character* develops: initiates are encouraged to imagine and embody historically constituted modes of habitual conduct.[13] In particular, in line with Velile's depiction, the experience builds "forbearance, courage, fortitude and strength" (Vincent 2008: 436). Initiates learn a conceptualisation of what a man is and does. And learn how to become a living example of this same conceptualisation. To this point, in isiXhosa, initiates are called *abakhwetha*, where '*aba*' means 'group' and *kwetha* means 'to learn'; the process is 'schooling' in the abstract sense. Velile proudly associated himself with this notion of moral personhood: he had faith that young Xhosa men could gain the necessary strength and freedom to endure the unpredictable challenges that would (surely) come their way.

Learners clearly had to overcome hardships and 'adult problems' before engaging with Xhosa initiation. As I have already suggested, the prevalence of such learning experiences motivated Ngomso staff and supporters to attempt to soften them with care. In turn, somewhat ironically given the school's mission, Velile insinuated that such care limited learners' ethical freedom to respond to the world by discouraging them from learning to care for themselves. Other interlocutors—learners, past pupils, and staff—explained a similar judgement by using the word "spoilt", meaning that Ngomso simultaneously spoilt learners with material gifts and spoilt their moral qualities by encouraging them to become dependent upon this charity.

As Velile intimated, the possibility that learners could "grow up soft" on account of the care given to them, materialised in an especially problematic moment when Ngomso terminated its care, which it did when past pupils left the Shelter or high school. To this point, Luzuko was concerned that learners who were "one-hundred percent spoilt" had "no future". In 2013, Velile himself was due to leave the Shelter when turning 18 and was worried about how he would 'fend for himself' (he had not graduated from grade seven to high school). Had he been spoilt or was he tough enough to endure the world out there? The Shelter made arrangements for him to stay a little longer and he began working in the pottery room. The gruesome irony of his situation, the moral bind of his predicament and that of some of his peers, is that the care he came to depend on was first offered to him by Ngomso and the Shelter when it was essential, perhaps life-saving, and not forthcoming from other parties. This realisation continues to trouble me because there is no quick-fix solution. Moreover, not all past pupils could be employed by the school and thus remain in this state indefinitely like Velile.

Ethical deliberations regarding the importance of *ukwaluka*, and the value of hardening into resilient, self-sustaining men more generally, were most evident when older learners were due to undergo initiation. This type of event most frequently presented itself following the instruction of enthusiastic parents or family members when they had access to the necessary funds.[14] At such moments, the school's policy to admit learners up to the age of 19 and customs regarding *ukwaluka* created space for predicaments. Unlike colonial missionaries, who objected to *ukwaluka* and pressed for it to be illegalised, which excluded many initiated men from mission schools (Mills 1995), Ngomso actively supported learners' decisions to undergo initiation.[15] However, in the past, learners had returned from initiation and demanded differential respect on account of their newfound adult status, which conflicted with staff efforts to give learners equal status.[16] Thus, at the time of my research, it was school policy that no learner could attend as an initiated Xhosa man. Regardless, many learners said that initiated men should not put their status at risk by attending schools that offered primary level education, although they could and did attend high schools. Therefore, when initiation beckoned, male learners at Ngomso encountered a dilemma: whether to stay in school and remain a Xhosa child, open to ridicule and belittlement by initiated 'age peers', or to permanently leave school for initiation.[17] Each option offered the promise of status and the attainment of a respected notion of moral personhood (i.e. 'Xhosa man' versus 'matriculant'). However, it was impossible for some individuals to pursue both opportunities.

Staff encouraged learners to defer their initiations until grade ten by promising to pay for them using funding from the Friends if they were delayed until such time, including the obligatory offerings of alcohol that cemented social ties. However, the efficacy of this technology of power was compromised because these young men knew that many Ngomso learners did not reach grade ten. In contrast, the status attained after initiation into Xhosa manhood was definable and somewhat guaranteed (although it could not be easily transferred to other contexts and other localities, unlike the claim that schooling and its qualifications enable individuals to 'go anywhere' (Moore 2011: 47–54)). There was also the possibility (or likelihood) that their families would not retain access to the necessary capital for them to complete the initiation process at a later date. Thus, if it did not happen at that moment, there was the chance it would never happen.

Although historical contexts and historically constituted possibilities of moral personhood, and the 'institutional specialness' of Ngomso, the 'commercialisation' of initiation ceremonies (e.g. the centrality of brandy), and generational orderings of power maintained in schools, created the room for such a dilemma, personal histories and ethical judgements determined outcomes. Samkelo left Ngomso without completing grade seven, primarily to undergo initiation, and did not (to my knowledge) become a bus driver as Betty (one of the sisters from the UK) had feared, while others intended to, and did 'stick it out' until grade ten. It may not have been a coincidence that Samkelo lived in the township, rather than the Shelter, where the value of the respect gained when becoming a 'Xhosa man' was greatest.

Learning About Justice

The possibility of being a 'tough, Xhosa man' was discordant with the possibility of sourcing protection, retribution, and justice from the State. Langa argued: "You can't go and open the case [when you have been] to the bush [i.e. initiation], you must do revenge." Dibana informed me that the police "[were] laughing" at those who did not take revenge. He said, "[It is only] women [who would] open the case". Fundani and Langa, elaborated, saying that opening a case brought accusations of "not [being] a man" but a "moffie" or "a gay". Siseko explained the word 'moffie' by saying "it is one of the names given to [those who are] too soft" (cf. Pascoe 2012; Ratele 2013).[18] As learners most frequently wished to avoid these accusations, for the same reason they wanted to avoid perceptions that they were a 'soft touch', each school day was littered with instances of learners testing each other's inclination to back down. This habitual practice is what Siseko meant when he said: "the small boy is not afraid of the bigger boy". Some female learners also interacted in this way.

The staff took steps to encourage them to act otherwise. Joyce once explained the school's efforts by saying "We are fighting a battle [against the immoral influences in learners' lives], it is an ongoing thing." To demonstrate the perpetual nature of this endeavour, I'd like to return to this book's opening ethnographic vignette: the scuffle between Sidima and Odwa that resulted from a cupboard being closed in the grade six classroom. In the first chapter of the book, I left the scene when Sidima said to Mary, "Look after me, mam", after a little deliberation regarding his options. This moment was not the end of the story, however. Instead, their interchange up until that point had merely served to reconstitute or refashion the power relation between them, and Sidima now looked set to continue his engagements with Mary and the school. Their conversation continued:

Mary: How am I going to look after you? What must I do?
Sidima: I don't know.
Mary: What have I done the past few days?
Sidima: Help me to have a future.
Mary: That is what. How [have I helped you]? Are you ready for me to tell you?

Sidima nodded in silence.

Mary: I have to discipline you. The 'how' is through discipline. Can you tell me some of the things about discipline that you might be needing?
Sidima: Respect?
Mary: Good. What else? What did you do in the classroom?
Sidima: I cheeked you.
Mary: That goes with respect.
Sidima: I can't remember.
Mary: You didn't speak the truth [afterwards]. You said that you couldn't remember [what happened with the fight], then you suddenly remembered.
Sidima: Can I ask you a question?
Mary: Yes.
Sidima: Was that bad?
Mary: Yes.

Sidima tutted to indicate his disapproval and said, "I am tired. You must suspend me; I have been standing [here for] a long time." Mary turned to Danny and me and said: "As soon as he gets to [the point of] changing his life, he runs away." She spoke to Sidima: "The truth is one of the most important things in life. If you can't tell the truth, that is what leads people [like you] to become criminals."[19] In response, without saying a word, Sidima attempted to dart out of the office. Mary shouted "Security", as she frequently did, and said, "If we don't pull him up now it will end in disaster." Danny offered an alternative: "Maybe he can just apologise?" "No", answered Mary, "he must face what is wrong [with what he did, in order] for him to be different in the future." Sidima was held by the security guards and returned to the Shelter with Danny until he was willing to discuss the matter again.

Actual events (and my notes) were more nuanced than this account; however, I hope it gives some sense of how maternalistic, agapeic ambitions translated into intricate forms of ethical contestation. During the initial altercation, think it is likely that Sidima fought back when challenged by Odwa because he did not want to lose respect (i.e. to appear soft). In line with a conceptualisation of moral personhood that she valued, Mary then attempted to transform his understandings of responsibility and respect. For Mary, he faced "disaster" if he continued to believe he could act immorally without taking responsibility for such actions, especially because a court of law can also locate responsibility. Instead, she wanted him to act morally in the first instance—that is, to continually take responsibility for his comportment and not reciprocate violence—to secure himself a more desirable future. Today's discipline is tomorrow's salvation. The exchange demonstrates the materialisation of the school's "mission", as stated in its Constitution. Most especially, Sidima was encouraged to learn "the value of self-discipline, self-awareness, good manners and courtesy". It was through such ethical interchanges that the ethical imaginations of staff and supporters materialised as practices of 'a loving education'.

In line with the related analysis offered in Chap. 4, such formations interweave with Foucault's (2008) theorisation of governmentality. Mary employed herself so that Sidima might be "different in the future". Her guidance might be understood through the lens of Foucault's (1982: 789–790) argument that the "exercise of power consists in guiding the possibility of conduct" or structuring "the possible field of action of others". Such processes are, I would argue, the key moral substance of schooling, and education more broadly. I draw particular attention to these two statements from Foucault because they both allow for indeterminacy. Education conditions the possible and probable but does not determine the materialisation of individualised or collective futures absolutely. In already having a moral habitus, Sidima encountered Mary's truth claims and pedagogic effort in a unique way (Asad 1993: 50). To reach a truce, they had to reach an agreement regarding his deportment and directionality or, at least, there had to be the appearance of compliance. Occasionally this did not happen, and a young man or woman never returned to battle with the staff again. In Sidima's case, he was at high school when I returned in 2013, intent that he would gain the respect of others upon matriculation.

BARRIERS TO LEARNING

Although Ngomso learners who were in the final stages of primary level schooling (i.e. grades six and seven) were generally committed to their studies and the possibility of matriculating, the majority did not complete high school, a scenario that is by no means case specific.[20] Past pupils gave several explanations for this fact. According to numerous accounts, and contra to government policy, modes of discipline at the local high schools regularly included corporal punishment.[21] Several past pupils informed me that they had boycotted particular lessons or high school more generally as a result. When Nitin complained about a learner who liked to jump the school fence to avoid attending lessons, a practice he attributed to his 'specialness' (see Chap. 2), he was speaking about Thembani. Thembani gave his version of events when speaking about another past pupil, who had missed a maths exam that morning:

Thembani: He never goes to maths. There is a gang of four of them who do not go; sometimes I am one of them too. If I have not done the homework, [because] maybe I don't understand it, and I know that the teacher will beat me, I go with them.
Oliver: He beats you for not doing the homework, so you don't go to the lesson?
Thembani: Yes, it's like that.

To my knowledge, such practices did not occur at Ngomso, increasing the need for challenging adjustments during transitions between the stages of schooling. As a past pupil named Dalumzi, who had left high school without matriculating, put it "When we reach high school we are not used to being beaten, so that's why we struggle very much." His friend Mzoxolo recommended that Ngomso should act illegally and use corporal punishment (like the high schools in question) to limit this struggle to adjust. As I discussed in Chap. 2, others have sought a different resolution when trying to stop such practices altogether. This unresolved political contestation, ostensibly concerned with learners' best interests, limited my interlocutors' engagements with school and the probability that an Ngomso learner would matriculate.

Individuals also spoke about the challenge of studying in English, which I witnessed during lessons at Ngomso and when helping past pupils with their homework. Learners, especially those in high school, also faced industrial strikes, instigated by the South African Democratic Teachers Union (SADTU), and teacher absenteeism more generally, resulting in lost classroom time and gaps in their curricular-related knowledge. Although the DoE offered their educators some training opportunities, they might also have suffered because staff at 'Black schools' during apartheid received little training (Morris and Hyslop 1991; also see Wright 2012). Outside of school, past pupils and Ngomso learners also experienced all manner of 'personal challenges' that compromised their schooling. For instance, heavy weather ruined the decrepit rented accommodation of a past pupil named Lindela, and he was absent from school when finding a solution.

In answer to my question "Do you guys think that where you live makes a difference to how well you do in high school?" Mzoxolo, another past pupil, captured several important issues:

> *Ja*, it does affect us man, when it comes to [living in] the poor family. Sometimes you do not concentrate at school because you know that, when you [get home, you are going to face the question]: 'What am I going to eat?' [Also], if I have to take off my uniform and go straight to town and start to beg to get some food, there is no chance for you to read your books after that. . . No one is working, so [during] the night, before we sleep, we are gonna sit at home and stare at each other [because there is nothing else to do]. And then the stomach is playing its noise [because you are hungry]. There is no time for you to read because the paraffin is about to be finished, so you have to sleep.

Bourdieu (2000: 224) argues that "powerlessness . . . breaks the relation of immersion in the imminent, [and] makes one conscious of the passage of time". Mzoxolo's account of hunger and boredom highlights such an experience. When working in London, my students were 'distracted' by impending court cases and the ambiguity of parental divorce. Given what I know about them, I would say that there is a strong chance that my interlocutors in South Africa experienced similar challenges, and, no doubt, more issues that I was not privy to.

I began to see that the students were icebergs: what I could see on the surface, or what they allowed me to see, was a small part of who they were. I thought of the invisible ice below the waterline as their dreams, fears, hopes, pains, memories, and regrets. On many occasions, chunks of ice flew up through the water's surface, into our shared, social world. A fight would erupt instantaneously, and I'd learn it was because neither student wanted to appear "shook", or scared. A student would walk out of class without saying a word, and I'd learn her mother was ill, and she wanted to go home to see her, or that she couldn't do the work and didn't want to be humiliated. A knife would appear in a bag, and afterwards, I'd learn its owner had to walk through an unwelcoming postcode to get to school. 'Special Educational Needs' began to mean something more than terminology.

Several interlocutors told me that drug use enabled them to alter their experiences of the passage of time with positive effect. In contrast, the consensus among members of staff, without notable exception, was that drug use (e.g. smoking marijuana or methaqualone) was incompatible with virtuous, moral lives and successful completions of schooling. They attempted to address all of these issues—that is, the special educational needs they attributed to societal marginalisation and poverty—with material and emotional support. However, such circumstances still limited learners' prospects of matriculation. Moreover, for young men such as Mzoxolo, a successful navigation of the schooling system, no matter how rare an achievement, did not necessarily equate to a reversal of economic fortunes. With a municipal youth (15–35 years old) unemployment rate of 42% (SSA 2011), his depiction of a household in which nobody had a steady income was commonplace.[22]

In addition to these contexts, which were salient and immediately visible to me because they dovetailed to some extent with my experiences of working in education in London, disparities of wealth were integral to another dynamic in the locality that conditioned learners' engagements with schooling. In 2011, I learnt that some past pupils concealed their high school uniforms when outside of school, fearing they were symbolic signifiers of success that incited jealousy and witchcraft. They were sure that other 'poppies', who were also not remarkably tall, yet less careful, were cut down. Additionally, one evening, when drinking with Madoda, one of the school's security guards, and his friends in the location one evening, I learnt that a couple had recently died in a house fire, just around the corner. Madoda's friends explained the events by saying their spaza (convenience) store had been making a lot of money. When I pushed back, asking what they meant by that, they asked me: how else do you explain why the door to the shop was locked from the inside so that they could not escape the fire? I was still scrambling for some clarity. One member of the group, a police officer who was, incidentally, the daughter of an educator at the school, told me that their deaths were the result of witchcraft. It wasn't the time for 'full anthropologist mode' so we left the discussion there, but the questions that had been sparked demanded attention.

Approximately two years later, one lunchtime in the pottery room, I was speaking with Velile about ancestral worship more generally when he said:

> [Ancestors] can protect you from the witch and those kinds of spells. When you have a new job, others have that jealousy; especially the Xhosa ones. Those Xhosa like money. [If] you are poor, and now [someone else] has money [that makes you jealous].

Seeing that I was keen to know more, David, the art educator took up the conversation:

> Success motivates the witches. [Other people] bewitch you because you have a big house. It sounds very silly, but it is true. Some people, especially neighbours [are doing witchcraft]; when you extend the house some will get ill and die. Even when they are building the foundations. Or something [else] bad happens and they don't finish the house.

I told them that I had been thinking about how witchcraft is related to education and asked if some young people did not attend school because they feared reprisals from jealous onlookers. In particular, I wanted to know if there was a causal connection between witchcraft and the high levels of absenteeism and 'school drop-outs' in the Eastern Cape. David responded to my query by saying:

> They are getting jealous [of people who are] at school. Some learners that are intelligent [are doing well at first] but then they have the problems, and they get ill [because of witchcraft].

He went on to tell me a story about a young woman living in the township who had "done well" and secured a place at the local university. However, her journey had been thwarted, as David explained: "Once she sets foot on campus [she gets ill]. But when she is in the township, nothing." He said there had been "talk in the area where she comes from that she is the only child [from that area] to go to the university, [which explains why some people are jealous and why witchcraft is preventing her from studying]." In what I read as an attempt to convince me that witchcraft was not the only barrier to educational success, he then emphasised the fact that residents of the location who pass matric rarely have the points necessary to attend university. He also said that such studies were prohibitively expensive for most. "Children are failing", he continued, "[because] they are not intelligent [enough to pass]." David seemed reluctant to have me believe that he fully endorsed the notion that witchcraft was the primary cause of 'schooling failures'. As he had said at the beginning, "it sounds very silly". However, perhaps because I gave him no indication that I thought it was silly, he returned to issue, saying: "But there is that jealousy of those that are achieving, [and there are] mothers that are witches who can see the children of others doing better in their schooling than their kids." He hadn't really told me if he believed young people were not attending school for this very reason, but I did now have a little more clarity, at least. I scribbled in my notebook: "there is a fear about being seen as successful". Perhaps some individuals had ceased to attend an educational institution of some kind for fear of reprisals. I don't know, for certain. However, such events would have something in common with Bornstein's (2005: 148) argument that "people [in Zimbabwe] had begun refusing positions of leadership at rural development sites" because "showing signs of success in relation to the position of others, made one vulnerable to the envy of neighbors, coworkers, and strangers". The salience of witchcraft certainly gave young men and women in the vicinity something to think about when they put their school uniforms on each morning.

Past pupils and Ngomso learners only spoke to me in private about their belief in witchcraft, which convinced me they were always evaluating alternative moral discourses. I learnt that the possibility of orienting their ethical projects in line with key moral discourses promoted at the school— that is, educational and economic success is to be celebrated and rewarded—had to be evaluated against the possibility of being 'taken down' at any moment for pursuing this directionality. It is my contention that this predicament demonstrates a fundamental cultural disjuncture: any emphasis on individualised competition—such as that found in most 'Western schools' (cf. Xu 2014)—contrasts with cooperative schemas, such as ubuntu (Metz 2007: 325).[23] Belief in witchcraft was neither taught nor encouraged at the school.[24] Instead, to varying degrees, educators worked to instil a counter-narrative, asserting the idea that economic and educational success does not open one up to acts of witchcraft.[25] Social contestation relating to these alternative moral possibilities is a long-standing, historically constituted dynamic of life in the locality (also see Mayer 1961; Wilson 1961).[26] Christian missionaries based in the eastern fringes of the Cape Colony during the nineteenth century "attacked" witchcraft (Ashley 1974: 201). However, given that alternative discourses are encountered with creativity and consciousness, such contestation is inventive (i.e. productive), rather than repetitive (reproductive).

Velile and David's explanations clearly demonstrate that witchcraft functions in response to, and is, perhaps, productive of, socio-economic distinctions and inequalities. Bornstein (2005: 147) similarly analyses witchcraft in Zimbabwe in terms of "the socially relational nature of evil: it results from someone's lack in relation to another's plenty". Velile also told me that the relation between inequality and witchcraft has a gendered quality, in the sense that mothers who do not have any male offspring can derail Xhosa initiations and transitions to manhood with acts of witchcraft resulting from their jealousy. This somewhat problematises the argument that jealousy-related enactments of witchcraft are responses to economic unevenness (cf. Bornstein 2005). It would be accurate to say that discourses of jealousy and witchcraft overlap with diverse hierarchies and formations of status and attainment. For Velile, the existential demands of this climate of suspicion were relentless:

> That's why I said, 'Don't trust anyone.' Because you can trust someone, but [then find out that] they are a big problem. You think, 'No, that guy [is ok, but then it turns out that he is not]. [You should] only trust a stone because a stone can't change. If you throw a stone, it will go in the direction that you throw it.

The existence and associated dangers of witchcraft were an integral and powerful component of the assemblage of public and institutional discourses that my interlocutors encountered each day. Like the promise of matriculation and graduation from university, witchcraft was both real and mythical; a descriptive and productive discourse that fashioned intersubjectivity and ethical imaginations, individual lives and modes of collectivity. Just like teacher strikes, a lack of lighting in the home, the inability to buy a school uniform, or any of the other scenario that served to condition the relative appeal of schooling and the probability of matriculation or graduation, witchcraft had to be navigated—acknowledged, judged, and responded to in some way. The unremitting prospect of illness or incapacitation had to be overcome, transformed, ignored, or absorbed into one's moral habitus, orienting everyday engagements and conduct. In addition to high rates of unemployment and low rates of matriculation, the threat of jealous parents was one more thing to worry about, perhaps the only thing worth worrying about.

Having spoken about the challenges that had to be overcome for one to matriculate, Mzoxolo went on to hypothesise how individuals might respond to such a predicament:

> That's why we are thinking 'No man, fuck this life. I have to go to town and [steal] a cell phone or a wallet or whatever, in order to get for myself something that I want.' And if you decide to do that, that is why you are going

to get arrested, and the whole thing that you were studying for is gone; just like that. When you come back from prison, you are [seen to be a] different person, you've got the criminal record, you can't work for the government, and you have another language.[27]

I would contend that the hypothetical moment when someone says "fuck this life" before making an effort, of one kind or another, to fashion an alternative one, is another example of what Zigon (2010: 9) has called moral breakdown. These are those instances when "some event or person intrudes into the everyday life of a person and forces them to consciously reflect upon the appropriate ethical response (be it words, silence, action or non-action)" (ibid.). When possible and probable responses are limited, such uncertainty and nervousness can give rise to opportunism. In an experiential melee conditioned by perceived and very real barriers, each and every option on the table demands consideration, no matter its moral quality. Mzoxolo's words and those of other interlocutors taught me that such events never transpire in a vacuum. Instead, actions that result from ethical judgements, as opposed to habitual, unthinking impulse, reflect the desirability that individuals see in various forms of moral personhood, whether criminalised or not and the evaluations they make about the probability of attaining them. In this way, an uneven distribution of material and economic resources, such as the food and paraffin Mzoxolo spoke of, and related modes of subjection, shape ethical processes of self-fashioning (Laidlaw 2010b: 376).[28] The same is true of those historical events that precede such processes, shaping the various moral discourses that are prominent in any one particular locality and the related freedom that individuals have to fashion their lives in particular ways (see Laidlaw 2002; Zigon 2010). Whatever limitations my interlocutors faced, they could exercise a degree of freedom when attempting to use their human agency to bring about an alternative state of affairs for themselves and those around them.

Unsurprisingly, among my interlocutors, it was no secret that one can steal from others. However, publicly and institutionally constituted moral discourses served to influence the frequency with which this possible course of action materialised (Zigon 2010). The decision to try to illegally obtain a cell phone or break into a house carried with it the prospect of becoming, to use Mzoxolo's words, a "different person". In this case, an ex-convict with a criminal record and mastery of the 'prison language', and not a 'clean' and complete school and employment record. When making such decisions, individuals are able to evaluate the potential consequences of acting otherwise, informing their ethical judgements with future-oriented, imaginary calculations. It is precisely these dynamics that the terminology of 'moral decay' or statistical models of correlating crime, education, and employment rates fail to capture. Those who did and did not finish school or engage in criminalised activity were united by their ability to act within a context of ethical possibility, even if their experiences of probability were conditioned to an objectionable extent.

THE (IM)MATERIALISATION OF HOPE

Bongani, the school's cook, had graduated from Ngomso and matriculated at the age of 22. As I helped him prepare some sandwiches, he told me he felt "proud" to have secured a job at the school. He had completed a valued stage of ethical transformation (Robbins, n.d: 10). Bongani presented himself as evidence of this when telling learners "[You] are not thugs. [You] are just like everyone else."[29] However, several weeks after our conversation, Bongani was stabbed during an altercation in the location. Upon his return from the hospital, he became a teaching assistant, as, to be frank, other members of staff did not rate his culinary skills. Despite this repositioning, he continued to come into conflict with 'the management' about his alcohol consumption and use of *dagga* outside of school. Soon after I returned to the UK, he permanently left Ngomso for an alternative, entry-level job in the private sector.

More generally, although several Ngomso learners had matriculated and secured full-time employment, a notable achievement given the challenges of high school and unemployment levels, it seemed there were no 'fully formed' exemplars (i.e. past pupils with lives that fulfilled the most extensive hopes of learners, educators, and supporters). I once asked Siseko "Do you know of anyone from Ngomso that you think is a *big* success story?" He instantly answered, "No; that is the problem." He spoke about a young man named Ntando, who went to Rhodes University to study art history before my time in South Africa. As I already knew, he had been within touching distance of high regard but 'dropped out' in his first year. As we chatted in his 'shack', Siseko and his friend Mzoxolo explained why:

Siseko: The moment you get into university, you experience another thing.
Mzoxolo: You are a higher person.

Siseko: *Ja.* You are eating very good, all that kind of stuff, and then you relax a lot. That is why you fail, [and why] you are not getting good qualifications. ... Everything is nice [there], and it is new [to you]. You see this room I am sleeping in? If I can get there [to a room on campus], I could sleep all day. In this one, I can't sleep all day. The wind will come in [through the cracks in the metal sheets] and say 'Wake up.'

Being in Siseko's shack was removed from my experiences on campus, and I had to readjust my comportment when moving between the environments; it makes sense that Ntando might have struggled with a similar endeavour. In Siseko's view, Ntando had taken his foot off the pedal when arriving at a more comfortable, higher destination, only to lose momentum and fall short of his final one.[30] Given knowledge of other Ngomso learners, I presume Ntando struggled for many years to meet the university's entry criteria. The idea that this same struggle tripped him up at university is tragic.

As I have mentioned already, Siseko himself was one of those rare individuals who transitioned from grade seven at Ngomso to complete high school. Having lived at the shelter during his teenage years because his parents were unemployed and drank heavily, he passed matric in 2010 at the age of 22. When we first met in Mary's office in 2011, she told him she had secured him a job with a local business. The warmth of the hug he gave her and the quiver in his voice as he said "Thank you" told me something about how important this was. He had been struggling to find employment for more than a year, and the atmosphere was one of celebration. Hope had been realised.

However, the job did not materialise as expected, as he explained: "I was working with people who had not been to school, they were doing hard labour, but the boss was paying me less than them. I said '*Eish*, this is not fair, this is unfair.'" Similarly, after matriculating, Luzuko left the job he had secured in a supermarket when ordered to clean shelves and stack boxes because this instruction conflicted with his sense of self and the value he placed on his exemplary performance at school. Both cases support Bourdieu's (2000: 217) more general claim that "the conditionings [of one's aspirations] imposed by the conditions of [their] existence are added to by . . . [various] educative interventions". In the case of Luzuko and Siseko, experiences of schooling structured expectations and intersubjective evaluations after matriculation (also see Hurtig 2008; Jeffrey 2010; Stambach 2000).

Weeks later, under a bare light bulb that hung in Siseko's 'cosy shack', his friends and I ate cold hot dogs smothered in watery ketchup. Siseko was adamant he would not work "hard labour" (i.e. construction) like those without matric certificates. He suggested he had once engaged in the kind of moralised education I have considered elsewhere in this book when recalling the words of one of his educators: "Siseko, if you can read books you are very clever, you can go anywhere."[31] Having done so, at least to the extent of passing matric, Siseko remained unenthusiastic about employment he could have secured without years of commitment to schooling. However, while unemployed, he was frustrated that he could not always repay friends without matric certificates who were working "hard labour" when they bought him drinks.[32] His position has much in common with the "educated idlers" of the 1860s, who concerned the colonial government because frustrations can morph into 'political disruption' (Ashley 1974: 207). Unlike other young South Africans (see Dawson 2014), however, to my knowledge, Siseko was not engaged in protest politics or revolutionary activity at this time. Instead, like male graduates in India who similarly compete for oversubscribed government jobs with favourable salaries and terms of employment (Jeffrey 2010), he pursued more education and training—in his case, a business management City & Guilds certificate and a driving licence, as he waited, hopeful and despairing, for a return on his investment in schooling.[33]

He had applied for positions as an office clerk and security guard, but individuals who were without qualifications were appointed. He did not judge this to be a fair outcome:

> If you finish grade twelve, what are they telling you? 'Write a CV; go out there and find a job.' But when you go out there, [there is] nothing. You just drop a CV and go home. Then you go to a rubbish bin and find your CV there. They put it there because it's [about] networks, family networks. He will say 'I know him', then you got the job.

Mzoxolo extended his argument: "But our families are working hard labour, so that is the choice that you have: 'My brother, can I be your friend and work in hard labour too?'" Siseko added: "And other people think 'He's from Ngomso [so I won't employ him].' [And] there's no one that can [speak up] for you and say '[You're wrong], he's good now.'"

Their words raise three points of interest. Firstly, their experience of the dearth of employment opportunities.[34] Secondly, securing employment depended on social connections and capital (Bourdieu 1986), as is also the case in India (Jeffrey et al. 2008: 4). Thirdly, stigma further restricted employment prospects, a gruesome double bind, as the school's unique qualities gave hope to many in the first instance. Siseko had tried to transform himself into a particular kind of moral person, to become "good", but felt that the actions and judgements of others, which were clearly beyond his control, nullified his efforts.[35] In short, his effort and investment in schooling had guaranteed neither employment nor fulfilment.

Fixing the Future

Months later, I filmed a music video for Siseko's hip-hop group. He fantasised about record deals and a world tour (also see Weiss 2002) while remaining reliant on the support of Ngomso and several members of the congregation at the city's cathedral, which he had attended while living at the Shelter. Together with a trickle of computer repair jobs, these networks were providing just enough income for him to sustain himself but left him with a feeling that he was not adequately providing for his six-month-old son.

After filming, Siseko explained how he had tried to hide his son from supporters at Ngomso and the cathedral, even though they would have offered financial assistance: "Because, I felt that 'this is my problem, *I have to fix it myself*.'" Zenzile agreed with his logic, saying, "Without your [own] money, you fail to show your child how much you love him, or her." Siseko then spoke of his failure in this regard: "It was killing me, that thing of having a child. *Joh*, [I was so surprised]. That's what makes me drink, just to [help me] sleep as well."

He told me that the mother of his child had informed his supporters at the cathedral about his son. The revelation caused more discomfort, as he explained:

Siseko: Now they are always asking 'How is he doing?' If he is not doing very well, I will tell them 'He is not doing very well', then they will have to pay. That's what I don't want. I am the problem.
Oliver: You don't want them to pay?
Siseko: *Ewe* [yes], that's not good, that's not fair.
Zenzile: Just because he is already the problem.
Siseko: I am already the problem.

These last five words, which I understood as an indication of Siseko's enthusiasm to take full responsibility for his life and that of his child, have stayed with me ever since. Recall the instruction of Dr Pienaar in the sports hall: "The youth must build their own futures: no one will build it for you." As though to reflect and highlight his embodiment of this instruction and moral discourses promoted at Ngomso more generally, Siseko was struggling to "fix" the problem—that is, to fashion a future for himself and his child with an alternative trajectory—while blaming himself for the difficulties he encountered while doing so. Moreover, he experienced ethical discomfort regarding the fairness of passing his responsibilities on to others. This internalisation of blame only added to his struggle; it was the *cause* of his inability to sleep and, consequently, his drinking.

When I returned to South Africa in 2013, Siseko and I sat on the kerb outside a small convenience store, eating samosas. He said there had been "ups and downs" since we last spoke but that he was now "in the middle". The computer repair work had dried up, and the hip-hop group had disbanded. In their absence, his life had become "too dark". In contrast to Lindela's words about how he was able to "see something" (i.e. an elevated future with school, further education, and employment) and the staff's hopes that His love would illuminate learners' lives, Siseko's life had lacked light, making it difficult to see forward. In response, he had turned to an opening he had previously shunned by asking a friend who was a local councillor to secure him a short-term contract working "hard labour", building houses for the government's Reconstruction and Development Programme (RDP). His new employer had not requested his matric certificate, City & Guilds qualification or driving licence. "It's not what you know, it's who you know," he said, with a smile that suggested he remembered our conversation from 2011.

He had been on strike for two weeks in a hopeful, ultimately fruitful, attempt to secure a 10% pay increase. We spoke about Marikana, where 34 striking miners were killed one afternoon by members of the South African Police Service. Siseko was now adding to the weight of political protest in the country, although he found the picket line as unstimulating as his wait for employment. He spoke about his parents, who remained unemployed and continued to drink heavily, saying "My family all think I am doing well and look [up] to me. 'No', I say, 'look at me, I am struggling.'"

Having had some interesting conversations with other interlocutors who made a link between misfortune and "witchcraft", I raised the subject with Siseko. We had never spoken about it before, and he first gauged my opinion on the topic. He then said his "whole family" were affected by "witchcraft" due to his father's (jealous) ex-lover, and that it had caused his father to lose his job and become an alcoholic. Before its influence, his father had been a "good man", he declared. (Several learners had already shared similar accounts of parental alcoholism, which encouraged me to question Siseko about "witchcraft".) Siseko then spoke about the learners at his high school who had, in his opinion, been unfairly rewarded, explaining "I was stronger than them [in class/exams], but now they are working for the police or the army." Siseko stopped eating his samosa while he collected his thoughts; ethically stepping away from himself and the world he shared with others momentarily, to contemplate what to think or say about his situation (Zigon 2009b: 261; also see Jackson 2012). He then concluded with "My family will always fail; we won't go anywhere."

According to the individualistic, meritocratic logic of schooling outlined earlier, those who perform well at school will fashion better lives for themselves. Why had this logic not held true for Siseko? I can understand how witchcraft provided him with an *explanation* for his misfortune (see Gluckman 1970: 84–85). Gluckman (1970: 86) argues that "witchcraft as a theory of causation embraces a theory of morals, for it says that witches are wicked people". I would argue that it is also moralistic in the sense that it maintains that (im)moral transformations can be brought about by witchcraft. Siseko held witchcraft responsible for his father's (im)moral transformation and the 'failure' of his family to better itself.

Siseko could have drawn upon explanatory discourses other than witchcraft. Other interlocutors spoke of how numerous other events/agents were responsible for such (mis)fortune, including "the legacy of apartheid", "failures of the ANC government", or "recession" (to paraphrase). As noted, Siseko and his friends were well aware of unemployment levels and discourses concerning corruption in recruitment processes. While these discourses all provide compelling explanations, which other individuals such as politicians, economists, and academics attempt to address, *in isolation* none explain why Siseko deserved his misfortune or should not have been more fortunate, especially given that these shared historical, economic, and political causal circumstances benefited others (see Laidlaw 2010a). Moreover, how might he have attempted to hold such perpetrators to account? With difficulty, no doubt. In contrast, Siseko believed that witchcraft can be countered with direct action: He wanted his father to visit a sangoma (diviner).[36]

As I understand it, if witchcraft was responsible for the failure and stagnation that had been "killing" him, the healing (i.e. fixing) offered by a sangoma was a mode by which he *hoped* to eradicate such predetermination. Thus, Siseko's belief in witchcraft not only offered an explanation for his misfortune, but it also enabled him to hope that he might fashion a better life for himself and that his family might be able to do likewise as a result of his father's action (i.e. a visit to a sangoma). This transformative potential contrasts with other antidotes to (overwhelming) misfortune that similarly provide a fix but have degenerative, unhealthy, and even deadly effects, including alcoholism, which Siseko had already turned to, and suicide, which has increased among young South African men. Migration away from the Eastern Cape, in search of improved employment prospects, provided another well-trodden option, which would have taken him away from family, friends, and the support network he had spent years building.[37]

Other members of Siseko's family had attributed their (mis)fortunes to witchcraft before he did. I asked him when he had begun to agree with their judgement. "I started to believe when I could see that life is too difficult", he replied.[38] We can understand the moment he described as another experience of what Zigon (2007: 138) calls "moral breakdown". When he could no longer encounter and fashion his life armed with the moral disposition he had had up until that point—one acquired during, and that had seen him through, his schooling—he had worked on himself to find hope again. Hence, coming to terms with his situation and the world he shared with others by transforming his "way of being in the world through conscious ethical work" (Jackson 2012; Zigon 2009b: 261). A lack of hope had necessitated a change of tack.

Siseko's transformation is comparable to that of other Ngomso learners and past pupils who were similarly drawn to new moral discourses and experiences at the school when they too were hoping to find hope. However, Siseko achieved his latest transformation by embracing a moral discourse that was promoted by his family (among others): the belief that witchcraft shackled their lives.[39] When realising that his agency was limited, that it was "too difficult" to build the life he had hoped for, this belief in witchcraft created or located agency of a different kind (see Laidlaw 2010a: 157).[40] Turning to punitive magic in an attempt to find the person/agent *responsible* for his struggles (ibid: 156), he now believed the (re)actions of others had caused his (mis)fortune and dismissed the possibility that he alone was responsible. His 'alternative' disposition relates to aforementioned moral discourses concerning "Afro-communitarianism" (Metz and Gaie 2010: 273); captured, in the South African context, by 'ubuntu', short for "*Umuntu ngumuntu ngabantu*; a person is a person through their relationship to others" (Swanson 2009: 11). While ubuntu has most frequently been examined with reference to harmonious social relations, belief in witchcraft similarly maintains that the thoughts and actions of others can influence your thoughts and actions and that you alone are not responsible for your being or for what befalls you.[41] In other words, it strongly recognises intersubjectivity. For example, Siseko said that when, on rare occasions, his father had "some money, he [thought] about [going to see the sangoma]". However, he said his father would "forget" about the sangoma and spend the money on alcohol instead. "That thing [the witchcraft] is working", he concluded. This assertion is important as it suggests some form of belief in the idea that witchcraft can compromise 'free will' and one's control of their cognitive functioning (also see Ashforth 2005). Such belief contrasts with my understanding of Siseko's previous position and struck me as being incommensurable with the educational discourses on offer at Ngomso, most especially discourses of individualised freedoms, responsibility, and attainment.

What explains this conflict? To my mind, the discourses offer competing *explanations* for what befalls individuals and their responsibility for it. In providing such explanation, they encourage individuals to understand that they can have a hand in shaping their being in the world, but by also recognising the agentive capacities of witchcraft or God, they account for the limits of such will (Jackson 2005: 127). "The ambiguity of human *existence*, in which we are acted upon *by* the world to the same extent that we act *on* the world, wherein we are both determined and free" makes such explanation necessary (Jackson 2012: 133, emphasis in original). Without it, individuals struggle to dwell comfortably in the world because they cannot comprehend and thus find it challenging to encounter the inherent uncertainty of their dwelling: the knowledge that they only have *some* control over their being and becoming. Due to the unevenness and unpredictability of South Africa's post-apartheid transition, Siseko and his peers appeared to be struggling for such control.

Learning to Hustle

I have suggested that past pupils were always in the process of becoming. I now want to discuss how their changeable fortunes impacted upon those following in their footsteps, highlighting individuals who did not matriculate and instead learnt an alternative possibility of moral personhood.

Siseko told me that his awareness of Ntando's journey to university had "pushed" him to finish school (before Ntando 'dropped out'). Mzoxolo then took up his line of discussion:

> [Ntando] was the one who inspired us to go to high school and to do strong at high school and pass grade twelve. Just because, we were thinking 'When we pass grade twelve, we will be the same as him.' But that turns wrong [i.e. he didn't finish his degree]. For me, I didn't pass grade twelve, I dropped out at grade ten, but for the others who did pass grade twelve, *eish* [it was a disappointing surprise].

Robbins (n.d: 29) suggests that "encounters with key values embodied in exemplary people and institutions . . . lend our lives a sense of moral purpose and of investment in the future, [because they provide] the pitched-forward quality of moving toward the good that is so crucial to our will to keep going". Siseko and Mzoxolo said something similar when explaining how they had been inspired and pushed by Ntando. However, as they also explained, exemplary people only supply a sense of moral purpose while they remain exemplary. Their catalytic influence diminishes the moment their propulsion falters.

As I have already argued, Ntando, Siseko, and Bongani all faltered when attempting to fashion exemplary lives. Younger learners lived in close proximately to them and other past pupils. In some cases, they were related. As a result, there was a feedback loop of information about the post-school reality that lay in wait for learners, and they could continually re-evaluate their educations in light of this knowledge. This is how my conversation with Siseko and Mzoxolo continued:

> Oliver: Do the [monthly] food parcels, and the money for rent [you get from Ngomso] encourage you to stay in [high] school?
> Siseko: *Ja*. It also encourages the younger boys to go to high school [in the first place] because they are thinking 'If we stay in high

school, we are getting more food.' They know they will get money for rent too, [meaning] you can stay out of your place [i.e. live independently]. [But] there is nothing else that encourages [you to stay in high school]. From my experience, nothing else. There is no [definitive] promise [of what will happen] if you pass grade twelve. What is going to happen to you? [You have no idea.] I think that [uncertainty] makes other children feel like 'Nah, [what's the point of staying in school]?'. [Learners are not] encouraged to think 'Look who is there [at university] now, [look at the positive things that happened to them] after they finished grade twelve' [because that example does not exist]. So [you already know] it's down, down [after grade twelve].

Mzoxolo: [It's the] end of the world [when you finish grade twelve].
Siseko: You're just going back to the street again.
Mzoxolo: *Ja*, that's why you have to hustle for yourself [because you cannot rely on schooling].
Siseko: [The younger ones see this and] they just start training for the hustle from grade eight. You have to go and hustle for yourself after grade twelve [anyway, so why not start early]?
Oliver: Do you guys agree?
Mzoxolo: I do agree, man. Because sometimes I used to ask myself 'What's the use of going [all the way] to grade twelve?' Because, at the end of the day, you are gonna work a contract [job] or hard labour or stuff like that, [no matter if you matriculate or not]. But [if you stayed in school, you'd be doing those jobs] at the same time [as being] well educated. [That would be hard to deal with.] You see? You would have to work at Pick n Pay [supermarket, having matriculated].

Given Luzuko's experiences, Mzoxolo's example was prophetic. Of interest here is the idea that the notable absence of 'fully formed' exemplars encouraged learners to pursue other endeavours, away from school. Although the food and rent money Ngomso gave to high school learners did encourage some individuals to attend school, as donors hoped, these 'carrots' were somewhat unique. A large number of learners without such incentives leave government-funded schools in the Eastern Cape each year, especially at grade ten. This process was true for Mzoxolo himself, who left at grade ten soon after Ngomso stopped supporting him after he stole from the school but did not reconcile with the staff. In line with my interlocutors' analysis, Jansen (2012: np), a prominent South African academic, has argued that the "value of education" has increasingly been negated by "the poorest communities of the country". In particular, he (ibid.) suggests, "the visible lack of connection between education and economic well-being" has resulted in a "lack of faith in education".[42] Like educators at Ngomso and their colleagues at the DoE and British and South African supporters, Jansen is troubled by this realisation. As the history I have detailed throughout this book confirms, such concern is not new.

The fact that some young South Africans lack faith in school educations is evidence of the "tendential law of human behaviours, whereby the subjective hope of profit tends to be adjudged to the objective probability of profit" (Bourdieu 2000: 216). This law of behaviour "governs the propensity to invest (money, work, time, emotion, etc.) in the various fields [of social action and activity]" (ibid.). As Bourdieu (ibid: 231) goes on to state, "A person can be durably 'held' (so that he can be made to wait, hope, etc.) only to the extent that he is invested in the game." Certainly, during my research, interlocutors restructured their investments of their selves having re-evaluated (im)probable events and reconfigured their hopes accordingly. Some knew there was no guarantee that investing themselves in schooling would deliver favourable employment, nor fulfilment more generally. This knowledge led some to abandon the pursuit of matriculation certificates for alternative pursuits. These events concur with Willis's (1977: 172) discussion of how "Settling for manual work . . . is felt, subjectively, as a profound process of learning: it is the organisation of the self in relation to the future." My interlocutors who left school 'early' did not necessarily learn to labour (although some did); however, in line with Willis's more general assertion, they did evaluate the future and embrace the present in a way that conflicted with educators' instructions.

As the reader may have spotted, Mzoxolo and Siseko spoke about one such possibility of ethical engagement: learning to "hustle". I have examined 'the hustle' throughout this book, without using this terminology. It is the moral habitus, or the 'immorality', that concerned staff and donors, a way of being in the world that jars with their ethical imaginations. I discussed one hustle or way of hustling, for example, in Chap. 2, when examining Jikela's claim that those who left Ngomso to 'beg in town' maintained misunderstandings that there were street children at the school by disingenuously claiming they were enrolled. I experienced it when talking to a young man named Lizo, as I walked home from a popular student pub one Sunday afternoon. He wanted "money for bread" (a common request). When I gave a non-committal response, he said his mother had died, forcing him to come to the town to earn money for rent, which was R40 a month and overdue. Adding depth to his story, he said his landlord had locked him out and was threatening to destroy his possessions, leaving him with no access to his school uniform and forcing him to spend the previous night "sleeping here in town". He said he did not want to repeat the experience, especially because it was raining. I suggested he come to Ngomso in the morning and ask Mary for help. Lizo didn't like this suggestion because he was sure Mary would accuse him of smoking *dagga*, as she had done before. In the end, we settled on the agreement that I would give him R20, half of what he wanted. Knowing this was "a bit of a punt" (to quote my field notes), I walked away and said I was looking forward to talking together at school.[43] Lizo said he'd be there and thanked me for the money.

Needless to say, the hustle worked. Lizo didn't come to school the following morning. However, my punt paid off too; it was the starting point of a genial relationship. I learnt that Lizo did not want to return to Ngomso because of the accusations of drug use and conflict with older learners. Instead, he frequently spoke about enrolling in a mainstream school in the location but never did. I think he was trying to keep me on his side by talking about such plans. Lucht (2015: 107) considers the hustling techniques of a Ghanaian migrant named Bobby, who describes his work: "We tell [our potential clients] stories. We are story-tellers." Similarly, Lizo was a keen storyteller. Much like Mary's fundraising presentations, he tailored narratives to his audience when eliciting money. The story of a young man kept from 'the promise of education' by a disgruntled landlord was surely a powerful one to convey to university students. Lizo delivered his stories with convincing, dramatic performances, occasionally wiping away tears that disappeared as soon as his audience was out of sight.

When a young man dropped into Joyce's office to tell her that he had lost both of his parents and wanted to enrol, he was also telling a story. He sat the entrance exam while Joyce phoned his previous school to berate them for not caring for him. It soon transpired that his parents were not dead. He walked back out of the gate. I guessed the young man was clever enough to know that such a story was exactly the kind of plight that Ngomso staff happily attempted to alleviate with material support. Relatedly, Joyce soon imposed a new rule, whereby newly enrolled learners had to wait two weeks before being given new uniforms, no matter how genuine their claims of need. Two years later, when the trustees of the Friends in the UK spoke of their concern that learners were selling their uniforms for profits soon after receiving them, which they had been in the past, Joyce confidently said this was not happening anymore.

Somewhat ironically, as I grew increasingly dubious about the truthfulness of Lizo's claims and lost confidence in his "confidence game" (Goffman 1952: 451), our conversations became more truthful. By the end of 2011, we were joking together about his continuous efforts to 'con me' and shared some 'true stories'. He told me he had moved out of the Shelter because the food portions were too small. He did not like to be locked behind gates at six p.m. either. Instead, as he put it: "I'm going to town to wash cars, to get money for supper, and then I will go home again." Clearly, he also was adept at 'begging', although he never used this term. He earned R50 a day, on average, or R100 on a good day; a wage similar to those working manual labour for ten hours. To me, it seemed that he did not attend school or live at the Shelter because he had made, quite understandable, judgements about the possibilities open to him and opted to live an alternative life; one with fewer rules and surveillance, and more food to eat and money to spend as he saw fit. Bordonaro (2012: 417) similarly discovered that her interlocutors 'migrated to the street' in search of "independence and [the] love of freedom" (also see Hecht 1998). Like 'street children' in Brazil (Hecht 1998) and 'day labourers' in Japan (Gill 1999), Lizo didn't want to be 'saved' by Christianised interventions that promised a long-term pay-off upon matriculation or at the gates of Heaven. He was busy living a 24-hour, present-oriented existence. He had honed his skills, and there was a real craft to his techniques; he was confident that he could enjoy the spoils of his efforts every night, with the group of friends that he lived with, and return to town to top up again in the morning. My fellow students and I helped provide him with easy pickings.[44]

Consider the thoughts of Siseko and friends:

Mzoxolo:	[Those who stay and work on the street] do have homes.
Dalumzi:	They do. But it's because of the life that they choose.
Mzoxolo:	They don't want to go to school. The parents [might] say 'Go to school.'
Dalumzi:	[But] they don't want to be forced [to go].
Mzoxolo:	[Instead], they look for money in town, get that money and that bread and milk [that people buy for them], and then go to the location to buy something to smoke, and then go back [to town].

Dalumzi: Easy life.
Oliver: When you say 'Easy life', what do you mean?
Dalumzi: When you choose to sleep under tunnels, that means, for you, it's an easy life. Like, you don't have anyone to force you [by saying] 'Do this and do this and do that.' It's like you are free. You are free to do anything you want to do.
Siseko: [In contrast], when you are reading the book [i.e. staying in school], you feel like 'No.'
Mzoxolo: I won't earn anything.
Dalumzi: I won't smoke, I won't drink [because I have no money]. No, no, no. That means that being in town is an easier life than to read a book.
Oliver: Because if you are reading the book, you are saying that you don't know what will happen at the end?
Dalumzi: *Ja* [yes].
Mzoxolo: *Ja*.
Siseko: You are not going to get any money. They know that when moving around in town and begging, at the end of the day, he is going to go out of town with some money, and it is buying what he feel like buying.
Mzoxolo: Buy what he feels like.
Dalumzi: Alcohol, drugs.
Mzoxolo: Everything.
Dalumzi: In our days of freedom, we can buy anything – even a girl. You see?

In sum, opting to be in town rather than school provided some individuals with a particular form of freedom, especially immediate access to drugs, alcohol, and women.[45] My interlocutors spoke about choices; however, these 'choices' were judgements given limited options, not evidence of absolute freedom (Laidlaw 2002). Hustling is, rather, a response to precarity and unpredictability (see Wacquant 2008: 62–69). Etymologically speaking, 'precarity' comes from the Latin root *prex* or *precis*, meaning 'to pray, to plead' (Casas-Cortés 2014). Whereas the staff encountered risky or uncertain situations by praying to Him, and learners were encouraged to do likewise, the hustle was a response to precarity that found hope in the adaptability of human creativity rather than the security of divine plans. In his track *Can't Knock the Hustle*, Shawn Carter, a.k.a. Jay Z, a rapper from New York, makes a related claim: "I'm making short term goals . . . [So while] y'all niggas [are] lunching, punching the clock, my function is to make much and lay back munching." In other words, he makes money in short spaces of time, without having to answer to anyone else, then sits back and enjoys his spoils.[46] By hustling, so runs the discourse, you thrive on your own endeavour and do not need anyone or anything else to help you find fulfilment; this is the promise. However, as with the promise of schooling, not every hustler is as successful as Jay Z.

Hustling is not only about making money in the 'rap game'. It is similar to *rasquachismo*, a habitus attributed to Chicano migrants adept at "making use of [scarce resources] . . . [and] coming up with imaginative solutions to unforeseen problems . . . [and] facing hardships with a resistant and resilient attitude of perseverance in the face of incredible adversity" (Spener 2007: 12). Like *rasquachismo* (considered in this quote as an art form), hustling is "a stance rooted in resourcefulness and adaptability" that enables "one to gain time, to make options, to retain hope" (Ybarra-Frausto 1991: 156).[47] To creatively survive and craft openings of hope, my hustling interlocutors robbed; dealt drugs; (illegally) sold alcohol; fixed computers and bikes; collected, stole, and sold 'scrap' metal; and washed and guarded cars. They also worked as day labourers (for cash and without union representation, healthcare, or pension contributions). These observations match Valentine's (1978: 23) ethnographic consideration of an American ghetto: "[Hustling] refers to a wide variety of unconventional, sometimes extralegal or illegal activities, often frowned upon by the wider community".[48] 'Begging in town' was another frowned upon activity.

On the railway line, en route to Siseko's place, Mzoxolo explained the direction he had taken: "I'm working, I'm self-employed." He then darted into the thicket, before emerging with a saw and a spanner he had hidden. With some friends, he had been using the tools to clear copper wiring from the railway, before selling it for R25 per kilogramme. (Recall, from Chap. 4, that Peter spoke about the Promised Land when he saw a group of past pupils selling scrap metal.) Mzoxolo explained what happened once they sold their 'recycled' metal: "We get this big money, and we smoke it all; for fun really." Sure enough, later that evening, he left Siseko's place for an hour to "visit a friend" and returned with glazed, reddened eyes. By way of explanation, he joked: "We were in my office, doing my other job." Moments later, when speaking about his life more generally, he said, "You must expect the unexpected, you can't control everything that comes your way."[49] This assertion is clearly antithetical to the educative discourses promoted at Ngomso that concerned human agency, responsibility and His power—that is, to succeed in school, learners had to know what to expect and meet the expectations of others, thus gaining some sense of mastery or control over their long-term progressions.

Desjarlais (1997: 128) describes similar disjuncture when writing of his research in a homeless shelter in Boston: "The dominant chronotope of the street was one of drifting unmoored... [People] did not so much do as have things done to them." In contrast, "[in the shelter] people were more the agents of their lives. They acted and moved in predictable, clearly defined expanses of time and space, with the 'whys' and 'wherefores' of such actions more readily at hand" (ibid.). In feeling there was not enough "structure" at Ngomso, despite the fact it was closer to Desjarlais's depiction of the shelter than the street, I presume Betty and Sally, the sisters from the UK would have experienced existential turmoil if forced to emulate Mzoxolo's temporal disposition and his relationship with futurity.

If you were hustling, you were 'off-grid', and, as such, considered (by others) to be marginalised from (their) society. However, in South Africa, 'the marginal' are not marginal by number. More broadly, "precarization is in a process of normalization" (Lorey, cited in Puar 2012: 164). Meaning that something similar to Mzoxolo's disposition, and his conceptualisation of futurity and causation, in particular, has become increasingly common as an increasing number find themselves with a similar degree, or lack of, economic and political power. Some (critics and interlocutors) consider such events as evidence of 'moral decay'. Indeed, Day et al. (1999: 21) suggest that 'marginal people' "can seem feckless or irresponsible in the eyes of their neighbours" on account of their "living in the present". Relatedly, such individuals might be denied "'the badges of success' by which mainstream society judges people" (ibid.)—that is, mortgages and car loans are unavailable. However, precarious predicaments and lacking moral sensibilities need not conjoin. For instance, Mzoxolo did not want to have a child because he believed he was in no position to care for another human being. Thus, while he acknowledged that he had relatively little power or control over what would befall him, he still morally considered the future and took steps to create a particular future for himself and others (cf. Bourdieu 2000: 221–3). A lack of predictability and determinability did not worry him; he was sure that he could navigate his way through or over whatever obstacles might arise, he just didn't think it was a good idea to submit the life of a newborn to the possibility he would fall short one day. Unlike members of staff and supporters, who were (relatively) economically secure and sure they had the power and skills to care for the children of parents who (in their judgement) did not have such resources, Mzoxolo cared for his unborn child by making sure that he/she was never born. Instead of being incapacitated by the existential turmoil of such limitations, he was busy living each day as a grasshopper, who liked to dance and sing (and smoke) every night.

In the introduction to their edited volume *Lilies of the Field: Marginal People Who Live for the Moment*, Sophie Day, Evthymios Papataxiarchis, and Michael Stewart (1999: 11) write:

> Representations of foraging [and gathering] and associated concepts of natural abundance are antithetical to the very idea of economy, which relies on notions of scarcity, saving, delayed consumption, and planning. To speak of 'economy' is to speak of a model of behavior according to which present actions should provide for the future. Gathering provides the opposite model, according to which there is no need for present action to provide for the future: The future is guaranteed instead by a generous, affluent, physical environment.

In being concerned with perpetuating, and preparing individuals for 'the economy', schooling relates to the first model. In contrast, Lizo, Mzoxolo, and their peers—that is, the 'street children' and 'school dropouts' who so concerned Ngomso staff and supporters—were oriented to the world according to the second model. In light of historical contestation between Christian missionaries and the Xhosa, such temporal disjuncture is nothing new. Peires (1989: 131) argues that the Xhosa had a "perception of the cyclical recurrence of natural phenomena and, ultimately, the cyclical nature of time itself", not unlike the notion of waking up each morning to enjoy 'the spoils of town'. Moreover, while "The Xhosa did have a conception of linear time, expressed through genealogies and the succession of *iziganeko* (significant happenings). . . . The annual cycle of stellar constellations . . . accustomed the Xhosa to expect every year the return of the circumstances of previous years" (ibid.). Missionaries of the colonial period tried hard to transform such cyclical temporal orientations and instil the belief that Christianised commitments in the present are a necessary precursor to prosperous futures. Individuals who propelled interventions that targeted Grahamstown's 'street kids' endeavoured to do the same work. Conflict with the targets of their efforts arose because many potential converts did not share their faith in the future. This contestation has been central to analysis throughout this book.

Notes

1. As was the case with engagements outside school and embodiments of moral possibilities more generally, learners' Christian faith was not solely influenced by the time they spent at Ngomso. Several learners attended churches at the weekend, although Zamekile was the most outwardly committed. Dumisa had a transformative experience—that is, he "felt" and first acknowledged His power—on a weekend away with his church, similar to the one Zamekile planned to attend. This experience was welcomed and praised by Mary and Joyce, and, during my research, Zamekile was the only learner to come into conflict with members of staff about engagements with other Christian institutions.
2. Although the speaker did not acknowledge his source, his words have much in common with those found in the book of Matthew (7: 24–27).
3. Her words come from the sixth book in the New Testament, Epistle to the Romans (6: 11).
4. In 2004, the Legal Resources Centre took the South African government to the High Court as there were no such schools in the Eastern Cape. During my research, one was available and maintained by the DoE. While legislated directives state that certain 'young offenders' should go to Reform Schools rather than prisons, the lack of such provisions has meant these targets have frequently been missed.
5. This exchange with Khuzani was the only time I saw Mary refuse to (re)admit a learner to the school, although Khuzani did later enrol at a high school with the support of Ngomso.
6. I have written and presented an unpublished paper dealing with drug use and conceptualisations of agency, however, it has not 'made the cut' into this book. Just briefly, as per Mary's instruction to Khuzani, members of staff were generally adamant that drug use could, and should be, countered with individualised effort. In contrast, learners valued drugs for various reasons and 'rehabilitation processes' were never clear-cut.
7. As per the missionaries that Stambach (2005: 212) came to know in Tanzania, staff did not insist that learners engage in prayer. However, they were praised if they decided to do so. In contrast, during the aforementioned Confirmation ceremony at the Cathedral, the Bishop informed those undergoing the initiation that they should pray every day in order to have a "direction line with Jesus Christ".
8. In Zigon's (2008: 52) analysis of the research Parish conducted with the Newar in Nepal, he writes "one of [their] main religious and moral concepts… is the heart, which they consider the seat of moral conscience and consciousness".

9. This vignette supports my argument in Chap. 4, which states that the most tightly surveilled movements and behaviours belonged to those living at the shelter.
10. Velile was the only learner who spoke about joining Ngomso because he wanted "to learn". However, even this claim was inseparable from his analysis of the situational context of this decision (i.e. the death of his mother). Only two of the past pupils who were extraordinarily committed to Christianity and schooling (i.e. Errol and Luzuko) said they had valued the prospect of matriculation before joining Ngomso.
11. In line with the analytical theme of justice and retribution, initiation is overseen by senior elders and, in some but not all cases occurs when 'stick fighting' is halted and initiates commit to the rule of law (i.e. that of Chiefdoms or what are now most often called "traditional courts").
12. An insight from Maurice Bloch (2011: np) is particularly relevant here: "All living things are caught in two processes, phylogeny and ontogeny. When we are dealing with our species we have to add a third process: that of history."
13. Thomas Alexander's (2013: 196, emphasis in original) reading of John Dewey inspired this sentence; he writes "character is our moral imagination in action" and dependent upon "the flexible ability to integrate the possibilities of the present by using the organized experience of the past in reconstructing present action".
14. The costs incurred during initiation can include animals for slaughter (e.g. goats or sheep), the services of a 'traditional surgeon', alcohol and food for the 'graduation' celebrations (which establish relationships), and new clothing (which mark transformations). One journalist (Bullock 2015: np) estimates the total cost to be R10,000 (£450) while an academic (Meel 2005: 58) estimates R3500–R5000. Despite being told how costly initiation was for my interlocutors and their families, I never asked them to estimate the total cost.
15. When the popularity of the rite among the Xhosa did not relent during the nineteenth century, missionaries who wanted to include the young men integral to their mission later compromised with them by selectively supporting 'initiation schools' that incorporated Christian teachings (Mills 1995).
16. During the nineteenth century, missionaries encountered a very similar problem: "Fighting and trouble in the mission schools was almost endemic as boys who had undergone the rite used *inkwenkwe* [uncircumcised boy] or similar disparaging forms of address with those who were not" (Mills 1995: 171).
17. Learners could not undergo initiation and then return to another primary school as they were always already too old to be considered eligible.

18. The *Oxford Dictionary* (2014: np) defines 'moffie' as, "A man regarded as effeminate" or "A male homosexual"; "Afrikaans, perhaps an abbreviation of *moffiedaai*, dialect variant of hermaphrodite 'hermaphrodite'." It would be a valuable and interesting exercise to explore the relationship between sexuality and initiation further, however, given the analytical focus of this chapter, I hope that the reader will forgive me for not doing so here.
19. Mary's exchange with Sidima was not explicitly oriented by Mary's faith. However, truth and truthfulness are integral to Christian discourses. For instance, "it is impossible for God to lie" (Hebrews, 6: 18) and "For we cannot do anything against the truth, but only for the truth" (2 Corinthians, 13: 8).
20. In the locality, the issue of unfinished school educations was not isolated to Ngomso and its past pupils. In 1999, for example, 79,000 learners enrolled in Eastern Cape schools. Thirteen years later, when they should theoretically have matriculated, only 28,000 sat but did not necessarily pass, matric exams. In the district encompassing Grahamstown, the respective figures are 3298 versus 1315, representing a 60% drop-out rate. (I recorded these figures during a presentation from the Eastern Cape Education Department in 2011.)
21. There was no 'special high school' and no Ngomso learner had ever transitioned to one of the private schools or former Model C schools (i.e. those that catered for Whites during apartheid and continue to be funded by a combination of private and government money) in the city that, to my knowledge, did not tolerate corporal punishment.
22. Importantly, such unemployment figures exclude the "not economically active population", which includes those categorised as "discouraged job seekers", of which there were approximately half-a-million in the Eastern Cape in 2010 (ECSECC 2011).
23. Robbins (2007: 297) follows Dumont when arguing that cultures possess "a paramount value that ultimately structures the relations between all the other values it contains and hence the overall structure of the culture as a whole". "When value-hierarchies break down", he (2009: 281) argues, "what were once fairly clear cut choices become difficult to make". Offering an interesting comparison with argument, Robbins (2004, 2009) suggests that the Urapmin of Papua New Guinea experience perpetual, somewhat debilitating, moral dilemmas, as the recently encountered values of Christian, *individualistic* sin are at odds with the *relationist* moral values the Urapmin that were prioritised before the arrival of Christian missionaries. Much like my interlocutors, the Urapmin, Robbins argues, are somewhat 'caught between' two cultural, moral systems.
24. Individuals can, of course, have both Christian and witchcraft beliefs. Relatedly, some churches and strains of Christianity recognise witchcraft

(Niehaus 2001). While some members of staff attended such churches, others spoke disparagingly about this. In particular, Mary was not supportive of a learner who asked her for money so that he might visit a sangoma and I know that she saw no value in such endeavours.
25. Bornstein (2005: 141–2) similarly examines such processes through the lens of a tension between "the Zimbabwean view of morally correct economic behavior that de-emphasized the success of individuals" and the view of the employees of Christian NGOs "who attempted to make the material success of individuals morally acceptable as they trained people to do well economically".
26. As I hope my analysis elsewhere indicates, by speaking of two 'alternative' moral possibilities, I am not suggesting that they were the only ones I encountered during my research or that life in the Eastern Cape is limited to navigations and invocations of them. Nor am I suggesting that my interlocutors lived in accord with one or the other, or that they all embraced them in uniform ways. Instead, I have offered a simplified, theorised, understanding of how my interlocutors were fashioning their lives. Such a depiction does not capture all that is worth knowing about them.
27. More generally, my interlocutors spoke about a "prison language" or a "gangster language", which were, as I understood it, one and the same. Stone (2002: 389) says that "the prison lexis" (e.g. Shalambombo or Flaaitaal (Ntshangase 2002: 409)) emerged in prisons during the early 1900s and "infiltrated delinquent lexis outside" from the mid-1970s onwards. It is, in general, only comprehensible to members of prison gangs and can be used to conceal information from 'outsiders', such as police officers, potential victims, and prison wardens (Manus 2011: 80).
28. The idea that someone may choose to steal a cell phone may have been hypothetical in Mzoxolo's account, but such responses to the marked inequalities in South Africa are not uncommon. For instance, reported instances of 'Robberies with aggravating circumstances' increased in Grahamstown from 44 in 2004 to 344 in 2011, in a city with a population of 70,000 (Crime Stats 2015). South Africa ranks seventh in the world for the number of robberies recorded per 100,000 population (HEUNI 2011).
29. Importantly, Bongani was a paid volunteer and not employed by the DoE. This role was potentially a source of stigma because other past pupils believed that such individuals had not fully transitioned from the care of the school and 'learner status'. One interlocutor suggested they were "paid with food" (i.e. free meals) and not money, meaning they did not have the freedom to live as they wished. Hence, although Bongani spoke of his sense of pride, some of his peers judged his status to be worthy of shame.
30. Drawing from public discourses of morality, Nyquist (1983: 3) referred to a *Middle Class Elite* in Grahamstown's township during apartheid, as the

"'high ones,' the *abaphakamileyo*". Such conceptualisations are productively understood in light of the idea that colonialism and practices of international development, including related processes of schooling, brought with them a framework of meaning that placed individuals against scaled criteria—that is, vertical topography of 'progress' or 'attainment'. In this view of the world and its dynamics, those with university educations are considered to have achieved a higher plane of accomplishment than those without one.

31. Bourdieu (2000: 217) suggests that educative interventions discourage "aspirations [that are] oriented to unattainable goals" and encourage "the adjustment of aspirations to objective chances [of materialisation]". In suggesting Siseko's power was limitless, the educator in question appears to have made no such adjustment.
32. Siseko and his friends were quite happy to drink cheaper brands of beer when we socialised in their homes, but they insisted that we drink more expensive bottles of Heineken during our visits to public taverns. I did not tell them that the efforts of my previous colleagues in London were clearly paying off (see Preface).
33. In India and South Africa, as former British colonies, the introduction of government-funded schools was tied to the labour demands of the colonial government. However, school enrolment levels have subsequently increased dramatically in both countries, without a respective increase in government-funded employment, which has compromised the notion that schooling provides a direct route to a government job.
34. The official "youth unemployment" level of the Makana Municipality (including Grahamstown) was 42.2% in 2011 (SSA 2011).
35. Goffman's (1963: 19–20) work predicts his experience: "[When the object of a stigmatised failing is corrected or repaired], what often results is not the acquisition of fully normal status, but a transformation of self from someone with a particular blemish into someone with a record of having corrected a particular blemish."
36. Jackson (2012: 131–133) offers an insightful consideration of how different explanations for (mis)fortune correlate with related modes of addressive action, which has informed my analysis here.
37. "The Eastern Cape has the highest net out-migration of any province in SA. [Moreover, in] the absence of high net out-migration the Eastern Cape's unemployment rates would be much higher than they currently are" (ECSECC 2012: 22). Relatedly, in 2012, Helen Zille, leader of the main opposition party and Premier of the Western Cape, infamously suggested that those leaving the Eastern Cape in search of better school educations in the Western Cape were "education refugees".

38. Isak Niehaus (2001: 192, 2012) similarly found that his interlocutors, living in a former Bantustan area of post-apartheid South Africa, invoked their belief in witchcraft when encountering "perplexing events" or "unspeakable misfortune" (also see Ashforth 2005).
39. I knew that he was visiting the cathedral less frequently and preferred to drink alcohol on Sunday mornings because "God was in church", but did not ask whether his belief in witchcraft indicated a shift in his Christian faith.
40. Niehaus (2012: 5) makes a similar point when treating "the sorts of frustrated expectations, social relations, and misfortunes encountered in contemporary South Africa as one possible context for witchcraft beliefs".
41. Ashforth (2005: 86) discusses witchcraft and "occult violence" in South Africa as forms of "negative ubuntu".
42. Jansen (2012: np) considers other influential factors that accord with those I have discussed: that is, "poor quality education; an unpredictable timetable; unreliable teaching; the shortage of basic resources (textbooks and basic science materials etc.); the lack of responsiveness from local, provincial and national education authorities".
43. I was experiencing what Tom Boylston (2015: np) terms "the anxiety of exchange" when asked for something as a 'wealthy anthropologist' while wanting to establish a relationship with a potential interlocutor and feeling he was probably playing/cheating me.
44. The extent of Lizo's 'support network' became clearer when a student friend phoned one afternoon, worried that Lizo was in trouble because he had been crying when speaking about an argument with his sister and the need to 'sleep rough'. I saw Lizo a few days later. He told me he was walking from his home to town; so either the problem was solved, or it never existed. Either way, my friend had given him money. Another friend gave Lizo his bike when he graduated from university. When Lizo asked me for an expensive takeaway Pizza, I said 'No' but assumed other students had bought one for him previously. I did give him money on one further occasion when it was freezing cold and pouring with rain because I believed him when he said he would go home if I did so.
45. See Mark Hunter (2010) for a fuller account of South Africa's 'sexual economy'.
46. I would guess that Carter uses the word 'lunching' to suggest those 'punching the clock' do so absent-mindedly, without thinking about their activity. In this sense, he is suggesting that he consciously hustles while others stupidly miss the opportunity to do so.
47. This quote from the art historian Ybarra-Frausto is relevant to my discussion because art is a craft embraced and produced in reference and response

to an artist's perception of the world, and humans similarly adopt a stance in reference and response to the world when crafting themselves.
48. Valentine also argues that welfare and forms of contracted 'hard labour' provided most residents of 'the ghetto' with other options, much like my findings in Grahamstown's location.
49. It is here that the relevance of Lévi-Strauss' (1962) discussion of 'bricolage' is perhaps most relevant. He (ibid: 11) informs us that the verb '*bricoler*' was "always used with reference to some extraneous movement", thus describing some motion extrinsic to the body in question. Likewise, Lizo was sure that his life moved in surprising directions that he did not control. In response, he was light-footed and flexible; unbeholden to long-term plans with definitive means and end points. This habitus has much in common with Strauss' (ibid.) assertion that, for the bricoleur, "the rules of game are always to make do with 'whatever is at hand'".

Bibliography

Alexander, T. (2013). *The Human Eros: Eco-ontology and the Aesthetics of Existence*. New York: Fordham University Press.
Asad, T. (1993). *Genealogies of Religion*. Baltimore: Johns Hopkins University Press.
Ashforth, A. (2005). *Witchcraft, Violence, and Democracy in South Africa*. Chicago: University of Chicago Press.
Ashley, M. (1974). African Education and Society in the Nineteenth Century Eastern Cape. In C. Saunders & R. Derricourt (Eds.), *Beyond the Cape Frontier* (pp. 199–212). London: Longman.
Bloch, M. E. (2011). The Blob. *Anthropology of This Century*, (1). Retrieved March 4, 2012, from http://aotcpress.com/articles/blob/
Bordonaro, L. I. (2012). Children's Geographies Agency Does Not Mean Freedom. Cape Verdean Street Children and the Politics of Children's Agency. *Children's Geographies, 10*(4), 413–426.
Bornstein, E. (2005). *The Spirit of Development: Protestant NGOs, Morality, and Economics in Zimbabwe*. Stanford: Stanford University Press.
Bourdieu, P. (1986). The Forms of Capital. In J. Richardson (Ed.), *Handbook of Theory and Research for the Sociology of Education* (pp. 241–258). New York: Greenwood.
Bourdieu, P. (2000). *Pascalian Meditations*. Stanford: Stanford University Press.
Boylston, T. (2015). On Ethnotragedy. *Anthropology of This Century*, (14). Retrieved December 12, 2015, from http://aotcpress.com/archive/issue-14/
Bullock, R. (2015). It's Hard to Be a Man: A Month with Three Initiates During the Xhosa Circumcision Ritual. *Africa Geographic Magazine* (Online).

Retrieved December 13, 2015, from http://magazine.africageographic.com/weekly/issue-48/xhosa-circumcision-ritual-south-africa-its-hard-to-be-a-man/

Casas-Cortés, M. (2014). A Genealogy of Precarity: A Toolbox for Rearticulating Fragmented Social Realities In and Out of the Workplace. *Rethinking Marxism*, 26(2), 206–226.

Crime Stats. (2015). *Crime Stats* (Grahamstown). Retrieved May 26, 2015, from http://crimestatssa.com/precinct.php?id=954

Dawson, H. (2014). Youth Politics: Waiting and Envy in a South African Informal Settlement. *Journal of Southern African Studies*, 40(4), 861–882.

Day, S., Stewart, M., & Papataxiarchis, E. (1999). Introduction. In S. Day, M. Stewart, & E. Papataxiarchis (Eds.), *Lilies of the Field: Marginal People Who Live for the Moment*. Oxford: Westview Press.

Desjarlais, R. (1997). *Shelter Blues: Sanity and Selfhood Among the Homeless*. Philadelphia: University of Pennsylvania Press.

Durham, D. (2008). Apathy and Agency. The Romance of Agency and Youth in Botswana. In J. Cole & D. Durham (Eds.), *Figuring the Future: Globalization and the Temporalities of Children and Youth* (pp. 151–179). Santa Fe: School of Advanced Research Press.

Eastern Cape Socio Economic Consultative Council (ECSECC). (2011). *Quarterly Economic Update, First Quarter 2011*. East London. Retrieved July 14, 2013, from http://beta2.statssa.gov.za/?page_id=993&id=makana-municipality

Eastern Cape Socio Economic Consultative Council (ECSECC). (2012). *Eastern Cape Development Indicators, 2012*. Retrieved April 13, 2013, from http://www.ecsecc.org/publication-details/1374/Eastern-Cape-Development-Indicators-2012

Foucault, M. (1982). The Subject and Power. *Critical Inquiry*, 8(4), 777.

Foucault, M. (2008). In M. Senellart (Ed.), *The Birth of Biopolitics: Lectures at the Collège de France, 1978–1979*. New York: Palgrave Macmillan.

Gill, T. (1999). Wage Hunting at the Margins of Urban Japan. In S. Day, E. Papataxiarchis, & M. Stewart (Eds.), *Lilies of the Field: Marginal People Who Live for the Moment*. Oxford: Westview Press.

Gluckman, M. (1970). *Custom and Conflict in Africa*. Oxford: Basil Blackwell.

Goffman, E. (1952). On Cooling the Mark Out. *Psychiatry*, 15(4), 451–463.

Goffman, E. (1963). *Stigma: Notes on the Management of Spoiled Identity*. New Jersey: Prentice Hall.

Hecht, T. (1998). *At Home in the Street: Street Children of Northeast Brazil*. Cambridge: Cambridge University Press.

HEUNI (European Institute for Crime Prevention and Control International Statistics on Crime and Justice). (2011). Countries Compared by Crime > Robberies. *International Statistics at NationMaster.com*. Retrieved February 11, 2018, from http://www.nationmaster.com/country-info/stats/Crime/Robberies

Hunter, M. (2010). *Love in the Time of Aids: Inequality, Gender and Rights in South Africa*. Bloomington: Indiana University Press.
Hurtig, J. (2008). *Coming of Age in Times of Crisis: Youth, Schooling, and Patriarchy in a Venezuelan Town*. New York: Palgrave Macmillan.
Jackson, M. (2005). *Existential Anthropology: Events, Exigencies and Effects*. New York: Berghahn Books.
Jackson, M. (2012). *Between One and One Another*. Berkeley: University of California Press.
Jansen, J. D. (2012, September 27). Seven Dangerous Shifts in the Public Education Crisis. Presidential Address, South African Institute of Race Relations. Retrieved June 23, 2015, from http://www.politicsweb.co.za/politicsweb/view/politicsweb/en/page71619?oid=328972&sn=Detail&pid=71616
Jeffrey, C. (2010). *Timepass: Youth, Class, and the Politics of Waiting in India*. Stanford: Stanford University Press.
Jeffrey, C., Jeffery, P., & Jeffery, R. (2008). *Degrees Without Freedom?: Education, Masculinities, and Unemployment in North India*. Stanford: Stanford University Press.
Laidlaw, J. (2002). For an Anthropology of Ethics and Freedom. *The Journal of the Royal Anthropological Institute, 8*(2), 311–332.
Laidlaw, J. (2010a). Agency and Responsibility: Perhaps You Can Have Too Much of a Good Thing. In M. Lambek (Ed.), *Ordinary Ethics: Anthropology, Language and Action* (pp. 143–164). New York: Fordham University Press.
Laidlaw, J. (2010b). Social Anthropology. In J. Skorupski (Ed.), *The Routledge Companion to Ethics* (pp. 369–383). London: Routledge.
Lambek, M. (2010a). Introduction. In M. Lambek (Ed.), *Ordinary Ethics: Anthropology, Language, and Action* (pp. 1–36). New York: Fordham University Press.
Lambek, M. (2010b). Toward an Ethics of the Act. In M. Lambek (Ed.), *Ordinary Ethics: Anthropology, Language and Action* (pp. 39–63). New York: Fordham University Press.
Lévi-Strauss, C. (1962). *The Savage Mind*. Chicago: University of Chicago Press.
Lucht, H. (2015). The Station Hustle: Ghanaian Migration Brokerage in a Disjointed World. In M. Jackson & A. Piette (Eds.), *What Is Existential Anthropology?* (pp. 104–124). New York: Berghahn.
Manus, V. B. (2011). *Emerging Traditions: Toward a Postcolonial Stylistics of Black South African Fiction in English*. Lanham: Lexington Books.
Mayer, P. (1961). *Townsmen or Tribesmen: Conservatism and the Process of Urbanization in a South African City* (with Contributions by Iona Mayer). Oxford/Cape Town: Oxford University Press.
Mayer, P. (1971). 'Traditional' Manhood Initiation in an Industrial City. The African View. In E. J. De Jager (Ed.), *Man: Anthropological Essays Presented to O.F Raum* (pp. 7–18). Cape Town: Struik.

Meel, B. L. (2005). Community Perception of Traditional Circumcision in a Subregion of the Transkei, Eastern Cape, South Africa. *South African Family Practice, 47*(6), 58–59.

Metz, T. (2007). Toward an African Moral Theory. *Journal of Political Philosophy, 15*(3), 321–341.

Metz, T., & Gaie, J. B. R. (2010). The African Ethic of Ubuntu/Botho: Implications for Research on Morality. *Journal of Moral Education, 39*(3), 273–290.

Mhlahlo, A. P. (2009). *What is Manhood? The Significance of Traditional Circumcision in the Xhosa*. Unpublished MPhil Thesis, Department of Sociology and Anthropology, the Stellenbosch University.

Mills, W. G. (1995). Missionaries, Xhosa Clergy and the Suppression of Traditional Customs. In H. Bredenkamp & R. Ross (Eds.), *Mission and Christianity in South African History* (pp. 153–171). Johannesburg: Witwatersrand University Press.

Moffie. (2014). *Oxford Dictionary* (Online). Retrieved September 29, 2014, from http://www.oxforddictionaries.com/definition/english/moffie

Moore, H. L. (2011). *Still Life: Hopes, Desires and Satisfactions*. Cambridge: Polity Press.

Morris, A., & Hyslop, J. (1991). Education in South Africa: The Present Crisis and the Problems of Reconstruction. *Social Justice, 18*(1/2), 259–270.

Ngxamngxa, A. N. N. (1971). The Function of Circumcision Amongst the Xhosa-Speaking Tribes in Historical Perspective. In E. J. De Jager (Ed.), *Man: Anthropological Essays Presented to O.F Raum* (pp. 183–204). Cape Town: Struik.

Niehaus, I. (2001). *Witchcraft, Power and Politics: Exploring the Occult in the South African Lowveld*. London: Pluto Press.

Niehaus, I. (2012). *Witchcraft and a Life in the New South Africa*. Cambridge: Cambridge University Press.

Ntombana, L. (2011). *An Investigation into the Role of Xhosa Male Initiation in Moral Regeneration*. Unpublished PhD Thesis, Faculty of Arts, Nelson Mandela Metropolitan University.

Ntshangase, D. K. (2002). Language and Language Practices in Soweto. In R. Mesthrie (Ed.), *Language in South Africa* (pp. 407–419). Cambridge: Cambridge University Press.

Nyquist, T. E. (1983). *African Middle Class Elite*. Grahamstown: Institute of Social and Economic Research.

Pascoe, C. J. (2012). *Dude, You're a Fag: Masculinity and Sexuality in High School*. Berkeley/Los Angeles: University of California Press.

Pattenden, O. (2015). Relations of Trust, Questions About Expectations: Reflections on a Photography Project with Young South Africans. *Anthropology in Action, 22*(3), 14–26.

Peires, J. B. (1989). *The Dead Will Arise: Nongqawuse and the Great Xhosa Cattle-Killing Movement*. Johannesburg: Ravan Press.
Puar, J. (2012). Precarity Talk: A Virtual Roundtable with Lauren Berlant, Judith Butler, Bojana Cvejić, Isabell Lorey, Jasbir Puar, and Ana Vujanović. *TDR/The Drama Review, 56*(4), 163–177.
Ratele, K. (2013). Masculinities Without Tradition. *Politikon: South African Journal of Political Studies, 40*(1), 133–156.
Robbins, J. (2004). *Becoming Sinners: Christianity and Moral Torment in a Papua New Guinea Society*. Berkeley: University of California Press.
Robbins, J. (2007). Between Reproduction and Freedom: Morality, Value, and Radical Cultural Change. *Ethnos, 72*(3), 293–314.
Robbins, J. (2009). Morality, Value and Radical Cultural Change. In M. Heintz (Ed.), *The Anthropology of Moralities* (pp. 62–81). Oxford/New York: Berghahn Books.
Sayed, Y., & Ahmed, R. (2011). Education Quality in Post-apartheid South African Policy: Balancing Equity, Diversity, Rights and Participation. *Comparative Education, 47*(1), 103–118.
Spener, D. (2007). *Cruces Clandestinos Y Movidas Rascuaches: Strategies of Migrant Resistance at the Mexico-U.S. Border.* Paper Prepared for Delivery at the 2007 Congress of the Latin American Studies Association, Montréal, Canada September 5–8, 2007. Retrieved July 02, 2013, from http://www.trinity.edu/dspener/clandestinecrossings/related%20articles/movidas%20rascuaches%20lasa%202007.pdf
Stambach, A. (2000). *Lessons from Mount Kilimanjaro: Schooling, Community, and Gender in East Africa*. New York: Routledge.
Stambach, A. (2005). Rallying the Armies or Bridging the Gulf: Questioning the Significance of Faith-Based Educational Initiatives in a Global Age. *Indiana Journal of Global Legal Studies, 12*(1), 205–226.
Stambach, A. (2010). *Faith in Schools: Religion, Education and American Evangelicals in East Africa*. Stanford: Stanford University Press.
Statistics South Africa (SSA). (2011). *Makana* (2011 Census). Retrieved January 12, 2012, from http://beta2.statssa.gov.za/?page_id=993&id=makana-municipality
Stone, G. L. (2002). The Lexicon and Sociolinguistic Codes of the Working-Class Afrikaans-Speaking Cape Peninsula Coloured Community. In R. Mesthrie (Ed.), *Language in South Africa* (pp. 381–397). Cambridge: Cambridge University Press.
Swanson, D. M. (2009). Where Have All the Fishes Gone? Living Ubuntu as an Ethics of Research and Pedagogical Engagement. In D. M. Caracciolo & A. M. Mungai (Eds.), *In the Spirit of Ubuntu: Stories of Teaching and Research* (pp. 2–22). Rotterdam: Sense.

Swartz, S., Harding, J. H., & De Lannoy, A. (2012). Ikasi Style and the Quiet Violence of Dreams: A Critique of Youth Belonging in Post-apartheid South Africa. *Comparative Education, 48*(1), 27–40.
Valentine, B. L. (1978). *Hustling and Other Hard Work: Life Styles in the Ghetto.* New York: Free Press.
Vincent, L. (2008). 'Boys Will Be Boys': Traditional Xhosa Male Circumcision, HIV and Sexual Socialisation in Contemporary South Africa. *Culture, Health & Sexuality, 10*(5), 431–446.
Wacquant, L. (2008). *Urban Outcasts: A Comparative Sociology of Advanced Marginality.* Cambridge: Polity Press.
Weiss, B. (2002). Thug Realism: Inhabiting Fantasy in Urban Tanzania. *Cultural Anthropology, 17*(1), 93–124.
Williams, B. (2006). *The Sense of the Past: Essays in the History of Philosophy.* Princeton: Princeton University Press.
Willis, P. (1977). *Learning to Labour.* Farnborough: Saxon House.
Wilson, M. (1961). *Reaction to Conquest: Effects of Contact with Europeans on the Pondo of South Africa.* Oxford: Oxford University Press.
Wright, L. (2012). Origins of the Eastern Cape Education Crisis. In L. Wright (Ed.), *South Africa's Education Crisis: Views from the Eastern Cape* (pp. 1–18). Grahamstown: NISC.
Xu, J. (2014). Becoming a Moral Child Amidst China's Moral Crisis: Preschool Discourse and Practices of Sharing in Shanghai. *Ethos, 42*(2), 222–242.
Ybarra-Frausto, T. (1991). Rasquachismo: A Chicano Sensibility. In T. McKenna & Y. Yarbro-Bejaran (Eds.), *Chicano Art: Resistance and Affirmation, 1965–1985* (pp. 155–162). Los Angeles: Wight Art Gallery, University of California.
Zigon, J. (2006). An Ethics of Hope: Working on the Self in Contemporary Moscow. *Anthropology of East Europe Review, 24*(2), 71–80.
Zigon, J. (2007). Moral Breakdown and the Ethical Demand: A Theoretical Framework for an Anthropology of Moralities. *Anthropological Theory, 7*(2), 131–150.
Zigon, J. (2008). *Morality: An Anthropological Perspective.* Oxford: Berg.
Zigon, J. (2009a). Phenomenological Anthropology and Morality: A Reply to Robbins. *Ethnos, 74*(2), 286–288.
Zigon, J. (2009b). Within a Range of Possibilities: Morality and Ethics in Social Life. *Ethnos, 74*(2), 251–276.
Zigon, J. (2010). Moral and Ethical Assemblages: A Response to Fassin and Stoczkowski. *Anthropological Theory, 10*(1-2), 3–15.
Zigon, J. (2011). *'HIV Is God's Blessing': Rehabilitating Morality in Neoliberal Russia.* Berkeley: University of California Press.
Zigon, J. (2013). Human Rights as Moral Progress? A Critique. *Cultural Anthropology, 28*(4), 716–736.

CHAPTER 8

The Way Forward?

Throughout this book, I have employed phenomenological analysis to consider the processes and experiences of learning and education that are integral to the construction of human lives across the world at any one moment in time, examining those moments when individuals learn about the multitude of possible and probable lives that await them and the various techniques with which they might endeavour to create them and examining how these events are conditioned and enabled by the political, environmental, economic, social, and cultural systems we collectively fashion and within which we live. In simple terms, I contend that our understanding of the world is most productively generated by way of our understanding of the format and formation of individualised, lived experiences, and not from methodologies that approach questions and concerns the other way around—that first aim to observe and understand systemic forms of change before employing knowledge of individual lives to support far-reaching and abstracted claims about what is happening in the world.

People *consciously* encounter educative experiences, and *ethically* engage with various notions of moral personhood. Education does not serve to push or channel human lives in definitive directions but is, more accurately, the processes whereby individuals learn about the directions that might be realisable. I would welcome more research that recognises that although we are most often not consciously aware of the embodied possibilities that guide our actions, we are aware of them at the moment when we first attain them (Zigon 2007: 135). This point of departure is important because it allows us to consider reflective and reflexive engagements with pedagogy. Methodologically, this direction allows for considerations of how individual lives materialise differently within shared social, cultural, political, spatial, environmental, and economic contexts. By taking up this line of scholarship, we can sidestep the idea that specific forms of education work in the same manner wherever they materialise in the world. We can also depart from the idea that systems of education take shape independently of the thought processes through which individuals encounter and construct them.

Such directionality can productively enable examinations of the transformative and reproductive qualities of various forms of education, schooling included. When the rightful place of any particular educative, moral discourse is not assumed as given, seemingly inconsequential, everyday interactions and events can reveal political and economic dynamics that serve to maintain relations of power and systems of differentiation. Accordingly, I have considered in the foregoing pages how various historically constituted moral discourses factored in processes of moral education at Ngomso and examined the reasons why certain parties keenly promoted and contested them. More broadly, it is my contention that through such attempts to understand how and why particular moral discourses are cemented and transformed we can better understand the productive qualities of educational institutions and experiences. Most specifically, we might learn more about how the content of moral pedagogy—that is, definable norms, aspirations, values, behaviours, expectations, and so on—is not *transferred* from one party to another, but *transformed* during efforts to relay and imbue such knowledge. By focusing our attention on such processes, we would be able to demonstrate how particular discourses come to have influence in the world through practices of education.

My interlocutors certainly *counted* some moral discourses and *discounted* others during their attempts to bring about particular states of affairs (see Zigon 2014: 747). For instance, when considering the court action and arguments surrounding corporal punishment, I examined human rights discourses, which have regularly underpinned the recent emergence of transnational forms of governmentality associated with schooling. I compared the viewpoints of those who attempted to hold up such moral criteria and those who were less convinced about claims of universal applicability. In doing so, I addressed Zigon's (2013) consideration of the transformative potential of human rights discourses. He (ibid: 732–3, emphasis in original) writes: "the human rights industry . . . ultimately works to foreclose alternative political possibilities for addressing the larger state of affairs of the situation that would make a *difference that matters* for the vast majority of those beings whose lives remain precarious". Zigon (ibid: 732) calls this "the fantasy of progress", meaning a "fantasy of overcoming without going beyond". Given the rather pessimistic tone of Chap. 7 and the fact that schooling cannot guarantee fulfilment, something akin to this fantasy may appear to be evident in the hope that undergirded Ngomso. More broadly, the industry that supports, and is supported by, human rights discourses that promote universal access to schooling as a moral good, can only ever attempt to overcome present inequalities in the world by improving and extending existing structures of governmentality.

As I have shown throughout this book, members of staff and their supporters, like those who worked for the Department of Education more directly, were sure, however, that learners would enjoy an improved state of well-being if they learnt to be attentive to moral conventions and fashioned particular embodied moralities, primarily because they hoped they would then be included in their moral world, as law-abiding and gainfully employed Christians, and the moral institutions of their society (e.g. churches, schools, and marriages).[1] These hopes, which were supported and informed by human rights discourses, do not 'go beyond' the current state of affairs because they are perceptions of what is probable rather than possible. Here, moral education is concerned with preparations for probable and proximal futures, rather than the facilitation of radical transformations. These efforts conjoin with the hope that He will ultimately bring an alternative world into being (Moore 2011: 139). There is, therefore, little to encourage attempts to 'go beyond' the current state of affairs because there is faith that an alternative state of affairs is already coming.

Lucht (2015: 120) suggests that "by putting one's life in the hands of powers beyond one's control (God or whatever name is given to the powers that one is sustained by), these powers are somehow morally obliged to respond, thus creating a moral structure and a sense of existential direction and empowerment in an otherwise unresponsive world." It is perhaps this notion of existential direction and empowerment that is captured by general usages of the word 'hope' and my employment of the same word in previous chapters. The embodied states of hopefulness I have examined were experienced when the individuals in question could see where they were going and felt powerful enough to take themselves there. Religion, like the education provided at Ngomso, provides individuals with clear direction on how to judge and respond to morally contentious and ambiguous situations evermore present in the precarity of today's world (Robbins 2010). The hope that drives Christian-oriented schooling and is taught to those who engage with it is thus not only an orientation to the future but a tool with which individuals might attempt to fashion it.

In detailing such exchanges, I have followed H. Moore's (2011: 80) encouragement that anthropology should be concerned with "the multiply constituted subject"—"accounting both for the workings of power and regimes of truth, and for practices of self-realization and creativity, the techniques of the self". Social practices concerned with constructions of the future never occur independently of relations of power, such as modes of domination and empowerment, but the interplay between politics and self-constituting effort is especially visible during processes of education. To some extent, this work represents a call for more studies that are attuned to the interplay between the intricacies of individualised human lives and globalised or transnational processes of governance that unfold in 'far-away' but intimately connected places. I have shown how the emphasis that Zigon (2007, 2009a, b, 2011) places on instances of 'moral breakdowns' is a relevant and productive theoretical starting point for such studies. His work resonated with my experiences in South Africa, as it was during moments of crisis that individuals most explicitly searched for ways out of, or beyond, their politically constituted predicaments. Of course, we must also recognise that individuals engage in ethically constituted forms of sociality outside of these 'troubling moments' (see Das 2012; Lambek 2010a, b). However, something interesting and important occurs when individuals encounter too many or too few moral possibilities, such that they have to respond to their uncertainty and discomfort by seeking some form of novel direction (see Zigon 2014). It is during these moments of ethical creativity that the intersubjectively constituted and consciously acquired nature of embodied morality is most observable. Such moments should, therefore, be at the heart of anthropological attempts to understand the moral and ethical qualities of human life.

As I hope is clear, interlocutors such as Siseko and Lizo always had a *degree* of ethical freedom to evaluate and navigate the numerous options and opportunities open to them, even if their experiences of socio-economic inequalities meant that they were not especially free to do (see

Laidlaw 2002, 2010). Moreover, learners enrolled with ideas about who they wanted to be and what they hoped the school might do for them. Additionally, despite clear moral boundaries (i.e. rules, policies, guidelines, etc.), they had some room to experiment when refashioning themselves (cf. Mattingly 2013). There was also space for ethics during to-and-fro exchanges between learners and members of staff, as individuals battled to construe and construct particular futures for themselves, each other, and others. One of this book's key arguments is, then, that it is misplaced to see schools as social spaces where ethical freedoms are stripped wholesale from individuals (also see Simpson 2003). Instead, in alignment with Zigon's (2011) analysis of an HIV clinic in Russia and Desjarlais's (1997) analysis of a homeless shelter in Boston, we should begin to see specialist education institutions, in particular, as spaces of inclusion/exclusion where individuals act out desires to live more comfortably or sanely in the world. Such contestation—that is, the nature of learners' educative experiences—relates not only to numerous important material or economic concerns but also the potential embodiment of all manner of moral values and related behaviours.

Collectively and generally, learners, students, pupils, disciples, and any other word that is employed to describe those who are subject to education are always encouraged to learn a possible way of living a moral life. In turn, my contention is that contestation arises within socially constituted fields of education because there are no guarantees that individuals will see this possibility of moral personhood as being appropriate or valuable for all occasions or evaluate it uniformly. As such, no two experiences of education are the same. As Heintz (2009: 9) writes: "the way in which different 'models' of moral life and public values are adopted or rejected by the individual depends on his life experience, with its lived moral dilemmas and personal encounters". In attempting to offer analytical brevity, I have not examined all the possibilities that my young interlocutors encountered. However, I have demonstrated that their experiences at Ngomso and other spaces of social interaction were constitutive of the habitual sensibilities with which they negotiated the world. This ethnography thus supports the claim that we are all *ethical subjects*, who are only ever able to constitute our personal transformations subject to our engagements with others, which are both enabling and constraining to varying degrees (Caduff 2011; Laidlaw 2002; Robbins 2012; Throop 2012). Importantly, these arguments hold true for all those implicated and encompassed by processes of education. We cannot decide who has power over who and in what ways before attempting to understand how individual lives are conditioned and enabled to varying degrees.

Instead, we should examine the modes of cohesion, cooperation, negotiation, exchange, conformity, compromise, rejection, and adherence that maintain and transform balances of power throughout the world (also see Heintz 2009: 11). Such forms of exchange are at the heart of processes of moral education and are only possible because human minds (i.e. one's thoughts, ideas, intentions, memories, etc.) can and do shape other minds.[2] By according the thoughts and words of my young(er) and old(er) interlocutors the same degree of respect, I have shown how the ethically considered judgements and actions of those who sit on the receiving end of internationally constituted, education-oriented, humanitarian interventions are no less influential than the judgements and actions of those parties that conceptualise the interventionalist projects that target them. Such an analytical lens enables us to pick apart hierarchical understandings of humanitarianism and education that conceptualise interventions as being constituted from the top and enacted downwards. We would do better to examine education and humanitarianism as a terrain of interdependent and overlapping ethical claims and balances.

If we are to better understand this terrain and the place and role of schools in today's world, we also need to extend the analytical lens of scholarship beyond the boundaries of classrooms and playgrounds. As earlier chapters have demonstrated, individuals learn, foster, contest, and problematise moralities outside of the school as well as within them. The legacy of these experiences does not dissolve when they walk through the school gate (also see Stafford 2006: 8–11). In this light, schools are clearly not bounded sites of education but spatially determined nexuses of transnational interchange. A major contention of this work is, therefore, that schooling provides just some of those experiences whereby young people learn of the multitude of possible lives that await them and the modes by which they might struggle to create them. Other, equally but differently transformative, educative experiences occur with all manner of individuals, in numerous locations.

Despite such claims, I should point out that schools are some of the most prominent and influential institutions to take responsibility for moral education, peer groups, families, and media outlets included. Whether financed by local or foreign governments, religious institutions of various faiths, or private monies, schools build nations, drive socio-economic development, and bring about various forms of positive (i.e. morally defended and defendable) cultural change. At least, this narrative is championed by those parties that seek to promulgate the idea that school-based educations offer viable and appealing solutions to the world's very visible imperfections. It is because this discourse remains so powerful and widely disseminated that anthropologically minded, or interpretively oriented, studies of this state of affairs are important. With this in mind, I would like to see more studies of the *relationship between* contextualised processes of moral pedagogy that occur inside and outside of schools. For instance, we could do more to examine how the hope offered by education and humanitarian interventions materialises as target beneficiaries traverse social, economic, political, and cultural terrains 'post-intervention'. In particular, we could increase our understanding of how hope is extinguished or refashioned as individuals experience various inequalities that hinder freedoms to traverse and navigate the world.

This analysis of how and why a large proportion of young South Africans do not finish school has rather uniquely focused on the ethical deliberations of young men and women who have, for various reasons, incomplete school educations. The nub of my argument is that those who leave school before its conclusion—adding to the mass of 'drop outs' that so concern those who fear widespread moral decay—do so because the possibility of investing themselves in schooling does not stack up against other options, given the limited fields of opportunity within which they operate. In learning to hustle instead, for example, they can orient themselves to precarity and unpredictability by 'going with the flow', without hoping to control it with the help of His guidance and influence. Such variable judgements of, and orientations to, the future are central to how various forms of economy are maintained in South Africa and in many localities throughout the world.

To better understand these dynamics, I believe we require more longitudinal research that follows young men and women through the processes of schooling and into the post-school reality. In particular, we need to engage ethnographically with those who experience schooling as an unenviable absence of freedom and power. However, it would be positive to also have studies of counter experiences: analysis of individuals who experience fulfilment and achievement through schooling and the post-school reality. Any related scholarship would also do well to attend to the 'feedback loops' of information regarding the struggles and achievements of previous beneficiaries (e.g. learners) that shape the decision-making processes of those presently engaged in humanitarian and education-oriented intervention. We would then be better placed to comprehend patterns of engagement and disengagement and would develop an understanding about how and why various forms of intervention materialise and breakdown as a consequence of these same dynamics.

In Chap. 1, I highlighted Appadurai's (2013: 5) call for "a robust anthropology of the future". With this book, I hope to have demonstrated how practices and sites of education are perfect focal points for such forms of inquiry because they revolve around morally and ethically conceived preparations for the future, including the future of one's own life, the life of others, and humanity as a whole (also see Hall 2017; Stambach 2017). These characteristics also ring true for practices and sites of humanitarianism, which are similarly concerned with the fashioning of collective and individual futures. In this territory of human engagement, we observe how employments of words such as assistance, love, care, intervention, support, donation, fundraising, and volunteering are descriptive of ethical engagements that are laced with potentiality.

Reflecting such observations, throughout this book, the various futures my interlocutors imagined, and the efforts they made to bring them to fruition are accorded a central place in the analysis. This arrangement constitutes an attempt to chart a course for how matters relating to futurity might be more productively addressed, most especially as relating to the fields of humanitarian and education and the overlaps between them. A key component of this directionality relates to the observation that conceptualisations of hoped-for futures never emerge independently of personalised past experiences and collective histories, and neither do the modes by which individuals may attempt to fashion them. Moreover, efforts to fashion alternative futures cannot materialise independently of historically constituted modes of societal (in)equality and uneven distributions of resources and technologies of power. For these reasons, this inquiry posits a historically informed framework of analysis.

More specifically, previous chapters have examined the continuing relationship between the UK and her former colonies. I have employed a methodological technique that has enabled me to follow individuals, discourses, finance, imaginaries, and imaginations backwards and forwards between these two distinct but united localities. I would welcome more 'dual-location' studies of the dynamics of educational and humanitarian funding, public/private intervention, and globalised projects of world-building.[3] Having said that, there were, of course, more than two locations in play during my fieldwork and no one location was somehow bounded nor separate from another. However, the time I spent conducting research in more than one geographical vicinity has enabled me to better conceptualise modes of isolation and enjoinment. This study, for instance, demonstrates how marketing activity can interlink individuals, institutions, and nations even when it is understood more readily through the discourse of fundraising. Similarly, the related movements and engagements of volunteers also strengthen such bonds. From one's reading of previous chapters, I hope it is clear that linkages and modes of mutual constitution that exist between the UK and South Africa are intimately intertwined with the ways that individuals living in the two localities conceptualise the lives of those who live north or south of where they do. It is individuals that collectively produce, cement, and refashion notions of separation and togetherness as they become dependent upon each other and incapable of maintaining forms of life in isolation of each other for various reasons.

Compared to those disciplines and methodologies that do not demand active engagement with the social phenomena under review (i.e. analysis of experiences lived alongside others), anthropologists can better understand the linkages and disjunctures between places united and separated in the world because they subject themselves to these same linkages and disjunctures and treat their own experiences as a source of ethnographic knowledge. Ethnographic knowledge of such dynamics enables us to better conceptualise how the transformative qualities of political epochs, understood through terminologies such as postcolonialism and post-apartheid, are fashioned by the engagements of transnational meshworks of ethically engaged individuals as much by government policies and official channels of diplomacy.

Within the professional fields of education and international development, such structures are most regularly conceptualised with modes of thought that account for individuals (e.g. life stages and personal development), groups (e.g. cohorts and next generations), nations (e.g. countries and governments), and internationally constituted entities (e.g. supranational organisations and collectives). In contrast, throughout this book, I have not employed such classificatory systems because this is not how my interlocutors conceptualised their shared world. Of course, they were capable of making such distinctions. However, these 'scales' of organisation blur into one another because every linked individual constitutes the life of others on account of their linkage to them. This mode of thinking shatters the illusion that definitive and neat conceptualisations of layered or tiered structures of such process are representative of the dynamics in question in such a way that they *are* them. Instead, we can focus on individualised conceptualisations and experiences of transnationally constituted education-oriented humanitarianism as a means to understand what it actually is.

Through such methodologies, we can also begin to develop forms of analysis that capture something of how '(local) worlds' are intimately intertwined both in the ways that they materialise and are constituted and in the ways that individuals imagine how their shared worlds and individual lives might be otherwise. In the case of Africa, these nuances and accuracies are especially important. If we simply assume to know about transnationally constituted forms of governmentality without learning about the locality and lives that constitute related transferences of finance and support, we gain only half the story. Africa is subject to the interventionist tendencies of an external populace, but individuals living on the content also have an ability to affect and fashion the lives of others with whom they may never meet.

This potentiality is clearly depicted in Chaps. 5 and 6, where I argue that the lives of those who supported and donated to the school were both implicated in and fashioned by the materialisations of humanitarianism and education that occurred in South Africa. In other words, their lives were fashioned to a certain extent by the learners and staff at the school, and the past pupils, police officers, government ministers, lawyers, and university students who folded into the activity at the school, as much as this relationship worked the other way around. By paying attention to the two sides of such coins, we can grasp a more full and rounded picture of the dynamics in question.

Throughout this book, I have also scrutinised the transformative capacity of schooling and humanitarianism, exploring both conceptual and practical limits, in order to state some broader arguments about the relationship between systems of intervention, inequality, marginality, and conceptualisations and productions of inclusion/exclusion. In particular, I have argued that attempts to bring about societal inclusion always depend upon historically, culturally, politically, and economically constituted judgements of specialness/abnormality. With such statements, I have built on the knowledge I gained while working in schools in London as well that which I acquired during the ethnographic fieldwork that more directly informs this work. In each locality, I came to see that efforts to bring about educational inclusivity, in particular, like enthusiasms for societal inclusion more broadly, always hinge upon discourses of normality.

Extending this further, I have put forward the argument that efforts to identify special educational needs most readily conjoin with hopes of bringing the world under control, especially when the special needs in question relate to behavioural conformity and disobedience. Such modes of identification—that is, the processes whereby some are separated from 'mainstream' others—are a means by which humans mark degrees and configurations of difference/specialness and attempt to delineate pathways or directionality towards the attainment of some form of end goal. On the surface, such points of conclusion might be achievements of matriculation or graduation, the securing of employment, or more abstract interpretations of human well-being or contentment. Yet, as this ethnography has demonstrated, such endpoints might also be individualised or collective salvation. In such a case, the channelling of human potentiality that takes places in and through education and humanitarian intervention is constitutive of conceptualisations of a collective alignment of directionality—that is, the notion that we are all moving towards a definitive endpoint, regardless of our positionality in this scenario. Such a situation can be contrasted with one whereby human freedom could be constituted in such a way that individuals became empowered to determine the nature of the possible and probable lives they hope to fashion. In this case, the shift would be from an education of cemented aims and milestones towards one of an education for adaptability, where the skills and resources required to roll with the unexpected are given primary importance. As we have seen, when individuals adopt the latter version, as in the case of those young men and women who learn to 'hustle' (Chap. 7), those most strongly tied to the first formation of advancement judge such an abandonment of predictability and finality as being constitutive of modes of exclusion. In other words, such individuals are considered to be living outside of the margins of a society that arranges and orients itself to the future in an antithetical way.

Although this study has focused on humanitarianism and special education, I do not intend for such analytical arguments to only resonant within these fields of human activity. Instead, I have examined mechanisms and productions of inclusion/exclusion in the hope of articulating something important and necessary about the human condition: that is, the idea that a preoccupation with dynamics of inclusion/exclusion represents a particular culturally and historically constituted configuration of thought and endeavour. The mechanism of separating individuals into categories—that is, those who are 'part of' and those who are 'not part of'—is, for example, an integral composite of the notion of civility. Certainly, without a notion of who is and who is not 'civil' (or moral/immoral, pure/impure, developed/backward, etc.) there could be no conceptualisation of a collective and aspirational notion of civility.[4] However, the exact format of this separation and the criteria against which judgements of inclusion/exclusion are made are not universal or ahistorical. Instead, as Zigon (2011: 227) points out, the notion of normality itself emerged post-Enlightenment as individuals responded to the realisation that the "world [could] not entirely [be] determined". Relatedly, individuals 'become special' against some criteria of normality when someone else identifies them as having some abnormal quality. Such modes of identification are always a component of attempts to address some sense of unease in the world. Thus, individuals who ostensibly attempt to assist others by highlighting their specialness inadvertently draw attention to potentially harmful judgements in order that they themselves might live more comfortably.

Through considerations of the multiple lives and voices that constitute such dynamics (e.g. police officer, psychologists, donors, learners, lawyers, and educators), this study illustrates an example of how the constitution and effect of such processes of identification play out in ways that serve to fashion both positive and negative experiences of the world. For instance, I tackled this theme by using theorisations of stigma, exploring not only experiences of stigma and attempts to deal with or overcome it, but also questions regarding how and why the conditions within which stigma emerges are constituted to some extent by the ethical imaginations of those who are attempting to assist these same individuals. Studies that solely consider the institutions and individuals that conceptualise and implement intervention programmes or those targeted by such actions, in isolation of each other, cannot hope to deliver a similarly layered understanding of this same dynamic.

The polyphonic nature of the analysis offered in this book also brings another quality to the forms of understanding that it puts forth: instead of a premeditated conceptualisation of inclusion/exclusion or the related notion of marginality, I have attended to an understanding of the modes by which individuals conceptualise such dynamics. By doing so, I have put forward an argument somewhat implicitly throughout the book: processes whereby exclusion and inclusion and related notions of marginality are conceptualised and mapped operate spatially (i.e. geographically and with reference to locations of physical presence) and vertically (i.e. hierarchically and according to some conceptual schema of differentiation).[5] To make this point clearer, it might help to think about conceptualisations of inclusion/exclusion as being 3D and not 2D. By this, I mean that (1) people conceptually place themselves and each other onto a map of places, spaces, sites, borders, cities, and continents (i.e. according to their conceptualisation of what the world looks like, spatially) and (2) people conceptually map themselves and each other according to positionality relating to hierarchically ordered scales, limits, indexes, and levels, including those that relate to material wealth (i.e. the polarities of rich and poor) and morality (i.e. the polarities of good and evil). In our everyday evaluations and attempts to place ourselves and others within a schema of differentiation, these two axes of conceptualisation do not operate independently of each other nor are they considered in isolation or combination in a two-dimensional manner. Instead, there is a process of '3D modelling' whereby individuals and collectives are placed within a schema of understanding where spatial and vertical modes of differentiation roll into one another to such an extent that such efforts to differentiate can only occur analytically.

This argument points to the deficiencies of other ways of conceptualising the dynamics of inclusion/exclusion. The graphs of economics that map income levels against country of residence, for example, are representations of some degree of differentiation and causation, but they can only fail to capture the modes of thought through which individuals conceptualise their world, their place in the world, and the potential futures that may materialise for themselves and their world. It is these modes of conceptualisation that are given meaning through the terms inclusion/exclusion and marginality, rather than a neatly ordered conceptualisation of earning power or financial wealth, for example. As the previous chapters have illustrated, in the case of my interlocutors' lives, there were numerous mechanisms of differentiation in play, which collectively constituted conceptualisations of inclusion/exclusion by competing, overlapping, and informing each other. For instance, there are those that operated as a spatialised, inside-outside type dynamic (mainstream/special, school/location, South Africa/UK, His Kingdom/Hell, town/location, etc.) and those that operated as a vertical, high-low type dynamic (rich/poor, moral/immoral, clean/dirty, intelligent/unintelligent, etc.).

Throughout previous chapters, I separated these distinctions from one another analytically, but my interlocutors' mapped various possibilities of spatial and vertical potentiality by attending to them in a less cohesive manner. In other words, it is impossible to adequately capture the formations of inclusion/exclusion that undergirded their endeavours and reactions to them. This observation is important because it should force us to ask questions, not about whether certain individuals or groups are or are not included or excluded, but also about *how* this is so. In other words, we are drawn into the territory of asking: how can we enhance our understanding of the mechanisms that create unevennesses in our shared world, which we cannot be comfortable with, by analytically separating out the various dimensions of spatial and vertical distinction that condition this state of affairs? This is a pragmatic endeavour. There is no impetus to seek a definitive answer or recommendation, but, rather, a desire to conceptually fashion depictions of how spatial and vertical modes of exclusionary politics serve to engender disharmony and unenviable experiences of hopelessness that would be visible to others. More broadly, the task is to understand how individuals make sense of our shared world so that we might better understand the unacceptable statuses of our shared world.

In addition to what has just been said, there is also the issue of temporal mechanisms of inclusion and exclusion. In other words, we must also be attentive to the processes whereby judgements are made regarding one's status relative to something that someone else has done in the past or might do in the future. The relevance of this claim is evident in the observation that individuals experience inclusion and exclusion subject to judgements of their past and plans for the future. One only has to think about how such processes work within the context of refugees and asylum seekers to understand how such processes are politically significant (see Cabot 2013). Likewise, in the case of my research, those included were included in a materialising collective future, and, perhaps, forgiven for their engagements or actions in the past. During such mundane interchanges, individuals are not only mapped according to some spatialised notion of inclusion nor some hierarchical schema but also with reference to a temporal framework of history and potentiality.

As such, this book has argued that individuals can experience forms of economic, political, cultural, and social exclusion on account of something that materialised in the past and over which they have no control going forward. Productions of inclusion and exclusion are therefore dynamics of readjustment and rebuilding. There are descriptive terms for fashioned interpretations of the past and imaginations of the future. For individuals, they are essential because they not only allow for judgements and engagements with others but also conceptualisations of one's own place within structurings of the past and future. Individuals are able to ask: How might I be included or excluded? How might I traverse away from the constitution of my past and supersede my present circumstances? How might I move on or move beyond? Who might I join with or who might join with me? I would contend that such modes of existential reflection fuel the scenarios of inclusion and exclusion that scholarship more readily reflects back upon as being a composite component of the world as already constructed. As such, future scholarship would do well to consider dynamics of inclusion/exclusion through the lens of a spatial, vertical, and temporal frame of reference.

These three modes of inclusion/exclusion—that is, spatial, temporal, and hierarchical—are tied to the notion of modernity, which functions as a differentiator of marginal and central statuses. To be modern is to be included in the world of the modern, to sit outside is to not have arrived yet or to be lagging behind. This line of argument has been explored by Ferguson (2006: 185), who argues, "The modernization narrative was a story not just about cultural difference, but also about global hierarchy and historical time, and it combined these three elements in a unique and powerful (if ultimately mistaken) way". Donors, volunteers, and supporters regularly invoked forms of historical comparison in order to conceptualise what they saw and experienced in South Africa, suggesting that such a scheme of thought continues to have resonance beyond the academy. However, Ferguson argues that the framework of modernity no longer dovetails with real-world events, if it ever did. In particular, he suggests that the framework makes a causal link between hierarchical advancement (i.e. positive shifts in status) and the passing of time that doesn't marry with increasing levels of inequality and economic disjuncture in the world. If we recognise this and depart from developmental notions of modernity, we are left in a position whereby individuals and nations are not linked by "developmental stairways" but separated by exclusionary "edge, walls and borders" (ibid: 189). Many of my interlocutors experienced such a transition, reflecting upon it before fashioning engagements with modes of future-making that are not captured by the modernisation framework. For instance, Siseko turned to a sangoma when he could see no other route into the modes of societal inclusion he had been seeking. I would argue that this shift in positionality is evidence of cultural plurality and his capacity to endure the experience of being excluded from the restructuring of wealth that has accompanied the post-apartheid period.

Once uncoupled from the temporally organised claim that everybody will advance in time with and through processes of development, hierarchically arranged modes of inclusion and exclusion associated with modernity become disentangled from promises of entitlement (ibid: 189). In other words, claims that everyone will come to enjoy the same economic standard of living in time, begin to look a little hollow. Ferguson (ibid: 190) contends that "the optimistic mood of a developmentalist era has – at least, in some specific social locations – given way to a much bleaker view that identifies 'Africa' with an unchanging future of hardship and suffering". Many of my interlocutors would recognise the conditions of their own lives in this statement. However, what I have endeavoured to show through my ethnography is that even in specific social locations multiple conceptualisations of the temporal conditions and potentialities of individual and collective lives can coexist and overlap. For some individuals in a locality, the future can appear bright; there is a sense that it will be different with time. However, for others, the scenario is more akin to repetition or regression. It is my contention that such conflicting frames of reference are powerfully constituted and transformed during processes of education and humanitarianism.

Whether or not particular frameworks of temporality are consolidated or dispensed with depends upon the relative power of those social processes that stand to embed them in arrangements of sociality. This dynamic was evident when the Xhosa took their time to acknowledge the validity of promises of salvation because their temporal horizons and conceptualisations of futurity meant that such discourses appeared ill-informed and irrelevant, to some extent at least. Schooling and humanitarianism must similarly work to shape temporal dispositions if they are to continue to be acknowledged as relevant. In the absence of such alignment, these endeavours would simply fall away, to be replaced by some other project of world-building.

I would argue that such a process may already be taking place. Ferguson (ibid: 186–7) has argued that "in a world where developmental patience has little to recommend it, the promise of modernization increasingly appears as a broken promise, and the mapped-out pathways leading from the Third World to the First World turn out to have been bricked up". My ethnography demonstrates that, for some, the modernising notion of schooling is very much experienced as a false hope or broken promise. Those who have already come to know that the guarantees of employment and betterment that are so central to discourses of schooling are not guaranteed to materialise are already sharing their dissatisfactions with those who are younger and following their lead. This dialogue threatens to unhinge the unrelenting rollout of schooling worldwide and upset those policies and programmes that harbour imaginations of full enrolment, the most modern of dreams.

Those who are engaged in constituting and promoting a model of educational and developmental uplift have not yet caught up with disengagements and distrust in the efficacy and validity of their framework for future-building. To some extent, they are peddling a solution that is, in the eyes of many, already premised upon a false logic. It is as though they have organised a party and can't figure out why so many people are leaving early even though the dance floor was never designed to accommodate everyone who wanted to dance. Nonetheless, they are already selling tickets for next year's event because they enjoyed similar parties when they were younger, and because they have faith that it will be an improved event for all. Some of the young people targeted are buying tickets, dressing appropriately, and learning the moves in preparation. However, others are one step ahead already, having witnessed the limits of the transformative capacity of schooling first hand, through their observations of loved ones and individuals living locally. They're pursing other options—husting from sunrise to sundown, writing their own music, and creating their own parties. The disruption they create inadvertently strengthens the resolve of those intent on bringing them inside. Backwards and forwards, in a state of precarity for all, the merry dance continues.

Notes

1. An insight from Williams (1993 [1985]: 47–8) sheds light on this line of analysis, he writes: "we [as adults] have much reason for, and little reason against, bringing up [our] children within the ethical world we inhabit" and "have little reason to believe that they will be happier if excluded from the ethical institutions of society". While it may be possible for an academic to step outside, or attempt to 'go beyond', the current state of affairs—in her thinking and analysis, if not in her broader engagements with the world—it would seem more controversial for children to be taught to do likewise at all times. For instance, a five-year-old would soon find herself in a precarious position if she was taught *always* to attempt to 'go beyond' socially constituted directives and moral discourses. Some parents who live such an existence—that is, those who consciously inhabit a revolutionary or anarchistic position counter to 'the mainstream'—may wish the same for their offspring.

However, this course of action would clearly represent a particular moral orientation to the world that would be open to critic, as with the encouragement that a child should attend school.

2. Jackson (2012: 2–3) offers a more articulate version of the claim that 'minds shape other minds' when he uses the term intersubjectivity to argue that "neither complete detachment nor complete engagement" from/with others "is a real ontological possibility". It is from this starting point that the rest of the paragraph takes shape.

3. Stambach (2010) employed a similar 'dual research site' technique when studying the relationship between American evangelicals and process of education in Tanzania. Likewise, O'Neill (2013) spent time in the US and Guatemala to better understand how mechanics of the Christianised charity that unites these two localities. Both of these studies illustrate the positive qualities of the kind of methodology that I am proposing.

4. This statement was informed by the work of Jeffery Alexander. He (2006: 55) writes: "just as there is no developed religion that does not divide the world into the saved and the damned, there is no civil discourse that does not conceptualize the world into those who deserve inclusion and those who do not".

5. To some extent, this conceptualisation of vertical and spatial configurations of inclusion and exclusion was informed by the analysis offered by Ferguson's (2006: 89–112) chapter on *Transnational Topographies of Power*. Although Ferguson is not so much explicitly concerned with configurations of inclusion and exclusion, he is attentive to distinctions between groups, most especially the lines drawn between agents of the state and civil society. His work got me thinking about how various conceptualisations of locality and power enable individuals to categorise initiatives and interventions as being attributable to certain parties when, in reality, such distinctions are often more conceptual than actual.

Bibliography

Alexander, J. (2006). *The Civil Sphere*. New York: Oxford University Press.

Appadurai, A. (2013). *The Future as Cultural Fact: Essays on the Global Condition*. London/New York: Verso.

Cabot, H. (2013). The Social Aesthetics of Eligibility: NGO Aid and Indeterminacy in the Greek Asylum Process. *American Ethnologist, 40*(3), 452–466.

Caduff, C. (2011). Anthropology's Ethics: Moral Positionalism, Cultural Relativism, and Critical Analysis. *Anthropological Theory, 11*(4), 465–480.

Das, V. (2012). Ordinary Ethics. In D. Fassin (Ed.), *A Companion to Moral Anthropology* (pp. 133–149). Hoboken: Wiley.

Desjarlais, R. (1997). *Shelter Blues: Sanity and Selfhood Among the Homeless*. Philadelphia: University of Pennsylvania Press.
Ferguson, J. (2006). *Global Shadows: Africa in the Neoliberal World Order*. Durham: Duke University Press.
Hall, K. D. (2017). Reflections on Student Futures and Political Possibilities: An Afterword. In A. Stambach & K. D. Hall (Eds.), *Anthropological Perspectives on Student Futures: Youth and the Politics of Possibility*. New York: Palgrave Macmillan.
Heintz, M. (2009). Introduction: Why There Should Be an Anthropology of Moralities. In M. Heintz (Ed.), *The Anthropology of Moralities* (pp. 1–19). Oxford/New York: Berghahn Books.
Jackson, M. (2012). *Between One and One Another*. Berkeley: University of California Press.
Laidlaw, J. (2002). For an Anthropology of Ethics and Freedom. *The Journal of the Royal Anthropological Institute, 8*(2), 311–332.
Laidlaw, J. (2010). Social Anthropology. In J. Skorupski (Ed.), *The Routledge Companion to Ethics* (pp. 369–383). London: Routledge.
Lambek, M. (2010a). Introduction. In M. Lambek (Ed.), *Ordinary Ethics: Anthropology, Language, and Action* (pp. 1–36). New York: Fordham University Press.
Lambek, M. (2010b). Toward an Ethics of the Act. In M. Lambek (Ed.), *Ordinary Ethics: Anthropology, Language and Action* (pp. 39–63). New York: Fordham University Press.
Lucht, H. (2015). The Station Hustle: Ghanaian Migration Brokerage in a Disjointed World. In M. Jackson & A. Piette (Eds.), *What Is Existential Anthropology?* (pp. 104–124). New York: Berghahn.
Mattingly, C. (2013). Moral Selves and Moral Scenes: Narrative Experiments in Everyday Life. *Ethnos, 78*(3), 301–327.
Moore, H. L. (2011). *Still Life: Hopes, Desires and Satisfactions*. Cambridge: Polity Press.
O'Neill, K. L. (2013). Left Behind: Security, Salvation, and the Subject of Prevention. *Cultural Anthropology, 28*(2), 204–226.
Robbins, J. (2010). On the Pleasures and Dangers of Culpability. *Critique of Anthropology, 30*(1), 122–128.
Robbins, J. (2012). On Becoming Ethical Subjects: Freedom, Constraint, and the Anthropology of Morality. *Anthropology of This Century*, (5). Retrieved March 19, 2014, from http://aotcpress.com/articles/ethical-subjects-freedom-constraint-anthropology-morality/
Simpson, A. (2003). *Half London in Zambia: Contested Identities in a Catholic Mission School*. Edinburgh: Edinburgh University Press.
Stafford, C. (2006). *The Roads of Chinese Childhood: Learning and Identification in Angang*. Cambridge: Cambridge University Press.

Stambach, A. (2010). *Faith in Schools: Religion, Education and American Evangelicals in East Africa*. Stanford: Stanford University Press.
Stambach, A. (2017). Introduction. In A. Stambach & K. D. Hall (Eds.), *Anthropological Perspectives on Student Futures: Youth and the Politics of Possibility*. New York: Palgrave Macmillan.
Throop, C. J. (2012). Moral Sentiments. In D. Fassin (Ed.), *A Companion to Moral Anthropology* (pp. 150–168). Chichester: Wiley.
Williams, B. (1993). *Ethics and the Limits of Philosophy*. London: Fontana Press.
Zigon, J. (2007). Moral Breakdown and the Ethical Demand: A Theoretical Framework for an Anthropology of Moralities. *Anthropological Theory, 7*(2), 131–150.
Zigon, J. (2009a). Hope Dies Last: Two Aspects of Hope in Contemporary Moscow. *Anthropological Theory, 9*(3), 253–271.
Zigon, J. (2009b). Phenomenological Anthropology and Morality: A Reply to Robbins. *Ethnos, 74*(2), 286–288.
Zigon, J. (2011). *'HIV Is God's Blessing': Rehabilitating Morality in Neoliberal Russia*. Berkeley: University of California Press.
Zigon, J. (2013). Human Rights as Moral Progress? A Critique. *Cultural Anthropology, 28*(4), 716–736.
Zigon, J. (2014). An Ethics of Dwelling and a Politics of World-Building: A Critical Response to Ordinary Ethics. *Journal of the Royal Anthropological Institute, 20*, 746–764.

Bibliography

Abdi, A. A. (2002). *Culture, Education, and Development in South Africa: Historical and Contemporary Perspectives*. Westport: Bergin and Garvey.

Abdi, A. A. (2006). Culture of Education, Social Development, and Globalization: Historical and Current Analyses of Africa. In A. Abdi, K. P. Puplampu, & G. J. Sefa Dei (Eds.), *African Education and Globalization: Critical Perspectives* (pp. 13–30). Oxford: Lexington Books.

Abdi, A. A., & Cleghorn, A. (2005). Sociology of Education: Theoretical and Conceptual Perspectives. In A. A. Abdi & A. Cleghorn (Eds.), *Issues in African Education: Sociological Perspectives* (pp. 3–24). New York/Basingstoke: Palgrave Macmillan.

Abebe, T. (2008). *Ethiopian Childhoods: A Case Study of the Lives of Orphans and Working Children*. Unpublished PhD Thesis, Norwegian University of Science and Technology, Faculty of Social Sciences and Technology Management, Department of Geography, Norwegian Centre for Child Research. Retrieved June 9, 2014, from http://www.diva-portal.org/smash/get/diva2:123904/FULLTEXT01.pdf

Abrahams, R. (1996). Vigilantism: Order and Disorder on the Frontiers of the State. In O. Harris (Ed.), *Inside and Outside the Law: Anthropological Studies of Authority and Ambiguity*. London: Routledge.

Abrahams, R. (1998). *Vigilant Citizens: Vigilantism and the State*. Oxford: Polity Press.

Abrams, P. (1988). Notes on the Difficulty of Studying the State (1977). *Journal of Historical Sociology, 1*(1), 58–89.

Abrams, L. (2001). Ideals of Womanhood in Victorian Britain. *BBC Online*. Retrieved September 24, 2015, from http://www.bbc.co.uk/history/trail/victorian_britain/women_home/ideals_womanhood_07.shtml

Admin. (2014). Rotten to the Core. *Herald Live* (online). Retrieved April 25, 2015, from http://www.heraldlive.co.za/rotten-to-the-core/

Agamben, G. (2005). *State of Exception*. Chicago: University of Chicago Press.

Alexander, J. (2006). *The Civil Sphere*. New York: Oxford University Press.

Alexander, T. (2013). *The Human Eros: Eco-ontology and the Aesthetics of Existence*. New York: Fordham University Press.

Allahyari, R. A. (2000). *Visions of Charity Volunteer Workers and Moral Community*. Berkeley/Los Angeles: University of California Press.

Allen, K. (2012). South Africa Education Crisis Fuels State School Exodus. *BBC Online*. Retrieved March 4, 2014, from http://www.bbc.co.uk/news/world-africa-17315157

Allman, J. (1994). Making Mothers: Missionaries, Medical Officers, and Women's Work in Colonial Asante, 1924–45. *History Workshop Journal, 38*, 23–47.

Anderson, K. (2005). Relatedness and Investment in Children in South Africa. *Human Nature, 16*(1), 1–31.

Anderson, K., Kaplan, H., Lam, D., & Lancaster, J. (1999). Paternal Care by Genetic Fathers and Stepfathers II: Reports by Xhosa High School Students. *Evolution and Human Behavior, 20*(6), 433–451.

Anderson-Levitt, K. (2003). A World Culture of Schooling? In K. Anderson-Levitt (Ed.), *Local Meanings, Global Schooling: Anthropology and World Culture Theory* (pp. 1–26). New York: Palgrave Macmillan.

Anonymous. Details omitted in order to maintain the anonymity of interlocutors.

Appadurai, A. (2013). *The Future as Cultural Fact: Essays on the Global Condition*. London/New York: Verso.

Apthorpe, R. (2011). Coda. With Alice in Aidland: A Seriously Satirical Allegory. In D. Mosse (Ed.), *Adventures in Aidland: The Anthropology of Professionals in International Development* (pp. 199–219). New York/Oxford: Berghahn Books.

Apthorpe, R. (2013). *Post-pieties Humanitarianisms, International Relations, Ex Ante Evaluation, and Anthropology*. Retrieved May 4, 2015, from http://www.raymondapthorpe.com/

Asad, T. (1993). *Genealogies of Religion*. Baltimore: Johns Hopkins University Press.

Ashforth, A. (2005). *Witchcraft, Violence, and Democracy in South Africa*. Chicago: University of Chicago Press.

Ashley, M. (1974). African Education and Society in the Nineteenth Century Eastern Cape. In C. Saunders & R. Derricourt (Eds.), *Beyond the Cape Frontier* (pp. 199–212). London: Longman.

Association of Christian Counsellors in South Africa. (2014). *ACC in SA (Homepage)*. Retrieved January 18, 2013, from http://www.accinsa.co.za/

Atkinson, D. (2007). Taking to the Streets: Has Developmental Local Government Failed in South Africa? In S. Buhlungu, D. Johnson, R. Southall, & J. Lutchman (Eds.), *State of the Nation South Africa*. Cape Town: Human Science Research Council Press.

άτακτους. (2015). *Glosbe, The Multilingual Online Dictionary*. Retrieved May 24, 2015, from https://glosbe.com/el/en/%CE%AC%CF%84%CE%B1%CE%BA %CF%84%CE%BF%CF%85%CF%82

Ballard, R., Habib, A., & Valodia, I. (2006). In R. Ballard, A. Habib, & I. Valodia (Eds.), *Voices of Protest: Social Movements in Post-apartheid South Africa*. Scottsville: University of KwaZulu-Natal Press.

Bank, L. (2011). *Home Spaces, Street Styles: Contesting Power and Identity in a South African City*. London: Pluto Press.

Barchiesi, F. (2003). Wage Labor, Precarious Employment and Social Inclusion in the Making of South Africa's Post-apartheid Transition. *African Studies Review*, 51(2), 119–142.

Barchiesi, F. (2011). *Precarious Liberation: Workers, the State and Contested Social Citizenship in Post-apartheid South Africa*. Scottsville: University of Kwa-Zulu Natal Press.

Barnett, C., & Land, D. (2007). Geographies of Generosity: Beyond the 'Moral Turn'. *Geoforum*, 38(6), 1065–1075.

Basopu, P. M. (2010). *Assessing Challenges of Corruption in the Eastern Cape Department of Education*. Unpublished MPA thesis, the University of Fort Hare. Retrieved February 04, 2018, from https://www.academia.edu/14886280/ ASSESSING_CHALLENGES_OF_CORRUPTION_IN_THE_EASTERN_ CAPE_DEPARTMENT_OF_EDUCATION

Bayaga, A., & Louw, J. (2011). Moral Degeneration: Crisis in South African Schools? *Journal of Social Science*, 28(3), 199–210.

BBC. (2006). The Spread of AIDS in Africa. *BBC Online*. Retrieved August 12, 2015, from http://www.bbc.co.uk/education/clips/zcdnvcw

BBC. (2012). South Africa Mine Strikes: Police Fire Tear Gas. *BBC Online*. Retrieved March 15, 2013, from http://www.bbc.co.uk/news/world-africa-20137096

BBC. (2013). 'Bongo Bongo Land': UKIP Bans Use of 'Outdated' Phrase. *BBC Online*. Retrieved April 5, 2015, from http://www.bbc.co.uk/news/ uk-23597233

BBC. (2014). Zuma's South African Nkandla Home Upgrade 'Unethical'. *BBC Online*. Retrieved June 24, 2015, from http://www.bbc.co.uk/news/ world-africa-26645400

Beier, A. (1987). *Masterless Men: Vagrancy Problem in Britain, 1560–1640*. London: Methuen.

Belial. (2014). *The Collins English Dictionary* (Online). Retrieved April 11, 2014, from http://www.collinsdictionary.com/dictionary/english/belial?showCoo kiePolicy=true

Bénit-Gbaffou, C. (2006). Police–Community Partnerships in Responses to Crime: Lessons from Yeoville and Observatory. *Urban Forum*, 17(4), 7–32.

Bénit-Gbaffou, C., Morange, M., & Didier, S. (2008). Communities, the Private Sector, and the State: Contested Forms of Security Governance in Cape Town and Johannesburg. *Urban Affairs*, 43(5), 691–717.

Bennell, P., & Monyokolo, M. (1994). A 'Lost Generation'?: Key Findings of a Tracer Survey of Secondary School Leavers in South Africa. *International Journal of Educational Development, 14*(2), 195–206.

Bernauer, J., & Mahon, M. (2006). Michel Foucault's Ethical Imagination. In G. Gutting (Ed.), *The Cambridge Companion to Foucault*. Cambridge: Cambridge University Press.

Besteman, C. (2008). *Transforming Cape Town*. Berkeley: University of California Press.

Bierschenk, T., Chauveau, J. P., & Olivier de Sardan, J. P. (2002). *Local Development Brokers in Africa: The Rise of a New Social Category*. Working Paper No. 13, Department of Anthropology and African Studies. Mainz, Germany: Johannes Gutenberg University.

Blackman, S. J. (2007). 'Hidden Ethnography': Crossing Emotional Borders in Qualitative Accounts of Young People's Lives. *Sociology, 41*(4), 699–716.

Blankenhorn, D. (1995). *Fatherless America: Confronting Our Most Urgent Social Problem*. New York: Basic Books.

Bledsoe, C. (1992). The Cultural Transformation of Western Education in Sierra Leone. *Journal of the International African Institute, 62*(2), 182–202.

Bloch, M. E. (1998). The Uses of Schooling and Literacy in a Zafimaniry Village. In M. E. Bloch (Ed.), *How We Think They Think. Anthropological Approaches to Cognition, Memory and Literacy* (pp. 171–192). Boulder: Westview Press.

Bloch, G. (2009). *The Toxic Mix: What's Wrong with South Africa's Schools and How to Fix It*. Cape Town: Tafelberg.

Bloch, M. E. (2011). The Blob. *Anthropology of This Century*, (1). Retrieved March 4, 2012, from http://aotcpress.com/articles/blob/

Bond, P. (2000). *Elite Transition: From Apartheid to Neoliberalism in South Africa*. London: Pluto Press.

Bonini, N. (2006). The Pencil and the Shepherd's Crook. Ethnography of Maasai Education. *Ethnography and Education, 1*(3), 379–392.

Bordonaro, L. I. (2012). Children's Geographies Agency Does Not Mean Freedom. Cape Verdean Street Children and the Politics of Children's Agency. *Children's Geographies, 10*(4), 413–426.

Bornstein, E. (2001). Child Sponsorship, Evangelism, and Belonging in the Work of World Vision Zimbabwe. *American Ethnologist, 28*(3), 595–622.

Bornstein, E. (2002). Developing Faith: Theologies of Economic Development in Zimbabwe. *Journal of Religion in Africa, 32*(1), 4–31.

Bornstein, E. (2005). *The Spirit of Development: Protestant NGOs, Morality, and Economics in Zimbabwe*. Stanford: Stanford University Press.

Bornstein, E. (2009). The Impulse of Philanthropy. *Cultural Anthropology, 24*(4), 622–651.

Bornstein, E. (2012). *Disquieting Gifts: Humanitarianism in New Delhi*. Stanford: Stanford University Press.

Bornstein, E., & Redfield, P. (2008). *Genealogies of Suffering and the Gift of Care: A Working Paper on the Anthropology of Religion, Secularism, and Humanitarianism.* New York: Social Science Research Council Working Papers.

Bostock, W. W. (2002). South Africa's Language Policy: Controlled Status Enhancement and Reduction. In S. Kossew & D. Schwerdt (Eds.), *Re-imagining Africa: New Critical Perspectives.* New York: Nova.

Bothma, M., Gravett, S., & Swart, E. (2000). The Attitudes of Primary School Teachers Towards Inclusive Education. *South African Journal of Education, 20*(3), 200–204.

Bourdieu, P. (1977). *Outline of a Theory of Practice.* London: Cambridge University Press.

Bourdieu, P. (1980). *The Logic of Practice.* Stanford: Stanford University Press.

Bourdieu, P. (1986). The Forms of Capital. In J. Richardson (Ed.), *Handbook of Theory and Research for the Sociology of Education* (pp. 241–258). New York: Greenwood.

Bourdieu, P. (2000). *Pascalian Meditations.* Stanford: Stanford University Press.

Bourdieu, P., & Passeron, J. (1977). *Reproduction in Education, Society and Culture.* Beverly Hills: Sage.

Bourdieu, P., & Wacquant, L. J. D. (1992). *An Invitation to Reflexive Sociology.* Chicago: University of Chicago Press.

Bourgois, P. (1996a). Confronting Anthropology, Education, and Inner-City Apartheid. *American Anthropologist, 98*(2), 249–258.

Bourgois, P. (1996b). *Search of Respect.* Cambridge: Cambridge University Press.

Bourgois, P. (2002). Understanding Inner-City Poverty: Resistance and Self-Destruction under U.S. Apartheid. In J. Macclancy (Ed.), *Exotic No More: Anthropology on the Front Lines* (pp. 15–32). Chicago: University of Chicago Press.

Bower, C. (2012). *Prohibition of Corporal and Humiliating Punishment in the Home.* Topical Guide (Prepared for PAN: Children). Retrieved April 15, 2013, from http://children.pan.org.za/sites/default/files/publicationdocuments/Prohibition of Parental Corporal Punishment Topical Guide.pdf

Boylston, T. (2015). On Ethnotragedy. *Anthropology of This Century*, (14). Retrieved December 12, 2015, from http://aotcpress.com/archive/issue-14/

Bradford, T. (2012). *Prophetic Identities: Indigenous Missionaries on British Colonial Frontiers.* Vancouver: University of British Columbia Press.

Bradlow, E. (1991). 'The Oldest Charitable Society in South Africa': One Hundred Years and More of the Ladies' Benevolent Society at the Cape of Good Hope. *South African Historical Journal, 25*(1), 77–104.

Brennan, Z. (2010). Sorry Bob, Band Aid Millions DID Pay for Guns: Charity's Man in Ethiopia Tells His Disturbing Story. *Daily Mail Online.* Retrieved March 3, 2013, from http://www.dailymail.co.uk/news/article-1259061/Sorry-Bob-Geldof-Band-Aid-millions-DID-pay-guns.html

Brogden, M. E. (1989). Origins of the South African Police – Institutional Versus Structural Approaches. In W. Scharf (Ed.), *Acta Juridica* (pp. 94–110). Cape Town: Faculty of Law, University of Cape Town.

Bullock, R. (2015). It's Hard to Be a Man: A Month with Three Initiates During the Xhosa Circumcision Ritual. *Africa Geographic Magazine* (Online). Retrieved December 13, 2015, from http://magazine.africageographic.com/weekly/issue-48/xhosa-circumcision-ritual-south-africa-its-hard-to-be-a-man/

Bundy, C. (2014). *Short-Changed? South Africa Since Apartheid.* Athens: Ohio University Press.

Burke, C. (2004). Theories of Childhood. In P. Fass (Ed.), *Encyclopedia of Children and Childhood: In History and Society* (p. 818). New York: Macmillan Reference.

Butler, P. (2011). Donations to Charity Fall 20% in a Year, Study Finds. *The Guardian* (Online). Retrieved March 3, 2013, from http://www.theguardian.com/money/2012/nov/13/charity-donations-fall-uk-survey

Buur, L. (2003). Crime and Punishment on the Margins of the Post-apartheid State. *Anthropology and Humanism, 28*(1), 23–42.

Buur, L. (2008). Democracy & Its Discontent: Vigilantism, Sovereignty and Human Rights in South Africa. *Review of African Political Economy, 35*(118), 571–584.

Buur, L. (2009). The Horror of the Mob: The Violence of Imagination in South Africa. *Critique of Anthropology, 29*(1), 27–46.

Cabot, H. (2013). The Social Aesthetics of Eligibility: NGO Aid and Indeterminacy in the Greek Asylum Process. *American Ethnologist, 40*(3), 452–466.

Caduff, C. (2011). Anthropology's Ethics: Moral Positionalism, Cultural Relativism, and Critical Analysis. *Anthropological Theory, 11*(4), 465–480.

Carl, A., & Johannes, D. (2003). Critical Elements in the Training of Teachers in Peace Education Within the Context of Outcomes-Based Education. *South African Journal of Education, 22*, 162–169.

Carter, R. T. T. (1857). *A Memoir of John Armstrong, D.D., Late Lord Bishop of Grahamstown.* Oxford/London: John Henry and James Parker.

Casas-Cortés, M. (2014). A Genealogy of Precarity: A Toolbox for Rearticulating Fragmented Social Realities In and Out of the Workplace. *Rethinking Marxism, 26*(2), 206–226.

Chauke, P. (2014). Union Won't Protect Corporal Punishers. *The Citizen* (Online). Retrieved December 19, 2015, from http://citizen.co.za/187784/no-union-protection-for-corporal-punishment-dismissals/

Cheney, K. (2007). *Pillars of the Nation: Child Citizens and Ugandan National Development.* Chicago: University of Chicago Press.

Cheney, K. (2010). Expanding Vulnerability, Dwindling Resources: Implications for Orphaned Futures in Uganda. *Childhood in Africa, 2*(1), 8–15.

Chisholm, L. (2002). Continuity and Change in Education Policy Research. In P. Kallaway (Ed.), *The History of Education Under Apartheid 1948–1994* (pp. 94–110). Pinelands: Pearson Education South Africa.

Chisholm, L. (2004). Introduction. In L. Chisholm (Ed.), *Changing Class Education and Social Change in Post-apartheid South Africa* (pp. 1–28). London/New York: Zed Books.

Chisholm, L. (2011). The Challenge of South African Schooling: Dimensions, Targets and Initiatives. In J. Hofmeyr (Ed.), *From Inequality to Inclusive Growth: South Africa's Pursuit of Shared Prosperity in Extraordinary Times*. Cape Town: Institute for Justice and Reconciliation.

Chisholm, L. (2012). *Corruption in Education: The Textbook Saga*. Paper Presented to a Symposium Hosted by the Public Affairs Research Institute (PARI) and Innovations for Successful Societies, Princeton University (at the University of the Witwatersrand, Johannesburg). Retrieved March 1, 2014, from http://pari.org.za/wp-content/uploads/Chisholm-Corruption-in-education.-The-textbook-saga-Aug20121.pdf

Chisholm, L. (2013). The Textbook Saga and Corruption in Education. *Southern African Review of Education, 19*(1), 7–23.

Chisholm, L., & Fuller, B. (1996). Remember People's Education? Shifting Alliances, State-Building and South Africa's Narrowing Policy Agenda. *Journal of Education Policy, 11*(6), 693–716.

Christie, P. (1985). *The Right to Learn: Struggle for Education in South Africa*. Johannesburg: Raven Press.

Christie, P. (1991). *The Right to Learn: The Struggle for Education in South Africa*. Johannesburg: Sached Trust & Ravan.

Christie, P. (1999). Inclusive Education in South Africa: Achieving Equity and Majority Rights. In H. Daniels & P. Garner (Eds.), *Inclusive Education*. London: Kogan Page.

Christie, P. (2006). Changing Regimes: Governmentality and Education Policy in Post-apartheid South Africa. *International Journal of Educational Development, 26*(4), 373–381.

Christie, P., & Collins, C. (1982). Bantu Education: Apartheid Ideology or Labour Reproduction? *Comparative Education, 18*(1), 59–75.

Christou, M. (2002). Who Needs Imagination? An Interview with Professor Paul Harris. *Harvard Graduate School of Education* (Online). Retrieved September 15, 2013, from http://www.gse.harvard.edu/news/features/harris03012002.html

Church of England. (2015). *Wholeness and Healing, Theological Introduction*. Retrieved September 18, 2015, from https://www.churchofengland.org/prayer-worship/worship/texts/pastoral/healing/healingintro.aspx

Cicognani, L. (2004). *To Punish or Discipline: Teachers Attitudes Towards the Abolition of Corporal Punishment*. Unpublished M.Ed. Research Report, School of Human and Community Development, University of the Witwatersrand.

Clissold, M. L. (2010). 'Pornography of Poverty': An Anthropological Perspective into Humanitarian Fundraising Campaigns. Unpublished MA dissertation, Social Anthropology of Development, SOAS, London. Retrieved January 14, 2014, from http://www.melissaclissold.com/uploads/2/5/8/8/25889170/2010_melissa_lara_clissold_soas_dissertation_pornography_of_poverty.pdf

Cobbing, J. R. D. (2015). South Africa, History. *Encyclopaedia Britannica* (Online). Retrieved April 12, 2015, from http://www.britannica.com/place/South-Africa/History#ref480694

Cole, T. (2012). The White-Savior Industrial Complex. *The Atlantic* (Online). Retrieved July 27, 2014, from http://www.theatlantic.com/international/archive/2012/03/the-white-savior-industrial-complex/254843/

Collier, J. (1973). *Alaskan Eskimo Education: A Film Analysis of Cultural Confrontation in the Schools*. New York: Holt, Rinehart and Winston.

Collis, V. (2013). *Anxious Records: Race, Imperial Belonging, and the Black Literary Imagination, 1900–1946*. Unpublished Ph.D. dissertation, Department of English and Comparative Literature, Columbia University. Retrieved July 23, 2014, from http://academiccommons.columbia.edu/catalog/ac:161742

Colson, E. (1960). *The Social Organization of the Gwembe Tonga*. Manchester: Manchester University Press.

Comaroff, J., & Comaroff, J. (1986). Christianity and Colonialism in South Africa. *American Ethnologist*, 13(1), 1–22.

Comaroff, J., & Comaroff, J. (1997). *Of Revelation and Revolution, Volume 2: The Dialectics of Modernity on a South African Frontier*. Chicago: The University of Chicago Press.

Comaroff, J., & Comaroff, J. (2005). Reflections on Youth. In F. De Boeck & A. Honwana (Eds.), *Makers & Breakers: Children & Youth in Postcolonial Africa* (pp. 19–30). Trenton: Africa World Press.

Comaroff, J., & Comaroff, J. (2007a). Popular Justice in the New South Africa: Policing the Boundaries of Freedom. In T. R. Tyle (Ed.), *Legitimacy and Criminal Justice: An International Perspective* (pp. 215–238). New York: Russell Sage Foundation.

Comaroff, J., & Comaroff, J. (2007b). Law and Disorder in the Postcolony. *Social Anthropology*, 15(2), 133–152.

Compretta, C. E. (2012). *Growing Gaps: Children's Experiences of Inequality in a Faith-Based Afterschool Program in the U.S. South*. Unpublished PhD Dissertation, College of Arts and Sciences (Department of Anthropology), University of Kentucky. Retrieved April 8, 2014, from http://uknowledge.uky.edu/anthro_etds/4/

Connolly, M. (1990). Adrift in the City. A Comparative Study of Street Children in Bogotá, Colombia and Guatemala City. *Child and Youth Services*, 14, 129–149.

Connolly, M., & Ennew, J. (1996). Introduction: Children Out of Place. *Childhood*, 3(2), 131–146.

Conran, M. (2011). They Really Love Me!: Intimacy in Volunteer Tourism. *Annals of Tourism Research, 38*(4), 1454–1473.

Cornerstone Institute. (2014). *Cornerstone: Learn to Change the World.* Retrieved October 1, 2014, from http://www.cornerstone.ac.za/about.php

Crais, C. (1992). *White Supremacy and Black Resistance in Pre-industrial South Africa: The Making of the Colonial Order in the Eastern Cape, 1770–1865.* Cambridge: Cambridge University Press.

Crais, C. (2011). *Poverty, War, and Violence in South Africa.* Cambridge: Cambridge University Press.

Crapanzano, V. (2014). Must We Be Bad Epistemologists? Illusions of Transparency, the Opaque Other, and Interpretive Foibles. In V. Das, M. Jackson, A. Kleinman, & B. Singh (Eds.), *The Ground Between: Anthropologists Engage Philosophy* (pp. 254–278). Durham: Duke University Press.

Crewe, E., & Axelby, R. (2013). *Anthropology and Development: Culture, Morality and Politics in a Globalised World.* Cambridge: Cambridge University Press.

Crime Stats. (2015). *Crime Stats* (Grahamstown). Retrieved May 26, 2015, from http://crimestatssa.com/precinct.php?id=954

Crossley, N. (1996). *Intersubjectivity: The Fabric of Social Becoming.* London: Sage.

Crouch, L. (1996). Public Education Equity and Efficiency in South Africa: Lessons for Other Countries. *Economics of Education Review, 15*(2), 125–137.

Cunningham, H. (2006). Re-inventing Childhood. *OpenLearn* (Open University Online). Retrieved March 28, 2015, from http://www.open.edu/openlearn/history-the-arts/history/re-inventing-childhood

Dahl, B. (2006). "Too Fat to Be an Orphan": The Moral Semiotics of Food Aid in Botswana. *Cultural Anthropology, 29*(4), 626–647.

Das, V. (2012). Ordinary Ethics. In D. Fassin (Ed.), *A Companion to Moral Anthropology* (pp. 133–149). Hoboken: Wiley.

Das, V., & Poole, D. (2004). State and Its Margins: Comparative Ethnographies. In V. Das & D. Poole (Eds.), *Anthropology in the Margins of the State* (pp. 3–34). Santa Fe: School of American Research Press.

Davies, S. (2010). *History in the Literary Imagination: The Telling of Nongqawuse and the Xhosa Cattle-Killing in South African Literature and Culture (1891–1937).* Unpublished PhD Thesis, St John's College, University of Cambridge. Retrieved August 9, 2012, from https://www.repository.cam.ac.uk/handle/1810/238313

Davies, J., & Spencer, D. (2010). *Emotions in the Field: The Psychology and Anthropology of Fieldwork Experience.* Stanford: Stanford University Press.

Davis, R. (2012). The Great NGO Funding Crisis, Part II. *Daily Maverick* (Online). Retrieved July 15, 2013, from http://www.dailymaverick.co.za/article/2012-10-23-the-great-ngo-funding-crisis-part-ii/#.VCFzAPldV8F

Dawson, H. (2014). Youth Politics: Waiting and Envy in a South African Informal Settlement. *Journal of Southern African Studies, 40*(4), 861–882.

Day, S. (2010). Ethics Between Public and Private: Sex Workers' Relationships in London. In M. Lambek (Ed.), *Ordinary Ethics: Anthropology, Language and Action* (pp. 273-291). New York: Fordham University Press.

Day, S., Stewart, M., & Papataxiarchis, E. (1999). Introduction. In S. Day, M. Stewart, & E. Papataxiarchis (Eds.), *Lilies of the Field: Marginal People Who Live for the Moment*. Oxford: Westview Press.

De Boeck, F., & Honwana, A. (2005). Introduction: Children & Youth in Africa. In F. De Boeck & A. Honwana (Eds.), *Makers & Breakers: Children & Youth in Postcolonial Africa* (pp. 1-18). Oxford: James Curry.

de Clercq, F. (1997). Effective Policies and the Reform Process: An Evaluation of the New Development and Education Macro Policies. In P. Kallaway, G. Kruss, A. Fataar, & G. Donn (Eds.), *Education After Apartheid: South African Education in Transition* (pp. 142-168). Cape Town: UCT Press.

de Klerk, M. (2012). Legacy of Selflessness. *Grocott's Mail* (Online). Retrieved, March 4, 2014, from http://www.grocotts.co.za/content/legacy-selflessness-08-11-2012

de Souza, M. L. (2009). Social Movements in the Face of Criminal Power. *City*, 13(1), 26-52.

de Waal, A. (2002). Anthropology and the Aid Encounter. In J. MacClancy (Ed.), *Exotic No More: Anthropology on the Front Lines* (pp. 251-269). Chicago: University of Chicago Press.

de Waal, M. (2012). Survival Times: Basic Education Wants Billions from Big Business. *Daily Maverick* (Online). Retrieved July 13, 2014, from http://www.dailymaverick.co.za/article/2012-04-12-survival-times-basic-education-wants-billions-from-big-business

de Wet, C. (2002). Factors Influencing the Choice of English as Language of Learning and Teaching (LoLT) – A South African Perspective. *South African Journal of Education*, 22(2), 119-124.

Dean, M. (2010). *Governmentality: Power and Rule in Modern Society*. London: Sage.

Deliwe, D. (1992). *Responses to Western Education Among the Conservative People of Transkei*. Unpublished MA Thesis, Department of Anthropology, Faculty of Humanities, Rhodes University.

Demissie, F. (2012). *Colonial Architecture and Urbanism in Africa*. Farnham: Ashgate.

Demuth, S., & Brown, S. L. (2004). Family Structure, Family Processes, and Adolescent Delinquency: The Significance of Parental Absence Versus Parental Gender. *Journal of Research in Crime and Delinquency*, 41(1), 58-81.

Dennis, M. (2005). *Happy New Year* (Television Programme). Britcom and Tiger Aspect Productions.

Department of Education (DoE). (1996). *South African Schools Act No. 84 of 1996*. Retrieved June 12, 2013, from http://www.education.gov.za/LinkClick.aspx?fileticket=aIolZ6UsZ5U%3D&tabid= 185&mid=1828

Department of Education (DoE). (2001). *Education White Paper 6: Special Needs Education, Building an Inclusive Education and Training System.* Retrieved June 16, 2014, from http://www.education.gov.za/LinkClick.aspx?fileticket=gVFccZLi/tI=

Department of Education (DoE). (2005). *Conceptual and Operational Guidelines for the Implementation of Inclusive Education: Full-Service Schools.* Retrieved March 14, 2013, from http://www.education.gov.za/LinkClick.aspx?fileticket=LgU29rjb2Hg%3D&tabid=452&mid=1036

Department of Education (DoE). (2010). *Guidelines for Full-Service/Inclusive Schools.* Retrieved March 12, 2013, from http://www.education.gov.za/LinkClick.aspx?fileticket=WbxRkIOFaok%3D&tabid=617&mid=2372

Department of Education (DoE) & MIET Africa. (2010). *National Support Pack.* Retrieved June 30, 2012, from http://www.education.gov.za/LinkClick.aspx?fileticket=TPD7RfXMw/U%3D&tabid=675&mid=2517

Department of Health. (2007). *HIV & AIDS and STI Strategic Plan for South Africa 2007–2011.* Retrieved October 24, 2014, from http://data.unaids.org/pub/ExternalDocument/2007/20070604_sa_nsp_final_en.pdf

Department of Health. (2013). *The 2012 National Antenatal Sentinel HIV & Herpes Simplex Type-2 Prevalence Survey in South Africa.* Retrieved May 22, 2014, from http://www.health-e.org.za/wp-content/uploads/2014/05/ASHIVHerp_Report2014_22May2014.pdf

Desai, A. (2002). *We Are the Poor: Community Struggles in Post-apartheid South Africa.* New York: Monthly Review Press.

Desjarlais, R. (1997). *Shelter Blues: Sanity and Selfhood Among the Homeless.* Philadelphia: University of Pennsylvania Press.

Desjarlais, R. (2014). Liberation Upon Hearing: Voice, Morality, and Death in a Buddhist World. *Ethos, 42*(1), 101–118.

DiFruscia, K. T. (2010). Listening to Voices: An Interview with Veena Das. *Altérités, 7*(1), 136–145.

Dixon, B. (2004). Community Policing: 'Cherry Pie' or *Melktert*? *Society in Transition, 35*(2), 251–272.

Dlanga, K. (2014). Change Town Names That Celebrate Our Oppressors. *Mail and Guardian* (Online). Retrieved December 30, 2014, from http://mg.co.za/article/2014-10-01-change-the-names-of-towns-that-celebrate-our-brutal-oppressors

Douglas, M. (1966). *Purity and Danger.* London: Routledge.

Douglas, M. (1984). *Purity and Danger: An Analysis of the Concepts of Pollution and Taboo.* London/New York: Routledge.

Drury, I. (2013). Wasted, the Millions Britain Has Poured into Aid for Congo: Damning Report Reveals EU Projects Have Failed to Deliver Any Results. *Daily Mail* (Online). Retrieved June 13, 2014, from http://www.dailymail.co.uk/news/article-2441580/Wasted-millions-Britain-poured-aid-Congo-Damning-report-reveals-EU-projects-failed-deliver-results.html

DSD, SASSA, & UNICEF. (2012). *The South African Child Support Grant Impact Assessment: Evidence from a Survey of Children, Adolescents and Their Households.* Retrieved February 12, 2014, from http://www.unicef.org/southafrica/SAF_resources_csg2012s.pdf

Dube, E. F. (1985). The Relationship Between Racism and Education in South Africa. *Harvard Education Review, 55*(1), 86–100.

Durham, D. (2008). Apathy and Agency. The Romance of Agency and Youth in Botswana. In J. Cole & D. Durham (Eds.), *Figuring the Future: Globalization and the Temporalities of Children and Youth* (pp. 151–179). Santa Fe: School of Advanced Research Press.

Dying to Be White. (2014). *Daily News* (University of Cape Town). Retrieved October 15, 2015, from http://www.uct.ac.za/dailynews/?id=8821

Eastern Cape Socio Economic Consultative Council (ECSECC). (2011a). *Service Delivery and Condition of Living in the Eastern Cape.* Retrieved March 17, 2015, from http://www.ecsecc.org/files/library/documents/ECSECCLivingStandardsJune2011.pdf

Eastern Cape Socio Economic Consultative Council (ECSECC). (2011b). *Quarterly Economic Update, First Quarter 2011.* East London. Retrieved July 14, 2013, from http://beta2.statssa.gov.za/?page_id=993&id=makana-municipality

Eastern Cape Socio Economic Consultative Council (ECSECC). (2012a). *Poverty Social Statistics 2012.* Retrieved July 14, 2013, from http://www.ecsecc.org/statistics-database

Eastern Cape Socio Economic Consultative Council (ECSECC). (2012b). *Access to Services 2012.* Retrieved December 16, 2014, from http://www.ecsecc.org/statistics-database

Eastern Cape Socio Economic Consultative Council (ECSECC). (2012c). *Eastern Cape Development Indicators, 2012.* Retrieved April 13, 2013, from http://www.ecsecc.org/publication-details/1374/Eastern-Cape-Development-Indicators-2012

Ebadolahi, M. (2008). Using Structural Interdicts and the South African Human Rights Commission to Achieve Judicial Enforcement of Economic and Social Rights in South Africa. *New York University Law Review, 83*(5), 1565–1606.

Eccelstone, K., & Hayes, D. (2009). *The Dangerous Rise of Therapeutic Education.* Abingdon: Routledge.

Educate. (2015). *Online Etymology Dictionary.* Retrieved January 11, 2015, from http://www.etymonline.com/index.php?allowed_in_frame=0&search=educate

Elisha, O. (2008). Moral Ambitions of Grace: The Paradox of Compassion and Accountability in Evangelical Faith-Based Activism. *Cultural Anthropology, 23*(1), 154–189.

Engelbrecht, P. (2006). The Implementation of Inclusive Education in South Africa after Ten Years of Democracy. *European Journal of Psychology of Education, 21*(3), 253–264.

Ennew, J. (1994). Parentless Friends. A Cross-Cultural Examination of Networks Among Street Children and Street Youth. In F. Nestmann & K. Hurrelmann (Eds.), *Social Networks and Social Support in Childhood and Adolescence* (pp. 409–426). Berlin: De Gruyter.

Ennew, J. (2002). Future Generations and Global Standards: Children's Rights at the Start of the Millennium. In J. MacClancy (Ed.), *Exotic No More. Anthropology on the Front Lines* (pp. 338–358). Chicago: University of Chicago Press.

Ennew, J., & Swart-Kruger, J. (2003). Introduction: Homes, Places and Spaces in the Construction of Street Children and Street Youth. *Children, Youth and Environments, 13*(1). Retrieved July 25, 2012, from http://www.colorado.edu/journals/cye

Enslin, P., & Horsthemke, K. (2004). Can Ubuntu Provide a Model for Citizenship Education in African Democracies? *Comparative Education, 40*(4), 545–558.

Epstein, A. (2010). Education Refugees and the Spatial Politics of Childhood Vulnerability. *Childhood in Africa, 2*(1), 16–25.

Erlank, N. (1999). Re-examining Initial Encounters Between Christian Missionaries and the Xhosa, 1820–1850: The Scottish Case. *Kleio, 31,* 6–32.

Escobar, A. (1997). Anthropology and Development. *International Social Science Journal, 49*(154), 497–515.

Fanon, F. (1967). *The Wretched of the Earth.* London: Penguin.

Fanon, F. (1969). *Towards the African Revolution.* New York: Grove Press.

Fanon, F. (1970). *Black Skin, White Masks.* New York: Grove Press.

Faranaaz, V. (2014). Our Courts are Schooling the State. *Mail & Guardian* (Online). Retrieved May 14, 2015, from http://mg.co.za/article/2014-03-14-our-courts-are-schooling-the-state

Fassin, D. (2007). Humanitarianism as a Politics of Life. *Public Culture, 19*(3), 499–520.

Fassin, D. (2010). Critique of Humanitarian Reason. *Public Lecture, Institute for Advanced Study, Princeton University* (Available Online). Retrieved July 15, 2013, from http://www.youtube.com/watch?v=jDT2mYg6mgo

Fassin, D. (2011). A Contribution to the Critique of Moral Reason. *Anthropological Theory, 11*(4), 481–491.

Fassin, D. (2012). *Humanitarian Reason: A Moral History of the Present.* Berkeley: University of California Press.

Fassin, D., & Rechtman, R. (2009). *The Empire of Trauma.* Princeton: Princeton University Press.

Faught, B. C. (2003). *Oxford Movement: A Thematic History of the Tractarians and Their Times.* University Park: Penn State University Press.

Fechter, A. (2014). 'The Good Child': Anthropological Perspectives on Morality and Childhood. *Journal of Moral Education, 43*(2), 37–41.

Ferguson, J. (1994). The Anti-politics Machine: 'Development' and Bureaucratic Power in Lesotho. *The Ecologist, 24*(5), 176–181.

Ferguson, J. (2006). *Global Shadows: Africa in the Neoliberal World Order*. Durham: Duke University Press.

Firth, R. (2011). *We the Tikopia: A Sociological Study of Kinship in Primitive Polynesia*. Abingdon: Routledge.

Fiske, E. B., & Ladd, H. F. (2004). *Elusive Equity: Education Reform in Post-apartheid South Africa*. Washington, DC: Brookings Institution Press.

Flanagan, J. (2014). South African President Jacob Zuma Must Pay Back £14 Million of Taxpayers' Money Used to Build a Swimming Pool, Football Pitch and an Amphitheatre at His Private Compound. *Daily Mail* (Online). Retrieved April 5, 2015, from http://www.dailymail.co.uk/news/article-2584611/South-African-President-Jacob-Zuma-pay-14-million-taxpayers-money-used-build-swimming-pool-football-pitch-amphitheatre-private-compound.html

Fleisch, B. (2008). *Primary Education in Crisis: Why South African Schoolchildren Underachieve in Reading and Mathematics*. Cape Town: Juta.

Flinn, J. (2000). Transmitting Traditional Values in New Schools: Elementary Education of Pulap Atoll. In B. A. U. Levinson (Ed.), *Schooling the Symbolic Animal: Social and Cultural Dimensions of Education* (pp. 123–136). Lanham: Rowman Littlefield.

Flouri, E. (2005). *Fathering & Child Outcomes*. Chichester: Wiley.

Foley, D. (1977). Anthropological Studies of Schooling in Developing Countries: Some Recent Findings and Trends. *Comparative Education Review, 21*(2/3), 311–328.

Foley, D. (1990). *Learning Capitalist Culture: Deep in the Heart of Tejas*. Philadelphia: University of Pennsylvania Press.

Fong, V. L. (2004). *Only Hope: Coming of Age Under China's One-Child Policy*. Stanford: Stanford University Press.

Foreman, J. (2013). How Your Money is Squandered on Foreign Aid. *Daily Mail* (Online). Retrieved November 19, 2014 from http://www.dailymail.co.uk/news/article-2255838/How-money-squandered-foreign-aid.html

Foucault, M. (1976). *Mental Illness and Psychology*. New York: Harper Colophon Books.

Foucault, M. (1977a). *Discipline and Punish: The Birth of the Prison*. London: Penguin.

Foucault, M. (1977b). The Political Function of the Intellectual. *Radical Philosophy, 17*(Summer), 12–14.

Foucault, M. (1982). The Subject and Power. *Critical Inquiry, 8*(4), 777.

Foucault, M. (1997). *Ethics: Subjectivity and Truth* (The Essential Works of Michel Foucault 1954–1984). In P. Rabinow (Ed.). New York: The New Press.

Foucault, M. (2008). In M. Senellart (Ed.), *The Birth of Biopolitics: Lectures at the Collège de France, 1978–1979*. New York: Palgrave Macmillan.

Fourchard, L. (2011). The Politics of Mobilization for Security in South African Townships. *African Affairs, 110*(441), 607–627.

Fraser, G. (2008). On the Genealogy of Morals, Part 4: Is Christianity Cowardly? *The Guardian* (Online). Retrieved May 11, 2012, from http://www.theguardian.com/commentisfree/belief/2008/nov/17/philosophy-religion

Freeman, L. E. (2001). *Knowledge, Education and Social Differentiation Amongst the Betsileo of Fisakana, Highland Madagascar.* Unpublished PhD Thesis, Department of Anthropology, London School of Economics and Political Science.

Freidus, A. (2010). 'Saving' Malawi: Faithful Responses to Orphans and Vulnerable Children. *NAPA Bulletin Special Issue: Intersections of Faith and Development in Local and Global Contexts, 33*(1), 50–67.

Freire, P. (1970). *Pedagogy of the Oppressed.* New York: Continuum.

Friedman, S. (2006). *Participatory Governance and Citizen Action in Post-apartheid South Africa.* Discussion Paper, International Institute for Labour Studies, Geneva. Retrieved September 14, 2013, from http://www.ilo.org/wcmsp5/groups/public/---dgreports/---inst/documents/publication/wcms_193613.pdf

Frost, N. (2005). *Child Welfare: Historical Perspectives.* Abingdon: Routledge.

Fry, C. M. (2012). *An Investigation into the Need for Introducing a Moral Education Programme to Adolescents in South African Schools.* Unpublished M.Ed. Research Report, Faculty of Humanities, University of the Witwatersrand, Johannesburg.

Gadda, A. (2008). *Rights, Foucault and Power: A Critical Analysis of the United Nation Convention on the Rights of the Child.* New Directions in Sociological Research Working Paper Series, The University of Edinburgh. Retrieved July 22, 2014, from http://www.cas.ed.ac.uk/__data/assets/pdf_file/0010/13015/WP31_Gadda.pdf

Gaitskell, D. (1990). Devout Domesticity? A Century of African Women's Christianity in South Africa. In C. Walker (Ed.), *Women and Gender in Southern Africa to 1945* (pp. 251–272). Cape Town: David Philip.

Gardner, R., Cairns, J., & Lowton, D. (2005). *Faith Schools: Consensus or Conflict?* New York: RoutledgeFalmer.

Garifzyanova, A. (2013). Research Emotions in the Field: The View from the Other Side. *World Applied Sciences Journal, 27*(8), 1079–1082.

Gates, B. (2005). Faith Schools and Colleges of Education Since 1800. In R. Gardner, J. Cairns, & D. Lowton (Eds.), *Faith Schools: Consensus or Conflict?* New York: RoutledgeFalmer.

Gay, J., & Cole, M. (1967). *The New Mathematics and an Old Culture: A Study of Learning Among the Kpelle of Liberia.* New York: Rinehart and Winston.

Geertz, C. (1968). Thinking as a Moral Act: Ethical Dimensions of Anthropological Fieldwork in the New States. *The Antioch Review, 28*(2), 139–158.

Giddens, A. (1984). *The Constitution of Society: Outline of the Theory of Structuration.* Cambridge: Polity Press.

Gill, T. (1999). Wage Hunting at the Margins of Urban Japan. In S. Day, E. Papataxiarchis, & M. Stewart (Eds.), *Lilies of the Field: Marginal People Who Live for the Moment*. Oxford: Westview Press.

Glaser, C. (1998). We Must Infiltrate the Tsotsis': Schools Politics and Youth Gangs in Soweto, 1968–1976. *Journal of Southern African Studies, 24*(2), 302–326.

Gluckman, M. (1958). *Analysis of a Social Situation in Modern Zululand* (The Rhodes-Livingstone Papers, 28). New York: Humanities Press.

Gluckman, M. (1970). *Custom and Conflict in Africa*. Oxford: Basil Blackwell.

Goffman, E. (1952). On Cooling the Mark Out. *Psychiatry, 15*(4), 451–463.

Goffman, E. (1959). *The Presentation of Self in Everyday Life*. London: Penguin.

Goffman, E. (1963). *Stigma: Notes on the Management of Spoiled Identity*. New Jersey: Prentice Hall.

Golde, P. (1986). *Women in the Field: Anthropological Experiences*. Berkeley/Los Angeles: University of California Press.

Graeber, D. (2004). *Fragments of an Anarchist Anthropology*. Chicago: Prickly Paradigm Press.

Green, M. (2011). Calculating Compassion: Accounting for Some Categorical Practices in International Development. In D. Mosse (Ed.), *Adventures in Aidland: The Anthropology of Professionals in International Development* (pp. 33–56). New York/Oxford: Berghahn Books.

Grindal, B. (1972). *Growing Up in Two Worlds: Education and Transition Among the Sisala of Northern Ghana*. New York: Holt, Rinehart and Winston.

Hall, K. D. (2017). Reflections on Student Futures and Political Possibilities: An Afterword. In A. Stambach & K. D. Hall (Eds.), *Anthropological Perspectives on Student Futures: Youth and the Politics of Possibility*. New York: Palgrave Macmillan.

Handley, A., Murray, C., & Simeon, R. (2008). Learning to Lose, Learning to Win: Government and Opposition in South Africa's Transition to Democracy. In E. Friedman & J. Wong (Eds.), *Political Transitions in Dominant Party Systems: Learning to Lose* (pp. 191–210). Abingdon: Routledge.

Hansen, T. B. (2006). Performers of Sovereignty: On the Privatization of Security in Urban South Africa. *Critique of Anthropology, 26*(3), 279–295.

Hansen, T. B. (2012). *Melancholia of Freedom: Social Life in an Indian Township in South Africa*. Princeton: Princeton University Press.

Harris, P. (2000). *The Work of the Imagination*. Oxford: Blackwell.

Harris, P. (2012). *Trusting What You're Told: How Children Learn from Others*. Cambridge, MA: Belknap Press.

Harrison, E., & Crewe, E. (1998). *Whose Development? An Ethnography of Aid*. London: Zed Books.

Heathen. (2014). *Oxford Dictionaries* (Online). Retrieved May 15, 2015, from http://www.oxforddictionaries.com/definition/english/heathen?q=heathen

Hecht, T. (1998). *At Home in the Street: Street Children of Northeast Brazil.* Cambridge: Cambridge University Press.

Hecht, T. (2008). Globalization from Way Below: Brazilian Streets, a Youth, and World Society. In J. Cole & D. Durham (Eds.), *Figuring the Future: Globalization and the Temporalities of Children and Youth* (pp. 223–243). Santa Fe: School of Advanced Research Press.

Heintz, M. (2009). Introduction: Why There Should Be an Anthropology of Moralities. In M. Heintz (Ed.), *The Anthropology of Moralities* (pp. 1–19). Oxford/New York: Berghahn Books.

Henderson, P. (2012). *A Kinship of Bones: AIDS, Intimacy and Care in Rural KwaZulu-Natal.* Scottsville: University of KwaZulu-Natal Press.

Hendricks, M. (2011). Eastern Cape Schools: Resourcing and Class Inequality. In G. Ruiters (Ed.), *The Fate of the Eastern Cape: History, Politics and Social Policy* (pp. 254–263). Scottsville: University of KwaZulu-Natal Press.

Herzfeld, M. (1985). *The Poetics of Manhood: Contest and Identity in a Cretan Mountain Village.* Princeton: Princeton University Press.

Herzog, J. (2013). *Father Hunger: Explorations with Adults and Children.* New York: Routledge.

Heugh, K. (1999). Languages, Development and Reconstructing Education in South Africa. *International Journal of Educational Development, 19*(4–5), 301–313.

HEUNI (European Institute for Crime Prevention and Control International Statistics on Crime and Justice). (2011). Countries Compared by Crime > Robberies. *International Statistics at NationMaster.com.* Retrieved February 11, 2018, from http://www.nationmaster.com/country-info/stats/Crime/Robberies

Hickel, J. (2015). *Democracy as Death: The Moral Order of Anti-liberal Politics in South Africa.* Berkley: University of California Press.

Higginbotham, P. (2012). *The Workhouse Encyclopedia.* Stroud: The History Press.

Hill, T., Jr. (2000). *Respect, Pluralism, and Justice: Kantian Perspectives.* Oxford: Oxford University Press.

Hlatshwayo, S. (2000). *Education and Independence: Education in South Africa, 1658–1988.* London: Greenwood Press.

Hodgson, J. (1983). *The God of the Xhosa: Study of the Origins and Development of the Traditional Concepts of the Supreme Being.* Oxford: Oxford University Press Southern Africa.

Hodgson, J. (1997). A Battle for Sacred Power: Christian Beginnings Among the Xhosa. In R. Elphick & R. Davenport (Eds.), *Christianity in South Africa: A Political, Social and Cultural History* (pp. 68–88). Los Angeles: University of California Press.

Holmwood, L. (2007). Dibley Criticised for Campaign Plug. *The Guardian* (Online). Retrieved March, 26, 2015, from http://www.theguardian.com/media/2007/jun/18/bbc.broadcasting1

Honwana, A., & De Boeck, F. (2005). *Makers and Breakers*. Oxford: James Curry.
Horowitz, R. (1983). *Honor and the American Dream: Culture and Identity in a Chicano Community*. New Brunswick: Rutgers University Press.
Horrell, M. (1963). *African Education, Some Origins and Developments*. Johannesburg: Institute of Race Relations.
Horrell, M. (1964). *A Decade of Bantu Education*. Johannesburg: SAIRR.
Hosegood, V. (2008). The Effects of High HIV Prevalence on Orphanhood on Living Arrangements of Children in Malawi, Tanzania, and South Africa. *Population Studies, 61*(3), 327–336.
Howard, A. (1970). *Learning to Be Rotuman: Enculturation in the South Pacific*. New York: Teachers College Press.
HST. (2011). Total Fertility Rate. *Health Systems Trust, Demographic Indicators* (Online). Retrieved, March 04, 2013, from http://indicators.hst.org.za/healthstats/5/data
Humphrey, C. (1997). Exemplars and Rules: Aspects of the Discourse of Moralities in Mongolia. In S. Howell (Ed.), *The Ethnography of Moralities* (pp. 25–48). London: Routledge.
Hunter, M. (1936). *Reaction to Conquest: Effects of Contact with Europeans on the Pondo of South Africa*. London: Oxford University Press.
Hunter, M. (2010). *Love in the Time of Aids: Inequality, Gender and Rights in South Africa*. Bloomington: Indiana University Press.
Hurtig, J. (2008). *Coming of Age in Times of Crisis: Youth, Schooling, and Patriarchy in a Venezuelan Town*. New York: Palgrave Macmillan.
Huxley, A. (2004). *Brave New World Revisited*. London: Vintage.
Hyslop, J. (1988). State Education Policy and the Social Reproduction of the Urban African Working Class: The Case of the Southern Transvaal 1955–76. *Journal of Southern African Studies, 14*(3), 446–476.
Hyslop, J. (2001). *Classroom Struggle: Policy and Resistance in South Africa 1940–1990*. Scottsville: University of KwaZulu-Natal Press.
Independent Online (IOL). (2007). *Councillors Pick a New Name for Grahamstown*. Retrieved October 21, 2014, from http://www.iol.co.za/news/politics/councillors-pick-a-new-name-for-grahamstown-1.370629#.VfrVIN9VhBc
Ingold, T. (2011). *Being Alive: Essays on Movement, Knowledge and Description*. Abingdon: Routledge.
Ingold, T. (2013). *Making: Anthropology, Archaeology, Art and Architecture*. Abingdon: Routledge.
Ingold, T., & Lucas, R. (2007). The 4 A's (Anthropology, Archaeology, Art and Architecture): Reflections on a Teaching and Learning Experience. In M. Harris (Ed.), *Ways of Knowing. New Approaches in the Anthropology of Experience and Learning* (pp. 287–306). Oxford: Berghahn.

Institute for Security Studies (ISS) and Africa Check. (2014). Factsheet: South Africa's Official Crime Stats Unpacked. *Mail and Guardian* (Online). Retrieved May 23, 2015, from http://mg.co.za/article/2014-09-22-factsheet-south-africas-official-crime-stats-unpacked/
Jack, M. (2011). Grahamstown Poised for Mass Protest. *The New Age (Online)*. Retrieved March 03, 2012, from http://www.thenewage.co.za/
Jackson, M. (1995). *At Home in the World*. Durham: Duke University Press.
Jackson, M. (2005). *Existential Anthropology: Events, Exigencies and Effects*. New York: Berghahn Books.
Jackson, M. (2012). *Between One and One Another*. Berkeley: University of California Press.
Jacobs, M. D. (2006). Indian Boarding Schools in Comparative Perspective: The Removal of Indigenous Children in the United States and Australia, 1880–1940. In C. Trafzer, J. Keller, & L. Sisquoc (Eds.), *Boarding School Blues: Revisiting American Indian Educational Experiences*. Lincoln: University of Nebraska Press.
Jacobs, M. D. (2009). *White Mother to a Dark Race: Settler Colonialism, Maternalism, and the Removal of Indigenous Children in the American West and Australia, 1880–1940*. Lincoln: University of Nebraska Press.
Jager, T. (2013). Guidelines to Assist the Implementation of Differentiated Learning Activities in South African Secondary Schools. *International Journal of Inclusive Education, 17*(1), 80–94.
Jamieson, L., & Mathews, S. (2013). *Submission on Amendments to the Children's Act: Corporal Punishment* (Policy Submission). Cape Town: Children's Institute. Retrieved June 25, 2014, from https://open.uct.ac.za/bitstream/item/3835/CI_policysubs_corporalpunishment_2013-07.pdf?sequence=1
Jansen, J. D. (2012, September 27). *Seven Dangerous Shifts in the Public Education Crisis*. Presidential Address, South African Institute of Race Relations. Retrieved June 23, 2015, from http://www.politicsweb.co.za/politicsweb/view/politicsweb/en/page71619?oid=328972&sn=Detail&pid=71616
Jeffrey, C. (2010). *Timepass: Youth, Class, and the Politics of Waiting in India*. Stanford: Stanford University Press.
Jeffrey, C., Jeffery, P., & Jeffery, R. (2008). *Degrees Without Freedom?: Education, Masculinities, and Unemployment in North India*. Stanford: Stanford University Press.
John, V. (2012a). Right to Education: Pupils Can Wait, Says Motshekga. *Mail & Guardian* (Online). Retrieved, May 26, 2013, from http://mg.co.za/article/2012-08-03-pupils-can-wait-says-motshekga
John, V. (2012b). Education in Crisis: Teaching Floored by Lack of Chairs. *Mail & Guardian* (Online). Retrieved, May 26, 2013, from http://mg.co.za/article/2012-10-19-00-teaching-floored-by-lack-of-chairs
Johns, L. M., & Dixon, B. (2001). *Gangs, Pagad & the State: Vigilantism and Revenge Violence in the Western Cape*. Centre for the Study of Violence and

Reconciliation, Violence and Transition Series, Vol. 2. Retrieved June 02, 2014, from http://www.csvr.org.za/docs/gangs/gangspagadstate.pdf

Kallaway, P. (2002). Introduction. In P. Kallaway (Ed.), *The History of Education Under Apartheid, 1948–1994: The Doors of Learning and Culture Shall Be Opened* (pp. 1–38). Cape Town: Pearson Education South Africa.

Kaplan, S. (2006). *The Pedagogical State: Education and the Politics of National Culture in Post-1980 Turkey.* Stanford: Stanford University Press.

Kennedy, D. (2006). *The Well of Being: Childhood, Subjectivity, and Education.* Albany: State University of New York Press.

Keto, C. (1990). Pre-industrial Education Policies and Practices in South Africa. In M. Nkomo (Ed.), *Pedagogy of Domination* (pp. 19–42). Trenton: Africa World Press.

Kilbride, P., Suda, C., & Njeru, E. (2000). *Street Children in Kenya: Voices of Children in Search of a Childhood.* Westport: Bergin & Garvey.

King, S., & Tomkins, A. (2003). *The Poor in England 1700–1850: An Economy of Makeshifts.* Manchester: Manchester University Press.

King's Norton History Society. (2004). *Timeline: Poor Laws, Workhouses, and Social Support, King's Norton.* Retrieved, September 6, 2013, from http://www.kingsnorton.info/time/poor_law_workhouse_timeline.htm

Kingfisher, C., & Maskovsky, J. (2008). Introduction: The Limits of Neoliberalism. *Critique of Anthropology, 28*(2), 115–126.

Kipnis, A. B. (2011). *Governing Educational Desire: Culture, Politics and Schooling in China.* Chicago: University of Chicago Press.

Kirsch, T. G. (2010). Violence in the Name of Democracy: Community Policing, Vigilante Action & Nation-Building in South Africa. In T. G. Kirsch & T. Grätz (Eds.), *Domesticating Vigilantism in Africa* (pp. 139–162). Oxford: James Curry.

Klees, S. J. (2008). A Quarter Century of Neoliberal Thinking in Education: Misleading Analyses and Failed Policies. *Globalisation, Societies and Education, 6*(4), 311–348.

Kleinman, S. (1991). Field-Workers' Feelings: What We Feel, Who We Are, How We Analyze. In B. Shaffir & R. Stebbins (Eds.), *Experiencing Fieldwork: An Inside View of Qualitative Research* (pp. 184–195). Newbury Park: Sage.

Kleinman, S., & Copp, M. A. (1993). *Emotions and Fieldwork.* Newbury Park: Sage.

Kohlberg, L. (1981). *Essays on Moral Development.* San Francisco: Harper & Row.

Kohlberg, L. (1984). *The Psychology of Moral Development: The Nature and Validity of Moral Stages.* San Francisco: Harper & Row.

Konanc, E. (1989). Street Children and Children Working in the Street: Preliminary Results of a Field Study in Turkey. *The Child Care Worker, 7*(11), 13–15.

Kross, C. (2002). W.W.M. Eiselen: Architect of Apartheid Education. In P. Kallaway (Ed.), *The History of Education Under Apartheid, 1948–1994: The*

Doors of Learning and Culture Shall Be Opened (pp. 53–73). New York: Peter Lang.

Kruss, G. (2002). 'Going Where the People Are': The Educational Philosophy of an African Indigenous Church Institute in the 1980s. In P. Kallaway (Ed.), *The History of Education Under Apartheid 1948–1994: The Doors of Learning and Culture Shall Be Opened* (pp. 288–303). New York: Peter Lang.

Kuper, A. (1999). *Culture: The Anthropologists' Account*. Cambridge, MA: Harvard University Press.

Laidlaw, J. (2002). For an Anthropology of Ethics and Freedom. *The Journal of the Royal Anthropological Institute, 8*(2), 311–332.

Laidlaw, J. (2010a). Agency and Responsibility: Perhaps You Can Have Too Much of a Good Thing. In M. Lambek (Ed.), *Ordinary Ethics: Anthropology, Language and Action* (pp. 143–164). New York: Fordham University Press.

Laidlaw, J. (2010b). Social Anthropology. In J. Skorupski (Ed.), *The Routledge Companion to Ethics* (pp. 369–383). London: Routledge.

Laidlaw, J. (2013). Ethics. In J. Boddy & M. Lambek (Eds.), *A Companion to the Anthropology of Religion* (pp. 171–188). Chichester: Wiley.

Laing, A. (2012). Jacob Zuma's £15m Home Upgrades Prompt Calls for Inquiry. *The Telegraph* (Online). Retrieved May 24, 2013, from http://www.telegraph.co.uk/news/worldnews/africaandindianocean/southafrica/9579538/Jacob-Zumas-15m-home-upgrades-prompt-calls-for-inquiry.html

Lambek, M. (2010a). Introduction. In M. Lambek (Ed.), *Ordinary Ethics: Anthropology, Language, and Action* (pp. 1–36). New York: Fordham University Press.

Lambek, M. (2010b). Toward an Ethics of the Act. In M. Lambek (Ed.), *Ordinary Ethics: Anthropology, Language and Action* (pp. 39–63). New York: Fordham University Press.

Landsberg, E. (Ed.). (2005). *Addressing Barriers to Learning: A South African Perspective*. Pretoria: Van Schaik.

Lang, S. (2011). Crime in Grahamstown – the Numbers. *Grocott's Mail* (Online). Retrieved, June 29, 2013, from http://www.grocotts.co.za/content/crimenumbers-08-09-2011

Lapsley, D. K. (2010). The Moral Ecology of South Africa's Township Youth (Review). *Journal of Moral Education, 39*(3), 403–405.

Larsen, H. B. (2003). *Children of the City: A Study of Street Children in Kathmandu, Their Social Practices and Territoriality*. Unpublished MPhil Dissertation, Department of Geography, University of Bergen. Retrieved March 02, 2012, from http://rua.ua.es/dspace/bitstream/10045/17395/1/STREET%20CHILDREN.pdf

Lawrence, D. H. (2011). *Studies in Classic American Literature*. Exeter: Shearsman Books.

Lawrence, J., & Starkey, P. (2001). Introduction: Child Welfare and Social Action. In J. Lawrence & P. Starkey (Eds.), *Child Welfare and Social Action in the Nineteenth and Twentieth Centuries: International Perspectives* (pp. 1–14). Liverpool: Liverpool University Press.

Lee, R., & Smith, D. M. (2014). *Geographies and Moralities: International Perspectives on Development, Justice and Place.* Chichester: Wiley-Blackwell.

le Roux, J., & Smith, C. S. (1998). Is the Street Child Phenomenon Synonymous with Deviant Behavior? *Adolescence, 33*(132), 915–925.

Leslie, H., & Storey, D. (2003). Entering the Field. In R. Scheyvens & D. Storey (Eds.), *Development Fieldwork: A Practical Guide* (pp. 119–138). London: Sage.

Lester, A. (2001). *Imperial Networks: Creating Identities in Nineteenth Century South Africa.* London: Routledge.

Lester, A., Nel, E., & Binns, T. (2000). *South Africa, Past, Present and Future: Gold at the End of the Rainbow?* Harlow: Pearson Education.

Levinas, E. (2002). Beyond Intentionality. In S. Hand (Ed.), *The Phenomenology Reader* (pp. 529–540). London: Routledge.

Lévi-Strauss, C. (1962). *The Savage Mind.* Chicago: University of Chicago Press.

Lewin, K. M., & Sabates, R. (2012). Who Gets What? Is Improved Access to Basic Education Pro-poor in Sub-Saharan Africa? *International Journal of Educational Development, 32*(4), 517–528.

Lewis, A. (1999). *Past and Present Perceptions Surrounding Mission Education: A Historical Metabletical Overview.* Unpublished D.Ed. Thesis, Stellenbosch University. Retrieved May 02, 2012, from http://scholar.sun.ac.za/handle/10019.1/16104

Lewis, D. (2005). Anthropology and Development: The Uneasy Relationship. *LSE Research Online.* Retrieved June 24, 2013, from http://eprints.lse.ac.uk/archive/00000253

Lewis, D., & Mosse, D. (2006). *Development Brokers and Translators: The Ethnography of Aid and Agencies.* Bloomfield: Kumarian Press.

Lewis, A., & Steyn, J. (2003). A Critique of Mission Education in South Africa According to Bosch's Mission Paradigm Theory. *South African Journal of Education, 23*(2), 101–106.

Lidchi, H. (1999). Finding the Right Image: British Development NGOs and the Regulation of Imagery. In T. Skelton & T. Allen (Eds.), *Culture and Global Change* (pp. 88–104). London: Routledge.

List of Countries by Vehicles per Capita. (2015). *Wikipedia.* Retrieved May 27, 2015, from https://en.wikipedia.org/wiki/List_of_countries_by_vehicles_per_capita

Lodge, T. (2002). *Politics in South Africa: From Mandela to Mbeki.* Cape Town: Kenilworth.

Lomofsky, L., & Lazarus, S. (2001). South Africa: First Steps in the Development of an Inclusive Education System. *Cambridge Journal of Education, 31*(3), 303–317.

Louw, J. M. (2009). *The Socio-Educational Implications of the Moral Degeneration of the South African Society: Towards a Solution.* Unpublished D.Ed. Thesis, University of South Africa. Retrieved June 22, 2012, from http://uir.unisa.ac.za/handle/10500/3087

Lucht, H. (2015). The Station Hustle: Ghanaian Migration Brokerage in a Disjointed World. In M. Jackson & A. Piette (Eds.), *What Is Existential Anthropology?* (pp. 104–124). New York: Berghahn.

Lutkehaus, N. (1999). Missionary Maternalism: Gendered Images of the Holy Spirit Sisters in Colonial New Guinea. In M. Taylor Huber & N. Lutkehaus (Eds.), *Gendered Missions: Women and Men in Missionary Discourse and Practice* (pp. 207–235). Ann Arbor: The University of Michigan Press.

MacKenzie, C. G. (1993). Demythologising the Missionaries: A Reassessment of the Functions and Relationships of Christian Missionary Education Under Colonialism. *Comparative Education, 29*(1), 45–66.

Madlingozi, T. (2007). Post-apartheid Social Movements and the Quest for the Elusive New South Africa. *Journal of Law and Society, 34*(1), 77–98.

Madonsela, T. (2014). Secure in Comfort: Report on an Investigation into Allegations of Impropriety and Unethical Conduct Relating to the Installation and Implementation of Security Measures by the Department of Public Works at and in Respect of the Private Residence of President Jacob Zuma at Nkandla in the KwaZulu-Natal Province. *Public Protector, South Africa.* Retrieved July 04, 2014, from http://www.publicprotector.org/library\investigation_report\2013-14\FinalReport 19 March 2014.pdf

Magazine, R. (2003). Action, Personhood and the Gift Economy Among So-Called Street Children in Mexico City. *Social Anthropology, 11*(3), 303–318.

Magubane, A. B. (1973). The 'Xhosa' in Town, Revisited Urban Social Anthropology: A Failure of Method and Theory. *American Anthropologist, 75*(5), 1701–1715.

Makoelle, T. M. (2012). The State of Inclusive Pedagogy in South Africa: A Literature Review. *Journal of Sociology and Social Anthropology, 3*(2), 93–102.

Malinowski, B. (1938). The Anthropology of Changing African Cultures. In L. P. Mair (Ed.), *Methods and Study of Culture Contact in Africa* (pp. vii–xxxviii). Oxford: Oxford University Press.

Malinowski, B. (1943). The Pan-African Problem of Culture Contact. *American Journal of Sociology, 48*(6), 649–665.

Malkki, L. (2010). Children, Humanity, and the Infantilization of Peace. In I. Feldman & M. I. Ticktin (Eds.), *In the Name of Humanity: The Government of Threat and Care* (pp. 58–85). Durham: Duke University Press.

Mangwana, T. (1992). Working with Street Children: Hints for Child Care Workers. *The Child Care Worker, 10*(5), 14–15.

Manne, R. (2004). Aboriginal Child Removal and the Question of Genocide, 1900–1940. In A. Moses (Ed.), *Genocide and Settler Society: Frontier Violence* and *Stolen Indigenous Children in Australian History* (pp. 217–243). New York/London: Berghahn Books.

Manus, V. B. (2011). *Emerging Traditions: Toward a Postcolonial Stylistics of Black South African Fiction in English*. Lanham: Lexington Books.

Manzo, K. (2008). Imaging Humanitarianism: NGO Identity and the Iconography of Childhood. *Antipode, 40*(4), 623–657.

Maphosa, C., & Shumba, A. (2010). Educators' Disciplinary Capabilities After the Banning of Corporal Punishment in South African Schools. *South African Journal of Education, 30*, 387–399.

Maqhina, M. (2011). School Transport Chaos. *Daily Dispatch* (Online). Retrieved June 03, 2012, from http://www.dispatch.co.za/news/article/321

Marais, M. (1995). The Distribution of Resources in Education in South Africa. *Economics of Education Review, 14*(1), 47–52.

Marais, L., Matebesi, S., Mthombeni, M., Botes, L., & Grieshaber, D. (2008). Municipal Unrest in the Free State (South Africa): A New Form of Social Movement? *Politeia, 27*(2), 51–69.

Mark, M. (2014). Get Your Africa Facts Right: Websites Seek to Stem Flow of Misinformation. *The Guardian* (Online). Retrieved September 24, from http://www.theguardian.com/world/2014/sep/27/africa-websites-fact-check-misinformation

Markus, B., & Free, W. (2008). Theoretical Reflections on the Life World of Tanzanian Street Children. *Anthropology Matters, 10*(2), 1–24.

Márquez, P. C. (1999). *The Street Is My Home. Youth and Violence in Caracas*. Stanford: Stanford University Press.

Marszalek, R. (2008). Introducing You to a New Website – Amasango. *Revising Reform*. Retrieved from http://hrht-revisingreform.blogspot.co.uk/2008_08_17_archive.html

Mason, R. (2013). Ukip MEP Godfrey Bloom Criticises Aid to 'Bongo Bongo Land'. *The Guardian* (Online). Retrieved June 29, 2014, from http://www.theguardian.com/politics/2013/aug/06/ukip-godfrey-bloom-bongo-bongo-land

Matlala, A. (2011). Teachers Quit over Lack of Discipline. *The Sowetan (Online)*. Retrieved April 25, 2013, from http://www.sowetanlive.co.za/news/2011/12/21/teachers-quit-over-lack-of-discipline

Matshiqi, A. (2010). The One-Party State and Liberation Movements in Africa: Lessons for South Africa. In N. Misra-Dexter & J. February (Eds.), *Testing Democracy: Which Way is South Africa Going?* (pp. 2–22). Cape Town: Idasa.

Mattingly, C. (2013). Moral Selves and Moral Scenes: Narrative Experiments in Everyday Life. *Ethnos, 78*(3), 301–327.

Mayer, P. (1961). *Townsmen or Tribesmen: Conservatism and the Process of Urbanization in a South African City* (with Contributions by Iona Mayer). Oxford/Cape Town: Oxford University Press.

Mayer, P. (1971). 'Traditional' Manhood Initiation in an Industrial City. The African View. In E. J. De Jager (Ed.), *Man: Anthropological Essays Presented to O.F Raum* (pp. 7–18). Cape Town: Struik.

Mayer, P. (1980). The Origin and Decline of Two Rural Resistance Ideologies. In P. Mayer (Ed.), *Black Villagers in an Industrial Society* (pp. 1–81). Oxford/Cape Town: Oxford University Press.

Mayer, P., & Mayer, I. (1970). Socialization by Peers: The Youth Organization of the Red Xhosa. In P. Mayer (Ed.), *Socialization: The Approach from Social Anthropology* (pp. 159–189). London: Tavistock.

Mazuri, A. (1993). Language and the Quest for Liberation in Africa: The Legacy of Franz Fanon. *Third World Quarterly, 14*(2), 348–365.

Mbazira, C. (2009). *Litigating Socio-Economic Rights in South Africa: A Choice Between Corrective and Distributive Justice*. Pretoria: Pretoria University Law Press.

Mbeki, T. (2005). Mbeki: Reply to Debate on the Presidency Dept Budget Vote 2005/2006. *The Presidency*. Retrieved June 03, 2014, from http://www.polity.org.za/article/mbeki-reply-to-debate-on-the-presidency-dept-budget-vote-20052006-26052005-2005-05-26

McAllister, P. A. (2006). *Xhosa Beer Drinking Rituals: Power, Practice and Performance in the South African Rural Periphery*. Durham: Carolina Academic Press.

McCarthy, M. R., Wiener, R., & Soodak, L. C. (2010). Vestiges of Segregation in the Implementation of Inclusion Policies in Public High Schools. *Educational Policy, 26*(2), 309–338.

McClay, W. M. (1994). *The Masterless: Self & Society in Modern America*. Chapel Hill: University of North Carolina Press.

McDermott, R. (1993). The Acquisition of a Child by a Learning Disability. In S. Chaiklin & J. Lave (Eds.), *Understanding Practice: Perspectives on Activity and Context* (pp. 269–305). Cambridge: Cambridge University Press.

McDermott, R., & Varenne, H. (1995). Culture as Disability. *Anthropology & Education Quarterly, 26*(3), 324–348.

McDermott, R., & Varenne, H. (1998). *Successful Failure: The School America Builds*. Oxford: Westview Press.

McHarry, K. E. (2013). *Sponsoring the Future: Marketizing Children's Potential in Senegalese Preschools*. Conference Presentation. The Anthropology of Potentiality in Africa (Panel), American Anthropological Association, Annual Conference, Chicago.

McKie, L. (2005). *Organisation Carescapes: Policies, Practices and Equality in Business*. Unpublished (Working) Paper. Presented at Public Policy and Equality Seminar, Cardiff. Retrieved June 19, 2014, from http://www.docs.hss.ed.ac.uk/education/creid/Projects/07xxvi_ESRC_Seminar3_PaperLMcKie.pdf

McMichael. (2013). Footsoldiers in a Social War: The Police, Crime and Inequality in South Africa. *Open Democracy* (Online). Retrieved October 23, 2014, from http://www.opendemocracy.net/opensecurity/christopher-mcmichael/footsoliders-in-social-war-police-south-africa

Meel, B. L. (2005). Community Perception of Traditional Circumcision in a Sub-region of the Transkei, Eastern Cape, South Africa. *South African Family Practice*, 47(6), 58–59.

Meintjes, H., & Giese, S. (2006). Spinning the Epidemic: The Making of Mythologies of Orphanhood in the Context of AIDS. *Childhood: A Global Journal of Child Research*, 13(3), 407–430.

Merseyside Maritime Museum. (2014). Child Emigration. *Merseyside Maritime Museum* (Online). Retrieved November 18, 2014, from http://www.liverpoolmuseums.org.uk/maritime/archive/sheet/10

Metz, T. (2007). Toward an African Moral Theory. *Journal of Political Philosophy*, 15(3), 321–341.

Metz, T., & Gaie, J. B. R. (2010). The African Ethic of Ubuntu/Botho: Implications for Research on Morality. *Journal of Moral Education*, 39(3), 273–290.

Mhlahlo, A. P. (2009). *What is Manhood? The Significance of Traditional Circumcision in the Xhosa*. Unpublished MPhil Thesis, Department of Sociology and Anthropology, the Stellenbosch University.

Mills, W. G. (1976). The Taylor Revival of 1866 and the Roots of African Nationalism in the Cape Colony. *Journal of Religion in Africa*, 8(2), 105–122.

Mills, W. G. (1995). Missionaries, Xhosa Clergy and the Suppression of Traditional Customs. In H. Bredenkamp & R. Ross (Eds.), *Mission and Christianity in South African History* (pp. 153–171). Johannesburg: Witwatersrand University Press.

Mitchell, C., Moletsane, R., & De Lange, N. (2007). Inclusive Education in South Africa in the Era of AIDS: Every Voice Counts. *International Journal of Inclusive Education*, 11(4), 383–386.

Mnisi, S. (2015). Traditional Courts Bill Contradicts Constitution. *Daily Dispatch* (Online). Retrieved December 29, 2015, from http://www.dispatchlive.co.za/news/traditional-courts-bill-contradicts-constitution/

Modisaotsile, B. M. (2012). The Failing Standard of Basic Education in South Africa. *Africa Institute of South Africa*, Briefing No. 72, 1–8.

Moffie. (2014). *Oxford Dictionary* (Online). Retrieved September 29, 2014, from http://www.oxforddictionaries.com/definition/english/moffie

Mokone, T., & Kgosana, C. (2011). Pretoria Takes Over EC Education. *Daily Dispatch* (Online). Retrieved July 26, 2013, from http://www.dispatch.co.za/news/news/article/620

Molteno, F. (1984). The Historical Foundations of the Schooling of Black South Africans. In P. Kallaway (Ed.), *Apartheid and Education: The Education of Black South Africans* (pp. 45–107). Johannesburg: Raven Press.

Moore, H. L. (2011). *Still Life: Hopes, Desires and Satisfactions*. Cambridge: Polity Press.
Moore, J. (2013). Kipling and Lord Roberts. *The Kipling Society* (Online). Retrieved February 6, 2015, from http://www.kiplingsociety.co.uk/rg_lordroberts_moore.htm
Morgen, S. (1989). Gender and Anthropology: Introductory Essay. In S. Morgen (Ed.), *Gender and Anthropology--Critical Reviews for Research and Teaching* (pp. 1–20). Washington, DC: American Anthropological Association.
Morrell, W. (1969). *British Colonial Policy in the Mid-Victorian Age: South Africa, New Zealand, the West Indies*. Oxford: Oxford University Press.
Morrell, R. (2001). Corporal Punishment in South African Schools: A Neglected Explanation for Its Persistence. *South African Journal of Education, 21*(4), 292–299.
Morrell, R. (2013). SA Broods Over Teen Pregnancies. *Mail & Guardian* (Online). Retrieved July 03, 2015, from http://mg.co.za/article/2013-04-12-sa-broods-over-teen-pregnancies
Morrell, R., Bhana, D., & Shefer, T. (2013). Pregnancy and Parenthood in South African Schools. In R. Morrell, D. Bhana, & T. Shefer (Eds.), *Books and Babies: Pregnancy and Young Parents in Schools* (pp. 1–30). Cape Town: HSRC Press.
Morris, A., & Hyslop, J. (1991). Education in South Africa: The Present Crisis and the Problems of Reconstruction. *Social Justice, 18*(1/2), 259–270.
Mostert, N. (1992). *Frontiers: The Epic of South Africa's Creation and the Tragedy of the Xhosa People*. New York: Knopf.
Motala, S., & Dieltiens, V. (2010). *Educational Access in South Africa: Country Research Summary*. Johannesburg: University of the Witwatersrand, Education Policy Unit (EPU). Retrieved March 03, 2013, from http://www.create-rpc.org/pdf_documents/South_Africa_Country_Research_Summary.pdf
Mother. (2014). *Glosbe: The Multilingual Online Dictionary*. Retrieved March 4, 2014, from http://glosbe.com/en/xh/mother
Mthanti, B., & Mncube, V. (2014). The Social and Economic Impact of Corporal Punishment in South African Schools. *Journal of Sociology and Social Anthropology, 5*(1), 71–80.
Musgrove, F. (1952). A Uganda Secondary School as a Field of Culture Change. *Africa: Journal of the International African Institute, 22*(3), 234–249.
Mustard Seed Foundation. (2015). *Overview*. Retrieved June 20, 2014, from http://msfdn.org/harveyfellows/overview/
Muthukrishna, N., & Ramsuran, A. (2007). Layers of Oppression and Exclusion in the Context of HIV and AIDS: The Case of Adult and Child Learners in the Richmond District, Province of KwaZulu-Natal. *International Journal of Inclusive Education, 11*(4), 401–416.
Muthukrishna, N., & Schoeman, M. (2000). From 'Special Needs' to 'Quality Education for All': A Participatory, Problem-Centred Approach to Policy

Development in South Africa. *International Journal of Inclusive Education,* 4(4), 315–335.

Naicker, S. (2006). From Policy to Practice: A South-African Perspective on Implementing Inclusive Education Policy. *International Journal of Whole Schooling,* 3(1), 1–7.

Nekhwevha, F. (2002). The Influence of Freire's 'Pedagogy of Knowing' on the South African Education Struggle in the 1970s and 1980s. In P. Kallaway (Ed.), *The History of Education Under Apartheid, 1948–1994: The Doors of Learning and Culture Shall Be Opened* (pp. 134–143). Cape Town: Pearson Education South Africa.

Ngcobo, J., & Muthukrishna, N. (2011). The Geographies of Inclusion of Students with Disabilities in an Ordinary School. *South African Journal of Education,* 31(3), 357–368.

Ngwane, Z. (2001). Real Men Reawaken Their Fathers' Homesteads, the Educated Leave Them in Ruins': The Politics of Domestic Reproduction in Post-apartheid Rural South Africa. *Journal of Religion in Africa,* 31(4), 402–426.

Ngxamngxa, A. N. N. (1971). The Function of Circumcision Amongst the Xhosa-Speaking Tribes in Historical Perspective. In E. J. De Jager (Ed.), *Man: Anthropological Essays Presented to O.F Raum* (pp. 183–204). Cape Town: Struik.

Nicholls, G. (2007). *A History of the English Poor Law in Connection with the State of the Country and the Condition of the People.* New Jersey: The Lawbook Exchange.

Niehaus, I. (2001). *Witchcraft, Power and Politics: Exploring the Occult in the South African Lowveld.* London: Pluto Press.

Niehaus, I. (2012). *Witchcraft and a Life in the New South Africa.* Cambridge: Cambridge University Press.

Niehaus, I. (2013). Anthropology and Whites in South Africa: Response to an Unreasonable Critique. *Africa Spectrum,* 48, 117–127.

Nietzsche, F. (1994). In K. Ansell-Pearson (Ed.), *On the Genealogy of Morality.* Cambridge: Cambridge University Press.

Nieuwenhuys, O. (2001). By the Sweat of Their Brow? 'Street Children', NGOs and Children's Rights in Addis Ababa. *Africa,* 71(4), 539–557.

Nina, D. (2000). Dirty Harry Is Back: Vigilantism in South Africa – The (Re)emergence of 'Good' and 'Bad' Community. *African Security Review,* 9(1), 8–28.

Nkosi, B. (2013). Motshekga Won't Retract 'Racist' Attack on Equal Education. *Mail & Guardian* (Online). Retrieved June 23, 2014, from http://mg.co.za/article/2013-06-19-motshekga-wont-retract-racist-attack-on-equal-education

Nolan, R. W. (2002). *Development Anthropology: Encounters in the Real World.* Oxford: Westview Press.

Ntombana, L. (2011). *An Investigation into the Role of Xhosa Male Initiation in Moral Regeneration*. Unpublished PhD Thesis, Faculty of Arts, Nelson Mandela Metropolitan University.

Ntombela, S. (2011). The Progress of Inclusive Education in South Africa: Teachers' Experiences in a Selected District, KwaZulu-Natal. *Improving Schools,* 14(1), 5–14.

Ntshangase, D. K. (2002). Language and Language Practices in Soweto. In R. Mesthrie (Ed.), *Language in South Africa* (pp. 407–419). Cambridge: Cambridge University Press.

Ntsimane, R. (2007). The Ukuhlonipha Code of Respect: Gender and Cultural Tensions Around the Zulu Nurses. The Case of the Emmaus Mission Hospital. *Studia Historiae Ecclesiasticae, XXXIII*(2), 115–133.

Nyamnjoh, F. B. (2012). Blinded by Sight: Divining the Future of Anthropology in Africa. *Africa Spectrum, 47,* 63–92.

Nyquist, T. E. (1983). *African Middle Class Elite.* Grahamstown: Institute of Social and Economic Research.

O'Meara, E. (1995). *Grahamstown Reflected.* Grahamstown: Albany Museum.

O'Neill, K. L. (2013). Left Behind: Security, Salvation, and the Subject of Prevention. *Cultural Anthropology, 28*(2), 204–226.

O'Neill, K. L. (2015). *Secure the Soul: Christian Piety and Gang Prevention in Guatemala.* Berkeley: University of California Press.

Olivier de Sardan, J. P. (2005). *Anthropology and Development: Understanding Contemporary Social Change.* London: Zed Books.

Onceya, T. (2013). No Consensus as Name-Change Workshops End. *Grocott's Mail* (Online). Retrieved January 28, 2015, from http://www.grocotts.co.za/content/no-consensus-name-change-workshops-end-28-01-2013

ONE. (2015). *About One.* Retrieved February 3, 2015, from http://www.one.org/international/about/

Oord, J. (2005). The Love Racket: Defining Love. *Zygon, 40*(4), 919–938.

Open Society Foundations (OSF). (2017). *Open Society Foundations (OSF).* Retrieved February 04, 2017, from http://www.osisa.org/open-society foundations-osf

Orgad, S., & Seu, B. (2014). Caring in Crisis – Why Development and Humanitarian NGOs Need to Change How They Relate to the Public. *Polis: Journalism and Society at the LSE* (Online). Retrieved March 02, 2015, from http://blogs.lse.ac.uk/polis/2014/07/08/caring-in-crisis-guest-blog/

Ortner, S. B. (2006). *Anthropology and Social Theory: Culture, Power and the Acting Subject.* Durham/London: Duke University Press.

Owen, S. (2012). South Africa: Briefing for the Human Rights Council Universal Periodic Review (13th Session, 2012). *Global Initiative.* Retrieved July 09, 2014, from http://lib.ohchr.org/HRBodies/UPR/Documents/session13/ZA/GIEACPC_UPR_ZAF_S13_2012_GlobalInitiativetoEndAllCorporalPunishmentofChildren_E.pdf

Panter-Brick, C. (2002). Street Children, Human Rights, and Public Health: A Critique and Future Directions. *Annual Review of Anthropology, 31*(1), 147–171.

Paquette, D. (2004). Theorizing the Father-Child Relationship: Mechanisms and Developmental Outcomes. *Human Development, 47*(4), 193–219.

Pascoe, C. J. (2012). *Dude, You're a Fag: Masculinity and Sexuality in High School.* Berkeley/Los Angeles: University of California Press.

Patel, L. (2005). *Social Welfare and Social Development in South Africa.* Oxford: Oxford University Press.

Pather, S. (2007). Demystifying Inclusion: Implications for Sustainable Inclusive Practice. *International Journal of Inclusive Education, 11*(5–6), 627–643.

Pather, S. (2011). Evidence on Inclusion and Support for Learners with Disabilities in Mainstream Schools in South Africa: Off the Policy Radar? *International Journal of Inclusive Education, 15*(10), 1103–1117.

Pattenden, O. (2015). Relations of Trust, Questions About Expectations: Reflections on a Photography Project with Young South Africans. *Anthropology in Action, 22*(3), 14–26.

Pauw, B. A. (1963). *The Second Generation: A Study of the Family Among Urbanized Bantu in East London.* Oxford: Oxford University Press.

Peires, J. B. (1979). Nxele, Ntsikana and the Origins of the Xhosa Religious Reaction. *The Journal of African History, 20*(1), 51–61.

Peires, J. B. (1982). *The House of Phalo: A History of the Xhosa People in the Days of Their Independence.* Los Angles: University of California Press.

Peires, J. B. (1987). The Central Beliefs of the Xhosa Cattle-Killing. *Journal of African History, 28*, 43–63.

Peires, J. B. (1989). *The Dead Will Arise: Nongqawuse and the Great Xhosa Cattle-Killing Movement.* Johannesburg: Ravan Press.

Peristiany, J. G. (1965). *Honour and Shame: The Values of Mediterranean Society.* London: Weidenfeld & Nicolson.

Peshkin, A. (1972). *Kanuri School Children: Education and Social Mobilization in Nigeria.* New York: Holt, Rinehart and Winston.

Pettman, C. (1913). *Africanderisms: A Glossary of South African Colloquial Words and Phrases and of Place and Other Names.* London: Longmans, Green and Co.

Pillay, J., & Di Terlizzi, M. (2009). A Case Study of a Learner's Transition from Mainstream Schooling to a School for Learners with Special Educational Needs (LSEN): Lessons for Mainstream Education. *South African Journal of Education, 29*, 491–509.

Piper, L., & Nadvi, L. (2010). Popular Mobilization, Party Dominance and Participatory Governance in South Africa. In L. Thompson & C. Tapscott (Eds.), *Citizenship and Social Movements: Perspectives from the Global South* (pp. 212–238). London: Zed Books.

Pithouse, R. (2011). On State Violence. *The South African Civil Society Information Service*. Retrieved July 19, 2014, from http://sacsis-org-za.win24.wadns.net/site/article/666.1

Pithouse, R. (2013). Durban Poison. *The South African Civil Society Information Service*. Retrieved March 04, 2014, from http://sacsis.org.za/site/article/1817

Pithouse, R. (2014). Four Bodies in Three Weeks. *The South African Civil Society Information Service*. Retrieved May, 23, 2015 from http://sacsis.org.za/site/article/1888

Pitt-Rivers, J. (1968). Honour. In D. L. Sills & R. K. Merton (Eds.), *International Encyclopedia of the Social Sciences* (pp. 503–511). London: Macmillan.

Pohlandt-McCormick, H. (2000). 'I Saw a Nightmare. . .': Violence and the Construction of Memory (Soweto, June 16, 1976). *History and Theory, 39*(4), 23–44.

Poland, M. (2013). Graham House – Fifty Year Jubilee. *St. Andrew's College* (Online). Retrieved September 23, 2015, from http://www.oldandrean.co.za/uploads/files/graham_house_brochure_50th_final_(low_res).pdf

Polat, F. (2011). Inclusion in Education: A Step Towards Social Justice. *International Journal of Educational Development, 31*(1), 50–58.

Pollock, M., & Levinson, B. A. U. (2011). Introduction. In B. A. U. Levinson & M. Pollock (Eds.), *A Companion to the Anthropology of Education* (pp. 1–8). Oxford: Wiley-Blackwell.

Popenoe, D. (1996). *Life Without Father: Compelling New Evidence That Fatherhood and Marriage Are Indispensable for the Good of Children and Society*. New York: The Free Press.

Posel, D., & Casale, D. (2011). Language Proficiency and Language Policy in South Africa: Findings from New Data. *International Journal of Educational Development, 31*(5), 449–457.

Potgieter, P. C. (1980). Moral Education in South Africa. *Journal of Moral Education, 9*(2), 130–133.

Prevost, E. E. (2010). *The Communion of Women: Missions and Gender in Colonial Africa and the British Metropole*. Oxford: Oxford University Press.

Prew, M. (2010). The South African Schools Act: Is It Time to Dump It? *The Centre for Education Policy Development* (Online). Retrieved July 20, 2012, from http://www.cepd.org.za/files/pictures/The South African Schools Act - Is it time to dump it by Dr Martin Prew.pdf

Prew, M. (2011). Socialism and Education: 'Peoples Education for Peoples Power': The Rise and Fall of an Idea in Southern Africa. In T. Griffi & Z. Millie (Eds.), *Logics of Socialist Education: Engaging with Crisis, Insecurity and Uncertainty* (pp. 133–153). New York: Springer.

Prinsloo, E. (2001). Working Towards Inclusive Education in South African Classrooms. *South African Journal of Education, 21*(4), 344–348.

Proctor, J. (1998). Ethics in Geography: Giving Moral Form to the Geographical Imagination. *Area, 30*(1), 8–18.

Puar, J. (2012). Precarity Talk: A Virtual Roundtable with Lauren Berlant, Judith Butler, Bojana Cvejić, Isabell Lorey, Jasbir Puar, and Ana Vujanović. *TDR/The Drama Review, 56*(4), 163–177.

Punch, S. (2012). Hidden Struggles of Fieldwork: Exploring the Role and Use of Field Diaries. *Emotion, Space and Society, 5*, 86–93.

Pupavac, V. (2001). Misanthropy Without Border: The International Children's Rights Regime. *Disasters, 25*(2), 95–112.

Qureshi, K. (2014). Sending Children to School 'Back Home': Multiple Moralities of Punjabi Sikh Parents in Britain. *Journal of Moral Education, 43*(2), 37–41.

Rabbitts, F. (2012). Child Sponsorship, Ordinary Ethics and the Geographies of Charity. *Geoforum, 43*(5), 926–936.

Rabbitts, F. (2013). *'Nothing is Whiter than White in This World': Child Sponsorship and the Geographies of Charity*. Unpublished PhD Thesis, University of Exeter.

Rabinow, P. (1997). Introduction: The History of Systems of Thought. In P. Rabinow (Ed.), *Ethics: Subjectivity and Truth* (The Essential Works of Michel Foucault). New York: The New Press.

Radcliffe-Brown, A. R. (1952). *Structure and Function in Primitive Society*. London: Cohen and West.

Raghaven, S. (2012). South Africa Loses Faith with the ANC. *The Independent* (UK, Online). Retrieved July 14, 2014, from http://www.independent.co.uk/news/world/africa/south-africa-loses-faith-with-the-anc-8303778.html

Rakometsi, M. S. (2008). *The Transformation of Black School Education in South Africa, 1950–1994: A Historical Perspective*. Unpublished PhD Thesis, Department of Humanities, Department of History, University of the Free State.

Ramphele, M. (2012). Time for Radical Change in Education. *The Star* (Online). Retrieved June 23, 2013, from http://www.iol.co.za/the-star/time-for-radical-change-in-education-1.1362669#.VgqLnN9VhBc

Ramusack, B. (1990). Cultural Missionaries, Maternal Imperialists, Feminist Allies: British Women Activists in India, 1865–1945. In N. Chaudhuri & M. Strobel (Eds.), *Western Women and Imperialism: Complicity and Resistance* (pp. 109–150). Bloomington: Indiana University Press.

Ramusack, B. (2005). Q&A: Barbara Ramusack (Conducted by Billie Dziech). *University of Cincinnati* (Online). Retrieved September 17, 2015, from www.uc.edu/news/NR.aspx?id=6579

Ratele, K. (2013). Masculinities Without Tradition. *Politikon: South African Journal of Political Studies, 40*(1), 133–156.

Reed, A. (2014). *Inkululeko: Youth, Non-governmental Organizations, and Discourses of Democracy in Post-apartheid South Africa*. Unpublished PhD Thesis, Department of Anthropology, University of California. Retrieved June 05, 2015, from http://escholarship.org/uc/item/7n75g82z

Religion in Brazil. (2014). *Wikipedia*. Retrieved January 19, 2014, from http://en.wikipedia.org/wiki/Religion_in_Brazil#Christianity

Republic of South Africa. (1996). *Constitution of the Republic of South Africa*. Pretoria: Government Gazette. Retrieved January 02, 2012, from http://www.gov.za/DOCUMENTS/CONSTITUTION/CONSTITUTION-REPUBLIC-SOUTH-AFRICA-1996-1

Republic of South Africa. (2003). *Health Professions Act 56 of 1974 Regulations Relating to the Registration of Registered Counsellors*. Retrieved June 24, 2013, from http://www.hpcsa.co.za/Uploads/editor/UserFiles/downloads/legislations/regulations/psychology/regulations/regulations_gnr1820_2003.pdf

Republic of South Africa. (2005). *Children's Act, No. 38 of 2005*. Retrieved March 28, 2012, from http://www.centreforchildlaw.co.za/images/files/childlaw/consolidated_childrens_act.pdf

Reuters. (2008). 'One Campaign' Stresses Voters to Focus on Africa. *Dawn* (Online). Retrieved 26 October 2012, from http://www.dawn.com/news/282686/one-campaign-stresses-voters-to-focus-on-africa

Richter, L., Chikovore, J., & Makusha, T. (2010). The Status of Fatherhood and Fathering in South Africa. *Childhood Education, 86*(6), 360–365.

Riley, L. (2013). Orphan Geographies in Malawi. *Children's Geographies, 11*(4), 409–421.

Rival, L. (2000). Formal Schooling and the Production of Modern Citizens in the Ecuadorian Amazon. In B. A. U. Levinson (Ed.), *Schooling the Symbolic Animal: Social and Cultural Dimensions of Education* (pp. 108–122). Lanham: Littlefield.

Rizvi, F. (2001). Postcolonialism and Globalization in Education. *Cultural Studies, 7*(3), 256–263.

Robbins, J. (2004). *Becoming Sinners: Christianity and Moral Torment in a Papua New Guinea Society*. Berkeley: University of California Press.

Robbins, J. (2007). Between Reproduction and Freedom: Morality, Value, and Radical Cultural Change. *Ethnos, 72*(3), 293–314.

Robbins, J. (2009). Morality, Value and Radical Cultural Change. In M. Heintz (Ed.), *The Anthropology of Moralities* (pp. 62–81). Oxford/New York: Berghahn Books.

Robbins, J. (2010). On the Pleasures and Dangers of Culpability. *Critique of Anthropology, 30*(1), 122–128.

Robbins, J. (2012). On Becoming Ethical Subjects: Freedom, Constraint, and the Anthropology of Morality. *Anthropology of This Century*, (5). Retrieved March 19, 2014, from http://aotcpress.com/articles/ethical-subjects-freedom-constraint-anthropology-morality/

Robbins, J. (n.d.). *Where in the World are Values? Exemplarity, Morality and Social Process*. Unpublished Manuscript.

Robins, S. L. (2008). *From Revolution to Rights in South Africa: Social Movements, NGOs and Popular Politics After Apartheid*. Scottsville: University of KwaZulu-Natal Press.

Rohner, R. P., & Veneziana, R. A. (2001). The Importance of Father Love: History and Contemporary Evidence. *Review of General Psychology, 5*(4), 382–405.

Rose, P. (2007). *NGO Provision of Basic Education: Alternative or Complementary Service Delivery to Support Access to the Excluded?* Create Pathways to Access, Research Monograph No.3, June 2007. Retrieved May 29, 2012, from http://sro.sussex.ac.uk/1830/1/PTA3.pdf

Ruiters, G. (2011). Inventing Provinces: Situating the Eastern Cape. In G. Ruiters (Ed.), *The Fate of the Eastern Cape: History, Politics and Social Policy* (pp. 19–41). Scottsville: University of KwaZulu-Natal Press.

Rydstrøm, H. (2003). *Embodying Morality: Growing Up in Rural Northern Vietnam*. Honolulu: University of Hawaii Press.

Sankore, R. (2005). Behind the Image: Poverty and 'Development Pornography'. *Pambazuka News*. Retrieved from http://www.pambazuka.net/en/category/features/27815

SAPA & M&G Online Reporter. (2012). Failure of State Teachers Boost Private Schools. *Mail & Guardian* (Online). Retrieved September 30, 2013, from http://mg.co.za/article/2012-07-22-failure-of-state-teachers-boost-private-schools

Save the Children (STC). (2005). *Ending Corporal Punishment of Children in South Africa*. Retrieved June 19, 2015, from https://test-za.savethechildren.net/sites/savethechildren.org.za/files/Ending%20Corporal%20Punishment%20of%20Children%20in%20South%20Africa.pdf

Sayed, Y., & Ahmed, R. (2011). Education Quality in Post-apartheid South African Policy: Balancing Equity, Diversity, Rights and Participation. *Comparative Education, 47*(1), 103–118.

Scheper-Hughes, N. (1992). *Death Without Weeping: The Violence of Everyday Life in Brazil*. Berkeley: University of California Press.

Scheper-Hughes, N., & Hoffman, D. (1997). Brazil: Moving Targets. *Natural History, 106*(61), 34–43.

Schernthaner, M. (2011). Coming of Age on the Streets: An Exploration of the Livelihoods of Street Youth in Durban. Paper Presented at the International RC21 Conference 2011 (Amsterdam), Session 30, Diversity and Space: Youth Geographies and Spatial Identities. Retrieved from http://www.rc21.org/conferences/amsterdam2011/edocs2/Session%2030/30-1-Schernthaner.pdf

Scherz, C. (2014). *Having People, Having Heart: Charity, Sustainable Development, and Problems of Dependence in Central Uganda*. Chicago: University of Chicago Press.

Schneider, J. (1971). Of Vigilance and Virgins: Honor, Shame and Access to Resources in Mediterranean Societies. *Ethnology, 10*(1), 1–24.

Schneider, J. (2015). Inside the White Saviour Industrial Complex. *New African* (Online). Retrieved August 16, 2015, from http://newafricanmagazine.com/inside-white-saviour-industrial-complex/

Schwandner-Sievers, S. (2001). The Enactment of 'Tradition': Albanian Constructions of Identity, Violence and Power in Times of Crisis. In I. W. Schröder & B. E. Schmidt (Eds.), *Anthropology of Violence and Conflict* (pp. 97–117). London: Routledge.

Scott, J. (1985). Everyday Forms of Resistance. In F. D. Colburn (Ed.), *Everyday Forms of Peasant Resistance*. New York: Routledge.

Scott, J. C. (2015). Everyday Forms of resistance. In F. Colburn (Ed.), *Everyday Forms of Peasant Resistance* (pp. 3–33). Abingdon: Routledge.

Seyer, I. (2002). *Smart on the Under, Wise to the Streets: Mapping the Landscapes of Urban Youth*. Unpublished PhD Dissertation, The School of Education, Stanford University.

Shaikhnag, N., & Assan, T. E. B. (2014). The Effects of Abolishing Corporal Punishment on Learner Behaviour in South African High Schools. *Mediterranean Journal of Social Sciences, 5*(7), 435–442.

Sharp, J. (1980). Two Separate Developments: Anthropology in South Africa. *RAI News, 36,* 4–6.

Sherman, J. (2014). Aid Group Mis-spent Flight Cash. *The Times* (UK, Online). Retrieved July 23, 2015, from http://www.thetimes.co.uk/tto/news/politics/article4138092.ece

Shindler, J. (2010). *Characteristics of Out-of-School Children of Compulsory School Age in South Africa: What the Community Survey 2007 Shows*. CREATE Working Paper No. 1. Retrieved September 21, 2012, from http://www.createrpc.org/pdf_documents/Working%20paper%201-%20Out%20of%20school%20children.pdf

Shipman, T., Cohen, T., & Chorley, M. (2013). UKIP Man in 'Bongo Bongo Land' Aid Row Storms Out of TV Interview After Channel 4 News Presenter Keeps Asking Him if He is a Racist. *Daily Mail* (Online). Retrieved, July 25, 2015, from http://www.dailymail.co.uk/news/article-2386488/Godfrey-Bloom-Sending-aid-Africa-treason-says-unrepentant-UKIP-man-Bongo-Bongo-land-storm.html

Shisana, O., Rehle, T., Simbayi, L. C., Zuma, K., Jooste, S., Zungu, N., Labadarios, D., Onoya, D., et al. (2014). *South African National HIV Prevalence, Incidence and Behaviour Survey, 2012*. Cape Town: HSRC Press.

Shizha, E. (2005). Reclaiming Our Memories: The Education Dilemma in Postcolonial African School Curricula. In A. A. Abdi & A. Cleghorn (Eds.), *Issues in African Education: Sociological Perspectives* (pp. 65–83). New York/Basingstoke: Palgrave Macmillan.

Simpson, A. (1999). The Labours of Learning: Education in the Postcolony. *Social Analysis: The International Journal of Social and Cultural Practice, 43*(1), 4–13.

Simpson, A. (2003). *Half London in Zambia: Contested Identities in a Catholic Mission School.* Edinburgh: Edinburgh University Press.

Sishana, O. (2008). *HIV/AIDS and Society* (Paper Prepared for The Presidency). Cape Town: HSRC Press.

Slack, P. (1974). Vagrants and Vagrancy in England, 1598–1664. *The Economic History Review, 27*(3), 360–379.

Slocum, S. (1975). Woman the Gatherer: Male Bias in Anthropology. In R. R. Reiter (Ed.), *Toward an Anthropology of Women* (pp. 36–50). New York: Monthly Review Press.

SlutWalk. (2014). About. *SlutWalk Toronto* (Online). Retrieved December 13, 2014, from http://www.slutwalktoronto.com/

Smit, M. (2013). Compatibility of Democracy and Learner Discipline in South African Schools. *De Jure, 1*(46), 345–365.

Smith, D. M. (1997). Geography and Ethics: A Moral Turn? *Progress in Human Geography, 21*(4), 583–590.

Smith, D. (2013). Jacob Zuma Accused of Corruption 'on a Grand Scale' in South Africa. *The Guardian* (Online). Retrieved June 14, 2014, from http://www.theguardian.com/world/2013/nov/29/jacob-zuma-accused-corruption-south-africa

Smith, N. R. (2015). Rejecting Rights: Rights and Violence in Post-apartheid South Africa. *African Affairs, 114*(456), 341–360.

Society for the Propagation of the Gospel (SPG). (1856). *The Global Missionary for 1856* (Vol. 6). London: Bell & Daldy.

Society for the Propagation of the Gospel (SPG). (1858). *The Global Missionary for 1858* (Vol. 8). London: Bell & Daldy.

Sokopo. (2010). Bad Start for Class of 2011. *Daily Dispatch* (Online). Retrieved June 15, 2013, from http://www.dispatch.co.za/news/news/article/226

Solomon, M. (2013). The Myth of Teenage Pregnancy and Child Support Grants. *Africa Check.* Retrieved January 24, 2014, from http://africacheck.org/2013/05/30/urban-myths-and-teen-pregnancy/

Soudien, C. (2002). Teachers' Responses to the Introduction of Apartheid Education. In P. Kallaway (Ed.), *The History of Education Under Apartheid, 1948–1994: The Doors of Learning and Culture Shall Be Opened* (pp. 211–223). Cape Town: Pearson Education South Africa.

Soudien, C., & Nekhwevha, F. (2002). Education Post-1948: A View from Below: Education, Tradition, and Change in the Apartheid Era, In P. Kallaway (Ed.), *The History of Education Under Apartheid 1948–1994* (pp. 259–269). Cape Town: Peter Lang Publishing Inc.

South African Democratic Teachers Union (SADTU). (2015). *Statement of SADTU NEC Following Its Meeting Held in Durban.* Retrieved October 14, 2015, from http://www.sadtu.org.za/show.php?id=3023

South African Press Association (SAPA). (2011). SADTU Block Court Entrance. *Times* (Live/Online). Retrieved, July 24, 2014, from http://www.timeslive.co.za/local/2011/03/14/sadtu-blocks-court-entrance#

South African Press Association (SAPA). (2012a). Public Schools Don't Match Private Schools. *Times* (Live/Online). Retrieved July 19, 2013, from http://www.timeslive.co.za/politics/2012/12/04/public-schools-don-t-match-private-schools

South African Press Association (SAPA). (2012b). Our Education System is in Crisis. *IOL* (Online). Retrieved November 12, 2012, from http://www.iol.co.za/news/south-africa/our-education-system-is-in-crisis-1.1355362

South African Press Association (SAPA). (2014). Tear Gas Used to Disperse Grabouw Protesters. *News 24* (Online). Retrieved June 25, 2014, from http://www.news24.com/SouthAfrica/News/Tear-gas-used-to-disperse-Grabouw-protesters-20140916

Southall, R. (2005). The Dominant Party Debate in South Africa. *Africa Spectrum, 39*(1), 61–82.

Spencer, D. (2010). Emotions in the Field and Relational Anthropology. *Emotions in Anthropological Fieldwork* (Online). Retrieved, April 02, 2012, from http://emotionsinanthropology.blogspot.co.uk/

Spener, D. (2007). *Cruces Clandestinos Y Movidas Rascuaches: Strategies of Migrant Resistance at the Mexico-U.S. Border*. Paper Prepared for Delivery at the 2007 Congress of the Latin American Studies Association, Montréal, Canada September 5–8, 2007. Retrieved July 02, 2013, from http://www.trinity.edu/dspener/clandestinecrossings/related%20articles/movidas%20rascuaches%20lasa%202007.pdf

Spicq, C. (2006). *Agape in the New Testament, Volume 2: Agape in the Epistles of St. Paul, the Acts of the Apostles and the Epistles of St. James, St. Peter, and St. Jude*. Eugene: Wipf and Stock.

Spiegel, A. D., & Becker, H. (2015). South Africa: Anthropology or Anthropologies? *American Anthropologist, 117*(4), 1–7.

Spiegel, A. D., & McAllister, P. A. (1991). Introduction. In A. D. Spiegel & P. A. McAllister (Eds.), *Tradition and Transition in Southern Africa* (pp. 1–10). Johannesburg: Witwatersrand University Press.

Spinage, C. (2012). *African Ecology: Benchmarks and Historical Perspectives*. Heidelberg: Springer.

Spreen, C. A., & Vally, S. (2006). Education Rights, Education Policies and Inequality in South Africa. *International Journal of Educational Development, 26*(4), 352–362.

Stafford, C. (2006). *The Roads of Chinese Childhood: Learning and Identification in Angang*. Cambridge: Cambridge University Press.

Stafford, C. (2010). The Punishment of Ethical Behavior. In M. Lambek (Ed.), *Ordinary Ethics: Anthropology, Language and Action* (pp. 187–206). New York: Fordham University Press.

Stafford, C. (2013). *Ordinary Ethics in China*. London: Bloomsbury Academic.
Stambach, A. (2000). *Lessons from Mount Kilimanjaro: Schooling, Community, and Gender in East Africa*. New York: Routledge.
Stambach, A. (2004). Faith in Schools: Toward an Ethnography of Education, Religion, and the State. *Social Analysis: The International Journal of Social and Cultural Practice, 48*(3), 90–107.
Stambach, A. (2005). Rallying the Armies or Bridging the Gulf: Questioning the Significance of Faith-Based Educational Initiatives in a Global Age. *Indiana Journal of Global Legal Studies, 12*(1), 205–226.
Stambach, A. (2010). *Faith in Schools: Religion, Education and American Evangelicals in East Africa*. Stanford: Stanford University Press.
Stambach, A. (2011). Education and Evangelism in Africa. *Public Lecture* (Available Online). Retrieved July 25, 2012, from https://www.youtube.com/watch?v=pl9AhRwLjIo
Stambach, A. (2017). Introduction. In A. Stambach & K. D. Hall (Eds.), *Anthropological Perspectives on Student Futures: Youth and the Politics of Possibility*. New York: Palgrave Macmillan.
Stambach, A., & Kwayu, A. (2013). Take the Gift of My Child and Return Something to Me: On Children, Chagga Trust, and a New American Evangelical Orphanage on Mount Kilimanjaro. *Journal of Religion in Africa, 43*, 379–395.
Stambach, A., & Ngwane, Z. (2011). Development, Postcolonialism, and Global Networks as Frameworks for the Study of Education in Africa and Beyond. In B. A. U. Levinson & D. Holland (Eds.), *Companion to the Anthropology of Education* (pp. 299–315). Hoboken: Wiley-Blackwell.
Stapleton, T. J. (1993). Reluctant Slaughter: Rethinking Maqoma's Role in the Xhosa Cattle-Killing (1853–1857). *The International Journal of African Historical Studies, 26*(2), 346–369.
Statistics South Africa (SSA). (2011a). *General Household Survey* (Statistical Release P0318). Retrieved July 10, 2014, from http://fraser.stlouisfed.org/docs/releases/e34/e34_19680629.pdf
Statistics South Africa (SSA). (2011b). *Makana* (2011 Census). Retrieved January 12, 2012, from http://beta2.statssa.gov.za/?page_id=993&id=makana-municipality
Statistics South Africa (SSA). (2012). *Census 2011 Statistical Release*. Retrieved July 19, 2013, from http://www.statssa.gov.za/publications/P03014/P030142011.pdf
Stewart, K. (2007). *Ordinary Affects*. Durham/London: Duke University Press.
Stofile, S. Y. (2008). *Factors Affecting the Implementation of Inclusive Education Policy: A Case Study in One Province in South Africa*. Unpublished PhD Thesis, Faculty of Education, University of the Western Cape.

Stone, G. L. (2002). The Lexicon and Sociolinguistic Codes of the Working-Class Afrikaans-Speaking Cape Peninsula Coloured Community. In R. Mesthrie (Ed.), *Language in South Africa* (pp. 381–397). Cambridge: Cambridge University Press.

Swanson, D. M. (2009). Where Have All the Fishes Gone? Living Ubuntu as an Ethics of Research and Pedagogical Engagement. In D. M. Caracciolo & A. M. Mungai (Eds.), *In the Spirit of Ubuntu: Stories of Teaching and Research* (pp. 2–22). Rotterdam: Sense.

Swanson, D. M. (2013). Neoliberalism, Education and Citizenship Rights of Unemployed Youth in Post-apartheid South Africa. *SISYPHOS Journal of Education, 1*(2), 194–212.

Swart, J. (1988). 'Street-Wise': Opening the Way to Self-Actualization for the Street Child. *Africa Insight, 18*(1), 33–41.

Swart, J. (1990). *Malunde: The Street Children of Hillbrow*. Johannesburg: Witwatersrand University Press.

Swart-Kruger, J., & Donald, D. (1994). Children of the South African Streets. In A. Dawes & D. Donald (Eds.), *Childhood and Adversity: Psychological Perspectives from South African Research* (pp. 107–121). Cape Town: D. Philip.

Swartz, S. (2009). *The Moral Ecology of South Africa's Township Youth*. New York: Palgrave Macmillan.

Swartz, S. (2010a). 'Moral Ecology' and 'Moral Capital': Tools Towards a Sociology of Moral Education from a South African Ethnography. *Journal of Moral Education, 39*(3), 305–327.

Swartz, S. (2010b). The Pain and the Promise of Moral Education in Sub-Saharan Africa. *Journal of Moral Education, 39*(3), 267–272.

Swartz, S. (2011). Going Deep' and 'Giving Back': Strategies for Exceeding Ethical Expectations When Researching Amongst Vulnerable Youth. *Qualitative Research, 11*(1), 47–68.

Swartz, S., Harding, J. H., & De Lannoy, A. (2012). Ikasi Style and the Quiet Violence of Dreams: A Critique of Youth Belonging in Post-apartheid South Africa. *Comparative Education, 48*(1), 27–40.

Sykes, K. (2009). Adopting an Obligation: Moral Reasoning About Bougainvillean Children's Access to Social Services in New Ireland. In M. Heintz (Ed.), *The Anthropology of Moralities* (pp. 1–19). New York: Berghahn Books.

Tabensky, P. (2012, January 27). *Reign of Thugs – The Easy Option. Grocott's Mail.* Grahamstown, p. 11.

Talented and Proud. (2012, August 14). Talented and Proud. *Grocott's Mail*, p. 10.

Tapscott, C. (2007). The Challenges of Building Participatory Local Government. In L. Thompson (Ed.), *Participatory Governance? Citizens and the State in South Africa* (pp. 81–94). Bellville: African Centre for Citizenship and Democracy, University of the Western Cape.

Terrio, S. J. (2004). Violence: Prosecuting Romanian Street Children at the Paris Palace of Justice. *International Migration, 42*(5), 5–33.

The Church of England. (2015). *Pastoral Services, Introduction*. Retrieved September 18, 2015, from https://www.churchofengland.org/prayer-worship/worship/texts/pastoral.aspx

The Presidency. (2015). *President Zuma Signs Special Investigating Unit Proclamation to Investigate Eastern Cape Department of Education*. Retrieved October 3, 2015, from http://www.presidency.gov.za/pebble.asp?relid=19986

The Salvation Army. (2014). *Social Work*. Retrieved March 23, 2012, from http://www.salvationarmy.org.uk/uki/HeritageSocialWork

Thessalonians 5:14. (2015). Bible Hub. Retrieved September 24, 2015, from http://biblehub.com/commentaries/1_thessalonians/5-14.htm

Throop, C. J. (2012). Moral Sentiments. In D. Fassin (Ed.), *A Companion to Moral Anthropology* (pp. 150–168). Chichester: Wiley.

Ticktin, M. (2006). Where Ethics and Politics Meet: The Violence of Humanitarianism in France. *American Ethnologist, 33*(1), 33–49.

Tisani, N. C. (2000). *Continuity and Change in Xhosa Historiography in the Nineteenth Century: An Exploration Through Textual Analysis*. Unpublished PhD Thesis, History Department, Rhodes University.

Tooley, J., & Dixon, P. (2006). 'De Facto' Privatisation of Education and the Poor: Implications of a Study from Sub-Saharan Africa and India. *Compare: A Journal of Comparative and International Education, 36*(4), 443–462.

Tools With A Mission (TWAM). (2014). *About Tools with a Mission*. Retrieved July 15, 2014, from http://www.twam.co.uk/aboutus.html

Turnball, B., Hernández, R., & Reyes, M. (2009). Street Children and Their Helpers: An Actor-Oriented Approach. *Children and Youth Services Review, 31*(12), 1283–1288.

Turner, V. (1974). *Dramas, Fields and Metaphors: Symbolic Action in Human Society*. Ithaca: Cornell University Press.

United Nations (UN). (1948). *The Universal Declaration of Human Rights*. Retrieved October 5, 2015, from http://www.un.org/en/documents/udhr/index.shtml

United Nations (UN). (2008). *Summary Prepared by the Office of the High Commissioner for Human Rights, in Accordance with Paragraph 15c of the Annex to Human Rights Council Resolution 5/1*. Retrieved April 14, 2013, from http://www.univie.ac.at/bimtor/dateien/southafrica_upr_2008_summary.pdf

United Nations Educational, Scientific and Cultural Organization (UNESCO). (1994). *The Salamanca Statement and Framework for Action on Special Needs Education*. Retrieved July 29, 2014, from http://www.unesco.org/education/pdf/SALAMA_E.PDF/

Valentine, B. L. (1978). *Hustling and Other Hard Work: Life Styles in the Ghetto*. New York: Free Press.

Vally, S. (1998). Spoil the Rod, Spare the Child. *The Educator's Voice, 2*(9), 4–5.
Vally, S. (2007). From People's Education to Neo-liberalism in South Africa. *Review of African Political Economy, 34*(111), 39–56.
Vally, S., Dolombisa, Y., & Porteus, K. (2002). Violence in South African Schools. *Current Issues in Comparative Education, 2*, 80–90.
van der Walt, J. L. (1992). The Culturo-Historical and Personal Circumstances of Some 19th-Century Missionaries Teaching in South Africa. *Koers, 57*(1), 75–85.
van Diemel, R. (2001). 'I Have Seen the New Jerusalem': Revisiting and Re-conceptualising Josiah T. Gumede and Jimmy La Guma's USSR Visit of 1927. *What Next? Marxist Discussion Journal* (Online). Retrieved June 13, 2014, from http://www.whatnextjournal.org.uk/Pages/History/Gumede.html
van Vuuren, C., & de Jongh, M. (1999). Rituals of Manhood in South Africa: Circumcision at the Cutting Edge of Critical Intervention. *South African Journal of Ethnology, 22*(4), 142–156.
Varenne, H. (2007). Difficult Collective Deliberations: Anthropological Notes Toward a Theory of Education. *Teachers College Record, 109*(7), 1559–1588.
Varenne, H. (2008). Culture, Education, Anthropology. *Anthropology & Education Quarterly, 39*(4), 356–368.
Vaughan, M. K. (1992). Women School Teachers in the Mexican Revolution: The Story of Reyna's Braids. In C. Johnson-Odin & M. Strobel (Eds.), *Expanding the Boundaries of Women's History* (pp. 278–302). Bloomington/Indianapolis: Indiana University Press.
Veriava, F. (2014). *Promoting Effective Enforcement of the Prohibition against Corporal Punishment in South African Schools.* Pretoria: Pretoria University Law Press.
Vincent, L. (2008). 'Boys Will Be Boys': Traditional Xhosa Male Circumcision, HIV and Sexual Socialisation in Contemporary South Africa. *Culture, Health & Sexuality, 10*(5), 431–446.
Vivian, L. M. H. (2012). *Psychiatric Disorder in Xhosa-Speaking Men Following Circumcision.* Unpublished PhD Thesis, Department of Psychiatry and Mental Health, University of Cape Town. Retrieved June 01, 2013, from http://uctscholar.uct.ac.za/PDF/91520_Vivian_L_M.pdf
Wacquant, L. (2008). *Urban Outcasts: A Comparative Sociology of Advanced Marginality.* Cambridge: Polity Press.
Wadesango, N., Chabaya, O., Rembe, S., & Muhuro, P. (2011). Source of Behavioural Problems That Affect the Realization of the Right to Basic Education Among Children: A Case Study of Schools in the Eastern Cape-South. *Journal of Social Sciences, 27*(3), 149–156.
Waghid, Y., & Engelbrecht, P. (2002). Inclusive Education, Policy and Hope: Mapping Democratic Policy Changes on Inclusion in South Africa. *International Journal of Special Education, 17*(1), 20–25.

Wang, C. (2013). Right or Wrong? A Taoqi Student in an Elite Primary School in Beijing. In C. Stafford (Ed.), *Ordinary Ethics in China today* (pp. 29–44). London: Bloomsbury.

Warden, T. (2013). Feet of Clay: Confronting Emotional Challenges in Ethnographic Experience. *Journal of Organizational Ethnography*, 2(2), 150–172.

Wark, M. (1995). Fresh Maimed Babies: The Uses of Innocence. *Transition, 65,* 36–47.

Waterhouse, S. (2007). Status of Corporal Punishment in the South African Children's Amendment Bill Law Reform Process. Cape Town. *Article 19, 3*(2), 1–3. Retrieved July 23, 2012, from file:///C:/Users/Oli/Downloads/Volume 3 Number 3 - December 2007 (2).pdf

Watson, K. I. (1999). *A History of the South African Police in Port Elizabeth, 1913–1956.* Unpublished PhD Thesis, History Department, Rhodes University.

Webb, V. (1999). Multilingualism in Democratic South Africa: The Over-Estimation of Language Policy. *International Journal of Educational Development, 19*(4–5), 351–366.

Weber, M. (1978). *Economy and Society: An Outline of Interpretive Sociology.* Los Angeles: University of California Press.

Weber, M. (1991). In H. H. Gerth & C. Wright Mills (Eds.), *From Max Weber: Essays in Sociology.* Abingdon: Routledge.

Weber, M. (2001). *The Protestant Ethic and the Spirit of Capitalism.* London: Routledge.

Weckesser, A. M. (2011). *Girls, Gifts and Gender: An Ethnography of the Materiality of Care in Rural Mpumalanga, South Africa.* Unpublished PhD Thesis, School of Health and Social Studies, University of Warwick.

Wedel, J. R. (2004, June 12). *Transactorship in Transition: The Shifting World of Aid and Advice in the U.S.-Russia Relationship.* Presentation, Conference on Comparative Transitions, London Business School. Retrieved April 14, 2016, from http://janinewedel.info/presentations_London04.html

Wedel, J. R., Shore, C., Feldman, G., & Lathrop, S. (2005). Toward an Anthropology of Public Policy. *The ANNALS of the American Academy of Political and Social Science, 600*(1), 30–51.

Weiss, B. (2002). Thug Realism: Inhabiting Fantasy in Urban Tanzania. *Cultural Anthropology, 17*(1), 93–124.

Weiss, B. (2009). *Street Dreams and Hip Hop Barbershops: Global Fantasy in Urban Tanzania.* Bloomington: Indiana University Press.

Wells, L. E., & Rankin, J. H. (1991). Families and Delinquency: A Meta-Analysis of the Impact of Broken Homes. *Social Problems, 38*(1), 71–93.

Wenzel, J. (2009). *Bulletproof: Afterlives of Anticolonial Prophecy in South Africa and Beyond.* Chicago: University of Chicago Press.

Whyte, W. F. (1969). *Street Corner Society.* Chicago: University of Chicago Press.

Williams, B. (1993). *Ethics and the Limits of Philosophy*. London: Fontana Press.
Williams, B. (2006). *The Sense of the Past: Essays in the History of Philosophy*. Princeton: Princeton University Press.
Willis, P. (1977). *Learning to Labour*. Farnborough: Saxon House.
Wilson, M. (1961). *Reaction to Conquest: Effects of Contact with Europeans on the Pondo of South Africa*. Oxford: Oxford University Press.
Wilson, M. (1969). Co-operation and Conflict: The Eastern Cape Frontier. In M. Wilson & L. Thompson (Eds.), *The Oxford History of South Africa* (pp. 233–271). Oxford: Oxford University Press.
Wilson, M. (1971). *Religion and the Transformation of Society*. Cambridge: Cambridge University Press.
Wilson, P., & Arnold, J. (1986). *Street Kids: Australia's Alienated Young*. Victoria: Collins Dove.
Winchatz, M. R. (2006). Fieldworker or Foreigner? Ethnographic Interviewing in Nonnative Languages. *Field Methods, 18*(1), 83–97.
Wolcott, H. F. (2003). *A Kwakiutl Village and School*. Walnut Creek: AltaMira Press.
Wolcott, H. F. (2011). If There's Going to Be an Anthropology of Education. In M. Pollock & B. A. U. Levinson (Eds.), *A Companion to the Anthropology of Education* (pp. 97–11). Chichester: Wiley-Blackwell.
Woods, B., & Shipley, D. (2004). *The Orphans of Nkandla* (Film). True Vision Productions Retrieved April 14, 2014, from http://truevisiontv.com/films/details/83/orphans-of-nkandla
Woolard, I., Harttgen, K., & Klasen, S. (2010). *The Evolution and Impact of Social Security in South Africa*. Paper Prepared for the Conference on "Promoting Resilience Through Social Protection in Sub-Saharan Africa", Organised by the European Report of Development in Dakar, Senegal, 28–30 June 2010. Retrieved April 28, 2013, from http://erd.eui.eu/media/BackgroundPapers/Woolard-Harttgen-Klasen.pdf
World Bank. (2009). *Gini Index*. Retrieved May 24, 2013, from http://data.worldbank.org/indicator/SI.POV.GINI/
Wright, L. (2012). Origins of the Eastern Cape Education Crisis. In L. Wright (Ed.), *South Africa's Education Crisis: Views from the Eastern Cape* (pp. 1–18). Grahamstown: NISC.
Xu, J. (2014). Becoming a Moral Child Amidst China's Moral Crisis: Preschool Discourse and Practices of Sharing in Shanghai. *Ethos, 42*(2), 222–242.
Ybarra-Frausto, T. (1991). Rasquachismo: A Chicano Sensibility. In T. McKenna & Y. Yarbro-Bejaran (Eds.), *Chicano Art: Resistance and Affirmation, 1965–1985* (pp. 155–162). Los Angeles: Wight Art Gallery, University of California.
Yende, S. (2005). Teacher Hit Kids, is Suspended. *News 24* (Online). Retrieved January 25, 2014, from http://www.news24.com/SouthAfrica/News/Teacher-hit-kids-is-suspended-20050908

Zeitlyn, B. (2014). The Making of a Moral British Bangladeshi. *Journal of Moral Education*, 43(2), 198–212.

Zigon, J. (2006). An Ethics of Hope: Working on the Self in Contemporary Moscow. *Anthropology of East Europe Review*, 24(2), 71–80.

Zigon, J. (2007). Moral Breakdown and the Ethical Demand: A Theoretical Framework for an Anthropology of Moralities. *Anthropological Theory*, 7(2), 131–150.

Zigon, J. (2008). *Morality: An Anthropological Perspective.* Oxford: Berg.

Zigon, J. (2009a). Hope Dies Last: Two Aspects of Hope in Contemporary Moscow. *Anthropological Theory*, 9(3), 253–271.

Zigon, J. (2009b). Phenomenological Anthropology and Morality: A Reply to Robbins. *Ethnos*, 74(2), 286–288.

Zigon, J. (2009c). Within a Range of Possibilities: Morality and Ethics in Social Life. *Ethnos*, 74(2), 251–276.

Zigon, J. (2010). Moral and Ethical Assemblages: A Response to Fassin and Stoczkowski. *Anthropological Theory*, 10(1-2), 3–15.

Zigon, J. (2011). *'HIV Is God's Blessing': Rehabilitating Morality in Neoliberal Russia.* Berkeley: University of California Press.

Zigon, J. (2013). Human Rights as Moral Progress? A Critique. *Cultural Anthropology*, 28(4), 716–736.

Zigon, J. (2014). An Ethics of Dwelling and a Politics of World-Building: A Critical Response to Ordinary Ethics. *Journal of the Royal Anthropological Institute*, 20, 746–764.

Zigon, J., & Throop, C. J. (2014). Moral Experience: Introduction. *Ethos*, 42(1), 1–15.

Zuma, J. (2012). *The Life and Times of Josiah Gumede.* Address by ANC President Jacob Zuma on the Occasion of the Memorial Lecture on the Life and Times of ANC Fourth President Josiah Tshangana Gumede, Durban, April 19, 2012. Retrieved March 23, 2013, from http://www.politicsweb.co.za/opinion/the-life-and-times-of-josiah-gumede--jacob-zuma

Index[1]

A

Abnormality, *see* Normality
Absenteeism, learner/pupil
 parental, 10, 16, 110
Addiction, *see* Drugs; Alcohol
Advertising, 2–5, 33, 61, 220, 244, 305
African National Congress (ANC), 27, 66, 75, 108, 123, 298–301, 307, 308, 319, 324–325n24, 364
Agamben, Giorgio, 192
Agency, 2–5, 11, 12, 72, 183, 232, 256, 311, 343, 345, 358, 365, 373
Aid, international, 169
AIDS/HIV, 13, 102, 103, 108, 113, 126, 145, 169, 201, 225, 226, 228–230, 246, 341, 393
Alcohol, 78, 100, 112–114, 244, 249, 348, 359, 366, 372, 373
Alcoholism, *see* Alcohol

Apartheid, 5, 9, 24–27, 29, 30, 32, 33, 61, 63, 68, 70, 72–74, 77–79, 83, 84, 103, 104, 124, 139, 140, 181, 255, 299, 301, 303, 304, 310, 312–314, 352, 364
Appadurai, Arjun, 16, 396
Appearance, 139, 140, 351
 See also Uniform, school
Ashforth, Adam, 88n25, 88n26, 203n5, 366, 381n38, 381n41
Attention Deficit Hyperactivity Disorder (ADHD), 6, 120, 154n36, 337

B

Bantu, education, 24, 26, 27, 304, 309, 316
Besteman, Catherine Lowe, 299
Bible, 32, 105, 311, 338

---

[1] Note: Page number followed by "n" refers to notes.

454 INDEX

Bornstein, Erica, 9, 19, 116, 169, 171, 183, 185, 192, 194, 197, 201, 209n41, 220, 227, 230, 231, 245, 247, 262n1, 279, 291, 296, 324n20, 340, 356, 357, 379n25
Bourdieu, Pierre, 10, 11, 238, 256, 266n30, 282, 313, 353, 360, 362, 369, 374, 380n31
Bourgois, Philippe, 39n21, 63, 73, 90n35, 119, 189

C

Cape Town, 11, 22, 23, 28, 69, 70, 189, 220, 235, 299, 306, 309, 315
Careers, 4, 11, 59, 126, 130, 185, 337
Charity, 4, 8, 9, 19, 27–29, 31, 34, 35, 118, 147, 174, 175, 223, 226, 236, 240, 241, 247, 261, 288–298, 302, 305, 307, 311, 343, 347
Cheney, Kristen, 9, 19, 20, 40n26, 117, 184, 188, 262n1, 264n19, 293, 326n36
Childhood, 77, 80, 115, 117–119, 124, 127, 132, 178–184, 189, 195, 232, 260, 275, 280, 309, 346
Child Support Grants (CSG), 68, 112–114
Christ, *see* Jesus
Christianity, 32, 109, 147, 183, 185, 188, 194, 196, 197, 259, 276, 279, 286, 287, 338, 345
Clothing, 106, 145, 198, 220, 241, 253
See also Uniform, school
Colonialism, 140, 304, 306
Comaroff, Jean, 30, 83, 90n33, 173, 182, 184, 195, 234, 242, 255, 265n23, 311, 312, 326n38
Comaroff, John, 30, 83, 90n33, 173, 182, 184, 195, 234, 242, 265n23, 311, 312, 326n38

Constitution, school, 182, 194
South African, 80, 315
Conversion, Christian, 185, 194, 208n35, 338
Corporal punishment, 33, 76–80, 141, 142, 351, 352, 390
Coventry, 226, 243, 279
Criminal, 70, 73, 82, 109, 111, 126, 181, 233, 350, 358

D

Dagga, 121, 339, 359, 370
Dahl, Bianca, 155n46, 227, 230, 231, 262n2
Day, Sophie, 137, 375
Death, 141, 182, 200, 237, 244, 283, 354
Democracy, 27, 28, 68, 76, 83, 124, 184, 308–310, 312, 313, 352
Department for International Development (DFID), 9, 291
Department of Education, *see* South African Department of Education (DoE)
Desjarlais, Robert, 12, 13, 37n11, 131, 138, 374, 393
de Waal, Alex, 240
Discipline, 2, 6, 10, 76–78, 80, 107, 123–125, 141, 172, 182, 233, 254, 255, 257, 258, 339, 351, 397
Douglas, Mary, 74, 109, 128, 129, 153n34
Drinking, 3, 59, 62, 69, 78, 85n7, 100, 107, 109, 110, 113, 123, 144, 145, 170, 189, 232, 248, 249, 305, 354, 361–363
Drugs, 5, 13, 71, 81, 100, 112, 126, 181, 187, 190, 193, 221, 224, 232, 237, 249, 261, 275, 340, 341, 345, 353, 370, 372, 373
Durham, Deborah, 12, 343

E

East London, 27, 29, 70, 73, 133, 280, 281
Employment, 24, 65, 73, 101, 103, 113, 129, 180, 184–196, 300, 312, 320, 342, 344, 358–363, 365, 369, 391, 396, 399, 404
Ennew, Judith, 105, 109, 114–116, 150n16, 169, 184, 188, 326n35
Ethnography, 9, 13, 14, 21, 25, 104, 121, 136, 182, 233, 244, 260, 291, 302, 317, 321, 349, 373, 393, 397–399, 404

F

Family, 5, 71, 72, 77, 99, 100, 103–106, 114, 115, 144, 145, 169, 171, 174–178, 187, 190, 200, 223, 226, 229, 233, 240, 249, 251, 254, 276, 280, 282, 296, 299, 303, 306, 318, 319, 343, 344, 347, 353, 361, 363–365
Fassin, Didier, 19, 189, 221, 227, 232, 279, 293, 294
Ferguson, James, 9, 251, 301, 302, 311, 312, 403, 404, 406n5
Forgiveness, 129, 180, 195, 277
Foucault, Michel, 12, 13, 15, 16, 36n1, 36n5, 87n23, 119, 179, 182, 183, 206n18, 207n28, 257, 351
Fundraising, 173, 220, 223, 224, 234, 236, 244–246, 273, 277, 282, 283, 286, 293, 310, 311, 322n7, 370, 396, 397
Future, *see* Temporality, future

G

Gluckman, Max, 14, 42n34, 364
God, 26, 70, 105, 167, 182, 184–197, 202, 233, 238, 243, 254, 275–281, 283, 287, 288, 290, 296, 319, 337–341, 343, 344, 366, 391
Goffman, Ervin, 102, 115, 121, 131, 137, 139, 283, 371, 380n35
Governmentality, 9, 183, 312, 316, 317, 351, 390, 391, 398
Graeber, David, 307
Grahamstown, 1, 7, 16, 17, 24, 25, 28–30, 63, 64, 66, 68, 69, 73, 75, 100, 122, 133, 141, 169, 174–176, 186, 188, 198, 220, 223, 239–244, 280, 282, 286, 290, 305, 306, 318, 375
Grey, Governor, 23, 185

H

Heart, 7, 9, 13, 70, 171, 224, 246, 281, 313, 341, 345, 392, 394
Heaven, 191, 338, 371
Hecht, 19, 27, 39n21, 112, 116, 118, 150n16, 233, 262n1, 371
Hip-hop, 59, 62, 69, 362, 363
Historical, *see* Temporality, historical
Homelands, 25, 27
Hope, 8, 9, 13, 22, 27, 33, 66, 73, 106, 129, 141–148, 192, 239–241, 245, 251–253, 260, 276, 284, 285, 288, 293, 297, 298, 312, 314, 321, 337–375, 391, 392, 395–397, 399, 400, 404
Housing, 24, 169
Humanitarianism, 4, 5, 9, 19, 34, 174–176, 183, 223, 230, 231, 245, 246, 250, 260, 261, 279, 290, 291, 296, 394, 396, 398, 399, 404
Human rights, 29, 33, 79, 80, 120, 123, 125, 197, 275, 308–316, 320, 343, 390, 391

456 INDEX

Hunter, Mark, 74, 78, 79, 86n14, 103, 113, 114, 313, 381n45
Hunter, Monica, 25, 78

I

Ingold, Tim, 20, 285, 316
Intersubjectivity, 14, 20, 21, 37n7, 131, 177, 342, 357, 360, 366, 392
Intervention, 8, 9, 19, 20, 115, 116, 121, 129, 130, 187, 189, 194, 196, 197, 201, 219, 221, 222, 227, 230–234, 237, 238, 241, 243–246, 249, 252, 260, 274, 277, 279, 281, 283, 288, 291, 296–298, 301, 307, 311, 318, 360, 371, 375, 394–396, 398–400, 406n5
Irresponsibility, 106
IsiXhosa, 18, 19, 30, 32, 60, 147, 172, 176, 280, 281, 338, 346

J

Jackson, Michael, 5, 20, 21, 140, 169, 240, 310, 316, 344, 364–366, 380n36, 406n2
Jesus, 31, 32, 275

L

Laidlaw, James, 12, 82, 207n28, 256, 343, 358, 364, 365, 372, 392, 393
Lambek, Michael, 10, 15, 37n10, 341, 342, 345, 392
Levinas, Emmanuel, 273
Lévi-Strauss, 115
Lewis, David, 5, 23, 36n2, 210n48, 284
Literacy, 5, 25, 118, 220, 242, 286, 315

London, 2, 3, 6, 7, 16, 61, 63, 74, 80, 101, 119, 129, 143, 175, 178, 186–189, 220, 224, 227, 228, 235, 236, 277, 284, 295, 313, 319, 353, 354, 398
Lutkehaus, Nancy, 173, 275

M

McAllister, Patrick, 25, 43n38, 43n40
McDermott, Ray, 119
Malinowski, Bronisław Kasper, 14, 38n16, 39n17, 115
Mandela, Nelson, 5, 27, 172, 305, 314, 325n28
Marginal, *see* Marginalisation
Marginalisation, 29, 34, 102, 183, 310, 354
Marijuana, 121, 122, 339, 353
Mattingly, Cheryl, 393
Mayer, Iona, 14, 25, 43n37, 43n40, 70, 73, 77, 78, 86n12, 87n20, 87n21, 88n24, 88n25, 104, 115, 123, 142, 181
Mayer, Philip, 25, 43n38, 123, 344, 346, 356
Media, 80, 220, 226, 230, 231, 238, 290, 291, 301, 303, 394
Military, *see* War
Missionary, 23, 42n32, 105, 110, 115, 147, 148, 155n49, 173–175, 177, 182, 185, 191, 194, 198, 204n7, 205n12, 205n15, 206n17, 207n26, 208n34, 210–211n48, 234, 238, 252, 253, 255, 278, 284, 286, 323n17, 325n28, 347, 356, 375, 376n7, 377n15, 377n16, 378n23
Modernity, 155n49, 249, 265n28, 304, 307, 403, 404
Moore, Henrietta, 16, 79, 238, 291, 302, 348, 391, 392

INDEX   457

Morality, 3, 7, 11–16, 25, 35, 37n9, 37n11, 38n12, 38n13, 81, 83, 86n15, 102, 104, 114, 123, 169, 173, 192, 197, 203n4, 207n28, 235, 255, 274, 318, 379n30, 392, 401
Mothering, 110, 173, 174, 178, 204n7, 289
Murder, 69, 187, 201, 260
Musgrove, Frank, 14, 15
Music, 4, 31, 59, 60, 62, 71, 75, 226, 362, 405

N
Neoliberalism, 251, 252, 265n26, 320
Ngwane, Zolani, 26, 78, 103, 120, 284
Niehaus, Isak, 42n34, 379n24, 381n38, 381n40
Nietzsche, Friedrich, 74, 188, 191, 196, 264n17
Normality, 12, 13, 34, 183, 184, 245, 399, 400

O
O'Neill, Kevin Lewis, 19, 180, 231, 238, 240, 243, 244, 247, 278, 279, 289, 406n3
Orphanhood, 117, 221, 262n1, 264n20, 295

P
Peires, Jeff, 22, 23, 25, 41n30, 42n32, 43n36, 147, 155n47, 155n49, 156n51, 156n52, 375
Police, 2, 16, 24, 44n43, 60–62, 70, 74, 78, 83, 84, 87n22, 89n31, 109, 126, 136, 140, 154n42, 167, 203n1, 294, 317, 345, 349, 354, 364, 379n27, 398, 400

Policy, 9, 40n23, 66, 87n18, 88n28, 101, 106, 126, 199, 201, 202, 210–211n48, 236, 239, 305, 308–310, 347, 348, 351
Port Elizabeth, 6, 45n55, 85n2, 113, 301
Poverty, 29, 63–67, 69, 85n2, 86n14, 116, 126, 138, 143, 149n2, 185, 197, 221, 222, 224–226, 228, 230, 233, 234, 237, 247, 251, 275, 297, 298, 343, 354
Power, 6, 10, 24, 33, 36n5, 38n13, 43n41, 61, 76, 79, 83, 87n23, 88–89n28, 118, 119, 121, 141, 155n49, 175, 176, 180–182, 192, 194, 195, 197, 202, 204n7, 208n32, 221, 222, 231, 233, 236, 242, 243, 251, 252, 257, 259, 260, 265n26, 275, 287, 288, 294, 298, 302, 307, 311–315, 317, 318, 320, 321n5, 324n21, 324n22, 325n28, 338, 340, 345, 348, 349, 351, 373, 374, 376n1, 380n31, 390–396, 401, 404, 406n5
Prayer, 32, 196, 280–283, 288, 290, 323n12, 323n15, 323n17, 324n18, 338, 340, 343, 376n7
Precarity, 372, 392, 395, 405
Prison, 2, 60, 70, 144, 192, 237, 243, 244, 358, 376n4, 379n27
Private school, 33, 36n3, 67, 71, 72, 74, 75, 107, 176, 178, 188, 207n22, 219, 223, 241, 257, 280, 282, 284, 378n21
Privatisation, 83, 87n17, 87n19, 90n33
Psychologist, 6, 11, 16, 108, 119, 187, 188, 317, 321n3, 400
Psychology, 36n6, 39n18, 118, 127, 149n6, 187, 208n31, 290, 321n3

Punishment, 6, 33, 76–80, 83, 87n20, 88n27, 88n28, 89n30, 89n32, 89n33, 120, 123–126, 141, 142, 151n23, 151n24, 152n25, 152n26, 152n27, 153n28, 155n44, 340, 352, 378n21, 390

R

Rabbitts, Frances, 226, 247, 289, 322n7, 322n8, 323n13
Race, 10, 30, 63, 206n17, 228, 317
Racism, 254
Radcliffe-Brown, Alfred Reginald, 39n17, 42n34
Rape, 112, 168, 224, 232, 238, 243, 244
Redemption, 187, 190, 192, 240
Respect, 38n16, 61, 76–80, 110, 111, 120, 139, 141, 142, 153n34, 197, 253, 255, 259, 265n28, 338, 348–351, 394
Responsibility, 1, 4, 29, 31, 35, 45n51, 77, 79, 82, 115, 124, 181, 182, 184, 189, 201, 203n1, 203n4, 249–251, 263n11, 265n26, 273–321, 339, 342, 343, 350, 351, 363, 366, 373, 394
Rights, *see* Human rights
Robbins, Joel, 79, 359, 367, 378n23, 392, 393

S

Salvation, 183, 187, 191, 192, 197, 209n37, 243, 248, 314, 351, 399, 404
Scheper-Hughes, Nancy, 115, 150n16
Scott, James, 294
Security, 31, 68, 69, 73, 83, 84, 86n9, 90n33, 90n34, 100, 101, 136, 140, 148, 149n1, 169, 207n27, 239, 243, 252, 254, 258, 259, 264n20, 313, 317, 350, 354, 361, 372
Segregation, 40n22
Self-esteem, 168, 182, 189
Sin, 118, 190, 191, 311, 326n39, 338, 343, 378n23
Sobriety, *see* Drinking
Social worker, 16, 73, 105, 108, 112, 180, 200, 201, 319, 320, 339
Soul, 195, 199, 339
South African Department of Education (DoE), 28, 120, 121, 125, 127, 150n9, 151n23, 153n33, 188, 197–201, 209n42, 210n43, 210n44, 210n45, 210n46, 210n47, 220, 240, 259, 293, 301, 307–310, 312–316, 318–320, 326n37, 327n41, 337, 339, 352, 369, 376n4, 379n29
Special Educational, 6, 7, 101, 120, 121, 210n46, 353, 354, 399
Stafford, Charles, 37n9, 81, 394
Stambach, Amy, 15, 17, 19, 20, 39n20, 40n21, 40n23, 105, 120, 124, 185, 197, 230, 247, 249, 251, 265n27, 284, 316, 338, 342, 360, 376n7, 406n3
Stigma, 130–141, 202, 229, 362, 379n29, 400
Street children, 27, 28, 34, 35, 105, 114–134, 150n15, 151n17, 151n18, 173, 183, 184, 221, 222, 224, 225, 233, 234, 236–239, 241, 262n1, 264n22, 275, 281, 369, 371, 375
Swanson, Dalene, 36n3, 39n16, 319, 366
Swartz, Sharlene, 11, 36n6, 37n8, 70, 86n11, 86n15, 109, 189, 343

T

Tattoos, 243
Temporality
  future, 16
  historical, 402
Tsotsi, 69–71, 76, 77, 82, 86n12, 104, 136, 234, 341

U

Ubuntu, 172, 182, 203n4, 203n5, 319, 320, 327n42, 356, 366
Unemployment, 65, 185, 244, 298, 312, 354, 357, 359, 364, 378n22
Uniform, school, 107, 108, 113, 122, 123, 150n8, 294, 354, 356, 357, 370

V

Varenne, Herve, 37n6, 39n19, 119
Violence, 6, 19, 33, 61, 69, 70, 80–82, 88n25, 89n29, 89n33, 111, 123, 126, 140–142, 144, 152n26, 168, 187, 190, 197, 203n1, 221, 225, 232, 244, 340, 351
Volunteer, 3, 4, 8–10, 16, 19, 31, 35, 44n48, 71, 114, 126, 132, 172, 173, 178, 198, 221, 223, 246, 252–254, 258, 259, 261, 263n8, 263n13, 274, 279, 281, 282, 285, 286, 289, 305, 322n6, 323n11, 379n29, 396, 397, 403
Voluntourism, *see* Volunteer

W

Wacquant, Loïc, 90n35, 313, 372
War, 22, 23, 42n32, 148, 174, 189, 204n8, 221, 259, 260, 265n29, 305
Warwick, 224–226, 262n4, 286
Weber, Max, 10, 31, 41n27, 197, 281–283, 309
Weiss, Brad, 39n21, 362
Wilson, Monica, 14, 182, 356
Witch, *see* Witchcraft
Witchcraft, 88n25, 147, 354–357, 364–366, 378n24, 381n38, 381n39, 381n40, 381n41
Wright, Laurence, 45n54, 264n23, 286, 304, 307, 352

X

Xhosa, 22–26, 30–32, 35, 41n29, 41–42n30, 42n32, 43n36, 43n37, 77, 85n8, 87n20, 87n21, 87n22, 88n27, 104, 105, 115, 120, 125, 138, 139, 142, 147, 148, 153n28, 154n38, 154n40, 155n47, 155n49, 155n50, 156n51, 156n52, 175–177, 181, 182, 191, 205n11, 205n12, 207n26, 210n48, 222, 242, 253, 254, 257, 259, 284, 306, 319, 320, 338, 344, 346–349, 354, 357, 375, 377n15, 404

Z

Zigon, Jarrett, 11–15, 37n11, 38n12, 38n13, 83, 109, 114, 131, 146, 148, 174, 180–182, 187, 196, 207n28, 261, 273, 274, 276, 278, 280, 281, 288, 298, 309, 311, 314–316, 326n39, 339, 341–343, 346, 358, 364, 365, 376n8, 390–393, 400
Zuma, Jacob, 87n18, 230, 301, 303, 325n28